MACROECONOMICS
FOR MANAGERS

MACROECONOMICS FOR MANAGERS

KNUT ANTON MORK

Norwegian School of Management
and Centre for Research in Economics
and Business Administration

WADSWORTH PUBLISHING COMPANY

Belmont, California
A Division of Wadsworth, Inc.

Economics Editor: Kristine Clerkin
Editorial Assistant: Nancy Spellman
Production: Ruth Cottrell
Designer: Janet Bollow
Print Buyer: Martha Branch
Copy Editor: Mary Roybal
Cover Photos: (left) The Image Bank/West, © 1991 Andy Caulfield;
(right) The Image Bank/West, © 1991 Romilly Lockyer
Cover: Vargas/Williams/Design
Signing Representative: Mark Francisco
Compositor: G & S Typesetters, Inc.

This book is printed on acid-free paper that meets Environmental Protection
Agency standards for recycled paper.

2 3 4 5 6 7 8 9 10—96 95 94 93 92

Library of Congress Cataloging-in-Publication Data

Mork, Knut Anton.
    Macroeconomics for managers / Knut Anton Mork.
      p. cm.
    Includes index.
    ISBN 0-534-13794-6 (alk. paper)
     1. Macroeconomics. 2. Macroeconomics—Problems, exercises, etc.
  I. Title.
HB172.5.M655 1991
339'.024658—dc20   91-23053
                                                     CIP

To Laila, who has chosen to endure life with an economist;
and to Erling and Knut, who have had to live with a father
who consistently refuses to use a Macintosh

CONTENTS

3 SOME FACTS ABOUT BUSINESS CYCLES AND INFLATION   51

6 THE IS-LM MODEL   139

7 AGGREGATE DEMAND, AGGREGATE SUPPLY, AND PRICE ADJUSTMENTS

8 INFLATION

PART III   EXTENSIONS OF MACROECONOMIC THEORY   223

9   INTERNATIONAL TRADE   227

10   THE ECONOMICS OF EXCHANGE RATES   245

11 ALTERNATIVE APPROACHES TO BUSINESS-CYCLE ANALYSIS

12 MACROECONOMIC POLICY MAKING 301

PART IV   **MONITORING AND FORECASTING THE ECONOMY**   333

PREFACE

Managers make decisions. Good decision making requires an adequate basis of information and knowledge. This book deals with that part of this basis which relates to the firm's external environment, as defined by the national and international economy. It deals with business cycles and inflation, with interest rates and exchange rates, with government policies, and with forecasting. Much of the book is devoted to macroeconomic *theory* because a sound theoretical framework is needed to put the real-world events in a proper and coherent perspective. In addition to introducing the conventional Keynesian analysis, this book introduces alternative and more recent approaches to macroeconomics—such as monetarism, rational expectations, and real-business-cycle analysis. The scope is international throughout, and two full chapters are devoted entirely to global interactions.

However, this book puts equal emphasis on the *practical* aspect of macroeconomics, explaining the virtual barrage of economic news that confronts the manager every day. No less than four chapters are devoted exclusively to this purpose. Yet another chapter provides guidance for dealing with macroeconomic forecasting services.

The exercises provide further practical insights. Many of them are "conventional" in the sense that they can be carried out with pencil, paper, a hand calculator, and occasionally an electronic spreadsheet. Others, however, involve manipulation of real-world macroeconomic data. The advent of user-friendly statistical computer software has put this type of manipulation within the practical reach of the nonexpert. The data on the special diskette that the publisher makes available to instructors using this book can be read into your (or your professor's) favorite software package. Chapter 2 reviews the tools that underlie such software packages; it is not intended to replace a solid one-semester course in statistics, but it should serve as an adequate review for those students who do not have statistical methods fresh in their minds. As an alternative, the book can be taught without the statistical exercises, in which case Chapter 2 can be safely skipped.

A practical course in macroeconomics is not complete unless the participants also follow the daily news about the economy. This book shows how such news items are presented in the *Wall Street Journal*. Alternative news sources include the other major newspapers, such as the

New York Times, as well as radio and television. Discussing these news reports in class along with the textbook material and the exercises will help to bring the material to life.

The material in this book is presented on a level that is usually referred to as intermediate in American colleges and universities. However, it is introduced in such a way as to be accessible to those students who have not previously taken the courses that make up the usual prerequisites for intermediate macro courses, such as principles of macroeconomics or money and banking. In my experience, many students enrolled in MBA programs find themselves in this kind of situation. The introductory material in Part I of the book should prove particularly useful to these students. However, this book may also be used by students with a much more solid background in economics, but they may not wish to read all the chapters. For example, a student with a good background in money and banking may skip the discussion of the monetary system in Chapter 4.

Although this book bears the name of only one author, that author has benefitted from the help of many other people. I received many constructive comments from my Vanderbilt colleagues Germain Böer, J. Dewey Daane, and William Lindsey. James Butkiewicz, University of Delaware; Michael Edgmond, Oklahoma State University; Lars Ljungquist, University of Wisconsin; Warren Matthews, Texas A&I University; James McCollum, Columbus College; David Meinster, Temple University; William Rohlf, Jr., Drury College; Mark Schaefer, Georgia State University; Nat Simons, Ohio State University; James Smith, University of North Carolina, Chapel Hill; and Pin Wang, Pennsylvania State University, University Park reviewed the entire manuscript, provided numerous suggestions for improvements, and forced me to stay current with the research and the events as well as to preserve rigor in the midst of simplicity. Kristine Clerkin, the editor for this project, did a marvelous job in coaxing and guiding me in the right direction, while at the same time encouraging me when things looked difficult. Last, but not least, my many MBA students, particularly those in the Vanderbilt Executive MBA Program, provided experience, inspiration, feedback, and encouragement. May their lives prove as useful to humankind as they have been to this book.

MACROECONOMICS
FOR MANAGERS

INTRODUCTION TO CONCEPTS, METHODS, AND INSTITUTIONS

PART I

PART I

The study of macroeconomics will take you through some sophisticated analyses of economic theory and data. To help prepare you for these tasks, the opening part of the book covers some necessary preliminaries. It offers an introduction to some concepts, facts, and institutions that will be used throughout the rest of the book. The facts relate to the performance of the U.S. economy and the world economy since World War II. The concepts are the key concepts of macroeconomic analysis and of elementary statistics. The institutions refer to central banking, particularly to the U.S. Federal Reserve System.

You may wonder why management students need to study macroeconomics. Perhaps you are on your way to a fast-track career in one of the functional areas of management, such as marketing or accounting, and have found to your unpleasant surprise that a course in macroeconomics is required for your management degree. Don't despair! Macroeconomics is much more important for the "bread and butter" of management than most students believe. Chapter 1 will tell you some reasons why; many more reasons will become apparent throughout the rest of the book.

A practical need for macroeconomics translates into a need for practical macroeconomics. Knowing elegant theories is poor consolation to the manager of a bankrupt company. Applied knowledge means real numbers, and manipulation of real numbers means statistical methods. In fact, a whole branch of statistics, referred to as **econometrics,** has been developed for the purpose of analyzing economic data. Perhaps the most important econometric technique is **regression analysis.** Just about every chapter of this book will present exercises with real data that require some use of such techniques; the last chapter is dedicated exclusively to the issue of econometric forecasting. Chapter 2 is a self-contained introduction to the econometric methods that will be useful for the study of the rest of the book. Many students no doubt will be familiar with this material already; others may want to use the book without doing the statistical exercises.

Whatever your reasons, you may bypass Chapter 2 without losing the continuity of the discussion of the macroeconomic substance.

Chapter 3 introduces the main concepts of macroeconomics and the salient facts about the U.S. economy and the world economy after World War II. The outline in this chapter frames the discussion presented in the rest of the book. If you feel confident about both the facts and the concepts (for example, if you already have had a good introductory course in macroeconomics), you may want to bypass this chapter, but you do so at your own risk. The risk is that you may start to think about economics in the abstract, perhaps merely as an interesting (or totally uninteresting!) collection of equations and diagrams. In order to benefit from the insights of macroeconomics in actual decision making, you will need a more practical mind-set.

A variety of institutions are involved in the study of macroeconomics, including manufacturing firms, financial institutions, and government agencies such as the U.S. Congress and the British Parliament, which levy taxes and decide on government spending. These institutions might be fairly familiar to you already. However, one particular group of institutions stands out as worthy of a special review—the **central banks,** found in almost every sovereign country. The central banks are important because they regulate the supply of money and credit to the economy and hence play a key role in the determination of interest rates and the business climate in general. In the United States, the functions of central banking are carried out by a network of institutions referred to collectively as the **Federal Reserve System.** This system and its operations are described in Chapter 4. The contents of this chapter may be known to those who have had a good course in money and banking. Note, however, that the information presented here is crucial for understanding most of the rest of the book.

1

MACROECONOMICS AND MANAGEMENT

A manager of a business organization must set objectives and determine strategies for achieving them. To do this effectively, he or she must understand and find a fit between the firm's internal environment and its external environment. The firm's internal environment consists of such components as its facilities, its personnel, its management, and its shareholders. While this environment is complex, most of it is fairly controllable.

The external environment, however, is even more complex and far less controllable. Those parts of the firm's external environment with which the manager is most familiar are suppliers, customers, and competitors. However, there is more to the external environment. It also includes the legal system, government regulations, and the overall economy. This last part—the manager's interaction with the overall economic environment—forms the focus of this book. It is our contention that an insufficient understanding and response to this part of the firm's environment make it difficult for a manager to succeed in his or her strategic initiatives. This chapter takes a preliminary look at the nature of this interaction. Let us start by considering an actual macroeconomic event, namely the drop in the prime lending rate in the United States in January 1990.

1.1 A DROP IN THE PRIME RATE

On January 8, 1990, most U.S. banks cut their prime lending rates from 10.5% to 10% per year. Most business leaders were pleased. The stock market had a good day as the Dow Jones Industrial Average rose by over 20 points.

WHAT HAPPENED?

In order to understand this response, we first need to understand what actually happened. The prime rate is an interest rate posted by the banks as a gauge for the overall levels of the interest rates that they charge for different kinds of loans. Although relatively few customers actually borrow at the prime rate, a number of other interest rates are tied to it, such as home equity lines, personal credit lines, auto loans, and many business loans. At the same time, a number of interest rates were not affected at all on this occasion. For example, mortgage lending rates had edged downward for some time before this drop in the prime rate. The same was true of the yields on bonds, which are a measure of the interest rates that government entities and businesses effectively pay when they borrow money by issuing bonds and selling them in the market. Finally, the interest rates on savings accounts and checking accounts were not affected by the drop in the prime rate. Therefore, the net effect was that some borrowing became cheaper and some stayed the same, while the returns on many savings arrangements remained unchanged.

THE CONTEXT   This was not the first cut in the prime rate during the late 1980s. As Figure 1.1 shows, it had declined through a number of steps since February of 1989. Before then, the prime rate mostly had been rising significantly since its 8.5% level in early 1988.

These movements had been part of a larger trend, which generally reflected **monetary policy** during these years. Monetary policy in the United States is conducted by the Federal Reserve, this country's central bank. At the center of monetary policy lies the control of the **supply of money.** A steady growth in the money supply has become usual. An acceleration in this growth is commonly referred to as a monetary **easing,** while a slowdown is called a monetary **tightening.**

We will get back to monetary policy in Chapter 4 and repeatedly throughout this book. For now we make the intuitive observation that an acceleration of the money supply makes funds available for lending more abundant and thus lessens the competition among borrowers. For this reason, interest rates can be expected to decline. Similarly, a monetary tightening usually is followed by an increase in interest rates. The conduct of monetary policy makes use of this insight by letting the movements in market interest rates serve as criteria for when monetary policy has eased or tightened enough, as the case might be. In particular, since the mid-1980s it has been well known that the Federal Reserve formulates its policies so as to keep one particular interest rate, called the federal funds rate, within rather narrow bands. When the Federal Reserve acts in this manner, it is said to use the federal funds rate as its **target** variable. The federal funds rate is the interest rate that banks pay each other for funds kept on account with the Federal Reserve. Because the Federal Reserve in the mid- and late 1980s was known to use this interest rate as its target, the movements in the federal funds rate can be read as a fairly direct indication of the direction of monetary policy.

In this perspective, the comparison of the prime rate and the federal funds rate in Figure 1.1 should make it clear that the movements in the prime rate by and large were driven by the Federal Reserve's monetary

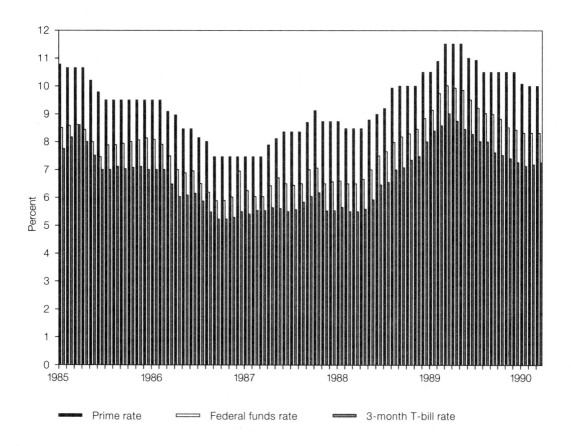

Percent

Prime rate   Federal funds rate   3-month T-bill rate

FIGURE 1.1

The performance of the prime lending rate, the federal funds rate, and the yield rate on 3-month Treasury bills, 1985–90.

policies. Usually, the tendency is for the prime rate to lie a little above the federal funds rate, perhaps reflecting the higher processing costs of loans to customers that are not themselves banks. However, the *movements* in the federal funds rate tend to be matched by corresponding movements in the prime rate. The last three months of 1989 came very close to being an exception to this rule, as the federal funds rate declined without a follow-up in the prime rate. Given this background, the prime-rate cut on January 8 was not surprising. If anything, it was just the final piece of an overall trend toward somewhat lower interest rates falling into place.

A further indication of the same effect is given by the third interest rate shown in Figure 1.1, namely, the yield rate on 3-month Treasury bills or, for short, the T-bill rate. This is the interest rate that the U.S. Treasury implicitly pays for funds it borrows in the bond market by issuing Treasury bills that can be exchanged for cash three months later. Except for a tendency to lie lower than both the prime rate and the federal funds rate, this rate follows the ups and downs of the federal funds rate. Its steady decline from March 1989 was a clear reflection of an overall easing in the U.S. credit markets. Other interest rates, such as home mortgage rates, edged down as well.

UNDERLYING FORCES

Why did the Federal Reserve start tightening the supply of money in early 1988 and then start easing it again in early 1989? A clue to the answer to this question can be found in Figure 1.2, which shows in the same graph the federal funds rate and the rate of inflation in consumer prices, as measured by the Consumer Price Index. Inflation had been extremely moderate in 1986—some months even experienced *de*flation, in other words, price declines. Inflation in 1987 stayed moderate as well, at least after an isolated burst in January of that year. However, 1988 saw a steady worsening of the inflationary picture. It wasn't that inflation rose to new heights every month; rather there were fewer and fewer months in between when it was negligible. It grew disturbingly high in early 1989 before it abated somewhat later that year.

FIGURE 1.2

The federal funds rate and inflation in consumer prices, 1985–90. The inflation in consumer prices is measured by the monthly changes in the Consumer Price Index, converted to annual rates.

The worsening inflation in 1988 had the Federal Reserve worried.

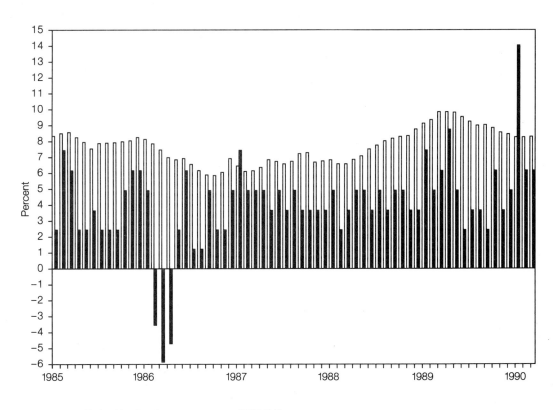

Federal funds rate ⬜   CPI inflation ⬛

They considered the control of inflation their primary responsibility. The option available to them for achieving this aim was to tighten the money supply, which they did through February of 1989. At that time, they felt that their policy had had the desired effect for the time being and allowed some easing again throughout 1989.

Figure 1.2 shows some of this effect, in that inflation slowed again in the middle of 1989. But how could the Federal Reserve already have perceived an effect in February or March? The answer to this question is seen in Figures 1.3 and 1.4, which match the federal funds rate with the monthly changes in two measures of production activity, namely, the monthly percentage change in the Index of Industrial Production and the monthly change in nonfarm employment, respectively. Both of these indicators suggested that a slowdown in production activity started in early 1989. Federal Reserve officials probably anticipated that the resulting softening in the markets for industrial goods as well as in the labor market would allow less room for price and wage increases. Thus, they could assume that inflation would slow down even though they

FIGURE 1.3

The federal funds rate and the growth in the Index of Industrial Production (converted to annual rates), 1985–90.

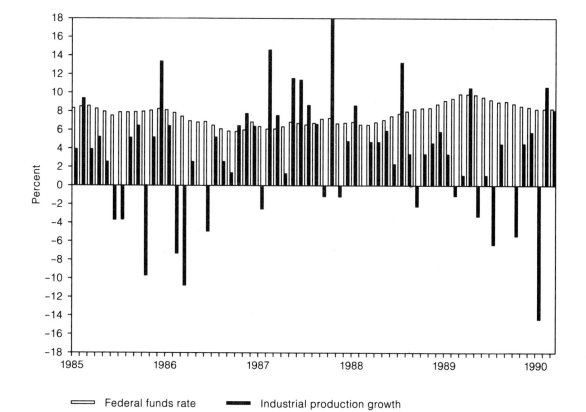

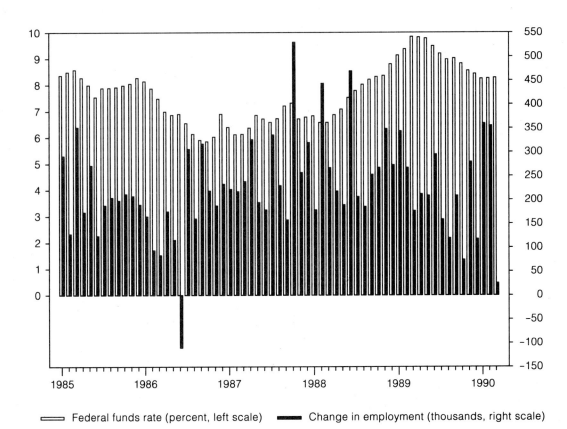

Federal funds rate (percent, left scale)   ▬ Change in employment (thousands, right scale)

FIGURE 1.4

The federal funds rate and the monthly changes in nonfarm employment (in thousands), 1985–90.

had not seen it yet. On this basis, they apparently decided that the need for further tightening had subsided for the time being.

The experience of 1988–89 followed in the wake of a number of similar episodes throughout the postwar period in which monetary tightening was followed by a slowdown in employment and production activity. To the people in the Federal Reserve, this experience served as a warning that further tightening could be followed by an outright. **recession,** a period in which the nation's output of goods and services actually declines. Because the Federal Reserve officials had signaled an intention to be careful to slow inflation without setting off a recession, they allowed monetary policy to be eased again.

APPARENT EFFECTS OF THE DROP IN THE PRIME RATE

The reduction in the prime rate was reported in all the media as being of great importance. What made it so important? A number of factors did. First, the lower cost of some kinds of borrowing made it cheaper to finance the purchase of a number of goods. This change was of immediate importance to businesses that were working on plans to expand or replace existing physical buildings or equipment, since such transactions are made for the longer term and often require outside financing. Therefore, the drop in the prime rate became a financial relief for many companies working on such plans, since now the financing costs of these projects would be lowered. This in turn raised the likelihood that the projects would be profitable, while at the same time reducing the financial risk of the company.

The cut in the prime rate had the potential for precipitating changes in business demand as well. For example, there seemed a good chance that the cheaper consumer loans could translate into higher consumer demand for items that need financing, such as automobiles and home improvements. Any company offering such goods or services would have reason to greet the prime-rate cut with cheer.

This scenario, however, was only the beginning of a longer story. Companies deciding to invest in new buildings and equipment would turn to other companies to fulfill this need. In doing so, they would create new business for companies in the construction industry, for example, and for manufacturing industries that make business equipment.

Still another round of effects might occur. As business picked up in certain industries, the people working there would earn more, new people would be hired, or both. As this happened, people would be likely to increase their individual purchases as well. In this way, demand and profits might rise in industries all over the economy.

A final effect would be more subtle. For the U.S. banks, the lower interest rates would mean a lower return on their loan portfolios. As an alternative, they might wish to invest their funds overseas. As it happened at the time, this incentive was amplified by rising interest rates in Europe and Japan. Now such transfers of funds overseas would translate into an increase in the market demand for foreign currency and a corresponding rise in the supply of U.S. dollars. In other words, there would be less foreign currency and more U.S. dollars available in the market. As a result, the dollar *exchange rate* could decline, an important occurrence because a fall in the dollar would have effects far beyond the banking industry. For example, it would mean that fewer Japanese yen could be bought for each dollar, or, to put it another way, the dollar would be worth less relative to the yen. This change would make Japanese imports more expensive. The same would be true of European imports, for similar reasons. Therefore, this development would be good news for U.S. producers trying to compete with foreign imports, because the prices of these imports effectively would rise. It would be equally good news for U.S. exporters. Why? With a lower dollar exchange rate, the prices they could obtain for their goods in foreign markets (in foreign currency) would translate into more dollars. With higher profits, they then could afford to market their goods more aggressively by cutting prices, investing their increased profits in improved quality or packaging, or increasing their advertising budgets.

Unfortunately, a fall in the dollar also implies some disadvantages for U.S. business. For example, a manufacturing company using foreign parts must pay more dollars for each such part. Similarly, foreign travel becomes more expensive when each dollar is worth less to local hotel and restaurant owners. Finally, the owners of assets denominated in U.S. dollars will suffer a loss, because these assets lose some of their value on the international market.

Of course, the interest rates are only one factor in the economy. Other factors, such as expectations of future profit opportunities, are equally important. As we have seen, the context surrounding this cut in the prime rate was not all rosy. Although the news was encouraging in itself, it came against the background of a much more sober trend. Growth in the U.S. economy had been slow all through 1989 and appeared likely to remain lethargic well into 1990. The cut in the prime rate was a sign that 1990 could turn out to be a little better than it would have been otherwise. At the time of this writing, the outcome remains uncertain.

LESSONS TO BE LEARNED

Understanding the ramifications of an event like this cut in the prime rate is an important ingredient in the overall portfolio of skills that a good manager possesses. The remaining chapters of this book will help equip you with the tools and the insights you need for this skill. For now, two lessons stand out from our example. The first is the importance of the general business climate and the forces affecting it, such as interest rates and monetary policy. Often these forces have broad indirect effects on business activity all over the economy—effects whose significance may surpass the impact on those companies most directly affected. The second lesson concerns the central role of *information*. Since the macroeconomic climate affects business decisions throughout the economy, managers, as the key decision makers, need to stay informed about this climate by paying constant attention to news releases and comments by the experts, both about what is happening at the moment and about what might lie ahead. Now let us look at both of these lessons in more detail.

1.2 BUSINESS CYCLES AND BUSINESS MANAGEMENT

A manager's ability ultimately tends to be measured by his or her contribution to the company's financial well-being. In short, a manager who makes money for the company is a good manager, while one who loses the company's money is not. Suppose, however, that you were a top manager in Ford Motor Company during the 1980s. In 1981 and 1982, your company reported net operating losses of $1 billion and $658 million, respectively.* Two years later, on the other hand, in 1984, these losses had been turned around to a net gain of $3 billion.**

If nothing had been known about the business-cycle situation during these years, you might have been criticized severely for mismanaging the company during 1981 and 1982. Or, if you had been brought on board after 1982, you might have been credited for the subsequent turnaround. Important changes no doubt did take place on the management level in the automobile industry during these years, and the turnaround at Ford Motor Company was indeed particularly remarkable. However, ascribing these changes to management skills alone would have been a major misunderstanding. A meaningful assessment of these figures is impossible without consideration of the fact that 1981 and 1982 were the years of one of the deepest **recessions** in the U.S. economy since World War II. As a result, many people were out of work. Despite the tax cuts initiated by the new Reagan administration, the average household saw its after-tax income decline, while interest rates rose to levels that were unprecedented for the postwar period. For most people, this was not the time to buy a new car. On the other hand, the recession reached bottom in late 1982, and by 1984 the U.S. economy was well into one of its most spectacular **recoveries** from recession. This recovery was the beginning of one of the longest-lasting **expansion** periods in the recorded history of the United States. Thus, much of the turnaround at Ford reflected this transition from recession to expansion!

Recessions and expansions are the main elements of **business cycles.** The business cycle is a term used to describe movements in economic activity that usually seem to be spread relatively uniformly throughout the various sectors of the economy. For example, if the automobile industry is in a recession, the steel industry, the rubber industry, and the glass industry usually are, too, because they supply raw materials and parts to the automobile industry. Furthermore, the income drops experienced by people engaged in these industries may put enough of a damper on their personal spending to send the retail industry, the apparel industry, the appliance industry, and so on into recession as well.

Recessions historically have been of varying depth, and expansions have been of varying duration. In fact, the term *cycle* is somewhat of a misnomer, because business cycles historically have shown none of the regularity typical of, say, radio waves. On the whole, they appear to be quite irregular phenomena. They also seem to be affected by a wide range of different forces. Consequently, both explaining and predicting business cycles have proved to be rather difficult tasks. Nevertheless,

---

* *Ward's Automotive Yearbook,* 1988, p. 239.
** Ibid.

the business cycles are a major fact of economic life. Together with inflation, they are the major focus of the study of macroeconomics. It is imperative that managers have a fundamental understanding of these factors and of how they affect their business.

Even if the frequency and amplitude of business cycles are irregular, they nevertheless appear to obey certain dynamics. For example, a recovery has followed every recession we have observed so far, even the Great Depression of the 1930s. The stabilizing forces in the economy that produce recoveries are part of the business-cycle dynamics. Stabilizing (or destabilizing) government policies are another factor to be reckoned with. If something undesirable happens to the economy, such as a recession or a period of high inflation, there will be political pressure from the business community as well as from the general public for the government to do something about it. On the other hand, policy actions sometimes appear to *cause* recessions. This outcome appears to be a possibility, for example, in situations when monetary policy is tightened in an attempt to slow inflation. Therefore, anticipating policy initiatives that affect the business cycle, as well as anticipating their effects, forms an important part of a manager's understanding of macroeconomics.

Business cycles strongly affect business profits, as the example from the automobile industry illustrated vividly. Managers need to know what to do as these cycles change. Although the business-cycle movements themselves may lie beyond the control of management, their effects on your company's health can be greatly influenced by how you as the manager respond to them.

The greatest challenge lies in how to respond to a *downturn* in the business cycle, in other words, a recession. For many in manufacturing, the first problem that a recession causes is an unexpected increase in inventories as sales fall off. The response often chosen is to close one or more plants temporarily while these inventories are being depleted. Such closings contribute further to the recession, of course, but may be the best thing that the company can do in the situation. However, it would be better if the problem could be prevented by avoiding an inventory pileup in the first place. Flexible manufacturing systems, such as just-in-time management, seek to eliminate or minimize inventories overall. Equally important are good predictions about likely turning points in demand.

The next issue that arises is how to survive through the rest of the recession. One way of responding is by cutting costs. For example, layoffs save costs in the short run, but they may be costly in the long run because totally new workers may have to be found once the recession is over. This problem becomes particularly acute for firms with well-trained workers who have a strong feeling of loyalty to the firm, because such workers are hard to replace. Flexible compensation plans, such as a system of bonuses tied to company profits, can help solve this problem. A second way of reducing costs is to cut the advertising budget. This alternative would make sense at a time when demand is low anyway. However, a trade-off exists here as well because advertising during the recession could keep potential customers aware of your company's presence and thus improve sales once the recession is over.

A third and common alternative is to postpone major investment projects. Major expansion or modernization projects aim toward the future and often can be postponed for a year or two without great difficulty. Such postponements allow you to economize your financial resources in difficult times and still have the new capacity in place when demand again picks up. Yet such decisions need to be made with caution. Failing to upgrade your equipment now may put you at a competitive disadvantage tomorrow. In fact, sometimes a recession provides an excellent opportunity to restructure your operations and turn your company into a leaner, more effective organization.

The correct decision about how to react to changes in the business cycle varies from case to case. Finding the right answer in each situation goes beyond the study of macroeconomics. That discussion belongs in courses on strategic management, operations management, marketing, and finance. However, macroeconomics is the right place to improve your understanding of the forces that shape the business-cycle movements. Such an understanding is an indispensable tool for adapting to today's rapidly changing business climate.

1.3   THE GLOBAL INFORMATION ECONOMY

Management planning for business-cycle turning points requires a constant stream of information. You need to follow the news on a regular basis in order to be up to date on the latest economic developments. Some such information comes from the daily movements in the financial markets. However, you also need to follow and understand the steady stream of data releases from government agencies at home and abroad. These data can give you a picture of where the economy is at any given moment. For the skillful reader, they also contain information about where the economy appears to be going.

To help prepare you for such information gathering, this book will introduce you to most of the relevant data series released regularly. Just as important, it will introduce you to a body of macroeconomic theory. With the help of this theory, you should be able to discern the forces at work in the economy at any given time. This understanding should enable you to make pretty good guesses about where the economy might be heading. To go beyond this level of understanding, you might want to turn to a professional macroeconomic forecaster for more specific predictions. The last chapter of this book is intended to prepare you for such contacts.

Although some people find macroeconomic theory exciting, others may find it rather dry. If you belong to the latter category, you may perceive it as a seemingly endless collection of curves and formulae that seem far removed from business reality. You may wonder about the point of going through all that if all you need to learn is just "what the numbers mean." Usually, however, raw numbers need to be put into a more suitable form before they take on any useful meaning. This "form" is what is needed to transform raw data into "in-form-ation." The study of macroeconomic theory helps you make such transformations. The following analogy with modern electronic hardware may illustrate this point.

A data disk is designed to store information. Most disks that you buy from the store, however, are not ready to accept information. They first need to be organized in a way that can enable them to "understand" the information you want to store on them. This organizing is called formatting, and you no doubt are used to formatting your disks before you use them. The point is that the human mind also benefits from some organizing—formatting, if you will—to help it put day-to-day macroeconomic information in the right context. Although some macroeconomic insights probably are obvious enough to be acquired without the help of rigorous theory, a body of theoretical insights can help you reach further.

You probably also are aware that macroeconomics is a field with competing theories. This book will introduce you to a number of them. In order to avoid confusing you with too many approaches at the same time, however, we will introduce them gradually. After first presenting a theoretical approach that has become known as neo-Keynesian, we will look at how parts of the analysis would change under other approaches. Although familiarity with more than one approach is useful, experience suggests that it is easier to grasp alternative approaches after you have become conversant with one of them.

The need for information has risen with the growing globalization of the economic environment. Beyond knowing his craft, the craftsman before the industrial revolution needed some rough information about the demand for his craft in his own community, but not much more. The industrial revolution introduced the regional and the national market, as well as the business cycle, and hence the need for information about the national economy. The international revolution has extended this information need to the global level. Even if your company produces strictly for the home market and is without foreign competition (for example, the real-estate industry), your business is affected in subtle but important ways by overseas events. A good example is interest rates, which can be influenced, say, by changes in the German discount rate or by the decisions of a Japanese industrial group to buy or not to buy U.S. Treasury bills.

In addition to giving you theoretical insights and access to current data, this book introduces some simple statistical tools that will enhance your ability to follow the signs of the times. Although this is not a textbook on statistics, the next chapter, a review of some basic statistical techniques, should be helpful.

2 STATISTICAL TOOLS

Statistical analysis forms the link between theory and reality in macroeconomics. Scholarly researchers use statistical techniques to test their theories against real-world data. Managers use them to extract information for decision making.

Macroeconomic analysis does not always rely on formal, statistical methods. People often use single experiences to support or illustrate their views, just as we used the case of a drop in the prime rate in Section 1.1 to illustrate some features of the economy.

Such examples can be quite useful for clarifying important issues, but they tend to hide the complexity of the real world, which may make many macroeconomic events look rather confusing and chaotic. This insight is important in itself and becomes clearest to those who work directly with statistical macroeconomic data. Furthermore, in order to detect patterns in this apparent chaos, you need a systematic approach. Macroeconomic theory and statistical methods form a natural pair of tools for this work.

This chapter provides an introduction to the statistical tools you will need for simple practical applications of macroeconomic analysis. Since the application of statistical methods in economics often goes under the name of **econometrics,** these tools also can be called basic econometric methods. We present only a brief summary of these methods, with an emphasis on practical applications rather than theoretical insights. The exposition is not mathematically rigorous—no proofs are provided.* Even so, the style is compact, so you probably will find it easier to read and comprehend this chapter if you already have had a full-semester course in probability and statistics. If you have not, this chapter will give you a brief and practical introduction to the tools you need to complete the data exercises in the rest of the book. You should be cautioned that a full appreciation of the value and the limitations of these tools requires both insight and experience. On the other hand, the availability of user-friendly computer software has placed them within the reach of people with minimal technical training. Used with caution, they can become powerful tools for managerial decision making.

---

* If you are interested in an exposition with mathematical rigor, you are referred to one of the many introductory textbooks in econometric methods, for example, J. Johnston, *Econometric Methods*, 3d ed. (New York: McGraw-Hill, 1988).

The exposition assumes that you are familiar with some basic statistical concepts, such as random variables (also called stochastic variables), probability distributions (including the normal distribution), and the expected value of a random variable. Beyond this, the chapter is technically self-contained. It contains a number of formulae that may be useful for reference; however, for macroeconomic analysis, developing a practical intuition for applications of the methods is much more important than memorizing the formulae.

2.1 MEANS, VARIANCES, COVARIANCES, AND CORRELATIONS

Consider a random variable y for which you have n observations, $y_1, \ldots, y_n$. The observations can be referred to as a **sample.** For macroeconomic variables, most samples are **time series;** that is, they are observations from time 1 through time n. The number of observations, n, also can be referred to as the **sample size** or—in time series—the **length** of the sample. As an example, we will use annual data for real Gross National Product (GNP) growth for the United States from 1958 through 1988. A complete definition of real GNP will be given in the next chapter. For now, it suffices to note that it is a comprehensive measure of the value of the country's output of goods and services. The term "real" means that, to compute the value, we use the prices prevailing in one particular year, so that the output measure is not influenced by inflation. Currently, 1982 prices are used to compute U.S. real GNP.

We work with growth rates of real GNP rather than its levels, because economists tend to consider the growth rate more descriptive of the state of the economy in relation to the business cycle. The growth rates are computed as percentage changes from year to year. Thus, if RGNP_t denotes the value of real GNP in year t and RGNP_{t-1} the corresponding level for the previous year, the growth rate for year t is computed as

$$y_t = 100 \times \frac{\text{RGNP}_t - \text{RGNP}_{t-1}}{\text{RGNP}_{t-1}}.$$

For example, since real U.S. GNP for 1987 and 1988 was 3,853.7 and 4,024.4 (billions of 1982 dollars), respectively, the growth rate for 1988 was

$$100 \times \frac{4,024.4 - 3,853.7}{3,853.7} = 4.43\%.$$

Based on this definition, our data sample now consists of y_1, the real GNP growth rate for 1958, which turned out to be -0.77% (that is, real

TABLE 2.1	REAL ANNUAL GNP GROWTH RATES FOR THE UNITED STATES, 1958–88.		
YEAR	GROWTH RATE (PERCENT)	YEAR	GROWTH RATE (PERCENT)
1958	−0.77	1974	−0.54
1959	5.84	1975	−1.26
1960	2.22	1976	4.89
1961	2.61	1977	4.67
1962	5.31	1978	5.29
1963	4.11	1979	2.48
1964	5.34	1980	−0.16
1965	5.79	1981	1.93
1966	5.79	1982	−2.55
1967	2.85	1983	3.57
1968	4.15	1984	6.78
1969	2.44	1985	3.35
1970	−0.29	1986	2.74
1971	2.84	1987	3.65
1972	4.98	1988	4.43
1973	5.19		

GNP declined by 0.77%), y_2, the real growth rate for 1959, 5.84%, and so on, until y_n, the real growth rate for 1988. The data are listed in Table 2.1 and shown graphically in Figure 2.1. This time-series sample consists of 31 observations, so $n = 31$.

THE MEAN

The **sample mean** (or just **mean**) of this series is defined as a simple arithmetic average of all the observations:

$$(2.1) \qquad \bar{y} = \frac{1}{n} \sum_{t=1}^{n} y_t.$$

The subscript t refers to the observation number. (Other expositions use i to index observations. The t index is natural when the data are time series, which is most commonly the case in macroeconomics.) The mean of a series gives information about its central tendency. In our example, it tells what GNP growth has been on average, namely 3.2%. Perhaps this figure can be interpreted as a "normal" growth rate. Unless you have had a lot of experience with data work, you should check this result by inserting the actual data in Table 2.1 into the formula. Normally, we use computer programs for such tasks. However, it often is a good idea for beginners to work the data through the formula at least once before allowing the computer to take over.

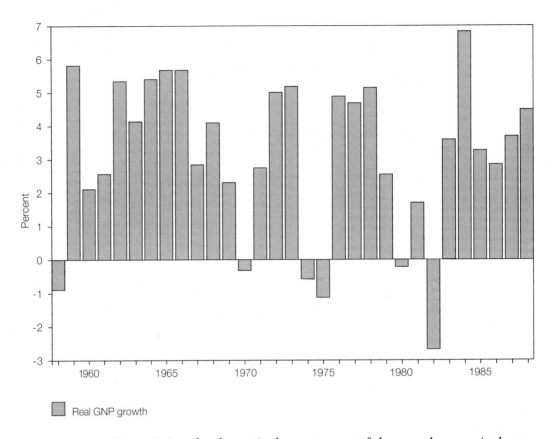

Real GNP growth

In statistics, the theoretical counterpart of the sample mean is the **expected value** (or **expectation**) of the variable, denoted μ_y:

$$(2.2) \qquad \mu_y = E y_t.$$

This formula implicitly assumes that all the observations have the same expectation. We will maintain this assumption in the following discussion.

The expected value indicates the central tendency of a distribution. Figure 2.2a illustrates this concept for an arbitrary random variable.

UNBIASEDNESS AND CONSISTENCY

While the sample mean is observable from actual data, the expected value is not; however, we can use the data to **estimate** it. A formula or a rule for constructing an estimate from the data is called an **estimator**, and the value of the estimator for a given data set is called an **estimate**. The sample mean is a common estimator for the expected value μ_y. It has the nice property of being **unbiased,** which means that the expectation of the sample mean $\bar{y}$ is equal to the expected value μ_y that we are trying to estimate.

FIGURE 2.2

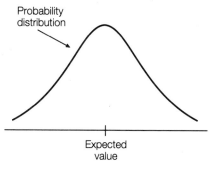

Probability distribution

Expected value

(a) Probability distribution and expected value for an arbitrary random variable.

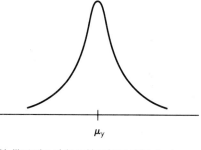

μ_y

(b) Illustration of the unbiasedness of the sample mean as an estimator for the theoretical expectation.

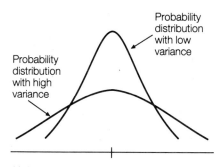

Probability distribution with low variance

Probability distribution with high variance

(c) Probability distribution of two variables with the same expected value, one with a low variance and one with a high variance.

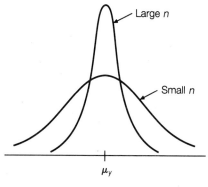

Large n

Small n

μ_y

(d) Illustration of the narrowing of the distribution for the sample mean as the sample size grows.

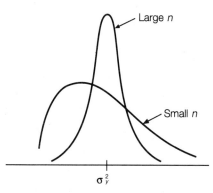

Large n

Small n

σ_y^2

(e) Illustration of the consistency and the small-sample biasedness of s_y^2 as an estimator of σ_y^2.

This result follows from the rule (which we will not prove) that the expectation of a constant times a sum equals the same constant times the sum of the expected values of each term going into the sum. In our case, the constant is $1/n$, so

$$(2.3) \qquad E(\bar{y}) = E\left(\frac{1}{n}\sum_{t=1}^{n} y_t\right) = \frac{1}{n}\sum_{t=1}^{n} Ey_t = \frac{1}{n}\sum_{t=1}^{n} \mu_y = \mu_y.$$

Unbiasedness does not guarantee that the estimator always gives the right answer. Typically, the estimate is sometimes too high and sometimes too small. However, an unbiased estimator cannot be *systematically* wrong in the upward or downward direction. If we can compute the sample means of many different samples for the same variable, then these estimates should equal the true value μ_y on average. This property is illustrated in Figure 2.2b.

If an estimator is unbiased, it is unbiased no matter how many observations arc in the sample. Intuitively, however, you may expect that a sample with many observations is more likely to provide the right answer than one with only a few observations. This notion corresponds to the concept of **consistency**. Essentially, *an estimator is consistent if the probability that the estimate differs from the true value becomes arbitrarily small as the number of observations grows toward infinity.*

In most cases of interest, the sample mean $\bar{y}$ is in fact a consistent estimate of the expected value μ_y, so that the probability of $\bar{y}$ being different from μ_y becomes very small in large samples. However, in order to develop an intuitive understanding of consistency, we first need to take a look at the concept of variance.

THE VARIANCE   The sample **variance** of y is defined as

$$(2.4) \qquad s_y^2 = \frac{1}{n}\sum_{t=1}^{n} (y_t - \bar{y})^2.$$

The sample variance provides information about how widely the observations are scattered around the sample mean. If all the observations are equal, they also will be equal to the sample mean, so the variance will be zero. The more they differ from each other, the larger the variance. The sample variance corresponds to a theoretical concept, also called variance, that is defined as

$$(2.5) \qquad V(y_t) = E(y_t - \mu_y)^2.$$

Sometimes we use the symbol σ_y^2 rather than $V(y_t)$ to denote the variance of y_t. As in the case of the expected value, formula (2.5) implicitly assumes that all the observations have the same variance σ_y^2. We will maintain this assumption.

Figure 2.2c illustrates the probability distributions of two random variables with the same expectation but different variances. The distribution of the variable with the higher variance is more stretched out (it has "thicker tails"), which indicates that the observations for this variable are more likely to be extremely large or extremely small.

In our example, the sample variance is 5.6. This is a somewhat awkward number, however, because it is expressed in units of squares of percentage points. For this reason, we often use the **standard deviation**, which is denoted s_y (σ_y as a theoretical concept) and defined as the square root of the variance. It thus is expressed in the same units as the observations—in our case, percentage points. For our example, the sample standard deviation is 2.4 percentage points. In a somewhat loose sense, this number may be interpreted as a typical deviation of the GNP growth rate from its mean.

For random variables whose behavior can be well approximated by the **normal distribution** (sometimes called the "bell curve" from its geometric shape), we can be more specific about the meaning of the standard deviation. For such a variable, there is a two-thirds probability that a given observation lies between one standard deviation below and one standard deviation above the expected value. In our example, one standard deviation below the mean is $3.2 - 2.4 = 0.8$ percentage points, while one standard deviation above is $3.2 + 2.4 = 5.6$ percentage points. Thus, we can expect two-thirds of the real GNP growth rates to lie between 0.8 and 5.6 percentage points. Normally distributed variables also have a 95% probability that any given observation lies between two standard deviations below and two standard deviations above the expected value, which in our example translates into the interval from $3.2 - 2 \times 2.4 = -1.6$ percentage points to $3.2 + 2 \times 2.4 = 8.0$ percentage points. A quick count of the data in Table 2.1 shows that 21 of the 31 observations in fact lie between 0.8 and 5.6 percentage points, while 30 out of 31 fall in the range between -1.6 and 8.0 percentage points. Thus, the data in the table follow the normal distribution very closely in this regard.

MORE ON CONSISTENCY

We can use the variance as a tool to help us understand the concept of consistency. Consider again the sample mean $\bar{y}$ as an estimator of the expected value μ_y. We already have found that the expected value of $\bar{y}$ is just μ_y itself, so $\bar{y}$ is an unbiased estimator. It also is a well-known result (although we will not prove it here) that the variance of $\bar{y}$ is σ_y^2/n, and the standard error consequently is $\sigma_y/\sqrt{n}$. Suppose again that the behavior of y can be approximated well by the normal distribution. Then we can apply the above discussion of the standard deviation to this formula, and we find that there is a 95% chance that the sample mean lies between $2\sigma_y/\sqrt{n}$ below and $2\sigma_y/\sqrt{n}$ above the true but unknown value

μ_y. For our example, this means that we can conclude, with 95% confidence, that the sample mean lies in a band between $2 \times 2.4/\sqrt{n} = 0.9$ percentage points below and 0.9 percentage points above μ_y, which we are trying to estimate.

Note that the width of this band is inversely related to the number of observations n. If n increases to 50, the band shrinks to 0.7 percentage points above and below μ_y; if $n = 100$, this number declines further to 0.5. The distribution of $\bar{y}$ *narrows* as the sample size grows, as illustrated in Figure 2.2d. Thus, if only we can find enough observations, we can be reasonably sure that the estimator $\bar{y}$ "hits the target" μ_y not only on average but *exactly*. This is the essence of consistency. The shrinking variance (and standard deviation) of the estimator $\bar{y}$ as the sample size grows illustrates what we mean when we say that $\bar{y}$ is a consistent estimator of μ_y.

We also can use the sample variance to illustrate another desirable property of consistent estimators. It is a well-known result (although, again, we will not show it here) that the expected value of s_y^2 is not σ_y^2, but $(1 - 1/n)\sigma_y^2$. Thus, s_y^2 is a *biased* estimator of σ_y^2. This is not a great problem, because it can be remedied simply by using $n - 1$ instead of n as the denominator in formula (2.4). However, it is worth noting that the magnitude of the bias, $(1/n)\sigma_y^2$, is inversely related to the sample size. In fact, since this quantity approaches zero as n grows to infinity, it is reasonable to state that *the bias disappears in large samples.*

The sample variance s_y^2 is a consistent estimator of the theoretical variance σ_y^2. The disappearance of the bias in large samples is not sufficient to prove this result; however, this observation nevertheless illustrates an important aspect of consistency. Consistent estimators hit the target in *large* samples even if they are off the target on average in *small* samples. Although unbiasedness in small samples is desirable, it often is even more important to be able to reach the truth "eventually" in large samples. The distribution of s_y^2 for various sample sizes is illustrated in Figure 2.2e.

COVARIANCE AND CORRELATION

Only exceptionally is statistical analysis in macroeconomics limited to one variable. Typically, we are interested in how the various macroeconomic variables influence *each other*. Information about such influence can be found in the degree to which the variables tend to move together. A measure of how two variables move together is called their **covariance.**

Suppose we study two variables, x and y. We will continue to use GNP growth as our y-variable. For our x-variable, we will use the growth rates in the real supply of money. As our measure of the money supply, we will use the relatively broad monetary aggregate M2. Roughly, M2 is the total of cash in circulation, the balances on most bank accounts, and money market funds. A more complete definition will be given in Chapter 4. The money supply is measured in dollars without adjustment for inflation. For reasons that will become apparent later in the book, such an adjustment can be made by dividing the money-supply figure for each year by a measure of the overall price level for that year. This process makes the resulting figure the "real" money supply. For this purpose, we use a measure of the overall price level called the GNP deflator, which we will study further in Chapter 3 as well as in Part IV. We construct growth rates for the real money supply in the same way as for real GNP. Table 2.2 presents the data for real GNP growth and real M2 growth together, and Figure 2.3 shows them together in the same graph. For reasons that will become apparent in Section 2.2, Table 2.2 also includes the observations for 1956 and 1957.

Let $\bar{x}$ denote the sample mean for x, defined in analogy with $\bar{y}$. The sample covariance between x and y then is defined as

$$(2.6) \qquad s_{xy} = \frac{1}{n} \sum_{t=1}^{n} (x_t - \bar{x})(y_t - \bar{y}).$$

Clearly, if GNP growth tends to be above average when the money growth is above average, and vice versa, then their covariance is posi-

TABLE 2.2   ANNUAL GROWTH RATES FOR REAL GNP AND THE REAL MONEY SUPPLY (M2) FOR THE UNITED STATES, 1956–88.

YEAR	REAL GNP	REAL M2	YEAR	REAL GNP	REAL M2
1956	2.06	−1.61	1973	5.19	3.08
1957	1.67	−0.82	1974	−0.54	−2.64
1958	−0.77	2.65	1975	−1.26	−0.43
1959	5.84	3.37	1976	4.89	6.28
1960	2.22	2.05	1977	4.67	5.55
1961	2.61	5.73	1978	5.29	1.14
1962	5.31	5.58	1979	2.48	−0.51
1963	4.11	6.75	1980	−0.16	−0.95
1964	5.34	6.19	1981	1.93	−0.15
1965	5.79	5.29	1982	−2.55	2.68
1966	5.79	2.89	1983	3.57	8.38
1967	2.85	3.95	1984	6.78	4.13
1968	4.15	3.12	1985	3.35	5.86
1969	2.44	0.71	1986	2.74	5.58
1970	−0.29	−1.37	1987	3.65	3.37
1971	2.84	6.14	1988	4.43	1.80
1972	4.98	7.47			

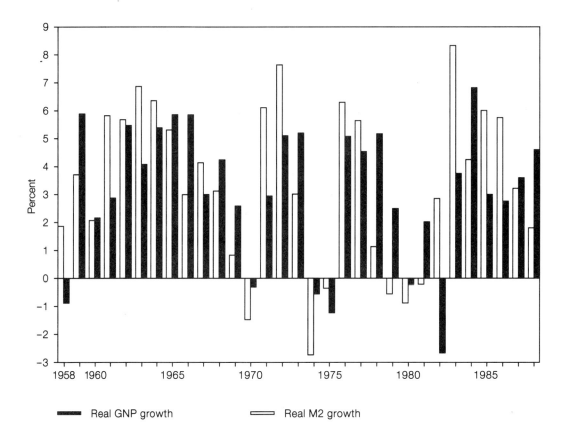

■ Real GNP growth   ▭ Real M2 growth

FIGURE 2.3

Annual growth rates in real GNP and the real money supply (M2) for the United States, 1958–88.

tive. Conversely, a negative covariance results if the GNP growth rate tends to be below average when the money growth rate is above average. In our example, the covariance is 3.7, indicating that real money growth and real GNP growth tend to move in the same direction. As is apparent from Figure 2.3, their comovement is somewhat irregular, but there is a *tendency* for the two variables to move in the same direction *on average*. When macroeconomic variables move together, it is mostly in this irregular, or *stochastic*, sense.

Corresponding to the sample covariance is the theoretical covariance. Let μ_x denote Ex_t. Then the definitional formula for the theoretical covariance can be written as

$$(2.7) \qquad \sigma_{xy} = E(x_t - \mu_x)(y_t - \mu_y).$$

You probably have suspected by now that the sample covariance is a consistent estimate of the theoretical covariance in most interesting cases.

Apart from its sign, the covariance says very little about the nature of the relationship between the two variables. More information can be obtained from the **correlation coefficient.** The sample correlation coefficient and the theoretical correlation coefficient are defined as

$$(2.8) \qquad r_{xy} = \frac{s_{xy}}{s_x s_y} \quad \text{and} \quad \rho_{xy} = \frac{\sigma_{xy}}{\sigma_x \sigma_y},$$

respectively. Since the standard deviation of a variable is always positive, the correlation coefficient shares the sign of the covariance. Thus, a positive covariance implies a positive correlation, and vice versa. Furthermore, it can be shown that the correlation coefficient always lies between 1 and −1. A value close to 1 or −1 indicates a close positive or negative relationship, respectively, while a correlation coefficient close to zero indicates that the relationship between the two variables is not very clear. When the correlation is zero, we say that the two variables are **uncorrelated** with each other.

In our case, the correlation coefficient is 0.56. This number is a rather clear indication that the two variables tend to move in the same direction but that the relationship is far from perfect.

The other way to transform the covariance into more useful information is to compute a **regression coefficient.** This coefficient tells something about *how much* the GNP growth rate is likely to change when the money growth rate changes. Regression analysis is our next topic.

2.2 REGRESSION THEORY

Regression analysis starts with the **regression model.** In general, a regression model specifies a stochastic variable as a linear function of another variable, except for random disturbances. To continue our example, we may specify real GNP growth as a linear function of real M2 growth plus a stochastic disturbance:

$$(2.9) \qquad y_t = a + bx_t + e_t.$$

Here, as before, y_t and x_t denote the real GNP growth rate and the real M2 growth rate, respectively, at date t. The new variable e_t denotes the **random disturbance** that may make y_t deviate from the linear function of x_t. It reflects the fact that the comovement is stochastic rather than exact. It also often is called the **residual** of the regression model, because the random variation in this variable represents a residual remaining after we have tried to explain the variation in y_t as the result of variation in x_t. The symbols a and b denote the **coefficients** or **parameters** of the model. It is common to refer to a as the **intercept** and b as the **slope** coefficient of the equation. The purpose of the regression analysis is to use the data for x and y to come up with numerical estimates for these parameters.

LEAST-SQUARES ESTIMATION

Regression analysis estimates the values of the coefficients a and b as **least-squares estimates.** The basic logic of least-squares estimation is as follows. Define the **sum of squared residuals,** S, as

$$(2.10) \qquad S = \sum_{t=1}^{n} e_t^2 = \sum_{t=1}^{n} (y_t - a - bx_t)^2.$$

Least-squares estimation chooses those values for a and b that minimize the sum of squared residuals for the given data for x and y. Since S is a simple, unweighted sum of squared residuals, this estimation method often is also called **ordinary least squares,** abbreviated **OLS.** Elementary calculus can be used to derive formulae for the OLS estimates as the values of a and b that minimize S. We write these estimates as $\hat{a}$ and $\hat{b}$. The appendix to this chapter shows that the formulae for computing the least-squares estimates $\hat{a}$ and $\hat{b}$ can be written as

$$(2.11) \qquad \hat{b} = \frac{s_{xy}}{s_x^2} \quad \text{and} \quad \hat{a} = \bar{y} - \hat{b}\bar{x}.$$

This formula shows that the slope coefficient is indeed a transformation of the covariance. Because the variance of x is always positive, the regression coefficient $\hat{b}$ always has the same sign as the covariance and the correlation coefficients.

For our example, the estimates are easy to compute using the formulae for $s_{xy}, s_x^2, \bar{x},$ and $\bar{y}$ from the preceding section (you may compute $\bar{x}$ and s_x^2 as an exercise). The results are $\hat{a} = 1.59$ and $\hat{b} = 0.47$. Thus, the estimated regression model is

$$(2.12) \qquad y_t = 1.59 + 0.47x_t + e_t.$$

The interpretation of this equation is as follows. For every percentage-point rise in the growth rate of real M2, the corresponding rate for real GNP rises by almost one-half a percentage point. If real money growth is zero, real GNP growth is likely to be 1.59%. However, it easily may deviate from this value because of the stochastic disturbance e_t.

Figure 2.4 shows the observed values of x and y in a diagram with x measured along the horizontal axis and y along the vertical axis. Such a diagram is called a **scatter plot.** The upward-sloping line is the graph of

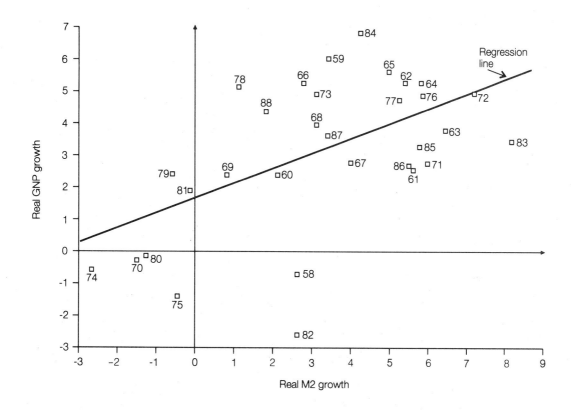

FIGURE 2.4

Scatter diagram with regression line for annual growth in real M2 and real GNP for the United States.

the estimated function in equation (2.12) (ignoring the error term) and is called the *regression line*. Geometrically, the least-squares method positions the regression line so as to minimize the sum of the squares of the vertical distances between this line and each observation point.

PROPERTIES OF LEAST-SQUARES ESTIMATES

The least-squares estimates are functions of the observed values of x and y, which are random variables, so the estimates are random variables as well. To understand them a little better, it is useful to go over some of their properties. Suppose the following assumptions are satisfied:

1. The error term e has an expected value of zero and is uncorrelated with the right-hand variable x.

2. The variance of the error term, denoted σ^2, is the same for all observations.

3. The error terms for different observations are uncorrelated with each other.

Assumption 1 means essentially that the stochastic disturbance e represents only those movements in the left-hand variable y that are unrelated to the right-hand variable x. Assumption 2 says that the error terms for different observations are equally likely to be small or large, so the respective observations for x and y carry similar amounts of information about the relationship between these two variables. Assumption 3 says that knowing, say, that the value of the error term was large for one particular year implies no suggestion as to the error term's likely value for the following year. Consequently, except for purely random movements in e, a change in the value of y can be fully ascribed to its relationship with x, which is what we are trying to estimate.

Given these assumptions, the OLS estimates can be shown to have the following properties:

1. They are unbiased and consistent in the sense discussed in Section 2.1. The unbiasedness implies that they can be expected to be correct on average, while the consistency implies that they should be "right on target" in large samples.

2. They are efficient in the sense that their variances are lower than those of other relevant alternative estimators. Thus, OLS is more likely than the alternatives to produce estimates that are close to the true values of a and b.

3. They are distributed according to the normal distribution. This property allows us to use the theory for normal distributions to analyze regression results. If the disturbance terms e_t are distributed normally themselves, this property is exact. Otherwise, it holds as an approximation provided the sample size is sufficiently large. A sample size of 30 or more usually is considered large enough for this purpose.

STANDARD ERRORS

Since the OLS estimators are random variables, they don't always hit their targets in small or medium-sized samples, such as 30 years. While a sample size of 30 may be large enough to make the coefficient estimates approximately normally distributed, it is usually not large enough to make them come out as equal to the true, unknown coefficient values we are trying to estimate. They sometimes turn out too high and sometimes too low. As for any stochastic variable, the tendency for these estimates to lie above or below their expected values is reflected in their *variances*.

To see this better, you might want to look back at Figure 2.2c and think of it as describing the distributions of OLS estimators. If the variance is small, the distribution is concentrated around the expected value, which, for an OLS estimator, is the true value of the coefficient. The likelihood is high that the estimate is close to its target. When this is the case, we may say that the estimate is reliable or "tight." Alternatively, if the variance is large, it is quite likely that the estimate has hit far from the target. In this case, the estimate gives us very little information about the value of the coefficient.

The appendix to this chapter derives the following formulae for the variances of the OLS estimates $\hat{a}$ and $\hat{b}$ of the slope and the intercept of the regression model, respectively:

$$(2.13) \qquad V(\hat{b}) = \frac{\sigma^2}{ns_x^2} \quad \text{and} \quad V(\hat{a}) = \frac{\sigma^2}{n}\left(1 + \frac{\bar{x}^2}{s_x^2}\right).$$

A few features of these formulae are worth noting. First, since the variance of the slope coefficient depends inversely on s_x^2, it is smaller the larger the variation in the observations of the x-variable over the sample. This is intuitive: it is easier to get a reliable picture of how y varies in response to changes in x if we have a wide range of observations for x. Second, the variances of both the coefficient estimates are proportional to the variance σ^2 of the residual term e_t. Intuitively, the less random "noise" from the residual term, the easier it is to get a reliable picture of the covariation between x and y. Third, the inverse relationship to the sample size n for both variances reflects the fact that larger samples provide more reliable information. As we saw in Section 2.1, this relationship reflects the consistency property.

Since the variance σ^2 of e_t is unknown, the variances of the estimates cannot be computed directly. However, a consistent estimate of σ^2 is available as

$$(2.14) \qquad s^2 = \frac{1}{n}\sum_{t=1}^{n} \hat{e}_t^2 = \frac{1}{n}\sum_{t=1}^{n} (y_t - \hat{a} - \hat{b}x_t)^2.$$

When s^2 is substituted for σ^2 in the variance formulae, we obtain consistent estimates of the variances for the OLS coefficient estimates. The square roots of these variance estimates are called the **standard errors** of the estimates. The term "standard error" is sometimes abbreviated s.e., so that s.e.$(\hat{b})$ is the standard error of $\hat{b}$. It is customary to report the standard errors together with the estimates (for example, in parentheses right under the estimated parameter values). The square root of s^2 also usually is reported as the **standard error of the regression (SER).**

In practice, the denominator n in formula (2.14) is often replaced by $n - 2$. The number 2 reflects the number of coefficients (slope and intercept). As in the case of the sample variance for the variable y in equation (2.4), this correction makes s^2 an *unbiased* estimate of σ^2. In large samples, it obviously does not make a big difference—if the sample size is 100, it doesn't matter much whether you divide by $n = 100$ or by $n - 2 = 98$.

Finally, it is customary to report the value of a statistic called the **co-**

efficient of determination. This coefficient is defined as the square of the correlation coefficient between the left-hand side variable y_t and the value of the linear function used to approximate it, namely $\hat{a} + \hat{b}x_t$. Since it is the square of a correlation coefficient, it usually is referred to by the shorter name R^2. It always lies between zero and 1. It can be interpreted as the *share of the variance of y that can be explained by the regression model*. With these additions, our regression can be reported as follows:

$$(2.15) \qquad y_t = 1.59 + 0.47\, x_t + e_t, \quad \text{SER} = 2.03, \quad R^2 = 0.31.$$
$$ (0.57) \quad (0.13)$$

Since the standard errors are consistent estimators of the square roots of the variances of the estimates, they provide information similar to the variances about the reliability of the estimates. A low standard error for an estimate indicates that the estimate of this parameter is "tight" or reliable, while an estimate with a large standard error is highly uncertain.

TESTING HYPOTHESES ABOUT REGRESSION COEFFICIENTS

The technique of statistical hypothesis testing is useful in a number of contexts. In regression analysis, it is indispensable. Its value may seem obvious in the case of scholarly research, but it also can be extremely useful for management decisions. Suppose, for example, you have reason to believe that the Federal Reserve will tighten its monetary policy in the sense that the real growth rate of M2 will decline, say by as much as 4 percentage points. According to equation (2.15), you then would expect a reduction in the real GNP growth rate of almost 2 percentage points. That reduction could bring the economy close to a recession, for which your company would need to prepare. However, suppose a colleague questions the relationship in (2.15) on the grounds that the regression coefficients are random, claims that the true slope coefficient is zero, and alleges that the fact that the estimate came out as large as 0.47 is just the result of chance.

The disagreement between your colleague and you obviously is of practical importance. If you are right, your company should prepare for leaner times; if your colleague is right, preparing for continued expansion is more appropriate. A natural question, then, is whether it is possible to determine objectively who is right. The answer is that statistical hypothesis testing can help you do so, at least in a probabilistic sense.

To check your colleague's claim, you can test the hypothesis that the true value of the slope coefficient b is zero. Suppose this hypothesis is true. From property 3 of the least-squares estimates, we know that $\hat{b}$ is distributed normally with expected value b. Under the hypothesis that $b = 0$ (that is, given that the hypothesis $b = 0$ is true), this means that $\hat{b}$ is distributed randomly around the expected value zero. From our discussion of variance and consistency in Section 2.1, we know that this property means there is only a 5% probability that the estimate comes out as more than 2 times its standard deviation above its expected value of zero or less than 2 times its standard deviation below this value. Actually, the exact measure here is 1.96 times the standard deviation. We can restate this insight in a more compact way as follows: There is only a 5% probability that the absolute value of the estimate exceeds 1.96 times its standard deviation.

Figure 2.5a illustrates what the distribution of the regression coefficient would be under the hypothesis that $b = 0$. The shaded region is that part of the distribution where the estimated coefficient exceeds 1.96 times its standard deviation in absolute value.

If you know this standard deviation, a simple way of checking if the estimate lies in this region is to divide the coefficient estimate by its standard deviation and see if the resulting ratio exceeds 1.96 in absolute value. If it does, you can conclude that the probability of this outcome is only at most 5% if $b = 0$ is true. With 95% certainty, you would know that your colleague is wrong. In statistical language, we would say that the hypothesis can be *rejected on the 5% level*. We also could say that $\hat{b}$ is *significantly different from zero on the 5% level*.

If the null hypothesis is true, the ratio of the coefficient to its standard deviation should be a *unit* normal variable, that is, a normally distributed variable with expectation zero and variance 1. A table of this distribution is reproduced in the back of this book. It confirms that the probability of such a variable exceeding 1.96 in absolute value is exactly 5%.

However, there is a hitch. Remember, we cannot compute the standard deviation of the coefficient estimate because the variance σ^2 of the error term is unknown. What we *can* compute is a *consistent estimate*, namely, the standard error. Suppose we divided the coefficient estimate by the standard error rather than by the unknown standard deviation.

FIGURE 2.5

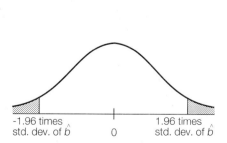

(a) Illustration of the probability distribution of the slope coefficient $\hat{b}$.

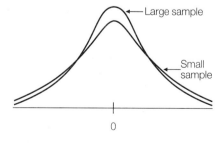

(b) Illustration of the *t*-distribution for different sample sizes.

Would the resulting ratio have a unit normal distribution? The answer is that it depends on the sample size. In most cases of interest, a sample size of 30 or more is large enough for the distribution of this ratio to be closely approximated by the unit normal. For smaller samples, this ratio is distributed according to the **t-distribution,** which also is tabulated in the back of this book. For this reason, the ratio of the coefficient estimate to its standard error is commonly referred to as the coefficient's **t-ratio** or **t-value.**

The table for the t-distribution is organized such that each row tabulates the distribution for a given number of **degrees of freedom.** For a simple regression like equation (2.9), the degrees of freedom are $n - 2$, where the number 2 again reflects the two coefficients—the slope and the intercept.

The main difference between the t-distribution and the unit normal is that the t-distribution graph has somewhat thicker tails. Thus, for small samples, the absolute value of the t-value needs to be a little more than 1.96 in order to justify rejection on the 5% level of the hypothesis that the true coefficient value is zero. However, for 20 or more degrees of freedom, the difference from the normal distribution usually is not large. As a rule of thumb, a coefficient value can be considered to be significantly different from zero on the 5% level if its t-value exceeds 2 in absolute value.

Since our sample has $31 - 2 = 29$ degrees of freedom, rejection of the hypothesis requires the t-value to be 2.05 or larger. In fact, it turns out to be 3.69, which exceeds 2.05 by a comfortable margin.* This result suggests that your friend's hypothesis can be rejected rather decisively.

Testing the hypothesis that the intercept is zero may be less interesting; however, it can be done in exactly the same way. Compute the t-value as the ratio of the intercept estimate and its standard error and check whether it exceeds 2.05 in absolute value. In our example, the t-value for the intercept is 2.79. Thus, this hypothesis can be rejected as well, although not quite as decisively as the hypothesis for the slope coefficient.

Occasionally, it is useful to test the hypothesis that a regression coefficient equals some value other than zero. For example, you might want

---

*If you compute this t-value directly from the estimates as presented in equation (2.15), you will get $0.47/0.13 = 3.62$ rather than 3.69. The reason for the slight difference is that the estimates presented in equation (2.15) have been rounded off to two decimal places. Thus, 3.62 is the ratio of two slightly inaccurate numbers, while 3.69 is the result of a more accurate computation. Most software packages present t-values that contain only a minimum of rounding errors. Whenever you have a choice, you should use these precomputed t-values, as we have done here and in the rest of this chapter.

to test the hypothesis that $b = 1$. The procedure then is to take the difference between the estimated and the hypothesized value and divide by the standard error of the coefficient: $(\hat{b} - b)/\text{s.e.}(\hat{b})$. With our data and the hypothesized value $b = 1$, this expression would be $(0.47 - 1)/0.13 = -4.00$. This number is the t-statistic for the hypothesis that $b = 1$. Thus, this hypothesis can be rejected quite decisively.

REGRESSION WITH A LAGGED VARIABLE

Suppose again that you are interested in how monetary policy affects real GNP growth. When you see new money-supply data being released, you want to form an idea about how the news is likely to affect GNP growth and hence the general business climate. Now, remember that the money-supply data that is released unavoidably covers a time period *before* the time you see the figures. For example, the money-supply figures for the year 1988 were released in January 1989. By that time, you probably would not be very interested in the effect on GNP growth for 1988, but you would care a lot about the effect on GNP growth for 1989. In order to estimate this effect, you need a model describing the relationship between real GNP growth at time t and real M2 growth at time $t - 1$. In other words, you need a model of the form

$$(2.16) \qquad y_t = a + bx_{t-1} + e_t.$$

[Note that a, b, and e_t in this equation are different from the corresponding symbols in equation (2.9).] The variable x_{t-1} is called a **lagged variable.** It shows the value of real M2 growth, but with a one-period (in this case, one-year) lag. In our example, for $t = 1$, y_t is the real GNP growth rate for 1958, whereas x_{t-1} is the real M2 growth rate for 1957. For $t = 2$, y_t is the real GNP growth rate for 1959 and x_{t-1} the real M2 growth rate for 1958, and so on. This is why the data for 1957 were included in Table 2.2.

Suppose we run this regression. It is done exactly the same way as above, except that the lagged variable x_{t-1} everywhere takes the place of x_t. The results are

$$(2.17) \qquad y_t = 1.20 + 0.60x_{t-1} + e_t, \quad \text{SER} = 1.66, \quad R^2 = 0.54.$$
$$ (0.45) \; (0.10)$$

The interpretation is as follows. For each 1-percentage-point change in the real growth rate of M2, real GNP growth is expected to change by 0.6 percentage points *the following year.* If real M2 growth happens to be zero, the expected real GNP growth rate for the following year is 1.2%. Again, both coefficient estimates are significantly different from zero on the 5% level. In fact, the significance for the slope coefficient is even stronger than in the previous regression. The magnitude of the estimated coefficient is greater as well, indicating that the effect on real

GNP growth may be even stronger the year after than the year the money growth takes place.

You may be able to see this feature of the data by inspecting the graph in Figure 2.3 once again visually. Notice the tendency for a change in the real money growth rate to be followed by a change in the real GNP growth rate in the same direction *the following year.*

MULTIPLE REGRESSION

Our discussion may have given you the impression that regression always involves only two variables, one on the left and one on the right of the regression equation. This is what we call **simple regression.** However, there is no need for regression to be "simple." **Multiple regression** generalizes the technique to many variables. In general, a multiple regression equation has the following form:

$$(2.18) \qquad y_t = a + b_0 x_{0t} + b_1 x_{1t} + \cdots + b_m x_{mt} + e_t.$$

Here, $x_{0t}, x_{1t}, \ldots, x_{mt}$ are the values at date t of $m + 1$ different variables, labeled x_0, x_1, and so on. For example, if y is real GNP growth as above, then x_0 might be the growth rate in M2, x_1 the growth rate in M3 (an even broader measure of money supply), and so on as far as you wish to include variables in the regression. In the multiple-regression case, the formulae for the parameter estimates and the standard errors become a good deal more complicated. Fortunately, however, there is no need for you to study them because the logic and the interpretation are precisely the same as in the case of simple regression. In particular, if assumptions 1–3 can be assumed to be true (and assumption 1 is generalized to hold for *all* the variables on the right of the equation), then properties 1–3 of the least-squares estimates continue to hold in the multiple regression case. Perhaps the most important property is the normality of the coefficient estimates, at least in large samples (30 observations or more). This means that the t-values can be used for hypothesis testing just as in the simple regression case. Tests of whether a coefficient value is zero are a useful tool in determining which variables to include or exclude in a given regression.

Obviously, the computation of multiple regression is more complicated than that of simple regression. However, you can safely leave this task to a computer package. It suffices here to note two related details. First, in the computation of the variance of the error term in multiple regression, it is customary to replace the denominator n in equation (2.14) by $n - k$, where k is the number of coefficients, including the intercept. This correction is a generalization of the division by $n - 2$, which we discussed for simple regression, to the case of multiple regression. Second, the number $n - k$ also defines the degrees of freedom for the appropriate t-distribution for testing of individual coefficients in a multiple regression.

As a practical example of multiple regression, consider regressing current real GNP growth on current *and lagged* M2 growth. Since we have found significant relationships between real GNP growth and both current and lagged real M2 growth in simple regressions, it may be interesting to see how they perform when we include them simultaneously in a multiple regression. The model then is

$$(2.19) \qquad y_t = a + b_0 x_t + b_1 x_{t-1} + e_t.$$

The data for this regression are contained in Table 2.2. Application of least squares yields the following estimates:

$$(2.20) \quad y_t = 0.66 + 0.26 \, x_t + 0.49 \, x_{t-1} + e_t, \quad \text{SER} = 1.54, \quad R^2 = 0.62.$$
$$\qquad\qquad (0.47) \quad (0.11) \qquad (0.10)$$

The interpretation is as follows. If this year's real M2 growth rate changes by one percentage point *and last year's real M2 growth rate was unchanged*, then this year's real GNP growth rate is likely to rise by about a quarter of a percentage point. On the other hand, if last year's real M2 growth rate rose by one percentage point *while this year's real M2 growth is unchanged*, then this year's real GNP growth rate is likely to rise by about one-half of a percentage point. If both this year's and last year's real M2 growth rates are zero, then this year's real GNP growth rate is likely to be two-thirds of one percent—the value of the intercept.

In this case, the intercept, whose *t*-value is 1.4, is not significantly different from zero. Both slope coefficients are significant, although the significance is more convincing for the lagged growth rate.

DISTRIBUTED LAGS

Quite often in macroeconomics we feel confident that one variable, such as real M2 growth, influences another variable, such as real GNP growth, but we are uncertain about the time it takes for this influence to make itself felt. Equation (2.20) suggests that, for these two variables, a significant part of the influence can be found during the same year the change in the money growth takes place. However, an even larger part of the influence seems to come the following year. This delayed effect became visible when we included the lagged variable in the regression. To see how long it takes before the *full* effect has occurred, we may include as additional variables the money growth rates of two and three years ago or more and see how many lags it takes before the coefficients of the more remote lags taper off to zero.

Such a model is referred to as a model with a **distributed lag.** It has the form

$$(2.21) \qquad y_t = a + b_0 x_t + b_1 x_{t-1} + \cdots + b_m x_{t-m} + e_t.$$

Here *m* is the length of the longest lag included, sometimes called the maximum lag length. Equation (2.19) is a simple example of a distributed lag model with maximum lag length 1.

For a slightly more general example, we might include one more lag, so that $m = 2$. (Note that now you will need the 1956 data in Table 2.2.) The results then become

(2.22) $y_t = 0.77 + 0.24\ x_t +0.52\ x_{t-1} - 0.05\ x_{t-2} + e_t,$
           (0.57) (0.12)   (0.13)   (0.12)

           SER $= 1.56,$ $R^2 = 0.62.$

Note that the estimated coefficient for the real money growth rate of two years ago is very small and not significantly different from zero. Thus, it appears that the influence on real GNP growth of a change in the money growth rate is felt only for the current year and the following year. To confirm this, we could have examined even longer lags than two years, but equation (2.22) should be sufficient to illustrate the principle involved.

THE *F*-TEST

A generalization of the *t*-test is available for the case of multiple regression. Suppose that, as in equation (2.22), you estimate the model in (2.21) for $m = 2$ and wish to test the hypothesis that the full effect of a change in the real M2 growth rate occurs within the same year. Then your hypothesis is that *both b_1 and b_2* are zero. One way to do this would be to look at their individual *t*-statistics; however, a more powerful procedure looks at both coefficients at the same time. This procedure generates a statistic called an **F-statistic.** Like the *t*-statistic, the *F*-statistic is tabulated in the back of this book. It can be computed as follows. First, run the regression with all the variables included; call this the **unconstrained** regression. Make a note of its R^2 value; call it the unconstrained R^2, or R_u^2. (Your software package also may print out an "adjusted" R^2; that is useful in other contexts, but not here.) Then run the regression again, but *without those variables whose coefficients you want to test.* Call this the **constrained** regression. In our case, this is equation (2.15). Make a note of its R^2 also, which you call the constrained R^2, or R_c^2. Now compute the *F*-statistic according to the following formula:

(2.23) $$F = \frac{(R_u^2 - R_c^2)/q}{(1 - R_u^2)/(n - k)}.$$

Here q is the number of coefficients you are testing (that is, the number of variables you are excluding from the constrained regression), k is the total number of coefficients in the unconstrained regression (*including* the intercept), and n is the number of observations as usual.

The tabulations for the *F*-statistic show different entries for different "degrees of freedom." The number of coefficients tested, q, is called the "degrees of freedom in the numerator"; the table contains a separate column for each value of q. The number of observations minus the total number of coefficients, k, is called the "degrees of freedom in the denominator"; the F-table has a row for each such degree of freedom shown. To find the correct entry for your problem, look up the cell for the appropriate combination of degrees of freedom. If the table does not show the exact combination of degrees of freedom you need, look for one close to it.

The numbers in these cells are the **critical values** on the 5% and the 1% significance levels, respectively. They have the following meaning: If the hypothesis being tested is true, there is only a 5% probability of observing an F-value greater than or equal to the 5% critical value. Similarly, there is only a 1% probability of observing an F-value greater than or equal to the 1% critical value. Thus, for example, if the F-statistic you compute exceeds the 5% critical value in the table, you can reject the hypothesis on the 5% significance level. In other words, you can conclude with 95% confidence that at least one of the parameters you have tested is different from zero. In contrast, if the computed F-value falls short of the 5% critical value, the hypothesis that all (or both) of them are zero cannot be rejected.

Applied to our example, we find the unconstrained R^2 in equation (2.22) to be $R_u^2 = 0.62$, while the constrained R^2 is shown in equation (2.15) to be $R_c^2 = 0.31$. Furthermore, note that $n - k = 31$ (observations) $- 4$ [coefficients in equation (2.22), including the intercept] $= 27$ degrees of freedom in the denominator, while $q = 2$ (the number of coefficients tested) degrees of freedom in the numerator. Substituting these values into formula (2.23), we obtain an F-value of 11.01, which greatly exceeds the 5% critical value of 3.35. Thus, we can safely reject the hypothesis that all the effect on real GNP growth of a change in the real M2 growth rate occurs within the same year that the change in the money growth takes place.

2.3 FORECASTING

Equation (2.17) states the empirical relationship between real M2 growth and the following year's real GNP growth as inferred from annual data for 1958–88. Suppose now that you find yourself in January 1989 and see the release of an estimate of real M2 growth for 1988 as 1.80%. Then you can substitute this number into the right side of equation (2.17) and obtain a **regression-based forecast** of real GNP growth for 1989:

$$y_{1989}^f = 1.20 + 0.60\, x_{1988} = 1.20 + (0.60)(1.80) = 2.3\%.$$

(The superscript f stands for *forecast*.) In other words, you can use the estimated regression equation together with the new data release for M2 to forecast that real GNP growth for 1989 will be 2.3%.

The actual real GNP growth rate for 1989 turned out to be 3.0%. Thus, the forecast was not perfect. It resulted in a **forecast error**—the difference between the actual and the forecasted value—of 0.7 percentage points. Nevertheless, the forecast was successful in predicting that the slowdown in the real money growth rate from 3.4% in 1987 to 1.8% in 1988 would be followed by a slowdown in the real GNP growth rate as well. This slowdown was apparent in the reduction in the real GNP growth rate from 4.4% in 1988 to 3.0% in 1989.

Forecasts can be generated by many methods other than regression. In a number of situations, however, a regression model presents the most efficient method of summarizing the information on which the forecast is based. In fact, it can be shown that, under assumptions 1–3 in the preceding section, regression-based forecasting is unbiased and efficient in the following sense. It is **unbiased** in that the expected value of the forecast error is zero. In other words, the forecast is accurate on average even if it never hits the target exactly. Errors on the upside tend to be balanced by errors on the downside. The regression forecast is **efficient** in that the variance of the regression forecast error is smaller than with any other forecast that can be constructed as a linear function of the right-hand variables involved. Of course, this efficiency property does not preclude the possibility that pulling additional variables—and hence additional information—into the analysis can improve the performance of the forecasts. What it means is that when additional information is used it should be put into a regression framework.

2.4 COMPLICATIONS IN REGRESSION ANALYSIS

You may feel that assumptions 1–3 for the validity of OLS estimation are rather strong. They are, and it is easy to find cases in which some of them are violated. This section discusses what to do in such cases. Consider first assumption 1. This assumption is essential for the unbiasedness and consistency of least squares. The most common example of a violation of this assumption in economic models is the case of **simultaneity,** which arises whenever y_t is a function of x_t at the same time as x_t is another function of y_t.

SIMULTANEITY

As a practical example, suppose as before that real GNP growth is a function of real money growth in the sense that higher money growth raises the real GNP growth rate. Suppose, however, that monetary policy also depends on what happens to real GNP. In particular, suppose that if real GNP declines or grows slowly the central bank will ease monetary policy in an attempt to stimulate the economy, so that the money supply will grow faster than usual. Conversely, very high growth in real GNP might make the central bank concerned about possible inflationary pressures, so that monetary policy is tightened and the money growth rate declines. However, suppose the central bank also looks at other criteria for monetary policy, which we for convenience can think of as random. Then we have not one but *two* equations characterizing the relationship between the two growth rates:

(2.24) $$y_t = a + bx_t + e_t, b > 0,$$

(2.25) $$x_t = A + By_t + E_t, B < 0.$$

Here the first equation is a reproduction of equation (2.9), while the second describes the influence of real GNP growth on monetary policy. The negative slope reflects the tendency, which we just assumed, for monetary policy to ease in the face of economic decline and vice versa. The new disturbance term E_t represents the other forces influencing monetary policy.

At first sight, these two equations might seem to contradict each other. While the first equation stipulates a positive relationship between the two variables, the second suggests that they move in opposite directions. However, on further thought you should realize that the two equations rather represent opposing forces that tend to balance each other. For any given combination of random disturbances e and E, there will be a growth rate in the money supply that (via the first equation) produces exactly the GNP growth rate that would make the central bank happy to implement the same money growth rate it started with.

Mathematically, such a solution is called a simultaneous solution to the system consisting of the two equations (2.24) and (2.25). Figure 2.6a illustrates the solution to this system when both the stochastic disturbances are zero. The upward-sloping line is the graph of equation (2.24), representing the assumed positive effect of real money growth on real

FIGURE 2.6

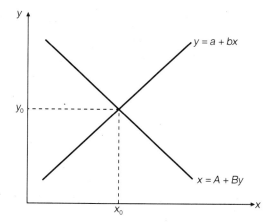

(a) Graph of a simultaneous equation system.

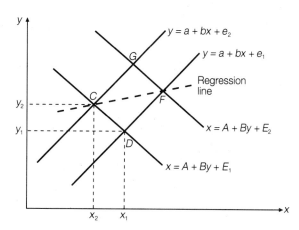

(b) Simultaneous equation model with stochastic disturbances.

GNP growth. Similarly, the downward-sloping line represents the negative effect of real GNP growth on the real money growth rate in equation (2.25). The solution is given by the coordinates x_0 and y_0 of the point at which the two curves intersect, which satisfies both equations.

Figure 2.6b illustrates how the solution values for x and y change as a result of stochastic movements in the error terms. Suppose first that the error term in equation (2.24) rises from e_1 to e_2 in the figure, while the other error term remains unchanged at E_1. Then the intersection of the two curves moves from the point labeled D to the point labeled C. The value of the real GNP growth rate rises from y_1 to y_2. This is what we usually expect from an equation like (2.24). Note, however, that the real money growth rate changes as well, declining from x_1 to x_2. But if a change in e results in a change in x, then *e and x cannot be uncorrelated.* Thus, assumption 1 is violated.

Figure 2.6b also illustrates what will happen if we try to regress y on x in this situation. As the two disturbances move from e_1 to e_2 and from E_1 to E_2, respectively, the solution of the system shifts between the points C, D, F, and G in the figure. These solutions are what we observe as data points. Thus, they define a scatter plot of the type shown in Figure 2.4. Figure 2.6b indicates the regression line that could be fitted to this scatter plot. You can see that it does not look at all like the graph of equation (2.24), which you are trying to estimate. It is much flatter because it is influenced by the second relationship between the two variables, which goes in the opposite direction. *The estimate of the slope coefficient is biased downward.*

Correcting a bias due to simultaneity can sometimes be quite difficult. Usually, some kind of *a priori* assumption is needed. An example of such an assumption would be if, in our case, we were willing to assume that $B = 0$ and that the two random disturbances e and E are uncorrelated. It should be clear from equation (2.25) that this assumption essentially amounts to saying that x is a random variable that is uncorrelated with e. Then assumption 1 for the validity of OLS estimation is satisfied, and equation (2.24) can be estimated by OLS without bias.

More sophisticated methods—which also use some sort of *a priori* assumptions—have been developed for the general case. They rely on a technique called instrumental variables, a technique that lies beyond the scope of this brief overview.

SERIAL CORRELATION AND HETERO-SKEDASTICITY

Consider now the possibility of assumption 2 or 3 being violated, while assumption 1 holds. The case in which assumption 2 fails to hold is referred to as **heteroskedasticity,** which is a Greek term for the fact that the variance of the disturbance term varies over time. If assumption 3 fails to hold, we have a case of **serial correlation** in the disturbance term; that is, the current disturbance is correlated with past disturbances.

For both cases, the following result is extremely important: *Although heteroskedasticity and serial correlation may affect the efficiency of ordinary least-squares estimation (property 2), OLS remains unbiased and consistent, and the estimates continue to be distributed normally.* Thus, OLS-based forecasts may miss more often and by larger amounts than necessary, but there is no systematic tendency to overpredict or underpredict.

The efficiency of OLS estimation and forecasting, however, does fail in these cases. In the case of heteroskedasticity, it fails because OLS gives equal weight to all observations, while an efficient procedure would give greater weight to the more reliable observations, namely, those whose disturbance terms have lower variances. In the case of serial correlation, past residuals can help predict current residuals and thus reduce the variance of the disturbance terms. OLS is inefficient in this case because it ignores that information.

Methods have been developed to improve on OLS in these cases as well. An important class of such methods goes under the name of Generalized Least Squares. Discussing these methods would take us beyond this simple survey; let us instead look briefly at an exception to the rule that serial correlation in the error term leaves OLS unbiased and consistent.

THE CASE OF A LAGGED DEPENDENT VARIABLE

Suppose your model postulates a relationship between a variable y and its own lagged value, y_{t-1}:

$$(2.26) \qquad y_t = a + by_{t-1} + e_t.$$

If you can also assume that the error term is uncorrelated with the lagged value of the dependent variable, y_{t-1}, OLS naturally retains its desirable properties. However, suppose the error term is serially correlated, so that e_t is correlated with e_{t-1}, and suppose the correlation is positive. Then a high value of e_t would make a high value of e_{t+1} likely as well. But we can also tell from equation (2.26) that a high value of e_t raises the value of y_t directly, so that y_t tends to be high when e_{t+1} is high. In other words, y_t is correlated with e_{t+1}, which also means that y_{t-1} is correlated with e_t. But we have already seen that a correlation between the residual and the variable on the right of a regression equation biases the coefficient estimates. Thus, *introducing a lagged dependent variable on the right of a regression in which the error term is serially correlated biases the OLS results.*

What OLS does in this case is produce an estimate for the slope coefficient that reflects not only this coefficient's true value but also the serial correlation in the error term. This combination represents a bias from the point of view of estimating the coefficient b. However, from the point of view of *forecasting* the next period's y-value, OLS does not result in a bias at all. The reason is that a good forecast based on this model should reflect *both* the influence of last year's y-value via the coefficient b *and* the information about this year's likely value of the error term that can be deduced from last year's error term. In this regard, OLS strikes exactly the right balance.

CHAPTER REVIEW

1. Statistical methods are helpful tools in the analysis of macroeconomic time series. The application of statistical methods to economic problems is called econometrics.

2. The mean of a series gives information about its central tendency, and the variance gives information about how widely the data are scattered around the mean.

3. Comovements between macroeconomic time series tend to be stochastic rather than exact. The direction of the comovement is measured by the covariance or the correlation, both of which always have the same sign. If the covariance between two series is positive, the series tend to move in the same direction, and if it is negative, the series tend to move in opposite directions. A zero covariance or correlation indicates no relationship between the series.

4. Regression estimation, also called estimation by ordinary least squares (OLS), is useful for evaluating parameter values in linear equations describing the relationship between data series. If the random disturbance is uncorrelated with the right-hand variables, OLS is unbiased and consistent. If, in addition, the disturbances have a constant variance and are uncorrelated with each other, OLS also is efficient.

5. A small standard error of a regression coefficient indicates that the estimate is highly reliable, while a large standard error indicates uncertainty about the coefficient estimate. If the *t*-ratio for a coefficient exceeds about 2 in absolute value, the coefficient is significantly different from zero on the 5% level, meaning that you can be 95% sure that it is different from zero. *F*-statistics can be used to test two or more parameter values at the same time in a multiple regression equation.

6. When regression equations have lagged variables on the right-hand side, they become useful tools for forecasting. The properties of regression-based forecasting with respect to unbiasedness and efficiency are similar to those of regression coefficients estimated by OLS.

7. The assumption that the regression residual is uncorrelated with the right-hand variables may be violated in simultaneous-equation models. In this case, OLS gives biased parameter estimates. Instrumental variables can be used to correct this bias.

8. Heteroskedasticity and serial correlation of the regression residual do not violate the unbiasedness and consistency of OLS, but they do make OLS inefficient and produce biases in the standard errors.

EXERCISES

1. Use a hand calculator and the data in Table 2.2 to compute the following.
   a. The sample means of the real growth rates of GNP and M2.
   b. The sample variances of the two series.
   c. The covariance of the two series.
   d. The regression coefficients *a* and *b* in equation (2.9).

   Whenever possible, use the results presented in the text as your answer guide.

2. Use a statistical software package to repeat the calculations in exercise 1.

3. Using a computer package, reproduce the results displayed as equations (2.17), (2.20), and (2.22) in the text.

4. Regress *quarterly* money growth rates of real GNP on real M2 growth rates for (a) the current quarter, (b) the previous quarter, and (c) both the current and the previous quarter. Comment on the differences from the corresponding results for the annual data.

5. With quarterly data on the real growth rates of GNP and M2, estimate distributed-lag models as in equation (2.21) with maximum lag lengths of 4 and 8, respectively. Carry out an *F*-test of the hypothesis that the true maximum lag length is 4. What do you conclude?

THINKING QUESTIONS

1. Assume that equation (2.9) satisfies assumptions 1–3. Suppose someone proposes another regression equation in which x is the variable on the left and y is the variable on the right. Can this equation satisfy assumptions 1–3 at the same time?

2. Explain in what sense equations (2.9) and (2.16) can be valid regression equations at the same time.

3. Explain the difference in the interpretation of the coefficient b for x_t in equation (2.9) and the corresponding coefficient b_0 for the same variable in equation (2.19).

4. Economic forecasters are often criticized because their forecasts frequently prove wrong. Is this the right way to criticize a forecaster? Why or why not?

5. Somewhat tongue-in-cheek, the average economist's motto has been described as "often wrong, but never in doubt." What does regression theory have to say about this attitude?

APPENDIX TO CHAPTER 2

This appendix derives the formulae for the OLS coefficients in a simple regression, as well as their expectations and variances.

FORMULAE FOR THE OLS COEFFICIENTS

The sum of squared residuals is

$$S = \Sigma\,(y_t - a - bx_t)^2.$$

The sum is assumed to be from 1 to n both here and in the rest of this appendix. To find the minimum of S, differentiate it with respect to the coefficients a and b and set the partial derivatives equal to zero. The estimates $\hat{a}$ and $\hat{b}$ must satisfy these equations:

(A.2.1) $\qquad \partial S/\partial a = -2\,\Sigma\,(y_t - \hat{a} - \hat{b}x_t) = 0,$

(A.2.2) $\qquad \partial S/\partial b = -2\,\Sigma\,(y_t - \hat{a} - \hat{b}x_t)x_t = 0.$

Let us divide both sides of (A.2.1) by $2n$ and sum up to get $-\bar{y} + \hat{a} + \hat{b}\bar{x} = 0$, which solves for $\hat{a}$ as $\hat{a} = \bar{y} - \hat{b}\bar{x}$. This is the second part of formula (2.11). Next, substitute this result into (A.2.2) and divide both sides by $2n$ to get $-(1/n)\,\Sigma\,(y_t - \bar{y} + \hat{b}\bar{x} - \hat{b}x_t)x_t = 0$, which solves as

(A.2.3) $\qquad \hat{b} = \dfrac{(1/n)\,\Sigma\,(y_t - \bar{y})x_t}{(1/n)\,\Sigma\,(x_t - \bar{x})x_t}.$

Note that

$$(A.2.4) \qquad s_{xy} = \frac{1}{n}\,\Sigma\,(y_t - \bar{y})(x_t - \bar{x}) = \frac{1}{n}\,\Sigma\,(y_t - \bar{y})x_t - \frac{1}{n}\,\bar{x}\,\Sigma\,(y_t - \bar{y})$$

$$= \frac{1}{n}\,\Sigma\,(y_t - \bar{y})x_t,$$

where the last equality follows because $(1/n) \Sigma (y_t - \bar{y}) = \bar{y} - \bar{y} = 0$. An analogous derivation shows that $s_x^2 = (1/n) \Sigma (x_t - \bar{x})x_t$. Substitution of these results into (A.2.3) gives $\hat{b} = s_{xy}/s_x^2$, which is the first part of formula (2.11).

EXPECTED VALUES OF THE OLS COEFFICIENTS

By an argument analogous to that for (A.2.4), it also follows that $s_{xy} = (1/n) \Sigma (x_t - \bar{x})y_t$. In this formula, substitute $a + bx_t + e_t$ for y_t to get

$$s_{xy} = \frac{1}{n} \Sigma (x_t - \bar{x})(a + bx_t + e_t) = b \frac{1}{n} \Sigma (x_t - \bar{x})x_t$$

$$+ \frac{1}{n} \Sigma (x_t - \bar{x})e_t = bs_x^2 + \frac{1}{n} \Sigma (x_t - \bar{x})e_t.$$

Substituted into the formula for $\hat{b}$, this result implies

$$\hat{b} = b + \frac{(1/n) \Sigma (x_t - \bar{x})e_t}{s_x^2}.$$

Define $w_t = (1/n)(x_t - \bar{x})/s_x^2$. Then the above formula can be written as

(A.2.5) $$\hat{b} = b + \Sigma w_t e_t.$$

Since x and e are uncorrelated, w and e are uncorrelated as well. Now we can use two well-known rules about expectations. First, the expectation of a sum is the sum of the expectations of the individual terms, so $E(\Sigma w_t e_t) = \Sigma E(w_t e_t)$. Second, the expectation of two uncorrelated variables equals the product of their expectations, so $E(w_t e_t) = Ew_t Ee_t = 0$ because e_t has a zero expectation. Thus,

(A.2.6) $$E\hat{b} = b + \Sigma Ew_t Ee_t = b,$$

which proves that $\hat{b}$ is unbiased.

Now substitute (A.2.5) into the formula for $\hat{a}$ to get

$$\hat{a} = \bar{y} - \hat{b}\bar{x} = \bar{y} - (b + \Sigma w_t e_t)\bar{x}.$$

Next, substitute $a + b\bar{x} + \bar{e}$ for $\bar{y}$ and define $v_t = \bar{x}w_t$, so that

(A.2.7) $$\hat{a} = a + b\bar{x} + \bar{e} - b\bar{x} - \Sigma v_t e_t = a + \bar{e} - \Sigma v_t e_t.$$

Since v_t is a function of x's only, it is uncorrelated with e_t. Thus,

$$E\hat{a} = a + E\bar{e} - \Sigma Ev_t Ee_t = a,$$

which proves that $\hat{a}$ is unbiased as well.

VARIANCES OF THE OLS COEFFICIENTS

We will derive the variance formulae only for the case in which x is a nonstochastic variable. Look at formula (A.2.5). First, we can apply the rule that the variance of a constant plus a stochastic variable equals the variance of the stochastic variable, so $V(\hat{b}) = V(\Sigma w_t e_t)$. Now, since x is a nonstochastic variable, w is nonstochastic as well. Furthermore, since the e_t are uncorrelated with each other (assumption 3 in the main text), the terms $w_t e_t$ are uncorrelated with each other as well. Then we can use the rule that the variance of a sum of uncorrelated terms is the sum of the variances of each term, so $V(\hat{b}) = \Sigma\, V(w_t e_t)$. Finally, use the rule that the variance of the product of a nonstochastic and a stochastic variable equals the square of the nonstochastic variable times the variance of the stochastic variable, so

$$V(\hat{b}) = \Sigma\, w_t^2 V(e_t) = \sigma^2 \Sigma\, w_t^2.$$

Now, from the definition of w_t,

$$\Sigma\, w_t^2 = \frac{1}{n^2 s_x^4} \Sigma\, (x_t - \bar{x})^2 = \frac{n s_x^2}{n^2 s_x^4} = \frac{1}{n s_x^2},$$

so

(A.2.8) $$V(\hat{b}) = \frac{\sigma^2}{n s_x^2}.$$

This is the first part of formula (2.13).

To find the variance of $\hat{a}$, note first from (A.2.7) and from the definition of the sample mean of e that

$$\hat{a} = a + \bar{e} - \Sigma\, v_t e_t = a + (1/n) \Sigma\, e_t - \Sigma\, v_t e_t = a + \Sigma\, (1/n - v_t) e_t.$$

The rules about variances we have just applied then imply that

$$V(\hat{a}) = \sigma^2 \Sigma\, (1/n - v_t)^2 = \sigma^2 \Sigma\, (1/n^2 + v_t^2 - 2v_t/n).$$

From the definition of v_t, we note that

$$\bar{v} = \bar{x}\bar{w} = (\bar{x}/s_x^2)(1/n) \Sigma\, (x_t - \bar{x}) = 0,$$

which makes the last term disappear. Furthermore,

$$\Sigma\, v_t^2 = \bar{x}^2 \Sigma\, w_t^2 = \frac{\bar{x}^2}{n s_x^2} \quad \text{and} \quad \Sigma\, \frac{1}{n^2} = \frac{1}{n},$$

so

(A.2.9) $$V(\hat{a}) = \sigma^2 \left(\frac{1}{n} + \frac{\bar{x}^2}{n s_x^2} \right) = \frac{\sigma^2}{n} \left(1 + \frac{\bar{x}^2}{s_x^2} \right).$$

This is the second part of formula (2.13).

3

SOME FACTS ABOUT BUSINESS CYCLES AND INFLATION

The histories of most industrialized economies show a combination of growth and fluctuations. Recessions and even depressions have interrupted periods of solid growth and then been followed by recoveries and expansions. Price stability has been replaced by inflationary periods. Economic slowdowns have often accompanied the curbing of inflation, while at other times they have coincided with accelerated inflation.

This chapter takes you on a brief journey through these movements as they have occurred since World War II. If your attention is directed toward business decisions for the future, you may wonder at first why you should be interested in this history. After a little further thought, however, you probably will realize that the recent past defines the context in which we attempt to make sense of the present and the future. More specifically, we can point to four reasons why the history of fluctuations in the economy should be studied.

First, this history provides us with the data that offer clues about the causes and effects behind the fluctuations. Economic theory can suggest reasonable hypotheses about the mechanisms at work, but factual data are indispensable tools for *testing* these hypotheses. Second, we can use the data to *predict the future*. Insights about the underlying causes and effects are useful for this purpose; if we can identify a cause in the present, we sometimes can predict its effects in the future.

Third, government authorities want to learn from the lessons of the past in order to develop suitable policies. Fourth, business managers are interested in the formation of economic policy because it affects them directly or indirectly. They may seek to influence the policy-making process by offering advice, by lobbying actively, or by participating in the public debate. At least as important, understanding the policy-making process can enable managers to anticipate their own government's or other countries' governments' next step. We will study the policy-making process in some detail in Chapters 4 and 12.

We start by studying the movements in the Gross National Product for the U.S. economy. These movements naturally lead us to consider the concept of **business cycles.** Business cycles are composed of recessions and expansions, characterized by decline and growth in real GNP, respectively. We look specifically at some of the postwar recessions in the United States. Next, we study the movements during the same period in the economies of West Germany and Japan as representative of the industrialized countries in Europe and Asia, respectively. We pay particular attention to the comovement of business cycles across national borders. As a third issue, we look in a little more detail at the behavior of consumption and investment activity in relation to business cycles. Fourth, we look at the history of inflation and how inflation and business cycles are related. The closing section summarizes the main events in terms of both business cycles and inflation over the last three decades.

3.1 BUSINESS CYCLES

The supreme indicator of business cycles is the Gross National Product, or GNP. It is natural to start with a definition of this concept.

DEFINING GNP

The **Gross National Product,** or **GNP,** of the United States can be defined as

> *the total value of final goods and services, evaluated at market prices, produced by U.S. factors of production within a specified period of time.*

The definition of GNP for other countries is analogous. The details of the definition are discussed further in Chapter 15 and need not concern us here. For the study of business cycles, the main point to note is that GNP is a dollar measure of the total output of the country's production activity. It sums up the value of production in agriculture, the automobile industry, the steel industry, financial services, fast-food restaurants, and so on. When GNP reaches new highs, the economy is doing well; if GNP stagnates, the economy has problems.

NOMINAL AND REAL GNP

If the definition is followed literally, we obtain what is called **nominal GNP.** Nominal GNP is problematic, because it is influenced by inflation in a somewhat awkward way. Suppose, for example, that no production volumes changed from one year to the next but all prices rose by 5%. Then, by the above definition, GNP would rise by 5% because it is "evaluated at market prices." Most of us, however, do not feel that such an increase means the economy is doing better in any real sense. Instead, we might say that inflation took away all the apparent improvement. To guard against such measurement problems, most analysts look instead at **real GNP.** Real GNP is defined in the same way as nominal GNP, except that the term "market prices" is replaced by "base-year market prices." By this term, we mean that in order to figure out the values of the production volumes in the various industries we use the prices of

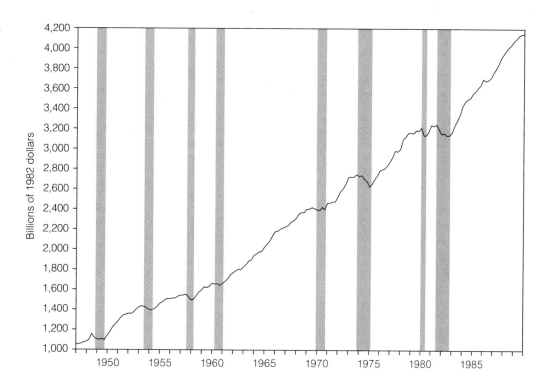

FIGURE 3.1

Real Gross National Product for the United States. Quarterly data for 1947–89. The shaded areas indicate recessions.

THE HISTORY OF REAL GNP IN THE UNITED STATES

the respective goods and services as they prevailed in some given year, called the **base year.** Because these prices are held fixed in the computation, changes in real GNP reflect only changes in quantities and not changes in prices. Currently, 1982 is used as the base year. This means that real GNP is expressed in 1982 prices, usually in units of billions of 1982 dollars.

Figure 3.1 illustrates the history of U.S. real GNP since World War II. The figure is based on *quarterly* data for GNP; therefore, it reflects fluctuations from quarter to quarter as well as over longer periods of time. The first feature to notice is a substantial and persistent growth over time. From 1946 through 1989, real GNP grew by a total of 278%, which averages out to 3.1% per year.* Part of the reason for this growth is the 76% growth of population during the same period, which means that more people were available to produce goods and services. However,

---

*This average is computed as the rate that would result in a 278% total improvement over 43 years if real GNP grew at this rate every year. It is different from 278% divided by 43, because, with a growing economy, the base for computation of the percentage growth rate changes from year to year.

real GNP growth outpaced population growth; there was an average improvement in real GNP *per capita* of 1.8% per year.

Growth in per capita GNP could be interpreted as an average improvement in the standard of living, although it should be clear that real GNP is not a fully satisfactory measure of the quality of life. For example, neither the pleasure of breathing clean air nor the value of work in the home is included in real GNP. For this reason, we will concentrate on real GNP as a measure of marketable production rather than of human well-being.

The second feature to note about the history of real GNP is that growth has not been uniform. Economic growth has been sometimes strong, at other times weak, and on some occasions negative. Periods of economic decline are called **recessions.** If real GNP declined for two calendar quarters in a row, most economists would call that event a recession. Sometimes, shorter declines are called recessions as well, provided the decline is sharp enough. However, there is no unambiguous rule that dictates when a decline should be called a recession and when it should not.

THE DATING OF BUSINESS CYCLES

Because of this ambiguity, it sometimes is difficult to reach agreement among the experts as to whether a particular event qualifies as a recession. In the United States, the task has been made easier by the fact that most experts defer to the judgment made by a standing committee of the National Bureau of Economic Research (NBER), a leading private economic research institution headquartered in Cambridge, Massachusetts. The committee is charged with determining when recessions begin and end—the so-called **peaks** and **troughs** of business cycles. Thanks to this committee, a universally accepted **business-cycle chronology** has been established for the United States. Table 3.1 lists this chronology for the recessions that have occurred since the end of World War II. In Figure 3.1, these recessions are marked as shaded areas. Table 3.1 also lists the duration of each recession as well as its depth, as measured by the percentage decline in real GNP and the increase in the unemployment rate. The average recession during this period lasted 11 months and reduced real GNP by 2.6%.

The recessions have exhibited a good deal of variation, however. The two recessions interrupting the long growth period from 1958 to 1973 were relatively shallow and brief. The two that occurred during the first 10-year period after World War II also were relatively short, but the second one, in 1953–54, was deeper than average in terms of real GNP decline (both were deeper than average in terms of unemployment). Many observers view these recessions as associated with the problems of adjusting from a wartime to a peacetime economy. The 1957–58 recession was brief, but it was the deepest between World War II and 1973.

The two recessions in 1973–75 and 1981–82 stand out as the longest

TABLE 3.1   U.S. RECESSIONS SINCE WORLD WAR II ACCORDING TO THE BUSINESS CYCLE CHRONOLOGY OF THE NATIONAL BUREAU OF ECONOMIC RESEARCH

MONTH RECESSION STARTED	MONTH RECESSION ENDED	DURATION IN MONTHS	DECLINE IN REAL GNP (PERCENT)[a]	RISE IN CIVILIAN UNEMPLOYMENT RATE[b]
November 1948	October 1949	11	2.0	4.2
July 1953	May 1954	10	3.0	3.4
August 1957	April 1958	8	3.6	3.3
April 1960	February 1961	10	1.1	2.0
December 1969	November 1970	11	1.1	2.6
November 1973	March 1975	16	4.3	4.4
January 1980	July 1980	6	2.4	1.9
July 1981	November 1982	16	3.4	3.6

[a] From the highest quarterly level before the recession to the lowest level during the recession.

[b] From the lowest monthly level during or immediately before the recession to the highest level during or immediately following the recession.

recessions since World War II. The 1973–75 recession also was the deepest, while the 1981–82 recession saw the highest unemployment rate since World War II (we will discuss the unemployment rate in more detail shortly). Section 3.4 introduces some attempts to explain these recessions. For now, we note that they roughly coincided with the sharp increases in the price of oil in the 1970s and 1980s and with the attempt to contain inflation by monetary tightening in the early 1980s.

REAL GNP GROWTH RATES

An alternative perspective is obtained by looking at the *growth rates* for real GNP. In Chapter 2, we defined the rate of growth for real GNP (denoted RGNP) from one year to the next (specifically, from year $t - 1$ to year t) as follows:

$$\text{Annual growth rate of real GNP} = 100 \times \frac{\text{RGNP}_t - \text{RGNP}_{t-1}}{\text{RGNP}_{t-1}}$$

(3.1)

$$= 100 \times \left(\frac{\text{RGNP}_t}{\text{RGNP}_{t-1}} - 1 \right).$$

We also could use this formula for the growth from quarter to quarter. We simply would need to redefine the subscripts t and $t - 1$ to refer to consecutive quarters instead of years. However, the quarterly growth rates we would get would have an average magnitude of only about one-fourth the typical year-to-year growth rate. Because many people find this difference inconvenient, it is customary to define quarterly growth rates, computed *at annual rates*, as the percentage change in real GNP that would have resulted if the actual growth for the quarter had con-

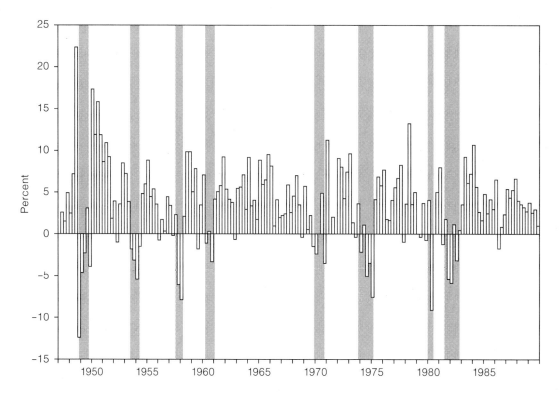

FIGURE 3.2

Growth in the real Gross National Product for the United States, 1947–89. Quarterly data at annual rates. The shaded areas indicate recessions.

tinued for four quarters in a row. The definition of this growth rate from quarter $t - 1$ to quarter t is as follows:

$$(3.2) \quad \frac{\text{Quarterly real GNP growth}}{\text{rate at annual rate}} = 100 \times \left[\left(\frac{\text{RGNP}_t}{\text{RGNP}_{t-1}} \right)^4 - 1 \right].$$

The conversion from quarterly to annualized rates thus is obtained by raising the ratio of this quarter's to last quarter's real GNP level to the power 4, because there are four quarters in a year. The analogy to the year-to-year growth rate becomes clear when you consider the formula that follows the second equal sign in equation (3.1); there the corresponding ratio implicitly is raised to the power 1.

If you are used to working with compound interest, you probably will notice that formula (3.2) is similar to the formula for compound interest. For this reason, we sometimes refer to the quarterly growth rates measured at annual rates as "including compounding."

The quarterly growth rates in U.S. real GNP since World War II are displayed in Figure 3.2. Not surprisingly, most of the negative growth rates show up in the shaded areas, that is, during recessions. In fact, all the recessions shown, except the one in 1980, have at least two quarters of negative growth. Occasionally, negative growth has occurred between recessions as well, but these have been isolated events with modest GNP declines and have not been followed by major changes in the business climate.

Another fact worth noting is the substantial variation in the GNP growth rate *between* recessions. In fact, the graph suggests that only a small part of the historical variation in real GNP growth is due to business-cycle movements. The rest is due to seemingly random movements from quarter to quarter. Many of these movements are difficult to explain or predict with existing theories. They also make the task of forecasting real GNP growth very difficult.

A third point worth noting is the convention of declaring a recession over as soon as it has "bottomed out" and the economy has started to grow again. This may seem natural if attention is focused on growth rates; however, if you focus on levels, as in Figure 3.1, you notice that the end of the recession does not necessarily mean that the economy's activity level is back to where it was before the recession. For example, in the second quarter of 1975, which was the first quarter after the 1973–75 recession, real GNP was 69 billion 1982 dollars lower than in the third quarter of 1973, which was the last quarter before the onset of the recession. Similarly, real GNP in the first quarter of 1983 was 78 billion 1982 dollars lower than in the third quarter of 1981.

The end of a recession *does* mean the beginning of the following **recovery.** The recovery implies a return to positive growth. Sometimes, spectacular growth rates can be observed during recovery periods, such as in 1958–59 or 1983–84. Such extraordinary growth is needed if the *level* of real GNP is to return to the growth path it was following before the recession, as illustrated in Figure 3.3, but the GNP level does not always

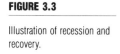

FIGURE 3.3

Illustration of recession and recovery.

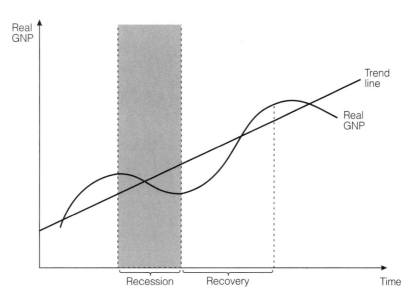

catch up in this manner after a recession. The experience after the 1970 downturn is a case in which no significant catch-up can be identified.

UNEMPLOY-MENT RATES

Table 3.1 indicates that the depth of a recession also can be measured by the associated increase in the **unemployment rate.** In fact, this measure seems to agree quite well with the percentage real GNP decline. The unemployment rate is computed as follows. First, the number of unemployed people is defined as the number of people 16 years of age and older who are available and looking for work but are not gainfully employed. Then the **labor force** is defined as the sum of the number of unemployed people and employed people. Finally, the unemployment rate is computed as the number of unemployed as a percentage of the labor force. We usually look at the civilian unemployment rate, which means that the armed forces are excluded from the numbers.

A graph of the monthly data for civilian unemployment for the United States since the late 1940s is shown in Figure 3.4. The shaded areas again identify business cycles. The main pattern is clear: The unemployment rate rises during recessions and peaks when a recovery starts. It declines gradually during the recovery period and then stays fairly stable until the next recession. The pattern of the unemployment rate is similar to that of real GNP growth (although with the opposite sign, for obvious reasons), with two exceptions. First, the unemployment rate does not fluctuate nearly as much between recessions as does the real GNP growth rate. In this sense, the unemployment rate is a somewhat more reliable indicator of business cycles than the real GNP growth rate. Its smoothness certainly makes it much easier to forecast. Second, the U.S. unemployment rate shows an upward trend during the 1970s and early 1980s that is unmatched by the real GNP growth rate. Except for the short recession in 1980, every new recession during this period raised the unemployment rate to a new high. Similarly, almost every new expansion period seemed less successful in bringing the unemployment rate down. This pattern was broken in the late 1980s. Even at the end of this decade, however, the unemployment rate hovered a little above 5%, well above the 3–4% range typical of the expansion periods before 1970.

A number of factors have been proposed as explanations for this long rise in the unemployment rate. One important factor is the demographic structure of the U.S. population. The "baby boom" has boosted the number of people competing for jobs. Furthermore, a growing number of women have joined the labor force since the 1950s, and women historically have had higher unemployment rates than men at all stages of the business cycle. Another factor is the realignment of industries that took place in the United States in the 1970s, with rising job opportunities in industries such as services and electronics combined with declin-

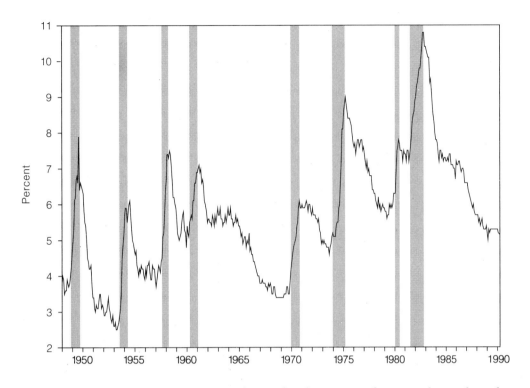

FIGURE 3.4

The civilian unemployment rate for the United States. Monthly data for January 1948–March 1990. The shaded areas indicate recessions.

ing employment in some traditional industries such as textiles and steel production. The adjustment problems associated with this realignment may have contributed to the high unemployment rates.

The experience of the late 1980s, however, suggests that this situation may be turning around. The "baby-boom" generation has grown older, and the growth in the number of female job seekers is slowing down. The realignment among industries also appears less dramatic now than during the seventies. Barring further disturbances such as a major recession, the unemployment rate again may dip below the 5% level in the 1990s.

BUSINESS CYCLES IN THE INTERNATIONAL ECONOMY

The U.S. economy does not exist in a vacuum. Many countries in Europe, North America, East Asia, and Australia are industrialized to about the same degree as the United States and have similar economic systems. It is both natural and important to ask whether the other industrialized countries experience business cycles as well and, if so, how these cycles are related to those in the United States.

To answer these questions, we could compare the behavior of real GNP over time for the United States and each other country, but given so many countries that would be a very cumbersome task. As a simpler alternative, we will look at West Germany and Japan as representative of the industrialized countries in Europe and Asia. Specifically, we will compare their real GNP growth rates and their unemployment rates with those of the United States and look for differences and similarities.

Quarterly GNP data did not become available for Japan and West Germany until the 1960s. Consequently, we base our comparison on the behavior of the *annual* real GNP growth rates. Figure 3.5 displays these rates for the United States, Japan, and West Germany in the same graph.

Two features stand out. First, overall growth in the postwar period has been much stronger in Japan than in the two other countries. West German growth also has been significantly stronger than that of the United States, especially in the 1950s and 1960s. Several reasons have been cited for these differences, one of the most prominent being that the U.S. economy was much more intact after World War II and thus started from a higher base. This was true in comparison not only with West Germany and Japan but also with most of the other industrialized countries, and these countries typically have experienced higher growth rates than the United States. Furthermore, Japan started from a particularly low base because industrialization came later in Japan.

FIGURE 3.5

Comparison of annual growth rates in real GNP for the United States, Japan, and West Germany, 1953–89. The shaded areas indicate U.S. recessions.

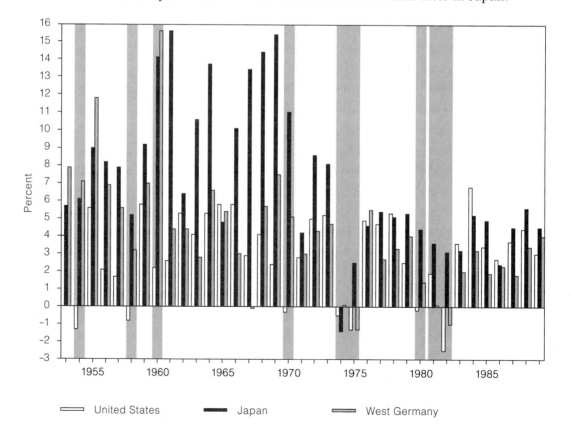

United States   Japan   West Germany

The second outstanding feature is that growth has been somewhat smoother outside the United States. The other countries also have experienced business cycles, but the recessions typically have not been as deep and the recoveries have been less dramatic. The next question is whether these business cycles, even if dampened, have coincided with those in the United States. To help answer that question, the shaded areas indicating recessions in the United States have been superimposed on Figure 3.5.

The evidence at this point turns out to be somewhat mixed. During some of the milder U.S. recessions, such as those in 1960–61 and 1969–70, the West German real GNP kept on growing more or less as usual. During the U.S. recessions of 1957–58 and 1980, West German growth took a pause but was not replaced by decline. However, during the deeper U.S. recessions of 1973–75 and 1981–82, West Germany—as well as the other European countries—experienced recessions as well. On the other hand, West Germany experienced a slight recession of its own in 1967. Furthermore, West German growth remained anemic for a long time after the 1982 recession, an experience representative of most of Western Europe, while the United States experienced a dramatic recovery.

The Japanese economy maintained positive real GNP growth throughout the postwar period, except for the important recession in 1974–75. It slowed down after 1973, but except for its one recession it has continued to maintain high growth rates by U.S. standards. At no point did the Japanese economy experience a recession of its own, although the relative slowdown in 1986 is worth noticing.

Figure 3.6 displays the monthly unemployment rates of the same three economies. This picture is strikingly different from that of Figure 3.5. Unlike the United States, the Japanese unemployment rate rose hardly at all during the 1974–75 recession. Despite a slight upward trend, the Japanese unemployment rate has remained extremely low throughout the postwar period. The West German unemployment rate started out even lower; it was elevated by the European recession in 1967 but returned to the 1% range shortly after. Then, after an increase to the 4–5% range around 1975, the West German unemployment rate declined very little during the expansion period of the late 1970s. This tendency was similar to what we already have observed for the United States, but more pronounced. The difference from the United States is seen even more clearly during the 1980s. After shooting up to the 9% range early in the decade, the West German unemployment rate has remained stuck at around 8%.

The lessons from these comparisons can be summarized as follows. Deep recessions tend to be world recessions, particularly in the case of recessions that coincide with international disturbances such as the oil

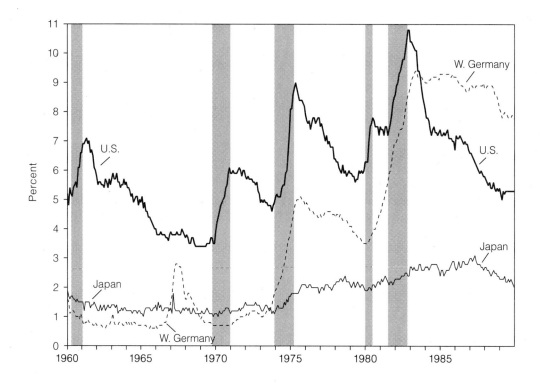

FIGURE 3.6

Comparison of monthly un-
employment rates for the
United States, Japan, and
West Germany, 1960–89.
The shaded areas indicate
U.S. recessions.

crises of the mid- and late seventies. Even in the absence of such global events, it seems plausible that recessions can spread because countries depend on each other as suppliers and customers. On the other hand, we noticed that the correlation is not perfect. The modern, global economy is a diverse economy, and events affecting the United States are not the only events that matter.

This diversity is evidenced even more clearly by the different behavior of unemployment rates. The mechanisms linking real GNP and unemployment seem to differ from country to country. Real GNP growth, therefore, appears to be a more reliable yardstick for evaluating and comparing economic performance.

3.2 GNP COMPONENTS AND THE BUSINESS CYCLE

Like most governments, the U.S. government maintains an accounting system, called the **National Income and Product Accounts,** to keep track of GNP and related variables. It breaks GNP down into four major **expenditure components:** Personal Consumption Expenditure, or consumption for short; Private Domestic Investment, or just investment; net exports; and government expenditure on goods and services.

Consumption refers to households' purchases of goods and services. The term **investment** in this context refers to the construction of new buildings, houses, machines, and other durable business equipment. It should not be confused with financial investment, which involves the acquisition of claims on assets that already exist. **Net exports** is the difference between exports and imports of goods and services. Thus, it can serve as a measure of the surplus or deficit in trade with other countries. Finally, **government expenditure on goods and services** includes purchases from the private sector by all levels of government, including diverse items such as B-2 bombers and school lunches. Wages and salaries paid to government employees are included as well. Excluded from this category of government spending on goods and services are **transfer payments,** such as checks sent to Social Security recipients, and interest payments on government debt.

It is common to denote the spending components of real GNP given above as C, I, X, and G, respectively, while real GNP is denoted as Y. The breakdown of GNP into spending components thus may be written as the equation

(3.3) $Y = C + I + X + G.$

Because these components are defined such that they add up to GNP, equation (3.3) always is true by definition. Equations that always must be true are referred to mathematically as identities. Thus, equation (3.3) has become known as the **GNP identity.**

The GNP components tend to behave rather differently over the business cycle. We will look at each of them in turn.

CONSUMPTION

Consumption is the largest GNP component. Typically, it makes up two-thirds to three-fourths of U.S. GNP. Thus, fluctuations in consumption are an important part of fluctuations in GNP. Figure 3.7 shows real consumption and real GNP for the United States in the same graph. The graph indicates first that consumption has shown a long-term growth pattern similar to that for GNP. This is not surprising; a steady growth in GNP means that consumers steadily have been able to afford to spend more.

When it comes to business-cycle movements, however, the two variables behave differently. Like GNP, consumption slows down in recessions and rises faster during recoveries, but the fluctuations in consumption are considerably more dampened than those of GNP. During some recessions, including the deep recession of 1981–82, consumption declined hardly at all but merely slowed its rate of expansion. A popular explanation of this phenomenon is that people realize that recessions come and go. If their income declines because of recession, they borrow or dip into their savings in order to maintain a reasonable standard of living, trusting that they will be able to make up the lost income later.

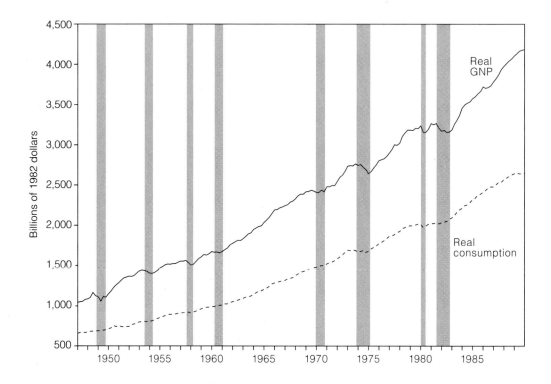

FIGURE 3.7

Comparison of the cyclical fluctuations in real GNP and real personal consumption expenditure. Quarterly data for the United States, 1947–89. The shaded areas indicate recessions.

Consumer spending can be broken down further into spending on **durable goods,** such as cars, furniture, and appliances; **nondurable goods,** such as food; and **services,** such as medical care, housing, and public transportation. It is interesting to note that consumer spending on durable goods fluctuates much more over the business cycle than does the rest of consumer spending, as illustrated in Figure 3.8. In fact, the graph shows that the expenditure on nondurable goods and services hardly responds to business-cycle movements at all, while durable-goods spending always declines in recessions and rises in expansions. A preliminary clue to understanding this relationship is the fact that most durable-goods purchases can be *postponed.* The trading of an old car for a new car is a good example. In contrast, it obviously is much more difficult to postpone food purchases.

INVESTMENT

Private U.S. domestic investment is graphed against GNP in Figure 3.9. This variable declines sharply in every recession and rises equally sharply in every recovery. In many ways, it behaves like the consumer-durables series, only it is even more volatile. This similarity is hardly surprising, because the purchase of a durable consumer good can easily be considered an investment decision in its own right. Faced with the

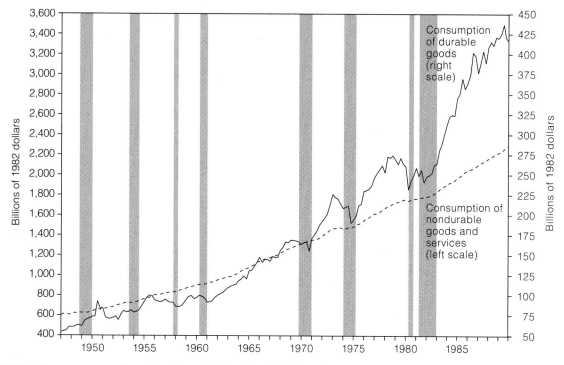

FIGURE 3.8

Comparison of the cyclical fluctuations in durable-goods consumption and consumption of nondurable goods and services. Quarterly real data for the United States, 1947–89. The shaded areas indicate recessions.

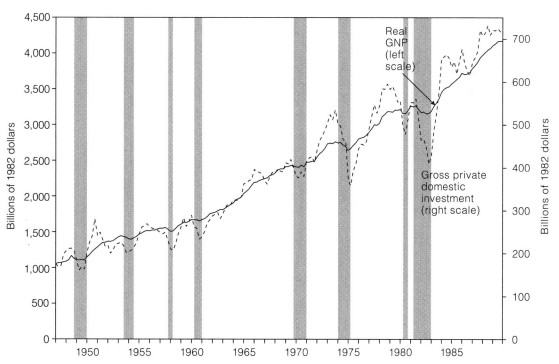

FIGURE 3.9

Comparison of the cyclical fluctuations in real GNP and real investment expenditure. Quarterly data for the United States, 1947–89. The shaded areas indicate recessions.

choice between carrying out an investment project during a recession or waiting until the recession is over, firms often have a strong incentive to wait.

A comparison of the components of private investment may be of some further interest. Figure 3.10 shows in one graph **nonresidential fixed investment** (that is, business buildings and machinery), **residential investment** (houses and apartment buildings), and **changes in business inventories.** If we compare the first two components, residential investment appears to be somewhat more sensitive to business-cycle movements in the economy. A possible explanation for this difference is that nonresidential fixed investment is maintained somewhat during recessions by the need to replace worn-out and outdated equipment, while this need is much weaker in the case of residential investment. With 50 years the typical lifetime for a house, only about 2% of the housing stock needs to be replaced each year.

Changes in business inventories are lower on average than the two other investment components. Note, by the way, that it is possible for this component to be negative, reflecting a drawdown rather than an increase in inventories. On the other hand, this component is highly sensitive to business cycles. Analysis of inventory behavior has proved

FIGURE 3.10

Comparison of the cyclical fluctuations of the components of real private domestic investment: residential investment, nonresidential fixed investment, and changes in business inventories. Quarterly data for the United States, 1947–89. The shaded areas indicate recessions.

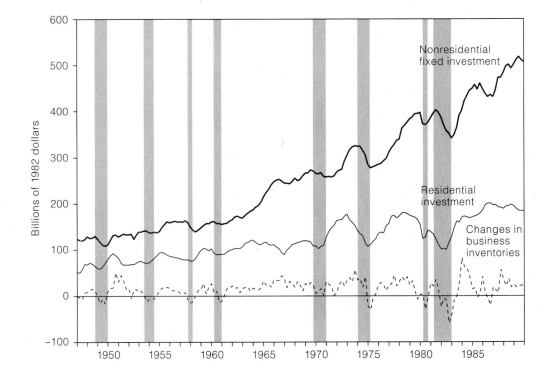

to be both difficult and controversial among economists. At least one relationship between business cycles and inventory behavior seems reasonably clear, however. When recessions start, they often take managers by surprise, and they suddenly find themselves unable to sell goods that already have been produced. Thus, inventories may pile up at the beginning of a recession, but as the recession continues, inventories are liquidated as production is curbed.

NET EXPORTS AND GOVERNMENT SPENDING

The last two expenditure components of GNP originate outside the private domestic sector. **Real net exports** for the United States, defined as the difference between real values of exports and imports, are shown in Figure 3.11. The cyclical behavior of this variable appears to be much more erratic than that of consumption and investment. It has increased during some recessions, declined during others, and shown an equally ambiguous pattern during expansion periods. However, a much more outstanding feature is the string of large negative values during the 1980s. These values reflect the **trade deficits** of that decade, which have received much attention in the public debate.

Figure 3.12 shows the behavior of U.S. **government spending on goods and services.** It is apparent from the graph that the behavior of this vari-

FIGURE 3.11

Real net exports for the United States. Quarterly data for 1947–89. The shaded areas indicate recessions.

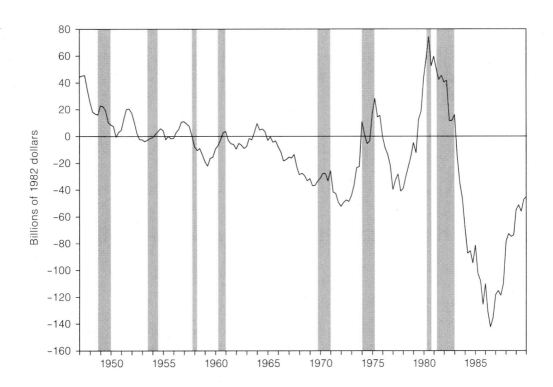

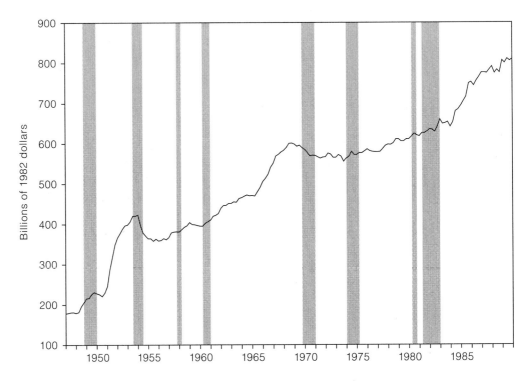

FIGURE 3.12

Real government purchases of goods and services. Quarterly data for the United States, 1947–89. The shaded areas indicate recessions.

able reflects U.S. military buildups more than it does business cycles. We can detect, for example, a peak during the Korean War in the early 1950s, a similar peak during the Vietnam War in the late 1960s, and evidence of the Reagan defense buildup in the 1980s. As to business cycles, the pattern is ambiguous for this component of GNP as well.

3.3 INFLATION

Inflation is a term used to describe the average increase in the prices of goods and services. If price increases are high on average, inflation is high. From a policy perspective, high inflation usually is considered undesirable, although the relationship between inflation and real economic growth in fact is rather ambiguous. The measurement of inflation offers some difficulties of its own. As a result, we have not one but at least three measures of inflation that are worth paying attention to.

THREE MEASURES OF INFLATION

The inflation measure that perhaps is easiest to understand is the **Consumer Price Index,** or **CPI.** The construction of the CPI starts with a shopping list that is constructed from a detailed survey of the buying habits of an average urban family. The list includes all types of goods and services that a typical family buys, including items such as housing, medical care, and imported products. Equipped with this list, the data collectors (in the United States, the field workers of the Bureau of Labor Statistics, or BLS) go out and seek to determine its current cost in the market. The resulting dollar figure is compared to a corresponding average figure for a **base period,** which for the United States currently is the period 1982–84. The ratio of the current cost to the base period cost, multiplied by 100 for convenience, is the current value of the consumer price index. Thus, the CPI is a measure of the current cost of a typical household shopping list relative to the cost of that shopping list in the base period.

The BLS constructs a CPI number for every month. This number can be thought of as an estimate of the overall **price level,** because it measures the average level of all prices relative to their base-period level. We use P_t as our symbol for the price level at time t. Given this measure, the **inflation rate,** denoted by the Greek letter π, is computed as the *rate of change in the price level:*

(3.4)
$$\pi_t = \frac{P_t - P_{t-1}}{P_{t-1}}.$$

For practical use, this rate is multiplied by 100 so that it becomes a percentage.

When this rate is released for a given month, it usually is stated as a *monthly* rate, that is, as the straight percentage change from the preceding month as defined in formula (3.4). Public discussions about inflation, however, often refer to inflation in terms of *annual rates.* That is, the monthly figures are "blown up" and presented as the percentage increase in the price level that would have resulted if the current monthly rate had persisted for 12 months. Analogous to quarterly GNP growth at annual rates in formula (3.2), the formula here is

(3.5)   Monthly inflation at annual rate $= 100 \times \left[\left(\frac{P_t}{P_{t-1}} \right)^{12} - 1 \right].$

The CPI is suitable for measuring the inflation in consumer prices; however, it is not necessarily representative of inflation in the prices of goods typically bought by businesses. A measure of inflation in the prices paid by businesses could serve as an indicator of *inflation in the cost of production.* The **producer price index,** or **PPI,** is such a measure. It measures inflation on the wholesale level rather than on the retail level, where consumers typically make their purchases. It is constructed monthly, like the CPI, and along similar principles. That is, a shopping list is defined, and its current wholesale cost is reestimated each month and compared to the cost in a base period. However, the task of composing the list is more difficult in this case. While the composition of the shopping list for the CPI is based on surveys of household spending patterns, the composition of the corresponding list for the PPI is based more on judgment.

The PPI is not as broad a measure of inflation as the CPI. In particular, it does not cover the prices of any services, only those of goods. Nevertheless, it is considered important as an early indicator of emerging inflationary trends. Quite often, new inflationary forces show up first on the wholesale level as increased costs. A few months later, these cost increases may be passed on as increases in consumer prices. This is not a firm rule. Retailers sometimes need to discount prices because demand is falling as wholesale prices are going up. It is a statistical fact, however, that changes in the PPI tend to foreshadow changes in the CPI.

The third and final measure of inflation that we consider is the **implicit GNP deflator.** It is constructed differently from the CPI and the PPI. The price level as measured by the GNP deflator is defined as the *ratio of nominal to real GNP* (multiplied by 100 for convenience). As for the CPI and the PPI, the inflation rate according to the GNP deflator is the percentage change in this measure of the price level. Because GNP is estimated quarterly rather than monthly, this inflation rate is reported quarterly, but at an annual rate, computed according to formula (3.5) with the exponent 4 rather than 12. This procedure is completely analogous to the construction of the annualized quarterly growth rate in real GNP given in formula (3.2).

The rationale behind the definition of the GNP deflator as the ratio between nominal and real GNP is as follows. If prices rise, then nominal GNP, which is evaluated at rising prices, rises faster than real GNP, which is evaluated at unchanging prices. Consequently, the GNP deflator rises, which suggests that a rising GNP deflator is an indication of inflation. As an example, suppose all prices rise by 5%, while the volume of all goods produced remains unchanged. Then, according to their respective definitions, nominal GNP rises by 5%, while real GNP is unchanged, so the ratio of nominal to real GNP rises by 5%. The GNP deflator then indicates 5% inflation, as it should. Suppose again that all prices rise by 5% but that all volumes rise at 3% rather than standing still. Specifically, suppose we start out with a nominal GNP of $4,000 billion and a GNP deflator of 100, so that nominal and real GNP at first are equal. The 3% rise in all production volumes then makes real GNP rise to 4,000 billion × 1.03 = 4,120 billion. However, because all prices are 5% higher, this output is currently worth not $4,120 billion, but 5% more, that is, $4,326 billion. The GNP deflator thus becomes 100 × 4,326/4,120 = 105. That simply means that the GNP deflator indicates 5% inflation, which again is what we would want it to do.

The way a price-level indicator is constructed makes a difference when different prices rise by different amounts or when different volumes produced grow differently. However, we defer that issue until Chapter 15.

THE HISTORY OF INFLATION IN THE UNITED STATES

Figure 3.13 shows a graph of all three measures of the overall price level for the United States—the CPI, the PPI, and the GNP deflator. The first point to note is that, by any measure, the price level has risen substantially since World War II. Moreover, inflation has been a persistent phenomenon. It is not possible to identify any prolonged period of zero or negative inflation since World War II.

Inflation has varied quite a bit, however. It was occasionally negative around 1950 and remained highly moderate during the 1950s. In the 1960s, too, inflation was moderate, but picked up speed as the decade went on. It picked up steam in the mid-seventies and then accelerated substantially until flattening out in the early 1980s.

These experiences were common to all three indices, but some differences are worth noting. In periods of moderate inflation, such as the 1950s and the 1960s, the moderation is by far strongest for the PPI. The slight dip in the PPI around 1950 and the more substantial dip in the mid-1980s, indicating negative inflation or *deflation*, are particularly noteworthy. Because the PPI does not cover services, the latter dip

FIGURE 3.13

Three indicators of the overall price level: the Consumer Price Index, the Producer Price Index for all goods, and the GNP deflator. Quarterly data for the United States, 1947–89. The shaded areas indicate recessions.

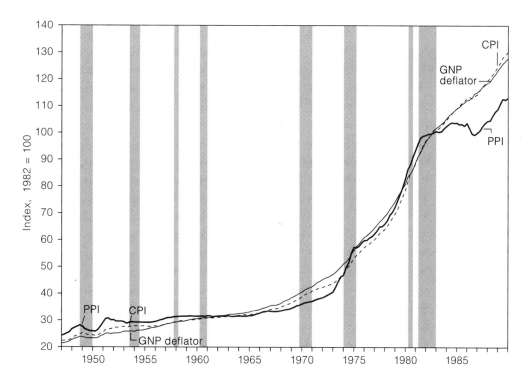

suggests that the prices of services rose faster than those of goods in the 1980s. In contrast, during the high inflation of the 1970s, the PPI also showed the strongest increases. Finally, it is worth noting that the GNP deflator has been slightly *smoother* than the two other indicators. This feature seems likely to reflect the fact that the GNP deflator covers a broader selection of prices—in fact, all items going into GNP—than either of the other two. Sharp movements in some individual prices tend to be offset by movements in other prices.

The behavior of inflation in relation to the business cycle is of particular interest because of the ongoing debate about whether inflation hurts real growth or is a negative side effect of strong growth. The empirical facts are illustrated in Figure 3.14, which shows the inflation rate (as opposed to the price level in Figure 3.13) as measured by the GNP deflator in a diagram where the shaded areas as usual indicate recessions.

The evidence is mixed. During most recessions, the inflation rate has declined and then picked up again during the following recoveries. Such observations would seem to favor the view that high inflation is a side effect of a strong growth performance. However, the 1973–75 and 1980 recessions are blatant exceptions to the rule; they were accompanied by the two highest peaks in the inflation rate since the late 1940s.

FIGURE 3.14

Inflation in the United States as measured by the GNP deflator, 1947–89. Quarterly data at annual rates. The shaded areas indicate recessions.

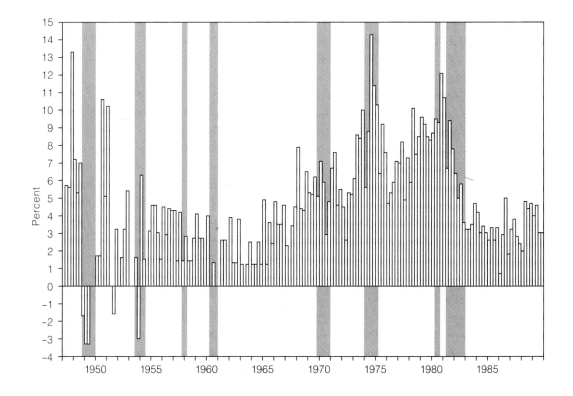

These observations, then, seem to favor the view that inflation hurts economic growth and that controlling inflation is good for business. In our discussion of macroeconomic theory in Part II, we will look for theories that can explain these seemingly contradictory observations. As a preview, we note that the theory of inflation we will study asks not only about the state of the business cycle but also about growth in the money supply, inflationary expectations, and external shocks such as the increases in the price of oil in the 1970s.

3.4 THREE DECADES OF BUSINESS CYCLES AND INFLATION

STRONG AND STABLE GROWTH IN THE 1960S

After the mild U.S. recession in 1960, the world entered a prolonged period of strong and stable growth. This period was particularly strong for the United States. In fact, the economy experienced an unprecedented expansion period, with no new recession until the recession of 1969–70, which also was mild (see Table 3.1 and Figures 3.1 and 3.2). Opinion is divided as to the causes of this expansion. The many technical advances and innovations introduced during this decade are one possible explanation. Another is the activity generated by the military buildup during the Vietnam War at the same time as the federal government was seeking to expand social programs.

This combination of a military buildup and expansion of social programs is an example of an **expansionary fiscal policy,** defined roughly as an increase in government spending unaccompanied by a corresponding increase in tax revenues, with the result that the government budgets go into deficit and new debt is incurred. Although opinion differs as to the effects of such a policy, an important school of thought predicts that it will result not only in high real GNP growth but also in inflation. According to this view, as well as others, the danger of inflation is much greater if the expansionary fiscal policy is accompanied by a **monetary expansion,** that is, by accelerated growth in the supply of money. Such an acceleration did, in fact, take place during the latter half of the 1960s.

As we have seen, the rate of inflation did rise over the decade. President Johnson was among those who became anxious to stem the expansionary fiscal policy in an attempt to improve on the situation. His proposal for a temporary income tax increase—called a surtax—was initially blocked by Congress but was passed in 1968. Even so, as we have seen, inflation continued to accelerate until the 1969–70 recession.

Growth in the sixties was strong in the rest of the world as well. The European countries experienced a slight slowdown in 1967, while growth in Japan took brief pauses in 1962 and 1965 (Figure 3.5). These slowdowns, however, were not strong enough to shake the image of the apparent health of the entire Western economic system. Although inflation was, on average, a little higher outside the United States, at the time this was mostly perceived as an acceptable side effect of strong economic growth. Optimism prevailed during this period; no end to the expansion seemed in sight.

EMERGING IMBALANCES IN THE 1970S

The expansion did end, however, and the 1969–70 recession was only the beginning of the end. Growth resumed after this recession, and rather strongly so, and inflation did not accelerate further at first. However, an important danger signal appeared: the Western economies started to show signs of shortages and tight supplies, especially of some important natural resources. Nowhere did the shortages become more visible than in regard to energy, as natural gas deliveries to many industrial customers were curtailed in the United States during every winter of the early 1970s. Many observers blamed these shortages on government price controls on the grounds that holding prices down served as disincentives to production. Government policies were not the only forces at work, however. World demand for oil rose persistently and was rapidly approaching capacity levels for the world's oil industry. Even more ominously, the world's known reserves of oil and natural gas showed signs of nearing physical depletion. At the same time, the world demand for food kept rising, aided by crop failures in the Soviet Union; U.S. agriculture, which traditionally had relied on government subsidies, was suddenly facing a seller's market.

Important events also took place on the supply side of the agricultural markets. The anchovy catch off the coast of Peru failed in 1973, raising the cost of fish meal, an important feed stuff, to U.S. farmers. Floods in the U.S. Midwest destroyed part of the 1973 soybean crop, adding to the price increases for feed stuff. Because these events took place in an already tight market, the result was a considerable increase in U.S. food prices. Since food is an important component of consumer spending, the U.S. CPI started to rise. Over the first six months of 1973, the CPI rose at an annual rate of 8.2%, compared to 2.9% the previous year.

THE FIRST OIL SHOCK AND THE 1973–75 RECESSION

But the worst was yet to come. The oil market had continued to tighten, and the United States, as well as western Europe and Japan, had become heavily dependent on oil from the Middle East. The governments of oil-exporting countries felt cheated out of what they considered fair profits. Moreover, a war was breaking out in the Middle East in which most Western countries sympathized with Israel, the enemy of some very important oil-exporting countries. The events that followed in the fall of 1973 were very dramatic. The Organization of Petroleum Exporting Countries (OPEC) decided unilaterally to raise the price of crude oil from about $3 to about $12 per barrel. Meanwhile, the Organization of Arab Petroleum Exporting Countries (OAPEC) imposed an *oil embargo* on the United States and some European countries as a protest against support of Israel. Oil and oil products, such as gasoline, suddenly went from plentiful and cheap to scarce and expensive. The U.S. CPI rose again, rising by 10.9% from June of 1973 to June of 1974. The drought that affected American agriculture in 1974 did not help the price increases.

The final event was the 1973–75 recession, which hit most of the Western nations. The cause or causes of this recession remain a matter of some dispute. The recession could have been the direct result of the rise in oil prices or an indirect result of the fact that monetary policy was tightened somewhat at the same time, apparently in an attempt to stem the inflationary tide. It is also possible that the disturbing factor was not so much the oil price increase per se as the problem of adjusting to the resulting realignment of industrial activity as some industries (most notably oil production) benefited from the oil price increase while others (such as the auto industry) suffered. Still other forces may, of course, have influenced the economy during this period. The main facts are that U.S. real GNP fell by 4.3% from the fourth quarter of 1973 to the first quarter of 1975 and that the unemployment rate hit a postwar high of 9.0% in May 1975. According to Table 3.1, this was the longest and most severe recession in U.S. postwar history. The slowdown was no less dramatic in most of the other Western economies.

RECOVERY AND INFLATION IN THE LATE 1970S AND THE SECOND OIL SHOCK

The recovery from the 1973–75 recession started in the United States in the second quarter of 1975. It was a strong recovery. However, the inflation rate, which had been driven to unprecedented levels before and during the recession, did not subside. The high inflation rate was accompanied by rising wages and high growth rates in the money supply. The result was what often is called an "overheated" economy, with a combination of high real GNP growth and high inflation. Thus, in the second quarter of 1978, U.S. real GNP growth reached 13.2% while the GNP deflator at the same time rose at an annual rate of 10.1%. Moreover, the strength of the recovery did not extend to all countries. Particularly in Europe, growth remained sluggish and unemployment remained high.

Then another political event stirred the oil market. As a result of the revolution in Iran, the export volume of oil from that country dropped from about 6 million barrels per day in 1978 to about one-tenth that in late 1979. Oil prices skyrocketed once more, this time led by forces in the open market rather than by OPEC. In late 1979, prices on the spot market passed the $40-a-barrel mark. In the United States, inflation as measured by the CPI peaked at an annual rate of almost 20% in March

1980. Again, monetary policy was tightened in an attempt to contain the inflationary pressures, and, again, recession hit. This recession, however, was much milder than that in 1973–75. Although growth was sluggish throughout 1979 (with growth rates of 0, −0.4%, 3.7%, and −0.8% for the four quarters, respectively), the only dramatic decline came in the second quarter of 1980, when real GNP declined at an annual rate of 9.1%. However sharp, this recession was brief. Growth recovered briskly in late 1980 and reached 8% in the first quarter of 1981.

Although the U.S. economy had been spared a major recession, inflation persisted. As late as the first quarter of 1981, inflation as measured by the GNP deflator was 10.7%. At this time, a consensus was reached between the new administration, led by President Ronald Reagan, and the Federal Reserve, led by Chairman Paul Volcker, that priority must be given to a serious attempt to reduce inflation.

The main strategy was to undertake a substantial tightening in the supply of money. The main reason why this route had not been followed before, at least not with the same resolve, was a fear that a strong monetary tightening would also set off a recession. The belief that a trade-off existed between inflation and growth in real GNP had been the mainstay of macroeconomic thinking among academics as well as policymakers throughout the sixties and much of the seventies. However, the seventies had also presented blatant evidence that inflation and recession could occur at the same time. Moreover, new ideas among economic researchers suggested that the alleged trade-off was an illusion, that inflation could not buy prosperity (certainly not in the long run), and that the economy would be better off getting rid of the yoke of inflation—the sooner the better. Even among those who refused to espouse the new theories, many argued that the risk of recession could be worth the prospect of reduced inflation.

ATTACK ON INFLATION AND THE 1981–82 RECESSION

The tightening operation was quite serious. M1, the narrowest measure of the supply of money (defined essentially as the sum of checking account balances and circulating cash), had grown by 7.5% from January 1979 to January 1980. By the period of April 1981 through April 1982, this rate had been cut to 4.9%. Moreover, success seemed indicated by a substantial slowdown in inflation. Between the first quarter of 1981 and the fourth quarter of 1982, inflation as measured by the GNP deflator declined from 10.7% to 3.6%.

However, a serious recession also occurred. It was as long as the recession in 1973–75 and almost as deep in terms of real GNP decline, and it drove the unemployment rate for November and December 1982 all the way up to 10.8%, a postwar high. It is, of course, impossible to tell with certainty whether this recession was caused by the monetary tightening operation or was, say, a delayed reaction to the second oil shock. What seems quite clear, however, is that this experience rekindled many analysts' belief that monetary tightening indeed involves a risk of slowdown and recession.

THE LONG EXPANSION PERIOD OF THE 1980S

The recovery from the 1981–82 recession was strong, with real GNP growth rates peaking at 10.7% in the first quarter of 1984. Moreover, inflation remained moderate after the recession, a sharply different experience from the recovery after the 1973–75 recession and, indeed, from most postwar recoveries. External shocks went the opposite way as in the seventies, as the oil market, hurt by overproduction by the OPEC countries and by reduced demand by the industrialized countries, collapsed in late 1985 and early 1986. During this period, the world price of crude oil dropped from about $30 per barrel to about $10, before settling down to a state of relative stability with occasional fluctuations between $13 and $20. Many observers expected this price decline to stimulate real growth, just as the earlier oil price increases apparently had led to recessions. However, evidence of such a boost proved hard to find. Instead, the U.S. unemployment rate *rose* from 6.7% in January 1986 to 7.2% in February, reportedly as a result of workers being laid off in the oil-producing regions of the country. Real GNP growth also failed to take off; in fact, for the last three quarters of 1986, it stayed within the rather sluggish bracket of between −2% and +2.5%. In comparison, 1987 was much stronger, while 1988 saw a return to real GNP growth in the 2.5% to 3.5% range.

In general, the recovery following the 1981–82 recession turned into a prolonged period of sustained expansion. At the time of this writing (late 1990), this expansion is showing some signs of weakening and perhaps ending. Even so, its length rivals that of the long expansion of the 1960s.

The 1980s differ from the 1960s in that the United States waged no major war (such as the Vietnam War) during the 1980s. However, one similarity to the sixties is worth noting. Even though no major war has been waged, fiscal policy clearly can be characterized as expansionary. Income taxes were cut early in the decade, military spending was increased, and the budget deficits of the federal government have consistently been many times larger than the largest deficits in the 1960s. Perhaps the U.S. economy has again been stimulated by fiscal policy.

Other countries also experienced recession and recovery in the 1980s. In Japan, the 1981–82 recession did not lead to much of a slowdown at all, and the subsequent expansion extended Japan's previous record. In Europe, the decline in 1982 was considerably milder than in the United States, but the European countries also had much more modest recoveries after the 1973–75 and 1981–82 recessions (see Figure 3.5). Most strikingly, European unemployment rates have not returned to their traditionally low levels (Figure 3.6). Whether this pattern will be reversed during the next decade remains to be seen.

CHAPTER REVIEW

1. Business cycles can be measured by real GNP growth as well as by the unemployment rate. The unemployment rate is less suitable for comparisons across countries.
2. Real GNP in the United States has grown significantly since World War II. However, the overall growth trend has been interrupted by several recessions with declines in real GNP. U.S. business cycles are dated by the National Bureau of Economic Research.
3. The unemployment rate rises during recessions and declines during recoveries. The unemployment rate moves much more smoothly than the real GNP growth rate. It also showed a long-term worsening during the seventies and early eighties; however, this tendency now appears to have turned around somewhat.
4. Business cycles have also occurred in Europe and Japan since World War II; however, they have been smoother than those in the United States. International business cycles tend to be coordinated, especially when they are associated with international disturbances.
5. Consumption moves much more smoothly over the business cycle than GNP. Expenditures on durable consumer goods, however, are much more volatile than expenditures on nondurable goods or services.
6. Business investment is even more volatile than purchases of consumer durables. Inventory changes are most volatile, and residential construction is fairly volatile; business fixed investment behaves somewhat more smoothly.
7. Inflation can be measured by the Consumer Price Index (CPI), the Producer Price Index (PPI), and the GNP deflator.
8. Inflation in the United States was low in the 1950s and 1960s. It accelerated sharply in the 1970s and abated during the 1980s.
9. Inflation behavior during recessions is mixed. While many recessions have brought lower inflation, the 1973–75 and the 1980 recessions were associated with record inflation rates.
10. The 1960s were a decade of exceptional expansion coupled with low inflation, although inflation worsened somewhat during the second half of the decade.
11. The 1970s experienced severe shortages and price shocks. On the macroeconomic level, inflation was very high. The recession of 1973–75 was severe, but the recovery in the late 1970s was quite strong. However, inflation remained very high during this recovery.
12. The 1980s saw two recessions, a brief one in 1980 and a long and deep one in 1981–82. Inflation abated, and the recovery from the 1981–82 recession was strong. The recessions were shallower in Europe and Japan, but the recoveries there were slower as well.

EXERCISES

1. For quarterly data of U.S. real GNP growth, compute means and standard deviations (a) for the entire period since World War II, (b) by decade, and (c) by political administration. Comment on your results. Also comment on any differences from the annual data that were analyzed in Chapter 2.
2. Repeat exercise 1 for the inflation rate as defined by the GNP deflator. Comment on these results.
3. Run a regression with the inflation rate (as defined by the GNP deflator) as the variable on the left and the real GNP growth rate on the right. Run the regression for the entire

postwar period and by decade. Can you infer anything from these results about the relationship (if any) between inflation and real GNP growth?

4. Compute the means and standard deviations of the GNP growth rates for the United States, Japan, and West Germany. Then compute the correlations among the three rates. Comment on the results.

THINKING QUESTIONS

Our discussion so far has not really equipped you with the tools to provide explanations for economic phenomena. However, to whet your appetite for the theory in Part II, you might try to answer the following questions.

1. Given the history of the last two decades, how would you describe the prospects for the U.S. economy in the 1990s?

2. Government policies were first credited with the stability of growth in the 1960s and then blamed for the instabilities of the 1970s. Try to assess the connections between public policy and macroeconomic performance during these two decades.

3. Try to explain why some recessions are associated with high inflation and some with low inflation.

4. Suppose it is correct that the policy efforts to stop inflation in the early 1980s also caused the 1981–82 recession. Do you consider stopping inflation worth this price? Why or why not?

5. Try to explain why Europe and Japan have experienced higher and smoother growth on average than the United States since World War II.

6. Can you think of any explanation why the European unemployment rates did not go back to normal after the recoveries from the recessions in the 1970s and 1980s, as they did in the United States?

THE MONETARY SYSTEM

Primitive economies do not need money, because they conduct trade by barter. Unfortunately, barter has the disadvantage that every person wanting to buy something must be able to offer something desirable for exchange at the same time. Finding such matches becomes increasingly difficult as an economy becomes more advanced and more specialized. Think of the difficulty a person with a management degree would face while grocery shopping if the only payment that person could offer was management consulting services for the supermarket! The availability of money as a mutually acceptable payment medium solves this problem. All you need to get your groceries is your wallet or checkbook. If the supermarket needs management consulting, it is free to buy it for money from any consulting firm, while you receive monetary payment for the work you do for your own employer.

In this sense, money is the solution to the *microeconomic* problem of facilitating trade. However, it also has major *macroeconomic* importance. First, as an asset, money is a key factor in the determination of interest rates, which in turn can influence investment, saving, and business cycles. Second, because prices are quoted in terms of monetary units such as dollars, money is of crucial importance for inflation. Third, because exchange rates are relative prices of monies from different countries, foreign trade and international capital markets depend on money as well.

The role of money in macroeconomic theory is explored further in Part II. This chapter introduces you to the **monetary system.** It starts by seeking an answer to the question of what money is, in a conceptual as well as an operational sense. The discussion then turns to central banks and what they do, with particular emphasis on the Federal Reserve System in the United States. Special attention is given to the mechanisms by which central banks control the supply of money.

4.1 WHAT IS MONEY?

In everyday use, the term *money* is synonymous with wealth or assets. If people want to say that someone is very rich, they might say that the person has a lot of money, even if all the person's wealth is tied up in stocks or real estate. In economics, the term *money* is used much more narrowly to refer to a class of very **liquid** assets that can be used for **payments.**

CONCEPTUAL DEFINITIONS

From a conceptual point of view, money can be defined by its functions. By money, we usually mean an asset or a group of assets that is readily acceptable as a *means of exchange*, that serves as a *unit of account*, and that is suitable as a *store of value*. We therefore can define money as an asset or group of assets that satisfy these criteria.

The function of money as a **means of exchange** goes right to the heart of money as the solution to the barter problem. To avoid the need to find matching pairs of desirable goods for every transaction, it is necessary to have an asset that is mutually acceptable as payment to everyone. This property of money is, in a loose sense, what we call **liquidity.** An asset is considered liquid if it can be either used directly as payment or converted quickly and at low cost into another asset that can be used as payment. Currency obviously is liquid, as is a balance on a checking account. The balance on a regular savings account is fairly liquid as well, although spending from such an account might require an extra trip to the bank. Stocks and bonds, on the other hand, are less liquid, because they need to be sold before the funds can be used for payment. Obviously, a house is an illiquid asset, because selling it can take months and may require the services of a real-estate agent.

It is not necessary that the same asset be used as payment and as a **unit of account,** but it is highly convenient. The old British custom of quoting the prices of horses in guineas (at 21 shillings per guinea) while making payment in pounds (at 20 shillings per pound) was feasible, but rather impractical. In the United States, the dollar serves both as a medium of exchange and as a unit of account. Using this unit helps avoid the old problem of "comparing apples and oranges." It is similar to having standard units of physical measurement, such as the meter, the kilogram, and the liter. However, in contrast to physical units, the dollar is less reliable for comparisons over time during periods of inflation.

Assets other than money may be more useful as **stores of value,** especially during periods of inflation. Nevertheless, this function of money is essential if money is to be useful in facilitating transactions. Finding matching pairs of desirable goods is only one part of the transactions problem. Another is that it usually is convenient to carry out different transactions at different times. For example, if you work in New York and are paid monthly, but you live in New Jersey, you may need money to cross the George Washington Bridge (a toll bridge) more than once a month. For transactions to be spread over time, money needs to keep a reasonable part of its value for this length of time.

This property of money becomes problematic during periods of very high inflation, because money then loses its value very quickly. Some countries in South America have recently gone through this kind of experience. Occasionally, newspaper articles describe how people in such situations try to make their purchases as soon after payday as possible.*

OPERATIONAL DEFINITIONS: THE MONETARY AGGREGATES

We could define money as the set of those assets that can fill all the functions just described. Such a definition would not be very precise, however, because disagreements about exactly which assets to include would be unavoidable. Fortunately, precise definitions have been worked out for what we call the **monetary aggregates** of the United States. These definitions are universally accepted and are used in the monetary statistics to measure the supply of money. The monetary aggregates are referred to as **M1, M2,** and **M3.** Their definitions are "concentric" in the sense that M1 is contained in M2, and M2 is contained in M3. Thus, M2 is defined as M1 plus some additional assets, and M3 is defined as M2 plus something else.

The narrowest aggregate, M1, is designed to include the most liquid assets in circulation. It is defined roughly as the sum of checking-account balances and currency held by the nonbank public. The technical term for a conventional checking account is a **demand deposit.** Such deposits earn no interest. However, in recent years, banks and thrift institutions have offered other accounts that both earn interest and can be drawn on with checklike documents; examples of such accounts are N.O.W. (Negotiable Order of Withdrawal), C.U.S.D. (Credit Union Share Drafts), and A.T.S. (Automatic Transfer from Savings) accounts. Accounts of this type are not subject to the strict legal rules surrounding conventional checking accounts. Thus, technically, they are not checking accounts, and the documents used to draw on them are not checks in the legal sense. In practice, however, they are just as convenient, and for this reason they are included in the official definition of M1.

Technically, M1 is defined as the sum of the following components:**

1. Currency held by the nonbank public

2. Traveler's checks

3. Demand deposits

4. Other checkable deposits (N.O.W. accounts, and so on.)

---

* For example, Roger Cohen, "Unfunny Money: Brazil's Price Spiral Nears Hyperinflation, Could Ruin Economy," *Wall Street Journal*, 8 December 1988.

** More detailed definitions of all the monetary aggregates can be found as footnotes to the monetary statistics in any issue of the *Federal Reserve Bulletin*, a monthly publication of the Board of Governors of the Federal Reserve System.

This definition is intended to capture the most liquid assets in the economy, those available for immediate spending by the public. Some other assets, however, are almost as liquid. They are included in M2, which is defined as the sum of the following:

1. All the components of M1

2. Savings deposits

3. Small time deposits

4. Money market deposits

5. Money market mutual fund shares (noninstitutional)

6. Overnight repurchase agreements with commercial banks

7. Overnight Eurodollar deposits

Time deposits sometimes are referred to as certificates of deposit or CDs. A time deposit account is considered "small" if it has a balance of less than $100,000. Money market deposits are a class of accounts allowed by recent regulatory changes. They earn market-determined interest and may be checkable, but they are subject to some restrictions. Money market mutual funds are investment funds offered by nonbank institutions, and in practice they have a high degree of liquidity. Those of such funds that are open to noninstitutional investors are included in M2 because they are close substitutes for bank deposits.

A repurchase agreement (sometimes abbreviated as "repo") is an arrangement whereby a business company buys securities from its bank with the understanding that the bank will repurchase the securities from the company at a later date. An interest rate is implicit in the transaction in that the agreed-upon repurchase price is higher than the price the company originally pays for the securities. For an overnight repurchase agreement, the repurchase date is the following day; otherwise, the agreement is called a term repurchase agreement. Repurchase agreements are close substitutes for depositing funds in a bank account.

The term *Eurodollars* refers to the balances of accounts in foreign banks that are denominated in U.S. dollars. Some of these accounts are "overnight" in the sense that the depositor may withdraw the entire balance the following day; otherwise, they are called term deposits. Such balances are included in M2 whenever they are deposited with foreign branches of U.S. banks and owned by U.S. residents.

M3 completes the picture. It includes a wider range of less liquid assets:

1. All the components of M2

2. Large time deposits ($\geq$ $100,000)

3. Shares in institutional money market mutual funds

4. Term repurchase agreements

5. Term Eurodollar deposits

In past years, discussions about monetary matters focused mostly on money in its narrowest sense, namely, M1. However, the 1980s saw an increase in the availability of close substitutes to assets included in M1, such as money market accounts and money market mutual funds. This availability made it difficult to predict the movements of funds between assets that were and were not part of M1. As a result, the movements in M1 became more volatile than in previous years. For this reason, the Federal Reserve now formally states its policy goals only in terms of M2 and M3, although some attention is paid to M1 as well.

4.2   CENTRAL BANKS

Most countries have established institutions, called **central banks,** that are charged with the task of managing the country's monetary system. The responsibility of a central bank is threefold. First, it serves as a "bankers' bank," where commercial banks can deposit funds and obtain loans. Second, it controls the supply of money. Third, it monitors and occasionally intervenes in foreign-exchange markets, where different countries' monies are traded against each other.

THE BANKERS' BANK

A central bank's first responsibility is to ensure the soundness of the banking system. With this purpose in mind, it provides some valuable services to the individual commercial banks. Individual banks are allowed to hold deposits with the central bank. These accounts bear no interest but are useful for the many interactions between the individual banks and the central bank. They are used, for example, as part of the central bank's **check-clearing** service. However, check clearing also can be done by private agencies, a practice common in the United States.

The accounts with the central bank also are useful for the central bank's function as the **supplier of currency** to the commercial banks. A bank in need of currency can simply obtain it from the central bank in return for a debit entry on its account.

The third purpose of central-bank accounts is to serve as a depository for **bank reserves.** Banks may be required by law to hold reserves, partly as security for their depositors and partly to facilitate central bank manipulation of the supply of money. Banks sometimes hold reserves beyond the legal requirements in order to smooth their financial flows. It should be noted, however, that the holding of reserves is costly because the central bank accounts earn no interest.

As a bankers' bank, a central bank also can extend **loans to individual banks.** This is, perhaps, the most important banking function of a central bank, for two main reasons. First, the interest the central bank charges on such loans, called the **discount rate** in the United States and in many other countries, serves as a signal for what the central bank thinks is a good range for market interest rates. Second, in times of financial distress, the central bank serves as the **lender of last resort.** By providing liquidity in a crisis situation, the central bank may be able to avert a potential breakdown of the entire financial system. The Federal Reserve's willingness to provide emergency loans after the stock market crash of October 19, 1987, has been cited as one reason why the effects of that event apparently were so mild.*

CONTROLLING THE SUPPLY OF MONEY

Central banks are responsible for controlling the supply of money. By doing so, they can influence interest rates, exchange rates, inflation, and business cycles. There are two basic methods for controlling the supply of money. Under the **metals standard,** the price of money is tied to a tangible commodity such as gold or silver, while the central bank supplies whatever quantities of money the public demands. The control of the money supply under this system relies on the fact that the public will demand only as much money as is worth its price in gold or silver.

No country currently follows a metals standard, although arguments for a return to it are occasionally heard. Instead, the supply of money is controlled by a variety of other instruments, the most important of which is the central bank's buying and selling of securities in exchange for money. The workings of this system are explained in Section 4.4.

MONITORING OF AND INTERVENTION IN FOREIGN-EXCHANGE MARKETS

A central bank also has external responsibilities that relate to the soundness of the market for **foreign exchange.** In this market, the country's currency is traded against other countries' currencies at prices called **exchange rates.** Exchange rates may be fixed at given levels or within narrow bands by government decree or international agreement, or they may be freely determined by market forces. If the exchange rate is fixed at a given level, the central bank is required to buy and sell foreign currency at that rate. If it is fixed within a band, as between the member countries of the European Monetary System, the central bank is com-

---

* The following statement was issued by Federal Reserve Chairman Alan Greenspan in the morning of October 20: "The Federal Reserve, consistent with its responsibilities as the Nation's central bank, affirmed today its readiness to serve as a source of liquidity to support the economic and financial system" (quoted here from the *Federal Reserve Bulletin,* December 1987, vol. 73, no. 12). A good journalistic analysis of the significance of this statement can be found in "Terrible Tuesday: How the Stock Market Disintegrated a Day After the Crash—Credit Dried Up for Brokers and Especially Specialists Until Fed Came to Rescue—Most Perilous Day in 50 Years," James B. Stewart and Daniel Hertzberg, *Wall Street Journal,* 20 November 1987.

mitted to buying or selling its own currency whenever its value in the market approaches the lower or upper end of the band, respectively. If the exchange rate is allowed to **float,** that is, to be determined by market forces (as is currently the case officially for the U.S. dollar), the central bank still may want to monitor the market and perhaps intervene by buying or selling foreign exchange in order to influence the market exchange rate.

With the growing globalization of the financial markets, as well as of the rest of the economy, the external function of central banking is becoming increasingly important. For many countries, especially small ones with fixed exchange rates, this function dictates their monetary policy, as we will see in Chapter 10. Larger countries may have some more freedom of maneuvering. Yet the foreign-exchange markets typically take up a large part of the agenda at top economic and financial meetings.

4.3 THE FEDERAL RESERVE SYSTEM

The central bank of the United States is the Federal Reserve System, created by an act of Congress in 1913. It is a slightly complex system, formally consisting of 12 regional Federal Reserve Banks (also called district banks), one for each Federal Reserve District, as well as a Board of Governors in Washington, D.C. The district banks are located in Boston, New York, Philadelphia, Richmond, Atlanta, Cleveland, Chicago, St. Louis, Kansas City, Minneapolis, Dallas, and San Francisco. Formally, each district bank is owned by the Federal Reserve member banks in its district, that is, by individual commercial banks that are members of the Federal Reserve System. National banks are required to be members; commercial banks chartered by individual states are given a choice. In practice, most commercial banks choose membership because of the privileges it implies. Membership requires that the commercial banks buy stock in their district's Federal Reserve Bank. Formally, then, the member banks are the owners of the Federal Reserve Banks. They also may choose two-thirds of its board of directors. However, they do not have the same powers as shareholders in other organizations; in particular, they have no real control over monetary policy.

THE BOARD OF GOVERNORS AND THE FEDERAL OPEN MARKET COMMITTEE

The central administration of the Federal Reserve in Washington, D.C., has two major policy-making bodies: the Board of Governors and the Federal Open Market Committee. The members of the **Board of Governors** are appointed by the president of the United States for a 14-year term upon confirmation by the Senate. The terms of individual governors are staggered (one term expires every two years) so that a wholesale replacement of all the members normally cannot take place.

One governor is designated as the Federal Reserve chairman and one as vice-chairman. Appointment of the chairman is made by the president of the United States for a four-year term upon confirmation by the Senate. In principle, the chairman is to be selected from among the seven governors as the first among equals. In practice, the chairmanship has developed into a highly powerful position of its own.

The chairman's four-year term begins and ends in the middle of the presidential term, a practice intended to add to the independence enjoyed by the Federal Reserve vis-à-vis the administration. Thus, a newly elected president may have to work with a chairman that was selected by the previous administration. On the other hand, chairmen can be reappointed. In this fashion, Chairman Paul Volcker was appointed by President Jimmy Carter, inherited by Ronald Reagan, and then reappointed by Reagan in the middle of the president's first term. When Volcker left at the end of his second term as chairman, an outsider, Alan Greenspan, was appointed.

The **Federal Open Market Committee** (**FOMC**), as the name suggests, issues directives about the Federal Reserve's sales and purchases of government securities in the open financial market. Under the leadership of the Federal Reserve chairman, its meetings currently take place eight times a year and are strictly closed to the public. Voting members are the seven governors, the president of the Federal Reserve Bank of New York (which carries out the open-market operations), and the presidents of four other regional Federal Reserve Banks, serving on a rotating basis. The presidents of the remaining regional banks may and do participate, but they do not vote.

THE FEDERAL RESERVE AS AN INDEPENDENT AGENCY

The Federal Reserve is an agency of the U.S. government. Although formally it is owned by its member banks, this ownership has little real consequence. The member banks receive a nominal return on their investment, but the substantial surplus generated by the Federal Reserve's open-market operations is handed over to the U.S. Treasury. Furthermore, the ownership entails no power over Federal Reserve decisions, which in practice are dictated by the Board of Governors or the FOMC.

Unlike most other government agencies, however, the Federal Reserve is quite independent of the other branches of government. The president or the secretary of treasury can confer with the chairman of the Federal Reserve and does so in practice, but neither can give the chairman orders. The chairman is required to testify before Congress at least twice a year and to state officially the Federal Reserve's policy goals. However, Congress has no power to give orders either, and the goals can be stated in rather broad terms. The only formal influence elected officials have on Federal Reserve policy is through the appointment and confirmation of the members of the Board of Governors and its chairman and vice-chairman.

The independence implied by this arrangement exists by design. It is intended to protect the Federal Reserve from pressure to make decisions that might be politically expedient but contrary to the country's best interest. However, this independence also enables the Federal Reserve to make decisions contrary to the country's interest without any opportunity for elected officials to reverse them. This state of affairs has been criticized from time to time, especially by members of Congress who have been dissatisfied with Federal Reserve decisions. In principle, the situation could be changed by new legislation. Legislation to limit the Federal Reserve's independence has in fact been proposed from time to time but not passed.

This is not the place to settle the dispute. It is an issue in most countries and has been solved in different ways at different times and in different places. However, given the importance of Federal Reserve decisions to the economy and the business climate, you should be aware of the tension that exists between the Federal Reserve and the elected branches of government. Both need to be reckoned with as independent forces shaping the nation's economic policy.

4.4   THE CONDUCT OF MONETARY POLICY

Central banks conduct monetary policy. This section gives a broad outline of how this task is organized in the United States. The appendix to this chapter gives a more detailed and technical presentation of an important part of the process called the money multiplier.

THE BALANCE SHEET OF THE FEDERAL RESERVE

The conduct of monetary policy in the United States is intimately tied to the Federal Reserve's disposition of its assets and liabilities. For this reason, our discussion starts with a look at the Federal Reserve's balance sheet. In simplified form, it looks something like the balance sheet shown in Table 4.1.

TABLE 4.1   SIMPLIFIED BALANCE SHEET FOR THE U.S. FEDERAL RESERVE SYSTEM

ASSETS	LIABILITIES
U.S. government securities	Currency held by the nonbank public
Loans to member banks	Currency held by banks as vault cash
Official reserves	Bank reserve deposits
Other assets	Other liabilities and net worth

The Federal Reserve's largest asset is its portfolio of government securities. This portfolio is useful when the Federal Reserve wants to carry out open market sales. The loan portfolio to member banks is more modest but also quite important. Member banks are allowed to borrow from the Federal Reserve if their own reserves are insufficient. The interest charged on these loans is called the **discount rate,** and borrowing from the Federal Reserve at this rate is called borrowing at the **discount window.** Borrowing at the discount window is a privilege rather than a right. The window is closed to nonmember banks and to other financial institutions that are not classified as banks. Moreover, the Federal Reserve approves loans at its own discretion, which it can use to impose discipline on the banks. A bank that is careless about its reserves may find itself cut off from loans at the discount window.

The official reserves include the central bank's portfolio of gold and of foreign currency, usually kept on account with other central banks. The foreign-currency part of these reserves is used for interventions in the foreign-exchange markets, as we will discuss below.

Currency is counted as a liability in keeping with the tradition of past years, when currency was a certificate redeemable in silver or gold. It is the Federal Reserve's largest liability. Currency is included in the monetary aggregates, but only that part of it that circulates among the nonbank public. The rest is held by banks as part of their reserves and is referred to as **vault cash.** Both vault cash and currency in circulation among the nonbank public are liabilities of the Federal Reserve. The other important liability item is **bank reserve deposits,** the deposits that private banks hold with the Federal Reserve as part of their reserves and as a vehicle for transactions between member banks and the Federal Reserve. The Federal Reserve's balance sheet can be used to define the **monetary base,** an even narrower definition of money than M1. It is defined as *the sum of currency and reserve deposits.* In other words, it is the sum of the first three entries on the liability side of the Federal Reserve's balance sheet in Table 4.1. Since banks have the choice of holding their reserves as vault cash or on account with the Federal Reserve, the last two of these entries also define total bank reserves. Thus, an alternative definition of the monetary base is *the sum of bank reserves and currency in circulation among the nonbank public.* The monetary base refers not to money available for spending by the public but rather to those assets that are under the most immediate control of the Federal Reserve. The nature of this control is the subject of the rest of this section. The relationship between the monetary base and the monetary aggregates is determined by the **money multiplier,** which we describe further below.

RESERVE REQUIREMENTS

Banks in the United States are required to hold reserves equal to at least certain percentages of their deposits. These percentages are called **reserve requirements.** They are determined by the Board of Governors of the Federal Reserve within fairly restrictive limits specified by the Depository Institution and Monetary Control Act of 1980. This act also extended the reserve requirements to all depository institutions (such as mutual savings banks, savings and loan associations, and credit unions), not just commercial banks. The reserve requirements vary by type of deposit, size of institution, how quickly the money can be withdrawn, and who owns the accounts (individuals or institutions). The strictest requirements are for checking accounts, for which the reserve requirement is 12% for large depository institutions. In contrast, the reserve requirement for savings account deposits owned by individuals is zero. Current reserve requirements are listed in Table 4.2.

If a bank finds itself short of reserves, it has various options in order to return to compliance with the reserve requirements. It can liquidate assets, such as government securities, or it can call in loans. However, such transactions can be costly and—especially in the case of calling in loans—send out embarrassing signals about the bank's financial soundness. A much more attractive alternative to resolve temporary reserve shortfalls is to *borrow* reserves. Banks have two opportunities to borrow reserves. The first is to borrow from other banks. The market in which commercial banks borrow and lend reserves among themselves is called the **federal funds market.** The interest rate charged in this market is called the **federal funds rate.** This rate is considered an important gauge

---

TABLE 4.2   LIST OF RESERVE REQUIREMENTS OF DEPOSITORY INSTITUTIONS AS OF APRIL 1990

TYPE OF DEPOSIT	PERCENT OF DEPOSITS
Checkable deposits (including non–interest-bearing checking accounts, N.O.W. accounts, and so on):	
First $40.4 million per institution	3
Additional funds	12
Savings accounts and time deposits not owned by individuals:	
With original maturity of less than $1\frac{1}{2}$ years	3
With original maturity of $1\frac{1}{2}$ years or more	0
Savings accounts and time deposits owned by individuals:	0
Eurodollar accounts:	0

SOURCE: *Federal Reserve Bulletin,* April 1990.

of overall interest-rate movements. It also plays a special role in monetary policy making, as we will see in the last section of this chapter.

The other borrowing opportunity is to borrow from the Federal Reserve at the *discount window*. Discount loans usually are cheaper because the Federal Reserve tries to make sure that the discount rate is a little lower than the federal funds rate. On the other hand, banks need to keep in mind that discount loans are granted at the Federal Reserve's discretion.

Because reserves can be borrowed, we distinguish between **nonborrowed reserves** and **borrowed reserves.** When banks borrow reserves from each other in the federal funds market, what is added to one bank's borrowed reserves is subtracted from the borrowed reserves of the lender bank. Thus, for the banking system as a whole, transactions in the federal funds market do not affect the amount of borrowed reserves. For the system, all borrowed reserves are borrowed from the Federal Reserve.

Banks arc free to hold reserves over the required amount. Such reserves are called **excess reserves** as opposed to **required reserves.** In practice, banks usually hold small amounts of excess reserves both in order to smooth transactions and as a buffer against running too low. However, since reserve assets earn no interest, whether as vault cash or on account with the Federal Reserve, the banks have a strong incentive to keep excess reserves as low as possible.

The reserve requirements originally were introduced to protect the depositors by ensuring that the bank would have a reasonable amount of liquid funds available to facilitate withdrawals. Today, however, the reserve requirements are much more important as part of the mechanism used by the Federal Reserve to control the supply of money. To see how this mechanism works, suppose there were no reserve requirements. Then banks would probably extend more credit to their customers than they do today, because reserves earn no return and loans to customers do. However, the recipients of these loans would not keep all they borrowed as cash in their pocketbooks. Instead they would use the money to pay bills to people or businesses who deposit their receipts back into the banking system. This increase in deposits would mean that the monetary aggregates had expanded. The banks would then like to lend and earn interest on the new deposits as well, so the process could go on for many more rounds. In this sense, reserve requirements help limit the supply of money.

Such a process does, in fact, take place every time a bank finds itself with excess reserves. A bank with excess reserves will attempt to increase its profits by lending the excess funds, and these same funds are likely to be redeposited in the banking system and thus generate a second round of excess reserves. Several rounds of this process may be repeated before all the excess reserves have been exhausted by the system. As we will see, the Federal Reserve influences the supply of money by manipulating bank reserves. The reserve requirements define the limits of this process and thus keep the money supply from getting out of hand.

THE TOOLS OF MONETARY POLICY

The Federal Reserve basically has four tools available for its conduct of monetary policy:

1. Open market operations

2. Changes in the discount rate

3. Changes in the reserve requirements

4. Interventions in the foreign-exchange markets

Open market operations involve purchases or sales of U.S. government securities, usually Treasury Bills, on the open market via private dealers in New York City. These operations are carried out almost every day by the Federal Reserve Bank of New York on directives from the Federal Open Market Committee.

Changes in the discount rate are less frequent and are considered to be more dramatic events. They are announced immediately through the media, with much fanfare. As we will see below, the same objectives that can be obtained by changing the discount rate often can be reached just as effectively via open market operations. However, changes in the discount rate are important exactly because they are announced with such fanfare. Because of their visibility, they can be used to signal the Federal Reserve's intentions.

Changes in the reserve requirements change the nature of the correspondence between reserves and deposits. Implementation of such changes, however, requires a substantial managerial effort by the entire banking system. As a result, this instrument is used rather infrequently. The most recent important case was a brief episode in 1980.

Interventions in the foreign-exchange markets involve purchases and sales of foreign currencies in exchange for dollars. Such interventions are carried out whenever the dollar exchange rate is perceived as moving too high or too low, which may happen rather frequently. In carrying out these actions, the Federal Reserve usually acts not at its own discretion but as an agent of the U.S. Treasury. Although the Federal Reserve currently disavows the use of this instrument for the purpose of controlling the supply of money, we will see in Chapter 10 that it is a central instrument for small countries seeking to maintain fixed exchange rates.

Open Market Operations Consider first an **open market operation.** To begin, think of an *open market purchase,* in which the Federal Reserve buys government securities in the open market. Specifically, suppose the Federal Reserve decides to buy 90-day Treasury Bills for $1 million from Citibank.* Payment is given in the form of a credit to Citibank's reserve account. Thus, the Federal Reserve's balance sheet shows an increase of $1 million in government securities on the assets side, matched by an equally large increase in reserve deposits on the liability side. By this rearrangement of its portfolio, the Federal Reserve has *added $1 million to bank reserves and hence to the monetary base.*

This is what we mean when we say that the Federal Reserve controls bank reserves and the monetary base. The control does not involve coercion. Instead, the Federal Reserve engages in voluntary trade of assets with the private sector in return for government securities. The private sector is willing to engage in such trade provided the Federal Reserve offers the right price. Determination of the right price is part of the effect of monetary policy on interest rates, which we will analyze much more comprehensively in Part II.

The Money Multiplier   The Federal Reserve's manipulation of bank reserves is only the beginning of the process whereby an open market operation affects the supply of money. Although Citibank's reserves have risen by $1 million in our example, the public's deposits in Citibank have not been affected by the change. Because reserve requirements are tied to deposits and no new deposits have been made, Citibank's *required* reserves have not changed, so the $1 million reserve increase represents *excess* reserves. From our discussion of reserve requirements, we know that the presence of excess reserves allows an expansion of bank lending and subsequently of customer deposits back into the banks. As a result, the level of deposits, and hence the supply of money as defined by the monetary aggregates, is likely to increase by several times the amount of the initial open market purchase. This is the **money multiplier** at work.

Detailed analysis of the money multiplier involves some tedious algebra that is presented in the appendix to this chapter. However, some insights can be gained without resorting to that amount of algebra. To simplify the argument, suppose there is only one type of deposit (say checking accounts) and that banks are required to hold reserves corresponding to a ratio r of these deposits. To begin with, suppose also that the banks have no desire to hold excess reserves. Then the required rela-

---

* In practice, the purchase is more likely to be made from a private investor that is not a bank. As this investor deposits the payments into a bank, however, the effect on bank reserves is the same as in the simpler case where the transaction is carried out directly between the Federal Reserve and a commercial bank.

tionship between reserves and deposits can be turned around and we can say that the deposits need to equal $1/r$ times the amount of reserves. Thus, for a given increase in reserves, say via an open market purchase, the money multiplier process will continue until deposits have risen by $1/r$ times the increase in reserves.

To find the effect on money supply, we must also consider changes in the public's holding of currency, because the money supply is the sum of currency in circulation and deposits. Suppose, however, as a somewhat extreme case, that the public does not change its holding of currency. In this case, the change in the money supply is just equal to the change in deposits, which we found to be $1/r$ times the change in reserves. Thus, the money multiplier is $1/r$. For example, if the reserve requirement is 10% ($r = 0.1$), then the money multiplier is $1/0.1 = 10$. In practical terms, this means that if reserves increase by, say, $1 million and the reserve requirement is 10%, then the money supply will increase by 10 times $1 million, or $10 million.

This simple result is complicated somewhat in the more realistic case in which the banks want to hold some excess reserves and the public wants to change its holding of currency when its total holding of money changes. The reason for the complication is as follows. Suppose, as an opposite extreme, that the public wants to keep all its money as currency. Then, even if an open market sale initially increases bank reserves and the entire amount is then lent out, none of the money finds its way back into the banking system as deposits. With no rise in deposits, no base is laid for a further increase in bank lending. Consequently, the initial increase in bank reserves is translated one for one into an increase in the public's holding of currency, and the increase in the money supply is limited to that amount. Thus, the money multiplier is 1, which obviously is a good deal less than 10.

In general, the public's desire to adjust its holding of currency creates a "leakage" in the monetary system such that some of the newly created money does not find its way back into the banks to be multiplied in the form of further lending of funds that are redeposited into the banks, and so on. Similarly, if the banks hold excess reserves, a given increase in bank reserves results in a smaller increase in lending, a situation which represents another "leakage" from the money multiplier process.

The appendix analyzes a case in which the banks want to hold a fixed ratio e of their deposits as excess reserves, while the public wants to hold a fixed fraction k of its money in the form of cash. The money multiplier then turns out to be

(4.1)
$$m = \frac{1}{r + e + k(1 - r - e)}.$$

In general, this multiplier lies between 1 and $1/r$, in other words, between the two extreme cases considered above. In the first case, we implicitly assumed $e = 0$ and $k = 0$. Then the denominator in equation (4.1) becomes $r + 0 + 0 \times (1 - r - 0) = r$, so that $m = 1/r$, just as we found. In the second case, the implicit assumption was $k = 1$, and the denominator in equation (4.1) reduces to $r + e + 1 \times (1 - r - e) = 1$, so that $m = 1$.

As a more realistic intermediate case, suppose, as above, that the reserve requirement is 10% ($r = 0.1$) but the banks hold 2% of their deposits as excess reserves ($e = 0.02$) and the public holds 25% of its money as cash ($k = 0.25$). Then the money multiplier is 2.94, which is greater than 1 but a good deal less than 10. Thus, in this case, an open market purchase of $1 million raises the money supply by a little less than $3 million.

Discount Rate Changes   A reduction in the discount rate would encourage banks to borrow from the discount window beyond their reserve requirements and to use the excess reserves to finance loans at a profit. The extension of such loans then would set off a multiplier process of the same kind as for open market operations. The discount rate change would differ from the open market operation by working via *borrowed reserves* rather than *nonborrowed reserves*. In terms of affecting the money supply, this difference is not significant, except that the central bank's control of borrowed reserves is a little less precise, as we will see in the next section.

If the same objective can be obtained either way, why does the Federal Reserve bother to change its discount rate? Basically, there are two reasons. First, as we mentioned above, discount rate changes are more visible than open market operations and thus can be used to signal the Federal Reserve's intentions. Second, the Federal Reserve has some interest in keeping the discount rate below the federal funds rate, because otherwise the member banks would have no incentive to borrow at the discount window. The Federal Reserve would then lose this instrument for imposing bank discipline. Of course, if the interest *differential* were the only concern, the Federal Reserve could engage in open market sales so as to create a scarcity of bank reserves and thus raise the federal funds rate. However, if the Federal Reserve does not want this to happen, simply reducing the discount rate will be much better. Adjusting the discount rate to align it better with market interest rates is sometimes referred to as a change "for technical purposes."

Changes in the Reserve Requirements   Both open market operations and discount-rate changes work directly on bank reserves. Their effects on the money supply follow from the relationship between reserves and deposits that is defined by the reserve requirements. The requirements limit the multiplier process and thus keep money supply down relative to reserves, and vice versa. Thus, if the Federal Reserve wants to reduce money supply, an increase of reserve requirements is an alternative method to those of open market sales and an increase in the discount rate. As mentioned above, however, changes in these requirements are used infrequently as instruments to change the supply of money.

Intervention in Foreign-Exchange Markets   An exchange rate is the price of the country's currency relative to that of some foreign currency. If these rates are perceived as too high, the central bank may react by selling its own currency in an attempt to drive the rates down again. Conversely, if they are perceived as too low, the central bank may buy its own currency in the open market. The Federal Reserve sometimes carries out such transactions on a substantial scale. However, it should be noted that the Federal Reserve usually intervenes as an agent for the Treasury and not as an independent agency.

The Federal Reserve currently does not use foreign-exchange interventions as a tool for controlling the supply of money. Nevertheless, the interventions have a direct effect on bank reserves and hence on the money supply. Suppose the Federal Reserve undertakes an intervention in the form of a sale of 1 million U.S. dollars to a U.S. member bank for the corresponding amount of Japanese yen. The Federal Reserve will then credit the member bank's reserve deposit for $1 million and in return receive the corresponding amount of yen from the bank. In terms of the Federal Reserve's balance sheet, this transaction involves an increase in official reserves worth $1 million, matched by an expansion in bank reserves by the same amount.

The latter part of this transaction is important, because it means that foreign-exchange interventions have consequences for bank reserves, and hence for the supply of money, similar to those of open market operations. In fact, on the Federal Reserve's liability side, the effect is identical to the $1 million open market purchase considered above. The only difference occurs on the asset side, where the Federal Reserve increases its official reserves rather than its holding of domestic government securities. Of course, the intervention also carries a message about the central bank's intentions in terms of exchange-rate policy that an open market operation would not have conveyed by itself.

The Federal Reserve can *undo* the effect on bank reserves by carrying out a matching open market *sale* of $1 million. Such neutralizing transactions are referred to as **sterilization.** However, the Federal Reserve may not want to sterilize. The point of selling U.S. dollars in the first place presumably is to make U.S. dollars less scarce in the market. What better way to reduce the scarcity of dollars than to increase the U.S. money supply?

4.5 TARGETS AND PRECISION

So far, we have discussed the mechanics of central bank control of the money supply. We have only touched upon why controlling the supply of money is worthwhile and have not discussed how accurate this control is in practice. This section discusses these issues. The purpose of controlling the money supply will become much clearer after we have studied the effects of monetary policy in Part II. However, it is useful to comment briefly on some of these issues before we close this chapter.

TARGETS IN MONETARY POLICY

Monetary policy potentially influences business cycles, is a major determinant of inflation, and affects interest rates and exchange rates on a day-to-day basis. In conducting monetary policy, the people at the Federal Reserve need to keep all these dimensions in mind. To help with this task, a substantial number of professional research economists are kept on staff at the Board of Governors in Washington as well as at each regional Federal Reserve Bank. These staff members are permitted and encouraged to engage in general macroeconomic research. However, an important part of their function is to advise the board and the presidents of the district banks about current economic developments. The members of the Federal Open Market Committee need such advice, because they seek to look at the overall health of the entire economy before issuing policy directives.

After the members of the Federal Open Market Committee have decided on the direction they want their policy to take, they must then determine how to carry it out. They need to choose among their tools: open market operations, discount rate changes, and changes in the reserve requirements. Furthermore, they also must determine which criterion to use to tell them when their policy has gone far enough. This is the role of **intermediate targets.**

A simple criterion is money supply itself, for example, M1, although the Federal Reserve recently has focused more on M2. At times, Federal Reserve officials have, in fact, declared that monetary policy would aim at controlling the monetary aggregates with little or no regard for the consequences for interest rates. The best-known recent example is the 1981–82 period, when the Federal Reserve worked hard to slow the rate of growth in the money supply in a successful attempt to curb inflation. In a statement to Congress, Chairman Volcker conceded that this policy could "contribute to exceptionally high interest rates for a time. But," he continued, "consider the alternative. If the supply of money is not restrained, the net result would surely be to acquiesce in an inflationary process." * In the face of the specter of continued high inflation, the Federal Reserve at that time decided not to let extreme interest rates distract their attention from the goal of curbing the growth in the monetary aggregates.

That episode, however, was somewhat of an exception. It has been more common for the Federal Reserve to keep its eye on interest rates as its intermediate target. This idea is sensible, because the link between money supply and interest rates should be a close one. Interest is the price paid for the temporary use of funds. This price depends on the scarcity of funds, and monetary policy affects this scarcity. Moreover, it can be argued that the movement in interest rates is more informative than the money-supply figures, because the interest-rate movements show the *effects* of monetary policy and not just mechanical movements in statistical aggregates whose definitions unavoidably contain elements of judgment. Also, interest rates can be studied daily and even hourly, while money-supply statistics are collected with a lag and are subject to measurement errors. In this context, it is not surprising to observe policy being directed at keeping key interest rates moving in a certain direction, with a particular band specified for the federal funds rate, rather than at having certain effects on the monetary aggregates themselves.

Specifically, since the mid-1980s, the Federal Reserve has used the federal funds rate as its intermediate target. The directives for open market operations, set forth by the Federal Open Market Committee, have identified specific target ranges for this interest rate for every six-week period between the meetings of this committee. Target ranges for the monetary aggregates M2 and M3 (but not M1) have been given as well, but they do not take the same central position in the directives. The choice of the federal funds rate is natural because it is the rate paid for funds that can be used directly as bank reserves. As such, it directly reflects the scarcity of reserves that are manipulated by the open market operations.

THE PRECISION OF THE FEDERAL RESERVE'S CONTROL

Another reason for targeting interest rates is the relative imprecision with which the Federal Reserve controls the supply of money. If the discussion in the previous sections of this chapter has left the impression of a very precise control, that impression is an artifact of the simplifying assumptions.

First, the Federal Reserve's control of bank reserves and hence the

---

* Paul A. Volcker, "Statement to Congress," *Federal Reserve Bulletin*, January 1981, vol. 67, no. 1, pp. 17–21.

monetary base is less precise than our discussion of open market operations indicated. It is true that the open market operations affect *nonborrowed* reserves directly and by the exact amounts of the open market operations. However, the control over *borrowed* reserves is less direct. Banks decide for themselves how much they want to borrow at the discount window. The Federal Reserve can encourage borrowing by offering an attractive discount rate, and vice versa, and it may limit the amount of borrowing by denying loan requests, but it cannot dictate the banks' decisions. Hence, because borrowed reserves are part of the monetary base, the Federal Reserve's control of reserves and the monetary base is inexact.

Second, the money multiplier process is unpredictable. It depends on bank behavior in regard to the holding of excess reserves. In the preceding section, we simplified this behavior by assuming that excess reserves are held in fixed proportion to deposits. In practice, this proportion is likely to be a function of interest rates as the banks' opportunity cost of holding reserves. Thus, the economists on the Federal Reserve staff might be able to make some predictions about the behavior of excess reserves, but not precise predictions.

Furthermore, the money multiplier process depends on the public's demand for currency. Again, we simplified by assuming that currency and demand deposits are demanded in fixed proportions. With some interest currently being offered on many demand deposits, variations in interest rates may again be relevant as the opportunity cost of holding currency. Even when this factor is taken into account, however, predicting the demand for currency has proved to be even more difficult in practice than predicting excess reserves.

Finally, in reality, there are different kinds of accounts that are subject to different reserve requirements and belong to different monetary aggregates. For example, whenever funds are transferred from a N.O.W. account to a time deposit, the reserve requirement for those funds may decline from 12% to 3%. At the same time, M1 declines by the amount of the transfer, while M2 stays unchanged. Such transfers are determined by the preferences of the public. Although Federal Reserve economists work hard to predict this behavior, their predictions can never be expected to be accurate.

Thus, in practice, the Federal Reserve's control over the supply of money is very inexact. Accidents are likely to happen where the monetary aggregates and interest rates move in the opposite direction of the policymakers' intentions. Because the deliberations of the Federal Open Market Committee are closed to the public, the participants in the financial markets are left to guess whether a surprising development is due to an unannounced change in policy or to a fluke in the system. This is part of what makes it exciting to watch economic indicators—the topic of Part IV.

CHAPTER REVIEW

1. Money is an important ingredient in modern economies because it removes the need to identify barter opportunities for every transaction.

2. The function of money is to serve as a means of exchange, a unit of account, and a store of value. Any asset or group of assets capable of filling all three functions could be called money.

3. In the United States, money is defined by the three monetary aggregates M1, M2, and M3. M1 essentially consists of currency and checking-account balances. M2 adds savings accounts, small time deposits, money market funds, and overnight repurchase agreements and Eurodollars. M3 adds large time deposits and term repurchase agreements and Eurodollars.

4. Central banks act as bankers' banks, accepting deposits, extending loans, and supplying cash; control the country's money supply; and monitor and intervene in the foreign-exchange markets.

5. The central bank of the United States is the Federal Reserve System. It consists of 12 district banks and a Board of Governors in Washington, D.C. The seven governors and five of the district bank presidents make up the Federal Open Market Committee. Although formally owned by its member banks, the Federal Reserve is an independent agency of the U.S. government.

6. The tools of monetary policy are open market operations, discount rate changes, changes in bank reserve requirements, and interventions in the foreign-exchange market. Open market operations and exchange interventions affect nonborrowed reserves, discount rate changes affect borrowed reserves, and changes in the reserve requirements affect the multiplier link between bank reserves and the monetary aggregates. Discount rate changes also signal the intentions of the Federal Reserve.

7. If banks hold no excess reserves and the public holds a fixed amount of currency, the money multiplier is the reciprocal of the reserve requirement ratio. If banks vary excess reserves with deposits and the public varies its currency holdings with its total money holdings, the multiplier is smaller, but greater than one.

8. The Federal Reserve's control of the money supply is inexact because borrowed reserves are not controlled directly and because the multiplier process depends on the unpredictable behavior of the public and of the banking system.

EXERCISES

1. Suppose the Federal Reserve buys government securities from a bank for $5 million. Assume that all deposits are demand deposits and that the reserve requirement ratio is 7%. Compute the money multiplier under each of the following two sets of assumptions.
    a. Banks hold no excess reserves, and the public does not want to change its holdings of currency.
    b. Banks hold excess reserves as 1.5% of their deposits, and the public wishes to hold 30% of its money as cash.

2. Consider the same situation as in exercise 1, but this time use the method derived in the appendix to trace the effects for the first five rounds as well as the total effects on bank reserves, bank lending, deposits, currency holding, the monetary base, and the money supply.

3. Repeat exercise 2, but assume that two banks are involved, bank A and bank B. The securities are bought from bank A, which lends money to a customer, but the deposit resulting from the loan is made in bank B. The second-round deposit is made in bank A, the third-round deposit in bank B, and so on. Compute the effects on reserves and deposits for each bank. When you add up the two banks, do you get a different answer for the banking system as a whole than you did in exercise 2? Why or why not?

4. Suppose the Federal Reserve buys govern-

ment securities for $5 million from an individual who has an account in bank A. How does this case differ from that in exercise 3?

5. Suppose that, as the effect of an increase in the discount rate, borrowed reserves decline by $2 million. Compute the same effects as in exercises 1 and 2 under the same alternative assumptions.

6. Using actual data for the United States, compute the growth rates (monthly at annual rates) for M1, M2, and the monetary base. Find their averages and standard deviations by decade and for the whole period for which data are available. Comment on the results.

7. Again using actual U.S. data, run a regression of the monthly changes in M1 on a distributed lag through six months of the changes in the monetary base. (In other words, run a regression with the monthly changes in M1 as the variable on the left, while the variables on the right are the corresponding change in the monetary base, the same change lagged one month, and so on through the same change lagged six months.) Explain what the results tell you about (a) the time pattern of the money multiplier process, (b) the total magnitude of the money multiplier, and (c) the predictability of the money multiplier.

8. Repeat exercise 7 for M2 instead of M1.

9. It might be expected that the demand for currency would have declined over time as a ratio of the money supply because other means of payments have become available. Are the data consistent with this expectation? Why or why not?

THINKING QUESTIONS

1. According to the explanation of the money multiplier process in Section 4.4, private banks contribute to the creation of money by lending to their customers. Yet every new loan is financed from funds that already exist within this bank. Where does the new money come from?

2. You may have noted that credit cards are not included in the definitions of the monetary aggregates, even though they can be used for payments. Can you explain why they are excluded? If they were to be included, how would you do it, and what do you think the consequences would be for the growth in the monetary aggregates?

3. Arguments sometimes are made that central banks should be abolished and the supply of money left to the private sector. Comment on the consequences of this proposal.

APPENDIX TO CHAPTER 4: THE MONEY MULTIPLIER PROCESS

Assume, for simplicity, that all deposits are demand (that is, checkable) deposits, so that the supply of money is defined unambiguously as the sum of currency and deposits. Use the following symbols:

$C:$ Currency held by the nonbank public

$D:$ Deposits

$R:$ Bank reserves

$B:$ The monetary base

By definition,

$$M = C + D,$$
$$B = C + R.$$

Also, define the money multiplier or, more specifically, the **base multiplier,** m, as the effect on money supply of a \$1 change in the monetary base, so that

$$m = \Delta M / \Delta B.$$

Assume that banks want to hold a constant fraction e as excess reserves in addition to the required ratio r, so that

$$R = (r + e)D.$$

Furthermore, assume that the public wants to hold a constant fraction k of its money as currency and the rest as deposits. Suppose now that, as an open market operation, the Federal Reserve buys Treasury Bills from a bank in the amount of ΔO. As we have seen, the initial effect is that bank reserves increase by just that amount as the payment for the Treasury Bills is made in the form of a credit to the bank's reserve account. Thus, initially, $\Delta R = \Delta O$.

Now the money multiplier goes to work. First, since nothing has yet happened to deposits, the bank will not change its reserves by requirement or by its own desire for excess reserves. Thus, the full amount ΔO is invested in a new loan. Second, the person receiving the loan wants to keep a fraction k of this amount as cash and to deposit the rest into a bank account. Thus, as a first-round effect, the increase in deposits is

(A.4.1) $$\Delta D_1 = (1 - k)\Delta O.$$

Banks now will keep the fraction $(r + e)$ of this amount as reserves and lend the rest. Then, in the second round, $(1 - r - e)\Delta D_1$ is lent. Again, a fraction $(1 - k)$ of this amount is redeposited, so that

(A.4.2) $$\Delta D_2 = (1 - k)(1 - r - e)\Delta D_1 = (1 - k)^2(1 - r - e)\Delta O.$$

Similarly, in the third round,

(A.4.3) $$\Delta D_3 = (1 - k)(1 - r - e)\Delta D_2 = (1 - k)^3(1 - r - e)^2\Delta O,$$

and, in general,

(A.4.4) $$\Delta D_i = (1 - k)(1 - r - e)\Delta D_{i-1} = (1 - k)^i(1 - r - e)^{i-1}\Delta O.$$

The total change in deposits is the sum of all these rounds, or

$$\Delta D = \Delta D_1 + \Delta D_2 + \Delta D_3 + \cdots$$

(A.4.5)
$$= [(1 - k) + (1 - k)^2(1 - r - e) + (1 - k)^3(1 - r - e)^2 + \cdots]\Delta O$$
$$= [1 + (1 - k)(1 - r - e) + (1 - k)^2(1 - r - e)^2 + \cdots](1 - k)\Delta O.$$

Here the expression in brackets is a geometric series with the common ratio $(1 - k)(1 - r - e)$. Using the standard formula for the sum of a geometric series, the total change in deposits becomes

$$(A.4.6) \quad \Delta D = \frac{1}{1 - (1 - k)(1 - r - e)}(1 - k)\Delta O$$

$$= \frac{1 - k}{r + e + k(1 - r - e)}\Delta O.$$

To find the change in money supply, we also must consider the change in currency holdings. The easiest way to find the total change in currency holdings is to use the assumption that people always want to hold a fraction k of their money as cash. Then the total change in currency holdings must equal k times the total change in money supply. Noting further that money supply is the sum of currency holdings and deposits, we obtain

$$(A.4.7) \quad \Delta C = k\Delta M = k(\Delta C + \Delta D).$$

Because ΔC occurs on both sides of this equation, we can solve to get

$$(A.4.8) \quad \Delta C = \frac{k}{1 - k}\Delta D.$$

Now we can find the change in the money supply as

$$(A.4.9) \quad \Delta M = \Delta C + \Delta D = \left(\frac{k}{1 - k} + 1\right)\Delta D$$

$$= \frac{1}{1 - k}\Delta D = \frac{1}{r + e + k(1 - r - e)}\Delta O.$$

From the definition of the monetary base, the change in this variable is

$$(A.4.10) \quad \Delta B = \Delta C + \Delta R = \left(\frac{k}{1 - k} + r + e\right)\Delta D$$

$$= \frac{k + (r + e)(1 - k)}{1 - k}\Delta D$$

$$= \frac{r + e + k(1 - r - e)}{1 - k}\Delta D = \Delta O.$$

Thus, the base multiplier is

$$(A.4.11) \quad m = \frac{1}{r + e + k(1 - r - e)}.$$

which is formula (4.1).

THE CORE OF MACROECONOMIC THEORY

PART II

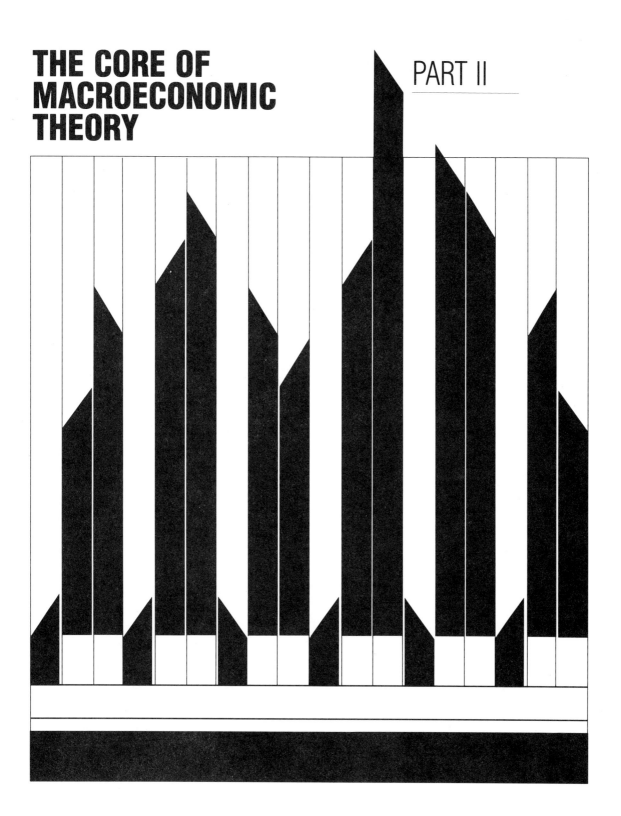

PART II

After having been introduced to the necessary preliminary material in Part I, you now should be ready to plunge into the conceptual framework that makes up the core of macroeconomic theory. In the language of Chapter 1, you are ready to be "formatted" like a computer disk, to be readied for the reading and interpretation of macroeconomic data as they appear from day to day in the news media.

The exposition of macroeconomic theory begins in Chapter 5 with an introduction to the market for goods and services. If you have studied microeconomics, the notion of a market should be familiar to you. However, the macroeconomic study of the market for goods and services is somewhat different from the microeconomic study of the market for, say, shoes. In the microeconomic case, at least part of the emphasis is on the choice between different kinds of commodities, such as the choice between shoes and sneakers or the choice between buying shoes and seeing a Broadway play. In macroeconomics, the emphasis is on the overall level of demand for *all* goods and services. In particular, we study how this demand level depends on income, which we will measure by GNP, and interest rates.

Chapter 6 expands the framework to include the financial markets. To keep the analysis simple, we represent these markets by a compact model of the supply and demand for money. When the market for goods and services and the money market are put together, we obtain the IS-LM model, a model of central importance for macroeconomic analysis in practice.

The IS-LM model, however, represents only one part of the economy, namely, the part we call aggregate demand. Chapter 7 extends the framework by introducing aggregate supply as that level of real GNP that firms would like to produce, given the current technology, the existing capital equipment, and that level of employment consistent with equilibrium between the demand and supply of labor.

A complete macroeconomic equilibrium results when aggregate supply equals aggregate demand. Economists disagree as to how quickly such an equilibrium is reached. Consequently, there are two basic approaches to studying fluctuations in the overall production level. These fluctua-

tions are what we call business cycles. The disagreement centers around whether these fluctuations should be analyzed as moving equilibria or as movements around a stable equilibrium.

Chapter 7 focuses on the overall price level as the force that can bring aggregate demand and aggregate supply together. Chapter 8 extends this focus by analyzing changes in this price level, in other words, inflation. The analysis covers both equilibrium and disequilibrium inflation. We will see that equilibrium inflation is a matter of growth in the money supply. In the short run, however, inflation may be driven by a disequilibrium mechanism known as the Phillips curve.

5 THE MARKET FOR GOODS AND SERVICES

Macroeconomic theory studies the balance between the demand and supply of goods and services in the economy as an **aggregate.** The term *aggregate* means that the focus is on the total level of demand (or supply) for *all* goods and services, rather than on individual goods, such as shoes. This chapter introduces the study of aggregate demand by analyzing the market for goods and services. Although the emphasis is on the total, we study the behavior of aggregate demand by considering four broad components. These components are the same as the expenditure components of GNP introduced in Chapter 3: consumption demand, investment demand, net export demand, and the government's demand for goods and services. In particular, we analyze how each of these demand components reacts to changes in aggregate income and interest rates. This discussion will enable us to construct a useful analytical tool called the "IS curve." In Chapter 6, the IS curve will be combined with another curve called the "LM curve." This combination will allow us to study the short-term determination of GNP and interest rates.

The IS and LM curves represent equilibria in the market for goods and services and the money market, respectively. Although we will think of equilibrium in the market for goods and services as a balance between production plans and spending plans, other accounts have been presented in terms of the balance between *I*nvestment and *S*aving, which is the background for the acronym IS. Similarly, LM stands for *L*iquidity and *M*oney in reference to equilibrium in the money market. This terminology was introduced by the twentieth-century British economist John Hicks in a now classic 1937 article.*

The analysis in this chapter focuses exclusively on *real* variables. We saw in Chapter 3 how real GNP is constructed by evaluating all goods and services at their 1982 prices, so that movements in real GNP reflect only quantity changes and not price changes. Similarly, when we study real consumption, investment, and so on, we study the behavior of the quantities purchased rather than the dollar amounts spent. The alter-

---

* John R. Hicks, "Mr. Keynes and the Classics: A Suggested Interpretation," *Econometrica*, 1937, vol. 6, pp. 147–59.

native would be to study *nominal* variables, whose movements partly or wholly reflect price movements and inflation. We introduce some important nominal variables in Chapter 6 and beyond.

We also distinguish between nominal and real *interest rates*. The *nominal* interest rate is the compensation a creditor receives for lending $1. The *real* interest rate is the compensation the creditor is left with after allowing for the fact that the real value of the principal may have been affected by inflation. The real, rather than the nominal, interest rate is the relevant concept for this chapter. Nominal interest rates enter the analysis in the next chapter.

After an initial overview of the market for goods and services, the investment and consumption components of aggregate demand are studied in particular detail in this chapter. This chapter also provides a preview of net export demand, while Chapters 9 and 10 give details about the relationship between the national and the global economy. Government demand is treated as an instrument of fiscal policy.

5.1 GOODS MARKET EQUILIBRIUM AND THE IS CURVE

Economic analysis usually centers around some kind of **equilibrium.** In this chapter, we study a simple kind of equilibrium, namely, one in which people's spending plans in terms of real goods and services just match the producers' planned output levels. We do not go into what determines the production plans; instead we make the rather simple (and not always realistic) assumption that firms seek to produce whatever the market buys. The emphasis is on spending decisions rather than production decisions. We refer to this type of equilibrium as "consistency of plans."

Spending plans and production plans do not have to coincide. If production plans are too optimistic, the companies making them will be unable to sell all their goods. As a result, inventories will pile up above what the managers had intended. Similarly, too pessimistic production plans result in involuntary inventory drawdowns. Equilibrium as the consistency of plans thus can be interpreted as a situation in which no involuntary pileups or drawdowns of inventories occur.

Real spending plans are represented by the demands for goods and services that arise from the four broad spending categories of consumption, investment, net exports, and government demand, which we denoted C, I, X, and G, respectively. In order to be consistent with production plans, the sum of these components must equal the level of planned production. Since overall production is measured by real GNP, which we denote Y, this equilibrium can be written as the following equation:

(5.1) $$Y = C + I + X + G.$$

Because this equilibrium condition refers to the production and spending plans for goods and services, equation (5.1) is also referred to as the condition for **equilibrium in the market for goods and services** or, for short, **equilibrium in the goods market.**

Although this equation has the same form as the GNP identity, equation (3.3), the interpretation is different. While the right side of equation (5.1) measures *planned* spending, the right side of the GNP identity reflects *actual* spending. If planned production exceeds planned spending, with the result that unintended inventories pile up, the National Income and Product Accounts treat this pileup as an investment in inventories. In other words, actual investment spending includes the inventory pileup, and planned spending does not. Because of this difference in interpretation, equation (5.1) is an equilibrium condition, which holds only in equilibrium, while equation (3.3) is an accounting identity that is always true by definition.

THE KEYNESIAN CONSUMPTION FUNCTION

In studying the equilibrium in the goods market, we start with some strong assumptions that simplify the analysis. Because these assumptions cannot be expected to be true, however, we will relax them later for improved realism.

Specifically, we assume initially that investment demand, net export demand, and government demand for goods and services are determined outside the model. In other words, we don't attempt to explain their behavior. In technical language, we say that we treat these spending components as **exogenous** variables. In contrast, we treat consumption and real GNP as **endogenous** variables, meaning that we try to explain them.

It seems reasonable to assume that the level of consumer spending is somehow related to people's *incomes.* Suppose this relationship is a very simple one, namely, that consumption in a given period is an increasing linear function of real income after tax during the same period. In macroeconomic terminology, real income after tax is called real **disposable income,** which we denote Y_d. The assumption that consumption is a linear function of disposable income then translates into the formula

(5.2)
$$C = a + bY_d.$$

The intercept in this function indicates the consumption level that could be expected if disposable income were zero. In such a case, we expect people to borrow or dig into their savings to maintain at least a minimal standard of living. Thus, we expect the parameter a to be positive, although it is worth noting that the case of a zero disposable income for a whole country is not very interesting. However, the slope coefficient b is important enough to have a name—the **marginal propensity to consume.** It indicates the change in real consumption that follows a $1 (in 1982 prices) increase in real disposable income. We will

FIGURE 5.1

The Keynesian consumption function.

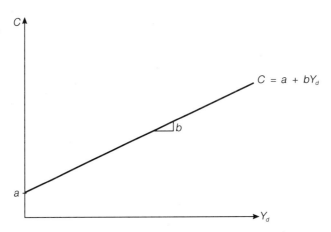

assume that this propensity is positive but less than 1. It is positive because people tend to consume more when their incomes go up and vice versa. It is less than 1 because, when people's incomes go up, they tend not to spend the entire increase but instead save some for a rainy day. Similarly, whenever people experience income declines, such as when they are laid off from work during recessions, they tend to dig a little into their savings in order to maintain their standard of living to some extent. As an example, the marginal propensity to consume might be 0.8, indicating that an increase in income of, say, $1,000 should result in a consumption increase of $800.

Equation (5.2) goes under the name of the **Keynesian consumption function** in reference to the famous British macroeconomist John Maynard Keynes (1883–1946). Although he did not explicitly formulate the consumption function, the relationship between income and consumption was one of the many topics he studied.* The consumption function is illustrated in Figure 5.1.

A SIMPLE GOODS MARKET EQUILIBRIUM

Remember that disposable income is income after taxes. Real income *before* taxes for the economy as a whole is the income that is generated by the production of GNP. In other words, it equals real GNP. This insight follows from the fact that whenever something is produced, it is also sold, and the sales revenue always ends up as someone's income.**

---

*Keynes's most influential work was his *General Theory of Employment, Interest, and Money* (New York: Harcourt Brace Jovanovich, 1935). This book summarized the insights Keynes had gained from studying the Great Depression in the 1930s.

**You might wonder what happens if something is produced but not sold. In the National Income and Product Accounts, this situation is handled by assuming that the producer sells the item to him- or herself as an investment in inventory. If the inventory increase was planned, this treatment is perfectly adequate. If it was not, the goods market is not in equilibrium. Thus, aggregate real income always equals real GNP in an accounting sense; in goods market equilibrium it also does so in a true sense.

Suppose now that we can approximate the tax system by a proportional tax on real GNP at the constant rate τ. For example, a 20% tax rate means that $\tau = 0.2$. Then disposable income can be written as $Y_d = (1 - \tau)Y$, and the Keynesian consumption function becomes

(5.2') $$C = a + b(1 - \tau)Y.$$

Now let us combine this function with the assumption that investment, net exports, and government spending are exogenous variables whose values are given outside the model. Then total planned spending can be written as

$$C + I + X + G = a + b(1 - \tau)Y + I + X + G,$$

where I, X, and G can be treated as constant parameters, as can the intercept a. This relationship tells us that *planned spending is an increasing function of real GNP.*

The equilibrium condition in the goods market, given by equation (5.1), now can be rewritten as

(5.3) $$Y = a + b(1 - \tau)Y + I + X + G.$$

The solution to this equation is a real GNP level that will make planned spending (on the right of the equation) just equal to that GNP level. When real GNP equals that level, which we call Y_0, the goods market is in equilibrium in the sense that spending plans equal planned production.

Figure 5.2 illustrates this equilibrium. Real GNP is measured along the horizontal axis, and planned spending and production are measured along the vertical axis. The 45° line shows planned production (PP in the graph) as equal to real GNP. The slightly flatter, upward-sloping line is the graph of the right side of equation (5.3), which shows planned spending (PS) as an increasing function of real GNP. At the point where the two lines intersect, labeled E, planned spending equals planned pro-

FIGURE 5.2

Equilibrium in the goods market.

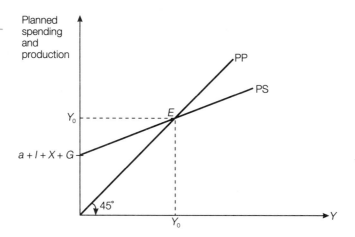

duction. This point represents equilibrium in the goods market. The equilibrium real GNP level is labeled Y_0 in the figure. This graph is often referred to as the Keynesian cross, after its crosslike shape and Keynes, who gave rise to the idea.

The algebraic solution to the Keynesian-cross model, Y_0, is the solution to equation (5.3), which is given by the formula

$$(5.4) \qquad Y_0 = \left[\frac{1}{1 - b(1 - \tau)} \right] (a + I + X + G).$$

THE SPENDING MULTIPLIER

Even though we so far have not tried to explain the behavior of investment, net exports, or government spending, it is interesting to ask what happens if one of these factors changes. Suppose, for example, that investment increases: Figure 5.3 shows what happens if the investment level rises from I_0 to I_1. Such an increase causes the line describing planned spending to shift upward from PS_0 to PS_1 because its intercept rises by the difference between I_1 and I_0. As a consequence, the goods market equilibrium shifts from E_0 to E_1, and the corresponding level of real GNP rises from Y_0 to Y_1.

You can probably see visually in the figure that real GNP rises by more than the investment increase, which is given by the vertical distance from PS_0 to PS_1. To see why, consider an increase in the demand for business computers as a practical example of an increase in investment demand. To meet this demand, the electronics industry will need to add to their staffs by hiring additional workers, so more people will be working. But more people working means more paid out in wages, so incomes rise. With higher incomes, people will want to consume more, as indicated by the consumption function. Thus, *planned spending rises*

FIGURE 5.3

The spending multiplier.

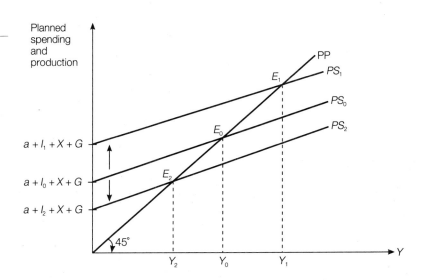

again, beyond the initial increase in investment demand. Perhaps the newly hired electronics workers will want to buy new cars. Then car production must increase as well to meet that demand. The auto industry will hire new workers, who will want to spend their new income on, say, household appliances. In this way, the increase in income and production activity may go on for several rounds. The end result is a production increase that exceeds the original demand increase.

This process is called the spending multiplier process. The **spending multiplier** is the ratio of the change in equilibrium real GNP to the initial change in planned spending. (Don't confuse this multiplier with the *money* multiplier introduced in Chapter 4, which describes the ratio of the change in the money supply to the initial change in bank reserves.) From what we have said, the spending multiplier exceeds 1. It also is called the **Keynesian multiplier,** again in reference to Keynes.

Algebraically, the spending multiplier is given by the coefficient $1/[1 - b(1 - \tau)]$ that in equation (5.4) multiplies those parts of planned spending we have assumed do not depend on income. Recall that we have assumed that b is positive but less than 1. The factor $(1 - \tau)$, which is the ratio of income left after tax, obviously also lies between zero and 1. You should be able to see that, under these circumstances, the multiplier is positive and *greater* than 1.

THE REAL INTEREST RATE

The assumption that all spending other than consumption is exogenous obviously is far from satisfactory. Intuitively, we expect that, at least, investment decisions are sensitive to interest-rate changes. Later in this chapter, we will find that it is sensitive to the *real* interest rate. Thus, before we proceed further in that direction, we need to grasp the concept of real interest rate.

Consider a simple society that produces only fish of a certain size and quality. In year 0, the price of a fish is $\$P_0$. During this year, you make a one-year loan of $\$P_0$ to your neighbor at an interest rate i, which means that your neighbor the following year (year 1) pays you back $\$P_0(1 + i)$. The interest rate i is a *nominal* interest rate, because it applies to the *dollar* amount $\$P_0$ rather than to the physical quantity (one fish) that this amount can buy.

You cannot eat dollars, however, you can only eat fish. Thus, when your neighbor has paid you back with interest, you will want to know how many fish you can buy for $\$P_0(1 + i)$ in year 1. The answer depends on how expensive fish have become by that time. Suppose the price per fish has risen to $\$P_1$. Then $\$P_1$ times the amount of fish you buy must equal the dollar amount you are paying, which is $\$P_0(1 + i)$. Thus, you can buy $(P_0/P_1)(1 + i)$ fish.

It seems natural to define the *real* interest on your loan as the percentage difference between the fish you can buy for your principal and interest in year 1 and the fish you could have bought for the principal in year

0, which was one fish. If we then call the real interest rate R, we can define it as

$$R = \frac{(P_0/P_1)(1 + i) - 1}{1} = \frac{1 + i}{P_1/P_0} - 1.$$

As in formula (3.4), we can define the inflation rate from year 0 to year 1 as

$$\pi = \frac{P_1 - P_0}{P_0} = P_1/P_0 - 1,$$

which can be solved as $P_1/P_0 = (1 + \pi)$. Substituting this solution into the formula for the interest rate, we obtain

$$R = \frac{1 + i}{1 + \pi} - 1 = \frac{i - \pi}{1 + \pi}.$$

In practice, it is useful to modify this formula in two ways. First, as long as inflation is reasonably low, we usually do not change the formula's value by very much if we ignore the factor $1 + \pi$ in the denominator. Second, at the time you make the loan, you might agree with your neighbor on the nominal interest rate, but you do not yet know what the inflation rate is going to be. For this reason, we usually define the real interest rate in terms of the *expected* inflation rate at the time the loan is extended. We denote this expected inflation rate by π^e. Thus, as an approximation, we define the real interest rate as *the difference between the nominal interest rate and expected inflation:*

(5.5) $$R = i - \pi^e.$$

For example, if the nominal interest rate is 11% and inflation is expected to be 4.5%, the real interest rate is 6.5%. Equivalently, the nominal interest rate can be written as the sum of the real interest rate and expected inflation:

(5.5′) $$i = R + \pi^e.$$

In real life, there are many types of interest rates—real as well as nominal—for different kinds of loans and bank accounts. Our analysis in the following section ignores this complication and proceeds as if there were only one nominal and one real interest rate. We will continue to denote them by i and R, respectively.

THE IS CURVE

When the real interest rate rises, the real cost of financing investment projects rises. Since in reality investment decisions are not exogenous but the result of careful comparisons between costs and revenues, we must expect that an increase in financing costs reduces investment de-

FIGURE 5.4

The IS curve.

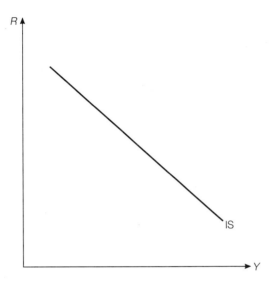

mands. We will see later that real-interest-rate changes also have similar effects on consumption demand and net export demand, but let us ignore that for now.

We then find that an increase in the real interest rate works via the spending multiplier as follows. First, the higher real interest rate reduces investment demand. This effect is illustrated as the downward shift in the planned-spending line from PS_0 to PS_2 in Figure 5.3. Next, consumption spending declines because workers are laid off in the industries producing investment goods and reduce their spending as their incomes go down. This spending decline leads to yet further layoffs and production cuts until a new equilibrium is reached at E_2 in Figure 5.3.

What we have just found is that *an increase in the real interest rate reduces the level of real GNP that corresponds to equilibrium in the goods market.* This inverse relationship can be shown graphically in the form of a downward-sloping curve in a diagram where the horizontal and vertical axes measure real GNP and the real interest rate, respectively. This curve, which has come to be known as the **IS curve,** is shown in Figure 5.4. Although it is useful to think of the real interest rate as the independent variable causing changes in real GNP, it has become customary to draw this curve in a diagram with real GNP (Y) on the horizontal axis and the real interest rate (R) on the vertical axis.

NET EXPORT DEMAND

Later in this chapter, we will see that consumption can also be expected to be influenced by the real interest rate, in the same direction as investment. We will also find that investment, like consumption, is apt to depend positively on the level of real GNP. A full description of the behavior of net export demand belongs in a discussion of the international linkages of the economy, which we take up in Chapters 9 and 10. However, because the behavior of net export demand influences the shape of the IS curve, we give a preview of that discussion here.

Net export demand is the difference between foreigners' demand for our exports and our demand for imports. Broadly speaking, export demand depends on the income level abroad, import demand depends on the income level at home, and both depend on the relative prices of foreign and domestic goods.

The foreign income level is a background variable for our analysis. We treat it as exogenous and do not include it formally in the analysis. Domestic income is, as we have seen, synonymous with our real GNP. We have already seen that an increase in this income raises consumption spending, and we have just noted that investment spending will probably rise as well. Some of this spending increase is likely to be directed toward imported goods. Thus, import demand depends positively on real GNP. Since the import component enters negatively into the computation of net exports, this relationship also means that *net export demand depends negatively on real GNP.*

This effect thus subtracts from the total effect of a change in real GNP on planned spending. However, the negative effect via net exports is not large enough to reverse the direction of the total effect. The reason is that even though some of the spending increase induced by a rise in income will be directed toward imported goods, a remaining part will always be directed toward domestic goods.

We have already noted that both export and import demand are influenced by the relative prices of domestic and foreign goods. If domestic goods become cheaper relative to foreign goods, it becomes desirable for people both at home and abroad to switch their purchases to goods made in this country. Thus, export demand will rise and import demand fall, with the result that net export demand rises.

In analyzing the relative prices of domestic and foreign goods, we need to consider the fact that different countries use different **currencies.** For example, while U.S. goods are priced in dollars, Japanese goods ultimately are priced in yen. In order to compare prices, we also need to consider the **exchange rate,** which we define as the price of our currency relative to the foreign currency. When this rate increases, foreigners need to pay more to obtain our currency, while we can get their currency more cheaply. For this reason, an increase in the exchange rate raises the price of domestic goods relative to that of foreign goods, so net export demand declines.

The exchange rate in turn *depends positively on the domestic real interest rate.* To see why, suppose the U.S. interest rate increases. Then international investors, such as the large banks, will normally want to move funds into dollar-denominated assets in order to earn this higher interest rate. Thus, the demand for dollar-denominated assets increases, which puts upward pressure on the dollar exchange rate. On the other hand, this mechanism would not work if the interest-rate increase were only nominal and not real, that is, if the interest-rate increase came from the expected-inflation term in formula (5.5') rather than from its real-interest part. Then, if the same investors bought dollars, they would have to expect to get stuck with a currency whose real value would be eroded by higher inflation. As a result, this nominal interest–rate increase would fail to increase both the demand for dollars and the dollar exchange rate. Thus, an increase in the *real* interest rate drives up the exchange rate and hence the relative price of domestic goods, which in turn discourages net export demand. Like investment, then, *net export demand depends negatively on the real interest rate.*

This result is important because it adds yet another reason for the IS curve to slope downward. However, you probably also noticed that the result depends on a number of mechanisms interacting with each other. Because each of these mechanisms is somewhat uncertain, the predictions we can make are approximations at best. This is one reason why the behavior of net exports appeared somewhat erratic in the graph in Figure 3.11.

5.2 INVESTMENT

So far, our discussion of the forces influencing real investment demand has been highly cursory. Because the fluctuations in investment demand are an important part of the movements in overall spending demand over the business cycle, we will now discuss these forces with more rigor.

When a manager considers an investment project, he or she needs to determine whether the project is likely to increase the company's profits. Profitable projects will probably be accepted and unprofitable projects rejected. The profitability of an investment project depends, in a broad sense, on the extra cash flow it generates compared to the cost of acquiring and financing the new asset.

A major portion of this cost is the *financing* of the up-front expenditures that are always involved in an investment project, such as the construction of a new office building. If such a project is financed by a bank loan at a nominal interest rate i, that interest rate represents the nominal financing cost. However, if inflation is expected, you can expect the value of the office building to appreciate, and the resulting capital gain will compensate you for the expected-inflation part of the interest rate. You are left with the real interest rate as the real cost of financing.

A bank loan is only one of many ways to finance an investment project. Bond financing, which is just a different way of organizing a loan, is similar. But what if the project is financed internally? The key to understanding this case is to note that the funds used to finance the project would be taken away from financial investment opportunities, where the same funds could have earned the market rate of return, which reflects the rate of interest. Thus, the interest rate reenters the picture as the **opportunity cost** of financing.

THE RENTAL PRICE OF CAPITAL

The purpose of investing in new capital equipment is to use it in the production of goods and services. The real interest rate is only part of the real cost of such use. Depreciation costs, for example, are important as well.

The real cost of using a piece of capital equipment is similar to the rent you would pay if you leased the equipment. Consequently, we refer to it as the **real rental price of capital.** In order to understand this price, we consider the profits of a leasing company that is buying a piece of capital equipment (say, an office building) in order to lease it to another company for a year.*

In year 0, the leasing company buys the building for $\$P_0$, which it finances completely with a loan at the nominal interest rate i. During that year, the leasing company also must consider the costs of physical depreciation in the form of wear and tear (we can think of it as maintenance cost). Suppose this cost comes to a fraction δ of the purchase price, so that the total depreciation cost is $\$\delta P_0$. In the year after, the leasing company receives rent at an amount we will call $\$V$ (the example becomes a little simpler by assuming that the rent is paid in arrears). In addition, the leasing company can sell the building in year 1 at the then prevailing price of $\$P_1$ and pay off the loan with interest at $\$P_0(1 + i)$.

Suppose it does. Then its profit from these transactions will be

$$P_1 + V - P_0(1 + i) - \delta P_0.$$

Let π_K denote the percentage change in the price of office buildings from year 0 to year 1, so that $P_1 = (1 + \pi_K)P_0$. Then the profit can be written as

$$V + P_0[1 + \pi_K - (1 + i) - \delta] = V - P_0(i - \pi_K + \delta).$$

Thus, in order to break even, the leasing company needs to charge a rent of

$$V = P_0(i - \pi_K + \delta).$$

---

*More details of this analysis can be found in Robert E. Hall and Dale W. Jorgenson, "Tax Policy and Investment Behavior," *American Economic Review,* June 1967, vol. 57, pp. 391–414.

This rent is expressed in nominal dollars. Suppose the overall price level for *all* goods is P, so that P buys the same amount of goods today as $1 bought in the base year. Using that amount as our unit of goods, we find that V today can buy $v = V/P$ such units, which we call the real rental price of capital. Furthermore, P_0 can buy $p = P_0/P$ units, which we call the real asset price for capital goods. Then the break-even real rental price of capital is

$$(5.6) \qquad\qquad v = p(i - \pi_K + \delta).$$

This price thus reflects not only the real interest rate (now expressed as $i - \pi_K$) but also the cost of depreciation δ and the price of capital assets p.

However, the real interest rate is expressed a little differently than in formula (5.5). Since the inflation rate applies to the prices of capital goods only, this real interest rate applies exclusively to the financing of capital investment and not, say, to consumer loans. In macroeconomics, we often ignore the differences in price developments for different goods and thus assume that the inflation rate for capital assets is the same as for the economy as a whole. Under that assumption, the real asset price p (the price of capital assets relative to other goods) becomes a constant, and we might as well choose units such that $p = 1$. Finally, note as in the last section that the rental rate needs to be set before next year's inflation is known and thus is based on the *expected* inflation rate. With these modifications, we can simplify the formula for the real rental price of capital so it becomes

$$(5.6') \qquad\qquad v = i - \pi^e + \delta = R + \delta.$$

The real rental price of capital is the sum of the real interest rate and the depreciation rate.

INVESTMENT AND THE DEMAND FOR CAPITAL

In Chapter 3, we looked at some data that described the behavior of investment. In particular, Figure 3.9 showed that overall investment fluctuates with GNP over the business cycle, a fact consistent with the idea that investment is an increasing function of GNP. However, we also found that investment fluctuates a good deal *more* over the business cycle than does GNP. Figure 3.10 further indicated that residential investment fluctuates more than business fixed investment. Some additional insights into this behavior can be gained by analyzing how investment demand is driven by the demand for capital as an input to production.

The purpose of real investment is to create new capital goods and replace old ones. Define the symbol K as the total stock of existing capital that exists at the end of the current year. Assume, as above, that a fraction δ of the capital stock depreciates every year. Then out of last year's capital stock, denoted K_{-1}, only the portion $(1 - \delta)K_{-1}$ is left today. In addition, this year's investment is added. Thus, at the end of this year, we have

(5.7) $$K = (1 - \delta)K_{-1} + I.$$

If this equation is solved for I and if ΔK is used to denote $(K - K_{-1})$, we obtain

(5.8) $$I = \Delta K + \delta K_{-1}.$$

The first term on the right of equation (5.8) is the net addition in the capital stock from this year to next, referred to as **net investment.** The second term is the investment needed to replace that part of the capital stock that is lost to depreciation; we call it **replacement investment.**

Firms use capital together with labor and other inputs to produce their individual outputs, which in the aggregate add up to GNP. Thus, the demand for capital is the demand for an input to production. Consistent with our discussion above of the real rental price of capital, we will think of this demand as a demand for *use* rather than for ownership. Common economic reasoning then leads us to expect that this demand will be lower the more expensive it is to use capital; in other words, it should be a decreasing function of the real rental price of capital.

Economists are often willing to assume that production takes place under what is called *constant returns to scale.* This technical term means that an increase in output can be obtained by increasing all inputs in the same proportion as the output level. Under this condition, it can be shown that the demand for capital as an input to production is proportional to the level of output, where the proportionality factor is a decreasing function of the real rental price of capital. Naturally, this year's production must rely on the capital available at the beginning of this year and hence at the end of last year, in other words, K_{-1}. Then the firm's desired relationship between capital and output can be written as

(5.9) $$K_{-1} = f(v)Y,$$

where f is a decreasing function of the real rental price v.

A similar relationship naturally will apply for next year, namely, $K = f(v^e)Y^e$, where the superscript e, as before, refers to the expected values for next year. If we subtract equation (5.9) from this expression, we obtain an interesting equation for *net investment:*

(5.10) $$\Delta K = f(v^e)Y^e - f(v)Y.$$

Three insights can be gleaned from this equation. First, investment demand depends not only on today's real GNP level but also on expectations about future GNP, because investment means to produce capital for future use. Second, net investment is a function of the *change* in real GNP rather than its level. This relationship, called the **accelerator prin-**

ciple, holds exactly whenever the real rental price is expected to remain unchanged over time, because then the right side of the equation becomes $f(v)(Y^e - Y)$. Otherwise, it holds as an approximation. The accelerator principle indicates that investment demand may fluctuate dramatically over the business cycle because the *changes* in real GNP fluctuate much more than its level. This is exactly what we observed in Figure 3.9.

Third, as expected, net investment depends on the real rental price of capital. Note, however, that the dependence here is also on the change rather than on the level. This result reflects the fact that investment decisions involve a choice not only about how much to invest but also about *when* to invest. Thus, if the real rental price is expected to decline, firms tend to postpone investment until the real rental price is low.

Now consider replacement investment. From equation (5.9), we can write it as

$$(5.11) \qquad\qquad \delta K_{-1} = \delta f(v)Y.$$

Thus, this investment component has the expected negative relationship with the real rental price and hence with the real interest rate.

Furthermore, replacement investment is proportional to the level of real GNP rather than to its change. Thus, it should be smoother than net investment over the business cycle. Also, the amount of replacement investment is proportional to the rate of depreciation. Since fast depreciation means a short life for the equipment, the investment figures for short-lived assets should contain a larger portion of replacement investment and thus be smoother over the business cycle than investment figures for long-lived assets.

This insight can explain the difference between residential investment and business fixed investment observed in Figure 3.10. Because business fixed investment contains a good deal of machinery and residential investment is dominated by houses and apartment buildings, which are longer lived, business fixed investment has the higher average depreciation rate. Thus, replacement investments are needed for this category even during recessions; this explains why it fluctuates relatively moderately.

THE *Q*-THEORY OF INVESTMENT

An alternative approach for analyzing investment demand is to look at the stock market rather than the credit market. As an introduction to this approach, look at equation (5.9). The right side of this equation represents the demand for capital, and the left side represents the supply. Suppose demand exceeds supply. Then the market will react by investing in new capital, so that equation (5.9) again can be satisfied. However, this process takes time, because the building of new capital equipment is a time-consuming, physical process. This feature is built into equation (5.9) because the supply of capital is limited to the capital stock available at the end of last year.

In the meantime, we can expect to see a different market reaction, namely, that the price of the *existing* capital will be bid up from the competition among those who want to own it. The market for ownership of existing capital is the stock market. Thus, other things equal, an increase in stock prices can be taken as an indication that investment activity is about to rise.

The caveat of "other things equal" refers to the price of *new* capital. Naturally, if this price rises, we should expect the stock market to rise as well, because new capital and existing capital are close substitutes. It is when stock prices rise faster than the prices of new capital assets that we can expect investment activity to pick up.

The ratio between stock prices and the price of new assets is usually denoted by the letter Q. That is why this approach is referred to as the Q-theory of investment. It predicts that investment activity is an increasing function of Q. You might also see this ratio referred to as "Tobin's Q," in reference to Professor James Tobin of Yale, who introduced the idea.[*] Tobin later was awarded the Nobel prize, partly for this contribution.

5.3 CONSUMPTION

In a fundamental sense, consumer spending is determined by income. People with comfortable incomes can afford to consume more than people of modest means. This is necessarily so, because households ultimately are bound by a **budget constraint:** They cannot spend what they don't have. The Keynesian consumption function reflects the link between consumption and income, but it simplifies this link to a one-to-one relationship that does not hold when we consider the time dimension of the budget constraint. If people save, they spend less than their income; if they live off prior savings or incur debt, they can spend beyond their income. As a result, people are able to maintain a reasonably stable standard of living even if their incomes go up and down. This section studies this relative stability, or *smoothness*, of consumption. It then attempts a more complete explanation of consumer spending, which goes under the name of the forward-looking theory of consumer behavior.

---

[*] See James Tobin and William Brainard, "Asset Markets and the Cost of Capital," in *Economic Progress, Private Values and Public Policy: Essays in Honor of William Fellner* (Amsterdam: North-Holland, 1977).

THE SMOOTHNESS OF CONSUMPTION

In Figure 3.7, we observed that consumption has followed the general development of real GNP since World War II. However, we also observed that the correlation between the two is much less exact over the business cycle. In particular, recessions are characterized by sometimes sharp declines in real GNP, while declines in real consumption are much milder, if present at all. This behavior is what we mean by the smoothness of consumption.

The Keynesian consumption function offers two explanations for this phenomenon. The first explanation is that the income tax system makes disposable income a little more stable than real GNP because the accompanying fluctuations in tax collections blunt the fluctuations in real GNP a little—if your income goes down, at least your taxes go down, too. However, consumption is even smoother over the business cycle than disposable income, as we can see from the comparison of these two variables in Figure 5.5. Here, the second explanation comes in. It says that because the marginal propensity to consume is less than 1, people save some of their income increases for a rainy day and dip a little into these savings when their incomes go down in recessions.

A subtle feature in the data, however, makes this explanation implausible. When we consider the total increase in income over the four

FIGURE 5.5

Historical data (quarterly 1947–89) for real disposable income and real consumption in the United States, showing that consumption has followed income in the long run but has been smoother over the business cycle. The shaded areas indicate recessions.

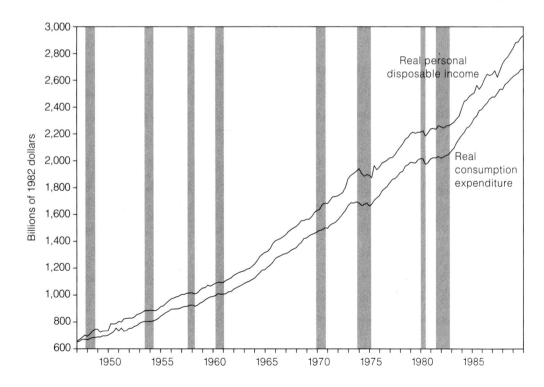

decades covered by the graph in Figure 5.5, we see that consumption has responded by increasing by almost the full amount of the income growth. In contrast, when disposable income has declined because of the onset of a recession, the consumption response typically has been much more modest. For example, while real disposable income declined by 69 billion 1982 dollars from the fourth quarter of 1973 to the first quarter of 1975, real consumption declined by less than 10 billion.

This difference in response suggests that *the marginal propensity is not a constant* but is influenced by the economic environment, such as the stage of the business cycle. Specifically, we can interpret the data in Figure 5.5 as indicating that, for long-term, or **permanent,** income changes, the marginal propensity to consume is close to unity. For short-term, or **transitory,** income fluctuations, it appears to be considerably smaller.

This seemingly minor difference actually is quite important, because the answers to a number of practical questions depend on the value of the marginal propensity to consume. For example, predictions of the effects of a tax cut would depend crucially on how much of the cut people are expected to spend and how much they will save. Similarly, if a recession has been forecast, retailers would like to know how severe a slowdown the recession will mean for their sales; then they are just asking about the marginal propensity to consume.

The Keynesian consumption function, because it postulates a constant propensity, is contradicted by the above observation. One of the purposes of constructing the forward-looking theory was to make sense of the variation in the marginal propensity to consume.

THE FORWARD-LOOKING THEORY OF CONSUMPTION

The basic premise of the **forward-looking theory of consumption** is an assumption that people make decisions about today's spending as part of a rational plan involving how much and when they want to spend in the future. Naturally, this plan is subject to a good deal of uncertainty about future income prospects and spending needs, but people are assumed to deal *rationally* with this uncertainty.

In Chapter 2, we studied the concept of the expectation of a stochastic variable. To emphasize the mathematical origin of this concept, we often refer to it as the *mathematical* expectation. Dealing rationally with uncertainty means that any subjective expectations formed are equal to the mathematical expectations of the relevant variables. Expectations formed in this manner are called **rational expectations.** Alternatively, rational expectations can be thought of as optimal forecasts, which we also studied in Chapter 2. The actual methods that consumers use may be less formal; nevertheless, it is assumed that the decisions people make are approximately the same as those that would be made if the appropriate statistical techniques in fact were applied.

The essence of the forward-looking theory, then, is as follows. When consumers make their decisions about how much they want to spend today, they look not only at their current income level but also at how much they expect to earn in the future. Given this information, they formulate a *financial plan* specifying how much they can afford to spend today and still afford a comparable life-style later in their lives.

To see how such a plan might work, consider first a person who expects to receive the same annual salary income (in real terms) for the rest of his or her life. For such a person, the solution is trivial: Unless needs change in a predictable way over time, the optimal plan is to consume just the amount earned each year. On the other hand, a person who expects to receive the same income on average but in a more irregular fashion—for example, as commission for real-estate sales—has no reason to behave any differently. To be sure, a real-estate agent needs to save a little to prepare for slow times; however, he or she has no need to plan a more *irregular* consumption pattern than the person who receives a steady income.* The point is that for predictable income the opportunity to save and borrow *breaks the immediate tie* between income and consumption.

Of course, this does not mean that consumption is always constant. Consumers make their plans based on the information they have available. Every time something new and unexpected happens, they need to *revise* their financial plans to fit the new environment. Thus, a person who is laid off unexpectedly will need to revise his or her spending plans downward. However, as long as there is hope of a recall, or at least another job some time in the future, consumption need not be reduced to a bare minimum even if income goes to zero in the short run. Similarly, the news of better job opportunities in economic recovery periods allows people to revise their consumption plans upward. If the good times are expected to be temporary, for example, construction work in a

---

*In one version of the forward-looking theory, known as the *permanent-income theory*, this phenomenon is interpreted as spending according to people's *permanent*, or "normal," income rather than their actual current income. The permanent-income theory was introduced by Milton Friedman of the University of Chicago in his book *A Theory of the Consumption Function* (Princeton: Princeton University Press, 1957), which helped him win the Nobel prize in economics in 1976. The other version of the forward-looking theory considers more explicitly the consumer's optimization problem and the implications for spending over a person's lifetime. This version is called the *life-cycle theory* and goes back to the work of Franco Modigliani of the Massachusetts Institute of Technology in a series of articles including Albert Ando and Modigliani, "The Life-Cycle Hypothesis of Saving: Aggregate Implications and Tests," *American Economic Review*, vol. 53, 1963, pp. 55–84. This work helped Modigliani win a Nobel prize in 1986. A major sharpening of this theory followed from its merging with the rational-expectations hypothesis. A pioneering contribution to this merger was made by Robert E. Hall in his article "Stochastic Implications of the Life Cycle–Permanent Income Hypothesis Under Rational Expectations: Theory and Evidence," *Journal of Political Economy*, December 1978, vol. 86, no. 6, pp. 971–87.

new oil field, the consumer would be well advised to spend only part of the new income and save some for the potentially leaner future. On the other hand, if the new jobs are permanent, there is no reason not to let consumption reflect that potential by spending the full amount of the new, higher income.

In this way, the forward-looking theory offers an explanation for the observed smoothness on consumption relative to disposable income. On the one hand, the long-term trend in income represents permanent changes, which are reflected fully in consumption. On the other hand, recessions represent temporary income reductions, which call for some reduction in consumption, but not to the same extent as the decline in income. Moreover, we also find a clue to predicting the effect on consumer spending of a given income change. Consider the example of a tax cut, which increases disposable income. If it is temporary, the effect on consumption should be minor, while a permanent tax cut should have a substantial effect.*

A simple algebraic description of the behavior implied by the forward-looking theory goes as follows. Let Y_d^e be a variable that summarizes the consumer's expectations about his or her future income levels. In practice, there will, of course, be many such levels, one for each remaining year the consumer expects to live. However, because the distinction between the near and the far future is not essential here, we catch the main idea by using one variable as a generic representation of the future. Furthermore, let z be a parameter whose value lies somewhere between zero and 1. Then the forward-looking theory can be used to modify the Keynesian consumption function as follows:

(5.12) $$C = a + b[zY_d + (1 - z)Y_d^e].$$

This equation expresses the main ideas of the forward-looking theory. If disposable income changes permanently, both current and future income levels (Y_d and Y_d^e) change by the same amount. Then, since z and $(1 - z)$ sum to 1, consumption changes by b times that amount. This result means that b must now be interpreted as the marginal propensity to consume out of permanent income changes, which should be close to 1. In contrast, suppose income changes temporarily, so that the expected future income level is unchanged. This would be the result, for example, of a temporary layoff due to a recession. Then consumption would change by only the smaller amount bz times the income change.

---

*In a recent paper, Alan Blinder and Angus Deaton of Princeton University examine the effects of a number of tax changes in the postwar period. See their article "The Time Series Consumption Function Revisited," *Brookings Papers on Economic Activity*, no. 2, 1985. Their findings offer some support for the forward-looking theory but also some conflicting evidence.

We can analyze reactions to tax changes more explicitly by including the tax rate in the formula, as in equation (5.2′). Let τ again symbolize today's tax rate, and use τ^e as a symbol for expected tax rates in the future. Then equation (5.12) can be written as

(5.12′) $C = a + b[z(1 - \tau)Y + (1 - z)(1 - \tau^e)Y^e].$

This formula implies that consumers will react much more strongly to a tax cut if tax rates are expected to stay low into the future. A temporary tax, however, will have a much more modest effect.

RICARDIAN EQUIVALENCE

An interesting question arises when a tax cut is not matched by a corresponding cut in government spending and thus leads to a deficit in the government's budget. Then the forward-looking theory can be used to argue that rational consumers understand the need for the deficit to be paid for in the form of higher future taxes. Thus, the reduction in the current tax rate τ will be matched by an increase in the future tax rate τ^e. Formula (5.12′) then suggests that the expectation of higher taxes in the future should dampen the boost to consumption of today's tax cut. In fact, it is possible to carry this argument further to say that consumers should save now exactly the amount needed to cover this future tax burden. This amount turns out to exactly equal the tax cut. Furthermore, if the consumers care about their descendants' well-being, it should not matter if the future tax increase can be expected to be implemented after their death. They should therefore save to leave an estate large enough to cover the higher tax when it is levied on their heirs. Thus, private saving should increase so as to match the government deficit exactly. This hypothesis is called **Ricardian equivalence** after the nineteenth-century British economist David Ricardo, who first voiced the idea.* After a fair amount of recent research, this view has gained a number of followers, yet many economists continue to regard it as a good argument carried to an absurd extreme.

EVALUATION OF THE FORWARD-LOOKING THEORY

Much research has been devoted to tests of the more basic implications of the forward-looking theory. As often happens in economics, the outcome of these tests has been somewhat ambiguous. What seems to be the case is that this theory describes the data reasonably well in an *approximate* sense. However, it does not seem to fit the data perfectly. Part of the reason for this less-than-perfect fit may be that the assumption

---

*The modern formulation of Ricardian equivalence was presented in a 1974 article by Robert J. Barro, then a professor at the University of Rochester (now at Harvard University). See Robert J. Barro, "Are Government Bonds Net Worth?" *Journal of Political Economy*, November–December 1974, vol. 82, pp. 1095–118.

about perfect rationality is too strong. Fully rational expectations may go beyond normal human capability. In fact, consumers might not even *try* to be rational all the time but instead let themselves be influenced by social norms and emotional whims.

Furthermore, the theory implicitly assumes that the consumers' financial plans can be made without constraints on borrowing. In particular, it assumes that a person who expects higher income later has no difficulty borrowing against that income in order to plan a smooth consumption path over time. If this is true, a business student should not need to wait until graduation to enjoy the prospects of a fat salary. In practice, however, the financial institutions may not always be willing to risk that these expectations will be realized, even though the person might have good reason to believe they will.

The forward-looking theory may not be the perfect answer to the shortcomings of the Keynesian consumption function, but it gives us some extremely important insights. In particular, analysts making predictions about consumer spending should pay special attention to people's expectations about the future. The link between income and consumption is fundamental, but its form is complex.

CONSUMER DURABLES

In Figure 3.8, we saw that expenditure on consumer durables roughly follows other consumption expenditure but is more volatile over the business cycle. More precisely, spending on durables responds to income changes in the same *direction* as nondurable consumption, but the responses are much stronger.

The key to understanding this relationship is the realization that the decision to buy a durable consumer good is essentially an investment decision. Thus, it is not surprising that the spending on consumer durables, like investment, fluctuates a good deal over the business cycle. As in the case of investment decisions, consumers decide not only *how much* to buy of consumer durables but also *when* to buy them. Thus, when a recession hits, durables purchases such as trading the old car for a new one tend to be postponed until after the recession. As a result, sales of new cars may drop significantly.

Because of this phenomenon, industries engaged in the production or sales of consumer durables tend to be highly sensitive to business-cycle fluctuations in the economy. However, the cycle has an upside as well as a downside. During a recession, a large number of households may wait patiently until times get better to replace their durables. When the economy turns around, these households represent a substantial pent-up demand for durable goods. This catch-up tendency in durable-goods markets explains the strong recovery for this spending component following each recession.

CONSUMP-TION, SAVING, AND INTEREST RATES

Saving is what is left of income after consumption. Thus, an explanation of consumption is at the same time an explanation of saving. According to the forward-looking theory, people save in order to smooth consumption over time. Thus, if incomes are good now but are expected to go down later, people save in preparation for the future decline. People therefore save for their retirement and for "a rainy day."* They may also save in order to leave bequests to their heirs.

Within this theory, the real interest rate reflects the cost of consuming now rather than later. If you don't expect to earn income until later but want to consume now, you can borrow funds to spend now. The price for being able to consume earlier is the real interest on the loan. Thus, an increase in the real interest rate will make borrowing to consume now seem less attractive. Economic theory classifies this effect as a **substitution effect:** People save more now because they substitute future consumption for current consumption.

A few complications are worth pointing out. First, some empirical evidence related to this substitution effect suggests that it may be small.** Second, the effect is likely to be temporary. If people cut down on spending now in order to spend later, they will not continue to save later. Third, interest-rate changes also have **wealth effects** apart from the substitution effect, which may be difficult to predict. For example, a person who has invested in a money market fund will feel wealthier from an interest-rate increase, because he or she will receive a higher yield on that financial investment. As a result, this person may consume more and hence *save less*. In contrast, a person with debt at a variable interest rate will feel worse off from an interest-rate increase and may save more. To protect themselves against these effects, people may invest in bonds with fixed coupons or borrow at fixed rates. Given these complications, the prediction that higher interest rates produce higher saving should be made with some caution.

The relationship between interest rates and consumption spending is much clearer when it comes to *durable goods*. Because the decision to buy a durable good is like an investment decision, it is affected negatively by an increase in the real interest rate in just the same way. This relationship strengthens the case for a negative link between interest rates and consumption and hence for a positive link between interest rates and saving.

---

*An interesting exploration of these implications of the forward-looking theory can be found in a recent article by John Campbell of Princeton University, titled "Does Saving Anticipate Declining Labor Income? An Alternative Test of the Permanent Income Hypothesis," *Econometrica*, November 1987, vol. 55, no. 6, pp. 1249–73.

**See Robert E. Hall, "Intertemporal Substitution in Consumption," *Journal of Political Economy*, April 1988, vol. 96, no. 2, pp. 339–57.

5.4 THE IS CURVE: ANALYSIS

Our analysis has identified the following determinants of the private (that is, nongovernment) demand for goods and services. First, according to equations (5.10), (5.11), and (5.12′), an increase in *current real income*, measured by real GNP, raises consumption as well as investment demand. It reduces net export demand. However, the negative effect on export demand is more than offset by the positive effect on consumption and income demand, because the latter two include the demand for both domestic and imported goods. The net effect of real GNP changes on total private demand can be interpreted as the **marginal propensity to spend on domestic goods.** Our analysis shows that this propensity is greater than zero. We will also continue to assume that the propensity is less than 1. This assumption is particularly appropriate under the forward-looking theory of consumption, as indicated by the low coefficient, $bz(1 - \tau)$, of current income in equation (5.12′).

Second, the demand for goods and services is influenced positively by *expectations about future real income* and production levels. This effect follows directly from the forward-looking theory of consumption in equation (5.12′) as well as from the dynamics of net investment demand in equation (5.10). Third, demand is affected negatively by the *real interest rate*. We analyzed this effect formally for investment [especially in connection with equations (5.6′) and (5.11)], where the real interest rate is the key component of the cost of capital services. We also noted an analogous effect with regard to the demand for durable consumer goods, because the decision to buy such goods is very similar to an investment decision. We found further that the substitution effect would pull in the same direction for other consumption, although the wealth effect is ambiguous. Finally, we noted that an increase in the real interest rate discourages net export demand by driving up the exchange rate. Thus, the private demand for goods and services is a decreasing function of the real interest rate.

Although some of these relationships appeared to be somewhat non-linear, our further analysis will be greatly simplified if we approximate the total effects on spending demand in the form of a linear function. Noting that the private demand for goods and services is the sum of consumption, investment, and net export demand, we can write this function as

$$(5.13) \qquad C + I + X = b_0 + b_Y Y + b_e Y^e - b_R R.$$

Here $0 < b_Y < 1$ is the marginal propensity to spend on domestic goods, and $b_R > 0$—together with the minus sign—describes the negative dependence on the real interest rate. The term $b_e Y^e$ reflects the influence of expected future income levels.

This function ignores taxes; however, equation (5.12′) suggests that an increase in current or future taxes should reduce the value of the co-efficients b_Y and b_e, respectively.

GOODS MARKET EQUILIBRIUM AND THE IS CURVE

Now substitute this demand function into equation (5.1), the equilibrium condition for the goods market. Then we see that this equilibrium condition can be described by the equation

$$(5.14) \qquad Y = b_0 + b_Y Y + b_e Y^e - b_R R + G.$$

The Y on the left of the equation represents production plans. The first four terms on the right summarize the behavior of consumption, investment, and net export demand, and the Y on the right side of the equation represents GNP—or income generated by the production of GNP—as it influences these demand components. The equation then states that the production plans must equal that income level that is derived from *actual* production and influences the private demand for goods and services.

Equation (5.14) is the equation for the IS curve, which we saw in Figure 5.4. It is also referred to as the **IS equation.** It defines those combinations of GNP levels and interest rates that are compatible with equilibrium in the market for goods and services.

Mathematically, solving the IS equation for GNP is easy. The solution can be written as

$$(5.15) \qquad Y = \left(\frac{1}{1 - b_Y}\right)\left(b_0 - b_R R + G + b_e Y^e\right).$$

If we graph this function, we obtain the IS curve, which was displayed in Figure 5.4 and is repeated as the curve IS_0 in Figure 5.6. In connection with Figure 5.4, we noted that the axes in this diagram are reversed so

FIGURE 5.6

The IS curve. The rightward shift from IS_0 to IS_1 could result from good news about future activity levels or an increase in government spending. The leftward shift from IS_0 to IS_2 could result from a tax increase.

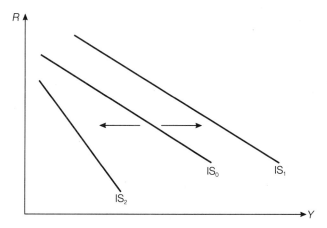

that the dependent variable Y is on the horizontal axis and the independent variable R on the vertical axis.

THE SLOPE OF THE IS CURVE

From equation (5.15), we see that an increase in R by the amount ΔR reduces Y by the amount $\Delta Y = -[b_R/(1 - b_Y)]\Delta R$. Thus, the slope of the curve is $\Delta R/\Delta Y = -(1 - b_Y)/b_R$, which is negative as long as b_Y, the marginal propensity to spend on domestic goods and services, is less than 1, which we have assumed. We then conclude that the IS curve defines a *downward-sloping relationship* between the real interest rate and real GNP. Thus, the higher the interest rate, the lower the GNP level that is compatible with equilibrium in the market for goods and services.

In the analysis of monetary and fiscal policy in Chapter 6 and later chapters, we will find that the effects of a given policy may depend on how steep the IS curve is. A relatively flat IS curve means that a given change in the real interest rate will have a large effect on the level of real GNP that corresponds to an equilibrium in the market for goods and services. Conversely, a relatively steep curve means that the effect is slight.

The steepness of the IS curve is reflected in the absolute value of its slope, $(1 - b_Y)/b_R$. As we might expect, this absolute value depends inversely on the parameter b_R, which reflects the sensitivity of the demand for goods and services to changes in the real interest rate. Thus, if this sensitivity is high, the IS curve is relatively flat, and vice versa. Furthermore, a large value of b_Y, the marginal propensity to spend on domestic goods, also tends to make the IS curve flat. To see why this is so, note that the initial spending effect of a decline in the real interest rate is multiplied by the spending multiplier. The secondary spending changes that go into this multiplier process are represented by the marginal propensity to spend on domestic goods. Thus, the larger this propensity, the larger the effect on real GNP of a given change in the real interest rate.

SHIFTS IN THE IS CURVE

The formula on the right of equation (5.15) also tells how the equilibrium in the goods market depends on expectations about future activity levels. Good news about future activity in the form of an increase in Y^e increases the value of Y without requiring a change in R. Thus, it shifts the IS curve to the right. This movement is displayed as the shift from IS_0 to IS_1 in Figure 5.6. In other words, good news about future activity raises the equilibrium level of GNP for any given interest rate. This result is intuitive; improved expectations make forward-looking consumers spend more and forward-looking managers invest more.

Equation (5.15) also indicates that equilibrium in the goods market depends on the level of government spending. This dependence should be expected from the simple fact that the government accounts for a substantial part of the demand in this market. An increase in government spending raises the equilibrium GNP level for any given interest rate and thus shifts the IS curve to the right, just like the shift from IS_0 to IS_1 in Figure 5.6. For this reason, an increase in government spending is considered to be an example of **expansionary fiscal policy.** From the multiplier analysis in Section 5.1, we can see that this shift involves an effect via the spending multiplier as well as an increase in government spending itself.

What about an increase in taxes? We noted above that an increase in the current income tax rate reduces the parameter b_Y. It then becomes apparent from equation (5.15) that such a change shifts the IS curve to the left, from IS_0 to IS_2 in Figure 5.6. (It also makes the curve steeper, but that result is less interesting here.)

The intuitive explanation for this case is that a tax increase reduces consumers' disposable income and hence makes them reduce their spending. This effect implies a reduction in aggregate demand. Moreover, a multiplier effect occurs in this case also. Thus, the IS curve shifts to the left by more than the initial decline in spending caused directly by the tax increase. A tax increase is an example of a **contractionary fiscal policy.**

Note, however, that this effect depends crucially on what is assumed about future tax rates. If the tax increase is temporary, the shift in the IS curve will be smaller than if it were permanent. Moreover, our discussion of Ricardian equivalence suggests that there are cases in which tax changes don't shift the IS curve at all.

The IS curve is useful, but it is insufficient as a tool for studying the determination of both real GNP and the interest rate in macroeconomic equilibrium. It must be combined with a model of financial markets that can help determine the interest rate. This model is summarized in the LM curve, which is introduced in the next chapter.

CHAPTER REVIEW

1. This chapter studies equilibrium in the market for goods and services in the form of consistency between production plans and spending plans. Total spending is composed of consumption, investment, net exports, and government spending on goods and services.

2. The link between consumption and income produces a multiplier effect for changes in other components of aggregate demand, such as investment.

3. The real interest rate is the difference between the nominal interest rate and the expected inflation rate.

4. Investment demand depends negatively on the real interest rate as the cost of financing and positively on expectations about the future levels of real GNP that the investment goods will help produce.

5. The accelerator principle makes investment demand a function of the rate of change in real GNP as well as its level. It

also explains why the components of investment behave differently over the business cycle.

6. The Keynesian consumption function focuses on current income, whereas the forward-looking theory emphasizes expectations. The forward-looking theory is more recent, but it may not fit the data perfectly.

7. The spending on consumer durables fluctuates more than other consumption over the business cycle because it can be postponed more easily.

8. The relationship between domestic interest rates and net export demand works via the foreign-exchange market. A higher real domestic interest rate raises the exchange rate, which makes domestic goods less attractive to foreigners and foreign goods more attractive domestically.

9. The total demand for goods and services depends negatively on changes in the real interest rate and positively on changes in real GNP, but such that the marginal propensity to spend on domestic goods is less than 1.

10. The combinations of interest rates and real GNP levels that are compatible with goods market equilibrium can be represented by the IS curve. The IS curve slopes downward. Increases in expectations about future activity shift this curve to the right.

11. The IS curve is shifted to the right by expansionary fiscal policy, such as an increase in government spending, and to the left by contractionary fiscal policy, such as a tax increase.

EXERCISES

1. Suppose you have the following information about the economy during periods 1 through 10:

Period	Y	i	π
1	4,000	0.15	0.12
2	3,900	0.12	0.12
3	3,800	0.10	0.10
4	3,800	0.05	0.05
5	3,850	0.06	0.04
6	3,900	0.07	0.05
7	3,950	0.08	0.05
8	4,000	0.08	0.05
9	4,050	0.09	0.05
10	4,000	0.08	0.05

Assume that $v = i - \pi^e + \delta$, where π^e denotes the expected inflation rate for the following period, and $f(v) = 0.53/v^{0.3}$. Assume $\delta = 0.1$. Suppose all expectations are correct in the sense of being equal to the actual variable values the following period. Using equations (5.7) and (5.9) to describe investment behavior, compute the behavior of investment and the capital stock over time. (You will probably find an electronic spreadsheet useful for this exercise.)

2. Suppose the forward-looking theory of consumption can be approximated by the following equation;
$C = 80 + 0.95[0.1(1 - \tau)Y + 0.9(1 - \tau^e)Y^e]$.
Assume that current and expected income both equal 4,000.

a. Compute the level of consumption with a tax rate of 30% ($\tau = 0.30$) that is expected to persist into the future.

b. Suppose the tax rate is cut to 20% currently, but the consumers expect it to return to 30% in the future. What happens to consumption?

c. Suppose instead that the tax cut in part (b) is expected to be permanent. What will be the effect on consumption then? Why is the answer different from part (b)?

d. Finally, suppose that a tax reduction to 20% now creates expectations about a tax increase to 31% in the future. What is the effect on consumption? Why?

3. Suppose again that consumption can be described as in exercise 2. The tax rate currently is 30%, and up until now you have seen no indication of future tax changes. Similarly, the income level is 4,000, and you have expected it to persist. However, an economic forecaster now tells you that a recession has become likely. The probability of recession is only 50%; however, if it occurs,

current income will drop by 5%. At this point, you don't know if income will rebound to its current level after the recession is over. You also don't know if the government will respond to the recession by enacting a future tax cut. Your company has been producing electronic equipment for the Defense Department but is now considering a major move into consumer electronics. What is your recommendation in regard to this move?

4. You are given the IS equation
$Y = 750 + 0.25Y - 10,000R + G + 0.6Y^e$.
Draw this curve to scale for $G = 600$ and $Y^e = 4,000$. Then show how the curve shifts in each of the following cases.
   a. Government spending increases to 650 or decreases to 550.
   b. Expected future income rises to 4,200 or declines to 3,800.

5. Define annual data for interest rates, inflation, and the price of investment goods as the 3-month Treasury-bill rate, the rate of change in the GNP deflator, and the ratio of the deflator for Gross Private Domestic Investment to the GNP deflator, respectively. Assuming $\delta = 0.1$, compute annual data for real interest rates and the user cost of capital. Make a graphical or printed display showing the nominal interest rate, the real interest rate, and the user cost. Compare these and comment on the differences. Compute means and variances by decades. Do you detect any interesting patterns? (Keep the data for the next exercise.)

6. As an illustration of the accelerator principle, use annual data to estimate a regression of the form
$I_t = b_0 + b_1 \Delta Y_t + b_2 Y_t$.
Comment on the results. Now use the data from exercise 5 to add the real interest rate or the user cost of capital (but not both) to the equation. Do the results make sense in light of the theory?

7. Construct quarterly data for "Tobin's Q" as the ratio of Standard and Poor's index of the prices of 500 common stocks to the deflator for Gross Private Domestic Investment. Regress data for real Gross Private Domestic Investment on this variable. What do the results tell you?

8. Using quarterly data, estimate the Keynesian consumption function (5.2) as a regression of (a) the level of real consumption on the level of real disposable income with a constant and (b) the *change* in real consumption on the *change* in real disposable income, with and without a constant. Compare the results and explain what they tell you about the relative merits of the Keynesian consumption function and the forward-looking theory of consumption. Why would you want to skip the constant in the second question?

THINKING QUESTIONS

1. Do you agree with the view of human rationality implicit in the forward-looking theory of consumption? Why or why not? What implications does your answer have for business marketing strategies?

2. Ricardian equivalence assumes (a) eventual government repayment of its debt and (b) a clear foresight of future taxes. Discuss whether these assumptions might or might not hold in real life.

3. The analysis of investment demand has avoided most of the controversy that has surrounded the research on consumer demand. Why do you think that is so?

4. In the discussion of fiscal policy, you might not have been surprised to see that tax increases are contractionary. However, some people have difficulty with the notion that government spending is expansionary. How would you formulate the logic behind this notion? How does it depend on the extent to which the resources used to produce goods and services for the government have been utilized by the private sector?

6 THE IS-LM MODEL

The previous chapter gave the rationale for the IS curve: If the real interest rate increases, the GNP level that is compatible with equilibrium in the market for goods and services decreases. It was silent, however, about what might make the interest rate move. This chapter fills this gap by describing how the interest rate and the GNP are determined and how they move in response to changes in the economic environment. Because the interest rate is the price for credit, our description requires an analysis of the **financial markets** as well as the market for goods and services. The financial markets are complex, as we saw in part in Chapter 4, and a more complete description belongs in a finance course rather than a course in macroeconomics. For our purpose, it is useful to construct a compact description of the financial markets that captures those elements most important for macroeconomic analysis. One such compact description that has proved to be particularly convenient is a simple specification of the **demand and supply of money.** We described the process behind the supply of money in Chapter 4. Let us now turn to the demand for money.

6.1 THE DEMAND FOR MONEY

Section 4.1, which discussed the functions of money in the modern economy, pointed out that the term money, as used in economic analysis, refers only to liquid assets that can be used as payment. Thus, even though the public's desire for wealth may know no limits, the demand for money is finite because it concerns only that portion of their wealth that people want to hold in liquid form. Section 4.1 emphasized the convenience value of money in allowing individuals and businesses to carry out transactions without having to look for a mutually desirable match for a barter transaction. This emphasis suggests that we can analyze the demand for money as a function of the need to carry out transactions.

The current value of transactions is a *nominal* concept; that is, it is measured in current dollars and rises with inflation. It is reasonable for the demand for money to depend on a nominal variable, because money itself is nominal. However, for the purposes of the rest of our macroeconomic analysis, it is important to be able to relate this nominal relationship to the *real* variables studied in Chapter 5.

A technique often used for this purpose is to carry out the analysis in terms of **real money.** Real money is money deflated by the overall price level, as in the statistical examples in Chapter 2. If M denotes money and P denotes the price level, then M/P is real money. To understand this formula, note that a current price level of P means that $\$P$ can buy the same amount of goods now as $\$1$ could in the base year. Thus, $\$M$ now can buy M/P times that amount. It follows that real money, M/P, is measured in units of real goods. Like real GNP, it can be expressed in 1982 dollars.

A prerequisite for carrying out the macroeconomic analysis in terms of real money is the assumption that the demand for money is proportional to the price level. That is, if we write down the demand for money, denoted M^D, as a mathematical function, we must be able to write it as

$$(6.1) \qquad\qquad M^D = PL(\cdot),$$

where $L(\cdot)$ is a function of other variables that will be specified below. This assumption is not controversial. Suppose you figure out that you need to carry $\$10$ in your pocketbook to be prepared for necessary transactions during the day. Suppose also that next year all prices have doubled, while nothing else has changed. Clearly, you will then need $\$20$ in your pocketbook to carry out the same transactions. As an even simpler example, suppose the U.S. government suddenly decided that the monetary unit would be the cent rather than the dollar. You would then need 100 times as many cents as you now need dollars because all prices would have risen by a factor of 100. Thus, the demand for money in cents obviously would be 100 times the money demand in dollars. We conclude that it is reasonable to assume that the demand for money is proportional to the price level. Having accepted this notion, we might as well divide both sides of equation (6.1) by the price level and write

$$(6.2) \qquad\qquad M^D/P = L(\cdot).$$

In other words, L is the demand function for real money.

The next question to consider is which variables influence real money demand. First, it obviously is affected, in a positive way, by the **real volume of transactions.** People who buy a high volume of goods need more money to carry out their transactions than people who buy lower volumes. Although this much is obvious, it is a little difficult to pin down a measure of the volume of transactions. We will follow most other textbook expositions in identifying the volume of transactions with *real GNP*, which we again denote Y. However, it should be pointed out that this measure is not ideal. On one hand, as a measure of *finished* goods and services, it excludes all intermediate transactions that also require the use of money. On the other hand, it gives equal weight to all transactions, even though payment methods may vary substantially. For example, the services provided at a public hospital probably involve a much more modest flow of liquid money than a comparable level of sales at a supermarket. In using real GNP to represent the volume of transactions, we ignore these complications.

The transactions demand for money is also influenced negatively by the *interest rate*. The interest rate matters as an *opportunity cost* of holding money. This relationship is most obvious in the case of the demand for money in the form of *currency*. A person holding currency forgoes the interest return that the same funds could have earned if invested in securities. If the interest rate is high, this person probably would be best off keeping as much of his or her funds as possible in interest-bearing assets and then selling them for cash in little bits and pieces when the cash is needed for transactions. Alternatively, if the interest rate is low, the convenience of not having to sell assets all the time might persuade the person to hold a larger reserve of cash. In this way, the demand for currency depends negatively on the interest rate.

Three points are worth noting about the role of other assets as alternatives to holding money. First, holding other securities is more attractive the less uncertainty is attached to the alternative investments. Thus, in times of uncertainty, such as those following dramatic international events, we may observe a surge in money demand beyond what we can explain by movements in interest rates, transactions volume, or the price level. We will not pursue this issue further here, however.

Second, the cheaper and easier it is to transfer funds between money and other assets, the less need people have for keeping large money balances for transactions purposes. Thus, an increase in brokerage fees for bonds could increase the demand for money. Similarly, financial innovations, such as the introduction of electronic funds transfers, may reduce the demand for money. We will get back to this issue in Section 6.4.

Third, we note that the *nominal* rather than the real interest rate influences the demand for money. To see this, suppose the nominal interest rate and the expected inflation rate rise by the same amount, so that the real interest rate is unchanged. Then people who hold interest-bearing assets are compensated for the higher inflation by the higher interest rate, while those who hold non–interest-bearing money see its purchasing power decline because of inflation. Thus, holding money becomes less attractive. This simply means that the demand for money is a function of the nominal interest rate.

As we saw in Chapter 4, M1 has some important components—such as N.O.W. accounts—that carry interest. The same is true of all the additional components that define M2 and M3. For these components, the opportunity-cost argument for a negative influence of interest rates is not quite as obvious as it is for currency. However, the interest rate each of them earns tends to be lower than that earned by a return to the less liquid assets that are not considered money, such as corporate bonds. The higher return on the nonmonetary assets is compensation for the lower liquidity of these assets. Thus, even interest-bearing components of money carry an interest-related opportunity cost of holding them.

From these considerations, we can conclude that the demand function for real money, $L(\cdot)$, is an increasing function of real GNP and a decreasing function of the nominal interest rate, i. It is convenient to specify these relationships in the form of a linear function. We can write it as

$$(6.3) \qquad M^D/P = L(Y,i) = k_0 + k_Y Y - k_i i.$$

The *nominal* demand for money is easily obtained from this equation by multiplying both sides by the price level P:

$$(6.4) \qquad M^D = PL(Y,i) = P(k_0 + k_Y Y - k_i i).$$

6.2 MONEY MARKET EQUILIBRIUM AND THE LM CURVE

Equations (6.3) and (6.4) summarize the important factors in the *demand* for money. Chapter 4 concluded that the *supply* of money is under the control of the central bank but that the control is imperfect. For simplicity, we will ignore this imperfection in our formal analysis. For further simplicity, we will also ignore the distinctions among the respective monetary aggregates and carry out the analysis as if the supply of money were one variable with an unambiguous definition. These simplifications allow us to specify the money supply as one exogenous variable, which we call M. The ratio M/P then denotes the real money supply. It should be noted that the central bank's control over the real money supply is even less perfect than its control over the nominal money supply, because the central bank cannot directly control the price level. Nevertheless, the real money supply is an important variable in macroeconomic analysis.

EQUILIBRIUM IN THE MONEY MARKET

It is much easier to define equilibrium in the money market than in the market for goods and services. We simply take it to mean the situation in which the demand for money equals its supply. The demand for money is specified in equation (6.4), and supply is the exogenous variable M. Thus, money market equilibrium can be described by the equation

$$(6.5) \qquad M = P(k_0 + k_Y Y - k_i i).$$

Alternatively, it can be described in terms of real money as

$$(6.6) \qquad M/P = k_0 + k_Y Y - k_i i.$$

Let us consider for a moment the process that makes the market for money reach this equilibrium. Suppose, for example, that the demand for money exceeds supply, so that some people would like to hold more money than they hold now. We would expect these people to try to obtain liquid funds by borrowing or by selling securities. If they try to borrow, their demand for borrowed funds will tend to drive up the interest rate. However, the higher interest rate will induce people to economize on their money holdings, with the result that the excess demand for money is diminished. We can expect this development to continue until people just want to hold the available supply of money. At such a point, equilibrium is restored.

Suppose that people instead try to obtain money by selling bonds. Then the price of bonds will be driven down. But a decline in bond prices is tantamount to an increase in the bond yield rate. To see this, note that the yield, y, of a one-year bond is the percentage difference between the current price of the bond, B, which the financial investor pays, and its face value, F, which the same investor receives when the bond matures a year from now:

(6.7) $$y = 100 \times (F - B)/B = 100 \times (F/B - 1).$$

Clearly, for a given face value, a decline in the price of the bond raises the yield rate. Furthermore, since bonds and loans are very close substitutes for both the borrowers and the lenders, the bond market makes sure that the bond yield rate and the interest rate follow each other closely. In fact, the yield rates on Treasury securities are considered among the most important interest rates in the United States. Thus, if people try to obtain more money by selling bonds, the interest rate as well as the bond yield rate will go up. Again, the demand for money is reduced and equilibrium eventually is restored.

Obviously, this scenario works equally well in reverse: If people hold more money than they would prefer, they will try to get rid of it by investing in other financial instruments or by paying off loans. As a result, the interest rate declines and equilibrium is restored.

We have not mentioned changes in real GNP or the price level as parts of this process. Even though these variables also affect the demand for money, the idea that an imbalance in the money market should lead to immediate adjustments in real GNP or the price level is less obvious. Once the interest rate has adjusted, real GNP may be affected via the demand for investment goods, consumer durables, and net exports. These adjustments are analyzed further below. However, when we analyze the market for money by itself, it is more convenient to think of real GNP and the price level as shift parameters and to study the effects on the interest rate of changes in these variables. Thus, we observe that *an increase in real GNP raises the demand for money and thus drives up the interest rate.* To see this, note from equation (6.5) or (6.6) that an increase in real GNP raises the demand for money in nominal as well as real terms. With a constant price level, the real as well as the nominal money supply is unchanged. The result is an excess demand for money. As we have just seen, in such a situation, the interest rate rises until equilibrium is restored.

Similarly, *an increase in the price level drives up the interest rate.* In nominal terms [equation (6.5)], a price level increase raises the demand for money without affecting supply, and the resulting excess demand drives up the interest rate. Alternatively [equation (6.6)], a rise in the price level reduces the real money supply. Again, the result is an excess demand for money, which is relieved by an increase in the interest rate.

THE LM CURVE

For given levels of the money supply and the price level, equation (6.6) can be solved as a relationship between real GNP and the interest rate:

$$(6.8) \qquad i = \frac{k_0 + k_Y Y - M/P}{k_i}.$$

However, from the point of view of the demand for goods and services studied in Chapter 5, we are more interested in relationships involving the *real* interest rate. We recall from equation (5.5) that the real interest rate R is the difference between the nominal interest rate i and the expected inflation rate π^e. Using this insight, we can rewrite equation (6.8) with the real interest rate on the left:

$$(6.9) \qquad R = \frac{k_0 + k_Y Y - M/P}{k_i} - \pi^e.$$

This formula leaves open the question of how people form their expectations about inflation. For the rest of this chapter, we bypass that question by treating expected inflation, like the price level, as a given parameter rather than trying to explain it. With this simplification, the money market equilibrium described in equation (6.9) provides an important link between the money supply—a nominal variable—and the real variables we want to study.

Given this assumption as well as a constant money supply, equation (6.9) defines an *upward-sloping* curve in the (Y,R)-plane, which is displayed in Figure 6.1. Its positive slope reflects the relationships just discussed. An increase in real GNP raises the volume of transactions and hence the demand for money. With money supply and the price level constant, however, the supply side in the money market is unchanged in nominal as well as real terms. Thus, the real GNP increase results in an excess demand for money, which drives up the nominal interest rate. For a given rate of expected inflation, the real interest rate then rises by the same amount.

FIGURE 6.1

The LM curve.

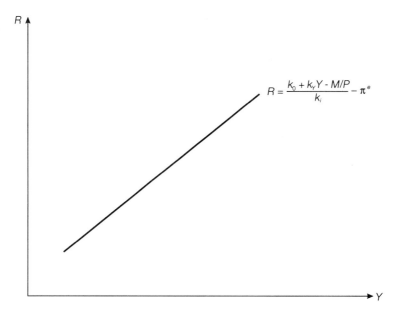

$$R = \frac{k_0 + k_Y Y - M/P}{k_i} - \pi^e$$

The curve defined by equation (6.9) goes under the name of the **LM curve.** As noted in the beginning of Chapter 5, the L in this name comes from "liquidity preference," which is an older term for the demand for money. (This is why we used the symbol L for the real money-demand function.) The M refers to the money supply. Thus, the name emphasizes the fact that this curve represents those combinations of real GNP and interest rates that are compatible with the equality of demand and supply—in other words, equilibrium—in the money market.

THE SLOPE OF THE LM CURVE

As we will see in Section 6.5, the effects of monetary and fiscal policy in the IS-LM model depend to some extent on how steep the LM curve is. A steep LM curve means that a given increase in real GNP must be matched by a large increase in the interest rate if equilibrium is to be maintained in the money market. Conversely, a relatively flat LM curve means that only a small increase in the interest rate is needed to match the same increase in real GNP.

The steepness of the LM curve can be read off its slope, which is given by the coefficient of Y, k_Y/k_i, in equation (6.9). This coefficient depends inversely on k_i, which reflects the interest sensitivity of the demand for money. The intuition is that if real GNP rises and the money demand is highly sensitive to interest-rate changes, then only a small increase in the interest rate is needed to offset the effect of the rise in real GNP on money demand. The coefficient k_Y/k_i also depends directly on k_Y, which reflects the sensitivity of money demand with respect to changes in real GNP. If k_Y is large, a given increase in real GNP affects money demand significantly and thus needs to be matched by a large interest-rate increase if equilibrium in the money market is to be maintained.

SHIFTS IN THE LM CURVE

The algebra in equation (6.9) should make it clear that an increase in the money supply (for a given price level and expected inflation rate) shifts the LM curve to the right, as illustrated by the shift from the curve LM_0 to LM_1 in Figure 6.2. Intuitively, the explanation for this shift is as follows. When the supply of money rises, the first effect is an *excess supply of money,* which, as we have seen, drives down the interest rate if the real GNP level and the price level stay constant. In other words, for a given real GNP and price level, the higher money supply corresponds to a lower equilibrium interest rate in the money market. Then, with a given expected inflation rate, the *real* interest rate is lower also. But that means that every point on the LM curve shifts downward, so the whole curve shifts downward as well. For an upward-sloping curve, a downward shift is equivalent to a rightward shift.

The rightward characterization of the shift also has an intuitive meaning of its own. Suppose the money supply is increased, resulting in an excess supply, but for some reason the interest rate does not rise. Then, if the real GNP is allowed to rise instead, the demand for money rises, so equilibrium can be restored at a higher real GNP level and at an un-

FIGURE 6.2

An increase in the supply of money shifts the LM curve downward and to the right (from LM_0 to LM_1), while an increase in the price level shifts it upward and to the left (from LM_0 to LM_2).

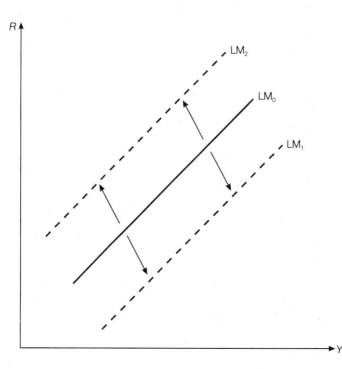

changed interest rate. In other words, each point on the LM curve shifts to the right, so the whole curve shifts to the right. Because the LM curve shifts to the right, an increase in the money supply is considered an *expansionary* monetary policy. In contrast, a reduction in the money supply is considered a *contractionary* policy move.

You may recall that in Chapter 3 we identified a monetary expansion with an increase in the growth rate of money supply, and a contraction with a decrease in that rate. Our earlier terminology can be reconciled with that in the preceding paragraph if we note that an increase in the growth rate of money will make the money supply increase *relative to what it would have been otherwise.* Thus, when we refer to increases and decreases in the money supply in the following discussion, you should think of the changes as relative to what otherwise would have happened, rather than as absolute changes over time. However, we will continue to carry out the analysis in terms of levels rather than growth rates, because it is simpler to do so.

It is apparent from formula (6.9), as well as from the entire analysis, that the relevant shift variable for the LM curve is the real rather than the nominal supply of money. Thus, an increase in the price level will have exactly the same contractionary effect as a reduction in the money supply, because it reduces the real money supply. This kind of shift is represented by the shift from LM_0 to LM_2 in Figure 6.2. We will consider this type of shift extensively in Chapter 7.

6.3 SIMULTANEOUS EQUILIBRIUM IN THE GOODS MARKET AND THE MONEY MARKET

In Chapter 5, we derived the IS curve as a representation of those combinations of real interest rates and real GNP that are compatible with equilibrium in the market for goods and services. As stated above, the points on the LM curve represent combinations of these same two variables that are compatible with equilibrium in the money market. Thus, if we can find an interest rate–real GNP combination that lies on *both* the IS and the LM curve, that combination would be compatible with equilibrium in both markets. In other words, we would find a **simultaneous equilibrium** in the goods and money markets. We define short-term **macroeconomic equilibrium** as this kind of simultaneous equilibrium.

Graphically, we find such a combination by putting both curves in the same diagram, as in Figure 6.3, and locating the point of intersection of the two curves. Because this point, marked *E* in the diagram, lies on both curves, it is both an equilibrium in the goods market and an equilibrium in the money market. In the following discussion, we will refer to diagrams such as the one in Figure 6.3 as an **IS-LM diagram.** The in-

FIGURE 6.3

The IS-LM diagram.

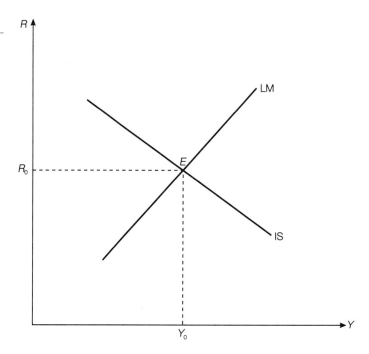

tersection point E will be referred to as an **IS-LM equilibrium.** The co-ordinates of this point in the diagram are the equilibrium values of real GNP and the interest rate, marked Y_0 and R_0, respectively.

It is worth noting here that an IS-LM equilibrium is defined for given levels of the price level and inflationary expectations. In a *full* macro-economic equilibrium, the price level is determined by the interaction between aggregate demand and aggregate supply, and inflationary ex-pectations are formed on the basis of people's notions about the future given this context. We extend our analysis to full macroeconomic equi-librium in Chapter 7.

Mathematically, the IS-LM equilibrium can be found as the simulta-neous solution to the IS and LM equations. Noting again that $i = R + \pi^e$, we now restate these equations, for convenience, in the following form:

(6.10a) $\qquad Y \;\; = b_0 + b_Y Y - b_R R + G + b_e Y^e \qquad$ (IS),

(6.10b) $\qquad M/P = k_0 + k_Y Y - k_i(R + \pi^e) \qquad$ (LM).

You can find the algebraic solution to this equation system in the appen-dix to this chapter. We illustrate its main features with a numerical example.

A NUMERICAL EXAMPLE

Suppose $b_0 + G + b_e Y^e = 3{,}250$, $k_0 - k_i \pi^e = -250$, and $M/P = 800$. Also, assume that $b_Y = 0.25$, $b_R = 10{,}000$, $k_Y = 0.3$, and $k_i = 6{,}000$. Then the IS-LM equation system is

(6.11a) $Y = 3{,}250 + 0.25Y - 10{,}000R$ (IS),
(6.11b) $800 = -250 + 0.3Y - 6{,}000R$ (LM).

To solve this system, it is convenient to first solve the LM equation for the real interest as a function of real GNP as follows:

$$R = (-250 + 0.3Y - 800)/6{,}000 = 0.00005Y - 0.175.$$

Then substitute this expression into the IS equation:

$$Y = 3{,}250 + 0.25Y - 0.5Y + 1{,}750.$$

Now solve this equation as

$$Y = (3{,}250 + 1{,}750)/(1 - 0.25 + 0.5) = 4{,}000.$$

Finally, you can substitute this solution into the solution of the LM equation for the real interest rate and obtain

$$R = (0.00005)(4{,}000) - 0.175 = 0.025.$$

Thus, the real interest rate is 2.5%. If we now add the assumption that expected inflation is 5%, we find that the nominal interest rate is 7.5%. These solution values correspond reasonably well to current values for U.S. real GNP in 1982 dollars and the 3-month U.S. Treasury bill rate. Of course, the example was constructed with these values in mind.

6.4 BUSINESS CYCLES IN THE IS-LM MODEL

Business cycles are composed of periods called recessions and expansions, during which real GNP declines and rises, respectively. Chapter 3 looked at the actual history of business cycles in the United States and elsewhere. We now look at how the IS-LM model can be used to explain them. As you will see in Chapter 11, this is not the only model that has been proposed for this purpose; however, you will probably find it easier to appreciate the other models after you have become reasonably well acquainted with the IS-LM model first. Out of many possible examples, we will look at how pessimism about the future may set off a recession and how a financial innovation such as the electronics revolution may set off an expansion.

PESSIMISM AND RECESSION

Suppose some bad news arrives that makes people less optimistic about future production levels. Such news could arrive in the form of an unexpectedly poor performance in government statistics, political instability in an important country in the world community, or an unexpected (and large) decline in the stock market. Whenever such news arrives, businesses will scale back investment plans because they realize that less capital will be needed for future production. Similarly, forward-looking consumers will cut spending in order to save for the leaner times they expect ahead.

The decline in expectations enters the IS-LM model in the form of a decrease in the variable Y^e, which occurs in the IS equation (6.10a). As we saw in Chapter 5, this variable represents consumer and investor expectations of future production and income levels. Algebraically, we see from equation (6.10a) that a decline in Y^e reduces the value of real GNP without an increase in the real interest rate being required. Thus, the IS curve is shifted to the left, as illustrated by the shift from IS_0 to IS_1 in Figure 6.4.

Intuitively, this shift happens as follows. At first, the lower expectations have a direct negative effect on investment and consumption demand, as noted above. Firms producing such goods respond to this demand reduction by contracting their operations and laying off people. Contractions and layoffs spell income reductions for the people involved, who then cannot afford to spend as much on consumer goods as they used to. Thus, consumption demand declines even further. Production

FIGURE 6.4

The effects of a worsening expectation of future income or a contractionary fiscal policy.

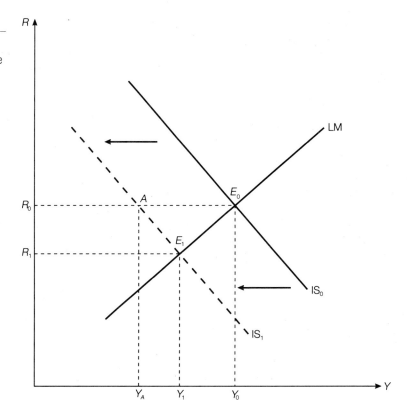

levels are then cut again, which makes income and hence consumption demand decline even more. This is the multiplier effect, discussed in Section 5.1, and which may go on for several "rounds." Eventually, the market for goods and services will settle down at a new equilibrium with a lower real GNP level. Note again that this decline takes place without any change in the real interest rate.

Graphically, the IS-LM equilibrium before the bad news broke was at the point E_0 in Figure 6.4, which represents the intersection of the LM curve and the initial IS curve, IS_0 in the figure. This point defines the initial equilibrium levels Y_0 and R_0 for real GNP and the real interest rate, respectively, before the new information was received. However, we just found out that at the initial real interest rate R_0, the new equilibrium output level in the goods market falls below Y_0 because of the bad news. In Figure 6.4, this lower level is labeled Y_A, which is the Y-value corresponding to point A in the diagram. However, since A represents a new equilibrium in the goods market, it must lie on the IS curve. This argument shows that the IS curve must have shifted to the left. The new IS curve, labeled IS_1, goes through A but not through E_0.

Now consider the LM curve. Mathematically, equation (6.10b) does not depend on Y^e, which suggests that the LM curve is unaffected. Intuitively, the demand for money is not influenced by the expectations of future production levels, because it is motivated by the need to carry out *current* transactions. Thus, nothing happens to the LM curve in this case.

That means that the point A is not on the LM curve and hence is not an IS-LM equilibrium. At point A, real GNP is lower than at E_0, while the interest rate is unchanged. Consequently, the demand for money is lower, resulting in an excess supply of money; pressures in the money market start to exert a downward influence on the interest rate. On the other hand, as the interest rate starts to decline, the cost of financing investment projects and consumer durables is reduced, which provides an incentive to increase spending a little. This stimulus comes via both investment and consumption, as well as from the net export component. As the interest rate declines, so does the exchange rate, which stimulates exports and discourages imports. Thus, a process is set off whereby the interest rate declines and real GNP rises relative to the value of either variable at A. Eventually, a new equilibrium is reached at E_1, where the new IS curve—IS_1—intersects the unchanged LM curve. At this point, real GNP, now at Y_1, is lower than its original level, Y_0. As real GNP has declined, a recession has been induced. The interest rate has also declined, from R_0 to R_1. Such declines in real interest rates often are observed during recessions.

For a numerical example, recall that the term $b_e Y^e$ in the analytical IS equation (6.10a) is included in the intercept in the corresponding numerical equation (6.11a). Therefore, we can model the change in expectations as a reduction in this intercept from 3,250 to, say, 3,000. Then you should be able to figure out that the equilibrium solution for real GNP declines from 4,000 to 3,800. This is a decline of 5%, which would be indicative of a severe recession. Similarly, the real interest rate would decline by 1 percentage point from 0.025 to 0.015, or 1.5%.

Not all recessions are the result of bad news regarding future activity.* However, many economists believe that the Great Depression of the 1930s was set off by an autonomous reduction in investment activity.** Others point to factors such as the reduction in the money supply that resulted from the way the Federal Reserve handled the many bank failures at the time. We study the effects of monetary policies in the next section.

A FINANCIAL INNOVATION

Now consider what would happen if a financial innovation reduced the need for money to carry out transactions. An example is increased availability of electronic transfers, which would allow people and businesses to maintain lower balances on their checking accounts. In such a situation, the demand for money would decline even if there were no changes in any of the determinants of money demand that we have considered. Such a decline occurred in the late 1970s, when the demand for money suddenly and persistently turned out to be lower than the predictions of money demand functions that had fit the data well in previous years.† Although the explanation of this decline was never quite clear, it seems reasonable to assert that it was related to the electronic innovations that took place in the financial system during this period.

Such a reduction in the need for money balances can be modeled as a reduction in the intercept parameter k_0 in the money-demand function, which makes up the right side of the LM equation (6.10b). Mathematically, it should be clear that this reduction shifts the LM curve down-

---

*In a recent paper, Matthew Shapiro of Yale and Mark Watson of Northwestern University analyzed the likely causes of U.S. recessions since World War II. Aggregate-demand disturbances, of which reactions to bad news are an example, were found to be responsible for only a fraction of all the movements in U.S. real GNP. Other contributors included changes in technology, oil price fluctuations, and changes in the labor force. Nevertheless, aggregate-demand disturbances were identified as the main contributors to the important U.S. recessions in 1957–58, 1960, and 1981–82. See Shapiro and Watson, "Sources of Business Cycle Fluctuations," in *Macroeconomics Annual 1988*, edited by Stanley Fischer (Cambridge, Mass.: M.I.T. Press, 1988).

**See, for example, the chapter by Robert J. Gordon and James A. Wilcox, "Monetarist Interpretations of the Great Depression: An Evaluation and Critique," in *Contemporary Views of the Great Depression*, edited by Karl Brunner (Hingham, Mass.: Martinus Nijhoff, 1981).

†See Stephen M. Goldfeld, "The Case of the Missing Money," *Brookings Papers on Economic Activity*, 3(1976): pp. 683–730.

ward because the solution value for the interest rate for a given level of real GNP becomes smaller.

The intuitive explanation is as follows. The reduction in the need for money balances leads to an excess supply of money. For a given level of real GNP, this excess supply leads to downward pressure on the interest rate as people seek to invest their excess liquid funds in less liquid, higher-yielding assets. Thus, at the old level of real GNP, the money market reaches a new equilibrium at a lower interest rate. This outcome means that the LM curve shifts downward. In contrast, the position of the IS curve is unchanged because the equilibrium in the market for goods and services does not depend on the demand for money in a direct sense, but only through the real interest rate.

This situation is depicted in Figure 6.5. Here the initial LM curve, labeled LM_0, intersects the IS curve at the initial equilibrium, E_0, corresponding to the equilibrium levels Y_0 of real GNP and R_0 of the real interest rate. Now consider the downward shift in the LM curve from LM_0 to LM_1. At the initial equilibrium GNP level, the real interest rate must fall to R_B in order to restore equilibrium in the money market after

FIGURE 6.5

The effects of an innovation in the financial system that shifts the demand for money or of an increase in money supply.

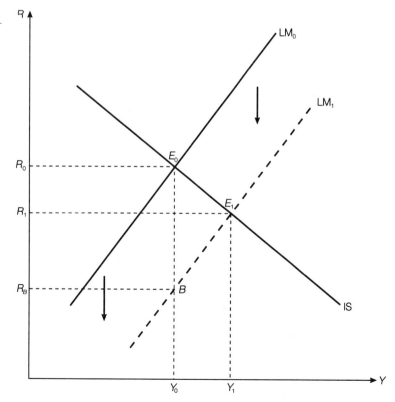

the innovations-induced decline in money demand. We know that this interest-rate decline restores equilibrium in the money market because the point B, corresponding to the coordinates Y_0 and R_B, lies on the new LM curve.

However, B is not on the IS curve and hence does not correspond to an equilibrium in the market for goods and services. From equation (6.10a), we see that a decline in the interest rate raises the demand for goods and services, which is the function on the right side of that equation. The reason for the rise is familiar: The demand for investment goods and consumer durables rises because these purchases become cheaper to finance. Also, the interest-rate decline makes the exchange rate fall, which stimulates export demand and discourages imports.

Thus, the reaction on the goods-market side is for demand to rise. Production increases in response to this rise. However, the increase in production volume, as measured by real GNP, raises the volume of transactions and hence the demand for money, which exerts upward pressure on the interest rate. Thus, there will be a tendency for real GNP to rise and also for the interest rate to start rising again from point B in Figure 6.5. This movement will continue until a new IS-LM equilibrium is restored at point E_1, where the new LM curve intersects the IS curve. The new equilibrium shows a real GNP level Y_1 that is higher than the old equilibrium level Y_0 and a real interest rate R_1 that is lower than the old equilibrium rate R_0 but higher than R_B.

As a numerical example, this financial innovation would take the form of a decline in the intercept term on the right side of the LM equation (6.11b). Suppose it declines from -250 to -300 while the intercept in the IS equation remains at 3,250. Then we find that the equilibrium solution for Y rises from 4,000 to 4,067, an increase of 1.7%, while the equilibrium real interest rate declines from 0.025, or 2.5%, to 0.02, or 2%.

This example shows how an autonomous decline in money demand can generate an expansion in the economy. The strong performance of real GNP in the United States in the late 1970s—especially in 1978—has, at least in part, been attributed by some to this change in money demand. Consistent with this explanation, real interest rates were low during this period as moderately high nominal interest rates were offset by quite high inflation.

6.5 MONETARY AND FISCAL POLICY IN THE IS-LM MODEL

The macroeconomic effects of monetary and fiscal policies can be analyzed naturally and intuitively in the IS-LM model. In fact, we have already done all the footwork for these exercises and can now concentrate on some interesting details.

MONETARY POLICY

First, consider the effects of an expansionary move in monetary policy, defined as an increase in money supply. From our analysis of the LM curve in Section 6.2, we know that an increase in the supply of money shifts the LM curve downward and to the right, as shown by the shift from LM_0 to LM_1 in Figure 6.2. Because we just found that an innovation-induced decline in money *demand* shifts the LM curve in the same direction, you may suspect that the effects of an increase in money supply are similar to the effects we found for such a decline in demand. That suspicion is correct. In fact, the two cases are so similar that we can again use Figure 6.5. However, it is useful to trace the whole story.

At the initial GNP level, Y_0, the increase in money supply means that there is more money in the market than people would like to hold. As they try to exchange some of this money for less liquid assets, such as bonds, the interest rate is bid down. Thus, equilibrium in the money market, at the initial GNP level Y_0, is restored at a point such as B, with a lower interest rate R_B. While point B represents an equilibrium for the money market, it represents a situation of excess demand in the market for goods and services because a decline in the real interest rate increases investment demand as well as consumption and net export demand. The production of goods and services is stimulated by this demand. At the same time, the higher activity level raises the volume of transactions and thus puts some renewed upward pressure on the interest rate. The new equilibrium, a point such as E_1 in Figure 6.5, is at a higher level of real GNP and a lower interest rate than initially. The positive effect on GNP is the reason such a policy is called expansionary.

For a numerical example, suppose the real money supply on the left side of equation (6.11b) rises from 800 to 890, while the other parameters are as shown in that equation. Then at the new equilibrium real GNP has grown to 4,120, while the real interest rate has declined from 0.025, or 2.5%, to 0.016, or 1.6%.

Before we leave this example, it is useful to tell the story a little more in line with the exposition of the monetary system given in Chapter 4. The first discrepancy is the assertion that the increase in the money supply finds people with more money than they actually want; in Chapter 4, all the parties involved did only what they wanted to do. To reconcile the two versions of our story, suppose the increase in the money supply is brought about by an open market purchase of Treasury bills, which are a kind of bond, by the central bank. In order to be able to buy these bills, the central bank needs to offer an attractive price. In other words, the price of Treasury bills is pushed upward by the open market purchase. However, as we saw in the discussion of formula (6.7) in Section 6.2 above, an increase in bond prices implies a decline in bond yields, which pull interest rates down with them. Furthermore, the subsequent expansion of the money supply via the money multiplier process implies several rounds of new bank lending. Again, in order to find new loan customers, banks have to offer favorable rates. Thus, the increase in the money supply and the decline in interest rates are two aspects of the same process. In practice, the money market does not really need to go out of equilibrium.

The other discrepancy between Chapter 4 and our story in this chapter concerns the central bank's intermediate target. Suppose the central bank bases its policy decisions on movements in the interest rate rather than on movements in money supply itself. We should now be able to see that this does not represent a problem. If central bank officials feel the interest rate is too high, they may direct their staff to go out and buy securities in the open market and thus raise the supply of money until the interest rate has declined enough. However, the central bank officials also need to look out for the next round of movements as the interest-rate reduction stimulates the demand for goods and services, because the resulting increase in activity is likely to bid the interest rate up again. This constant monitoring of the financial markets as well as the rest of the economy is, in fact, a routine part of central banking.

FISCAL POLICY

Toward the end of Chapter 5, we analyzed how fiscal policy, that is, changes in taxes or government spending, affects the IS curve. We found that expansionary fiscal policies—tax cuts or spending increases—shift the IS curve to the right. Similarly, contractionary fiscal policies—tax increases or spending cuts—shift the IS curve to the left. A contractionary fiscal policy thus has effects similar to those of a decline in the expectations about future activity levels. As in that case, fiscal policy changes also do *not* affect the LM curve, because they do not affect the financial markets other than via whatever they might do to the overall transactions volume (as measured by real GNP) or the interest rate. Thus, we can use Figure 6.4 to illustrate the effects of contractionary fiscal policy. As the figure shows, such a policy move reduces both real GNP and the interest rate. Conversely, an expansionary fiscal policy raises both real GNP and the interest rate. The effects of such a policy move are shown in Figure 6.6.

Let us consider a story that might lie behind Figure 6.6. Suppose the expansionary policy move consists of an increase in the government's demand for goods and services in the form of the design and production of Stealth bombers, without a corresponding tax increase or cuts in other spending categories. Such a move obviously would reduce the government's surplus or raise its deficit, as the case might be. Thus, the government would need to draw down its financial assets or increase its borrowing. We will comment shortly on the long-term consequences of a government deficit. For now, let us consider the short-term consequences, which are all the IS-LM model can give us.

FIGURE 6.6

The effects of an expansionary fiscal policy.

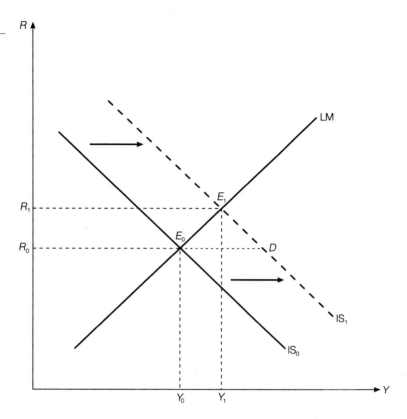

In response to the government's new demand for bombers, activity rises in the defense industry; more workers are hired, and incomes rise. This rise in incomes then sets off a new round of demand increases, this time for consumer goods, as the people engaged in the defense industry spend their new income. If the interest rate stays constant, several such rounds could take place. The net effect then would be an increase in the real GNP level that is compatible with equilibrium in the market for goods and services at the initial interest rate. This increase, however, means that the IS curve shifts to the right, as illustrated by the shift from IS_0 to IS_1 in Figure 6.6.

The LM curve is unaffected by this move. Thus, point D in the figure, which represents the new GNP level that is compatible with goods market equilibrium at the old real interest rate R_0, does not lie on the LM curve. In fact, it is doubtful that the economy will ever reach point D. Rather, as soon as output starts to rise in response to the demand increase, the transactions demand for money rises as well, and upward pressure is exerted on the interest rate. Thus, the movement from E_0 goes in the upward as well as the outward direction. This interest-rate increase obviously puts a damper on the expansion in the demand for goods and services. Thus, the new equilibrium E_1, the point at which the new IS curve crosses the LM curve, corresponds to a somewhat lower GNP level than does point D. Nevertheless, the expansionary fiscal policy results in a net increase in real GNP, albeit with an accompanying interest-rate increase.

The dampening of private demand by the rise in the interest rate is commonly referred to as **crowding out,** because the increase in public spending "crowds out" some private spending due to its financial effects. A different way of looking at the same effect comes from the observation that the increase in government spending is accompanied by an increase in government borrowing. When the government thus enters the bond market, it crowds out private financing needs, which puts a damper on private investment.

We should also note that investment is not the only private demand component that can be crowded out. The demand for consumer durables is also affected negatively by higher interest rates, and this negative effect counteracts the stimulative effect of higher income levels. Furthermore, higher interest rates must be expected to raise the exchange rate of the country's currency, which would make the country's products less attractive in world markets while making imported goods cheap. Through this mechanism, net exports can be crowded out as well. This process will become much clearer after we have studied international linkages in Chapter 10.

Obviously, our analysis of fiscal policy depends crucially on our assumptions about consumer behavior, particularly the marginal propensity to consume. The multiplier effect of defense purchases occurs as households spend a part of their increased income. This effect, of course, is stronger the larger the marginal propensity to consume. If we view this effect in light of the forward-looking theory of consumer behavior, we see that the effect of fiscal policy will be stronger for a permanent policy change, such as a new weapons program, than for a temporary change, such as a one-time tax rebate.

Our discussion of Ricardian equivalence in Section 5.3, however, suggests an intriguing possibility. It predicts that an increase in the government deficit should *reduce* consumer spending, because the consumers realize that the higher government spending generates a deficit that will increase the future tax burden. Their response then is to set aside just enough money to cover this future burden on themselves or their heirs. In fact, the increase in public spending should be offset exactly by the decline in private spending. Total demand should not be affected. The IS curve should not shift, and nothing should happen to real GNP or to the real interest rate.

As we noted in Chapter 5, the hypothesis of Ricardian equivalence is a long way from enjoying general acceptance among economic researchers. Nevertheless, the contrast between the predictions generated by this hypothesis and the Keynesian consumption function serves as an important reminder that crucial uncertainties remain with regard to the short-run effects of fiscal policy changes.

MONETARY AND FISCAL POLICY AND THE SLOPES OF THE IS AND LM CURVES

The effects of monetary and fiscal policy that we just studied are robust in the sense that the *directions* of the predicted changes in real GNP and the real interest rate are unambiguous implications of the IS-LM model. However, the *magnitude* of each such change depends on the slopes of the IS and LM curves. In particular, it turns out that *monetary policy is more effective in terms of real GNP changes the flatter the IS curve,* whereas *fiscal policy is more effective the flatter the LM curve.* We discussed the slope of the IS curve briefly in Section 5.4 and that of the LM curve in Section 6.2. We now apply those insights to show the result just stated.

Before we start, it is worth noting that we are not implying that government or business can *choose* the slopes of these curves. Rather, the slopes are part of the economic environment where these parties operate. Thus, we are studying how this environment affects the consequences of monetary and fiscal policy.

Figure 6.7 shows an IS-LM diagram with two alternative IS curves, one relatively steep, labeled IS^S, and one relatively flat, labeled IS^F. They have been drawn such that both cross the initial LM curve, LM_0, at the same initial equilibrium point E_0, corresponding to a real GNP level of Y_0 and a real interest rate of R_0. Now consider the effects of an expansionary monetary policy. As in Figure 6.5, such a policy shifts the LM curve downward and to the right from LM_0 to LM_1. Whether the IS curve is steep or flat, real GNP will rise. Thus, the direction of this effect does not depend on how steep the IS curve is.

However, the magnitude of the effects does. Suppose the IS curve is like the relatively steep IS^S. Then, the new equilibrium point is E_1^S, corresponding to the new levels of real GNP and the real interest rate of Y_1^S and R_1^S, respectively. Alternatively, if the IS curve is like the relatively flat IS^F, the movement is to the point E_1^F with coordinates Y_1^F and R_1^F. It is clear from the figure that the expansion in real GNP is stronger the flatter the IS curve is.

To see why, recall from our earlier discussion that the immediate effect of an expansionary monetary policy is a drop in the interest rate as the money market regains equilibrium at the old GNP level. As in Figure 6.5, this immediate effect is reached at the point labeled B in Figure 6.7, with the corresponding lower interest rate R_B. The eventual effect on real GNP now depends on how much a given interest-rate decline affects the equilibrium real GNP level in the goods market—in other words, on how steep the IS curve is.

As we saw in Section 5.4, the IS curve is relatively flat if the demand

FIGURE 6.7

Comparison of the effects of
a monetary expansion with a
flat and a steep IS curve.

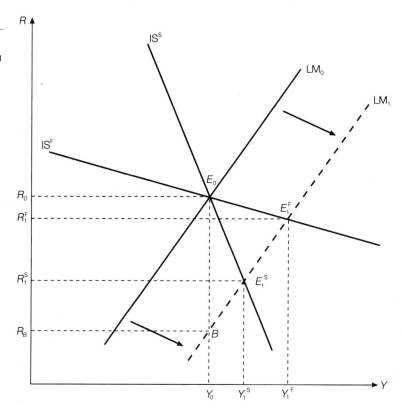

for goods and services is highly sensitive to interest-rate changes (so
that b_R is large) or if the marginal propensity to spend on domestic
goods (b_Y) is large. As noted there, a high value of b_R means a large initial effect of the interest-rate decline, whereas a high value of b_Y means a
large secondary effect via the spending multiplier. Either way, the flatter IS curve gives the most powerful effect on real GNP.

An extreme case with a nearly vertical IS curve arises when the demand for goods and services is barely influenced by changes in the real
interest rate, so that b_R is close to zero. In that case, real GNP is essentially determined in the goods market alone without any interaction
with the money market. The IS-LM model is then more or less equivalent to the simple Keynesian-cross model, which we studied briefly in
Section 5.1. Although the Keynesian-cross model can be useful as an introduction to macroeconomic equilibrium, most analysts consider it
inadequate for today's economy. Nevertheless, it is sometimes viewed
as approximately representative of an extremely depressed economy,
where prospects of future profits are so slim that investment demand
responds only marginally to improved incentives in the form of lower
interest rates.

FIGURE 6.8

Comparison of the effects of a fiscal expansion with a flat and a steep LM curve.

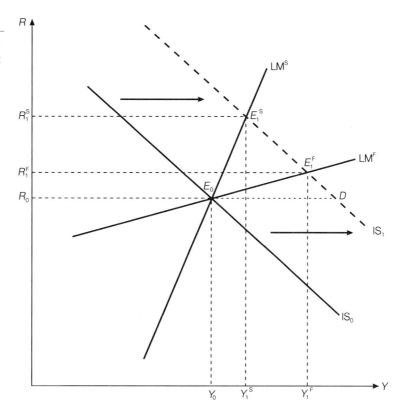

Figure 6.8 presents a similar comparison of the effects of an expansionary *fiscal* policy with a steep and a flat LM curve. The analysis here is like the one surrounding Figure 6.6. The expansionary fiscal policy shifts the IS curve to the right from IS_0 to IS_1 so that, if the real interest rate does not change, the economy will find itself at point D in the diagram. However, as we noted in connection with Figure 6.6, point D is unlikely to be reached in practice because as soon as production activity starts to expand, upward pressure will be put on the interest rate via the money market, and this interest-rate increase will crowd out some private spending.

The question now is how much private spending is crowded out, and the answer depends on the slope of the LM curve. With the relatively flat LM curve LM^F, crowding out is modest, so the net effect on real GNP is a relatively large increase. In contrast, the steep LM curve LM^S results in much more crowding out and a correspondingly smaller net effect on real GNP.

The crowding out occurs in response to the interest-rate increase that is induced by the production increase raising money demand. The magnitude of the crowding-out effect depends directly on how much the real interest rate rises. This rise will be large if a given increase in real GNP produces a large increase in money demand, or if the money demand depends only slightly on interest-rate changes, so that the interest rate will have to rise a lot to offset the activity-induced surge in money demand. Mathematically, a given increase in real GNP means a large increase in money demand if the parameter k_Y is large, whereas the money demand depends only slightly on interest-rate changes if k_i is small. We saw in Section 6.2 that these two conditions are exactly the ones that imply a steep LM curve.

A fair amount of attention traditionally has been directed toward the case where money demand is extremely sensitive to interest-rate changes, which implies a very flat LM curve. As we just have seen, fiscal policy is very powerful in this case. In contrast, however, monetary policy is very *in*effective because it takes only a very small initial decline in the interest rate to restore equilibrium in the money market (at the original GNP level) when money supply is increased. Consequently, the added interest incentive for investment, consumption, and net export demand becomes very modest, thus rendering the policy rather ineffective.

It has become common to refer to this case as a "liquidity trap." The central bank is trapped in the sense that whatever it does to the supply of money matters very little for the economy's activity level. Keynes believed this case was representative of a deeply depressed economy because people then, because of the uncertainty surrounding other assets, would be motivated to hold any amount of liquid money that the central bank would care to supply, without needing much encouragement in terms of lower interest rates. For this reason, he proposed using fiscal rather than monetary policy to get the economy out of the depression of the 1930s.

MONETARY AND FISCAL POLICY IN THE LONG RUN

Our analysis so far seems to suggest that expansionary policies are always desirable because they raise real GNP. However, policymakers such as the Federal Reserve Governors are often quoted in the press cautioning against such policies. Why this caution? The answer is that the analysis of this chapter covers only *short-term* macroeconomic equilibria and thus only the *short-run* effects of monetary and fiscal policy. The long-run effects may be quite different.

For expansionary *monetary* policy, the main long-term concern is inflation. Although a monetary expansion may stimulate real production activity in the short run, the long-run result is likely to be inflation. We address this issue further in Chapters 7 and 8. This result does not mean that undertaking a monetary expansion should never be expected. In particular, policymakers are likely to consider it as a way to pull the

CHAPTER 6 THE IS-LM MODEL **163**

economy out of a recession. However, central bankers tend to be cautious about allowing monetary expansions in times when the economy is already doing well on its own.

The long-term concerns about *fiscal* policy are primarily related to the crowding out of private investment. This effect prevents the economy's capital stock from being maintained or expanded as it otherwise would have been. Thus, the economy's *productive capacity* is damaged in the long run.

This prediction depends on two important assumptions, however. First, it assumes that the fiscal expansion does not build the nation's capital stock, either because it does not sufficiently raise expectations of future activity to offset the crowding-out effect on private investment or because all the government spending is for current needs. This assumption would have to be modified if we were studying, say, a public investment in transportation infrastructure, such as airports, highways, or high-speed railroads. We return briefly to these issues in Chapter 12. The second assumption is that Ricardian equivalence does not hold. If it did, private saving would increase to meet the government's new borrowing demand, so interest rates would not be affected and investment would not be crowded out. Unfortunately, however, the validity of this hypothesis remains uncertain, and this uncertainty has left a number of analysts concerned about the long-term consequences of government deficits.

CHAPTER REVIEW

1. The demand for money is driven primarily by the need to carry out transactions. It is proportional to the price level and is an increasing function of the transactions volume, approximated by real GNP. It is a decreasing function of the nominal interest rate as the opportunity cost of holding money.

2. The market for money is in equilibrium when the demand for money equals the supply of money as determined by the central bank.

3. The LM curve represents those combinations of interest rates and real GNP levels that are compatible with equilibrium in the money market. It slopes upward because an increase in real GNP means a higher transactions volume, which results in upward pressure on the interest rate. Expansionary monetary policy (an increase in money sup-

ply) shifts the LM curve downward and to the right, while a contractionary monetary policy shifts it upward and to the left.

4. Short-run macroeconomic equilibrium is defined as a simultaneous equilibrium in the money market and the market for goods and services. Mathematically, it is described as the simultaneous satisfaction of the equation describing equilibrium in the goods market (the IS equation) and the equation describing equilibrium in the money market (the LM equation). Graphically, it is represented by the intersection of the IS curve and the LM curve in the IS-LM diagram.

5. The IS-LM model can be used to analyze business cycles. Bad news causing pessimism among businesses and consumers shifts the IS curve to the left and thus leads to a recession. A financial innovation reducing the de-

mand for money shifts the LM curve to the right, resulting in an expansion.

6. An expansionary monetary policy shifts the LM curve to the right and thus raises real GNP and lowers the interest rate in the short run.

7. An expansionary fiscal policy—increased government spending or lower taxes—shifts the IS curve to the right and raises real GNP as well as the interest rate in the short run. Because of the interest-rate increase, it crowds out part of private investment and net exports.

8. In terms of real GNP changes, monetary policy is more effective the flatter the IS curve, while fiscal policy is more effective the flatter the LM curve.

9. In the long run, a monetary expansion runs the risk of inflation, while a fiscal expansion may reduce the economy's production capacity.

EXERCISES

1. Carry out on your own all the numeric exercises in the text of this chapter.

2. Using the numerical IS-LM model developed in this chapter, suppose that an income tax cut raises the marginal propensity to spend on domestic goods (b_Y) from 0.25 to 0.3. Discuss whether this specification of a tax cut makes sense and compute the effects on real GNP and the interest rate.

3. Suppose the fiscal expansion in exercise 2 is supplemented by an increase in the real money supply from 800 to 950. Compute the effects of this policy combination. What kind of light does this exercise shed on the performance of the U.S. economy in the mid-1980s?

4. Repeat the last part of exercise 3 in Chapter 2 in which you used annual data for real GNP and real money supply (M2 deflated by the GNP deflator) and regressed the growth rate in real GNP on the growth rates for real money supply for this year, last year, and two years ago. Discuss whether these results are consistent with the IS-LM model. Also,

run the same regression for the levels rather than the growth rates of the same variables. Can you think of an economic or statistical reason for why working with growth rates is preferable?

5. The government deficit is often used as an indicator of fiscal policy, because expansionary policies tend to raise this deficit. Get real annual U.S. data for this deficit as well as for GNP (you can use the GNP deflator to deflate the nominal deficit data). Construct annual changes for either variable (for any variable x_t, the annual change is simply $x_t - x_{t-1}$.)

   a. Regress the real change in GNP on the real change in the deficit for the same year. Do the results support the predictions of the IS-LM model? If not, what would you conclude about the likely effects of fiscal policy? Can you think of a reason other than the failure of the IS-LM model for its apparent contradiction? [Hint: Even though expansionary policy may stimulate the economy, recessions tend to raise the deficit, because tax revenues and transfer payments depend on income.]

   b. Now, as one multiple regression, regress the change in real GNP on the real deficit changes from a year ago, two years ago, and three years ago (do not include the real deficit change for the current year this time). Do the results differ from part (a)? If so, can you explain the difference?

   c. Can you think of a reason why we used the straight changes in the deficit rather than their growth rates in this exercise?

THINKING QUESTIONS

1. What kind of effect would the IS-LM model predict for natural disasters like earthquakes and hurricanes? How do you reconcile this answer with the cost you would incur if you owned a business whose facilities were damaged or destroyed? What does this example tell you about the limitations of the IS-LM model?

2. Suppose the central bank uses the interest rate as its intermediate target. Does that mean we can gauge the effects of monetary policy by regressing real GNP on the interest rate? Why or why not?

3. From inside as well as outside the United States, the argument has been made repeatedly that the U.S. government needs to reduce its deficit from the high levels of the 1980s. Yet such a move would represent a contractionary fiscal policy. Against this background, would you advocate deficit reduction? Why or why not?

APPENDIX TO CHAPTER 6:
ALGEBRAIC SOLUTION TO THE IS-LM MODEL

This appendix solves the IS-LM equation system [equations (6.10a) and (6.10b)] algebraically for real GNP and the real interest rate as functions of the remaining variables. The equations are

(6.10a) $Y = b_0 + b_Y Y - b_R R + G + b_e Y^e$ (IS),

(6.10b) $M/P = k_0 + k_Y Y - k_i(R + \pi^e)$ (LM).

Start by adding $k_i(R + \pi^e)$ to and subtracting M/P from both sides of the LM equation, (6.10b), to obtain

$$k_i(R + \pi^e) = k_0 + k_Y Y - M/P.$$

Then divide both sides by k_i and subtract π^e to obtain a solution for R in terms of Y:

(A.6.1) $R = (k_0 + k_Y Y - M/P)/k_i - \pi^e.$

Now substitute this expression into the IS equation, (6.10a), to obtain

$$Y = b_0 + b_Y Y - b_R[(k_0 + k_Y Y - M/P)/k_i - \pi^e] + G + b_e Y^e$$
$$= b_0 + b_Y Y - b_R k_0/k_i - (b_R k_Y/k_i)Y + (b_R/k_i)M/P + b_R \pi^e + G + b_e Y^e.$$

Collect terms for Y and move them to the left of the equation:

$$Y(1 - b_Y + b_R k_Y/k_i) = b_0 - b_R k_0/k_i + (b_R/k_i)M/P + G + b_R \pi^e + b_e Y^e.$$

Next divide by the factor multiplying Y to obtain the solution for Y:

(A.6.2) $Y = \mu[b_0 - b_R k_0/k_i + (b_R/k_i)M/P + G + b_R \pi^e + b_e Y^e],$

where μ is shorthand notation for $1/(1 - b_Y + b_R k_Y/k_i)$. Now substitute this solution into (A.6.1) to solve for R:

$$R = k_0/k_i + (k_Y/k_i)\mu[b_0 - b_R k_0/k_i + (b_R/k_i)M/P + G + b_R \pi^e + b_e Y^e]$$
$$- (1/k_i)M/P - \pi^e$$
$$= k_0/k_i + (k_Y/k_i)\mu(b_0 - b_R k_0/k_i) + (k_Y/k_i)\mu(G + b_e Y^e)$$
$$- (1/k_i)(1 - \mu k_Y b_R/k_i)M/P - (1 - \mu k_Y b_R/k_i)\pi^e.$$

Note from the definition of μ that

$$1 - \mu k_Y b_R / k_i = (1 - b_Y + b_R k_Y / k_i - k_Y b_R / k_i)/(1 - b_Y + b_R k_Y / k_i)$$
$$= (1 - b_Y)/(1 - b_Y + b_R k_Y / k_i),$$

which is between zero and 1. Call this expression λ. Then the solution for R becomes

(A.6.3)
$$R = k_0 / k_i + (k_Y / k_i)\mu(b_0 - b_R k_0 / k_i)$$
$$+ (k_Y / k_i)\mu(G + b_e Y^e) - (\lambda / k_i)M/P - \lambda \pi^e.$$

7 AGGREGATE DEMAND, AGGREGATE SUPPLY, AND PRICE ADJUSTMENTS

Throughout our analysis in Chapters 5 and 6, we treated the price level as **predetermined,** that is, as determined by a sluggish process driven by past rather than current forces. Since price-level movements are important parts of the macroeconomic reality, it is now time to study this determining process. The purpose of this chapter is to present a model in which the price level and the inflation rate are determined as endogenous variables. Obviously, the price level is a nominal variable because it changes with inflation—in fact, it *defines* inflation. Thus, we can expect the mechanism determining the price level to be slightly different from those determining the real variables, such as real GNP. Not surprisingly, the money supply, another nominal variable, takes on a special importance; however, the relationship between the money supply and the price level is not necessarily simple. In particular, adjustments in the price level typically involve a considerable amount of *interaction* between the nominal and the real variables. A good deal of this interaction already was apparent in the analysis in Chapter 6, where we found that monetary policy could have important **real effects,** that is, effects on real variables such as real GNP and the real interest rate.

This chapter pursues such interactions further. We will study, in particular, how real GNP and the price level are determined simultaneously in the same model, which goes under the name of the **aggregate demand–aggregate supply** model. The demand side in this model is derived from the IS-LM model, while the supply side is determined by the resources available in the economy. Price adjustments form the link between aggregate demand and aggregate supply. The mechanism that produces these adjustments is commonly referred to as the **Phillips curve.**

7.1 THE AGGREGATE DEMAND CURVE

Our first task is to determine how changes in the price level affect the aggregate demand for goods and services for a given (nominal) money supply. From now on, we will think of aggregate demand as the equilibrium real GNP level in the IS-LM model. It may seem odd to associate the IS-LM model with the demand side in the economy, considering the fact that the supply of money and the production of goods and services play important roles in this model. The reason we do so is that the IS-LM analysis ignores the more fundamental supply constraints arising from the scarcity of resources, such as labor and capital, used in the production of goods and services. If we reserve the term *aggregate supply* for these fundamental resource constraints, it becomes natural to think of the IS-LM model as a model of aggregate demand.

THE PRICE LEVEL AND THE REAL MONEY SUPPLY

The only explicit role played by the price level in the IS-LM model is as a deflator for the money supply. In the LM equation, (6.10b), the money supply and the price level appeared only as the ratio M/P, which denotes the real money supply. As we showed in our analysis of Figure 6.2, an increase in the price level shifts the LM curve to the left because, for a given supply of money in nominal terms, it *reduces the real money supply*. Thus, the formal analysis of a price-level increase in the IS-LM model is exactly like the analysis of a monetary contraction. In other words, we can use the analysis in Figure 6.5 in reverse. Such a diagram is presented in Figure 7.1. The contraction in real money supply shifts the LM curve upward and to the left, resulting in an interest-rate increase and a contraction in real GNP.

FIGURE 7.1

An increase in the price level from P_0 to P_1 contracts the real money supply from M/P_0 to M/P_1, which shifts the LM curve to the left and reduces the equilibrium level of GNP in the IS-LM model.

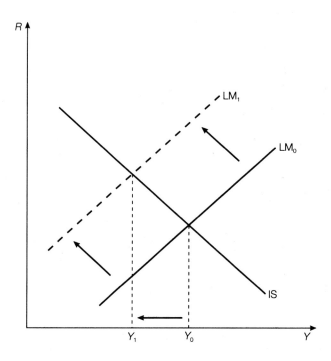

FIGURE 7.2

The aggregate demand curve.

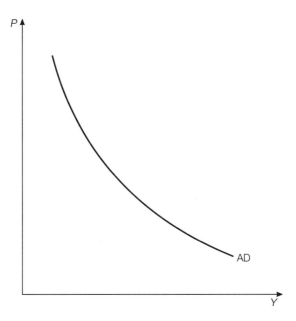

What we have found is an inverse relationship between the price level and the equilibrium real GNP level in the IS-LM model. Because we identify this GNP level with aggregate demand, we have also found an inverse relationship between aggregate demand and the price level. We can illustrate it by a downward-sloping curve in a diagram with real GNP on the horizontal axis and the price level on the vertical axis, as presented in Figure 7.2. We call such a curve the aggregate demand curve or, for short, the **AD curve.**

It is instructive to analyze this curve in more intuitive terms as well. Think of the demand and supply of money in nominal terms. Remember that the nominal demand for money is proportional to the price level because of the close tie between the price level and the dollar value of transactions. This means that an increase in the price level raises the demand for money. However, the nominal supply of money, M, is unchanged during this exercise. The result is an excess demand for money, which drives up the interest rate. The next step takes place in the goods market, where investment demand, net export demand, and the demand for consumer durables are all discouraged by the higher interest rate. This decline is amplified by the multiplier process, whereby the lower production levels are translated into reduced income and hence even lower spending. On the other hand, the decline in demand is mitigated somewhat via the money market as the reduced level of activity reduces the transactions demand for money, which allows interest rates to recede a little. The net effect, however, is a higher interest rate than initially and a lower level of aggregate demand. In short, a rise in the price level reduces aggregate demand, which means that the aggregate demand curve slopes downward.

A COMMON MISCONCEPTION ABOUT THE AGGREGATE DEMAND CURVE

The shape of the AD curve is very appealing, because it looks just like the microeconomic demand curve for an individual good except that the variable on the vertical axis in Figure 7.2 is the overall price level instead of the relative price of a particular good. Because of this similarity, you might be tempted to bypass the IS-LM analysis and simply state that the demand for goods and services is reduced because real incomes decline when the price level rises.

Why can't we just use this story directly to justify the downward slope? The answer to this question is that an increase in the price level is guaranteed to reduce real income only if nominal income stays constant or declines at the same time. However, no such assumption is made in the IS-LM model. Rather, the effect on nominal GNP of a change in the price level can be derived in that model as the change in the product PY when P changes. Using the methods of the appendix to Chapter 6, you should be able to verify that an increase in the price level in general *raises* nominal income in the IS-LM model.* As the preceding analysis shows, this increase is not large enough to make real GNP rise. However, in order to find the effect on real GNP, it is necessary to go through the entire IS-LM analysis.

SHIFTS IN AGGREGATE DEMAND

In the last chapter, we studied a number of factors that could affect the equilibrium solution in the IS-LM model. We found that a decline in real GNP could result from declining expectations about future production activity or from a contractionary monetary or fiscal policy. In contrast, an innovation-induced decline in money demand or expansionary monetary or fiscal policies were found to result in higher GNP levels.

Each of these examples assumed that the price level was unaffected by the events. Since the level of aggregate demand is the solution to the IS-LM model, we can make the following inference: Any disturbance that, according to the IS-LM model, reduces real GNP for a given price level also reduces the level of aggregate demand for that price level. But this means that the same negative disturbances must *shift the aggregate demand curve to the left*. Figure 7.3 illustrates such a leftward shift as the movement from AD_0 to AD_1. Similarly, any positive disturbance that

---

* There is a special case in which nominal GNP in the IS-LM model is independent of the price level. It arises if the real money demand function does not depend on the interest rate and does not have an intercept, so that $k_0 = 0$ and $k_i = 0$. In this case, which you may recognize from Section 6.5 as one with a vertical LM curve, nominal GNP is proportional to the money supply. Arguments supporting this case have been made by economists adhering to the monetarist view, which we discuss further in Chapter 11.

FIGURE 7.3

Changes in the economic environment that change the equilibrium level of real GNP in the IS-LM model shift the aggregate demand curve by the same amount as the change in equilibrium GNP. Changes in the environment that might have such effects include changes in expectations about future income levels, innovations in the financial system, and monetary and fiscal policy moves.

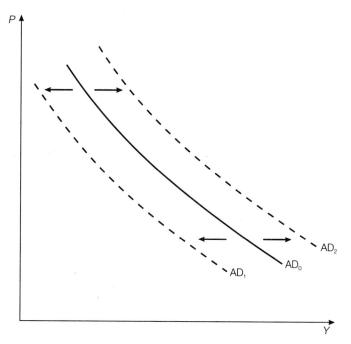

makes real GNP rise in the IS-LM model (at a given price level) shifts the aggregate demand curve to the right. Such shifts are illustrated by the movement from AD_0 to AD_2 in Figure 7.3.

7.2 AGGREGATE SUPPLY

When we speak about aggregate supply in macroeconomics, we think of the constraints on economic activity defined by the availability of productive resources in the economy. The most important such resources are the labor force and the stock of capital equipment, although we will make some reference to energy resources as well. Other natural resources are also important for long-run growth. However, since they seem to have played a minor role in business cycles so far, we will ignore them in our analysis.

THE AGGREGATE PRODUCTION FUNCTION

In the theory of the firm, the physical constraints on production possibilities are often summarized in the form of a **production function.** This analytical tool is useful in the aggregate as well; when used in this context, it is referred to as the *aggregate* production function. It describes the amount of goods and services that can be produced at varying levels of employment and capital services. As before, let the symbol K denote the capital stock available for current use in production. In Chapter 5, we used the symbol K_{-1} for this purpose in order to emphasize the time it takes to build new capital. We can allow ourselves to ignore that refinement here, but we should note that the capital stock K is given by past investment and cannot be changed instantaneously. Also, we use H as a symbol for employment, measured in hours. Then the aggregate production function can be written as

(7.1) $$Y = A(t)F(K, H).$$

The factor $A(t)$ is an indicator of productivity, which we will discuss shortly.

Figure 7.4 graphs the production function for a given level of the capital stock. Its upward slope indicates that more can be produced with higher employment. Note, however, that the curve also tends to flatten out as it increases. This flattening out occurs because the curve is drawn for a given capital stock, that is, given the available buildings and machinery. Then additional workers have no more equipment to work with. Thus, the more worker hours added, the more modest becomes the additional amount of output that results from adding another hour of work.

PRODUCTIVITY

Figure 7.4 shows an upward shift in the production function. Such a shift is indicative of improved **productivity,** which means that more output can be produced with the same levels of input or, equivalently, that the same output can be produced with lower inputs of labor and capital. The adjustment factor $A(t)$, which we included in the produc-

FIGURE 7.4

Graph of the aggregate production function for a given capital stock. The upward shift represents a productivity improvement.

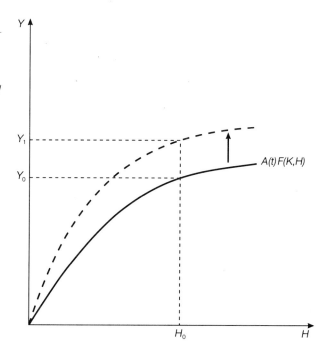

tion function (7.1), is intended to represent productivity changes. It is written as a function of time, t, because we usually think of productivity as exhibiting an upward trend over time. We can interpret the function F as representing the combined input levels of labor and capital, while changes in A represent changes in output above what results from changes in the input levels.

Productivity is usually measured in terms of growth rates. Define y, a, and f as the growth rates of real GNP, the productivity indicator $A(t)$, and the function F, respectively. Then a can be called the productivity growth rate, while f can be interpreted as the average growth rate in labor and capital inputs. Since the growth rate of a product is simply the sum of the growth rates of each factor,* we have

$$y = a + f.$$

The growth rate in real GNP can be observed from government statistics. Since employment and capital stock can be observed, the average growth rate f of factor inputs can be observed as well. (The weights used for this average are usually the shares in total production costs for the respective inputs.) We can then compute the productivity growth rate a as

(7.2) $$a = y - f.$$

Productivity growth computed according to this definition is called **total factor productivity** because it reflects productivity improvement for labor as well as capital.

Unfortunately, the measurement of physical capital always has to rely on certain assumptions about depreciation. Employment data, however, do not contain this ambiguity. For this reason, data for **labor productivity** have become much more widely available than data for total factor productivity. Labor productivity is defined simply as output per worker hour. Now, since the growth rate of a product is the sum of the growth rates, the growth rate of a ratio must be the difference between the growth rates. Thus, if we use the symbols p and h for the growth rates in labor productivity and worker hours, respectively, the growth in labor productivity is

(7.3) $$p = y - h.$$

---

* Suppose that, from year 0 to year 1, $A(t)$ and $F(K, H)$ grow at rates a and f from A_0 and F_0 to $A_1 = (1 + a)A_0$ and $F_1 = (1 + f)F_0$, respectively. Then the growth rate in Y over the same year is

$$y = (Y_1 - Y_0)/Y_0 = [(1 + a)A_0(1 + f)F_0 - A_0F_0]/A_0F_0$$
$$= (1 + a)(1 + f) - 1 = a + f + af.$$

As long as the growth rates a and f are small (< 0.1), their product af is much smaller (< 0.01) than each of them. For this reason, we ignore it in practice and treat the growth rate of a product simply as the sum of the growth rates.

TABLE 7.1   PRODUCTIVITY GROWTH RATES FOR THE TOTAL BUSINESS SECTOR FOR THE UNITED STATES AND SOME OTHER LEADING COUNTRIES

COUNTRY	TOTAL FACTOR PRODUCTIVITY			LABOR PRODUCTIVITY		
	PRE-1973	1974–79	1980–86	PRE-1973	1974–79	1980–86
United States	1.5	−0.1	0.1	2.2	0.3	0.7
Japan	6.3	1.8	1.7	8.8	3.2	2.8
West Germany	2.6	1.8	0.8	4.7	3.4	2.0
France	3.9	1.8	1.2	5.6	3.2	2.4
United Kingdom	1.9	0.2	1.0	3.3	1.3	1.9
Italy	4.8	1.6	0.7	6.6	2.4	1.3
Canada	2.3	1.1	−0.3	3.0	2.0	1.1

SOURCE: *OECD Economic Outlook*, December 1988.

Comparing formulae (7.2) and (7.3), we find that they coincide if labor and capital inputs grow at the same rate, so the average growth rate is the same as the growth in labor productivity. If the capital stock grows faster than employment (in hours), the average factor growth rate f is greater than h, so labor productivity grows faster than total factor productivity. Conversely, if employment grows faster than the capital stock, total factor productivity is the faster-growing productivity measure.

Table 7.1 presents some data for labor productivity and total factor productivity for the United States as well as for some other leading countries in the world economy. The table demonstrates the problem of relying on labor productivity alone. For example, virtually all the growth in labor productivity in the United States in the 1980s can be explained as the result of capital investments. The table also reveals the weak international position of the United States in terms of productivity growth, especially after 1974. On the other hand, most countries experienced a slowdown in productivity growth at about that time. That the *level* of productivity remains high in the United States is also part of the story. By most measures it is still the world's highest.

AGGREGATE SUPPLY AND EQUILIBRIUM IN THE MARKETS FOR LABOR AND CAPITAL

In general, the aggregate production function describes how much can be produced, in terms of real GNP, from given input levels of labor and capital. Our primary interest here, however, is how the function can be used to derive aggregate supply. We use this term to mean the level of real GNP that can be produced with the labor and capital input levels that workers and capital owners want to supply and that firms want to buy. In other words, *aggregate supply is the level of real GNP that can be produced from the equilibrium levels of employment and capital use.*

Determining the equilibrium level of capital usage is trivial, because the current capital stock is given unambiguously by past investment and because no capital owner would prefer to have a piece of equipment stay idle if it could be put to profitable use.

The determination of the equilibrium employment level is more subtle. Here we must consider both the demand for labor by firms and the supply of labor by workers. The demand side is the simpler part in this instance. In order to make a profit, firms need to compare the output produced by their employees with the cost of employing them. This cost can be summarized by the **real wage,** which is the hourly wage measured in terms of the amount of goods that an hour's wage can buy. We can think of it as wages measured in 1982 dollars. If the real wage is low, firms can afford to hire many workers; if it is high, they need to look for ways to cut their work force. Thus, *the demand for labor is a decreasing function of the real wage.** In Figure 7.5, this relationship is represented as a downward-sloping demand curve for labor, labeled HD.

The *supply* of labor arises from workers' choices about the use of their time. They might choose to seek work that will pay them a wage they can spend on goods and services. The alternative is to spend their time on other activities, such as caring for the household or fixing the house, that may be useful but do not pay. The supply of labor is the outcome of this trade-off.

The supply of labor depends on the real wage, but in a somewhat ambiguous way. According to the *substitution effect*, an increase in the real wage makes work a more attractive activity because its reward has risen relative to, say, homemaking. According to the *income effect*, on the other hand, a higher real wage makes it possible to work fewer hours and still maintain or increase one's income level. Thus, in the case of a real wage increase, the substitution and income effects pull in the direction of higher and lower labor supply, respectively. Because they counter each other, the *net* effect is ambiguous.

It should be added that the labor supply decision concerns not only *how much* a person wants to work but also *when* a person wants to work. Thus, if people see a decrease in the real wage but expect it to be temporary, they may choose to stay out of work for a while until condi-

---

* This conclusion follows from the curvature of the production function, that is, from the way it flattens out, as we saw in Figure 7.4. We noted in connection with that figure that the rate of increase in the graph of the production function reflects the additional amount of production volume generated by an additional hour of work. Economists call this additional amount of production volume the *marginal product of labor*. The flattening out of the curve means that the marginal product of labor is a decreasing function of employment. It will be profitable for a firm to hire additional workers as long as their marginal product per hour exceeds the cost per worker hour measured in goods, in other words, the real wage. If the wage is low, this criterion can be satisfied at high levels of employment. If it is high, the curvature of the production function means that it can be satisfied only at low employment levels.

FIGURE 7.5

Supply, demand, and equi-
librium in the labor market.

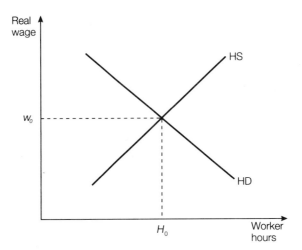

tions pick up again. This dimension of the problem makes it a little more likely that the substitution effect will dominate.

If it does, the supply of labor will be an increasing function of the real wage. In other words, the labor supply curve will slope upward, like the labor supply curve shown in Figure 7.5 and labeled HS. Regardless of the slope of the labor supply curve, however, equilibrium in the labor market can be found where demand equals supply or, in the diagram, where the labor supply and labor demand curves intersect. The **equilibrium real wage,** then, is determined as the real wage at which the supply and demand for labor are equal, w_0 in the diagram. The equilibrium level of employment (measured in hours) is the common level of labor supply and demand at this real wage level, H_0 in the diagram.

Now that we have found the equilibrium level of employment, we can put it into the aggregate production function (7.1), together with the available capital stock, to determine the level of aggregate supply, which we now denote as Y^S:

(7.4) $$Y^S = A(t)F(K, H_0).$$

7.3 AGGREGATE SUPPLY AND AGGREGATE DEMAND IN THE SHORT AND THE LONG RUN

The discussion of the labor market in the preceding section implicitly assumes that equilibrium is always reached, so the supply of labor always equals demand. This means that everybody who wants a job can find the job and the hours he or she wants and that firms never face labor shortages. Economists are far from agreement over whether this type of equilibrium describes the labor market accurately. Keynesian economists tend to view the variation in employment over the business cycle as a result of temporary **disequilibria** in the labor market, a situation in which some people who look for work cannot find any. Classical or equilibrium economists, on the other hand, argue that unemployment rises during recessions because some workers choose not to work during recessions, because the wages they can earn are too low to make working worthwhile.

This disagreement, which we will get back to soon, is important for the short-term analysis of business cycles. However, most economists tend to agree that equilibrium equality of supply and demand reasonably describes the labor market in the *long run*.

MACRO-ECONOMIC EQUILIBRIUM IN THE LONG RUN

In order to be able to analyze aggregate demand and aggregate supply simultaneously, we need to find out how long-run aggregate supply depends on the price level. Let us go through the steps again and see what role, if any, is played by this variable. First, the price level obviously is irrelevant for the production function, which is a relationship among real variables entirely. Second, the price level is irrelevant for the capital stock because this variable is given by past investment. Third, the supply and demand for labor both depend on the real wage—another real variable. In the short run, it is possible that the real wage may be affected by the price level if the nominal wage is fixed, say, by contract, so that the real wage varies inversely with the price level. However, in the long run we assume that the real wage is free to adjust so that equilibrium is reached (for example, because contracts are renegotiated). This means that nominal factors such as the price level are irrelevant for the determination of the equilibrium level of employment.

These insights together clearly indicate that all the factors determining aggregate supply are independent of the price level. Thus, aggregate supply can be represented by the vertical line in Figure 7.6. This line is labeled AS and is presented together with the aggregate demand curve, labeled AD.

The intersection E of these two curves represents the long-run equilibrium of the economy. At this equilibrium, aggregate demand equals aggregate supply, and the price level is just what it needs to be in order to fix aggregate demand at the same level as aggregate supply. The equilibrium levels of real GNP and the price level are marked Y_0 and P_0, respectively. Note that the level of real GNP is determined entirely by aggregate supply in this equilibrium. This is consistent with the way most economists think about the long-run behavior of the economy. The only long-term role of aggregate demand is to determine the price level. Thus, in the long run, real production is a supply phenomenon, and inflation is a demand phenomenon.

FIGURE 7.6

Aggregate demand (AD), aggregate supply (AS), and long-run macroeconomic equilibrium.

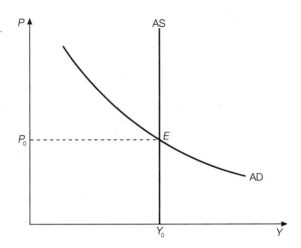

FIGURE 7.7

Aggregate growth and inflation in the long run.

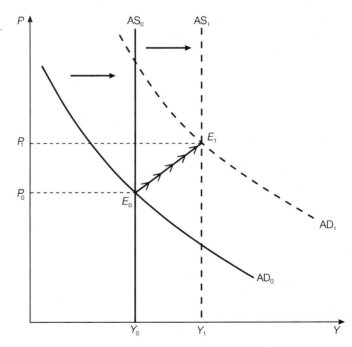

Although Figure 7.6 presents the long-run equilibrium as one point, this equilibrium is likely to move over time as conditions change. An example of such movement is shown in Figure 7.7. As the labor force grows, as new investment is added to the capital stock, and as productivity improves, the aggregate supply curve shifts to the right, as shown by the shift from AS_0 to AS_1 in Figure 7.7. Similarly, if the money supply is allowed to grow, the real GNP level implied by the IS-LM model increases for any given price level. In other words, the aggregate demand curve moves to the right, from AD_0 to AD_1. The result of these movements is a growth in real GNP from Y_0 to Y_1. The price level may rise or fall depending on whether aggregate demand grows faster or slower than aggregate supply. In the case illustrated in Figure 7.7, aggregate demand grows a little faster, which gives rise to some inflation of the price level, from P_0 to P_1.

The arrow connecting E_0 and E_1 in the diagram illustrates how the macroeconomy moves in normal times. However, during periods of recession or rapid expansion, the economy may deviate from this pattern. The short-term analysis of economic fluctuations occupies most of macroeconomic analysis. We now turn to that issue; note before we start, however, that opinions here are rather sharply divided. The disagreement is mainly over the short-term behavior of aggregate supply. We discuss two opposing views and then use one of them as the basis for further analysis.

THE EQUILIBRIUM VIEW OF THE SHORT RUN: REAL BUSINESS CYCLE THEORY

The equilibrium view of business cycles uses the notion of economic equilibrium as its basic paradigm. This means that all markets are analyzed under the assumption that the observed prices and quantities always reflect intersections of demand and supply curves. In particular, the level of real GNP is determined by the intersection of the aggregate demand and aggregate supply curves. Since this relationship is assumed to hold at all times, there is no difference between long-run and short-run analysis.

Given this view, we can use the analysis we just developed for the long run to describe the behavior of the economy in the short run as well. In particular, we can use the diagram in Figure 7.6 to conclude that the economy always reaches an equilibrium like the point labeled E in that graph. This means that, *even in the short run*, the level of economic activity is determined by aggregate supply. Aggregate demand influences only the price level and not the level of real activity as measured by GNP.

In Chapter 6, we saw how the IS-LM model could be used to study business cycles. Since the aggregate demand curve is derived from the IS-LM model, the analysis in Chapter 6 implicitly explained business cycles as the effects of disturbances to aggregate demand. How can the equilibrium view account for business cycles? The answer is simple: *Business cycles are the result of disturbances to aggregate supply.*

The supply disturbances that give rise to recessions and expansions are usually modeled as negative and positive shocks to *productivity*. In equation (7.1), these shocks can be represented as spontaneous shifts in the productivity factor $A(t)$. During periods of disappointing productivity, the wages offered by firms fall to such low levels that some workers prefer to be unemployed. Thus, unemployment rises and the economy enters a recession. Conversely, good news about productivity leads to expansion periods with low unemployment. Because business cycles in this case are caused by disturbances to *real* variables, this view of business cycles is usually referred to as the **real-business-cycle** view.

Figure 7.8 illustrates the real-business-cycle analysis of a recession. The economy starts out before the recession with aggregate demand and aggregate supply curves marked AD_0 and AS_0, respectively. The intersection of these curves, labeled E_0, defines the initial equilibrium real GNP Y_0 and price level P_0. Then an adverse productivity shock shifts the AS curve leftward to AS_1.

This shift represents not only the productivity shock itself but also the effect this shock has on the equilibrium level of employment. Because the shock has reduced the productivity of labor, firms will offer their workers reduced wages. Graphically, as illustrated in Figure 7.9, this means that the labor demand curve shifts downward from HD_0 to HD_1. Then, provided the substitution effect is large enough to make the labor supply curve slope upward, equilibrium employment declines from H_0 to H_1. Since the aggregate production function depends on the productivity term $A(t)$ both directly and indirectly via employment, the shift in the curve from AS_0 to AS_1 in Figure 7.8 represents the sum of both these effects.

However, chances are that the aggregate demand curve will shift to the left as well. The reason for this shift is that the productivity shock affects the future outlook of the economy. We saw in Chapter 6 that bad

FIGURE 7.8

Illustration of a "real business cycle." A negative productivity shock causes simultaneous recession and inflation in AD-AS equilibrium.

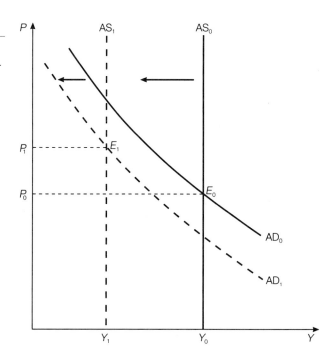

FIGURE 7.9

A downward shift in the demand for labor and in employment as the result of a negative productivity shock.

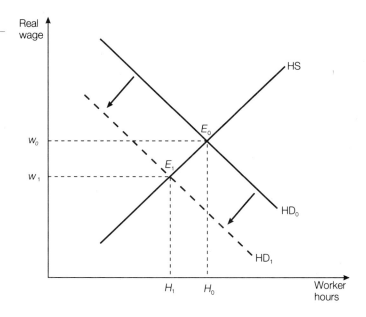

news implying lower future real income levels than previously anticipated causes a leftward shift in the IS curve and thus reduces the equilibrium level of real GNP in the IS-LM model. Consequently, since the aggregate demand curve represents the solutions to the IS-LM model, that curve must shift left as well. There are two reasons for the expectations about future income levels to decline. First, it may not be realistic to expect productivity to bounce right back after the initial shock, so future productivity is affected as well. Second, and more subtly, a recession now, even if temporary, will result in reduced investment and capital formation, which affects future aggregate supply adversely through the capital input in the aggregate production function. However, if the productivity shock is temporary, the leftward shift in the aggregate demand curve is likely to be smaller than that of aggregate supply.

This is the situation shown in Figure 7.8. At the new equilibrium, real GNP is lower than before (it has fallen from Y_0 to Y_1), which illustrates the arrival of a recession. At the same time, the price level has risen from P_0 to P_1.

The real-business-cycle theory has been quite successful in explaining actual business-cycle movements in the U.S. economy.* However, two

---

* See Finn E. Kydland and Edward F. Prescott, "Time to Build and Aggregate Fluctuations," *Econometrica*, September 1982, vol. 50, no. 6, pp. 1345–70. Starting from a more agnostic point of view, Matthew Shapiro and Mark Watson also find that a good deal of real GNP movement can be explained by productivity shocks. Their paper "Sources of Business Cycle Fluctuations" is published in *Macroeconomics Annual 1988*, edited by Stanley Fischer (Cambridge, Mass.: M.I.T. Press).

weaknesses are worth pointing out. First, although the theory relies on shocks in the form of sudden deteriorations and improvements in productivity, its proponents so far have failed to come up with a definite idea about the nature of these shocks. Some authors have pointed to the strong fluctuations in oil prices, particularly during the 1970s, as real, production-related disturbances.* But it seems fair to point out that the problem seemed to be that the energy resources became more expensive rather than that they became less productive. Moreover, although oil shocks might have been important in the 1970s, they seem too isolated to form the basis for a general theory of business cycles.

The second problem lies in the explanation of inflation. This problem is illustrated in Figure 7.8, in which the adverse productivity shock increases the price level at the same time as it reduces real GNP. In other words, it creates a combination of recession and inflation. This combination, sometimes called "stagflation," could serve as a good description of the economy in the two recessions in the 1970s. However, as we saw in Chapter 3, most other U.S. recessions since World War II, including the important U.S. and world recession in 1981–82, have been associated with a substantial *decline* in the inflation rate. The real-business-cycle theory has some difficulty explaining this fact.

The theory of real business cycles is a new research area in macroeconomics. We will discuss it in greater detail in Chapter 11. For now, we should note that it is too early to tell whether it will become a temporary interest or the new mainstream view. For the rest of this chapter, we base our analysis on what until now has been considered the conventional view of business cycles, which focuses on disequilibria between aggregate demand and aggregate supply. This view admits that business cycles can be caused by fluctuations in aggregate supply as well as aggregate demand but puts particular emphasis on aggregate-demand fluctuations. Central to this view is the contention that rigidities in prices and/or wages often keep the economy from reaching a full macroeconomic equilibrium. The price level adjusts in response to the resulting disequilibria, but does so only gradually over time. This price-adjustment mechanism has become known as the Phillips curve.

RIGIDITIES AND DISEQUILIBRIUM IN THE SHORT RUN

The conventional view also models aggregate supply as the level of real GNP that will be produced when the labor market is in equilibrium. However, equilibrium in the labor market is viewed as an ideal, long-term situation that is not realized at all times. In particular, recessions

---

*Of particular interest here are two articles by James D. Hamilton of the University of Virginia: "Oil and the Macroeconomy since World War II," *Journal of Political Economy*, April 1983, vol. 91, no. 2, pp. 228–48, and "A Neoclassical Model of Unemployment and the Business Cycle," *Journal of Political Economy*, June 1988, vol. 96, no. 3, pp. 593–617.

are associated with excess supply in the labor market (that is, with large numbers of workers who want jobs but can't find any), because various rigidities in the system prevent the real wage from adjusting fast enough to ensure a continuous equilibrium. Similarly, rapid expansions may result in labor shortages. The fluctuations in the demand for labor result mainly from corresponding fluctuations in aggregate demand. *Business cycles are viewed primarily as a result of disturbances to aggregate demand.*

Because equilibrium in the labor market is viewed as an ideal, long-term situation, the aggregate supply curve, in the conventional view, is identical to the long-run aggregate supply curve studied above. Thus, it remains a vertical line in the (Y, P) plane. However, unlike the situation in the equilibrium view, it usually does not move around so as to generate business cycles but rather defines a level of normal activity, referred to as **potential GNP.** Business cycles then are generated as aggregate-demand disturbances that cause actual GNP to *fluctuate around* potential GNP. *Actual GNP follows aggregate demand* in these fluctuations. Thus, for example, business cycles are mainly caused by the type of aggregate-demand disturbances studied in Chapter 6.

The reason that actual GNP follows aggregate demand is that the price level, like wages, is "sticky" in the short run and responds only slowly to differences between aggregate demand and supply. Similarly, the level of employment is not determined by equilibrium in the labor market but is simply the level needed to produce the actual level of real GNP.

The determination of real GNP according to the conventional view is illustrated in Figure 7.10. The aggregate supply curve, labeled AS, defines potential GNP, which is denoted Y^*. Initially, the aggregate demand curve, labeled AD_0, intersects the aggregate supply curve at E_0. Suppose the economy starts out from such a long-run equilibrium, but because of some negative disturbance to aggregate demand (say, a contractionary policy) the aggregate demand curve shifts to the left. The new aggregate demand curve is labeled AD_1 and intersects the aggregate supply curve at E_1. This point represents the new long-run equilibrium.

However, the economy does not necessarily reach this equilibrium within a short period of time, such as a year, because the price level adjusts slowly. Suppose it stays at its original level P_0, which is higher than the new equilibrium level P_1. Then aggregate demand is Y_D, corresponding to the point D on the new aggregate demand curve. This demand falls short of potential GNP and thus represents a *dis*equilibrium. The conventional view assumes that *actual GNP is determined by aggregate demand.* Thus, actual real GNP equals Y_D. Since this level falls short of potential GNP, the economy is in a recession—aggregate demand falls short of aggregate supply.

FIGURE 7.10

The conventional view of aggregate demand and supply.

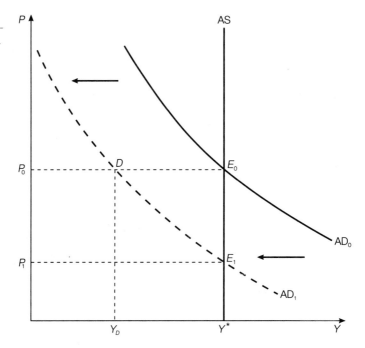

Aggregate supply can move according to this view as well, but this movement is expected to reflect mostly long-run changes, such as population growth, capital accumulation, and trend changes in productivity. These forces determine the long-term path of economic growth. They are influenced by business cycles; for example, growth in the capital stock is slowed by a decline in investment activity. However, the business cycles themselves primarily represent fluctuations *around* this path.

7.4 THE PHILLIPS CURVE

When the price level is too high, aggregate demand falls short of aggregate supply. However, since this situation is a disequilibrium, we expect it to activate an adjustment mechanism that will work to restore equilibrium.

Let us consider how such a mechanism would have to work. Suppose the economy finds itself at the disequilibrium point D in Figure 7.10, where aggregate demand falls short of aggregate supply, so that actual real GNP lies below potential GNP. In this situation, the price level P_0 is higher than the equilibrium price level P_1. Then the price adjustment mechanism should bring the price level down. Conversely, if actual GNP lies above potential GNP* and the price level is *lower* than the equilibrium price level, the price level should adjust upward.

To specify such a mechanism, define the **GNP gap** as the percentage difference between actual and potential real GNP, $(Y - Y^*)/Y^*$. Thus, if actual GNP lies below potential GNP, the GNP gap is negative, and vice versa. Furthermore, as long as actual GNP is determined by aggregate demand in the short run, a negative GNP gap, such as that in Figure 7.10, means that the price level is too high for a complete macroeconomic equilibrium, and vice versa. Therefore, the price level should fall when the GNP gap is negative and rise when it is positive. However, to emphasize the notion that this process is somewhat sluggish, we assume that the price-level movement this period is determined by *last* period's GNP gap. Again using the subscript -1 to denote last period's values, we can specify the price adjustment that satisfies these criteria as

$$\frac{P - P_{-1}}{P_{-1}} = \gamma \, \frac{Y_{-1} - Y^*_{-1}}{Y^*_{-1}} \, ,$$

where γ is some positive constant indicating the speed of the price adjustment process.

In the analysis of price adjustments, we often ignore the changes in potential GNP over time and let Y^* denote potential GNP in all periods. Moreover, the percentage change in the price level in the formula above is simply the *inflation rate*, which we previously denoted π. Thus, the price adjustment mechanism just specified can be written as

(7.5) $\pi = \gamma(Y_{-1} - Y^*)/Y^*.$

We will refer to equation (7.5) as the formula for the Phillips curve, which is illustrated graphically in Figure 7.11. It contains at least the beginnings of a theory of inflation by indicating that a positive GNP gap leads to inflationary pressures and that deflationary tendencies are the result of a negative GNP gap. As a theory of inflation, it is consistent with the popular notion that an "overheated" economy breeds inflation, because the term *overheating* usually is used in reference to an excessive activity level and hence a positive GNP gap.

It is worth noting that formula (7.5) is not the original Phillips curve. The original version of this curve can be found in a 1957 article by A. W. H. Phillips that presented evidence of a negative correlation between the rates of change in nominal *wages* and the *unemployment*

---

*It may seem odd that actual GNP can exceed potential GNP. However, potential GNP does not define an upper limit for how much can be produced. Rather, it represents the level of GNP that will be produced under balanced, equilibrium conditions, as discussed in the main text. In this sense, the term "potential GNP" is somewhat of a misnomer. However, since it has become established among macroeconomists, we will use it.

FIGURE 7.11

The Phillips curve.

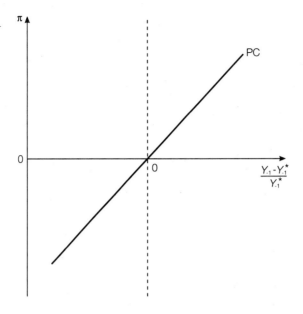

*rate.** However, the two versions capture the same main idea, namely, that an unusually high activity level puts upward pressure on wages and prices, and vice versa. Although larger-scale models of the Phillips curve seek to explain wage changes and unemployment rates in addition to price-level changes, the simpler formulation in equation (7.5) is adequate for our purposes.

DYNAMIC ADJUSTMENT WITH THE PHILLIPS CURVE

Figure 7.12 illustrates how shifts in aggregate demand and price-level adjustments interact over time. The left panel of this diagram shows the aggregate demand curve and aggregate supply in the form of potential GNP. The right panel shows the Phillips curve. Suppose that, initially, aggregate demand is given by the curve labeled AD_0. Suppose also that the economy has had enough time to reach the long-run equilibrium E_0, so that the initial price level is P_0 and real GNP is initially equal to potential GNP. We finally assume that the price level has been at P_0 for at least one period, so that initial inflation is zero.

Now suppose that in year 0 the aggregate demand curve shifts outward from AD_0 to AD_1. Since the aggregate demand curve represents solutions to the IS-LM model, this shift must represent some change

---

*A. W. H. Phillips, "The Relationship between the Unemployment Rate and the Rate of Change in Money Wage Rates in the United Kingdom, 1861–1957," *Economica*, November 1957, pp. 283–99.

that implied an increase in the equilibrium solution for real GNP in the IS-LM model. As an example, we assume that the shift was the result of an increase in the money supply. In period 0, this shift makes the economy move to point A_0 in the left panel of the diagram, and actual GNP rises from Y^* to Y_0. Thus, within this period, the entire effect is on the quantity side, because the price level takes a period to react.

However, the GNP gap during period 0 changes from zero to $(Y_0 - Y^*)/Y^*$, denoted g_0 in the diagram on the right of Figure 7.12. So according to the Phillips curve, the inflation rate in period 1 rises from zero to π_1, as shown in the right panel. This means that the price level is higher in period 1, because a positive inflation rate means a rise in the price level. The real effect of this change can now be read off the aggregate demand curve AD_1 in the left panel. Between period 0 and period 1, the nominal money supply is constant by assumption, so the aggregate demand curve does not shift further. However, the price-level increase implies a contraction in the real money supply, which makes the economy climb back up along AD_1 to point A_1; actual GNP contracts from Y_0 to Y_1.

As a result, the GNP gap for period 1 is smaller than it was for period 0, so the upward pressure on the price level has been reduced. On the Phillips curve, this reduction in upward pressure is reflected as a lower inflation rate, π_2, for period 2. However, even this inflation rate is positive, so the price level continues to rise to P_2. For this reason, the process

FIGURE 7.12

Dynamic effects of a positive shift in aggregate demand on inflation, the price level, and real GNP.

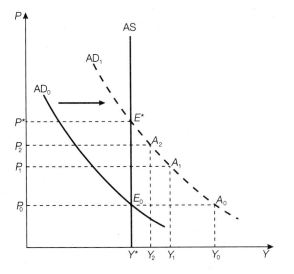

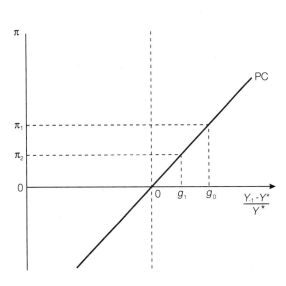

for the determination of real output repeats itself during period 2. The economy continues to move back up along the aggregate demand curve, this time to A_2. Actual real GNP contracts again, from Y_1 to Y_2.

This process continues until the economy comes to rest at the new long-term equilibrium, E^*. At this point, real GNP is back to its potential level. At the same time, the adjustment process has moved the price level from its initial value, P_0, to the new equilibrium level, P^*. According to this model, the monetary expansion has no long-term effect on real GNP. In the long run, the entire effect is an increased price level. The long-run properties of this model are exactly like those of the equilibrium model considered in the previous section, because the economy eventually reaches the same equilibrium. However, this long-term picture masks an intervening process whereby real GNP first rises, then recedes gradually; the same is true of inflation.

This example could be run in reverse to show the effect of a monetary contraction. The effects are completely symmetric. The contraction first makes real GNP decline. Then the price level starts to decline. As it falls, real GNP is gradually restored to its old level. This reversed story demonstrates the **stabilizing role of prices.** Recessions do not last forever. When the economy enters a recession, stabilizing forces are activated that eventually get the economy back on its feet again. The decline in the price level is the stabilizing force that eventually pulls the economy out of recession.

EXPANSIONARY MONETARY POLICY—IS IT ALWAYS BAD?

Our analysis may have left the impression that expansionary monetary policies, despite their promising effects in the IS-LM model, are always inadvisable because they raise the price level and give no ultimate benefit in terms of a higher level of real GNP. However, that impression arises mainly because the example studied started from a long-run equilibrium.

As an alternative example, suppose the economy finds itself in a recession because of a negative shift in expectations about future activity levels. Thus, the aggregate demand curve has shifted to the left and the economy finds itself in a position like that represented by point D in Figure 7.10. If in this situation the money supply is increased, the resulting expansion of aggregate demand will bring real GNP back toward aggregate supply. The recession will be shortened, because the adjustment process will have a shorter distance to go before it again reaches equilibrium.

The trick, then, is to know exactly when the economy needs a boost to restore equilibrium and when a monetary expansion will lead to "overheating" and upward pressure on the price level. This dilemma is an important part of the art of monetary policy making, which we discuss further in Chapter 12.

ARGUMENTS OVER THE PHILLIPS CURVE

From the press or from other courses in economics, you might be aware that the Phillips curve is a somewhat controversial concept. The controversy centers mainly around the notion, implicit in formula (7.5), that inflation is always the result of high economic activity. Inflation is the side effect of good times, so to speak. Thus, it may be argued—and indeed has been argued in the past—that macroeconomic policy making can be reduced to making trade-offs between real GNP growth and inflation.

This view has met with two objections. The first is that the apparent policy trade-off is an illusion, because an attempt to stimulate the economy beyond its potential will be futile in the long run. The analysis carried out above largely agreed with this judgment, even within the Phillips curve model itself. In Chapter 8, we will see that this argument becomes even stronger when the analysis includes the effects of inflationary expectations.

The second objection is the empirical observation that inflation does not always seem to be a side effect of good times. This view naturally became popular in the stagflationary times of the seventies. That experience led many Phillips-curve analysts to modify their models in ways that could account for stagflation. We look at one such modification below. First, however, another and even more recent empirical fact is worth noting. After the substantial monetary tightening in the early eighties, the economy entered another severe recession, and inflation subsided. Thus, the experience of the early 1980s is much closer to the Phillips curve model, especially when we include inflationary expectations in the analysis, as we do in the next chapter.

INFLATIONARY SHOCKS IN THE PHILLIPS CURVE MODEL

Economists who believed in the Phillips curve initially had some difficulty rationalizing the events of the 1970s. However, it soon became clear that oil price increases could be modeled as *external inflationary shocks*, which raise the price level above what would have been indicated by the simple Phillips curve formula in equation (7.5).

Specifically, we can add a shift variable, denoted s, to the Phillips curve to account for such shocks. Then the formula becomes

$$(7.6) \qquad \pi = \gamma(Y_{-1} - Y^*)/Y^* + s.$$

This modification of the model admittedly is somewhat ad hoc. However, it does illustrate an interesting point.

Figure 7.13 illustrates the effects of an external inflationary shock on real GNP and inflation in this model. The economy starts out at the aggregate demand–aggregate supply equilibrium E with a stable price level. Then the external inflationary shock *shifts the Phillips curve upward* from PC_0 to PC_1 in the Phillips curve diagram on the right side of the figure. As a result, the price level increases abruptly from P_0 to P_1.

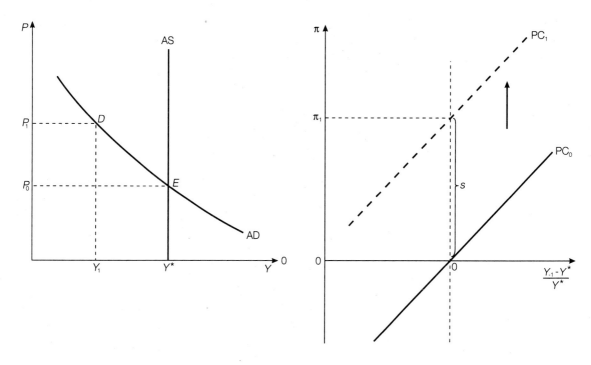

FIGURE 7.13

Effects of an external inflationary shock in the Phillips
curve model.

However, because this price level increase comes from outside, it is not
the result of an increase in the money supply. On the contrary, with an
unchanged nominal value of the money supply, the price-level increase
contracts the *real* money supply, sending aggregate demand climbing
up the aggregate demand curve from the equilibrium point E to the re-
cessionary disequilibrium D. Thus, the inflationary shock sets off a recession.* The augmentation made to the Phillips curve model enabled it
to account for stagflation.

Figure 7.13 also suggests an explanation for how the economy eventually recovers from this kind of recession. Since the GNP gap is negative, there will be downward pressure on the price level over time. As

---

*This analysis suggests that external *deflationary* shocks should lead to economic boom.
Thus, the collapse of the oil market in late 1985 and early 1986 should have been followed
by a substantial economic expansion. In fact, growth in the U.S. economy slowed slightly
in 1986. This experience suggests that the effects of oil price shocks may be *asymmetric*,
that is, price declines do not have positive effects similar to the negative effects of price
increases. The slowdown in 1986 may have been caused by the adjustment problems associated with businesses and people moving out of the oil industry and the oil-producing
regions and seeking opportunities elsewhere. This adjustment problem parallels that of
the opposite movements in 1974–75 and may account for the asymmetry. For a compact
discussion of this issue, see Knut Anton Mork, "Oil and the Macroeconomy When Prices
Go Up and Down: An Extension of Hamilton's Results," in *Journal of Political Economy*,
June 1989, vol. 97, no. 3, pp. 740–44.

the price level responds to this pressure, real GNP starts to increase until the economy again returns to the original equilibrium, *E*.

This adjustment story is broadly consistent with the relative slowdown in inflation in the United States in 1976. However, it does not explain the continued inflation in the second half of the seventies. That story must wait until the next chapter.

THE PHILLIPS CURVE AND HYSTERESIS

The Phillips curve model in equation (7.5) contains a subtle yet important feature concerning how GNP eventually returns to its potential level after a disturbance. According to this formula, the economy does not come to rest until real GNP has converged to potential GNP. The system cannot get stuck at any other GNP level.

U.S. data seem to support this idea reasonably well. When recessions are over, real activity tends to settle down at a normal level. This is apparent, for example, from the fact that the unemployment rate after a recession tends to return to approximately the same level as before the recession. However, this pattern is not universal. We saw in Figure 3.6 that the West German unemployment rate, after rising from about 1% to about 5% in the 1974–75 recession, did not decline much for the rest of the decade. Then the recession of the early eighties sent it toward the 10% range, from which it recovered only slightly over the rest of that decade. Table 7.2 presents similar data for France and the United King-

TABLE 7.2   UNEMPLOYMENT RATES SHOWING EVIDENCE OF HYSTERESIS IN EUROPE, BUT NOT IN THE UNITED STATES

YEAR	WEST GERMANY	FRANCE	UNITED KINGDOM	UNITED STATES
1973	1.3	2.7	2.1	4.9
1974	2.7	2.8	2.2	5.6
1975	4.8	4.0	3.4	8.5
1976	4.6	4.4	4.5	7.7
1977	4.5	5.0	4.8	7.1
1978	4.4	5.2	4.7	6.1
1979	3.8	5.9	4.3	5.9
1980	3.9	6.3	5.4	7.2
1981	5.6	7.4	8.5	7.6
1982	7.7	8.1	9.9	9.7
1983	9.2	8.3	10.7	9.6
1984	9.1	9.7	11.1	7.5
1985	9.3	10.2	11.3	7.2
1986	8.9	10.3	11.4	7.0
1987	8.9	10.5	10.0	6.2
1988	8.8	10.1	8.2	5.5

dom and compares the data to those of the United States for the same period. The pattern for the two other European countries is similar to that for West Germany. Every recession has apparently lifted the unemployment rates for these countries permanently. In contrast, the surges in the unemployment rates for the United States appear to have been more temporary.

The apparent persistence of the unemployment rates in Europe is sometimes referred to as a case of **hysteresis,** a technical term used to describe a dynamic system in which temporary disturbances have lasting effects. How does hysteresis arise in the economy? A common explanation refers to the relationship between *insiders* and *outsiders* in the labor market.* The insiders are people who already hold jobs, while the outsiders are the unemployed. The insiders negotiate wages with the employers based only on their own desires for employment and income. The outsiders would like to offer their services at lower wages in order to become employed. However, since they are not represented at the negotiation table, their voice is not heard. Every time the economy is shaken by a recession, more people are laid off and become outsiders. Since their preferences play no role in the negotiations, they remain outsiders once they have been relegated to that status.

There is reason to believe that even an economy with an "insider-outsider" labor market will eventually return to full employment and potential GNP. Although the outsiders are not included in negotiations, they do represent a pool of potentially cheap labor that can become an effective competitor to the insiders over time. However, the European experience of the 1980s suggests that this adjustment process can drag out quite a bit.

CHAPTER REVIEW

1. Aggregate demand is the equilibrium level of real GNP in the IS-LM model. Aggregate supply is the real GNP level that is implied by the constraints defined by the supply of capital and labor.

2. Aggregate demand is a downward-sloping function of the overall price level, because a rise in the price level reduces the real money supply.

3. Aggregate supply is determined by the aggregate production function, with the existing capital stock and the equilibrium level of employment as inputs. Changes in productivity shift this function.

---

*For a more detailed discussion of the hysteresis phenomenon and the insider-outsider argument, see Olivier J. Blanchard and Lawrence H. Summers, "Hysteresis and the European Unemployment Problem," in *NBER Macroeconomics Annual 1986*, edited by Stanley Fischer (Cambridge, Mass.: M.I.T. Press). A book-length analysis of the same problem is contained in Assar Lindbeck and Dennis J. Snower, *The Insider-Outsider Theory of Employment and Unemployment* (Cambridge, Mass.: M.I.T. Press, 1989).

4. Aggregate supply is independent of the overall price level, which means that the aggregate supply curve is a vertical line in the (Y, P) plane. In the long run, this curve shifts gradually to the right because of growth in the capital stock, the labor force, and productivity.

5. The real-business-cycle view holds that business cycles are due to short-term fluctuations in aggregate supply. The conventional view regards business cycles mainly as resulting from fluctuations in aggregate demand around a smoothly growing aggregate supply.

6. If aggregate demand differs from aggregate supply, the price level starts to move to restore equilibrium, but with a lag. The Phillips curve describes this adjustment process.

7. Oil shocks may be modeled as supply shocks in the real-business-cycle model or as external inflationary shocks in the Phillips curve model. Either analysis predicts a recession combined with inflation.

8. Hysteresis describes a situation in which the economy does not return to its original equilibrium after a disturbance. European unemployment rates in the 1980s show signs of hysteresis.

NUMERICAL EXERCISES

The following numerical IS-LM model represents aggregate demand:
(IS) $Y = 150 + 0.75Y - 10{,}000R + G + 0.25Y^e$,
(LM) $M/P = 50 + 0.3Y - 6{,}000R$.

1. For this model, derive the aggregate demand function and draw the aggregate demand curve to scale for $G = 600$, $M = 800$, $Y^e = 4{,}000$.

2. Draw to scale the shifts in the aggregate demand curve for the following parameter changes.
   a. G rises from 600 to 700.
   b. M declines from 800 to 700.
   c. Y^e rises from 4,000 to 4,200.

3. Solve the IS-LM model for *nominal* GNP and explain how the solution for this variable depends on the price level. What does the answer tell you about why the aggregate demand curve slopes downward?

The next two exercises ask you to analyze simultaneous equilibria between aggregate demand and aggregate supply. For these exercises, use the aggregate demand function implied by the IS-LM model above and assume $G = 600$.

4. Suppose that, from year 0 to year 1, the money supply grows from $M_0 = 800$ to $M_1 = 880$. At the same time, aggregate supply grows from $Y^S_0 = 4{,}000$ to $Y^S_1 = 4{,}100$, and further to $Y^S_2 = 4{,}200$ in year 2. Assume that people have rational expectations about future income levels in the sense that $Y^e_0 = Y^S_1$, and so on. Compute the rate of inflation from period 0 to period 1.

5. Suppose you start from the same level of $Y^S_0 = 4{,}000$, with the same expectation for $Y^S_1 = 4{,}100$, and with the same money supply $M_0 = 800$. However, an unexpected productivity shock then reduces Y^S_1 to 3,800 and leaves Y^S_2 at 3,900, while the money supply again grows to $M_1 = 880$. Compute inflation and the real GNP growth from period 0 to period 1.

Exercises 6 and 7 combine the IS-LM model above with the Phillips curve model
$\pi = (Y_{-1} - Y^*)/Y^*$.
Now assume that $Y^* = 4{,}000$ and $Y^e = 4{,}000$ for all periods. Assume also that the economy starts from a situation with $P = 1$, no inflation, and no GNP gap. Also assume $G = 600$ throughout.

6. Suppose the money supply in period 0 is raised from 800 to 880 and stays there. Compute the path of real GNP, real GNP growth, the price level, the inflation rate, and the real interest rate for 10 periods. Present your results in the form of numbers as well as graphs showing the paths of each variable. What does this exercise tell you about the effects of monetary policy over time? (You will probably find an electronic spreadsheet helpful for the computations as well as for drawing the curves.)

7. Suppose instead that, in period 0, Y^e declines from 4,000 to 3,400 and stays at the lower level indefinitely. First, compute the paths of real GNP, real GNP growth, the price level, the inflation rate, and the real interest rate for 10 periods under the assumption that the money supply stays unchanged at $M = 800$. Then suppose that, in year 1, the money supply is raised to $M = 880$ and stays there. Again, present your results graphically as well as numerically. What do these results suggest about the usefulness of monetary policy in stabilizing the economy?

DATA EXERCISE

1. Construct potential GNP for the United States as an exponential trend fitted to real GNP, and use this construct to compute GNP gaps for the U.S. economy. Regress inflation on the GNP gap for the entire post-war period as well as for subperiods defined as decades. How do the results fit the Phillips curve model?

THINKING QUESTIONS

1. Look at a data series for U.S. labor productivity. You will probably find that productivity declines in recessions and improves in expansion periods. Supporters of real-business-cycle theories take this phenomenon as support for their view that productivity shocks cause recession; others argue that it happens just because firms hold on to overhead labor during recessions. Can you suggest what kind of information would be needed to resolve this controversy?

2. Some people argue that the reduction of the U.S. inflation rate in the early 1980s caused the 1981–82 recession but was still worth it. Do you agree?

8 INFLATION

The previous chapter introduced the concept of inflation and showed how a shift in aggregate demand or aggregate supply could change the price level in equilibrium. We also saw how a *dis*equilibrium between aggregate demand and aggregate supply could generate inflation via the Phillips curve. The discussion might have left the impression that inflation is a disequilibrium phenomenon and that inflation cannot occur unless the economy is running in high gear with a positive GNP gap. This chapter rectifies this impression.

The simple Phillips curve studied in Chapter 7 is a special case of inflation analysis. Although we will see again in this chapter that a disequilibrium can *contribute* to inflationary forces, inflation is in fact a much more general phenomenon. Most, if not all, countries have experienced at least some inflation almost continually both before and after World War II. A theory that attempted to explain such a general phenomenon as the result only of temporary disequilibria would not be very satisfactory. Fortunately, we can do better.

In this chapter, we start by analyzing inflation as an *equilibrium* phenomenon. After finishing that analysis, we resume the thread from the Phillips curve analysis and see how the two approaches can be put together. The result is the *expectations-augmented* Phillips curve. We use this new model to analyze how an expansionary monetary policy can generate persistent inflation and how that process interacts with real variables, such as real GNP, over the business cycle. Last, we try to see whether inflation is good or bad for the economy.

8.1 EQUILIBRIUM INFLATION

In order to study inflation as an equilibrium phenomenon, we need an equilibrium model. As in Chapter 7, we use the aggregate demand–aggregate supply model. However, we now focus on the situation in which aggregate demand *equals* aggregate supply. Since aggregate supply does not depend on the price level, real GNP will be determined by the supply side, and in our study of inflation we can concentrate on aggregate demand and treat real GNP as given. In fact, most of the time it turns out that a study of equilibrium inflation that is limited to the supply and demand for money is satisfactory.

MONEY AND INFLATION

The only way the price level appears in the IS-LM model is as a deflator for the money supply. Because the money supply is a nominal variable, we must deflate it in order to study its interactions with real variables. That is, we need to divide it by the price level in order to express the money supply in units of real goods and services that the money supply can buy at the current prices. This is how we get the real money supply, M/P. Movements in the real money supply have real effects, as we saw in Chapters 6 and 7. However, the same is not necessarily true for the *nominal* money supply. If the price level moves at the same time and in the same proportion as nominal money supply, then the real money supply is unchanged and no real effects occur.

This observation provides our first and in some ways our most fundamental insight about inflation. Proportional changes in the money supply and in the price level are perfectly consistent with a macroeconomic equilibrium in which real GNP stays constant. Proportional changes in the money supply and in the price level mean that their relative (percentage) rates of change are equal. The relative rate of change in the price level is the rate of inflation, for which we have already introduced the symbol π. Let m stand for the relative rate of change in the money supply, in other words, the money growth rate. (Note that this notation is different from that in Chapter 4, where we used m to denote the money multiplier.) Then equilibrium inflation with a constant real GNP level is

(8.1) $$\pi = m.$$

The rate of inflation, which is a purely nominal variable, is determined by another nominal variable, namely, the money growth rate. *Inflation is a monetary phenomenon.*

HOW DOES MONEY DRIVE INFLATION?

The result above shows the particular combination of inflation and money growth consistent with a macroeconomic equilibrium with a constant level of real GNP. However, it does not specify the *mechanism* by which an increase in the money supply raises the price level.

Although the nature of this mechanism isn't quite clear in the equilibrium model, an example can illustrate it. In earlier times, the value of money was tied to gold, so that a dollar was defined as a certain fraction of an ounce of gold. This arrangement is known as the **gold standard.** Under the gold standard, money in a sense *was* gold. The gold rush of 1849 took place during such a period. Since money was gold, the gold rush increased the supply of money. The people who mined the new gold sold it for dollars at the fixed price that defined the value of the dollar in terms of gold. Then they went out to spend their newfound wealth on goods and services. However, the discovery of gold did not by itself produce any other new resources that could be used to produce the goods and services the gold miners wanted. So the gold miners' demands had to compete with other people's ordinary demands. In other words, *aggregate demand rose*. The suppliers had no more goods to offer, but they soon found that this higher demand allowed them to charge higher prices for the goods they had. The result was a solid round of inflation.

Today's mechanism for translating money growth into inflation is probably a good deal more complicated. It may, for example, involve some interaction with real variables, with the result that a monetary expansion may first lead to an expansion of real GNP in response to the higher level of aggregate demand before the effect shows up in the price level. These interactions are the focus of the Phillips curve, to which we return in Section 8.3.

MONEY, INFLATION, AND GROWTH

The assumption of a constant real GNP level is convenient for the sake of simplicity, but it is not realistic for a long-run analysis. Let us now examine how we can integrate our equilibrium model of inflation with a model of a growing economy. We will continue to assume that the real GNP level is determined by aggregate supply, but that growth in productivity, population, and the capital stock allows real GNP to grow over time. It is easiest to think of this growth as being steady in the sense that the growth rate is approximately constant over time.

In order to keep the analysis simple, we start by making a simplifying assumption about the form of the money-demand function, which was introduced in Section 6.1. We argued that the demand for money should be proportional to the price level, an increasing function of real GNP as an approximate measure of the volume of transactions, and a decreasing function of the nominal interest rate as the opportunity cost of holding money. We wrote this function as

$$M^D = PL(Y, i)$$

and interpreted the function L as the real money demand.

Let us make two simplifying assumptions about this function. First, assume that the real money demand is proportional to the volume of transactions carried out. This assumption allows us to write the function L as

(8.2) $$L(Y, i) = Y\ell(i),$$

where ℓ is a decreasing function of the nominal interest rate. Second, assume for now that the interest-rate effect on the demand for money is weak enough to be ignored. (From Section 6.2 you should be able to recognize this case as one with a vertical LM curve, but that fact is not important here.) Then we can treat ℓ as a constant.

Given these assumptions, equilibrium in the money market is written as

$$M = \ell PY,$$

which solves for the price level as

$$(8.3) \qquad\qquad P = (1/\ell)M/Y.$$

Suppose that, in some year that we call year 0, real GNP and the money supply are Y_0 and M_0, respectively. Then if these variables grow at the respective rates y and m, their values in the following year, year 1, are $Y_1 = (1 + y)Y_0$ and $M_1 = (1 + m)M_0$, respectively. Since ℓ is a constant, equation (8.3) now implies that the inflation rate is

$$(8.4) \qquad \begin{aligned} \pi &= \frac{P_1 - P_0}{P_0} = \frac{(1/\ell)(1 + m)M_0/(1 + y)Y_0 - (1/\ell)M_0/Y_0}{(1/\ell)M_0/Y_0} \\ &= \frac{1 + m}{1 + y} - 1 = \frac{m - y}{1 + y}. \end{aligned}$$

Since the real growth rate y is usually small, this result can be approximated as

$$(8.5) \qquad\qquad \pi = m - y.$$

Formula (8.5) gives meaning to the well-known adage that inflation is the result of "too much money chasing too few goods." Inflation is the result of growth in the money supply, but only to the extent that this growth exceeds that of the real amount of goods being produced.

This insight adds an important element to the mechanism by which money growth drives inflation, which we attempted to outline above. Although an increase in the price level raises aggregate demand, such an increase is not inflationary unless the aggregate demand rises faster than the aggregate supply. If money growth just matches real GNP growth, it simply generates the demand needed to sell the larger supply at the old price level. In that case, inflation is zero. A case of matching growth in real GNP and money supply is illustrated in Figure 8.1, which shows the AD curve and the AS curve shifting right by the same amount. As a result, the price level is unchanged, meaning that inflation is zero. Money growth by itself is not necessarily inflationary. It is inflationary if it exceeds the growth in real GNP.

EQUILIBRIUM INFLATION WITH RATIONAL EXPECTATIONS

The result given by equation (8.5) also generalizes to the more realistic case in which the demand for money depends on the nominal interest rate, provided the growth rates in real GNP and the money supply are constant over time. In other words, the result holds for long-term inflation but not necessarily over the business cycle, even if the economy stays in equilibrium as in the real-business-cycle model.

FIGURE 8.1

A case of equal-sized right-ward shifts in aggregate demand and aggregate supply, which leave the price level unchanged.

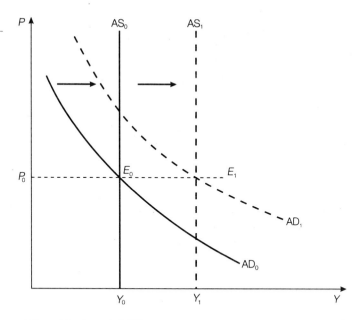

Provided real GNP grows at a constant rate, it can be shown that the real interest rate R is constant as well,* so variations in the *nominal* interest rate, $i = R + \pi^e$, can come only from expected inflation. Suppose now that these expectations are formed as *rational expectations*. Then, as we saw in Chapter 5, people make efficient use of all the available information, which must mean that their expectations are equally as sophisticated as the model we study. In other words, we can simply assume that the expected rate of inflation is just that inflation rate that the model predicts for the next period. Then the nominal interest rate is

$$i = R + \pi_{+1},$$

where the subscript $+1$ indicates the model's prediction for next period's inflation rate. Putting this formulation into the real money-demand equation (8.2), we can now write equilibrium in the money market as

(8.6) $$M = PY\ell(R + \pi_{+1}),$$

---

*This result may seem to contradict the IS equation. The way we stated that equation, in formula (5.15), for example, suggests that a growing real GNP would require an ever-declining real interest rate. However, remember that this formula is a linear approximation of a more general underlying formula. From the theory of long-term growth, it can be found that the true form of the IS equation is more like the formula
$$Y = bY^e/R^\alpha,$$
where α is a constant exponent. Clearly, this formula, like the one in equation (5.15), depends negatively on the real interest rate. However, if real GNP growth is constant, such that Y and Y^e grow at the same rate, this formula implies that the real interest rate is constant.

which solves for the price level as

(8.7) $$P = (M/Y)/\ell(R + \pi_{+1}).$$

Let us see if this equation can be satisfied by the solution that the rate of inflation equals the difference between the real GNP growth rate and the money growth rate [equation (8.5)]. To see this, we need to check whether the actual inflation in the model turns out to be the same as this proposed solution.

Look again at year 0 and year 1. In year 0, real GNP and the money supply are Y_0 and M_0, respectively. Between that year and year 1, they grow at the respective rates y and m. If the solution in equation (8.5) holds, the next year's inflation rate is $m - y$. Substituting Y_0, M_0, and this expected inflation rate into equation (8.7), we find the price level in year 0 to be

$$P_0 = (M_0/Y_0)/\ell(R + m - y).$$

Now consider the price level in year 1. Recall that $M_1 = (1 + m)M_0$ and $Y_1 = (1 + y)Y_0$. Note also that the value of the function ℓ stays constant over time because its arguments do not change. Then the computation of the inflation rate from year 0 to year 1 becomes exactly like that in equation (8.4). This result shows that, in a situation of steady growth, the inflation rate is given by the difference between the money growth rate and the real GNP growth rate whether or not the demand for money depends on the interest rate.* As a description of long-run inflation, this result is quite general.

8.2 EVIDENCE ABOUT THE RELATIONSHIP AMONG MONEY GROWTH, REAL GNP GROWTH, AND INFLATION

Is it true in practice that the rate of inflation equals the difference between the money growth rate and the real GNP growth rate? Figure 8.2 seeks to shed some light on this issue by presenting a scatter diagram of annual data for the United States from 1955 to 1989. The horizontal axis measures the difference between money (M2) growth and real GNP growth, while the vertical axis measures inflation (as represented by the GNP deflator). If the theory holds exactly, the variables along the two axes should be equal to each other at all times, and all the observations should lie straight along the 45° line in the graph.

This graph offers some support for the theory in that we seem able to

---

*The mathematically minded reader will have recognized the equilibrium condition in equation (8.6) as a differential equation. Like most differential equations, it has more than one solution. However, it can be shown that the solution we discuss is the only one that is stable.

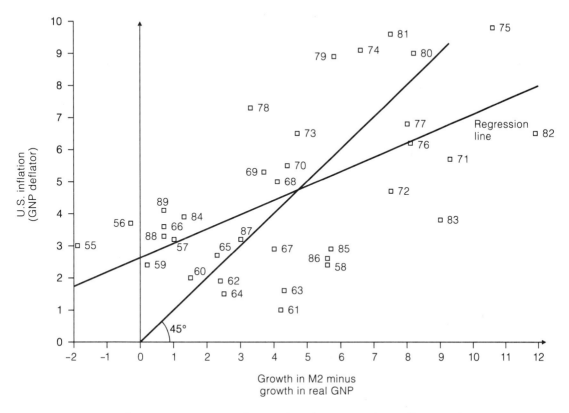

FIGURE 8.2

Scatter diagram and regression line for annual inflation data for the United States. The horizontal axis measures the difference between the growth rates in M2 and real GNP, the vertical axis the inflation rate as measured by the GNP deflator. The 45° line is the regression line predicted by the theory.

detect a positive relationship between the difference between money growth and real GNP growth on one hand and inflation on the other. However, the fit is not good. The data points are scattered widely around the 45° line. If we use these data to estimate a regression line, we get

$$\pi_t = 2.63 + 0.44(m_t - y_t) + e_t, \quad \text{SER} = 2.08, \quad R^2 = 0.34.$$
$$(0.59) (0.11)$$

These results indicate a significantly positive relationship, since the t-statistic of the slope coefficient is $0.44/0.11 = 4$, which is well above 2. However, to match the 45° line, this slope should be 1, and in fact it is much less than 1. Moreover, the intercept is significantly different from zero, even though the theoretical equation (8.5) has no intercept. Finally, the R^2 value of about 0.3 indicates that the model explains only about a third of the variation in annual inflation.

This somewhat negative result is not very surprising. Remember that when the demand for money depends on the interest rate the simple rule in equation (8.5) holds only in a long-term equilibrium of steady real GNP growth. Because the postwar period has seen many recessions and other disturbances to real GNP growth, we should not be surprised to find that this simple formula does not hold exactly.

FIGURE 8.3

Scatter diagram and regression line for annual price-level data for the United States. The horizontal axis measures the ratio of M2 to real GNP, the vertical axis the price level as measured by the GNP deflator. Both variables are normalized to equal 100 in 1982. The 45° line is the regression line predicted by the theory.

Remember, however, that equation (8.5), which gives the hypothesized formula for the inflation rate, is derived from equation (8.3), which states an equilibrium relationship between the price level and the levels of the money supply and real GNP. Equation (8.3) is also consistent with the case in which money demand depends on the nominal interest rate, because we just found that the value of the function ℓ is constant in the long run.

The relationship between levels in equation (8.3) can also be tested empirically. Although the theory does not suggest a value for ℓ, we can bypass this issue by normalizing the data for both P and M/Y so that both variables equal 100 in 1982. Then, for equation (8.3) to hold in 1982, ℓ must be 1, so the data should lie along the 45° line in this case as well.

These data are shown in another scatter diagram in Figure 8.3. Clearly, the price-level data conform much more closely to the theory, as they all lie very close to the 45° line. If we fit a regression line, it becomes:

$$P_t = 0.004 + 0.97(M_t/Y_t) + e_t, \quad \text{SER} = 0.02, \quad R^2 - 0.995.$$
$$(0.008) \quad (0.01)$$

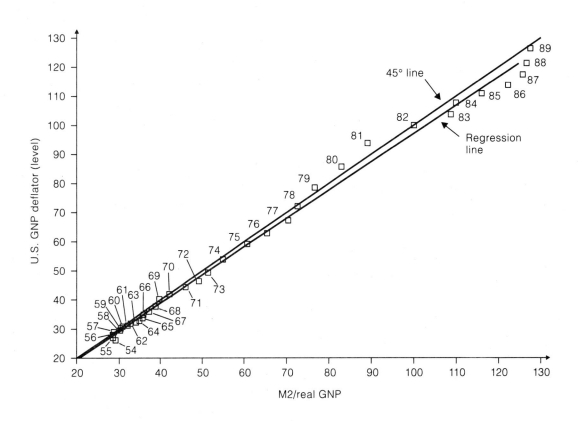

Here the slope is very close to 1 and the intercept very close to zero, just as the theoretical equation (8.3) suggested. Furthermore, the high R^2 value indicates that the equilibrium inflation theory can explain most of the variation in the price level over time.

How can the levels adhere so closely to the theory when the growth rates perform so poorly? The answer is that the price level changes in response to changes in money supply and real GNP. However, because business cycles and other disturbances interfere, it does not necessarily respond right away. The delay causes the growth rates to deviate substantially from the theory. However, the levels soon catch up and follow the theory very nicely. Thus, the price *level* never deviates far from the long-run equilibrium theory, even though the inflation rate does.

Figure 8.4 presents yet another piece of evidence supporting the long-run validity of the relationship between inflation, money growth, and real GNP growth. The data in Figure 8.4 are growth rates averaged over the 15-year period 1971–85 for a number of different countries. As in Figure 8.2, the horizontal axis measures the difference between money growth and real GNP growth, while the vertical axis measures inflation.

FIGURE 8.4

Scatter diagram and regression line for average inflation data, 1971–85, for 23 different countries. The horizontal axis measures the average difference between the growth rates in "money plus quasi-money" (similar to M2) and real GDP, the vertical axis the inflation rate as measured by the GDP deflator. The 45° line is the regression line predicted by the theory.

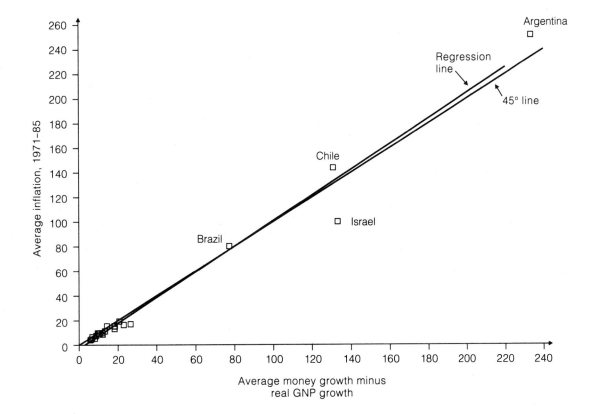

TABLE 8.1 INTERNATIONAL DATA FOR THE GROWTH RATE IN MONEY SUPPLY, REAL GDP GROWTH, AND INFLATION, AVERAGES OF ANNUAL DATA 1971–85.

	MONEY GROWTH	REAL GDP GROWTH	DIFFERENCE BETWEEN MONEY GROWTH AND REAL GDP GROWTH	INFLATION
United States	9.6	2.7	6.9	6.7
Canada	12.8	3.9	8.9	7.6
Australia	12.9	3.3	9.6	9.9
Japan	12.6	4.4	8.2	5.7
France	12.7	2.7	10.0	9.7
West Germany	8.1	2.2	5.9	4.6
Italy	17.3	3.1	14.2	15.8
Switzerland	7.6	1.3	6.3	5.0
United Kingdom	15.3	2.0	13.3	11.7
Kenya	15.6	5.0	10.6	10.0
Nigeria	26.0	2.9	23.1	16.9
Tanzania	21.2	2.6	18.6	15.4
India	16.2	4.1	12.1	9.1
Indonesia	33.4	6.9	26.5	17.6
South Korea	26.6	8.1	18.5	15.8
Pakistan	17.4	5.5	11.9	9.9
Israel	137.4	4.2	133.2	100.2
Kuwait	19.0	−1.9	20.9	19.5
Saudi Arabia	31.2	7.0	24.2	17.0
Argentina	234.3	0.7	233.6	251.3
Brazil	83.4	6.1	77.3	80.4
Chile	132.8	1.8	131.0	144.1
Venezuela	20.6	2.4	18.2	13.8

The data underlying Figure 8.4 also are displayed in Table 8.1. Note that real growth here is measured in terms of Gross Domestic Product, or GDP, which is closely related to GNP but measures the value of goods and services produced within the country rather than those produced by the country's factors of production. For small countries, GDP often is used as the preferred measure of overall production.

These data provide considerable support for the theory. When we compare countries over an extended period of time, we find indeed that the countries with high money growth relative to real GNP growth have the high inflation rates, and vice versa. The evidence is particularly telling when we look outside the big cluster of data points in the lower left corner of the diagram at the outlying observations representing Argentina, Brazil, Chile, and Israel, all of which have experienced inflation so high that it is called "hyperinflation." All cases of hyperinflation in this graph can be accounted for as the result of extremely high growth in the money supply.

The regression line in this case is

$$\pi_i = -3.29 + 1.04(m_i - y_i) + e_i, \quad \text{SER} = 8.88, \quad R^2 = 0.98,$$
$$\quad (2.23) \quad (0.03)$$

where the subscript i indicates individual countries. The slope here is very close to 1, just as suggested by the theory. The estimated intercept does not quite match its hypothesized value of zero. However, since its t-statistic is $-3.29/2.23 = -1.48$, which is less than 2 in absolute value, it is not significantly different from zero. The high R^2 value indicates that, on average for this 15-year period, the growth in money and real GNP can account for virtually all the international variation in inflation.

8.3 THE EXPECTATIONS-AUGMENTED PHILLIPS CURVE

Having studied equilibrium inflation in both theory and practice, we can now integrate this analysis with the Phillips curve analysis in Chapter 7, in which inflation resulted from macroeconomic *dis*equilibrium. The analytical tool we use for this integration is the **expectations-augmented Phillips curve.**

THE PHILLIPS CURVE AS DEVIATION FROM TREND

Suppose the economy has reached equilibrium with a steady inflation rate. Think of this rate as a *trend* inflation rate. Then suppose monetary policy is eased in the sense that growth in the money supply is accelerated. In other words, the supply of money rises by more than the amount needed to sustain the current trend inflation. Then the equilibrium model predicts that the inflation rate should accelerate immediately as well, to correspond to the higher money growth rate.

Suppose, however, in the spirit of the simple Phillips curve in Chapter 7, that the inflation rate does not react immediately. Then, just as in Chapter 7, the price level will not adjust fast enough to maintain equilibrium between aggregate demand and aggregate supply. The acceleration in the money growth rate will make aggregate demand grow faster than aggregate supply, so a positive GNP gap arises. Thus, real GNP growth accelerates as well. However, a positive GNP gap means a disequilibrium, which will activate forces to restore equilibrium. Since the faster money growth now requires higher inflation in equilibrium, an acceleration of inflation is needed to restore equilibrium. In general, a positive or negative GNP gap will produce inflation rates above or below trend, respectively. If we write trend inflation as π^*, this argument justifies the following formula for the augmented Phillips curve:

$$(8.8) \qquad\qquad \pi = \pi^* + \gamma(Y_{-1} - Y_{-1}^*)/Y_{-1}^*.$$

Formula (8.8) specifies inflation as consisting of two components. First, it follows its own long-term trend. Second, a positive or negative GNP gap makes the inflation rate deviate from that trend. Inflation eases in recessions and picks up during expansions. However, the *trend* inflation rate is independent of the stage of the business cycle.

TREND AS EXPECTATION

It is common to identify the trend inflation rate in equation (8.8) with *expected* inflation. There are two justifications for this practice. First, if expectations are rational, people will expect future inflation to be whatever is predicted by the model. Suppose the acceleration of the money supply that we discussed happens unexpectedly. Then before it happened rational people would have expected future inflation to follow its past trend. Thus, in this case, it would be correct to identify the past trend with rational expectations.

Second, a number of pragmatic arguments can be made that suggest that expectations play an important role when people set prices and wages in the economy. Suppose, for example, that you are the manager of a mail-order company that markets consumer goods. When you send your catalog to the printer, you do not know what the market conditions for your product will be when the catalog reaches your potential customers. You also may not know what wages you will need to pay your workers to deliver your products. So you decide on the prices in your catalog on the basis of the expectations you have about these factors. The prices you set reflect your inflationary expectations.

Such behavior is not confined to mail-order companies. Many goods—especially intermediate goods—are sold under contract, and the parties' inflationary expectations influence the contract price. Even in the absence of formal contracts, many firms prefer to review their prices at discrete intervals, in which case their prices depend on their inflationary expectations for those intervals. Finally, wages are a major determinant of prices via the cost of production. In a number of countries, wages tend to be set for at least a year at a time, whether by formal negotiations between labor and management or unilaterally by management. In either case, decisions about wages need to take into account the amount of real goods and services that the wages will buy a little into the future; in other words, wage determination is influenced by inflationary expectations. These pragmatic arguments, then, also support the notion that, in the absence of pressures from a positive or negative GNP gap, inflation tends to be what people expect it to be.

Specifically, we identify trend inflation as the inflation rate that people last period expected to prevail for this period. We denote this expected inflation rate as π^e_{-1}. With this modification, the expectations-augmented Phillips curve can be written as

$$(8.9) \qquad \pi = \pi^e_{-1} + \gamma(Y_{-1} - Y^*_{-1})/Y^*_{-1}.$$

As long as aggregate demand and aggregate supply remain in balance, actual inflation and expected inflation are the same. Their common value is determined by the growth in the money supply relative to the growth in real GNP. However, a positive GNP gap generates demand pressures that accelerate inflation above its expected rate. Similarly, a negative GNP gap means weakness in aggregate demand, which decelerates inflation.

HOW ARE EXPECTATIONS FORMED?

So far in this chapter, we have assumed that people hold *rational* expectations. As we have stated before, the rational way of forming expectations is to make use of all the information available and to apply sophisticated analysis in order to make optimal predictions. This assumption fits naturally into the equilibrium model for two reasons. First, if the equilibrium model is interpreted as a model of the long-term trend, it seems reasonable to assume that people indeed recognize long-term trends correctly after they have been visible for some time. Second, the equilibrium model itself suggests a certain degree of rationality from the way in which it assumes that people react quickly to change in the environment. For example, prices do not take a long time to change in the equilibrium model but are adjusted to a new equilibrium right away. Rationality in expectations is a natural extension of this view of the world.

Some important contributions to the literature have analyzed the role of the Phillips curve under the assumption that expectations are formed rationally. We study some of that analysis in the next section and again in our discussion of alternative approaches to business-cycle analysis in Chapter 11.

However, there are also some good reasons to study the Phillips curve in the case in which people are not completely rational in the way they form their expectations. For one thing, such a study is considerably easier. For another, forming rational expectations is an extremely demanding task that requires both the effort to gather the relevant information and the time to analyze it. This dilemma is familiar to all managers: everybody wants to make better decisions, but the time and cost involved make many people rely on less accurate rules of thumb.

For these reasons, we carry out most of our analysis in the next section under the assumption of **adaptive expectations.** Adaptive expectations mean that people base their expectations on only a subset of the information available to them. In particular, people form their expectations about a certain variable, such as inflation, on the basis of the recent past behavior of that same variable. Expected inflation, then, is modeled as a weighted average of recent past inflation rates.

The simplest case of adaptive expectations occurs when this average includes only the most immediate past experience. In this case, people always expect the present to continue into the future. Expectations formed in this way are referred to as **static expectations.** In the case of inflation, static expectations mean that the expected inflation rate for this year just equals last year's inflation, that is, $\pi^e_{-1} = \pi_{-1}$. With this specification, equation (8.9) becomes

$$(8.10) \qquad \pi = \pi_{-1} + \gamma(Y_{-1} - Y^*_{-1})/Y^*_{-1}.$$

Note that the inflation rate, and hence the price level, is determined entirely by past variables in this model, just as in the simple Phillips curve model in equation (7.5). This is different from the situation in a rational-expectations model, in which the current inflation rate depends on the model's solution for *next* period's inflation rate and you need to solve the model simultaneously for the present as well as the future. However, because the model in equation (8.10) does not have this feature, we can study its solution period by period, just as we did for the simple Phillips curve in Chapter 7. The next section performs this exercise for some illustrative cases.

8.4 DYNAMICS WITH THE EXPECTATIONS-AUGMENTED PHILLIPS CURVE

The Phillips curve model with static or adaptive expectations implies a sluggish adjustment in response to shifts in aggregate demand. This sluggishness means that the economy suffers temporary disequilibria, which are characterized by some important interactions between the nominal and the real variables of the model. Therefore, monetary policy has real effects in the model, albeit temporary ones. A monetary tightening, for example, can lead to a recession. Thus, this analysis is potentially important for understanding the conventional view of business cycles.

The analysis also predicts a relationship between inflation and the stage of the business cycle. With the expectations augmentation, this relationship is no longer one-to-one. However, it remains true within this model that stopping or slowing inflation requires a slowdown or decline in real GNP.

In order to keep the analysis simple, we assume throughout this section that the aggregate supply curve stands still, so that there is no underlying tendency for growth in the economy. This assumption allows us to treat potential GNP, Y^*, as fixed over time. However, you should note that we make this assumption for convenience only. Relaxing it would not invalidate the analysis but only make it messier to follow.

A ONE-SHOT INCREASE IN THE MONEY SUPPLY

In Section 7.4, we used the Phillips curve to study the dynamic response to a one-time increase in the money supply. Let us repeat that analysis, but with the augmentation by static expectations introduced in equation (8.10). For simplicity, we start from a situation with zero inflation and no past trend growth in the money supply. The analysis is illustrated in Figure 8.5, which shows the aggregate demand–aggregate supply diagram on the left and the Phillips curve on the right, as in Figure 7.12.

The story begins as in Chapter 7. The monetary expansion shifts the aggregate demand curve to the right, and the entire effect during year 0 comes in the form of an increase in real GNP. Period 1 is also unchanged from Chapter 7. Because expected inflation for period 1 is actual inflation in period 0, which we assumed to be zero, inflation is not yet influenced by expectations in period 1. As before, inflation in period 1 can be

FIGURE 8.5

Dynamic effects of a one-shot increase in the money supply.

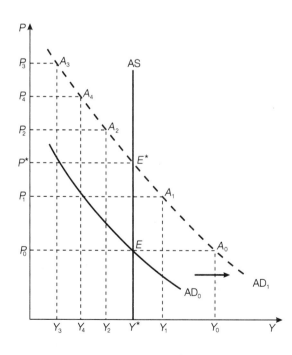
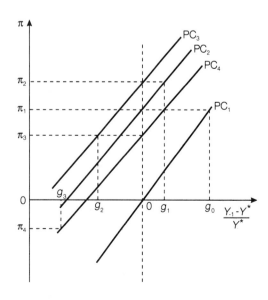

read off the Phillips curve labeled PC_1, the price level in period 1 is P_1, and real GNP contracts to Y_1.

Now consider how inflation is determined for period 2. First, the Phillips curve *shifts* to reflect the inherited inflation from period 1, which spills over into inflation in period 2. Equation (8.10) tells us that, if the GNP gap for period 1 had been zero, inflation in period 2 would have just equaled inflation in period 1. But this means that the Phillips curve for period 2 has shifted upward so that its new π-coordinate is π_1 for a zero value for last period's GNP gap. This new Phillips curve is marked PC_2 in the diagram. In fact, however, the GNP gap for the first period was positive. It is marked g_1 in the diagram; the inflation rate for period 2 can now be read as the height of the PC_2 curve at g_1. This inflation rate is higher than in the model without inflationary expectations. In fact, it is higher than inflation in period 1. In this sense, inflation becomes *entrenched* in the model that uses the expectations-augmented Phillips curve.

As a consequence of this high inflation rate, the price level in period 2 becomes so high that real GNP contracts to a level *below* potential GNP, marked Y_2 in the diagram. Thus, we again have an example of stagflation, characterized by a combination of inflation and real GNP decline. However, this time the stagflation experience is caused not by a supply shock or an external inflationary shock but rather by the entrenchment of inflation due to slowly changing expectations.

In period 3, two opposing forces work on the inflation rate. On one hand, inflationary expectations shift the Phillips curve upward once again, this time to PC_3, which passes through π_2 at the point where the GNP gap is zero. This shift adds to inflation. On the other hand, the actual GNP gap for period 2, marked g_2, was negative, which eases the inflationary pressure. The result is an inflation rate, π_3, that is positive but lower than in the two previous periods. However, positive inflation means that the price level again rises and consequently contracts real GNP even more, to Y_3.

Finally, in period 4, things start to turn around. The Phillips curve shifts downward to PC_4 because π_3 was lower than inflation in the previous periods. The substantial negative GNP gap in period 3 adds to this effect to produce a slightly *negative* inflation rate in period 4. With negative inflation, the price level finally starts to stabilize. It declines to P_4, which allows real GNP to approach potential GNP again.

The process does not stop here, but the major insights have become clear. Inflationary expectations allow inflation to become entrenched so that prices continue to rise for a while even after GNP has fallen *below* potential GNP. However, eventually the inflation rate stabilizes at the zero rate that is consistent in equilibrium with the zero growth rates for the money supply and real GNP. The price level gravitates toward P^* and real GNP gravitates toward Y^* as the new long-term equilibrium.

ACCELERATION IN THE GROWTH RATE OF MONEY SUPPLY

Our example of a one-shot increase in the money supply is unrealistic, for two reasons. First, monetary policy in practice is conducted not in the form of one-time increases or decreases in the money supply but rather by easing or tightening in the form of increases or decreases in the money *growth rate*. Second, when the entrenchment of inflation following the one-shot money-supply increase leads to overshooting in the form of a decline in real GNP, the central bank would probably face some pressure to increase the money supply again in order to avoid this adverse effect.

In order to add some realism to our discussion, we now study a case of *acceleration in the growth rate* of the money supply rather than a discrete increase in its level. In order to keep the analysis as simple as possible, we assume that we start from an equilibrium of zero money growth and zero inflation but that the money supply then starts to grow at a constant, positive rate. Thus, the example starts out with an increase in the money supply, as in the case we just studied, but we now assume that the initial increase is followed by similar increases in the periods following.

The analysis is illustrated in Figure 8.6. As before, the aggregate

FIGURE 8.6

Dynamic effects of an acceleration in the money growth rate.

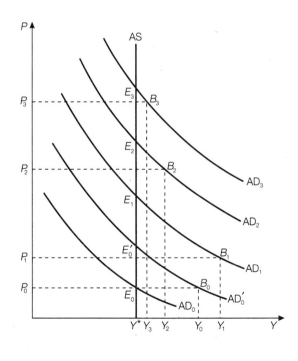

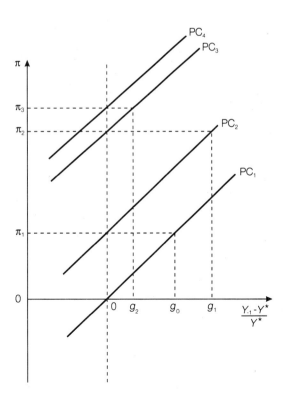

demand–aggregate supply diagram is shown on the left, with the shifting Phillips curve shown on the right. The example starts with the first increase in the money supply in period 0, which shifts the aggregate demand curve from AD_0 to AD'_0. The price level does not yet move, because the economy so far does not have any history of past GNP gaps or past inflation for the current price level to react to. Consequently, the economy moves from the initial equilibrium E_0 to the disequilibrium point B_0, with the price level unchanged at P_0 and with an increase in real GNP from Y^* to Y_0. So far, the monetary acceleration has had a positive real effect and no effect on inflation.

In period 1, two things happen. First, because of the positive GNP gap in period 0, the inflation rate rises from zero to π_1, which moves the price level upward to P_1. This movement parallels the one-shot case. However, the second change is different from the previous example. Because the money supply now continues to rise, the aggregate demand curve shifts by an amount similar to that in period 0, from AD'_0 to AD_1. Thus, the price-level increase and the monetary expansion pull in opposite directions. While the price-level increase puts a damper on real activity, the monetary expansion stimulates it. Because the price-level adjustment is somewhat sluggish, the expansionary force dominates. The economy moves to point B_1 in the diagram, and real GNP grows again to Y_1.

In period 2, inflation rises, for two reasons. First, the Phillips curve shifts from PC_1 to PC_2, as in the previous example, because the inflation in period 1 is expected to continue. Second, the GNP gap was even larger in period 1 than in period 0. The combined effect is a considerably higher inflation rate in period 2 than in period 1, moving the price level up to P_2 in the left part of the diagram.

Again, the continued growth in the money supply has an expansionary effect in period 2, moving the aggregate demand curve to AD_2. However, this time the contractionary effect from the price-level increase dominates, because inflation responds not only to the equilibrium force from the monetary expansion but also to the disequilibrium force in the form of the large, positive GNP gap. The net result is a movement to point B_2 and a corresponding decline in real GNP from Y_1 to Y_2.

Period 3 repeats the movements. The Phillips curve shifts again, this time to PC_3, because people expect the inflation from period 2 to continue. However, since the GNP gap for period 2 was lower, it does not add much to inflation. The price level rises to P_3, while the aggregate demand curve moves to AD_3. As you can see from the diagram, this solution is not far from the equilibrium solution, E_3, that corresponds to this aggregate demand curve. In period 4, the shift in the Phillips curve is minimal. Moreover, because the period 3 GNP gap was very small, period 4 inflation is very similar to that in period 3.

What we seem to be observing is that the economy is about to settle down at a steady inflation rate. This inflation rate is just high enough for the price level to rise every period by the same amount as the shift in the aggregate demand curve due to the continued growth in the money supply.

The primary lesson to be learned from this exercise is the same as that in the previous example. An easing in monetary policy at first has real effects, but the long-term effect is inflation and inflation only. The continued growth in the money supply avoided overshooting and stagflation; however, the entrenchment of inflation is now much more serious. Because it is supported by growth in the money supply, the initial disequilibrium inflation is translated over time into equilibrium inflation, and this inflation does not go away just because the real GNP expansion comes to an end.

STOPPING INFLATION

Running this example in reverse shows us how a monetary tightening can be used to stop inflation. As a by-product, we obtain this model's predictions about the real effects of such a policy. As we will see, a temporary decline in real GNP is unavoidable in this model if inflation is to be reduced.

The dynamics of this problem are illustrated in Figure 8.7. The graph is based on the assumption that the economy starts from a history of steady, positive growth in the money supply and a matching inflation rate. The steady money growth has continually pushed the aggregate demand curve outward. However, in the period that we call period 0, this growth comes to an abrupt halt. After having reached the position labeled AD in the graph, the aggregate demand curve shifts no more. Because past inflation has been of the equilibrium kind, the economy in period 0 finds itself at the equilibrium point E, with a price level P_0 and with real GNP equal to potential GNP, Y^*.

However, people derive their expectations from their recent inflationary experience, so they expect past inflation to continue. Moreover, there was no negative GNP gap in period 0 to pull down inflation in period 1. Therefore, inflation continues at the same rate in period 1 as in period 0, as shown in the Phillips curve in the right side of Figure 8.7.

Note that this inflation happens without a matching increase in the money supply. So as the price level rises from P_0 to P_1, the real money supply declines, and the economy climbs up along the aggregate demand curve to the disequilibrium point D_1. The economy goes into a recession as real GNP declines from Y^* to Y_1.

In period 2, inflationary expectations still have not changed, because inflation was the same in period 1 as in period 0. However, the negative GNP gap in period 1 makes the inflation rate slow down to the lower yet still positive rate π_2 in the graph on the right, so the price level rises

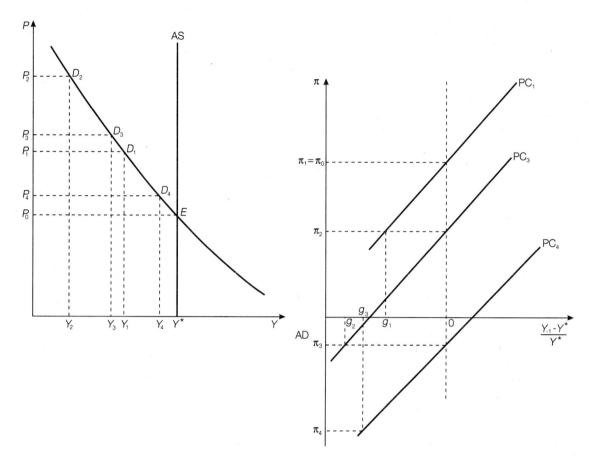

FIGURE 8.7

Dynamic effects of an attempt to use a slowdown in money growth to stop inflation.

further to P_2. The economy goes deeper into recession as real GNP declines to Y_2.

In period 3, the Phillips curve finally shifts down from PC_1 to PC_3 as people adjust their expectations downward in light of the actual experience of inflation in period 2. This downward shift interacts with the negative GNP gap to produce a *negative* inflation rate in period 3. As the price level declines from P_2 to P_3, the economy starts to recover from the recession. Period 4 essentially repeats the same movements and brings the economy back toward its equilibrium, E.

Three lessons can be learned from this exercise. First, the operation to stop inflation was effective. When the economy settles down at its new equilibrium, inflation will remain at the zero level indicated by the zero equilibrium growth rates in money supply and real GNP. Second, the same operation drove the economy into a recession. Inflation can be stopped, but at a cost. Third, since the price level overshoots its equilibrium level P_0, the inflation rate must turn negative before it settles down at zero. To some extent, this result stems from our assumption that the new equilibrium inflation rate is exactly zero. When such operations are performed in practice, the money supply usually continues at a faster rate than real GNP, but slower than before. What our result says, then, is that inflation will slow down to a rate even *lower* than the new, lower equilibrium inflation rate before it settles down to the rate at which it will remain. For a while, therefore, it might look as if the operation was more successful than hoped for.

RATIONAL EXPECTATIONS AND THE LUCAS CRITIQUE

The conclusion of the analysis above may have seemed overly pessimistic. Is it really impossible to stop inflation without also inducing a recession? The answer is that our result depended crucially on the assumption made about how people form expectations. Because we assumed that they look only at past inflation when they form their expectations and because expected inflation drives actual inflation, the price level continued to rise after the money supply had ceased rising; it was the resulting fall in the real money supply that set off a recession.

Suppose instead that people hold *rational* expectations. Then they use the knowledge that a halt to the growth in the money supply brings down inflation. This insight leads us to suspect that rational people immediately revise their inflationary expectations down to zero when they hear about the stop in money growth. Remember, however, that rational expectations also need to be consistent with the model. Thus, before we conclude that rational inflationary expectations drop to zero right away, we should check that this is indeed what the model with rational expectations predicts.

Suppose expectations do drop to zero. Then, since expected inflation drives actual inflation, actual inflation in period 1 would also drop to zero in the example above. Potentially, it could have been affected by a nonzero GNP gap; however, since the economy started from an inflationary equilibrium in period 0, the GNP gap was zero. Now, if inflation is zero in period 1, the price level stays at P_0 in Figure 8.7, which allows the economy to remain at its new equilibrium, E. Once it has reached this equilibrium, no further forces will pull it away. So the expectation of zero inflation has been fulfilled, which proves that such an expectation was indeed rational.

The outcome of this model is obviously very different from that of the adaptive-expectations model. Although it shares the view that inflation will be brought down effectively, *the rational-expectations model does not predict a recession from the slowdown in inflation.* Thus, no painful policy dilemma arises. If the central bankers want to get rid of inflation, they can do so by simply reducing the growth in the money supply.

The rational-expectations model was launched in the 1970s, when inflation was high and the debate over how to stop it was intense. It was met by an apparently convincing counterargument, namely, that models of the Phillips curve that assumed adaptive rather than rational expectations fit the data very well. Thus, it was argued that after years of inflation it would likely take a long time to break people's expectations about continued high inflation. Consequently, a braking operation for money supply would likely set off a recession.

In a famous paper, Professor Robert E. Lucas of the University of Chicago presented a powerful conceptual critique of this argument.* Lucas argued that people had been slow to change their inflationary expectations in the past not because they were slow to learn but because the monetary policies affecting inflation had been slow. People had formed their expectations rationally. However, because of the policy climate in the fifties and sixties, the changes in these expectations over time had very closely matched those slow changes that researchers would have expected from *adaptive* expectations. Thus, an economic researcher looking at the data might not notice the difference between adaptive and rational expectations.

Lucas argued that the appearance of adaptive expectations was not an inherent feature of human behavior but a simple result of the pattern of economic policies during the fifties and sixties. Thus, an analyst who estimated a Phillips curve model on data from this period would obtain a model whose structure was in part the result of the policies conducted. Then, Lucas argued, that model would not be a useful tool to predict the effects of *changes* in those same policies. Specifically, the model would predict a recession as the result of a monetary tightening, while in fact no recession would take place.

In another paper, Lucas presented his own alternative to the Phillips curve.** His model not only assumed rational expectations but also explained the positive relationship between output and inflation as an equilibrium outcome of profit-maximizing behavior rather than price rigidity and disequilibrium. We discuss this model further in Chapter 11. Here the main point is that rational expectations about inflation remove the danger that anti-inflationary policies will trigger a recession.

Lucas's critique of the models in use at the time was well taken. It stands to reason that a model whose structure depends on a certain

---

* Robert E. Lucas, "Econometric Policy Evaluation: A Critique," in *The Phillips Curve and Labor Markets*, edited by Karl Brunner and Allan H. Meltzer, Carnegie-Rochester Conference Series on Public Policy, 1976.

** Robert E. Lucas, "Some International Evidence on Output-Inflation Tradeoffs," *American Economic Review*, vol. 68, 1973, pp. 326–34.

policy pattern cannot be useful in predicting the effects of a change in that pattern. At the same time, it is worth noting the empirical fact that when U.S. monetary policy eventually was tightened in the early 1980s, a severe recession followed. Because this tightening was not a controlled experiment, we cannot conclude with certainty that it caused the recession. However, the experience does suggest that the rational-expectations model might not have been correct after all. If the inflationary expectations were *not* rational, then the structure of the expectations-augmented Phillips curve model did not depend on the policy pattern. Thus, Lucas's critique, while perfectly valid in general, may not have applied as directly to the Phillips curve model as it originally appeared.

8.5   DOES INFLATION HELP OR HURT ECONOMIC PERFORMANCE?

Toward the end of Chapter 3, we raised the question of whether inflation helps or hurts economic growth. From Figure 3.14, we saw that the empirical evidence was mixed. On one hand, the inflation rate has shown signs of abating during most recessions and has picked up again during the subsequent recoveries, especially during the late stages of each expansion. On the other hand, the 1973–75 and 1980 recessions coincided with drastic run-ups in inflation.

DIFFERENT SHOCKS CREATE DIFFERENT RECESSIONS

The theory we have studied in this chapter and in Chapter 7 should help take the mystery out of these apparently conflicting observations. Inflation and real activity are not simple causes of each other but are determined jointly in a complex, dynamic system in which many different forces are at work. Thus, when a recession is followed by deceleration of inflation, the whole event can be explained as the result of a shortfall in aggregate demand. Conversely, when inflation and recession occur at the same time, they can be explained in terms of supply shocks or external inflationary shocks.

IS THERE A POLICY TRADE-OFF BETWEEN INFLATION AND ECONOMIC GROWTH?

When we first introduced the Phillips curve in Section 7.4, we also mentioned that the Phillips curve has been interpreted as a trade-off between inflation and growth in real GNP. This tradeoff sometimes is also referred to as a **policy menu.** This idea suggests that the policymakers should be able to choose a point on the Phillips curve that represents an ideal trade-off between real activity and inflation. A government that puts a high premium on price stability could follow a tight monetary policy in order to obtain low inflation but would have to be willing to accept lower real GNP growth. On the other hand, a government that is less afraid of inflation could use monetary and fiscal policies to stimulate the economy and obtain higher real activity, at the cost of somewhat higher inflation.

Our analysis of the expectations-augmented Phillips curve presented the argument against this view—the menu interpretation of the Phillips curve. One important message of that model is the futility of attempting to stimulate real activity by means of monetary acceleration *beyond the potential defined by aggregate supply*. The long-run effect of such acceleration is inflation. Only in the short run will real activity exceed its potential; in the equilibrium (rational-expectations) version of the model not even that happens.

We should also note, however, that a short-run real expansion can be valuable. For as long as it lasts, it results in increased production levels of real goods and services. Moreover, because a monetary easing tends to reduce real interest rates, part of the real expansion should come in the form of higher investment. This investment is added to the capital stock and thus *expands aggregate supply*. Our discussion of monetary acceleration in Section 8.4 ignored this effect for the sake of simplicity. Figure 8.8 reproduces the aggregate demand–aggregate supply diagram in Figure 8.7 but adds shifts in the aggregate supply curve that result each period from the higher investment activity in the preceding

FIGURE 8.8

Dynamic effects of monetary acceleration when higher investment activity increases aggregate supply.

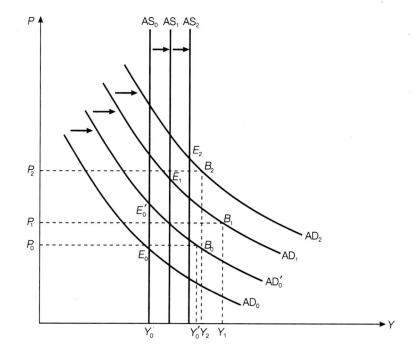

period. (The lag occurs because of the time it takes to produce and implement new capital equipment.) In this case, real GNP is increased somewhat in the long run, though still at the cost of higher inflation.

Thus, as long as the economy does not follow the equilibrium version completely, a policy trade-off remains. It is a complicated trade-off, however, between long-run inflation on one hand and an elevated activity level in the short run and somewhat higher production levels in the long run on the other. Moreover, the trade-off goes both ways. Once inflation has become entrenched, stopping it runs the risk of triggering a recession. Part of the effect of such a recession is likely to be lower investment activity, with corresponding long-run effects on the capital stock.

Furthermore, the conventional version of the expectations-augmented Phillips curve leaves open the possibility that expansionary policy measures can be successful in stabilizing an economy that has been thrown into recession by a demand shock. If a negative GNP gap exists, measured expansionary policies can close this gap, shorten the recession, and put the economy back on track. Again, long-run benefits may result as investment is stimulated by the expansionary policies. Some observers argue that a long-run benefit results on the labor side as well. Because unemployed workers do not keep up their job training and tend to become demoralized, a stimulating policy that reduces unemployment should avoid this negative effect. However, expansionary policy measures also present the risk that the policy may overreact and in fact set off an acceleration of inflation.

WHAT IS BAD ABOUT INFLATION?

The arguments above should explain why so many people are skeptical about the wisdom of implementing policies whose real effects are ultimately dissipated by inflation. However, they do not explain why people dislike inflation in the first place. In macroeconomic equilibrium, real variables should be determined by real forces and not by monetary phenomena such as money growth and inflation. Then why do people fear inflation?

First, let us point out that there is no reason to fear inflation just because it makes prices go up. Rising prices sometimes are identified with declining real incomes, but rising prices reduce nominal incomes only if nominal income does not keep pace with inflation. Our analysis emphasized that long-term inflation is an equilibrium phenomenon; in macroeconomic equilibrium, real income is determined by aggregate supply.

However, more sophisticated arguments can be presented to the effect that equilibrium inflation can create *distortions* to aggregate supply, especially if the economy's institutions are not equipped to function in an inflationary environment. One example of such a distortion is the tax system, especially as it concerns the taxation of capital income.

Consider the following example. With a 15% tax rate, a 10% before-tax return on financial investment is reduced to an 8.5% after-tax return. If there is no inflation, the 10% and the 8.5% will also be the *real* before-tax and after-tax returns, respectively. This effect of the tax system is intended. It need not represent any distortion, given the fact that a government is needed and must be paid for. Suppose instead that inflation is 5%. Then the real return before tax is 10% − 5% = 5%, while the real after-tax return is 8.5% − 5% = 3.5%. Thus, with 5% inflation, the 15% tax reduces the real return by 30% rather than 15%. Meanwhile, if the same tax rate applies to, say, labor income, no such distortion occurs there. Thus, inflation raises the effective tax rate on investment income relative to that on other income. This is a distortion to the incentives for saving that may have an adverse effect on the formation of real capital. Many people have argued that in the 1970s this distortion kept many investors away from the stock market and contributed to its lackluster performance.

The purpose of pointing out inflation-induced distortions is to explain the fundamental difficulty involved in making policy decisions. The prospect of long-term inflation can be more than a nuisance; it can be a real disadvantage. The policy choices are not easy. We discuss them at greater length in Chapter 12.

CHAPTER REVIEW

1. Inflation is not just a result of macroeconomic disequilibrium. Equilibrium inflation in the long run is equal to the difference between the rate of money growth and the growth rate in real GNP.
2. Time-series data for inflation rates do not entirely support the long-run equilibrium model of inflation. However, data for long-term trends, such as time series of the price level and international comparisons of average inflation rates, fit the theory quite well.
3. Equilibrium inflation and the Phillips curve can be reconciled in the expectations-augmented Phillips curve.
4. With adaptive expectations, the expectations-augmented Phillips curve predicts that a monetary expansion will have positive real effects in the short run but only inflationary effects in the long run. A monetary tightening can stop inflation, but at the cost of a recession.
5. The expectations-augmented Phillips curve with rational expectations predicts, in contrast to that with adaptive expectations, that inflation can be stopped without a recession. The Lucas critique questions the empirical support for the adaptive-expectations hypothesis. Nevertheless, the experience of the recession following the monetary tightening in the early 1980s does not support the rational-expectations position.
6. A trade-off between inflation and real activity may exist. However, choices regarding this trade-off are complicated.

NUMERICAL EXERCISES

As in Chapter 7, derive the aggregate demand function from the following numerical IS-LM model:

(IS) $Y = 150 + 0.75Y − 10,000R + G + 0.25Y^e,$

(LM) $M/P = 50 + 0.3Y − 6,000R.$

Specify aggregate supply as follows:
- Expectations-augmented Phillips curve with an additional term for external price shocks:
$$\pi_t = \pi_t^e + (Y_{t-1} - Y^*)/Y^* + s_t \quad (\gamma = 1)$$
- Adaptive inflationary expectations:
$$\pi_t^e = 0.4\pi_{t-1} + 0.3\pi_{t-2} + 0.2\pi_{t-3} + 0.1\pi_{t-4}$$
- Assume $Y^* = 4,000$ for all periods.

Initially, assume also that $Y_t^e = 4,000$, $G_t = 600$, $M_t = 800$, and $s_t = 0$ for all periods. Assume a history of no inflation and stable real GNP unless otherwise noted.

The following five exercises give you an opportunity to explore the dynamic properties of the expectations-augmented Phillips curve model with adaptive expectations. You will probably prefer to use an electronic spreadsheet. For each case, solve the model for 30 periods. Think of each period as a quarter of a year. Inspect and interpret the numerical results. For further clarity, use the spreadsheet package to construct graphs that illustrate the solutions. Even though the model is a highly stylized representation of reality, you should try to compare the results with the actual economic events suggested in each exercise. If you find major discrepancies between model and reality, try to think of factors that can explain them.

1. Solve the model with the initial parameter values. Explain why the solution has a stable GNP and no inflation.
2. Suppose Y^e declines by 600 from period 0 to period 1 and stays at the lower level indefinitely. Compare the results to U.S. data for the 1958 recession.
3. Suppose $s_1 = 0.05$, $s_2 = 0.03$, and $s_t = 0$ for all other periods. Compare the results with the 1973–74 oil price shock and the ensuing recession.
4. Suppose G is elevated by 100 for all periods starting in period 1. Compare the results to data for the years following the escalation of the Vietnam War.
5. Assume that the economy's history through period 0 shows steady inflation of 2.5% per quarter (roughly 10% per year), made possible by growth in the money supply at the same rate. In period 0, the money supply

just reaches $M_0 = 800$, and the price level is $P_0 = 1$. Simulate the model under the assumption that the growth in the money supply is stopped abruptly after period 0 and never resumes. Compare the results to data for the U.S. economy in the early 1980s.

DATA EXERCISES

1. Look at the international data for average inflation for 1971–85 analyzed in the text, but this time look only at the data for those countries that have not experienced hyperinflations. (You may define hyperinflation as, for example, average annual inflation exceeding 50%.) Do the data still support the equilibrium-inflation hypothesis?
2. Look at international data for inflation, money growth, and real GDP growth in one particular year, including all the countries listed in Table 8.1. Does the pattern in the data coincide with the average data for 1971–85? Why or why not?
3. Try to estimate a Phillips curve model with time-series data for one country that has experienced hyperinflation, such as Brazil or Israel. Use the difference between the real GDP growth rate and its historical average as an approximation of the GNP gap. Assume static expectations. Does the estimated Phillips curve have the right slope? What does your result tell you about the validity of the Phillips curve under hyperinflations?
4. As in the data exercise in Chapter 7, construct potential GNP for the United States as an exponential trend fitted to real GNP, and use this construct to compute GNP gaps for the U.S. economy. Use the rate of change in the GNP deflator to represent inflation. Furthermore, augment the Phillips curve model with (a) static expectations and (b) adaptive expectations in the form of a distributed lag of past inflation rates. Estimate the model for the entire postwar period as well as for subperiods defined as decades. How do the results fit the expectations-augmented Phillips curve model?

THINKING QUESTIONS

1. During the 1988–90 period, the Federal Reserve tried to engineer a "soft landing," by which inflation is reduced without inducing a recession. Judging from subsequent events, do you think such a policy can be successful?

2. The way people form expectations obviously matters to the central bankers and others who formulate policies about inflation. However, as a business manager, does this issue affect your decisions? If so, how?

EXTENSIONS OF MACROECONOMIC THEORY

PART III

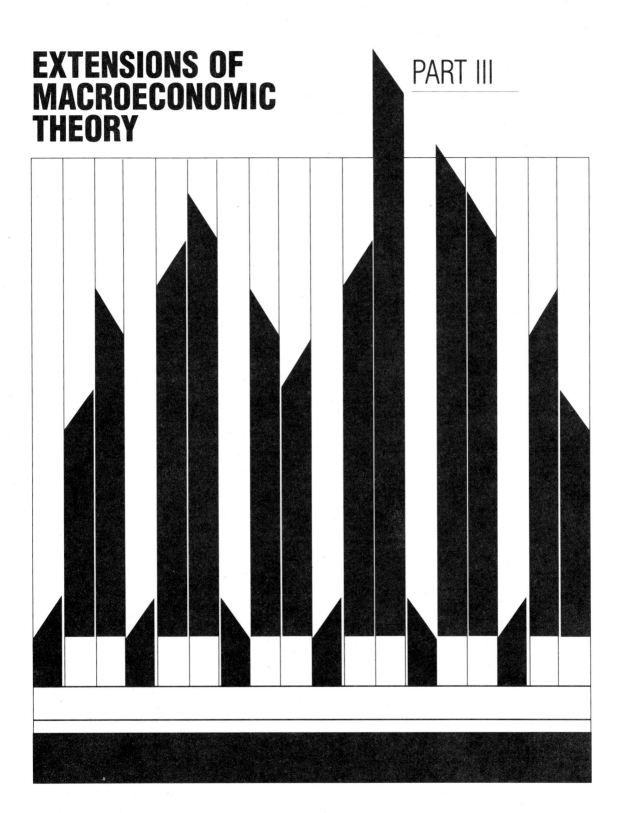

PART III

The preceding chapters have acquainted you with the basic elements
of macroeconomic theory: the IS-LM
model, aggregate demand and aggregate
supply, the Phillips curve, and inflation
analysis. In this part of the text, we go on
to study some additional issues. Chapters 9
and 10 deal with the international linkages that tie the economies of different
countries together. Chapter 11 addresses
the various schools of thought in macroeconomics, and Chapter 12 takes a closer
look at macroeconomic policy making.

Chapter 9 takes a brief look at the economic theory of international trade. On
one hand, this theory seeks to explain the
existing pattern of trade. On the other, it
addresses the issues of trade balance and
imbalance for individual countries. Chapter 10 looks at the international monetary
system, in particular, the market for foreign exchange. It concludes with an analysis of macroeconomic policies under fixed
and floating exchange rates.

Controversies are commonplace among
macroeconomists. The neo-Keynesian approach, which dominated the analysis in
Part II, is only one of several approaches
to macroeconomic analysis. Chapter 11
provides a critical survey of alternative
approaches and seeks to evaluate how a
manager can make use of macroeconomic
analysis in the presence of these competing theories.

Finally, Chapter 12 takes a closer look at
macroeconomic policy. Although business
managers rarely have an opportunity to
formulate public policy, the policies can
have substantial effects on business. Thus,
understanding how the policies are made
and how they work can be quite valuable
for business planning. This chapter makes
extensive use of the theory presented in
the preceding chapters but seeks at the
same time to view the policies in a practical perspective.

9 INTERNATIONAL TRADE

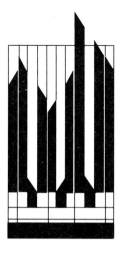

The globalization of American business became a popular topic in the 1980s. However, countries have interacted economically with each other all through recorded history. After World War II, the United States played a leading role in the international economic community as an exporter, an investor nation, and the dominant power in economic policy making. To a considerable extent, however, this position was more visible abroad than at home. This asymmetry is underscored by the fact that the U.S. position was powerful enough to often enable this country to make its decisions unilaterally, while other countries were forced to accept the terms given to them by the Americans.

An important change during the 1970s and 1980s was the decline in American dominance. The U.S. map has become studded with the subsidiaries of Asian and European multinationals, even as a number of American industries have been challenged by foreign competition. From 1950 to 1989, the portion of U.S. spending going to imports almost tripled, from 4.4% to 12.9%, while the share of U.S. production being exported more than doubled, from 5.0% to 12.0%. Every day, the U.S. financial markets deal in foreign securities and interact with overseas markets. Finally, the power in economic policy making is now shared more equally between the United States and its major competitor nations, such as Japan, Germany, and the other members of the European Community. Against this background, the story of macroeconomics would be severely lacking without a discussion of the global economic interactions.

In order to discuss these interactions, we first take a brief look at the main attempts to explain the existing patterns of international trade. We then study the demand for a country's exports and imports from a macroeconomic perspective. We end the chapter with a presentation of the balance of payments and a discussion of trade deficits.

9.1 THE PATTERN OF INTERNATIONAL TRADE

Why does the United States export grain and import textiles, while the European countries buy and sell cars from each other? Economists provide a two-part answer to this question. First, trade may result when different countries have different *comparative advantages*, which explains why the United States trades grain for textiles. Second, trade may result from *economies of scale*, making large-scale production to world markets more profitable than small-scale production for domestic markets, which explains why the Europeans trade cars among themselves.

COMPARATIVE ADVANTAGE

The concept of **comparative advantage** is central to the economic theory of international trade. To keep matters simple, we start with a stylized example with two countries, A(lphastan) and B(etastan), both of which can produce two goods, i(ce cream) and j(elly).

In this example, we assume that both countries use only labor in their respective production processes. Alphastan uses a technology where the production of one liter (1 ℓ) of ice cream uses 2 worker hours of labor, while the production of one kilogram (1 kg) of jelly uses 4 worker hours. Then, 4 worker hours can be used to produce 2 ℓ of ice cream or 1 kg of jelly. Since ice-cream production and jelly production compete for the same labor resources in Alphastan, this relationship can be interpreted by saying that $\frac{1}{2}$ kg of jelly needs to be given up for each liter of ice cream produced in that country. Thus, we can say that the production of 1 ℓ of ice cream costs $\frac{1}{2}$ kg of jelly. Because ice-cream production thus means a lost opportunity for jelly production, we say that the **opportunity cost** of ice-cream production in Alphastan is $\frac{1}{2}$ kg of jelly per liter of ice cream. If we now use C as the symbol for this cost and use subscripts for countries, we can write this fact as $C_A = \frac{1}{2}$.

The first column of Table 9.1 summarizes this information for Alphastan. The first row states the number of worker hours needed to produce 1 ℓ of ice cream and the second row the number of worker hours needed to produce 1 kg of jelly. The third row shows the opportunity cost, defined as the ratio between the entries in the first and second rows, respectively.

Betastan has a different technology, which is summarized in the second column of Table 9.1. Specifically, this technology needs 6 worker hours for each liter of ice cream produced, but only 3 hours for each kilogram of jelly. Because ice-cream production and jelly production

TABLE 9.1   DESCRIPTION OF PRODUCTION TECHNOLOGIES FOR ALPHASTAN AND BETASTAN: FIRST EXAMPLE

	ALPHASTAN	BETASTAN
Labor resources needed to produce one unit of output:		
Ice cream	2	6
Jelly	4	3
Opportunity cost of ice cream:	$\frac{1}{2}$	2

compete for the same labor resources in Betastan as well, this means that the same 6 worker hours can be used to produce 1 ℓ of ice cream or 2 kg of jelly. For each liter of ice cream produced in Betastan, the Betastanians have to give up 2 kg of jelly. In other words, the opportunity cost of ice cream in Betastan is 2 kg of jelly, as listed in the lower right corner of Table 9.1.

In this example, Alphastan has a lower opportunity cost of ice cream than does Betastan. For this reason, we say that Alphastan has a comparative advantage over Betastan in ice-cream production. The theory of comparative advantage predicts that *each country will produce and export goods in which it has a comparative advantage and import those in which it does not.* In the example just given, Alphastanians can sacrifice 1 kg of jelly, use the 4 worker hours thus freed up to produce 2 ℓ of ice cream, and offer this ice cream to the Betastanians at a relative price of, say, 1 kg of jelly per liter of ice cream. If the Betastanians accept, the Alphastanians will have traded the 2 ℓ of ice cream for 2 kg of jelly. But the Alphastanians gave up only 1 kg of jelly of their own production. Thus, by specializing in ice-cream production, the Alphastanians end up with more jelly even if they keep the same amount of ice cream for their own consumption.

Will the Betastanians accept? The answer is yes, and for the following reason. Because of this trading opportunity, the Betastanians can produce 2 ℓ less ice cream, thus freeing up 12 worker hours, which can be used to produce 4 kg of jelly. Two of these 4 kg are needed as payment for the imported ice cream, while the remaining 2 kg are available for additional consumption. Both countries profit. Trade is mutually beneficial, and the theory predicts that mutually beneficial trades are those that in fact take place.

DOES EVERY COUNTRY HAVE AN ADVANTAGE?

In the example just given, Alphastan could produce ice cream more efficiently than Betastan in the sense that the Alphastanian technology needed only 2 worker hours per liter, while the Betastanian technology needed 6. In contrast, Betastan could produce jelly more efficiently than Alphastan. We can say that Alphastan has a higher *productivity* in ice-cream production than does Betastan, while Betastan has a higher productivity in the production of jelly. As another way of expressing the same relationship, we can say that Alphastan has an **absolute advantage** in ice-cream production, while Betastan has an absolute advantage in jelly production.

In such a situation it is easy to see that trade is mutually beneficial. But suppose the Betastanian technology was less productive for *both* ice-cream *and* jelly production. Then Betastan would have no absolute advantage, and you might be tempted to conclude that Betastan would not benefit from trading with Alphastan because the Betastanians would have nothing attractive to offer.

TABLE 9.2 DESCRIPTION OF PRODUCTION TECHNOLOGIES FOR ALPHASTAN AND BETASTAN: ALTERNATIVE EXAMPLE

	ALPHASTAN	BETASTAN
Labor resources needed to produce one unit of output:		
Ice cream	2	10
Jelly	4	5
Opportunity cost of ice cream:	$\frac{1}{2}$	2

However, such a conclusion would be false, as the alternative example in Table 9.2 illustrates. In this example, Betastan uses more labor in the production of both ice cream and jelly and thus has no absolute advantage in anything. However, Betastan still has a *comparative* advantage in jelly production. To see this, note that the *opportunity costs* of the two countries are just the same as in the first example, namely $C_A = \frac{1}{2}$ and $C_B = 2$. Thus Alphastanians still want to trade ice cream for jelly. But that also means that they want to buy jelly from Betastan. Betastan still has a comparative advantage in jelly production.

Specifically, the Alphastanians can, as before, sacrifice 1 kg of jelly, use the 4 worker hours thus freed up to produce 2 ℓ of ice cream, and offer this ice cream to the Betastanians at 1 kg of jelly per liter of ice cream. As in the first example, the Alphastanians then end up with 2 kg of jelly in return for the 1 kg that they sacrifice. The Alphastanians are still happy with the trade.

The Betastanians remain happy with the trade, too. Again they can give up 2 ℓ of ice-cream production. This time they free up 20 rather than 12 worker hours, but the 20 hours freed are needed to produce the same 4 kg of jelly as in the previous example. Having used 2 of these 4 kg as payment for the imported ice cream, the remaining 2 kg are again available for additional consumption. Trade is no less mutually beneficial than when Betastan had an absolute advantage in jelly production.

This example illustrates that the key to comparative advantage is not to have a superior productivity in terms of the use of labor or other resources, but to have a lower opportunity cost in terms of other goods. The opportunity cost of producing jelly in Betastan is not measured in worker hours, but in the amount of ice cream that needs to be given up for jelly production; in other words, $1/C_B = \frac{1}{2}$, which is less than $1/C_A = 2$ because $C_A < C_B$.

This example can be generalized to any number of countries and any number of goods. Of course, the opportunity cost could be the same in all countries, in which case no comparative advantage would exist. However, *if one country has a comparative advantage in something, the other countries must have a comparative advantage in something else.*

This is the good news for a low-productivity country with no absolute advantage. The bad news is that its standard of living is lower. A country's real income is a direct reflection of the value of the goods it produces. A country having difficulty producing large amounts of goods and services with the resources it has available necessarily also ends up with a low real income and a correspondingly low standard of living. The theory of comparative advantage promises such a country a market for those goods that it produces the most efficiently compared to other goods. However, the same theory makes no guarantee about the income that the sale of these goods generates. The pattern of trade reflects comparative advantage, but international differences in real income reflect productivity differences.

SOURCES OF COMPARATIVE ADVANTAGE

The simplest case of comparative advantage arises when technological or other differences create **differences in productivity** among countries, as in the examples just presented.* Although modern societies tend to have access to similar technologies, important differences in productivity exist in practice. For example, Japan developed a comparative advantage in the production of steel in the 1970s by its early adoption of the oxygen furnace. An equally important source of comparative advantage among industrialized countries is **differences in resource endowments.** Thus, the opportunity cost of growing grain is quite low in the United States because of its wide areas of fertile farmland, Canada has a comparative advantage in lumber production because of its wide forest lands, and Saudi Arabia has an obvious comparative advantage in the production of crude oil. In general, developing countries tend to have a comparative advantage in the production of labor-intensive goods, such as textiles and apparel, because their populations are large relative to their capital stocks. In contrast, rich nations like the United States and Japan have large amounts of capital relative to labor, which gives them an advantage in the production of such capital-intensive goods as airplanes and automobiles.**

---

*A model of this type, with only one input to production (labor), is referred to among economists as the Ricardian model, in honor of the nineteenth-century British economist David Ricardo, who used the logic of this model to argue for the repeal of the British Corn Laws. These laws had prevented the importation of grain into Great Britain after the Napoleonic wars. Incidentally, this is also the Ricardo of Ricardian equivalence, which we studied briefly in Chapter 5.

**The standard model of trade resulting from differences in resource endowments is referred to as the Heckscher-Ohlin model, after the twentieth-century Swedish economists Eli Heckscher and Bertil Ohlin, who first launched the idea. Bertil Ohlin was awarded the Nobel prize in economics in 1977.

ECONOMIES OF SCALE AND INTRA-INDUSTRY TRADE

The theory of comparative advantage predicts that the goods that a country exports and imports will be *different goods*. A country will produce and export goods for which it has a comparative advantage and import goods for which it does not. Thus, the theory can account for U.S. exports of grain and airplanes and U.S. imports of textiles from labor-abundant developing countries. This kind of trade can be called **interindustry trade,** because the goods imported and exported are produced by different industries.

However, a large share of world trade cannot be accounted for in this manner, namely, the trade in similar goods between similar, industrialized countries. For example, Germany exports Volkswagen automobiles to Italy while at the same time importing Italian-made Fiats. This is an example of **intraindustry trade,** because Volkswagen AG and Fiat S.p.A. belong to the same industry, namely, the automobile industry. Current trade statistics offer a large number of such examples, in which similar manufactured goods are traded back and forth across the same borders.

Trying to explain trade in goods this similar as the result of comparative advantage does not seem reasonable. To say that Germany has a comparative advantage in Volkswagen production and Italy a comparative advantage in Fiat production seems strained, and an alternative explanation should be sought. The alternative that has been offered in the research literature on international trade points to the importance of *economies of scale* and *product differentiation*.

The term **economies of scale** means that the cost per unit of producing large quantities of a product is lower than that of producing smaller quantities. Thus, if economies of scale apply, a company can make more money if it can sell to a large market. In many countries, especially small ones, the domestic market is too small to generate a worthwhile profit. The obvious solution is to expand the market by exporting. Then, as in the case of comparative advantage, the export marketing is motivated by a desire to exploit a special cost advantage. However, unlike the previous case, the cost advantage now comes from economies of scale rather than from some kind of inherent comparative advantage for a specific product. Which brands are produced where, or **product differentiation,** may be a matter of historical accident rather than the result of deep economic forces. The point is that each company has the opportunity to specialize, which gives rise to product differentiation. At the same time, international trade means that the consumers in both countries can benefit from wider choices, because they are not restricted to buying only domestic brands. Thus, consumers as well as producers in both countries benefit from having a larger, international market.* This

---

*This idea is spelled out in an article by Paul Krugman, "Intraindustry Specialization and the Gains from Trade," in *Journal of Political Economy*, October 1981, vol. 89, no. 4, pp. 959–73.

type of benefit is an important part of the impetus behind the efforts to create a unified internal market in the European Community by the end of 1992.

9.2 IMPORT AND EXPORT MARKETS

The theory of international trade predicts the trade *pattern* that will arise in unregulated markets. However, from a macroeconomic perspective, we are usually more interested in the *overall movements in exports and imports* for a particular country. The mechanisms behind these moves are the familiar forces, prices and incomes. Because different countries are involved, we will distinguish between domestic and foreign incomes. To keep matters simple, we will mostly pretend that there are only two countries, a "home" country and a "foreign" country.

INCOME AND NET EXPORT DEMAND

Import demand in the home country obviously depends on domestic income, which can be measured by home-country GNP. As we noted in Chapter 5, a higher domestic income level will, other things being equal, tend to raise the demand for *all* goods, including imported goods. Thus, an increase in real GNP raises import demand. The demand for exports from the home country is influenced similarly by changes in the foreign income level. Of more interest to our analysis is whether the demand for the home country's exports is also influenced by changes in *home-country* income. Here the connection is more subtle. An increase in the domestic income level, since it raises import demand, could also stimulate other economies and thereby raise the demand for the home country's exports. However, because this link is indirect, it is reasonable to expect it to be somewhat weaker. Since net export demand is the difference between export demand and import demand, we can therefore conclude that *an increase in domestic real GNP reduces net export demand.*

THE RELATIVE PRICES OF DOMESTIC AND FOREIGN GOODS

In order to determine the effects of price changes, we first need to clarify the relevant price concepts for foreign and domestic goods. Consider first a single good, such as a particular brand of women's shoes. Call this item good i and write its domestic price, in terms of the domestic currency, as P_i. The foreign price of the same pair of shoes, P_i^*, is denominated in the foreign currency. For example, the domestic price could be $150 and the foreign price DM300, where DM stands for deutsche mark or D-mark, the German currency. In order to compare these two prices, we need to know how many marks a dollar is worth, or vice versa. In other words, we need to know the *exchange rate* between the dollar and the D-mark. We denote this exchange rate by E and define it as the price of the domestic currency in terms of the foreign currency.* For example, if each dollar is worth 2 D-mark, we have $E = DM2/\$$. Then the domestic price, expressed in the foreign currency unit, is the product $E \cdot P_i$. This means that, for a foreigner to buy this pair of shoes in the home country (for example, for a German to buy it in the United States), she will first have to buy the home currency at a rate of E per unit of the foreign currency (for example, DM2 per dollar) and then use the home currency to pay for the shoes. This price can then be compared to the foreign price, P_i^*.

The **relative price** for a foreigner buying the shoes in the home country rather than in the foreign country is the *ratio* of the price $E \cdot P_i$ of buying the shoes here to the price P_i^* of buying them in her home country. In other words, the relative price is the ratio $E \cdot P_i/P_i^*$. If this relative price is less than 1, it will be advantageous (ignoring transportation and other indirect costs) for foreigners to buy these shoes in the home country (that is, for Germans to buy them in the United States); in other words, it is advantageous to *import* them from the home country rather than to buy them from their own suppliers.

Home-country customers face a similar choice. They can buy the shoes at home at the price P_i. Alternatively, if they want to buy them abroad, they first need to buy foreign currency at a price of $1/E$ per unit of the domestic currency (for example, if $E = 2$ so that each dollar is worth DM2, then each D-mark is worth \$0.5, or 50¢, so the price of the D-mark is $1/E$). Equipped with this foreign currency, they can buy the shoes abroad at P_i^*. The cost in the domestic currency thus is $(1/E) \cdot P_i^*$ and the price of buying at home relative to that of buying abroad is $P_i/(1/E) \cdot P_i^*$, or $E \cdot P_i/P_i^*$. In other words, foreign and domestic customers face the same relative price, so it is also true of domestic customers that they would rather buy the shoes at home than import them from abroad if the relative price is less than 1. In general, a low relative price makes home-country goods cheap at home as well as abroad, while a high relative price makes them expensive.

Although the prices of individual goods may move independently of each other, the general price movements in the home and the foreign markets can be captured by the overall price-level indices P and P^*, respectively. Thus, in an aggregate sense, $E \cdot P/P^*$ represents the relative price of domestic to foreign goods. An increase in $E \cdot P/P^*$ reduces export demand and raises import demand for the home country. In other words, *an increase in $E \cdot P/P^*$ reduces net export demand.*

We defer a detailed discussion of the determinants of the exchange rate

---

* Some other texts define the exchange rate as the price of the *foreign* currency. This difference does not affect the substance of the discussion.

to the next chapter. Here we note a relationship between exchange rates and net export demand that is commonly referred to as the **J curve.**

THE J CURVE

It may be worth noting that the relationship stated above was between relative prices and net export demand in *real* terms. However, the effect on *nominal* net exports may go in the opposite direction, especially as a short-run phenomenon. In units of the home currency, the nominal value of net exports is

(9.1)
$$X_N = P \cdot EX - (P^*/E) \cdot IM,$$

where *EX* and *IM* are the volumes of exports and imports, respectively. It is easy to see that $P \cdot EX$ is the nominal value of exports in the domestic currency. Moreover, since $1/E$ is the domestic price of the foreign currency, $(1/E) \cdot P^* = P^*/E$ is the price of imports in the domestic currency. Thus, $(P^*/E) \cdot IM$ is the nominal value of imports in the domestic currency.

Suppose the relative price $E \cdot P/P^*$ rises because of an increase in the exchange rate *E*, while the two price levels *P* and P^* stay unchanged. Then we expect the volume of export demand, *EX*, to decline, while the volume of import demand, *IM*, should rise. However, because less is paid for each unit of imports, nominal net exports may rise overall. This possibility is particularly strong in the very short run, because then the export and import volumes may not yet have had time to adjust to the price change, so the direct effect of the import prices dominates. Similarly, a *decrease* in $E \cdot P/P^*$ may at first reduce net exports in nominal terms and then raise them later. Figure 9.1 shows a graph of the behav-

FIGURE 9.1

The J curve.

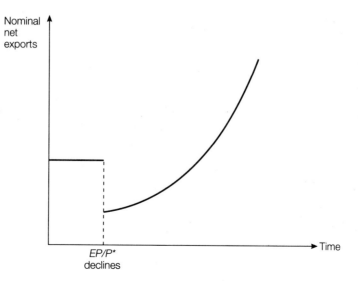

Nominal net exports

EP/P*
declines

Time

ior of nominal net exports over time for this case. Because the curve bears some resemblance to the letter *J*, it is usually called the J curve.

9.3 TRADE BALANCES AND IMBALANCES

Balanced trade means that the value of imports equals the value of exports. When trade is balanced between two companies, neither company ends up owing the other company money, because the value of one company's deliveries to the other exactly matches the value of the other company's deliveries to the first. Likewise, when trade is balanced between countries, the citizens of neither country, as a group, end up owing money to the citizens of the other country. All imports are paid for in kind, that is, in the form of exports of other goods.

When ice cream is traded for jelly in a simple exchange, international trade is balanced, because all the ice cream is paid for with jelly, and vice versa. However, if the value of a country's exports exceeds that of its imports, its trade is not in balance but shows a *surplus*. Conversely, if imports exceed exports, the country is running a trade *deficit*. In practice, trade is rarely exactly balanced for any country over any period of time, and sometimes we observe large imbalances, such as the U.S. trade deficits in the 1980s.

Imbalanced trade sometimes makes eminent sense. Suppose, for example, that a country faces exceptional investment opportunities that promise to pay off greatly in the future. Such opportunities were faced, for example, by Norwegian companies when the world price of oil skyrocketed shortly after large oil reserves were discovered in the North Sea. In this situation, it made perfect sense for Norway to run a trade deficit while importing oil drilling equipment, because oil revenues could be expected to more than cover the payments of interest and principal for the foreign loans needed to finance the investment expenses.

This example demonstrates that trade imbalances are not problems by themselves. However, people often become concerned about trade deficits when they are large and no prospect of quick improvement is apparent. The reason for the concern is that large deficits can have ripple effects for the whole economy. We return to these concerns toward the end of this chapter. First, however, we look at the accounting system used to organize information about foreign trade and international capital movements—the system known as the **balance of payments.**

THE BALANCE OF PAYMENTS

The balance of payments consists of two parts, the *current account* and the *capital account*. The balances on these accounts, as well as some of their components, carry useful information that is released regularly in the media and compiled in public statistics.

As the name indicates, the **current account** registers current trade in goods and services. *Exports* enter positively and *imports* negatively. In addition, the current account contains information on **unilateral transfers.** For example, a U.S. grant to the Polish government is entered as a *negative* item on the current account for the United States. Because the transfers component is usually small for industrialized countries, the balance on the current account essentially indicates the difference between exports and imports for a specified period. It is *conceptually equivalent to net exports,* although differences in definitional details may cause small discrepancies in the official statistics.

The left side of Table 9.3 shows in broad outline how the current account is organized. Exports and imports are divided into **merchandise trade** and **trade in services.** Merchandise trade is the easiest component to keep track of, because it goes through customs. For this reason, the merchandise trade balance is published monthly in the United States and many other countries, while the entire current-account balance is typically released quarterly and with a lag. However, trade in services is important, too. Exports and imports of **capital services** cover interest and dividend payments for home-country investments abroad (an example of exports of capital services), as well as the corresponding yields on foreign investments in the home country (imports of capital services). For a country with a large foreign debt, the deficit in capital services can be a significant item. This situation is very familiar to the large debtor countries in Latin America and Africa.

TABLE 9.3   OUTLINE OF THE BALANCE OF PAYMENTS

BALANCE OF PAYMENTS	
Current Account: Merchandise trade balance 　(Merchandise exports − Merchandise 　imports) Balance on trade in services 　(Exports of services − Imports of services) Net unilateral transfers 　(Unilateral transfers in − Unilateral 　transfers out)	Capital Account: Net nonofficial capital inflows 　(Capital inflows − Capital outflows) Net reduction in official reserves 　(Sales of official reserves − Purchases of 　official reserves)
Current-Account Balance	Capital-Account Balance
Current-Account Balance + Capital-Account Balance = 0 (except for statistical discrepancy)	

The **capital account,** outlined on the right side of Table 9.3, reflects international capital movements. **Capital inflows** are entered with a positive sign. Such inflows include merchandise credit issued to domestic importers by foreign suppliers, increases in the balances on bank accounts that foreigners hold in the home country, borrowing from foreign banks, bond sales (corporate or government) to foreigners, stock sales to foreigners, and direct investment in home-country companies and real estate. **Capital outflows,** entered negatively, include the same types of transactions but going the other way.

All these capital movements can be referred to as **nonofficial capital transactions.** The term **official transactions** is reserved for increases and decreases in the **official reserves** of the central bank, which are usually kept in the form of accounts with other central banks, denominated in foreign currencies. To the extent that central banks hold gold reserves, these holdings are also included. A sale of official reserves is classified as a capital inflow, because the sale produces a flow of payments into the country, as does borrowing from or direct investment by foreigners. Similarly, acquisitions of official reserves are considered capital outflows.

In today's markets, the typical cases of official transactions are central-bank **interventions** in foreign-exchange markets. If the U.S. Federal Reserve buys dollars to support the value of the dollar in the international market, payment is made in the form of foreign exchange, which means that the Federal Reserve is selling official reserves. Conversely, dollar sales, undertaken to bring down the value of the dollar, represent Federal Reserve purchases of official reserves.

The balance of payments accounts are based on the principle of double-entry bookkeeping. This means that every transaction should be entered twice, once with a positive sign and once with a negative sign. As one example, consider the importation of a shipment of Toyota cars into the United States. The shipment enters as a merchandise-import item with a negative sign in the current account. The payment is a financial transaction that is recorded positively in the capital account as a capital inflow—say, in the form of an increase in the balance of Toyota's dollar account in some U.S. bank when Toyota deposits the check issued as payment by the U.S. importer. Next consider the purchase of Macintosh computers by a Japanese publishing company. This transaction enters the current account positively as an export item. In analogy with the first example, the payment represents a capital outflow and is entered negatively in the capital account.

As a third example, suppose a European company takes over a U.S. corporation for cash, paid as dollar-denominated checks to the stockholders. Because this is a direct investment, it is a capital inflow, entered with a positive sign in the U.S. capital account. The cash payment, on the other hand, implies a reduction in the European company's holdings of U.S. bank accounts—a capital outflow. Thus, this transaction leaves the capital-account balance unchanged. This is a common occurrence; the gross volume of international *financial* transactions typically far exceeds the volume of trade in goods and services.

The double-entry bookkeeping principle implies that the current-account balance and the capital-account balance always sum to zero. In practice, imperfections in the data-collection process usually keep this from happening. The difference is referred to as a "statistical discrepancy." In principle, however, a current-account deficit always implies a net capital inflow of the same magnitude. It should be clear from all the examples above that a capital inflow in one way or another always implies an increase in the claims that foreigners hold on the home country. In this sense, *a trade deficit is equivalent to foreign borrowing.* Let us look a little more closely at this issue.

TWO USEFUL ACCOUNTING IDENTITIES

One useful perspective on trade deficits comes from the National Income and Product Accounts. This perspective starts from the **GNP identity,** which is the identity that breaks down GNP into its familiar spending components, namely, consumption, investment, net exports, and government spending. We introduced the GNP identity as equation (3.3) and used it (or rather an equation that looks like it) as an equilibrium condition in equation (5.1). We restate it here:

$$(9.2) \qquad Y = C + I + X + G.$$

Remember that we can identify (at least in principle) net exports with the current-account surplus, which we write as *CAS*. With *CAS* taking the place of *X* in the GNP identity, that identity can be solved for the current-account surplus as

$$(9.3) \qquad CAS = Y - (C + I + G).$$

The sum of consumption, investment, and government expenditure can be interpreted as total **domestic spending.** With this interpretation, equation (9.3) says that the current account is in surplus if and only if the value of the country's production exceeds domestic spending. Stated a little differently, *a current-account deficit is the result of the country spending more than it makes.*

This relationship can also be expressed another way. Remember that GNP also represents the income generated by the country's production activity. The difference between income (Y) and spending for current needs by consumers and their government ($C + G$) can then be interpreted as **domestic saving.** This saving consists of two parts: private saving, which we denote S, and public saving, which is defined as the difference between the government's revenues and expenses. In other words, public saving is the same as the government's surplus. Because the surpluses of the U.S. government have recently been large negatively, it is more convenient to say that domestic saving is the difference between private saving and public *dis*saving, that is, the difference between private saving and the government deficit. Denoting this deficit as *GD*, we can write

$$Y - (C + G) = S - GD.$$

Let us substitute this expression into equation (9.3). For convenience, let us also use *CAD* as a notation for the current-account *deficit*, which is obviously the negative of the current-account surplus, that is, *CAD* = −*CAS*. Then after a little rearrangement, we find that

(9.4) $$I + GD = S + CAD.$$

This equation has an interesting interpretation. On the left side are investment and the government deficit, items that both need financing. On the right side are the available financing *sources*. The first and obvious source is private saving. However, the fact that a current-account deficit is tantamount to foreign borrowing makes that deficit an alternative financing source.

To clarify the role of the current-account deficit as a financing source, note that whenever goods are imported to the United States the foreign suppliers typically accept payment in U.S. dollars, which they take to a bank in their home country in exchange for their own currency. The bank can do one of two things with the dollars. If the imports to the United States are matched by exports of equal value, the bank can sell the dollars to importers who use them to pay for the American goods. In this case, trade (the current account) balances, and there is no net accumulation of claims across borders. However, suppose the U.S. imports are *not* matched by exports. Then the foreign bank will sell the dollars to a foreign investor who uses them to buy U.S. securities, real estate, or ownership in U.S. companies. Thus, a U.S. current-account deficit always results in an accumulation by foreigners of some kind of claim on the U.S. economy.

During the 1980s, the magnitudes involved in equation (9.4) were such that private saving roughly matched investment. The equation then implies that the government deficits during this decade were roughly matched by equally large trade deficits. In the public debate, this match in the numbers has given rise to the phrase "twin deficits," which is used to describe simultaneous deficits in the government's accounts and in foreign trade.

It is important to note that equation (9.4) is only an accounting identity. In order to claim a causal relationship between government deficits and current-account deficits, we need a theory that links their behavior.

We return to this issue in the next chapter, in which we study the theory of fiscal policy under fixed and floating exchange rates. Before we close this chapter, however, we look briefly at why so many people think that trade (or current-account) deficits are a problem.

WHY ARE PEOPLE CONCERNED ABOUT TRADE DEFICITS?

A deficit on the current account means that a net stream of financial capital is running into the country in the form of loans, stock ownership, or direct investment in real estate or production facilities. Is such a stream a reason for concern? This question has become especially acute in the United States recently as a result of this country's large and consistent current-account deficits in the 1980s.

A number of people think there is no cause for concern. They argue that, for example, if a U.S. corporation wants to borrow in the world capital market, it is a normal business decision of no government concern. Furthermore, they point out that the international credit is extended quite willingly, which must mean that foreign investors feel they obtain a good return on their capital in the U.S. market at an acceptable risk. The very fact that foreigners want to invest in U.S. assets must mean that they have a high level of confidence in the health of the U.S. economy. Thus, from this perspective, the U.S. trade deficit is read as a stamp of approval rather than a danger sign.

Not everyone shares this sanguine view, however. The skeptics point out that the inflow of capital is not only the result of the attractiveness of American assets but also is influenced by the American demand for credit. Moreover, they argue that this demand is the result not of increased investment activity in physical capital but of a people living beyond its means. While the American life-style is currently being sustained by overseas financing, it shifts the burden to future generations of Americans, who collectively will be left with a large debt.

Is this an issue for the *government*? After all, if the American people spend too much and leave an unfair debt burden to their children, that should be a private decision. To this question the critics answer a partial yes but add that the private sector should share in the responsibility. At the same time, the government is part of the problem, because the large U.S. government deficits subtract substantially from total domestic saving.

Furthermore, critics of the trade deficit are concerned about what might happen if the foreign creditors should decide to pull out of the U.S. capital market. Although these creditors currently seem confident about the safety of their investments in the United States, that sentiment could turn around if a perception should arise to the effect that American debtors—public or private—were having difficulty meeting their obligations.

If that were to happen, the adjustment problems for the U.S. economy could potentially become severe. For example, if foreigners were no longer willing to finance a trade deficit, production resources would have to be redirected from producing for the domestic market, such as services, to export production, mainly manufacturing. The critics of the trade deficit would consider such a transition healthy over the long run. However, they also fear that production and employment might decline in the short run as jobs are lost in one industry before they are gained in the next. Thus, it might be preferable to reduce the risk of this situation ever arising by seeking to reduce the trade deficit now.

CHAPTER REVIEW

1. International trade comes from two sources. Interindustry trade is driven by comparative advantage, and intraindustry trade is driven by economies of scale and product differentiation.

2. The relative price of domestic goods in the world market is the product of the exchange rate and the ratio of the domestic and foreign price levels $(E \cdot P/P^*)$. Net export demand depends negatively on this relative price and on domestic real GNP.

3. The J curve indicates that a decline in the exchange rate may at first reduce net exports in nominal terms but is likely to reduce the deficit later.

4. The balance of payments is made up of the current account and the capital account. The balance on the current account shows the difference between exports and imports of goods and services minus net transfers out. The capital account records inflows and outflows of capital. A current-account deficit is equivalent to borrowing from the rest of the world.

5. A trade deficit results when domestic spending exceeds domestic production (GNP) or, equivalently, when private domestic saving is insufficient to finance domestic real investment and the government deficit.

6. Opinion is divided as to whether trade deficits are reason for concern. Different people view them alternatively as evidence of foreign investors' confidence in the domestic economy or as a long-term problem of overspending and excessive borrowing.

EXERCISES

1. Two countries (the home country and the foreign country) can produce two products, wine and cheese. Labor is the only available input to production. For each kilogram of cheese produced in the home country, 10 worker hours are needed, while the foreign country can produce the same amount with 8 worker hours. For wine production, the home country needs 25 worker hours per liter, while the foreign country needs 15. In which good does the home country have a comparative advantage? Does it have any absolute advantage? Which country do you think is richer?

2. The U.S. Bureau of the Census collects detailed data for U.S. foreign trade by country and by type of commodity. From one of its publications, collect data for trade patterns between the United States and (a) one developing country and (b) one industrialized country. For either case, try to determine to what extent the trade pattern can be explained in terms of comparative advantage.

3. Construct quarterly data for the relative price $E \cdot P/P^*$ (the latter variable can be constructed as an average vis-à-vis the most important countries or vis-à-vis one important trading partner, such as Japan or Germany). Also, find data for U.S. net exports (in current as well as constant dollars) and U.S. real GNP. Run a regression of net exports *in constant dollars* on current and lagged values of real GNP and the relative price. Are

the results consistent with the theory? Repeat the exercise for net exports in *current dollars*. Do you find evidence of a J curve?

THINKING QUESTIONS

1. Through negotiations, the United States has sought reductions in other countries' import restrictions. One objective of this policy has been to reduce the deficit on the U.S. current account. Bearing in mind what such a deficit implies about domestic spending and saving, do you think this strategy is likely to succeed? Can you suggest a better alternative?

2. After having heard some arguments from both sides of the debate over the U.S. trade deficit, what are your own thoughts about the issue? Do you think it should affect your managerial decisions, and if so how? What about your personal decisions?

10

THE ECONOMICS OF EXCHANGE RATES

Exchange rates provide one of the most important linkages between the economies of the world. We saw in the previous chapter how these rates help determine the relative prices of goods traded on the world market. However, an equally important function of exchange rates is to influence the relative returns on investments in financial assets denominated in the various currencies. This function provides a close link between exchange rates and interest rates in different countries.

Through this function, the exchange rates play the important role of linking domestic interest-rate movements with the supply and demand for exported and imported goods. Net exports are one of the components of aggregate demand; therefore, the exchange-rate mechanism is important to the internal as well as the external functioning of an economy.

This chapter starts by reviewing the institutional arrangements for international currency transactions, which together are called the **international monetary system.** We describe how exchange rates have sometimes been traded freely in the market, while at other times the governments or the central banks have sought to maintain a system of fixed exchange rates. Against this background, we then go on to study how each of these systems works. Finally, we discuss the likely future trends in the international monetary system.

10.1 THE INTERNATIONAL MONETARY SYSTEM

What we call the international monetary system is the interplay of the national monetary systems for the various individual countries of the type studied in Chapter 4. Today, this interplay takes on a variety of forms; some exchange rates are more or less fixed, while others float more or less freely. The historical background of this heterogeneous system is worth a brief review.

THE BRETTON WOODS SYSTEM OF FIXED EXCHANGE RATES

In the period between the two world wars, depression and protectionism had all but broken down the international financial markets, as well as the market for international trade. As World War II drew to a close, leading economists and policymakers were concerned that the world economy would fall back into the same pattern. To prevent this situation, they sought to design an international economic system with enough flexibility to allow a variety of trade and yet enough structure to provide stability. The agreement for such a system was drawn up in the town of Bretton Woods, New Hampshire, in 1944; the agreement, as well as the system to which it gave rise, came to bear the name of that town.

Under the Bretton Woods agreement, each country except the United States pledged to fix the value of its own currency vis-à-vis the U.S. dollar. The value of the U.S. dollar, in turn, was fixed in terms of gold at US$35 per ounce. The individual central banks committed themselves to supply foreign currency at these rates to people and businesses in their respective countries in order to facilitate trade. These currency supplies were to come out of the central banks' official reserves. For those occasions when individual central banks ran out of reserves, the agreement set up a procedure whereby they could borrow reserves from the **International Monetary Fund,** which was established as part of the Bretton Woods agreement. The agreement also set up a mechanism for readjusting the individual exchange rates in exceptional cases in which the existing rates were deemed inviable. These readjustments were called **devaluations** or **revaluations** depending on whether the value of the currency was adjusted down or up relative to the U.S. dollar. However, such readjustments were not intended to be part of the central banks' daily business.

BREAKDOWN OF BRETTON WOODS AND FLOATING EXCHANGE RATES

The Bretton Woods system functioned smoothly throughout the 1950s and most of the 1960s. As time went by, however, repeated episodes occurred in which the individual central banks ran low on official reserves. Maintaining a healthy supply of official reserves was important in this system because by using some of these reserves to buy their own currency in the open market a country's central bank could boost its demand artificially whenever its exchange rate showed signs of sagging in the private market. With official reserves low, however, individual currencies became subject to **speculative attacks.** Such attacks happened when private investors feared that low official reserves would render the central bank incapable of supporting the official exchange rate and thus force it to devalue. Because the devaluation of a currency implies losses for those holding it, expectations of an upcoming devaluation would send a stream of investors to the central bank asking to convert their funds into foreign currencies before it was too late. Such conversions obviously would drain the official reserves even more. In this way, relatively minor weaknesses could quickly destabilize a currency and force its devaluation.

Although the Bretton Woods system was designed to accommodate such exchange-rate realignments, it only gave prescriptions for the adjustment of one exchange rate at a time *vis-à-vis the U.S. dollar.* Thus, when the U.S. dollar itself became subject to a speculative attack in the early 1970s, the system faced a problem it was not equipped to handle. The problem was that *a devaluation of the U.S. dollar required a simultaneous revaluation of all the other currencies.** Such a simultaneous revaluation was actually undertaken in December 1971 as the result of an international agreement, called the Smithsonian agreement because the talks leading to the agreement were held in the Smithsonian Institution in Washington, D.C.

However, the Smithsonian agreement did not end the speculative attacks on the dollar. After repeated difficulties, the Western countries gave up defending the fixed exchange rates in March 1973. Since then, the major currencies have been allowed to **float;** that is, their relative exchange rates have been determined by the market. The foreign-exchange market has subsequently become a major commercial undertaking, with the large commercial banks as its major players. Because currencies are traded in all the major financial centers, which are located in different time zones, a virtually continuous, worldwide market in foreign exchange now exists.

MANAGED FLOAT, PEGGING, AND REGIONAL SYSTEMS

The fact that exchange rates are allowed to float does not mean that the central banks and the ministries of finance around the world have lost interest in exchange rates. They remain, in fact, the subject of intense and continuous scrutiny. Policy moves are influenced by the exchange-rate movements; and policy moves designed to influence these rates are undertaken regularly. Central banks intervene regularly in the foreign-exchange markets in order to maintain the values of their currencies within desired limits. Especially since the mid-1980s, concerted efforts to align the major currencies within relatively narrow bands have been a regular agenda item for the meetings of the so-called **Group of Seven,** or G7, which consists of the United States, Japan, Germany, Canada, France, Italy, and the United Kingdom. These activities are reminiscent of those undertaken to support the fixed rates under the Bretton Woods system. The differences are that the target ranges for the exchange rates are less well defined and that the coordinated efforts are undertaken somewhat informally in the absence of an umbrella agreement like that reached at Bretton Woods.

Some countries have gone further. Most developing countries have decided to **peg** their currencies to that of some industrialized country,

---

*You might think that the dollar could be devalued by an increase in the official dollar price of gold. However, since the prices of gold in the other currencies were fixed as the product of the dollar price and the individual exchange rates, such an adjustment would raise the price of gold in *all* currencies, which would have no effect on the exchange rates.

such as the U.S. dollar, the British pound, or the French franc. The choice of currency is sometimes guided by the country's colonial history; for example, former French colonies may peg their currency to the French franc. Other countries, including developing countries as well as some small industrialized countries, peg their currencies to an *average* of the currencies of the countries with which they trade the most. This practice is called pegging to a *basket* of currencies rather than to a single currency. An intermediate arrangement between pegging and floating is the so-called **crawling peg,** whereby the exchange rate is set by the central bank but adjusted frequently, for example, in response to inflation.

Perhaps the most important steps toward reestablishing fixed exchange rates have been taken by the members of the **European Monetary System** (**EMS**). These countries, which include Germany, France, Italy, and, starting in 1990, Great Britain, have agreed on a system of fixed or near-fixed exchange rates *among themselves.* This means that these currencies float as a group vis-à-vis the U.S. dollar and the Japanese yen, while maintaining stable rates among themselves. All the members of the EMS are also members of the **European Community** (the **EC**). Plans for a common EC currency are currently being negotiated. We return to these plans in Section 10.4.

Another region worth mentioning in this context is Eastern Europe. Because the governments of these countries until recently have not favored private markets, their currencies have not been **convertible;** that is, private trade in these currencies has been prohibited. Trade with the west as well as within Eastern Europe has been undertaken through government-owned companies, which have either worked out barter arrangements or received special allocations of "hard" (that is, Western) currency from the government. With the recent political changes in many of these countries, major revisions in this system are now under way. The most dramatic change is the monetary union between East and West Germany and the subsequent unification of Germany, which we discuss further in Section 10.4.

10.2 THE ECONOMICS OF FLOATING EXCHANGE RATES

Like any other market, the foreign-exchange market is governed by supply and demand. However, the supply and demand for a currency are driven by different forces than, say, the supply and demand for toothpaste. First, it is important to bear in mind that exchange rates are the relative prices of different *monies.* Because the money is used to buy and sell real goods and services, its value is influenced by the goods and services it can buy. This insight has led to the hypothesis of **purchasing** power parity (**PPP**), which says that exchange-rate movements are governed by relative rates of inflation.

Since currencies are also *assets*, however, exchange rates should be influenced by forces similar to those behind other asset prices. This perspective has given rise to the so-called **asset approach** to exchange-rate analysis, which emphasizes international differences in interest rates and expectations about future exchange-rate changes. This approach has proved to be particularly useful for the understanding of short-term movements in the foreign-exchange market, while purchasing power parity is useful as a guide for long-term trends.

PURCHASING POWER PARITY (PPP)

The PPP hypothesis starts with the notion that identical products should cost the same everywhere. Thus, a pair of women's shoes that costs \$200 in the United States should cost DM400 in Germany if the dollar is worth DM2. Mathematically, this idea is represented by the equation $P_i^* = E \cdot P_i$. The PPP hypothesis generalizes this idea to all goods, so the same equation holds for the overall price levels at home and abroad as well as for the individual prices. In other words, $P^* = E \cdot P$, which implies the PPP equation,

$$(10.1) \qquad\qquad E = P^*/P.$$

When this condition holds, the exchange rate reflects the purchasing power (in terms of real goods and services) of the home currency relative to that of the foreign currency.

This hypothesis is intuitively appealing, but does it hold true in practice? Figure 10.1 provides some evidence related to this question by plotting the exchange rate of the dollar vis-à-vis the deutsche mark since 1960 against the relative price levels in the United States and West Germany, as measured by their respective consumer price indices. This graph does show a common downward trend in the two series, which suggests that the total decline in the dollar over the past 20 years is related to the higher average inflation in the United States.

However, the match of the *short-run* movements in the graph is not good at all. An important reason for the short-term failure of the **PPP** appears to be that the foreign-exchange market adjusts much more quickly than the markets for goods and services. Foreign-exchange transactions can take place electronically in a matter of seconds, and the exchange rates themselves may change equally fast. In contrast, real goods and services need to be produced, and changes in their prices are undertaken much more cautiously. Because of this difference, we should not expect adjustments in the exchange rate to wait for price-level changes. Rather the short-run functioning of the foreign-exchange market is very much like that of other financial-asset markets, such as stocks and bonds.

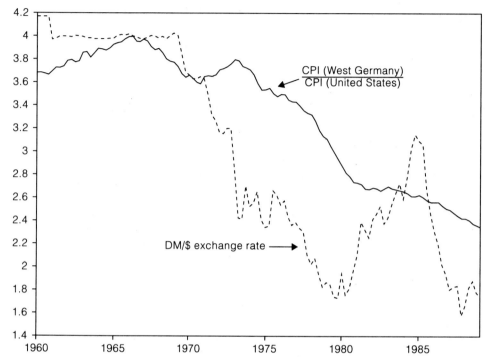

FIGURE 10.1   Evidence related to the PPP hypothesis for the United States and West Germany. The price indices have been scaled such that their ratio exactly equals the exchange rate for the first quarter of 1970. This scaling is needed because the price levels are expressed as indices whose absolute values are arbitrary. Of course, the fact that the scaling makes the exchange rate and the relative price level coincide for the first quarter of 1970 does not imply that PPP fit particularly well at that time.

THE ASSET APPROACH TO THE FOREIGN-EXCHANGE MARKET

The asset approach starts from a comparison of the nominal returns on financial investments at home and abroad. At home, this return is approximated by the nominal home interest rate, i. For investments abroad, the return consists of two parts: the foreign interest rate, i^*, and the expected appreciation of the foreign currency over the term of the investment. For a one-year investment, for example, an investor in the home country first needs to buy the foreign currency in order to undertake the investment and then needs to sell it a year later in order to enjoy the proceeds. If the value of the foreign currency rises over this period, the investor earns a capital gain, which is part of the return on the investment. At the time the investment is made, the future exchange rate is unknown, so the investor's decision must be based on *expected* changes. Moreover, because we have defined the exchange rate as the value of the *domestic* currency, the expected rate of increase in the value of the foreign currency is the expected rate of decline in the exchange

FIGURE 10.2

The rates of return on financial investments at home and abroad and the equilibrium exchange rate.

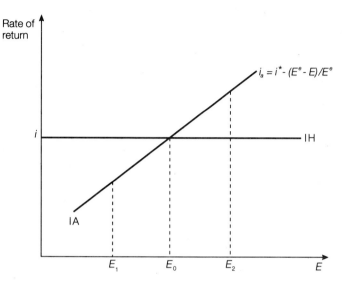

rate. Letting E^e denote the expected future exchange rate and i_a the rate of return on investment abroad,* we can write this return as

(10.2) $i_a = i^* - (E^e - E)/E^e.$

Because the formula on the right of this equation can also be written as $i^* - 1 + E/E^e$, we see that the return on investment abroad is an increasing function of the exchange rate, given the foreign interest rate and the expected future exchange rate. The reason for this relationship is that if the exchange rate rises now it will have a shorter distance to go to reach its expected future level. Therefore the expected increase in the exchange rate over time is lower, but then the expected rate of increase in the *foreign* currency is *higher,* which adds to the rate of return of investing abroad.

The upward-sloping curve labeled IA in Figure 10.2 shows the relationship between the exchange rate and the nominal return on financial *investment abroad* implied by equation (10.2). The exchange rate is measured along the horizontal axis, while the vertical axis measures rates of return. The curve is drawn for a given foreign interest rate i^* and a given expected future exchange rate E^e. The horizontal line labeled IH shows the return on *investment at home,* which is the nominal domestic interest rate i.

This diagram can be used to illustrate how the foreign-exchange mar-

---

*It may seem curious that the change is written as a percentage of the expected future value as opposed to the current value. The difference matters very little in practice, but the form used here simplifies some of the subsequent formulae.

ket reaches equilibrium. Suppose the exchange rate is E_1 in figure 10.2. Then the return on investments abroad falls short of that on investments at home (i). Assuming the two investment alternatives are about equally risky, we then expect all investors to transfer their funds to the home country in order to take advantage of the higher return. By doing so, they raise the demand for the home currency and drive up its price, which is the exchange rate. Similarly, if the exchange rate were higher, say E_2, the rate of return would be higher for investing abroad, so the investors would have an incentive to move funds abroad. These movements would increase the supply of the home currency and thus drive down the exchange rate. However, when this rate reaches the level E_0 in the figure, the IH and the IA curve intersect, so the rates of return on the two types of investment are equal. Then no investor has any further incentives to move his or her funds, and the international capital market is in equilibrium. The condition for this equilibrium is that the domestic interest rate equals the rate of return on financial investment abroad. This condition is known as the **interest parity** condition and can be written as follows:

(10.3) $$i = i^* - (E^e - E)/E^e.$$

For given expectations, the interest parity condition relates the exchange rate to the international **interest differential**, $i - i^*$. To see this, solve equation (10.3) for the current exchange rate:

(10.4) $$E = E^e(1 + i - i^*).$$

The message of this formula is as follows. If the domestic interest rate rises above the rate abroad, capital will flow into the home country to take advantage of the higher return. This flow translates into a higher demand for the domestic currency, which drives up its price. Similarly, if interest rates rise abroad with no matching change at home, capital will flow out and the exchange rate will be driven down.

To complete this story, we need to add some explanation about how exchange-rate *expectations* are formed. In the previous subsection, we saw that PPP provides a reasonable approximation to exchange-rate movements in the long run. People holding rational expectations would naturally like to take advantage of this insight. But this means that, as an approximation, we can replace the expected exchange rate with the expected relative price levels. Specifically, because the condition $E = P^*/P$ given in equation (10.1) can be used as a good predictor of long-term exchange-rate movements, we specify exchange-rate expectations as $E^e = (P^*/P)^e$. Substituting this expression into the right side of equation (10.4), we obtain

(10.5) $$E = (P^*/P)^e(1 + i - i^*).$$

This formula shows how the PPP hypothesis and the asset approach can be combined to obtain an exchange-rate model that fits both the short and the long run. This formula suggests that if the future expectations move somewhat more slowly than interest rates, the short-run movements in exchange rates will be driven primarily by interest-rate differentials. In the long run, however, international interest-rate differentials tend to be smoothed out, with the result that exchange rates are governed by the relative rates of inflation.

OVERSHOOTING AND VOLATILITY

As we saw in Figure 10.1, exchange rates tend to fluctuate quite a bit. At least part of this volatility can be explained by the interaction of PPP and interest parity described in formula (10.5). Such volatility is referred to as **overshooting**.* It occurs in response to changes in monetary policy in the home country. For a simple analysis of overshooting, we consider the case of a one-shot increase in the money supply from a situation of zero trend money growth and no growth in aggregate supply.

The IS-LM and AD-AS analysis of this situation is shown in Figure 10.3. As usual, the monetary expansion shifts the LM curve and the AD curve to the right. In the IS-LM diagram, we see that the real interest rate is reduced as the economy moves from A to B. Following the Phillips curve model of sluggish price adjustment, we see in the AD-AS diagram that real GNP rises at first, as the economy moves from the old equilibrium point F to the disequilibrium point D. In the longer run, however, we expect the Phillips curve to raise the price level to P^e as the economy eventually moves along the new AD curve to the new equilibrium G. Rational consumers will foresee this movement and adjust their expectations about the future price level accordingly.**

Over time, as just noted, the price level will start to rise. As the real money supply is reduced by the price-level increase, the LM curve will start to move gradually backward to its original position, LM_0. However, the price level itself will be permanently higher.

---

* The idea of exchange-rate overshooting was introduced by Professor Rudiger Dornbusch of the Massachusetts Institute of Technology. See R. Dornbusch, "Expectations and Exchange Rate Dynamics," *Journal of Political Economy*, December 1976, vol. 84, no. 6, pp. 1161–76.

** The expected rise in the price level actually also affects the LM curve via the expected-inflation component of the nominal interest rate. From equation (6.9), we see that the increase in inflationary expectations adds another downward shift in the LM curve. This shift occurs because, with higher inflationary expectations, a given decline in the nominal interest rate implies an even larger decline in the *real* interest rate, which is the variable used to draw the LM curve. In Figure 10.3, we have not attempted to draw the two shifts in the LM curve separately. Instead, you can interpret the shift from LM_0 to LM_1 as the total effect of both shifts.

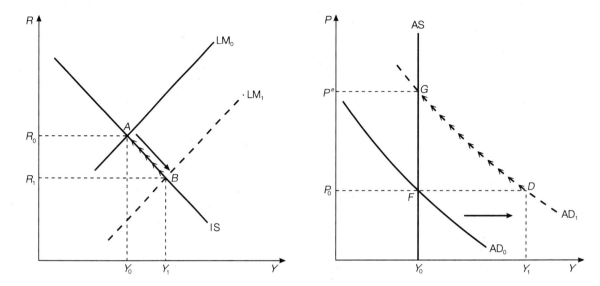

FIGURE 10.3

IS-LM and AD-AS analysis
of a one-shot monetary
expansion.

The effects of these movements on the exchange rate are illustrated in
Figure 10.4. In this diagram, both the IH and the IA curves shift. First,
as we saw in the IS-LM model, the domestic real interest rate declines.
The effect on the *nominal* interest rate is more ambiguous, because the
price level is expected to rise, and this rise pulls the expected-inflation
component of the nominal interest upward. However, because it seems
more likely that in practice the nominal interest rate will decline as
well, we focus our analysis on this case. The decline in the nominal interest rate from i_0 to i_1 then shifts the IH curve down from IH_0 to IH_1 in
Figure 10.4.

The second shift takes place in the IA curve, which represents the return on investment abroad. Because the price level is expected to increase, the purchasing-power-parity argument for the long run implies
that the expected future exchange rate will drop, say, from E_0^e to E_1^e. But
then, for any given current exchange rate, the expected exchange-rate
decline over time will be that much larger. This result means that the
value of the foreign currency can be expected to *appreciate* that much
more, adding to the return on investments abroad for any given current
exchange rate. Thus, the IA curve shifts upward from IA_0 to IA_1.

The movements in the exchange rate can now be traced in Figure
10.4. Starting from the original equilibrium at *H*, the market moves to
the new short-run equilibrium at point *J*, the intersection of the shifted
curves IH_1 and IA_1, immediately after the increase in the money supply.
As a result, the exchange rate drops from E_0 to E_1. This drop has two
causes: the drop in the domestic interest rate and the downward adjustment of the expected future exchange rate. However, as the economy
starts to move back toward a new equilibrium, the exchange rate starts

FIGURE 10.4

Exchange-rate overshooting following a one-shot monetary expansion.

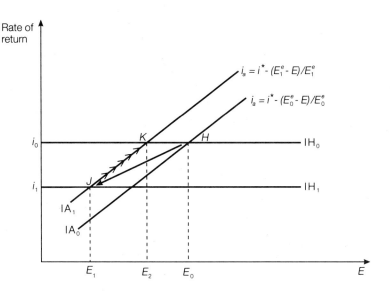

FIGURE 10.5

Effects of exchange-rate overshooting over time on the domestic interest rate, the domestic price level, and the exchange rate.

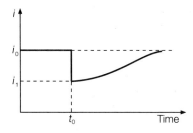 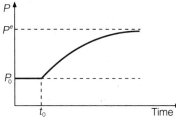 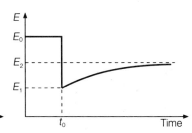

to move, too. As the LM curve in Figure 10.3 moves back toward its original position LM_0, the IH curve moves with the domestic interest rate back to *its* original position, IH_0. However, the price level has been increased permanently, so the IA curve does not shift back. In the long run, the international capital market therefore comes to rest at K, the point of intersection between the original IH curve IH_0 and the new IA curve IA_1. Here the exchange rate, E_2, is higher than the value E_1 to which it dropped at first but still lower than its original value, E_0.

Figure 10.5 illustrates how the domestic interest rate, the domestic price level, and the exchange rate will move over time in response to the monetary expansion, which is assumed to take place at time t_0 in the diagram. The interest rate first declines and then returns to its original level. The price level at first does not move but then moves gradually to its new level. The exchange rate first drops, then rises, and finally settles down at a lower level than where it started. Thus, *the negative effect on the exchange rate is larger in the short run.* Many analysts believe that this phenomenon contributes to the volatility of exchange rates.

THE REAL INTEREST DIFFERENTIAL AND THE RELATIVE PRICE OF DOMESTIC GOODS

In Chapter 5, we made the claim that net export demand, like investment demand and the demand for consumer durables, is a function of the *real*, rather than the nominal, interest rate. In support of that claim, formula (10.5) can be transformed to show that the relative price of domestic goods in the world market is a function of the difference between the real interest rates at home and abroad.

To see this, note first that expected domestic inflation, π^e, makes the domestic price level grow from its current level P to the expected future level $P^e = P(1 + \pi^e)$. Similarly, expected foreign inflation gives $P^{*e} = P^*(1 + \pi^{*e})$. These two results transform (10.5) into

$$(10.6) \qquad E = (P^*/P)\left(\frac{1 + \pi^{*e}}{1 + \pi^e}\right)(1 + i - i^*).$$

As long as each interest rate and inflation rate is small, we can approximate the product of the last two terms in parentheses as[*]

$$\left(\frac{1 + \pi^{*e}}{1 + \pi^e}\right)(1 + i - i^*) = 1 + (i - \pi^e) - (i^* - \pi^{*e}).$$

But the two expressions in parentheses on the right of this equation are just the domestic and foreign real interest rates, R and R^*. If we substitute this result back into equation (10.6) and multiply both sides by the price-level ratio P/P^*, we should obtain the following approximate expression for the relative price of domestic goods:

$$(10.7) \qquad E \cdot P/P^* = 1 + R - R^*.$$

Thus, the relative price of domestic goods in the world market is indeed determined by the international real-interest differential.

MANAGING THE EXCHANGE RATE

From a policy point of view, a low exchange rate is attractive because it reduces the relative price of domestic goods. Thus, it stimulates exports and discourages imports, which improves the current-account balance

---

[*] Start by adding and subtracting 1, so that
$$(1 + \pi^{*e})(1 + i - i^*)/(1 + \pi^e)$$
$$= 1 + (1 + \pi^{*e})(1 + i - i^*)/(1 + \pi^e) - 1.$$
Then put the last two terms over a common denominator:
$$1 + [(1 + \pi^{*e})(1 + i - i^*) - (1 + \pi^e)]/(1 + \pi^e).$$
Now multiply out to get
$$1 + [1 + i - i^* + \pi^{*e} + \pi^{*e}(i - i^*) - 1 - \pi^e]/(1 + \pi^e)$$
$$= 1 + [i - i^* + \pi^{*e} + \pi^{*e}(i - i^*) - \pi^e]/(1 + \pi^e).$$
Note first that all the terms in the numerator of the last fraction are growth rates or products of growth rates. Thus, they are small, and their magnitudes are not affected much if we replace the denominator $(1 + \pi^e)$ with 1. Second, if the growth rates are small (for example, < 0.1), then their products are even smaller (< 0.01), so we can ignore the product term $\pi^{*e}(i - i^*)$. A little rearrangement then gives the formula in the text.

and stimulates aggregate demand at the same time. On the other hand, a stimulus to aggregate demand means not only GNP growth but also rising inflationary pressures. Some of these pressures come directly from the decline in the exchange rate in the form of higher import prices.

The overshooting analysis showed how the exchange rate can be affected by changes in monetary policy. However, attempts to influence exchange rates as reported in the media are usually in the form of direct *intervention* in the exchange market. If American authorities want the U.S. dollar to rise, the Federal Reserve will buy dollars in the open market in exchange for yen, D-mark, or other foreign currencies. At the same time, critics often claim that such interventions at most have extremely short-lived effects. What does economic analysis have to say about the likely effects of interventions?

Economic analysis says that interventions work whenever they affect the supply of money. To see the connection between interventions and money supply, consider the central-bank balance sheet in Table 10.1. The asset side of this balance sheet is more simplified than those we looked at in Chapter 4 in that the central bank's holdings of government securities and loans to commercial banks have been consolidated into "domestic credit." The interesting portion of official reserves is the central bank's holdings of foreign exchange. Other assets are ignored. The main items on the liabilities side are currency in circulation and the reserves of commercial banks (held as vault cash or as deposits with the central bank), just as in Chapter 4. The sum of either side of the balance sheet equals the monetary base. Chapter 4 analyzed how a change in the monetary base translates into a change in money supply via the money multiplier process.

Consider now an intervention in which the central bank purchases its own currency, offering foreign exchange as payment. Table 10.2 shows the effects of such an intervention, with the Federal Reserve buying $500 million in the foreign-exchange market in exchange for the corresponding amount of Japanese yen. Since the yen are drawn from the U.S. official reserves, these reserves are reduced by $500 million.

TABLE 10.1 SIMPLIFIED BALANCE SHEET OF A CENTRAL BANK

ASSETS	LIABILITIES
Domestic credit Official reserves	Currency Bank reserves
Monetary base	Monetary base

TABLE 10.2   EFFECTS ON THE CENTRAL BANK'S BALANCE SHEET OF AN EXCHANGE-MARKET INTERVENTION

ASSETS		LIABILITIES	
Domestic credit	(no change)	Currency	(no change)
Official reserves	−$500 million	Bank reserves	−$500 million
Monetary base	−$500 million	Monetary base	−$500 million

TABLE 10.3   EFFECTS ON THE CENTRAL BANK'S BALANCE SHEET OF A STERILIZED EXCHANGE-MARKET INTERVENTION

ASSETS		LIABILITIES	
Domestic credit	+$500 million	Currency	(no change)
Official reserves	−$500 million	Bank reserves	−$500 million
			+$500 million
Monetary base	(no change)	Monetary base	(no change)

The people buying the yen pay by checks drawn on commercial banks, and the Federal Reserve cashes in on these checks by charging $500 million against the reserve accounts of these commercial banks. Thus, the decline in official reserves is matched by a corresponding decline in bank reserves. Currency in circulation and domestic credit are unaffected. The result is a $500 million reduction in the monetary base. (If the payments had been made in cash, the decline on the liability side would have come in the currency component, but the effect on the monetary base would have been the same.) As the decline in the monetary base is translated into a change in the money supply, the domestic interest rate rises; the resulting interest differential (as well as the decline in inflationary expectations) then boosts the exchange rate, as we saw above. In other words, *the intervention is effective because it changes the money supply.*

The reason for the widespread skepticism about the effectiveness of interventions, then, must be a belief that the monetary effects of the intervention are negated by opposite moves in domestic monetary policy, called **sterilizations.** Table 10.3 shows how such moves work. Suppose, as above, that the central bank sells $500 million of its official reserves in order to support the exchange rate of its own currency. Thus, official reserves and commercial bank reserves again both decline by $500 million. However, in order to avoid a decline in the money supply, which would be contractionary, the central bank at the same time buys domestic government securities in the open market. Then, as we saw in Chapter 4, domestic credit is increased by $500 million, matched by an equal increase in bank reserves. That means that bank reserves in the end are unchanged. On the central bank's asset side, the decline in official reserves is offset by the increase in domestic credit. Thus, the monetary base is unchanged. This analysis, therefore, suggests that *sterilized interventions are ineffective.*

Real-world cases can have room for more nuances. For example, interventions might signal an intention by the central bank regarding future policies. This signaling effect can be particularly powerful when the interventions are carried out in concert by several central banks—such as the G7 group—and perhaps accompanied by public statements. As another example, even sterilized interventions can be effective in the very short run, that is, for the few hours that the foreign exchange is actually dumped on the market. Sometimes that may be enough to change an adverse market psychology. Basically, however, interventions need to be followed up by more fundamental changes in monetary policy in order to be effective.

POLICY CONFLICTS WITH FLOATING EXCHANGE RATES

Governments and central banks usually like to aim for high and growing levels of economic activity, price stability, and a reasonable balance in the current account. Achieving all three goals at the same time can be difficult, however.

An *expansionary monetary policy* helps increase real activity, as we saw in Chapter 6. However, this gain tends to be lost in the intermediate and long run as the higher activity level puts upward pressure on the price level, as indicated by the analysis in Chapters 7 and 8. Consider now the effects of a monetary expansion on the exchange rate and the current account. We have seen that the exchange rate overshoots in the downward direction, producing a quick decline in the prices of imported goods. This effect adds an extra element to the inflationary process and is likely to start earlier than the inflation in domestic prices. The effect on the current account is ambiguous. On one hand, it is improved by the decline in the exchange rate, because domestic goods become cheaper and foreign goods more expensive. On the other hand, the increase in real GNP raises the demand for imported goods via the income effect, which tends to worsen the current account. Although the current account is likely to improve on balance, it seems clear that *the effects of a monetary expansion become much more complicated when the international aspects are taken into account.*

A *fiscal expansion* will have conflicting effects. Again, the positive effect on real activity is unambiguous, if somewhat short-lived, but the effect on the current account is equally unambiguously negative. By raising domestic interest rates, a fiscal expansion raises the exchange rate and thus makes domestic goods more expensive and foreign goods cheaper. Moreover, the rise in domestic income raises import demand even further. Thus, the current account unambiguously declines.

This insight can shed some light on U.S. fiscal policies in the 1980s. On one hand, a low-tax policy combined with high defense expenditures resulted in large government deficits. This policy has been credited by some analysts with contributing to the long expansion period during this decade. On the other hand, the fiscal expansion also appears to have had the predicted effect on the current account, namely, large and persistent deficits.

This result is the analytical argument behind the common criticism of the *twin deficits* in the United States in the 1980s. It adds strength to the argument presented toward the end of Chapter 9, which stated that the current-account deficit is a *political problem* and not just the result of the inherent attractiveness of the U.S. financial markets. In fact, according to the IS-LM analysis, part of this attractiveness comes from the high interest rates that result from the fiscal expansion.

The graph in Figure 10.6 shows the performance of the government deficit and the current-account deficit (measured in the form of net ex-

FIGURE 10.6

Deficits of the U.S. government and net exports of the United States during the 1980s, in current dollars. Budget deficits are shown as negative surpluses.

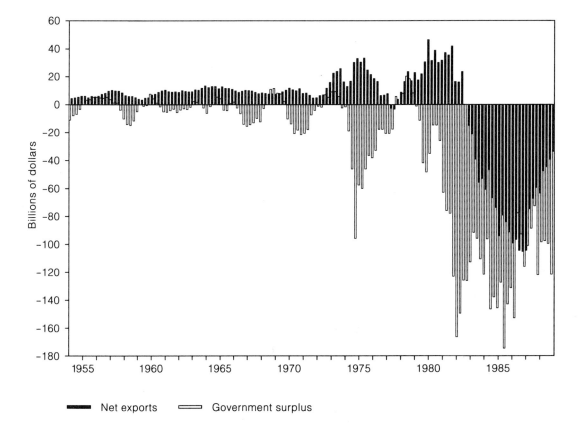

Net exports   Government surplus

ports) over time. Although the correlation between them is far from perfect, the simultaneous occurrence of large deficits in both areas during the 1980s clearly stands out. The policy dilemma goes both ways, however. Just as a fiscal expansion improves domestic activity at the cost of a worsening current account, so also a fiscal contraction improves the current account at the cost of a decline in domestic activity. Thus, if the U.S. government deficit is to be reduced, avoiding a negative effect on real GNP may be very difficult.

A further complication for an open economy is vulnerability to foreign policy changes. For example, a *monetary* expansion by a foreign central bank increases the interest differential and hence the exchange rate for the home country. The rise in the exchange rate has the usual negative effect on the home country's net export demand. However, this negative effect may be offset by the rise in foreign income, which should raise net export demand for the home country. Thus, the net effect is ambiguous.

An expansionary *fiscal* policy abroad raises the demand for exports from the home country, because foreign income rises and because the home country's exchange rate is lowered through a reduction in the interest differential. The result is a stimulation of real activity in the home country, accompanied by rising interest rates and a stimulation of inflation. These effects have been among the reasons behind the complaints by America's trading partners about the expansionary U.S. fiscal policy in the 1980s.

10.3   THE ECONOMICS OF FIXED EXCHANGE RATES

A credible commitment to a fixed exchange rate implies an expectation that the future exchange rate will remain the same as the current rate. It then follows immediately from equation (10.3) that the domestic interest rate is dictated from abroad. No interest differential can exist in equilibrium; if it did, capital would flow into or out of the country until equilibrium was reestablished. *The domestic interest rate becomes exogenous.* This situation has the further implication that the central bank *loses control over its own money supply.*

EXOGENOUS INTEREST RATE AND THE LOSS OF CONTROL OVER MONETARY POLICY

To see how this mechanism works, look again at the central bank's balance sheet given in Table 10.1. Suppose the central bank has increased the monetary base by buying domestic credit (via open market operations), with the (temporary) effect of reducing the domestic interest rate to a level below the foreign interest rate. As soon as investors perceive the interest differential, they will want to move their capital out of the country in order to earn the higher foreign interest rate. They do this by buying foreign exchange from the central bank. The central bank is not

FIGURE 10.7

The ineffectiveness of monetary policy under a fixed exchange rate.

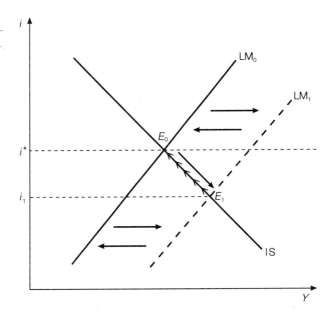

in a position to refuse, because if it did the exchange rate would be bid down below the level that the central bank is committed to defend. However, as official reserves are sold, the monetary base is again reduced, causing the interest rate to rise. This process will continue until the money supply has returned to its original level and interest parity is reestablished.

This analysis illustrates a fundamental insight. Because money is an artificial commodity created by the central bank to facilitate trade, its value must be protected by special means. This protection can take one of two forms: either a direct control over the supply of money or a fixation of the exchange rate backed up by whatever money supply is needed to protect that rate. The central bank must choose one form or the other; it cannot choose both at the same time.

Figure 10.7 illustrates the situation described above in the IS-LM model. Initially, the LM curve is at LM_0. The domestic nominal interest rate equals the foreign interest rate i^*, so the domestic *real* interest rate equals the nominal rate minus expected inflation. However, in this case we can allow ourselves to treat expected inflation as fixed, because the price level turns out to be unaffected. Then we might as well treat the expected inflation rate as zero, so the nominal and the real interest rates are equal. This is the reason why this IS-LM diagram has been drawn with the *nominal* interest rate along the vertical axis.

As the central bank attempts to raise the money supply via open market operations, the LM curve shifts to the right to LM_1; the domestic interest rate momentarily declines to i_1. However, as investors observe the

FIGURE 10.8

Fiscal policy under a fixed
exchange rate.

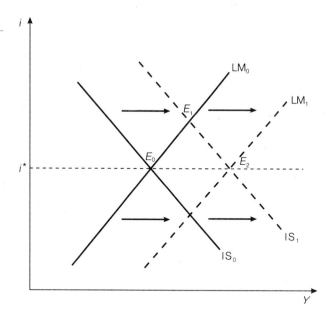

interest differential, they start to buy official reserves from the central
bank. The resulting decline in the monetary base shifts the LM curve
back toward the left again. This process goes on as long as the domestic
interest rate stays below i^*; thus, it does not stop until the LM curve is
back at LM_0.

INCREASED POWER OF FISCAL POLICY

Consider an expansionary fiscal policy under a fixed exchange rate. This
situation is illustrated in Figure 10.8. Again, we assume that expected
inflation is zero. As in Chapter 6, an expansionary fiscal policy shifts the
IS curve to the right from IS_0 to IS_1. If the exchange rate had been variable, the new equilibrium would now have been at E_1, with a higher
GNP but also a higher interest rate. However, with a fixed exchange
rate, an elevated domestic interest rate will set off capital flows *into* the
country as investors seek to take advantage of the higher interest rate.
They can buy domestic currency from the central bank, which again has
no choice but to accept the transactions. This time, official reserves *rise*,
and hence the monetary base also rises. As a result, the LM curve shifts
to the right from LM_0 to LM_1, that is, until the domestic interest rate
again equals the world interest rate. This means that the GNP effect of
the fiscal expansion is enhanced. Investment is not crowded out, because the interest rate is maintained at the world level. On the other
hand, the current account is affected adversely because of the income
effect on import demand. The twin-deficit phenomenon is not avoided
under fixed exchange rates either.

DEVALUATIONS AND EXCHANGE CONTROLS

Suppose a country is experiencing a combination of sluggish real activity and a deficit on the current account. If the exchange rate had been floating, both problems could have been ameliorated by an expansionary monetary policy, provided the net effect on the current account was positive. With a fixed exchange rate, the government finds itself in a bind; as we just saw, fiscal policy would have opposite effects on real activity and the current account.

Another opportunity remains, however, namely to *devalue* the exchange rate. A **devaluation** is a discrete reduction in the official exchange rate announced by the central bank. It does not imply floating, because the central bank guarantees that the new rate will be as fixed after the devaluation as the old rate was before. A similar discrete *increase* in the exchange rate is referred to as a **revaluation.**[*]

The immediate effect of a devaluation is to make imports more expensive at home and exports cheaper abroad, so the current account is improved. Because this effect is not induced by an interest-rate change, as it would have been with a floating exchange rate, it is natural to model the resulting increase in net export demand as a rightward shift in the IS curve, from IS_0 to IS_1 in Figure 10.9. This shift tightens the money market and drives up the interest rate from i^* to i_1. However, the resulting interest differential cannot persist with a fixed exchange rate. As investors seek to transfer funds into the country in order to take advantage of the higher rate, they sell foreign exchange to the central bank at the new exchange rate. Official reserves thus rise, and the monetary base rises with it. The LM curve consequently shifts to the right from LM_0 to LM_1, which is just enough to bring the domestic interest rate back in line with the world interest rate. Both objectives have been attained: real GNP has been increased, and the current account has been improved.

In fact, these effects are the same as the effects of an expansionary monetary policy under floating exchange rates, which we studied in Section 10.2. In this sense, devaluations and revaluations are a substitute for monetary policy for a country whose exchange rate is fixed. Unfortunately, they also have all the disadvantages of monetary policy. A devaluation is inflationary, first raising the prices of imported goods and then setting off inflationary pressures in the domestic markets by raising aggregate demand. In the long run, a devaluation has no more real effects than a monetary expansion. In particular, it does not affect the relative price of domestic and foreign goods, $E \cdot P/P^*$, in the long

---

[*]Note that the words *devaluation* and *revaluation* are used only with regard to discrete changes in exchange rates that otherwise are fixed. They should be distinguished from the words *depreciation* and *appreciation*, which are used to describe market-determined changes in floating exchange rates.

FIGURE 10.9

Devaluation in the IS-LM
model.

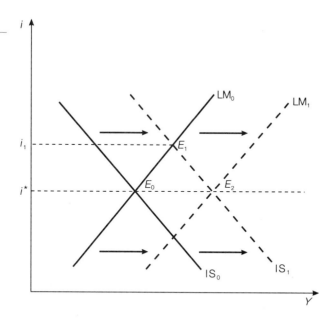

run, because the domestic price level will eventually rise by the same percentage as the devaluation of the exchange rate.

A devaluation also has an additional dynamic complication that can be quite serious. If a central bank devalues its currency, it reneges on its commitment to keep it fixed. Such a move can easily make investors suspect that devaluations may happen again, which would make the expected future exchange rate fall short of the current rate. To prevent an outflow of capital, the central bank would need to maintain a *higher* interest rate at home than abroad, as suggested by formula (10.3), until its reputation was reestablished. In terms of Figure 10.9, this means that the LM curve would not shift all the way to LM_1, a situation that would put a damper on the boost to real activity.

Another way for a central bank to circumvent its inability to control the money supply under fixed exchange rates is to impose **exchange controls.** Such controls have been widely used by less-developed and East-bloc countries, as well as elsewhere. Simply put, they limit the public's opportunity to buy and sell foreign exchange from the central bank. The central bank thus regains some control of its foreign reserves and hence the monetary base. Because investors are restricted, they are unable to move enough funds to eliminate interest differentials. Monetary policy can thus be used, but at the cost of restricting capital movements that could have led to a better allocation of productive resources. This cost is one important reason why most Western countries have given up exchange controls.

A DOMINANT COUNTRY UNDER FIXED EXCHANGE RATES

If control over monetary policy is unavailable under fixed exchange rates, how did the U.S. Federal Reserve conduct an active and independent monetary policy during the years of the Bretton Woods agreement? The answer is that the United States, as the leader of that system, was not bound by the fixed exchange rates. All the other countries were obliged to keep the values of their own currencies fixed vis-à-vis the U.S. dollar, which left the United States "off the hook." If the United States opted for monetary expansion, as it did in the late 1960s and early 1970s, the other countries were forced to keep their exchange rates at the agreed-upon levels by increasing their money supplies as well.

In today's situation, Germany's position in the European Monetary System is the most important example of a dominant power in a system of fixed exchange rates. Because of the importance of the German economy, the other EMS members essentially have delegated the conduct of monetary policy to the Bundesbank.

10.4 THE FUTURE OF THE INTERNATIONAL MONETARY SYSTEM

Modern economic history has seen movements back and forth between systems of fixed and floating exchange rates. As we saw in Section 10.1, the postwar period started with fixed exchange rates under the Bretton Woods system, which was subsequently taken over by a system of floating exchange rates. More recently, however, important steps have been taken in the direction of fixed exchange rates. Before we leave this issue, it is reasonable to ask what the next step is likely to be. The clue lies in the advantages and disadvantages of fixed and floating exchange rates.

ADVANTAGES AND DIS-ADVANTAGES OF FLOATING EXCHANGE RATES

The main advantage of floating exchange rates is their flexibility. The governments are relieved of the obligation to manage the foreign-exchange market, and the private sector is relieved of some government interference. Moreover, each country retains full control of its monetary policy and can use it freely for domestic needs.

The second advantage is in the area of crisis management. The speculative attacks discussed in Section 10.1 simply do not occur, because the central bank has no obligation to buy or sell official reserves. Furthermore, international crises, such as the oil price shocks of the 1970s, can be managed by each country separately, without the need for cumbersome international policy coordination.

On the other hand, when each country can control its monetary policy, there is a temptation to use it counterproductively. For example, individual countries might attempt expansionary monetary policies in order to stimulate their economies and to keep their exchange rates low and thus obtain a competitive advantage. Of course, the real stimulation from a monetary expansion is bound to be short-lived, and it is impossible for all exchange rates to decline relative to each other at the same time. Thus, the advantages are likely to be short-lived, while the long-run effects are likely to persist in the form of higher inflation.

In terms of the domestic economy's reaction to shocks and policy moves in other countries, flexible exchange rates can be both an advantage and a disadvantage. The activity level in a country with a flexible exchange rate can be quite sensitive to, say, the level of optimism among foreign managers for two reasons. First, if increased pessimism dampens foreign production activity (as in the example in Section 6.4), it also reduces the demand for imports from the home country because the foreign income level declines. Second, the resulting decline in foreign activity also reduces the foreign interest rate, which makes the home country's exchange rate increase and thus raises the relative price of goods from the home country. Foreign fiscal policy would have similarly double effects, rendering the home country vulnerable to swings in other countries' fiscal policies, as mentioned toward the end of Section 10.2.

On the other hand, the discussion in Section 10.2 also indicated that the sensitivity to unwanted fluctuations in foreign *monetary* policies is more ambiguous. While a foreign monetary tightening hurts the home country's net export demand by reducing the foreign income level, it also reduces the relative price of home-country goods by raising the foreign interest rate and hence the exchange rate. However, as mentioned above, all countries eventually suffer the inflationary consequences if each consistently tries to improve its competitive position by following a more expansionary monetary policy than its neighbors.

ADVANTAGES AND DIS-ADVANTAGES OF FIXED EXCHANGE RATES

Whereas floating exchange rates allow policy abuses, fixed exchange rates provide discipline. Remember that a country with a fixed exchange rate loses control of its monetary policy. Of course, the money supply can be increased if the increase is carried out in unison by all countries, and a dominant country has the privilege of forcing its policies on the follower countries. However, for most countries most of the time, a fixed exchange rate means that monetary policy cannot be used. While the loss of a policy instrument may be frustrating, it also supplies an element of discipline that can prevent counterproductive policies.

An older argument for fixed exchange rates is that they provide predictability and stability in the world economic system. This view has been challenged repeatedly, because the fixed exchange rates of the Bretton Woods system were accompanied by a number of crises. Furthermore, no monetary system can eliminate the inherent risk of doing business.

A particular instability problem arises when the dominant country's monetary policies hurt the interests of the other countries in a system of fixed exchange rates. A monetary tightening in the dominant country hurts activity in all countries, not only via the income effect on the dominant country's import demand (as in the case of flexible rates), but also because the resulting increase in the dominant country's interest rate spreads to the other countries under fixed exchange rates. At the same time, the offsetting relative-price effect that we observed in the case of flexible exchange rates disappears when exchange rates are fixed. Similarly, expansionary monetary policies in the dominant country unambiguously stimulate activity everywhere in the short run, whereas in the longer run they equally unambiguously breed inflation everywhere. Thus, in the late 1960s and early 1970s, the European members of the Bretton Woods system complained that they had to suffer the inflationary consequences of the expansionary monetary policy of the United States.

On the other hand, fixed exchange rates put somewhat of a damper on the international effects of fiscal policy moves or changing expectations in the dominant country. As in the case of flexible rates, increased pessimism or a fiscal contraction in a dominant country reduces its import demand because its income declines. However, with fixed rates the relative-price effect on this demand disappears and, as a counteracting effect, the implied decline in the dominant country's interest rate spreads abroad, where it has a stimulating effect.

Current policy debate emphasizes an entirely different advantage of fixed exchange rates, namely that they eliminate the need for *foreign-exchange management* by the private sector. Even if the foreign-exchange market functions efficiently, it is a complicated machinery. It requires a good deal of management talent that perhaps could be used more productively. As an extreme example, think of the additional burden on business that would be created if the 50 American states each had freely floating individual currencies, which American business would have to juggle in their daily transactions. Many companies operating today in Europe, with all its different national currencies, face an environment that is not entirely different from this hypothetical situation.

One type of exchange cost for European business would also remain if the respective currencies were tied permanently to each other with fixed exchange rates—the cost of actually exchanging currency each time a transaction takes place. This cost is particularly annoying for business travelers, who always need to use the local currency. This problem could be solved by going beyond fixed exchange rates to a *common currency.*

RECENT DEVELOPMENTS

During recent years, a number of countries have taken steps in the direction of again fixing exchange rates or at least making them less variable. The first example of such steps being taken was the monetary union between East and West Germany, which preceded by a few months the political unification of the two Germanies in late 1990. The formation of this monetary union differed somewhat from the typical case of fixing the exchange rate between two market economies. On the one hand, it was made somewhat easy by the strong national and cultural ties that existed between the two former countries despite 45 years of separation. At the same time, it had to contend with the adjustment problems of transforming the former East Germany from a centrally controlled economy to a market-oriented economy. Nevertheless, an important motivation for the German monetary union was to avoid the transaction costs of having to exchange the two types of mark for each other whenever a transaction between the former East Germany and the former West Germany was to take place.

The same theme recurs in the work toward a European Monetary Union (EMU) among the member countries of the EC.* Since 1979, the central banks of most of these countries have cooperated in a somewhat looser exchange-rate system known as the European Monetary System (EMS). The United Kingdom, after having declined to cooperate in the earlier efforts, joined this system in 1990. The system defines a set of central exchange rates among the member-country currencies *relative to each other* but not relative to other world currencies, such as the U.S. dollar or the yen. Whenever an exchange rate approaches a level of 2.25% up or down from its central rate, the central bank is supposed to intervene in the exchange market or manipulate domestic credit (for example, through discount-rate adjustments) to keep the exchange rate in line. In practice, this system has come to be dominated by its strongest economic power, Germany. Thus, it is not much of an exaggeration to call the EMS a D-mark–based system, whose monetary policies are determined in the Frankfurt headquarters of the German central bank, the Bundesbank.

The EMU, if realized, will be a more comprehensive system. Current plans identify three stages in building this union. The first stage consists of the removal of all exchange controls among the EC member states. This step was completed in July 1990. The second stage is a transition period intended to result in completely and permanently fixed relative exchange rates and monetary policy coordination. The third and final

---

* The member countries of the European Community are Belgium, the Netherlands, Luxembourg, France, Italy, Germany, the United Kingdom, Ireland, Denmark, Greece, Spain, and Portugal.

stage will replace the national currencies with a common European Currency Unit (ECU) and establish one common central bank, perhaps modeled after the Federal Reserve system. The ECU already exists as a unit of account defined as a weighted average of EC currencies, and it is used for some transactions. The goal of the EMU as currently proposed is to make it the only legal tender of the EC.

The third development worth noting in the world economic system is the consultations among the G7 countries. Although agreement is not always reached, the very fact that the consultations are being held is indicative of a desire to maintain some control over the exchange rates among the major world currencies. The governments of the leading economic powers are not necessarily happy about freely floating exchange rates. Market interventions have become heavy and frequent, and the exchange-rate fluctuations seem to have been somewhat more damped since these consultations became a regular phenomenon in the mid-1980s.

These tendencies have led some observers to predict that we will soon have a common *world currency*. At this stage, such predictions obviously are pure speculation. However, further developments in the international monetary system are well worth watching.

CHAPTER REVIEW

1. The international monetary system has evolved from the Bretton Woods system of fixed exchange rates into a world market of government-monitored floating exchange rates, mixed with a variety of local and regional arrangements to limit exchange-rate movements.

2. The movements of exchange rates can be explained reasonably well by purchasing power parity in the long run and interest parity in the short run. Overshooting behavior produces volatility. The relative price of domestic goods is determined by the real-interest-rate differential.

3. A floating exchange rate can be managed with official interventions provided the interventions are backed up by overall monetary policy. Sterilized interventions are much less likely to succeed.

4. Under floating exchange rates, an expansionary monetary policy increases activity and (probably) improves the current account. Its inflationary effects come in part from abroad, partly—and later—from the home markets. An expansionary fiscal policy stimulates activity but produces deficits on the current account. An open economy is also influenced by policy changes abroad.

5. Under fixed exchange rates, the interest rate is exogenous and monetary policy is ineffective. In contrast, fiscal policy is more powerful than under floating rates but has the same conflicting effects on real activity and the current account as under floating rates.

6. Devaluation of a fixed exchange rate is a substitute for monetary expansion. However, it is inflationary and can create expectations of further devaluations, which will necessitate higher interest rates at home than abroad.

7. A dominant country in a system of fixed exchange rates usually is free to conduct mon-

etary policy despite the fixed rates. This situation described the United States under the Bretton Woods system and characterizes Germany under the European Monetary System.

8. Recent developments, such as the EMS, the planned EMU, and the G7 consultations, suggest a movement toward fixed or less variable exchange rates. A major motivation is the cost of managing and operating the foreign-exchange market.

NUMERICAL EXERCISES

1. Consider the following IS-LM model of an open economy under a floating exchange rate:

$C + I = 2,790 + 0.3Y - 6,000i$,
$X = 3,960 - 0.05Y - 4,000E \cdot P/P^*$,
$E \cdot P/P^* = 1 + i - i^*$,
$M/P = 50 + 0.3Y - 6,000i$.

Assume zero inflationary expectations at home and abroad, so that nominal and real interest rates can be used interchangeably.
a. Construct and explain the IS equation.
b. Solve the model for real GNP, the domestic interest rate, the relative price of domestic goods, and net exports given $M/P = 800$, $G = 600$, and $i^* = 0.10$.
c. For the same variables that you solved for in part (b), compute the effects of an expansionary monetary policy in the home country that raises M/P to 1,020. Identify the ambiguity in the effect on the current account.
d. Similarly, compute the effects of a domestic fiscal expansion that raises G to 800. Identify the conflict between internal and external goals.

2. Suppose you have the following model for an open economy under a fixed exchange rate:

$C + I = 2,790 + 0.3Y - 6,000i$,
$X = 3,960 - 0.05Y - 4,000E \cdot P/P^*$,
$M/P = 50 + 0.3Y - 6,000i$,
$i = i^*$.

Assume zero inflationary expectations at home and abroad, so that nominal and real interest rates can be used interchangeably.
a. Construct and explain the IS equation.
b. Solve the model for real GNP, the money supply, and net exports given $G = 600$, $i^* = 0.075$, $E = 0.975$, $P = 1$, and $P^* = 1$. Do you find this model easier or harder to solve than the model with a floating exchange rate in exercise 1? Why?
c. Find the effects on the same variables as in part (b) of a fiscal policy in the home country that raises G from 600 to 800. Why does real GNP rise by more than in the case in which the exchange rate floats (exercise 1d)? Why does the money supply rise?
d. Suppose the exchange rate is devalued by 5%. Compute the effects on real GNP, the money supply, and net exports. Why does the money supply rise? What do the results say about the arguments for and against the use of this policy instrument?

DATA EXERCISES

1. Use data for comparable interest rates for the United States and another country (for example, the rates on short-term government debt) as well as the exchange rate between the U.S. dollar and the other country's currency to compare the actual returns to U.S. residents on financial investment at home and abroad. Has there been any systematic difference? Why or why not?

2. Formula (10.3) can be solved for E^e. Use this formula, as well as data for a U.S. and a foreign interest rate and the dollar exchange rate, to compute estimates of expected future exchange rates. Compare these estimates to the exchange rates that subsequently were realized. Write a brief memo stating what you think this evidence says about the theory.

3. Compare U.S. data for trade, business cycles, and inflation before and after the floating of the dollar. Use this evidence together with other relevant information to write a memo expressing your views concerning the broad economic significance of the international monetary system.

THINKING QUESTIONS

1. It is often claimed that the international currency markets are driven more by market psychology than by rational economic decisions. If this view is correct, the rational expectation of the future exchange rate should be more correct on average than the market's expectation. In such an environment, how could you use this insight to make a profit? In practice, would you recommend such a strategy for your company?

2. From the point of view of business inside as well as outside Europe, discuss the advantages and disadvantages of a European Monetary Union, particularly the introduction of a single European currency (the ECU).

11 ALTERNATIVE APPROACHES TO BUSINESS-CYCLE ANALYSIS

Macroeconomists are known to disagree. The spectrum of disagreement is probably no wider than in many other scholarly disciplines, but it gets highlighted because the disagreements tend to follow familiar political divisions and because the matters discussed are important to business and the public.

A cynical view of these disagreements holds that after 50 years of study macroeconomists have gained no scientifically valid insights and rely instead on political demagoguery under the guise of academic language. Although it should be admitted that this view is not completely unfounded, it is probably too strong. Some disagreements undoubtedly reflect differences in political views and cannot be expected to be resolved. However, a healthier type of controversy, which arises as a result of new empirical evidence or new intellectual ideas, also exists. Although such developments might be confusing to people used to the established views, they constantly add new life to the discipline.

An alert observer of macroeconomists nevertheless faces the difficult challenge of sorting out which views seem to make sense and which do not. This chapter is intended to offer some help in meeting this challenge. The discussion centers on the long-standing controversy between Keynesian and classical macroeconomics. However, because both schools have evolved over time, we also discuss monetarism and the new classical school of macroeconomics as well as recent contributions to Keynesian and more eclectic approaches to macroeconomics. We conclude by considering the managerial implications of the presence of so many competing schools of thought.

11.1 THE FOUNDATIONS OF THE KEYNESIAN–CLASSICIST DEBATE

The difference between the Keynesian and the classical approaches centers around the issue of **equilibrium,** specifically, the question of *whether or not aggregate demand equals aggregate supply in the short run*. In Figure 11.1, the point *E* represents such an equilibrium. Classical analysis

FIGURE 11.1

Equilibrium and disequilibrium between aggregate demand and aggregate supply.

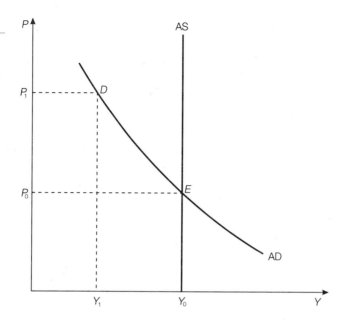

focuses on such equilibria in the short run as well as the long run. In contrast, Keynesian analysis, while agreeing that aggregate demand and aggregate supply will reach equilibrium in the long run, focuses its attention on points such as *D* for the short run. This point represents a **disequilibrium,** a situation in which the economy has a production level below aggregate supply; the latter is interpreted as potential GNP. According to Keynesian analysis, this shortfall occurs because *price rigidity* (possibly aided by *wage rigidity*) keeps the price level from adjusting to its new equilibrium level in the short run.

Classical economists may have insisted on the equilibrium assumption to different degrees and in different ways at different times. For example, **monetarism,** which is now considered an older version of classicism, might allow for short-term deviations from equilibrium but would focus on the equilibrium solution as the basis for policy discussions. The **new classical school,** which gained popularity in the 1970s, represents a return to the insistence on equilibrium even in the short run. Because price adjustments are the mechanism that makes the economy reach equilibrium, the new classical school starts from an assumption of *price flexibility* rather than price rigidity. This school has given rise to two distinct approaches. The rational-expectations approach with incomplete information, which was particularly popular during the seventies, insisted on equality between aggregate demand and aggregate supply. However, it added that aggregate supply could deviate from its normal, long-run level in the short run, not because of price rigidity but because people do not have the right information. Most recently, the real-business-cycle approach has maintained that aggregate demand equals aggregate supply but that shocks to aggregate supply generate business cycles.

Because the classical and the Keynesian schools obviously seek to explain the same empirical phenomena, their theories frequently result in similar predictions. However, they often differ when it comes to the *policy implications* of economic analysis. In general, Keynesian economists tend to advocate an *active role of government*, while classical economists tend to advocate a more *passive* or measured role. An active role makes sense if the economy has trouble finding equilibrium on its own, as in the Keynesian view of the world. In contrast, if the economy manages well when left to itself, as in the classical view, government meddling is useless at best and harmful at worst.

It should be noted that the general issue of government involvement in the economy extends beyond the question of whether the economy reaches equilibrium on its own. An equilibrium, even if reached, isn't necessarily ideal. It can involve unfair or unproductive competition, monopolistic exploitation of consumers, congestion and pollution, and an inequitable distribution of income and wealth. Most classical economists acknowledge these problems. In continuing to resist government attempts to address them, they do not deny the problems but simply fear that government action will make the problems *worse* rather than better. In particular, they argue that the government should be viewed not as a neutral and unselfish protector of all its citizens' interests but as an agency dominated by competing special-interest groups. The political system in which the interaction among such groups takes place may be even less perfect than the economic markets. Keeping the government out of the economy as much as possible, then, should prevent the problems of government from spreading to the economy.

11.2   MONETARISM

The monetarist school was the main competitor to Keynesian analysis in the 1950s and 1960s. Its popularity among academic researchers has given way to new classical analysis, but monetarist views continue to be held by many practicing economists in government and industry.

As the name indicates, this school emphasizes the importance of money. However, it is worth pointing out from the outset that its followers do *not* recommend an active use of monetary policy as an instrument to spur growth or stabilize activity. While monetarists certainly believe in the effectiveness of monetary policy, they tend to distrust the abilities of monetary policy*makers*. They argue that, because monetary policy can be used to do bad as well as good, the active use of monetary policy is likely to be *de*stabilizing. As an alternative, they prefer a policy *rule* that specifies a fixed growth rate in the money supply. As we saw in Chapter 8, such a rule should ensure a stable inflation rate in the long run.

THE MONETARIST ALTERNATIVE TO IS-LM ANALYSIS

In order to characterize monetarism analytically, it is useful to look at the monetarist alternative to the Keynesian IS-LM model. Even more than as indicated in our discussion in Chapter 6, this alternative highlights the demand for money as a *transactions demand* and hence as driven primarily by the volume of transactions. Thus, the role played by the interest rate in the money-demand function is deemphasized. In terms of the money-demand functions in formulae (6.3) and (6.4), this emphasis translates into a belief that the coefficient k_i for the interest rate is small or zero. In practice, the intercept term k_0 is ignored as well, so the money demand function simplifies to

$$(11.1) \qquad M^D = k_Y PY.$$

In words, the demand for money is proportional to *nominal GNP* (the price level, P, times real GNP, Y). When the money market is in equilibrium, so that the demand for money (M^D) equals the supply of money (M), nominal GNP is then proportional to the money supply:

$$(11.2) \qquad PY = (1/k_Y)M.$$

This formula summarizes a key monetarist tenet called the **quantity theory of money.** This theory highlights the importance of money by hypothesizing that its supply singularly and proportionately determines the nominal value of GNP. The relationship between the money supply and nominal GNP is summarized in a measure called the **velocity of money,** denoted as V and defined as the ratio of nominal GNP to the money supply: $V = PY/M$. If nominal GNP is interpreted as the nominal transactions volume, the velocity of money measures how many transactions of $1 each per year are carried out for each dollar of money supply. In other words, it indicates how many times the money supply "goes around" to various transactions during the course of a year. The quantity theory of money implies that this velocity is constant and equal to $1/k_Y$.

If the demand for money—contrary to the monetarist position—depends significantly on the interest rate, the formulae in Chapter 6 should make it clear that velocity becomes an increasing function of the interest rate.* Although most monetarists would concede that interest-rate

---

* Intuitively, if people want to economize on their money holdings because of higher interest rates, they try to get rid of their money faster, for example, by investing it in financial securities, so the money supply "goes around" faster than before. In other words, a higher interest rate raises velocity. Mathematically, in money market equilibrium, $M = M^D = k_0 + k_Y Y - k_i i$, so $V = PY/(k_0 + k_Y Y - k_i i)$. If $k_i > 0$, the last formula depends positively on i.

movements and other factors make the velocity of money fluctuate some-what in the short run, they are anxious to emphasize its stability for long-run developments and policy considerations.

The quantity theory of money serves primarily as a tool for explain-ing the monetarist view on inflation. If real GNP is determined by the equality of aggregate demand and aggregate supply, equation (11.2) can be solved for the price level to show that it is proportional to the money supply:

$$(11.3) \qquad P = M/(k_Y Y).$$

Suppose equilibrium implies that real GNP grows at a steady rate, at least in the long run. Then this formula implies that *the rate of inflation is determined by the rate of growth in the money supply.* As a remedy for inflation, monetarists would like to fix money growth to a low rate permanently.

You have probably noticed that this view of inflation parallels the analysis of inflation undertaken in Section 8.1. In Chapter 8, the velocity of money was the reciprocal of the function ℓ, which we found to be con-stant in a long-run equilibrium of constant growth in real GNP and the money supply. However, the last qualifier is worth noting; namely, the simple relationship between money and inflation in equation (11.3) holds only in a long-run equilibrium. This insight highlights the fact, often stressed by monetarists themselves, that monetarist analysis is more concerned with the long run than with the short run.

Formula (11.2), because it describes equilibrium in the money market under the monetary approach, can also be interpreted as the monetarist LM equation. Monetarists might feel somewhat uncomfortable about the assumption of a given price level that underlies the IS-LM model, because they would emphasize the link between money and inflation. However, if we keep the price level constant as a thought experiment, it becomes clear that the monetarist LM curve is a vertical line located at

$$(11.4) \qquad Y = M/(k_y P).$$

This curve is drawn on the IS-LM diagram in Figure 11.2.

Consider the effects of fiscal policy in this diagram. If the IS curve shifts outward from IS_0 to IS_1—an expansionary fiscal move—the inter-est rate rises from R_0 to R_1. However, *real GNP does not change at all.* The reason is that, with a vertical LM curve, *crowding out is complete.* The crowding out occurs for reasons similar to those in the Keynesian analy-sis. The increase in government spending (or tax-cut-induced private spending) raises the demand for money, thus putting upward pressure on the interest rate and dampening the interest-sensitive components of aggregate demand, namely, investment, consumer durables, and net ex-ports. However, under the monetarist assumption, the interest-rate in-crease puts no damper on the demand for money, because money de-

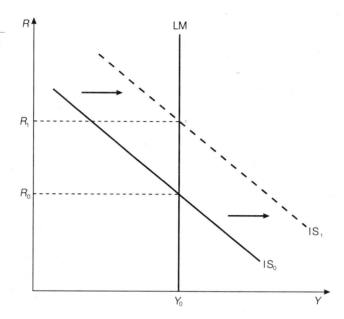

mand is not influenced by the interest rate. Thus, the crowding-out effect is allowed to go on until the demand for goods and services returns to the level it occupied before the fiscal expansion. Only then does the money market regain equilibrium.

You may have been able to recognize the similarity between the monetarist view of crowding out and the case of fiscal policy with a steep LM curve in Section 6.5. In fact, the vertical LM curve in Figure 11.2 is nothing but an extreme version of the steep LM curve in Figure 6.8, reflecting the assumption that the sensitivity of money demand to interest-rate changes is completely absent rather than just weak.

UNPREDICTABLE LAGS AND DESTABILIZATION

Such pessimism about the effectiveness of fiscal policy stood in particular contrast to the Keynesianism of the early postwar years, which strongly advocated fiscal policy as a stabilization tool. Modern-day Keynesians share this pessimism to a considerable extent. However, the two schools remain at odds over *monetary* policy. In the case of a monetary expansion, Keynesians predict an increase in real GNP in the short run, as analyzed in Chapter 6, possibly followed by an inflationary surge that eventually brings real GNP back to its potential, as analyzed in Chapters 7 and 8. Thus, in their view, monetary policy should be useful for making temporary adjustments in economic activity.

The monetarist prediction has a different emphasis. Of course, there is agreement that nominal GNP will increase when the money supply does. However, a monetarist would add that the exact timing and nature of this effect is uncertain. First, although the proportionality in (11.2) is the main rule, the effect of a money-supply change on nominal GNP may be delayed by short-run adjustment problems, and the exact timing of these adjustments may be hard to predict in each individual case. This uncertainty is important, because it can throw off the timing of monetary policy relative to the underlying business cycle. For example, if the monetary expansion comes in response to a recession and the lag is longer than expected, the monetary expansion may take effect just as the economy starts to recover on its own. The likely result in such a case is overheating and inflation.

This danger of **destabilization** makes monetarists fear the active use of monetary policy. It is the main reason why monetarists prefer a rule fixing the growth rate in the money supply to some low number once and for all. The alternative to applying such a rule is called **discretionary policy,** in which the policymakers react to each new situation as it arises. We return to the subject of rules versus discretion in policy making in the next chapter.

11.3 RATIONAL EXPECTATIONS WITH INCOMPLETE INFORMATION

The concept of *rational expectations* was introduced in Chapter 5 as part of the forward-looking theory of consumer behavior. It was also discussed in regard to the expectations-augmented Phillips curve in Chapter 8. In its basic form, it is a hypothesis that seeks to explain how people form expectations about the future values of economic variables such as income levels or inflation rates. People hold rational expectations if they (1) make use of all the relevant information available to them, (2) put this information into the correct theoretical framework, and (3) use efficient statistical techniques to process the information within this framework.

The requirement to use the correct model of the economy may seem to represent an ambiguity as long as there is disagreement over what the appropriate model is. In practice, however, rational expectations are always analyzed within the context of a particular model that implicitly is postulated to be correct. Rational expectations, then, are the predictions of the model being studied.

The assumptions underlying the rational-expectations hypothesis may seem overly rigorous; introspection might suggest that very few expectations are formed completely rationally. However, introspection might not be the right guide if in fact the expectations people hold in practice are *like* rational expectations. What matters to economic analysis is not the nature of the mental thought process but the outcome of that process. Thus, if people act *as if* their expectations are rational, the rational-expectations assumption is useful.

A reinforcing argument says that people with less-than-rational expectations tend to make wrong predictions more often than necessary and thus are at a disadvantage in the market. Consequently, market equilibria should be determined by people who do not make such mistakes, in other words, people with rational expectations.

A CLASSICAL ACCOUNT OF THE PHILLIPS CURVE

The assumption of rational expectations was a key ingredient in a highly influential paper published by Robert E. Lucas of the University of Chicago in 1973.[*] The background for the paper was a decade and a half of Keynesian literature on the positive empirical correlation between inflation and real activity and on the Phillips curve model as an analytical explanation for this correlation. The policy implication of the literature was that monetary expansions should have positive *real effects* (in other words, should stimulate real GNP) in the short run. Although monetary expansions ultimately could result in inflation, the Phillips curve presented a "menu" for monetary policy, offering a choice between higher growth now at the cost of a little more inflation later and vice versa, as discussed at the end of Chapter 8.

Lucas's model was constructed such that *unexpected* increases in the money supply would raise both real GNP and inflation, while *anticipated* increases would affect only inflation. Thus, the model reproduces the positive empirical correlation between real GNP and inflation as a result of policy *surprises*. However, if the central bank tries to use this correlation as a policy menu in the model, it will be disappointed. The problem is that any attempt to use monetary policy in a systematic way would come to be anticipated by the market, and anticipated policy changes have no real effects in Lucas's model.

THE LUCAS SUPPLY CURVE

The emphasis in Lucas's model is on the supply side. The economy consists of many sectors, and the suppliers in each sector follow normal producer behavior in that they want to supply more when the real price of their product is high, and vice versa. The real price is defined, as usual, as the nominal (dollar) price divided by the overall price level. The nominal prices of their own products are, of course, known to the suppliers. However, an important assumption in Lucas's model is that the suppliers' current information is limited to what goes on in their own sector. Therefore, the overall price level—and hence the real prices

---

[*] Robert E. Lucas, "Some International Evidence on Output-Inflation Tradeoffs," *American Economic Review*, vol. 68, 1973, pp. 326–34.

of their own products—remains unknown until the government releases its price-level statistics.

The suppliers manage this problem in the best way possible. Although the price level is unknown, supply decisions can be based on the *rational expectation* of what the price level is at the moment. Whenever the nominal price rises by more than the rational expectation of the rise in the price level, the supplier concludes that the real price has risen and responds by raising his or her output level. If it rises by less, the supplier reduces the output level.

Because the overall price level is simply a weighted average of the individual nominal prices, the outcome of this rule for the economy as a whole is that aggregate supply rises whenever the price level rises by more than its rational expectation. The **Lucas supply curve** represents this relationship. Its equation can be written as

(11.5) $$Y^S = Y^*[1 + \beta(P/P^e - 1)],$$

where β is a positive parameter. The formula can be interpreted as follows. If the price level P just equals its rational expectation P^e, then $P/P^e = 1$, so aggregate supply, Y^S, just equals potential GNP, which as before is denoted Y^*. As in the Keynesian model of aggregate supply, potential GNP is considered fixed in the analysis (or as growing slowly over time), so business cycles take place as *fluctuations around potential GNP.** Such fluctuations take place if the overall price level deviates from the rationally expected price level. If the price level rises more than expected, so that $P/P^e > 1$, then aggregate supply exceeds potential GNP, and vice versa.

As a technical point, we should note that P^e here denotes *today's* expectation of *today's* price level. This formulation differs from the models we studied earlier, in which the expectations variables represented today's expectations about the future or yesterday's expectations about today. The difference arises because not only the future is unknown in the Lucas model but the present as well.

Equation (11.5) postulates an upward-sloping relationship between the price level and real GNP; therefore, it performs the role of the Phillips curve in the Lucas model. To see this relationship mathematically, note first that, since the price level rises at the rate of inflation, π, this period's price level, P, and last period's price level, P_{-1}, are linked by the relationship $P = P_{-1}(1 + \pi)$. Similarly, if we use π^e to denote this period's expectation about today's inflation rate, we can write the *expected*

---

*Lucas's paper refers to Y^* as the "natural" rather than the "potential" output level. However, this difference is mainly semantic, so we continue to use the terminology introduced in Chapter 7.

price level as $P^e = P_{-1}(1 + \pi^e)$. These relationships clearly imply that $P/P^e - 1 = (1 + \pi)/(1 + \pi^e) - 1 = (\pi - \pi^e)/(1 + \pi^e)$, which is approximately equal to $\pi - \pi^e$. Thus, as an approximation, equation (11.5) can be rewritten as

$$(11.5') \qquad\qquad Y^S = Y^*[1 + \beta(\pi - \pi^e)].$$

In words, aggregate supply exceeds potential GNP whenever actual inflation exceeds expected inflation, and vice versa. Let us solve this equation for the inflation rate, π. Then, if we also use Lucas's assumption that the economy is always in equilibrium so that actual GNP, Y, equals aggregate supply, Y^S, we obtain

$$(11.6) \qquad\qquad \pi = \pi^e + (1/\beta)(Y - Y^*)/Y^*.$$

This formula looks very much like the inflation-augmented Phillips curve formula (8.9). The fact that the parameter γ is replaced by $1/\beta$ is immaterial and means only that γ and β are inversely related. It is equally immaterial that the expectation of today's inflation in (11.6) is formed today while that in (8.9) was formed last period, because both represent expectations about today's inflation rate. Much more important is the fact that π^e in (11.6) denotes expected inflation as derived from rational expectations, while (8.9) leaves the expectations mechanism open for further discussion. Finally, it should be noted that *no lag is involved* for the output term on the right of (11.6), so inflation is hypothesized to be related to *this* period's GNP gap. In contrast, (8.9) implies that economic activity as reflected in the GNP gap affects inflation with a lag.

UNEXPECTED VERSUS ANTICIPATED POLICY CHANGES

Figure 11.3 illustrates the interaction between aggregate demand and aggregate supply in the Lucas model. The aggregate demand curve (AD) slopes downward as usual. Potential GNP, labeled Y^*, is indicated by a dashed vertical line. The Lucas supply curve, labeled LS, slopes upward according to equation (11.5). Because the expected price level P^e is a variable on the right side of equation (11.5), every LS curve is drawn for a given level of P^e.

Suppose aggregate demand and aggregate supply initially are represented by AD_0 and LS_0, respectively. As it happens, these curves cross at E_0, the point at which actual GNP equals potential GNP. Suppose now that the money supply rises *unexpectedly*, for example, because of an unanticipated rise in the money multiplier, shifting the aggregate demand curve to the right from AD_0 to AD_1. Since this policy move is unexpected, its effect on the price level must be unexpected by the suppliers as well, so the expected price level, P^e, is unaffected. Thus, the Lucas supply curve *does not shift for an unexpected policy move*. As a result, the equilibrium between aggregate demand and aggregate supply

FIGURE 11.3

Expected and unexpected changes in monetary policy under rational expectations with incomplete information.

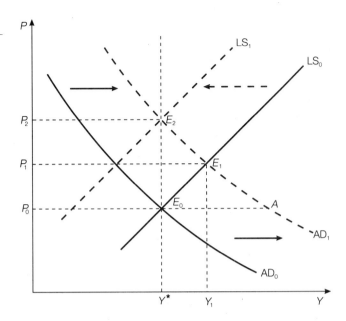

now moves from E_0 to E_1, where the new aggregate demand curve AD_1 intersects the unchanged Lucas supply curve LS_0. At this point, *both real GNP and the price level have risen* from Y^* and P_0 to Y_1 and P_1, respectively.

Although this outcome is similar to the Keynesian prediction, the mechanism by which real output changes is unique to the Lucas model. Recall that before government statistics are issued the suppliers can only observe the nominal prices of the goods they themselves supply. Thus, all that each of them observes is a nominal increase in the price of the good he or she supplies. Each supplier then has to apply rational reasoning to determine whether this increase is likely to have been a real increase in the price of the particular product or the result of over-all inflation. Since there is no expectation of an increase in the money supply, at least some probability exists that the price increase for each good is real, so each supplier acts to increase output. In hindsight, this decision turns out to have been a mistake, because in fact the money supply did increase, with the result that *all* nominal prices rose while all the *real* prices stayed unchanged. Nevertheless, the decision was ra-tional given the limited amount of information available. It is the *com-bination of rational expectations and incomplete information* that gives rise to the real effect of an unexpected money-supply increase.

As a comparison, consider the effects of an equally large *anticipated* money-supply change. The anticipation may have been the result of a prior announcement or simply of a consistent and predictable pattern of central-bank policies. Starting again from E_0 in Figure 11.3, the shift in the AD curve would be as before. However, because the policy move is anticipated, the suppliers, by applying rational expectations, correctly anticipate its effect on the price level. Thus, the expected price level, P^e, changes to exactly the same level as the new equilibrium price level, P, changes to. Their common new level is labeled P_2 in Figure 11.3. But this means that the suppliers are not "fooled" into believing that their respective real prices have increased, and consequently they do not change their supply levels. This result can be read directly from equation (11.5): If the actual and expected price levels move in tandem, aggregate supply is not affected.

This formula also suggests that an anticipated policy move shifts the LS curve to the left, because a higher expected price level, P^e, reduces the aggregate supply level Y^s for any given actual price level P. In Figure 11.3, this effect is shown as the shift in the Lucas supply curve from LS_0 to LS_1. Because we have already found that real GNP does not move away from potential GNP as a result of this policy move, we can conclude that this shift is just large enough to make AD_1 and LS_1 intersect at the point at which real GNP equals potential GNP. This point is labeled E_2 in the graph.

FUTILITY OF INFLATIONARY POLICIES

The rational-expectations model with incomplete information combines empirical predictions and policy recommendations neatly within the classical tradition. Empirically, it correctly predicts a positive correlation between inflation and economic activity, driven by the unexpected changes in money supply. However, *this correlation is not translated into a policy "menu."* Whenever the central bank attempts to use monetary expansions systematically in order to stimulate real economic activity, the economy fails to respond. Although the data give the *appearance* of a policy trade-off between real growth and inflation stability, real growth will prove elusive if the central bank seeks to promote it by systematic expansionary policies. The reason is simply that policy used systematically becomes predictable, and predictable policies in this model have only inflationary effects and no real effects.

The role played by incomplete information in this model is central and should be noted. If complete information were available freely and instantaneously, the Phillips curve correlation between inflation and real activity would disappear, because then no supplier could be "fooled" by inflation. This feature of the model has made some critics remark that it could perhaps help explain business cycles in earlier times, when information flows were modest and slow, but that it is less adequate as a description of today's information society.

Another area of criticism centers around the empirical correlation between real GNP changes on one hand and unanticipated and anticipated money-supply changes on the other. Some researchers claim to have found a significant correlation between real GNP changes and *anticipated* changes in the money supply, which would be contradictory to the predictions of the Lucas model. Others question the validity of a correlation between money growth and real GNP growth altogether, which would represent another contradiction. We return to these findings when we evaluate the various models in Section 11.6. Such criticisms made many classical researchers move their attention away from money as the 1980s began. This shift in emphasis gave rise to real-business-cycle analysis, which we discuss next.

11.4   REAL BUSINESS CYCLES

We discussed real-business-cycle analysis briefly in Chapter 7. Because this approach represents the current state of the art in classical macroeconomics, we go over its main elements again here.

THE "BACK-TO-BASICS" OF CLASSICAL MACRO-ECONOMICS

Real-business-cycle analysis represents the most relentless and consistent effort to date in terms of insisting on an *equilibrium* approach to macroeconomic analysis. Unlike monetarism, it postulates that the state of the macroeconomy at any instant—no matter how "short run"—can be interpreted as an intersection of aggregate demand and aggregate supply. Although the real-business-cycle model relies heavily on the assumption of rational expectations, there is no reliance on incomplete information as a mechanism for differentiating aggregate supply behavior with respect to expected and unexpected policy actions.

The real-business-cycle analysis, however, goes further by studying only *real* causes of business cycles, such as shocks to the productivity of capital and labor as inputs to production. In contrast, *nominal* factors, such as the money supply, are explicitly ignored as sources of business-cycle fluctuations. This attitude obviously differs sharply from the monetarist approach as well as from the approach based on rational expectations with incomplete information, although all three approaches agree that money and monetary policy are major forces in determining *inflation*.

In many ways, the real-business-cycle approach represents a return to the *original* classical approach, which represented the mainstream view prior to the Keynesian revolution in the 1930s. In that approach, short-term deviations from equilibrium were acknowledged as possibilities, and monetary disturbances were counted among the forces that could cause them. However, the temporary and transitory nature of such disequilibria was always emphasized, implying that economists would be better off studying equilibria than the process of reaching them.

Real-business-cycle analysis is a return to this approach. The basic question asked is to what extent the business-cycle fluctuations in the economy can be explained within a model in which all movements go directly from one equilibrium to another, without intervening adjustment periods. The model is based exclusively on the basic assumptions of economic analysis, namely, the equilibrium of supply and demand. "Arbitrary" elements, such as price or wage rigidities, which are not implied by these assumptions, are to be excluded from the analysis—the prices and wages in the model are simply those that produce equilibrium between supply and demand.

BUSINESS CYCLES AS SHIFTS IN AGGREGATE SUPPLY

Earlier analysis, classical as well as Keynesian, had taken for granted the idea that aggregate supply needed to be modeled as a stable, predictable relationship between the inputs to production (capital and labor) and the level of output (real GNP). Chapter 7 summarized this relationship in an **aggregate production function** that took the following form:

$$(11.7) \qquad Y^S = A(t)F(K, H_0).$$

As in Chapter 7, K stands for the capital stock that exists and is available at any given time, and H_0 stands for the employment level (measured in hours of work) that is determined by supply and demand in the labor market. The term $A(t)$ reflects the level of productivity. Because it can be assumed to grow over time as productivity improves, it is written as a function of time, t.

Earlier analysis had also always taken it for granted that productivity growth was smooth and predictable. Because the capital stock also tends to grow smoothly, business-cycle fluctuations in aggregate supply would be possible only in the form of fluctuations in the equilibrium level of employment. Such fluctuations would have to come from either the supply or the demand for labor. Of these possibilities, spontaneous fluctuations in labor supply would seem implausible. In the famous words of M.I.T.'s Franco Modigliani, it would have been necessary to explain the Great Depression in the 1930s as "a severe attack of contagious laziness!" * Fluctuations in labor demand would be consistent with aggregate demand fluctuations. Yet one would still have to explain why workers are so willing to resign their positions during recessions rather than take pay cuts and remain on their jobs.

Suppose, however, that productivity fluctuates unpredictably because

---

* This remark can be found on page 6 in Franco Modigliani, "The Monetarist Controversy or, Should We Forsake Stabilization Policies?" *American Economic Review*, March 1977, vol. 67, no. 3, pp. 1–19.

it is subject to some kind of random shock. Then all the arguments just presented evaporate, because such fluctuations clearly could generate equally random and unpredictable fluctuations in aggregate supply. *Provided productivity fluctuates enough, business cycles can be explained entirely as the results of shifts in aggregate supply.*

The logic of the real-business-cycle model can be illustrated in the AD-AS model in a highly straightforward way. Because this exercise was carried out in Chapter 7, it will be repeated here only briefly.

Figure 11.4 reproduces Figure 7.8. In this graph, the economy starts at the equilibrium point E_0, with the corresponding values Y_0 and P_0 for real GNP and the price level, respectively. Then a negative shock shifts the aggregate supply curve leftward from AS_0 to AS_1. This shift represents both the productivity shock itself and its likely negative effect on equilibrium employment. Furthermore, the aggregate demand curve shifts somewhat to the left as well, from AD_0 to AD_1, because the shock also hurts the prospects of future economic activity and thus leads people to cut down on consumption and investment. However, for a temporary shock, the shift in aggregate demand is likely to be smaller than that for aggregate supply. As the economy attains the new equilibrium E_1, the result is a decline in real GNP from Y_0 to Y_1, in other words, a recession.

It is apparent from the graph that this recession also raises the price level from P_0 to P_1. That means, of course, that the real-business-cycle approach has some difficulty explaining the positive overall correlation between real GNP growth and inflation. This is one of the weaknesses of

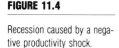

FIGURE 11.4

Recession caused by a negative productivity shock.

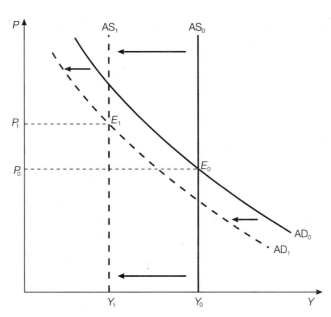

this approach that we discuss further in Section 11.6. Another weakness is the problem of identifying the productivity shocks with observable events that might precede business-cycle movements. This is another area that requires further work in real-business-cycle analysis.

POLICY IMPLICATIONS

Real-business-cycle analysis takes the laissez-faire classical policy implications to the extreme. The assumption of a vertical and spontaneously shifting aggregate supply curve, combined with the insistence on equilibrium between aggregate demand and aggregate supply, immediately precludes any stabilizing role for monetary policy. Monetary policy in this view affects only the price level (and hence, of course, inflation). Thus, the real-business-cycle approach goes further than the Lucas model by predicting that *no* changes in money supply—expected or unexpected—affect real GNP.

11.5 RECENT ADVANCES IN KEYNESIAN MACROECONOMICS

While all these changes have been taking place in classical macroeconomics, Keynesian analysis has not stood still. Like classical analysis, it has evolved and has, in fact, benefited greatly from the advances made by scholars using other approaches. The Keynesian–monetarist debate helped clarify the crowding-out problem of fiscal policy as well as the overall significance of monetary policy. The assumption of rational expectations has proved helpful in both Keynesian and classical analysis. Most recently, the concept of real business cycles has helped Keynesian analysts focus on aggregate supply as well as aggregate demand as a possible source of fluctuations.

Furthermore, important advances have taken place within the Keynesian school itself. These advances include analyses of price and wage rigidity, of the role of sectoral imbalances for business cycles, and of coordination failures in economics. Some contributors to these research efforts would probably object to having their work classified as "Keynesian." Perhaps *eclectic* would be a better word. The best justification for including these advances under a Keynesian label is that Keynesian analysis itself has become more and more eclectic over the years.

WAGE CONTRACTS AND BUSINESS CYCLES

Our analysis of the demand and supply of labor in Chapter 7 identified the equilibrium real wage as the wage that made the demand for labor just match the supply. If the real wage went above that level, firms would curtail production levels and lay off workers because of the high labor costs. But production curtailments and layoffs are exactly the stuff that recessions are made of. Thus, perhaps recessions can be explained as the result of too high wages. Such an explanation of recessions is offered by the contract-wage theory of business cycles.

This theory assumes that wages are set in advance for at least a year at a time. The wage may have been negotiated by a union, in which case it is a true contract wage, or it may be the result of an implicit understanding between employer and employee, which would make it an *implicit* contract wage.

Suppose, as is common in practice, that the contract or implicit contract specifies a *nominal* wage for the year ahead. Then the aggregate supply curve will no longer have its familiar vertical shape. If a firm's nominal price goes up and the nominal wage is fixed, the firm's nominal profit will rise. In particular, the price will more than cover the cost of producing additional goods or services, so the firm can earn even higher profits by producing more. Because this situation will apply to all firms, overall production will increase when the price level rises. In other words, *the aggregate supply curve slopes upward.*

The left side of Figure 11.5 shows such a supply curve. It is labeled $AS(W)$ to remind us that it is drawn given the nominal wage rate, W. If this wage should rise, the firms would need higher nominal prices to cover their costs at any given output level, so the aggregate supply curve would shift upward. The diagram shows such an upward shift to the curve labeled $AS(W')$. We will return to the significance of this shift shortly.

FIGURE 11.5

Business cycles under nominal contract wages.

Figure 11.5 also shows a set of aggregate demand curves. These curves are derived in the usual way. The different curves correspond to different levels of the money supply. This model assumes that equilibrium is

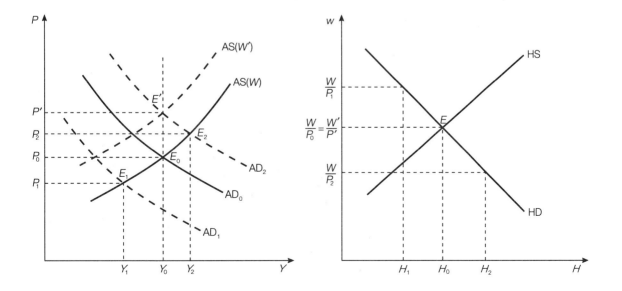

reached in the *goods* market, so aggregate demand always equals aggregate supply. However, the contract rigidity for the wage can result in disequilibrium in the *labor* market.

The right side of Figure 11.5 illustrates the labor market. The vertical axis measures the real wage, as usual. However, since the contract determines the nominal rather than the real wage, we note that the actual real wage is given as the ratio of the nominal contract wage to the overall price level, W/P. Thus, if the price level rises in the middle of the contract period, the real wage declines, and vice versa.

Suppose aggregate demand starts out at AD_0. Together with the aggregate supply curve $AS(W)$, this curve defines an equilibrium at E_0 in the left side of Figure 11.5. Suppose this was the aggregate demand level that workers and employers expected when they negotiated the wage. Then the corresponding price level, P_0, must be just the right level for the resulting real wage, W/P_0, to ensure equilibrium in the labor market.

However, suppose the money supply is now contracted, so that the aggregate demand curve shifts left to AD_1. Then the price level declines to P_1, which raises the real wage to W/P_1. The demand for labor contracts to H_1, because the real labor costs have risen. The model now assumes that employment is determined unilaterally by the number of workers firms want to hire, so employment declines from the equilibrium level H_0 to H_1 as real GNP declines from Y_0 to Y_1. The monetary contraction has had a negative real effect. Conversely, if the money supply is increased so that aggregate demand shifts to AD_2, the price level rises to P_2, the real wage declines to W/P_2, and firms seek to expand their employment to H_2. If employment is again determined by the demand for labor, employment rises to H_2 as real GNP rises to Y_2. The monetary expansion has a positive real effect.

This model essentially represents the logic of the contract-wage theory as presented in two articles by Stanley Fischer of the Massachusetts Institute of Technology and John Taylor of Stanford University.* These models were able to identify the long-standing Keynesian assumption of wage rigidity with a well-known institutional fact in the labor market. Moreover, they did not rest on an assumption of nonrational expectations. Workers and employers can be perfectly rational in these models by negotiating the contract wage so as to make it correspond to the equilibrium real wage given the expected price level. However, monetary policy implemented after the wage was negotiated would still have

---

* Stanley Fischer, "Long Term Contracts, Rational Expectations, and the Optimal Money Supply Rule," *Journal of Political Economy,* 1977, vol. 85, pp. 163–90; and John B. Taylor, "Aggregate Dynamics and Staggered Contracts," *Journal of Political Economy,* 1980, vol. 88, pp. 1–24.

real effects. Of course, these effects would be short-lived, because next time the wage was renegotiated it would be adjusted to the new realities.

Figure 11.5 illustrates such an adjustment for the case in which the money supply has been increased and kept at the new, high level. Then the next renegotiation raises the wage in order to keep up with inflation. By rational negotiation, the wage is set at just the right level to restore equilibrium in the labor market. Thus, the new nominal wage W' divided by the new price level P' equals the original equilibrium real wage rate, W/P_0. The wage increase shifts the aggregate supply curve upward to AS(W'), as noted above. Since we know that employment has now returned to its equilibrium level, real GNP must also have returned to its original level, Y_0. But then the shift in aggregate supply must have been just enough for the new aggregate supply curve AS(W') to intersect the new aggregate demand curve AD$_2$ at that level of real GNP.

This model was quite popular among Keynesian economists during the late seventies and early eighties. Unfortunately, however, it has flaws. Theoretically, some analysts have argued that contract rigidity should not make aggregate demand shifts have real effects, because the contract prices are not actual transactions prices but rather define installments of the total amount due under the contract. Therefore, according to this argument, they should not play the usual roles as incentives for supply and demand.* Empirically, the model is in trouble because it explains the decline of employment during recessions as a result of rising real wages. However, real wages do not usually rise in recessions, nor do they decline during expansions. In fact, the correlation between real wage changes and real GNP growth in the United States is essentially zero.

These observations have led a number of Keynesian researchers to look for cases of rigidities other than labor contracts. Moreover, they have sought to explain such rigidities as the result of people working for their own self-interest rather than as unexplained institutional facts.

THEORY AND EVIDENCE OF PRICE RIGIDITY

Theoretically, the assumption of price rigidity has been challenged repeatedly by the classical school as being "arbitrary," that is, an ad hoc assumption that does not follow from people's attempts to promote their own best interests. Empirically, it seemed odd to focus on stagnant prices during periods of high inflation such as occurred during the 1970s.

However, high overall inflation rates do not imply that all individual prices change quickly. As an example, a well-known recent study by Stephen Cecchetti took a detailed look at newsstand magazine prices in

---

* Robert Barro, "Long-term Contracting, Sticky Prices, and Monetary Policy," *Journal of Monetary Economics*, 1977, vol. 3, pp. 305–16.

the United States.* The infrequency with which the prices of major magazines have been adjusted was found to be quite striking. Between 1953 and 1979, the price of *Reader's Digest* had been adjusted only six times, while the price of *Time* and *Newsweek* had been changed nine times during the same period. Because the factors affecting the supply and demand of magazines must have undergone many small and perhaps some large changes during these years, this evidence suggests rather strongly that sluggish adjustments of individual prices are a fact of life.

The main explanation for price rigidity has been to allow for a *cost of price adjustments*. This category of cost has come to be called **menu costs,** because the standard example given is the cost to a restaurant of rewriting the prices on its menu.** Of course, the idea is that this type of cost exists in many industries, which would be necessary for it to be of macroeconomic significance. Retail trade is an obvious example, as demonstrated by the evidence related to magazine prices.† Moreover, industrial suppliers might want to minimize the frequency of price adjustment in the interest of maintaining good customer relationships.

The presence of menu costs does not imply that prices are rigid in any absolute sense, nor does it imply that it necessarily takes a long time for prices to change. However, since changes are costly, they will be undertaken at *infrequent intervals* rather than in response to every little change in demand or supply. Consequently, a considerable margin may exist within which aggregate demand can change before prices start to adjust. Shifts in aggregate demand can have real effects. By the same token, monetary and fiscal policy can be used to stabilize the economy, at least within limits. Of course, the menu-cost hypothesis does not address the monetarist concern that discretionary policy might be carried out in the wrong way and *de*stabilize the economy, but it does open the door for a meaningful discussion of the proper stabilization role of monetary and fiscal policy.

SECTORAL IMBALANCES

Both Keynesian and classical analysis until recently have been focused on the economy as a whole, while the study of individual sectors has been relegated to microeconomics. However, realignments among the

---

*Stephen Cecchetti, "The Frequency of Price Adjustments: A Study of the Newsstand Prices of Magazines, 1953 to 1979," *Journal of Econometrics*, 1986, vol. 31, pp. 255–74.

**A relatively simple analysis of the macroeconomic implications of menu costs can be found in N. Gregory Mankiw, "Small Menu Costs and Large Business Cycles: A Macroeconomic Model of Monopoly," *Quarterly Journal of Economics*, 1985, vol. 100, pp. 529–37.

†Interestingly, the significance of this example diminishes as bar codes take over the role of price tags. The implications of this technology for price rigidity and macroeconomic stability obviously are intriguing.

sectors of the economy may be associated with adjustment problems that can have significant effects for the overall economy. An important example of such an association is the adjustment that takes place in response to a large change in the price of oil. When the oil price quadrupled in the world market in late 1973, the increase set off a massive movement of resources out of sectors that relied heavily on energy consumption, such as the automobile industry, and into sectors that either contributed to energy production or were lighter users of energy. However, a resource transfer of this magnitude appears to be subject to important *frictions* that can delay the process and lead to temporary imbalances between the sectors. Because moving unemployed auto workers to the Texas oil fields is not a simple matter, many workers in Michigan remained idle despite a boom in the oil industry in the U.S. Southwest. The analysis in Chapter 7 suggested that the recession in 1974–75 could be explained by the *aggregate supply shock* or *inflationary shock* caused by the oil price increase. However, sectoral imbalances may have contributed to its depth. Some analysts have even suggested sectoral imbalances as the main force behind this recession.*

Credibility is added to this explanation by the experience following the precipitous decline in the price of oil in 1985–86. As expected, business in the oil region of the United States suffered greatly. Significantly, however, this decline was not offset by expansion in industries benefiting from the oil-price reduction. As a result, real U.S. GNP grew at the low average annual rate of 0.4% for the last three quarters of 1986, compared to 3.6% for all of 1985; the second quarter even saw a *decline* of 1.8%. This slowdown is difficult to explain in terms of the price-shock scenario of Section 7.4. The sectoral-imbalance hypothesis, however, can explain it as a result of friction involved in the movement of resources, this time out of the oil patch and back into the rest of the economy.**

This hypothesis does not rest on any particular assumption regarding price rigidity or equilibrium. The frictions can be described as the result of disequilibria, for example, rigid wages may lead to layoffs in the automobile industry when the oil price goes up, even though lower wages could have enabled the automobile manufacturers to keep their workers on the job. They can also be described as the result of real costs, which would be relevant in any equilibrium, such as the cost of moving, re-

* David M. Lilien, "Sectoral Shifts and Cyclical Unemployment," *Journal of Political Economy*, 1982, vol. 90, pp. 777–93.

** For further comments, see Knut Anton Mork, "Oil and the Macroeconomy When Prices Go Up and Down: An Extension of Hamilton's Results," *Journal of Political Economy*, June 1989, vol. 97, no. 3, pp. 740–44.

training, or searching for a new job. In either case, sectoral imbalances can have important macroeconomic effects.

COORDINATION FAILURES

Sectoral imbalances can be viewed as an example of a **coordination failure:** The resources needed in one sector are available, but in the wrong place and at the wrong time. The problem of coordinating the needs of the various sectors leads to a decline in overall activity.

Some recent studies have analyzed coordination failures as a more general issue. The main idea behind this literature is that a recession may be the result not of a decline in aggregate demand or aggregate supply but of a failure to match the individual levels of demand and supply in the economy.

Because this literature so far has tended to operate on a very high level of abstraction,* summarizing it in simple terms is difficult. However, some basic assumptions are worth noting. First, coordination-failure models typically study *equilibria*, but these equilibria tend to be associated with **imperfect competition,** such as oligopoly or monopolistic competition. These settings differ from, say, the Lucas model, where the business managers look only at the prices of their products (and their own guesses about the overall price level), which they take as given by the market, in order to decide how much to supply. Under imperfect competition, market prices cannot be taken as given but are the results of a complicated interaction among competing firms and their customers. Thus, a business manager needs to be concerned about what all the competing firms will do and how they will react to the manager's decision. This type of behavior, which should be familiar to any real-world manager, is referred to in technical language as **gaming behavior,** and *game theory* plays an important part in the study of coordination failures.

The gaming environment provides the context for the second assumption of coordination-failure models, namely that a concept known as **positive externalities** plays an important role. This concept describes a situation in which one company's decision to increase production influences another company to do the same. One example of such an externality is the case in which an increase in one sector's output generates income and hence demand for the output of other sectors, so that the profitability of one sector depends positively on activity elsewhere. In this sense, the coordination-failure models mimic the Keynesian spending multiplier, studied in Section 5.1.

Third, imperfect competition and positive externalities typically in-

---

* For a good but technical survey, see Russell Cooper and Andrew John, "Coordinating Coordination Failures in Keynesian Models," in *Quarterly Journal of Economics*, August 1988, vol. 103, no. 3, pp. 441–63.

teract to produce more than one possible equilibrium for the economy. These **multiple equilibria** can be interpreted as different states of the economy, with low-activity equilibria corresponding to recessions and high-activity equilibria corresponding to expansions.

So far, this literature has not attempted to explain the shifts that make the economy move from a high-activity to a low-activity equilibrium. However, it offers some intriguing thoughts on how and why the economy may "get stuck" in low-activity equilibria. Such equilibria are suboptimal, because all agents would prefer a higher activity level. This is the essence of the positive externality. However, because the economy is in equilibrium at the low activity level, no single agent has an incentive to change the situation on his or her own because increasing production for one firm will not be profitable unless the other firms increase theirs. This describes the coordination problem in a nutshell: Nobody wants a recession, but if the economy ends up in one, nobody has an incentive to produce more.

Although the policy implications of this analysis remain to be worked out, the existence of a coordination problem does seem to point to the potential benefit of an agency that can take the role of coordinating everybody's activity. This should be a role for government, but it could be rather different from the traditional role of administering proper doses of monetary and fiscal policy.

11.6   AN EVALUATION

With so many approaches to macroeconomic analysis being taken, it is natural to ask which approach is right or, at least, which approach comes closest to the truth. Naturally, there is no simple answer to this question, for if there were all analysts would already have agreed. Nevertheless, some meaningful comments can be made about the plausibility of the various hypotheses and about the prudent application of competing theories to managerial decision making.

HOW MUCH CAN THE DATA TELL?

The ultimate test of a scientific hypothesis is whether or not it is contradicted by empirical data. In the physical sciences, such data are obtained from experimentation. Because controlled experiments cannot be—or at least are not—carried out in macroeconomics, we must rely on nonexperimental historical data. This circumstance handicaps any attempt to test macroeconomic theories. Nevertheless, some important findings are worth pointing out.

First, the extreme monetarist contention of a constant velocity of money is not supported. At the same time, the effect of interest-rate changes on the demand for money is not necessarily strong. Furthermore, the demand for money appears to have shifted unpredictably from time to time.* These results have contributed to the decline of monetarism on one hand. On the other hand, they serve as a caution against excessive confidence in our ability to predict the effects of monetary policy.

Second, the rational-expectations model with incomplete information has inspired a number of tests of the hypothesis that changes in real GNP are positively correlated with preceding unexpected changes in the money supply but not at all with expected changes. Some early studies produced results that seemed strikingly consistent with this hypothesis.** However, a subsequent set of studies, which allowed for longer lags in the money-GNP relationship, pointed in the direction of significant correlations between real GNP changes on one hand and expected as well as unexpected monetary changes on the other.† A third set of studies has questioned the validity of the money-GNP relationship altogether. Although the simple correlation is clear, the relationship is weakened considerably if an interest rate is included as an additional variable in a multiple regression equation. Although interest rates can also be construed as instruments of monetary policy, some authors have interpreted these results as support for the real-business-cycle approach.††

This hypothesis, because it explains business cycles as the results of productivity shocks, predicts a procyclical movement in productivity: Productivity should decline in recessions and rise in recovery. This correlation is, in fact, strongly supported by the data. It was known long before real-business-cycle analysis and probably helped inspire it. However, this observation proves nothing by itself, because business cycles could make productivity move just as easily as the other way around.§ A more readily testable hypothesis is the implication that busi-

---

*For a recent study of the demand for money, see Robert L. Hetzel and Yash P. Mehra, "The Behavior of Money Demand in the 1980s," *Journal of Money, Credit, and Banking*, November 1989, vol. 21, no. 4, pp. 455–63.

**Robert J. Barro, "Unanticipated Money, Output, and the Price Level in the United States," *Journal of Political Economy*, 1977, vol. 86, pp. 549–80.

†Frederic Mishkin, "Does Unanticipated Money Matter? An Econometric Investigation," *Journal of Political Economy*, 1982, vol. 91, pp. 22–51.

††For a presentation of the evidence as well as the controversy, see Martin Eichenbaum and Kenneth J. Singleton, "Do Equilibrium Real Business Cycle Theories Explain Postwar U.S. Business Cycles?" in *NBER Macroeconomics Annual*, 1, edited by Stanley Fischer (M.I.T. Press, 1986); and David E. Spencer, "Does Money Matter? The Robustness of Evidence from Vector Autoregressions," *Journal of Money, Credit, and Banking*, November 1989, vol. 21, no. 4, pp. 442–54.

§Consider, for example, *labor hoarding*, whereby firms hold on to some workers during recessions so they will not need to start looking for new, perhaps untrained, workers when the recession is over. Then labor productivity, defined as output per worker, would decline in recessions because the workers who are kept on the job have less work to do.

ness cycles should not be correlated with the forces that drive fluctuations in aggregate demand, such as changes in the money supply. However, we have already noted that the results with regard to this point are rather ambiguous.

These findings, together with the ongoing intellectual debate, currently seem to have produced a consensus to the effect that monetarism and the rational-expectations model with incomplete information are dormant if not dead as leading contenders for an overall macroeconomic paradigm. So are the simplistic versions of Keynesianism. The remaining active contenders are real business cycles, sophisticated Keynesianism (for example, with menu costs), and eclectic approaches such as coordination failure. However, as the research frontier continues to expand, this consensus is subject to constant change.

WHAT MAKES A THEORY "MAKE SENSE"?

If the data cannot determine what we should believe, does that mean that anything goes in macroeconomics? Fortunately, this is not the case. Some very helpful criteria can be used to at least establish whether a theory makes sense.

First, the theory needs to be *logically consistent*. Most of Chapters 5 through 8 was devoted to the development of the logic of Keynesian analysis, just as most of this chapter studied the logic of the classical approaches. The emphasis on logic safeguards against nonsense predictions. For example, within the IS-LM model, it would be illogical to claim that an expansionary fiscal policy reduces GNP in the short run, even though the interest rate rises, because the model shows that crowding out can at most bring GNP back to where it came from. Since all the theories discussed in this book are consistent with their own assumptions, the criterion of logical consistency does not help us discriminate among them.

Second, for a theory to be plausible, it must *agree with well-established facts* about the economy. Thus, any respectable theory should be able to account for the strong procyclical fluctuations in employment, consumption, and investment, as well as for the positive correlation between real activity and inflation, or at least unexpected inflation. The real-business-cycle analysis is in trouble on the latter point, although an attempt to reconcile it with the data should be noted.*

Third, a good theory relies on *plausible mechanisms* to generate its implications. This criterion admittedly is somewhat subjective, because different people have different ideas about what is plausible. Sometimes, it might mean that people let their political preferences deter-

---

* Robert King and Charles Plosser, "Money, Credit and Prices in a Real Business Cycle," *American Economic Review*, June 1984, vol. 74, pp. 363–80.

mine their beliefs about how the economy works. At other times, this criterion is applied more objectively. As an example, it seems fair to point out that the real-business-cycle analysts have not yet provided a satisfactory story describing why or how productivity is subject to random shocks. It might be easy enough to think of technological breakthroughs or new management principles that *improve* productivity; however, how productivity can deteriorate enough to create recessions is far from clear.

A BALANCED PORTFOLIO OF APPROACHES

Management decisions often need to rely on estimates of the likely course of the overall economy, such as the demand for a consumer durable, that may depend heavily on the course of the business cycle. These estimates are the implications of macroeconomic theory, and we have seen in this chapter how widely they can vary depending on the approach taken. In the case of the marketing of a durable good, demand for the good may be in question if the central bank has shown signs of tightening its monetary stance. A real-business-cycle analyst would ignore this fact altogether, because monetary policy should have no effect on business-cycle movements or on other real variables, such as the real interest rates, influencing the demand for durable goods. This sanguine attitude would stand in obvious contrast to that of both Keynesian and monetarist analysts, who would warn against recession as well as higher interest rates. To whom should management listen?

The first step, obviously, is to check the empirical evidence and the plausibility of the various approaches, as discussed above. When these possibilities are exhausted and the verdict is still ambiguous, the manager's problem is not unlike that of an investor choosing a portfolio of risky securities. Rather than betting all the money on one alternative, a prudent investor would reduce his or her risk by choosing a balanced portfolio. Similarly, it usually pays off to choose a balanced portfolio of approaches to macroeconomics, that is, to pay some attention to all the schools of thought. Since we cannot be sure that any one of them is right, it is a good idea to listen to all the advice and make contingency plans for areas in which their predictions differ. Thus, in the example above, it might be prudent to make contingency plans for continued recovery following a monetary contraction even if many analysts predict a recession.

Professional disagreements may bring frustration to anyone who is forced to act on the professionals' advice. However, it is important to understand and accept that such disagreements need not be signs of weakness or confusion in the profession but rather an indication that knowledge is evolving and that professional knowledge is limited by the clarity of the evidence. Once these difficulties are understood, professional opinion can contribute important insights into the decision process that are too valuable to ignore.

CHAPTER REVIEW

1. The fundamental difference between the Keynesian and the classical schools of thought is that classical economists analyze macroeconomic events as equilibria in the sense of equality between aggregate supply and aggregate demand, while Keynesians explicitly incorporate price rigidities and disequilibria into their analysis.

2. Since the 1950s, the classical school has evolved from monetarism into new classical macroeconomics, which includes the rational-expectations approach with incomplete information and, most recently, the real-business-cycle approach.

3. Monetarists emphasize the central role of the money supply as a determinant of nominal GNP. While they recognize the possibility that monetary policy can have real effects in the short run, they caution against its discretionary use in the fear that it might prove to be destabilizing.

4. The Lucas model assumes rational expectations but incomplete information. It implies that unexpected monetary changes have real effects but that anticipated policy moves do not. It contains the Phillips curve as an empirical regularity but not as a policy menu.

5. Real business cycles are hypothesized as driven by random shocks to productivity that cause shifts in potential GNP. Because the economy reaches equilibrium on its own, public policy can do nothing to improve upon business cycles.

6. Recent advances in Keynesian macroeconomics include the contract-wage theory of business cycles, the rationalization of price rigidity as the result of menu costs, the sectoral-imbalance approach to analyzing aggregate fluctuations, and models of coordination failure.

7. Monetarism and the rational-expectations model with incomplete information have declined in popularity in the 1980s, leaving the modern Keynesian school and the real-business-cycle school as the main contenders for leadership in macroeconomics. The data are not clear enough to allow an unambiguous choice. A prudent manager would do well in listening to all the relevant schools of thought.

NUMERICAL EXERCISES

1. Consider the following IS-LM model:
   (IS) $Y = 1,150 + 0.75Y - 10,000R + G$,
   (LM) $M/P = 0.2Y(0.075/R)^a$.
   Assume $M/P = 800$ and $G = 600$ initially.
   a. For $a = 1$, solve the model for real GNP and the real interest rate given the initial values for government spending and the real money supply. Then find the effects on GNP of an expansion of government spending to $G = 700$. Also find the effects of an increase in the money supply to $M/P = 900$.
   b. Repeat the analysis for $a = 0$. What does the comparison tell you about monetarist versus Keynesian policy analysis?

2. Consider the following Lucas-type aggregate demand–aggregate supply model:
   (AD) $Y = 2,250 + 2.5M/P$,
   (LS) $Y = 800 + 3,200P/P^e$.
   a. Solve the model for Y and P given $M = 700$ and $P^e = 1$.
   b. Derive the effects on real GNP and the price level of an unexpected increase in the money supply from 700 to 750.
   c. Derive the same effects under the assumption that the money-supply change is fully anticipated.
   d. Suppose you observe such an increase in the money supply but don't know whether or not it was anticipated by the market. What would you predict the effects to be?

DATA EXERCISES

1. Using annual data for M2, real GNP, the price level, and the 3-month Treasury bill rate, run a regression to estimate a money-demand function of the form
   $M/P = k_0 + k_Y Y - k_i i$.
   Do the results support the hypothesis that the demand for money is only weakly dependent on the interest rate?

2. Using the same data as in data exercise 1, regress the velocity of money on the T-bill rate. What do these results say about the hypothesis that velocity is constant?

3. With quarterly data, regress the real GNP growth rate on the M2 growth rate, lagged one through four quarters, as well as the real GNP growth rate itself with a one-quarter lag. Carry out an F-test of the hypothesis that the coefficients of M2 growth are all zero. What does the result say about the real-business-cycle claim that money supply has no effect on real GNP growth? Now include the 3-month Treasury bill rate, lagged one through four quarters, as an additional variable. With this addition, carry out a new F-test of the same hypothesis. Also test the hypothesis that all the interest-rate coefficients are zero. Does this modification change your conclusion?

4. With quarterly data, regress real GNP growth on the rate of change in the price of oil, lagged one through four quarters, plus a one-quarter lag of the real GNP growth rate itself. Carry out an F-test of the hypothesis that the coefficients of the oil-price changes are all zero. What does this result say about the real-business-cycle hypothesis? Next include the 3-month Treasury bill rate as an additional variable, with lags from one through four quarters. Run the same F-test again. Does the result change?

THINKING QUESTIONS

1. Suppose you manage an aluminum smelting plant. Two of the plant's three potlines have been closed down for six months because of low prices. News of a 10% price rise for aluminum ingots makes you consider reopening one of the lines. However, your associate warns you that labor and other costs are likely to rise as well, because she believes the aluminum price increase is part of a new wave of inflation. How would you analyze the situation, and what action would you take?

2. Suppose you manage an automobile distributorship. You hear repeated reports to the effect that the Federal Reserve is tightening the supply of money. However, the media commentators belong to different schools of thought and disagree as to the likely effects of this tightening. You know that your company has a considerable inventory of cars. Should you offer special incentives to liquidate it?

3. In 1980–82, the Federal Reserve tightened monetary policy with the intention of reducing inflation. This episode has been characterized as an experiment in monetarism, because the monetary aggregates, rather than any interest rate, were used as intermediate targets. Do you agree with this characterization?

4. In Chapter 7, we mentioned the claim that the oil shocks of the 1970s do not qualify as examples of productivity shocks because these price changes did not change the technology that determined how much output could be produced with every given level of input. Do you agree or disagree?

12 MACROECONOMIC POLICY MAKING

Macroeconomics can be studied from two perspectives—the management perspective and the public-policy perspective. In the *management* perspective, which is the basis for this book, the main purpose of studying macroeconomics is to become acquainted with the broad economic environment of business decision making. In contrast, in the *public-policy* perspective, the overriding concern is to find out how the economy can be controlled, or at least influenced, by public policy. However, the perspectives interact. In particular, public policy is important for private-sector managers even if they don't *make* the policy, because business is affected by public policy in crucial ways. A recession induced by a policy designed to slow inflation obviously affects business, as do policy efforts to manipulate interest rates and exchange rates. Therefore, a proper understanding of the basics of public policy making is essential for making prudent managerial decisions.

12.1 WHAT IS MACROECONOMIC POLICY?

Macroeconomic policy is part of the broader concept of *economic* policy, which covers a variety of policy areas, including antitrust, health and safety regulation, environmental regulation, research and development, farm policy, and financial-market regulation. Macroeconomic policy is defined more narrowly in terms of its two main instruments, monetary policy and fiscal policy.

MONETARY POLICY

Monetary policy essentially refers to the activities of the central bank. In Chapter 4, we studied how the central bank can influence the money supply via open market operations, discount-rate changes, and adjustments to the commercial banks' reserve requirements. In Chapter 6, we saw how monetary policy moves can have rather direct effects on the interest rates in private capital markets. For this reason, monetary policy in practice is often identified with interest-rate movements. In the United States, the focus has been on the federal funds rate, the interest rate banks pay each other for funds that can be used to satisfy reserve requirements. Considerable attention is also given to the yields of

3-month Treasury bills as well as Treasury bonds of various longer maturities. However, it seems clear that since the mid-1980s the Federal Reserve has used the federal funds rate as the immediate target for its policies. By fine-tuning its open market operations, the Federal Reserve "controls" this interest rate.

Monetary policy is also closely linked to exchange-rate movements. As we saw in Chapter 10, this link is somewhat more indirect in that exchange rates respond not only to interest-rate changes but also to other factors, such as inflationary expectations. However, the indirectness disappears when a central bank intervenes directly in the foreign-exchange market by buying or selling its own currency. The analysis in Chapter 10 made it clear that such interventions, unless sterilized, also influence the money supply—and hence interest rates.

In a wider sense, monetary policy also includes the regulatory framework of the financial markets. Of special recent importance in the United States was the liberalization of the rules regulating the lending practices of savings and loan associations. This liberalization allowed these institutions to expand their lending volume and to assume greater risks during the 1980s. The effects of this expansion are likely to have been similar to a conventional monetary expansion and may have contributed to the strength of the 1980s expansion in the United States. Unfortunately, however, a great many of the recipients of these loans were unable to repay their debts. As a result, a large number of savings and loan associations failed or needed an infusion of new capital from the government. The investigations of the failures also uncovered a number of cases of fraud. In hindsight, this liberalization proved quite costly, both to the federal government and to the economy in general.

FISCAL POLICY

Fiscal policy manipulates government expenditures and receipts. In Chapter 5, we saw how government expenditures on goods and services influenced aggregate demand not only directly by being part of it but also indirectly via the spending multiplier. Other government expenditures, called *transfer payments*, include important programs such as Social Security, Medicare, and veterans' benefits in the United States. From the point of view of macroeconomic policy making, it is convenient to analyze transfer payments as *negative taxes*, because they put money into people's pockets rather than taking it out. Transfer payments together with those payments we are used to calling taxes make up *net taxes* paid to the government. Chapter 5 showed how a reduction in net personal income taxes could stimulate consumer spending, although the possibility of Ricardian equivalence made this prediction somewhat ambiguous.

Other tax instruments are also available, such as the corporate income tax. This instrument has most commonly been used somewhat indirectly by manipulation of the rules stating which expenditures can be deducted from taxable corporate income. In particular, the rules for depreciation of investment expenditures for tax purposes and the investment tax credit have been used to influence investment demand. The investment tax credit, which allowed U.S. businesses to subtract a certain percentage of their investment expenses from their tax liabilities, was abolished in 1986.

COORDINATION OF MONETARY AND FISCAL POLICY

If monetary and fiscal policies are not coordinated, they can fail to achieve their desired effects. In the IS-LM diagram in Figure 12.1, fiscal policy is aimed at stimulating activity, perhaps to pull the economy out of a recession, as indicated by the rightward shift in the IS curve from IS_0 to IS_1. The goal is to move the economy from the initial equilibrium E_0 to E_1, with a higher GNP level, even though the cost is higher interest rates. Suppose money supply is contracted at the same time, however, so that the LM curve shifts leftward from LM_0 to LM_1. Then the GNP gain disappears, and the interest rate is driven even higher.

This example also illustrates the contrast between monetary and fiscal policy in their effects on interest rates. While a fiscal expansion can be expected to raise real interest rates, a monetary expansion reduces them. This difference is important for two reasons. First, because an interest-rate reduction stimulates investment activity, a monetary expansion can do a better job of building the capital stock that will be needed to meet future production challenges. Second, an interest-rate

FIGURE 12.1

Conflicting policies in the IS-LM model: expansionary fiscal policy and contractionary monetary policy.

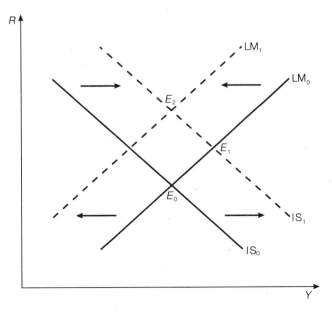

reduction, by inducing a decline in the exchange rate, also stimulates net export demand. If there is a perceived need to stimulate economic activity, the choice of the desired *mix* of monetary and fiscal policy should be influenced by both the country's external balance and its need to build its capital stock.

Macroeconomic theory tends to discuss monetary and fiscal policy in the abstract, without explicit reference to the people or the institutions that develop and carry out the various policies. In practice, however, the institutional arrangement can be quite important. Although the arrangement varies from country to country, monetary and fiscal policy are usually handled by different agencies. Consequently, problems of **policy coordination** often arise.

The **independence of the central bank** is honored by most countries, although in varying degrees. It is rather weak in the United Kingdom, where the Bank of England largely respects the directives of the Chancellor of the Exchequer. It is stronger in Germany and taken very seriously in the United States, where the Federal Reserve jealously guards its independence from politicians and private business alike.

The purpose of this independence is to protect the central bankers from political pressures to make short-sighted decisions that could be politically expedient but are detrimental to the long-term well-being of the economy. An example of such a decision is a monetary expansion to lower interest rates and raise incomes in the short run at the cost of inflation in the long run. On the other hand, institutional separation can lead to conflicting policies. Many analysts view the combination of fiscal expansion and monetary contraction in the United States in the early eighties as an example of such conflict.

The coordination problem is not limited to the monetary-fiscal policy mix. Fiscal policy has some coordination problems of its own due to the often conflicting demands made by different agencies and their respective constituencies. These conflicts, which seem to be particularly acute in the United States, are discussed further in Section 12.5.

INTER-NATIONAL POLICY COORDINATION

Coordination of the policies of different countries presents additional challenges. For example, the United States complained repeatedly during the 1980s that its European and Asian allies hurt U.S. export demand and hence the U.S. current-account balance by failing to stimulate their economies; at the same time, the allies complained about high interest rates created by the large U.S. budget deficits. This interdependence suggests that all countries could benefit from some coordination of policy.

A number of attempts have been made. An important example is the Bretton Woods system, which fixed the exchange rates of the Western economies after World War II. As explained in Chapter 10, this system also made it difficult for the member countries to conduct independent monetary policies. The exception to this rule was the United States, whose leadership position enabled the Federal Reserve to more or less set the monetary policy course for the entire group.

Another example is the European Community (EC), whose coordination attempts so far have been concentrated in *trade* policy. However, important aspects of fiscal policy have been involved as part of the effort to harmonize tax rates. Most EC members also participate in the European Monetary System (EMS), which seeks to maintain fixed exchange rates among its member countries. Unlike the Bretton Woods system, the EMS does not have a designated leader country, nor does it have a formal mechanism for coordination of monetary policy moves. In practice, the German Bundesbank has a leadership role in the sense that the other EMS central banks usually feel compelled to follow its monetary policy initiatives. As discussed in Chapter 10, further steps in the direction of monetary cooperation are on the EC agenda for the next decade, including the possibility of a European Monetary Union, with a common currency and a common central bank.

International policy coordination is also promoted by regular discussions at summit meetings among the leaders of the top industrial powers, such as the Group of Seven (G7), consisting of the United States, Japan, Germany, France, Great Britain, Canada, and Italy. However, these discussions have the character of consultations only and are not part of a binding system. Finally, regular consultations take place through the Organization of Economic Cooperation and Development (OECD). The staff at its Paris headquarters issues annual reports evaluating the policies of each of the 24 member countries.*

12.2 WHAT CAN MACROECONOMIC POLICY HOPE TO ACCOMPLISH?

Common goals of economic policy include high and sustained growth in real GNP, business-cycle stability, low and stable inflation, an equitable distribution of income, and stability in the external balance. Let us look at each of these goals and how they relate to each other.

---

*Members of the OECD are, in alphabetical order, Australia, Austria, Belgium, Canada, Denmark, Finland, France, Germany, Greece, Iceland, Ireland, Italy, Japan, Luxembourg, the Netherlands, New Zealand, Norway, Portugal, Spain, Sweden, Switzerland, Turkey, the United Kingdom, and the United States.

LONG-TERM ECONOMIC GROWTH

This goal concerns the performance of the economy on average. It is a goal not about the business cycle but about how the economy's resources can best be mobilized to benefit the population's needs over the long haul. Figure 12.2 illustrates the effects of a successful growth policy. Implemented at time t_0, it lifts the long-term growth path from Y_0^* to Y_1^*.

Our analysis of monetary policy suggests that this policy instrument is far from ideal in promoting long-term growth. Toward the end of Chapter 8, we noted that a monetary expansion can have long-run real benefits by encouraging investment activity that will add to the economy's productive capacity in years ahead. However, the clearest long-run effect of an acceleration in the growth of the money supply is inflation.

Nonmonetary policy instruments are likely to be more effective. The *perestroika* policy of the U.S.S.R. and the wholesale restructuring of most of Eastern Europe outside the U.S.S.R. are examples, as are the integration efforts of the European Community. The governments of many successful Asian countries have made a conscious effort to spur investment in research and development and to assist in the coordination of the growth efforts of private industry.

Government support of private research and development usually falls under *fiscal* policy, in the form of subsidies, tax incentives, or defense contracts. However, fiscal policy is also important in a more general sense. Government purchases of goods and services include the provision of **public goods and services,** which can contribute to the efficient allocation of resources in the economy. Examples of such public goods

FIGURE 12.2

Illustration of the effects of a successful policy promoting long-term growth.

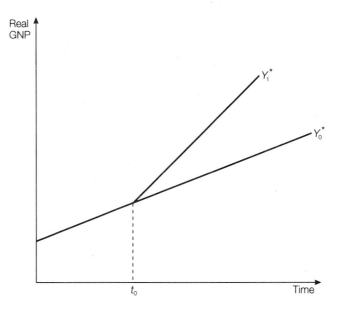

and services include law enforcement, public education, and investments in transportation infrastructure. Law enforcement provides the economy with a reasonably safe and predictable environment as well as procedures for conflict resolution. Public education plays an economic role by preparing people for the workplace. Transportation infrastructure facilitates commerce over long distances. A recent study suggests that such investments have been crucially important for the long-term performance of the U.S. economy.*

Fiscal policy is also charged with finding efficient ways to finance public expenditures. Part of this task consists of designing a *tax system* that provides the desired revenue and distributes the tax burden equitably while at the same time distorting incentives for work, saving, and production as little as possible. Another part of the task is to distribute the tax burden *over time*, for example, to determine whether budget deficits are allowed to defer the tax burden to a later time or perhaps to future generations.

STABILITY OF REAL OUTPUT AND EMPLOYMENT

Even more than long-term growth, the *stabilization* role of monetary and fiscal policy has been the traditional focus of macroeconomic policy. Figure 12.3 illustrates the effects of attempts to stabilize real output. Real GNP, Y, is shown as fluctuating around potential GNP, Y^*, which is assumed to grow smoothly. Stabilization policies implemented at time t_0 make real GNP leave its fluctuating path Y_0 in favor of the smoother path Y_1. The policies "fill in the valleys" and "smooth out the peaks."

This view of stabilization policies is typical of the mainstream Keynesian philosophy, which views the vagaries of the business cycle as an unnecessary evil against which the government should protect its citizens. It is also representative of the views of many "pragmatic" analysts who hesitate to espouse any particular philosophy but still prefer to see policy used to stabilize economic activity.

According to Keynesian analysis, monetary as well as fiscal policy can be used for this purpose. If the economy is showing signs of going into recession, it can be stimulated either by an easing in monetary policy or by a fiscal expansion in the form of a tax cut or increased spending, for example, on a "jobs program." Conversely, when the economy returns to an expansion, these measures should be pulled back.

Naturally, this view is not shared by real-business-cycle analysts, who consider business cycles as fluctuations *in* potential GNP rather than *around* it. As long as the supply shocks causing these fluctuations are

---

* David A. Aschauer, "Is Public Expenditure Productive?" unpublished paper, Federal Reserve Bank of Chicago, June 1988.

FIGURE 12.3

Illustration of the effects of successful and unsuccessful stabilization policies.

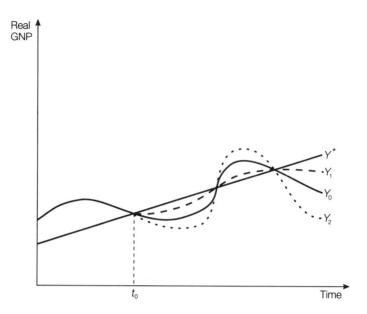

beyond the control of government, any attempt to change them will be a wasted effort.

The monetarist position does not dispute the view of business cycles as fluctuations around potential GNP. However, monetarists warn that human errors and political expediency could easily lead to a policy that in practice destabilizes rather than stabilizes. Thus, discretionary policies could lead the economy to a more unstable path, like that labeled Y_2 in Figure 12.3.

PRICE-LEVEL STABILITY

A stable price level has intuitive appeal to most people as a policy goal. Yet the rational reasons for this appeal are not always clear. Toward the end of Chapter 8, we emphasized that inflation is primarily a nominal phenomenon, on which account it should cause no concern, but that it can also cause real distortions, which *are* cause for concern. We mentioned the interaction between inflation and the tax system as one example of such a distortion. As another example, consider the effect of inflation on a country's *international competitiveness*. Recall from Chapter 9 that the relative price of a country's goods in the world market can be written as $E \cdot P/P^*$, where E is the exchange rate, P the domestic price level, and P^* the foreign price level. If inflation is higher at home than abroad, P rises faster than P^*. Then, for a given exchange rate, the relative price $E \cdot P/P^*$ rises, which makes it difficult for the home country to compete in the world market. In other words, the country's net export demand declines. This problem would be avoided if the exchange rate moved so as to compensate exactly for the change in the relative price level P/P^*, in other words, if purchasing power parity held. However, we found in Chapter 10 that purchasing power parity cannot be expected to hold at all times, whether the exchange rate is fixed or floating. Then domestic inflation in excess of world inflation typically can create a competitiveness problem.

Finally, inflation makes comparisons of prices over time difficult and uncertain. This uncertainty adds an extra complication to business planning. It could be solved without stabilizing the price *level* if the *inflation rate* were made stable and predictable. With a stable inflation rate, planning is simple as long as the accountant has a calculator that can do exponential functions! Needless to say, however, reducing the inflation rate to zero—in other words, stabilizing the price level—would solve the problem of uncertainty even more fundamentally.

EQUITABLE DISTRIBUTION OF INCOME AND WEALTH

Other things being equal, most people seem to favor an even distribution of income and wealth over an uneven distribution. This preference is based on the common ideal of fairness and justice that also forms the philosophical basis for a democratic political system.

However, an equitable income distribution also has other advantages. People who are well fed and financially secure have more physical and mental energy that can be used for productive work. In this sense, equity can also support long-term growth. Similarly, an even income distribution can save resources that otherwise would be devoted to relief efforts or law enforcement.

Finally, and perhaps most importantly, an equitable society is more likely to be a stable society, one in which people tend to trust each other and are willing to work hard without coercion. The problem of mistrust of the ruling or privileged classes has been a major obstacle to development in many less-developed countries.

EXTERNAL BALANCE

A country seeking to maintain a fixed exchange rate must watch its *official reserves*. If the inflow of private capital falls short of the current-account deficit, the central bank needs to draw on these reserves in order to defend the exchange rate. If the reserves are drawn down too much, the central bank needs to tighten its monetary policy so that higher domestic interest rates encourage capital inflow.

This problem can be avoided by letting the exchange rate float. However, a freely floating exchange rate is not without problems either. As discussed toward the end of Chapter 10, a stable exchange rate can free up management resources that otherwise would be needed to manage exchange risk and to run the foreign-exchange market. For these reasons, many governments, even if they do not fix their exchange rates completely, seek to *manage* their exchange rate. But then they cannot avoid the need to watch their official reserves.

External balance usually is also taken to mean a reasonable balance in the *current account*. As discussed toward the end of Chapter 9, opinion is divided as to the need for the government to have a goal with respect to the current account, because it is not clear that foreign borrowing by private companies or individuals should concern the government. However, we have also seen that the current-account balance is likely to be tied intimately to *fiscal policy*, which is definitely a policy concern of the government. Moreover, because a current-account deficit now means a foreign debt burden later, policymakers may consider that they have a responsibility to keep private decision makers from leaving an undue debt burden to the country's future citizens.

12.3 CONFLICTS AMONG POLICY GOALS

Unfortunately, the policy goals just discussed tend to conflict with each other. It rarely happens that all of them can be fulfilled at the same time. Part of the reason for this conflict is that the policy instruments available are too few to accomplish the many separate policy goals.

Nowhere is the shortage of instruments more apparent than in the case of monetary policy. Monetary policy is usually called upon to stabilize the price level, fight recessions, keep interest rates low, and stabilize the exchange rate, all at the same time. Yet monetary policy is fundamentally a *one-dimensional* instrument. All it can do is tighten or ease the supply of money. Then it could only be by luck that all the purposes this policy is called upon to serve are achieved at the same time.

As a rule, we cannot expect to be that lucky. It is normal for situations to arise in which one policy goal must be traded off against another. Let us look at some of these conflict dilemmas.

STABILIZATION OF REAL ACTIVITY AND INFLATION

This conflict represents the conventional trade-off in macroeconomic policy making. We discussed it in connection with the Phillips curve, and it shows up regularly in the popular debate. Both monetary and fiscal policies are involved in this trade-off, because both can influence aggregate demand. However, the close link between money and inflation has caused the debate to be focused more on the monetary side.

In one sense, the management of inflation is the most basic goal of monetary policy. Money is an artificial commodity and keeps its value only because its supply is limited, equally artificially, by the central bank. Because the price level summarizes the price of all other goods and services in terms of money, the value of money—relative to the other goods and services—is inversely proportional to the price level. Thus, preservation of the value of money means controlling the price level.

However, focusing one-sidedly on inflation means giving up on stabilizing real activity. Worse, once inflation has taken off, it may take a recession to bring it back under control again. A policy-induced recession typically results in the temporary loss of millions of jobs and numerous wasted business opportunities.

If macroeconomic policy were designed carefully enough, wouldn't it be possible to stabilize *both* inflation *and* real activity? An optimistic response to this question would be to say that policy should be expansionary during recessions and contractionary whenever the economy shows signs of overheating and inflation. Monetary policy in the United States in the second half of the 1980s appears to have been consistent with this view. Money supply was allowed to grow rapidly as long as inflation did not seem to be a problem. Then, when inflation showed signs of becoming persistent in 1988, monetary policy was tightened, and the slowdown in inflation in late 1989 appeared to open the door for renewed expansion. This expansion paused again when inflation bounced back in the winter and spring of 1990, but it was restarted in the fall of that year when the economy showed signs of slowing down.

However, policymakers are not always this lucky. In late 1973, the Western economies were subjected to a round of very high inflation, apparently triggered by the quadrupling of the world price of crude oil. At the same time, they plunged into a very deep recession. In this situation, Keynesian theory still suggests that a sufficient dose of monetary expansion could have aborted the recession. The reader is encouraged to carry out this analysis with the model given for the numerical exercises in Chapter 8. Not surprisingly, however, such an expansion would have *worsened* rather than improved the already difficult inflationary situation.

This problem is not limited to external inflationary shocks. If the economy has been stimulated by expansionary policies for some time, inflation is likely to rise gradually but steadily, as it did in the United States in the late 1960s and early 1970s. As it becomes ingrained in people's expectations, it becomes harder to stop. Although entrenched inflation can be stopped by a monetary contraction, an extra sharp tightening might be needed.

STABILITY AND GROWTH: THE PROBLEM OF TIME CONSISTENCY

The conflict between inflation and stabilization is part of a wider issue, namely, the trade-off between short-term costs and long-term gains, and vice versa. We have already noted that inflation can have negative real effects in the long run. However, similar conflicts are faced elsewhere as well. For example, the Soviet policy of *perestroika* represents a restructuring that appears to cause painful transition problems but is expected to improve the economy in fundamental ways in the long run. The unification of the economies of the two Germanys has presented a similar trade-off between short-run adjustment problems and the promise of long-term gains. Third, the efforts by the European Community to create a unified internal market by the end of 1992 have been predicted to ultimately produce a gain in efficiency of perhaps 6% of the member countries' combined GNP. However, because much of this gain is projected to come in the form of restructuring of industries and individual companies, the short-run adjustment problems in terms of bankruptcies, plant closings, and unemployment can be considerable.

The research literature has described this dilemma as a problem of **time consistency.** A policy plan is time consistent if the decision for tomorrow that appears desirable today remains desirable tomorrow after today's decisions have taken effect. In the case of monetary policy, a steady restraint might be optimal in a long-term perspective because it avoids inflationary distortions and does not result in occasional and hazardous efforts to stop inflation. However, it is not necessarily time consistent. If restraint has been exercised in the past, so that inflation is not a problem, then the central bankers will be tempted to deviate from the plan at any given time in order to provide a little extra stimulus. Once this pattern has started, however, it might be costly to stop inflation again.*

The proposed remedy for this problem is to tie the government's hands, so to speak, by committing it once and for all to a *rule* of action that prevents it from yielding to the temptation to stimulate the economy. In terms of *fiscal policy*, this argument implies that the government's budget making should be concerned with the long-term allocation of resources and not with short-term efforts to counteract business cycles. A constitutional amendment to balance the budget could, for example, pull the budget process in this direction. In terms of *monetary policy*, the time-consistency issue provides support to the traditional monetarist proposal to replace discretionary monetary policy with a rule that raises the money supply by a certain percentage each year. The time-consistency argument adds sophistication to this proposal by focusing not only on the timing of monetary policy and its effects but also on the effects of that policy on people's *expectations*.

Let us look at the expectations issue a little more carefully. A one-time stimulation of the economy by monetary policy can be quite effective, because it can be introduced as a surprise. But after it has been tried two or three times, the private sector may start to expect it to be repeated. We saw in Chapter 8 that continued growth in the money supply

---

*The classical reference for dynamic consistency is Finn Kydland and Edward Prescott, "Rules Rather than Discretion: The Inconsistency of Optimal Plans," in *Journal of Political Economy*, June 1977, vol. 85, no. 3, pp. 619–37.

will result in inflation, while a failure to continue the growth might result in a recession. Real effects of monetary policy are most likely obtained when the policy change comes as a surprise. If policy has been restrained in the past, surprising the economy is not difficult. However, this very action takes away the surprise element the next time the policy is tried and at the same time makes the policy very difficult to stop.

The argument against policy rules is that they become too rigid. A rule can function well as long as no major changes take place in the environment. Once in a while, however, it will be appropriate to modify the rules in light of recent developments. An example in terms of *fiscal policy* is the recent thaw in superpower relations, which has given rise to a major reassessment of the need for defense spending on both sides.

In terms of *monetary policy,* it is worth noting that all the theoretical results related to policy rules rest implicitly on the assumption that the demand for money has a stable relationship to the price level, real GNP, and the nominal interest rate. Suppose this relationship were to change, for example, as the result of a financial innovation of the type discussed in Section 6.4. We saw then from the IS-LM model that maintaining a steady money supply would probably stimulate real activity in the short run; an extension of the analysis to the AD-AS model would have indicated an increase in the price level in the long run. It seems fair to ask whether it would have been preferable for the central bank to have sufficient flexibility to make a downward shift in money supply in that situation.

A more practical recent example for monetary policy is the Federal Reserve's reaction to the major decline in the stock market on October 19, 1987. The decision to make additional liquidity available on the day after the market decline has been credited by some as the reason why this break in the market was not followed by a recession or a depression, as was the decline in 1929. Even though this view cannot be proven and might be wrong, it would seem imprudent to ignore the possibility that this view might be correct. Then it should also be prudent to allow the central bank sufficient flexibility to carry out such actions.

Movements in the business cycle are not normally examples of such changes in the environment. However, it is very difficult in practice to draw a clear line between what constitutes a change in the environment and what constitutes a normal event within the existing environment. Making these distinctions requires human judgment.

If human judgment is brought back into the analysis, however, the way back to the traditional Keynesian argument for discretionary policies is very short. According to this view, recessions are the result of aggregate demand falling short of aggregate supply, and using monetary policy to stimulate aggregate demand in these situations is not falling to temptation but instead is the appropriate response to an unexpected imbalance in the economy. A monetary expansion applied in this manner is not inflationary, provided the central bank pulls back before inflationary pressures start to build up. In the language of Chapter 8, a monetary expansion is a suitable instrument for bringing the GNP gap up to zero, but it should not be used to produce a *positive* GNP gap.

Unfortunately, this last caveat is easier said than done. No central bank knows what the GNP gap is at every moment. Consequently, discretionary policy always risks errors and unintended destabilization. At the same time, replacing monetary policy making by a simple arithmetic rule might make about as much sense in practice as replacing the board of AT&T with an answering machine. An ever-changing reality always offers a stream of new challenges that so far only real people, making real decisions, have been able to counter.

INTERNAL VERSUS EXTERNAL BALANCE: A DILEMMA FOR FISCAL POLICY

Most governments prefer to maintain a reasonable balance in the current account with the rest of the world. Unfortunately, this goal of external balance may conflict with the stabilization of real GNP. In particular, a fiscal stimulus—used, for example, to counteract a recession—discourages net export demand by raising the domestic income level. We saw in Chapter 10 that this effect is particularly strong with a fixed exchange rate, because then the interest rate does not change, so there is no crowding out. On the other hand, with a floating exchange rate, the interest rate and hence the exchange rate will rise, which hurts net export demand from the price side. Thus, the conflict is not avoided with floating exchange rates either.

Expansionary fiscal policies are not used only to get an economy out of recession. In the early 1980s, the Reagan administration in the United States proposed dramatic tax reductions for the purpose of promoting long-term growth. At the same time, the administration sought increases in defense spending. It proposed cuts in some areas of domestic spending but was unable to obtain approval by Congress. As a result, fiscal policy took a major expansionary turn. The federal deficit reached record highs that did not go away when the U.S. economy recovered from the 1981–82 recession.

Just as predicted by the theory cited above, the current-account deficit rose as well. This simultaneous increase in the two deficit measures gave rise to the phrase "twin deficits." In Figure 10.6, we presented a graph of these two deficits. There seems little doubt that their simultaneous rise during the 1980s was both spectacular and unlike any other episode since World War II.

We discussed in Chapter 9 the future burden that results from a current-account deficit. Moreover, our analysis makes it quite plausible that the large U.S. current-account deficits in the 1980s were directly related to the expansionary fiscal policy. Thus, a genuine policy dilemma seems to exist. The expansionary fiscal policy may have stimulated the U.S. economy during the 1980s and contributed to the length of the cyclical expansion in that decade. However, that policy also appears to have resulted in a substantial future burden of foreign debt. This debt will need to be repaid some time in the future in the form of increased taxes, reduced government services, or both. Ironically, though the tax cuts had been introduced to promote long-term growth, they ended up creating other long-term problems that perhaps are more serious than those they were intended to solve.

FIXED, FLOATING, OR MANAGED EXCHANGE RATES

As a final policy dilemma, let us consider the choice between a fixed and a floating exchange rate. In this case, a number of intermediate options are also available in the form of some kind of *managed* float.

Fixed or stable exchange rates have many advantages because they make international transactions easier and more predictable. However, as we saw in Chapter 10, these advantages are bought at the price of giving up the other uses of monetary policy. If a fixed exchange rate is chosen, then monetary policy must be devoted to the goal of maintaining this exchange rate and to that goal only. For individual countries with fixed exchange rates (other than the dominant country of an area of fixed exchange rates), monetary policy is unavailable as a tool for stabilization of domestic activity or control of domestic inflation.

In this sense, the decision about the exchange rate is one of the most fundamental decisions regarding monetary policy. If the exchange rate is fixed, discretionary monetary policy is impossible. Therefore, *deciding to fix the exchange rate is an example of committing to a policy rule.* In some ways, this rule is much more interesting than a rule to fix the growth of the money supply, because keeping the exchange rate fixed in fact is currently practiced by a number of central banks.

Discretionary efforts to tighten or ease monetary policy can be carried out as a *coordinated* effort among countries that maintain fixed exchange rates among each other, such as the members of the EMS. Such an effort could reduce all countries' interest rates while keeping them equal to each other. Furthermore, a large country might be able to take such policy steps unilaterally and effectively force the other countries to follow their example.

The United States currently is not committed to a fixed exchange rate vis-à-vis any other currency. Even so, since 1985 steps have been taken in cooperation with the other leading world economies to keep exchange rates within reasonable, though undefined, bounds. As long as this goal is being pursued, the United States is not completely free to conduct its own monetary policy, because it currently lacks the power to force its policies on the other Western countries. Thus, unilateral tightening by the United States is very likely to lead to a rise in the dollar, which means a deviation from exchange-rate stability. Such a unilateral move was undertaken as part of an effort to stem the emerging inflation in 1988–89, and the dollar did indeed rise for some time. Coordinated efforts subsequently were undertaken to bring it back down. However, the basic conflict between the external and internal goals of monetary policy was not resolved.

12.4 MONETARY POLICY IN PRACTICE

The centerpiece of monetary policy making in the United States is the meetings of the Federal Open Market Committee (FOMC). The voting members of this committee are the seven governors of the Federal Reserve System, the president of the Federal Reserve Bank of New York, and four other presidents of Federal Reserve district banks, on a rotating basis. The presidents of the remaining district banks participate in the meetings but are not allowed to vote. Senior staff members are present to brief the committee on recent developments. The meetings are held eight times a year, approximately every six weeks. They are closed to the public; however, the minutes of each meeting are made available in a press release shortly after the completion of the following meeting six weeks later.

The FOMC meeting starts with the staff briefings, summarized in three briefing books, which have been named after the colors of their respective covers. The "Beige Book" is a compilation of reports on the economic developments in the regions served by each Federal Reserve district bank. It is based on public statistics as well as the individual district banks' industry contacts. This report is available to the public.

The "Green Book" contains a survey by the staff of the Federal Reserve Board of all the current aspects of the economy. Although intended as an objective analysis, this book sometimes contains elements of the staff's policy recommendations. For this reason, the Green Book is not available to the public. Finally, the "Blue Book" contains the Federal Reserve Board staff's assessment of how monetary policy relates to the various market variables. This book is most definitely an internal document.

The discussion at the FOMC meetings evaluates the information from the briefings and seeks implications for policy over the next six weeks, called the "intermeeting period." The discussion culminates in the passing of a **policy directive.** This directive is issued to the Federal Reserve Bank of New York, which is responsible for the implementation of the Federal Reserve's open market operations.

The directive starts with a brief summary of the current situation. The directive issued at the November 14, 1989, FOMC meeting begins as follows:

> The information reviewed at this meeting suggests continuing expansion in economic activity, though at a somewhat slower pace than earlier in the year. Total nonfarm payroll employment increased appreciably in October, but on balance its growth has been more moderate over the past several months, especially in the private sector. The civilian unemployment rate has remained around 5¼ percent. Strike activity and other disruptions depressed industrial production noticeably in October. Retail sales fell appreciably in October, reflecting a sharp drop in purchases of motor vehicles, but some upward revisions were made for August and September. . . . Consumer prices have risen more slowly on balance since midyear, partly reflecting sharp reductions in energy prices, but the latest data on labor compensation suggest no significant change in prevailing trends.*

After this survey, the directive states the general objective of Federal Reserve policies:

> The Federal Open Market Committee seeks monetary and financial conditions that will foster price stability, promote growth in output on a sustainable basis, and contribute to an improved pattern of international transactions.**

This statement is obviously quite general. In recent years, many Federal Reserve representatives have indicated that they consider price stability their top priority. Some have advocated a more precise inflation goal, such as a return to zero inflation in five years. However, these proposals remain controversial due to fear that the tightening needed to reduce the inflation rate that much could hurt real activity too much.

The Federal Reserve's general goals, regardless of their nature, must be translated into specific criteria for those variables the Federal Reserve uses as its *target* variables. These targets include the percentage rates of growth in the monetary aggregates. Of more current operational interest, however, is the target range for the federal funds rate. The following specific recommendations are stated at the end of the November 14, 1989, directive:

> In the implementation of policy for the immediate future, the Committee seeks to maintain the existing degree of pressure on reserve positions. Taking account of progress toward price stability, the strength of the business expansion, the behavior of the monetary aggregates, and developments in foreign

---

*Federal Reserve press release, 22 December 1989, pp. 12–13.

**Ibid., p. 13.

exchange and domestic financial markets, slightly greater reserve restraint might or slightly lesser reserve restraint would be acceptable in the inter-meeting period. The contemplated reserve conditions are expected to be consistent with growth of M2 and M3 over the period from September through December at annual rates of about $7\frac{1}{2}$ and $4\frac{1}{2}$ percent, respectively. The Chairman may call for Committee consultation if it appears to the Manager for Domestic Operations that reserve conditions during the period before the next meeting are likely to be associated with a federal funds rate persistently outside a range of 7 to 11 percent.*

The main point here is the commitment to *maintain* the current policy position. In practice, this means keeping the federal funds rate near recent levels. However, deviations from this rule are not ruled out, as seen in the statement that "slightly greater reserve restraint *might* or slightly lesser reserve restraint *would* be acceptable in the intermeeting period" (emphasis added). The choice of the words *might* and *would* is important and indicates that the committee members are more open to an easing than to a tightening. However, before any major changes are undertaken during the intermeeting period, the chairman must consult with the committee members by telephone. Such consultations are not unusual, but they are somewhat infrequent. For example, a large decline in the stock market, creating exceptional demands for liquidity, might occasion consultations during the intermeeting period.

The directive then goes to the Federal Reserve Bank of New York. Specifically, it is up to the manager of its Open Market Desk to implement the policy by undertaking the right amounts of open market buying and selling of government securities, mainly Treasury bills. Buying such securities will add nonborrowed reserves to the banking system and thus ease the demand for borrowed reserves. Consequently, the federal funds rate will decline or remain steady. Conversely, open market sales tend to tighten the federal funds market. By watching this market and drawing on long experience, the manager of the Open Market Desk comes close to carrying out just the right amounts of open market sales and purchases.

12.5 FISCAL POLICY IN PRACTICE

Fiscal policy is more cumbersome to manage than monetary policy because it involves a number of decisions made by a number of agencies and affecting a number of people in different ways. Nevertheless, it remains an important force in the determination of economic activity.

---

*Federal Reserve press release, 22 December 1989, pp. 13–14.

THE BUDGET PROCESS

Fiscal policy is conducted by the formulation and eventual passage of a government budget. This process is slow and cumbersome because of all the detail involved and all the special interests that are affected. The problem appears to have become particularly acute in the United States, where it now seems the exception rather than the rule to pass the annual budget on time before the beginning of the fiscal year.

The budget process in the United States starts with a *budget proposal* being worked out by the administration. This effort is coordinated by the Office of Management of the Budget, but important contributions come from the Department of the Treasury as well as the other cabinet departments. The Council of Economic Advisers counsels the President on budget policies as well as on economic policies in general.

After the proposal has been approved by the president, it is presented to Congress. In the meantime, the congressional budget committees will have done their own work to prepare the budget, facilitated by the Congressional Budget Office. The budget is next discussed separately by the Senate and the House of Representatives, who typically end up passing different versions. The disagreements between the two houses are negotiated in a conference committee. These negotiations can be lengthy and difficult, especially when the respective majorities in the two houses are held by different political parties, which was the case throughout much of the 1980s. When agreement has been reached between the two houses, the budget is sent to the president, who has the choice of signing it or vetoing it. Thus, a three-party agreement eventually needs to be worked out between the House, the Senate, and the president. Again, problems arise when the president comes from a different party than the congressional majority.

Party ideology, however, is not the only source of conflict. For one thing, with each senator representing a single state and each representative a single district, regional conflicts abound. Furthermore, all members of Congress as well as the administration are under constant pressure from all kinds of special-interest groups. A separate subdiscipline of economics, called **public choice,** is devoted to the analysis of the interactions among such forces. The insights gained from these analyses often are not flattering to the democratic process.*

All these conflicts make firm decisions difficult. As a final conflict, budget makers are faced with the attractiveness of favoring the constituencies represented to the detriment of the one constituency that is not represented, namely, the future generations who will be stuck with

---

* One of the leaders of this subdiscipline, Professor James Buchanan of George Mason University, was awarded the Nobel prize in economics for 1986. For a survey of his contribution to economics, see Agnar Sandmo, "Buchanan on Political Economy: A Review Article," *Journal of Economic Literature*, March 1990, vol. 28, no. 1, pp. 50–65.

the debt burden of today's deficits. Some institutional reforms have been proposed to overcome this problem. A **constitutional amendment** to balance the budget was supported by President Reagan but never passed. However, the **Gramm-Rudman-Hollings** Balanced Budget and Emergency Deficit Control Act was passed and signed into law in 1985. This act imposes proportionate cuts in all expenditure items unless the federal deficit is removed over time according to a specific schedule. Both these initiatives seek to remove deficit spending as an option. At the time of this writing, it is too early to judge the final impact of the Gramm-Rudman-Hollings Act, although the growth in federal spending indeed has shown signs of slowing since its passage. Nevertheless, it seems clear that any attempt to tie the government's hands will suffer from a weakness similar to that inherent in the proposal to replace monetary policy with an arithmetic rule. It solves the problem of unwise policies but makes it more difficult to adapt to changes in the economic environment.

A less drastic proposal is the so-called **line-item veto,** which would give the president the power to veto individual spending items while accepting the rest of the budget. This mechanism obviously could be used to discipline a spendthrift Congress. However, it also makes it more difficult for the members of Congress to trade one budget item against another as part of an overall compromise. Also, it provides no mechanism for disciplining a president and a Congress that agree on high spending levels.

Many of the difficulties inherent in this system become much less serious under the **parliamentary system** of government, which is used by most other democratic countries. Under this system, only the Parliament is elected, usually as one chamber or with one chamber holding the real power, such as the British House of Commons. The administrative branch—"the government"—is organized around the cabinet, led by a prime minister. The prime minister is not elected directly and needs to retain the confidence of Parliament to remain in power.

This system eliminates the need for compromises, both between the legislative chambers and between the legislative and executive branches. Because the government already enjoys the confidence of Parliament, the budget that is passed is usually the government's own proposal, perhaps with minor changes. In the absence of such confidence, the government must resign, and a new government is formed from the majority supporting the budget.

The regionalism that is so pronounced in the U.S. Congress does not disappear under the parliamentary system. However, it is weakened because of the stronger role of the political parties that is necessary for forging a stable parliamentary majority. This role can be strengthened further by proportional representation and by an at-large representation used as a supplement to the regional system.

The conventional reason given for the rejection of the parliamentary system in the United States is that this system takes away the checks and balances that are built into the U.S. system. These checks and balances are presumed to guarantee against an excessive centralization of power in one branch of government.

In practice, the main weakness of the parliamentary system rather appears to be its tendency to become deadlocked if no single party holds the majority and if forging a stable coalition is difficult. Proportional representation tends to aggravate this problem by encouraging the formation of many small parties. The frequent changes of government in Italy appear to be an important reason behind that country's seemingly chronic budget deficits.

SHOULD FISCAL POLICY BE ABANDONED AS A STABILIZATION TOOL?

Our discussion of the problems of fiscal policy may have left the impression that this tool is not very suitable for purposes of economic stabilization. Should fiscal policy then be abandoned?

In answering this question, we should first note that the budget cannot be abandoned even if stabilization is given up as a conscious objective. In the process of passing a budget, a government may very well end up conducting fiscal policy inadvertently. For example, the U.S. budget deficits in the 1980s are more likely to have been the results of difficult budget compromises than a conscious effort to stimulate the economy. If fiscal policy thus cannot be avoided, it might as well be carried out consciously.

Second, we should keep in mind that monetary policy is unavailable as a stabilization tool for small countries seeking to maintain fixed exchange rates. Even a large country with a floating exchange rate, such as the United States, might find its hands tied by a perceived need to maintain a stable exchange rate. Given these constraints on monetary policy, it seems unwise to reject offhand the only other policy instrument available.

The difficulties involved in the making of public policy are not unlike those involved in private decision making. Many obstacles stand in the way of a company's success, and many companies fail. Nevertheless, we would all be worse off if nobody tried. The same appears to be true of macroeconomic policy.

12.6 BUSINESS MANAGEMENT AND PUBLIC POLICY

Although macroeconomic policy is made in the public sector, the private sector cannot ignore it. Along with all other forces influencing the economy, business managers need to keep informed about policy decisions so they can prepare for the consequences. Furthermore, because business interests are affected by public policy, managers may need to formulate and state company views related to it. Finally, business managers have a number of opportunities to participate in and influence the policy-making process.

HOW DOES MACRO-ECONOMIC POLICY AFFECT BUSINESS?

A successful macroeconomic policy usually is one that is good for business. Like workers and consumers, business companies benefit from a high and stable level of economic activity by enjoying steady demands for their products as well as healthy and predictable profits. Keeping inflation under control benefits business by removing inflation-induced distortions and making business planning easier. Internationally, stable and predictable exchange rates make trade easier and free multinational companies from unpleasant surprises.

It should be equally clear that unsuccessful, inefficient, and destabilizing policies work against the business interest. Furthermore, businesses must realize that active, discretionary policy making implies a prominent role for government in the economy. Thus, a company wishing to enjoy the benefits of active policies must also accept this role of government. A strong government presence does not imply a socialist economy, because no public ownership of business is involved. Nevertheless, this presence does mean that the government becomes somewhat of a partner in business decisions.

The choice of a preference in regard to the economic role of government to some extent boils down to a political choice. However, a choice made for a public statement on a company's behalf is different from the private choice the same manager expresses in the voting booth. When speaking on behalf of the company, the manager represents the interests of the company's owners and must keep their interests in the forefront. Private convictions do not always coincide with the company's best interests.

BUSINESS PARTICIPATION IN THE POLICY PROCESS

We have already pointed out that public policies in a democratic society reflect a complex interaction of many forces. Business is one of these forces. Many opportunities exist for business managers to influence public policy in directions that can be advantageous to their companies.

In the United States, this opportunity is most evident in regard to fiscal policy. Industry associations as well as individual companies can influence budget decisions through organized lobbying efforts. Lobbying is expensive because it usually involves both the hiring of expensive professional lobbyists and a good deal of top executives' time. Nevertheless, many organizations and companies have found that it pays to maintain good relations with key legislators.

Contact with the executive branch is equally important. In addition to lobbying, the contact with executive agencies involves a good deal of activity on the *professional* level. Many companies find it desirable to hire personnel with government experience. Business executives can act as informal advisors and can serve on presidential commissions to study special problems of national importance. Other executives might be asked to take a leave from their business positions to serve the administration in some capacity. Such appointments allow the administration to draw on a rich pool of talents and give business executives unique opportunities to apply their skills in an area of wider significance. They also contribute in important ways to the general communication between the public and private sectors.

The opportunity to serve includes the Federal Reserve System. Its chairman and governors often (though not always) are recruited from private industry. Once they are inside the Federal Reserve, however, these people are expected to cut their ties with private business in the interest of central-bank independence. Nevertheless, good business sense is usually considered a prerequisite for becoming a good central banker.

Business managers seeking to influence public policy would do well to remember that business is not the only interest influencing policy. Legitimate conflicts are likely to arise between companies and workers, producers and consumers, and industry and environmentalists. Fair play among all these forces is needed in order for a democratic system to function soundly.

12.7 TWO RECENT CASES IN U.S. MACROECONOMIC POLICY

It is instructive to look at two episodes of policy making in the United States during the 1980s. Both episodes concern attempts to slow inflation by monetary tightening. However, they differ in terms of willingness to risk recession as well as in regard to the fiscal policies conducted during the respective periods.

INFLATION FIGHTING AND RECESSION IN 1980–82

The United States had had a problem of creeping inflation since the late 1960s. With the oil price shock in 1973, the problem became acute, and in the late 1970s inflation became rampant, frequently exceeding annual rates of 10%. Double-digit inflation became a major political problem; the distortions it introduced were believed to put a significant damper on long-term growth.

After the Carter administration's unsuccessful attempts to stem inflation with a program of voluntary wage and price guidelines, the Federal Reserve decided in early 1980, with the approval of the administration, to use monetary restraint. During the two months from February to

April 1980, M1 declined by more than 1.5% as the federal funds rate rose from 14.1% to 17.6% (Figure 12.4). At the same time, consumer credit was tightened by activation of the provisions of the Credit Control Act of 1969. As if by textbook prediction, real GNP declined at an annual rate of 9% during the second quarter, although in retrospect it is not clear how much of this decline was due to the monetary tightening and how much to the second oil price shock that followed the Iranian revolution in 1979. The price of stopping inflation was deemed too high, especially in an election year, and the tightening was called off for the time being.

The election of a new president brought new resolve and new optimism. The Federal Reserve, under Chairman Paul Volcker, tightened money again. The tightening was more gradual this time in terms of money supply. Both M1 and M2 were allowed to continue to grow, but the growth rate in M1 was reduced somewhat. In November of 1981, M1 stood 4.7% above the prior-year level, compared to 8.1% in 1980, 7.3% in 1979, and 8.2% in 1978, as shown in Figure 12.5. This figure also shows that the growth in M1 was highly uneven throughout 1981. However, in terms of interest-rate effects, this tightening was not gradual at all. From July 1980 to January 1981, the federal funds rate rose from 9.0% to 19.1% (see Figure 12.4).

FIGURE 12.4

The U.S. federal funds rate, 1977–82.

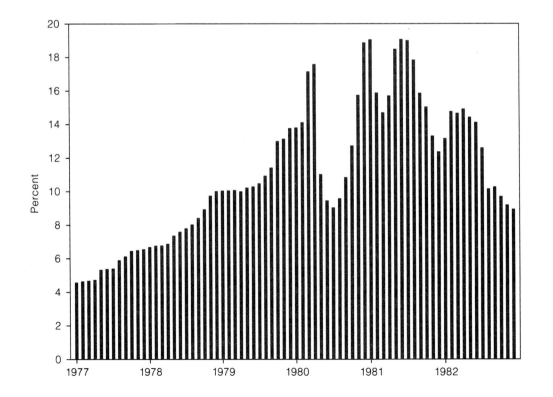

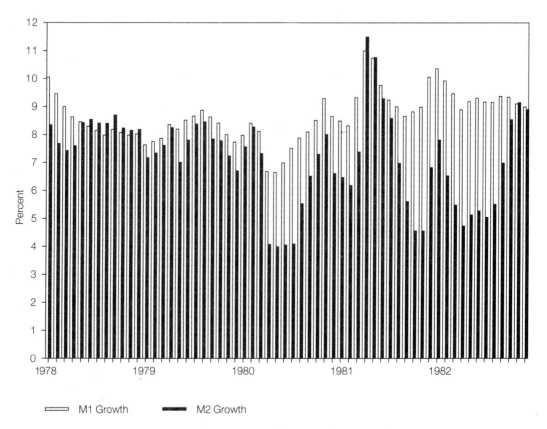

The U.S. monetary aggregates M1 and M2, 1978–82. Monthly data showing growth from the same month a year earlier.

Monetary policy was not the only factor influencing interest rates during this period, however. The election of President Reagan ushered in a new era in *fiscal policy*. The president's intentions were to increase defense spending, reduce taxes, and balance the budget by deep cuts in domestic spending, a great many of which were to come from social programs. However, these cuts were resisted by Congress, which also wanted to balance the budget, but at the cost of defense spending. The compromise that eventually was worked out gave something to everybody. The tax cut and the defense increase were enacted, and the domestic cuts were limited. However, balancing the budget was abandoned for all practical purposes. The federal deficit, which had been a modest $40 billion in the fiscal year 1979 (October 1978–September 1979), rose to $79 billion in fiscal 1980, $127.9 billion in fiscal 1981, and $208 billion in fiscal 1982.

This fiscal policy was highly expansionary and thus on a collision course with monetary policy. While compounding the rise in interest rates, this policy had the opposite effect on real activity. This situation is illustrated in Figure 12.6, which shows a leftward shift in the LM curve due to the monetary contraction and a rightward shift in the IS curve

FIGURE 12.6

Stylized illustration of U.S. monetary and fiscal policies in the early 1980s.

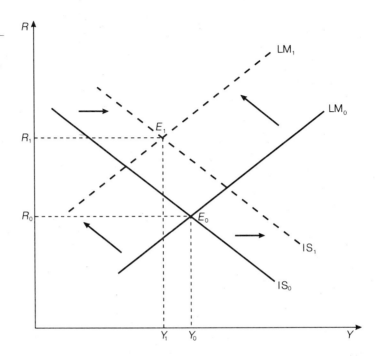

due to the fiscal expansion. If the recession that followed had anything at all to do with these forces, the monetary contraction must have been the stronger force. Real GNP fell by 2.6% from 1981 to 1982, down to a level below that of 1979. This recession proved to be quite deep, with unemployment approaching 11% of the civilian labor force for the first time since World War II.

Nevertheless, in terms of slowing inflation, the tightening maneuver by the Federal Reserve was a success. As shown in Figure 12.7, this slowing took some time—not until the second half of 1981 did inflation as measured by the Consumer Price Index (CPI) drop below 5%. The sluggishness of this response was, of course, quite consistent with the predictions of the Keynesian Phillips curve model, as was the fact that the economy entered a recession before inflation started to abate.

THE QUEST FOR A "SOFT LANDING," 1988–90

Inflation remained moderate as the economy recovered from the 1981–82 recession. The collapse of OPEC's pricing scheme in late 1985 pushed it further down and actually produced some *deflation* in the Consumer Price Index in 1986 (see Figure 12.7). Although positive inflation resumed later, some optimistic observers claimed that inflation had been whipped for good, that the Phillips curve was dead, and that macroeconomic policy henceforth could concentrate solely on the stimulation of real activity.

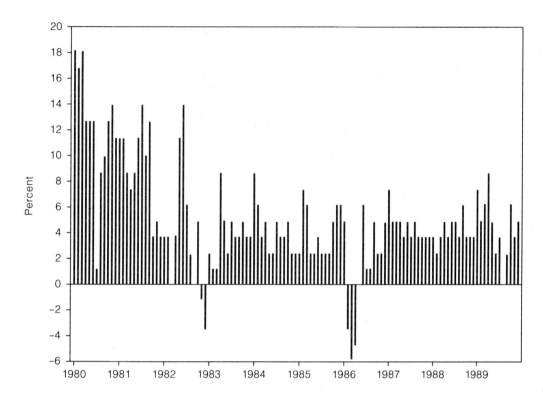

FIGURE 12.7

Monthly changes (at annual rates) in the Consumer Price Index for the United States, 1980–89.

More cautious observers pointed to the length of the expansion since the last recession (Figure 12.8) and reminded people of the inflationary pressures that had built during similar or shorter expansions in the past. Even though fiscal policy had become slightly less expansionary as the decade proceeded, they feared that "bottlenecks" in individual sectors could set off pressures for renewed inflation.

In the beginning of 1988, these predictions appeared to come true as inflation returned to the 4–5% range. The Federal Reserve responded with a tightening in the spring of 1988. Because the Federal Reserve used the federal funds rate as its policy target during this period, the tightening can be read fairly directly off this rate. As shown in Figure 12.9, it rose from about 6.5% to almost 10% over the calendar year 1988, pretty strong evidence of tightening.

Alan Greenspan replaced Paul Volcker as Federal Reserve chairman in the middle of this tightening. Greenspan was known to share Volcker's aversion to inflation but also to favor a more cautious and gradual approach to policy than his predecessor. In particular, he was anxious to slow inflation without setting off a recession. This objective came to be known as a "soft landing."

The movements in the federal funds rate (Figure 12.9) reflect this objec-

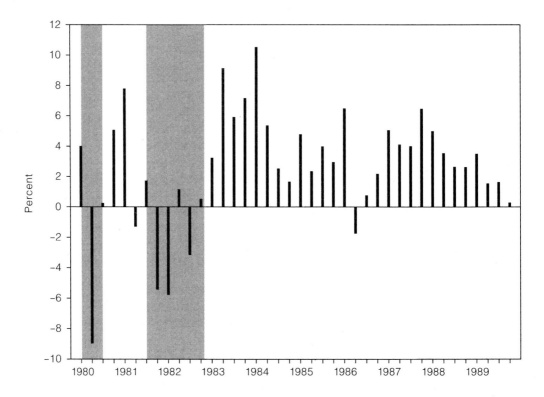

FIGURE 12.8

Real GNP growth by quarter (at annual rates) for the United States, 1980–89. Recessions are marked as shaded areas.

tive. It was increased in 1988, but not to the levels of the early 1980s, and was allowed to decline again throughout 1989, apparently before any recession dangers could develop. As a consequence, the effects on real activity were modest, except in the construction sector, which showed a substantial decline. Real GNP continued to grow throughout 1989 (Figure 12.8), although at moderate rates. (The high growth rate in the first quarter was generally regarded as a one-time recovery of the farm sector from the 1988 drought.) Employment continued to grow modestly as well, even though manufacturing employment declined toward the end of 1989, as did the index of industrial production. So far at least, the Federal Reserve seemed to have been successful in avoiding a recession.

Figure 12.7 indicates some success with inflation as well. Interestingly, this effect occurred earlier than the corresponding dampening effect on inflation of the 1980–82 tightening. This observation may be related to the fact that the tightening took place before inflation had become deeply entrenched.

At the time of this writing, the probability of recession appears to have grown, although the ultimate success of the soft-landing operation remains an open question. What does seem clear, however, is that inflation remains a force to be reckoned with in the American economy. The optimists of the mid-1980s who claimed that inflation had been

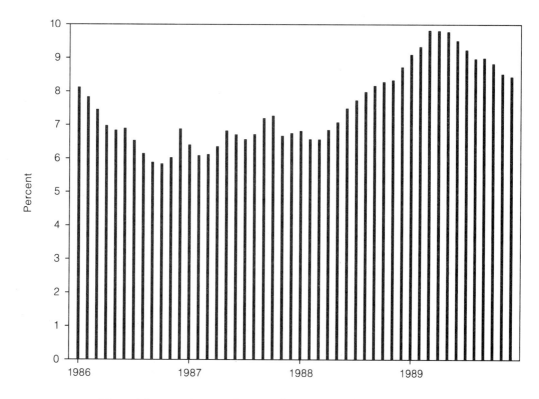

FIGURE 12.9

The U.S. federal funds rate, 1986–89.

whipped for good turned out to be wrong. The Phillips curve appears to be alive: economic expansion always runs the risk of setting off renewed inflation. Moreover, the Federal Reserve remains ready to fight inflation with monetary tightening.

The consequences of this resolve will depend on the way the fighting is carried out. If, as until now, it is done in an off-and-on manner, monetary policy can be expected to contribute to economic fluctuations throughout the 1990s, although the fluctuations might turn out to be modest. An alternative has been suggested in the form of a gradual but persistent tightening until inflation has been brought down to zero by the middle of the decade. That alternative, by being predictable, may bring more stability, but it also risks tightening too much and setting off a full-scale recession.

CHAPTER REVIEW

1. Macroeconomic policy includes monetary and fiscal policy. Monetary policy manipulates bank reserves, the money supply, interest rates, and exchange rates. Fiscal policy determines taxes and government spending. The coordination of monetary policy and fiscal policy is difficult given the traditional independence of the central bank. International policy coordination is becoming increasingly important in a global environment.

2. The main goals of macroeconomic policy include long-term growth, output stability, price-level stability, equitable distribution of income and wealth, and balance in foreign transactions.

3. A number of conflicts arise in macroeconomic policy making. Of special importance is the conflict between long-term growth and short-term stability, which involves the problem of time consistency. This problem leads to an argument for replacing discretionary monetary policy making with a policy rule. However, such a rule could become an impediment to the ability to respond to changes in the economic environment.

4. Monetary policy in the United States is made by the Federal Open Market Committee, which meets behind closed doors eight times a year. The meeting results in a directive to the Open Market Desk in New York, where the policy is implemented.

5. The institutional setup for U.S. fiscal policy is extremely cumbersome. Various reforms have been proposed.

6. Despite the problems of fiscal policy, it is important as the only remaining policy tool for a country wishing to fix or stabilize its exchange rate.

7. An active use of macroeconomic policy may be beneficial to business if successful, but it also means that the government becomes an active player in the economy. Business managers have a number of opportunities to participate in the policy-making process.

8. In the beginning of the 1980s, an expansionary fiscal policy and a contractionary monetary policy produced unusually high interest rates. In terms of real activity, the monetary contraction appeared to dominate and to produce the 1981–82 recession. The contraction was successful in regard to its stated goal of stopping inflation.

9. In the late 1980s and early 1990s, U.S. monetary policy has sought a "soft landing," whereby inflation is slowed without a reces-

sion. This trade-off sends a signal that inflation and attempts to slow it are likely to remain part of life for the 1990s.

EXERCISES

1. The minutes of the meetings of the Federal Open Market Committee (FOMC) are published in a monthly periodical called the *Federal Reserve Bulletin*. Go through the minutes for the meetings of the past year. Try to identify (a) the variables used as intermediate targets, (b) the school of thought dominating the discussion, (c) the overriding policy concerns for the FOMC during that year, and (d) how the FOMC typically responds to news about the economy. What do these insights suggest for the likely course of monetary policy in the months ahead?

2. Run a regression of quarterly M2 growth on lagged values of various variables that you think might influence monetary policy. Experiment with inflation, real GNP growth, the unemployment rate, and a short-term interest rate. What do these results tell you about the determinants of monetary policy? How do they compare to the insights from the FOMC minutes in exercise 1?

3. Get a copy of the president's most recent budget proposal for the federal government. Write a memo outlining its likely consequences for interest rates, exchange rates, inflation, and real growth in the short run. Add some thoughts about the long-run consequences of this budget.

THINKING QUESTIONS

1. The independence of the central bank is a matter of continuing discussion. The main argument for independence is that it protects monetary policy from being influenced by political expediency. The main argument against independence is that monetary policy is not subject to democratic control. Discuss these arguments and present your own views on this issue.

2. Whenever it is time to appoint a new governor of the Federal Reserve, the question of what kind of background the new person should have is usually raised. For example, should the person come from academia, from public service, or from private business? The choice involves a judgment not only about the relevance of the various backgrounds but also about the proper role of monetary policy. Present your thoughts on these issues.

3. Opinions vary as to which variable the central bank can or should control, such as real GNP, inflation, or the exchange rate. From our discussion of policy conflicts, what are your views as to the goal or goals toward which you think monetary policy should strive?

4. In this age of global interactions, it is sometimes argued that the governments of single countries, such as the United States, have lost the ability to control their own economies. From our discussion of fixed versus floating exchange rates, to what extent do you believe this is true? Can you present any proposals to improve the situation?

MONITORING AND FORECASTING THE ECONOMY

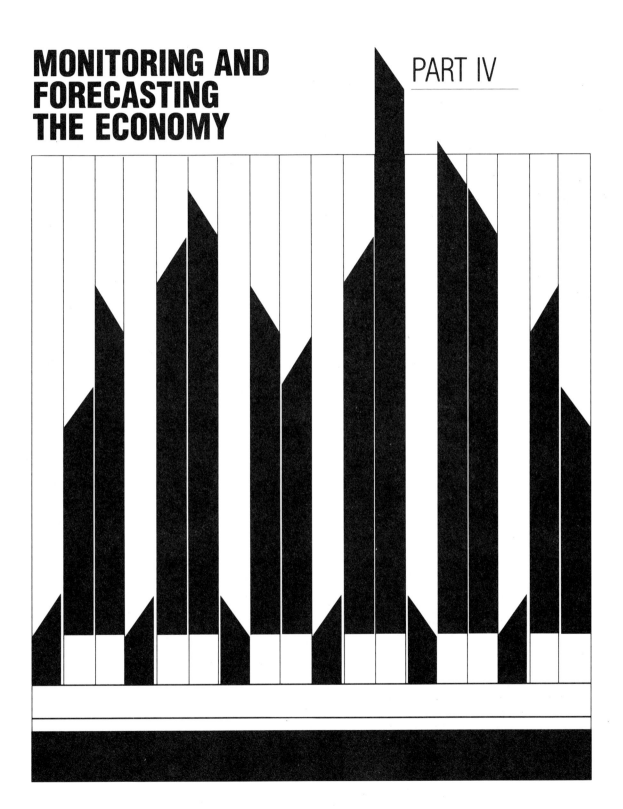

PART IV

Managers need to go beyond a theoretical understanding of the workings of the economy. In order to benefit from their insights, they need to watch the economic events as they unfold from day to day and react to them as they arrive. Knowing what is going on helps a manager understand the current direction as well as the likely future movements in the important economic variables, an understanding crucial for designing and implementing an effective business strategy. Today's news media facilitate this process by continuously reporting on new economic data as they are released.

This part of the book is devoted to the monitoring and forecasting of these economic signs of the times. Chapter 13 starts out with a survey of how macroeconomic information affects the various functional areas of management. It goes on to explain how to interpret current economic data releases as *signals* of upcoming trends and changes.

Macroeconomic data arrive in different forms and at different times. Chapter 14 provides a survey of those data that arrive at the highest frequency. These data include the daily stream of information from the financial markets—stock prices, bond prices, exchange rates, and commodities prices—as well as data that arrive weekly, such as the U.S. money supply and new claims for unemployment insurance. They also include the data for U.S. automobile sales, which are released every 10 days.

Chapter 15 explores the information contained in the National Income and Product Accounts, which include data on the Gross

National Product (GNP) and its major components, such as consumer spending, investment spending, and foreign trade. Some of these data are published monthly and some quarterly, but new information tends to arrive monthly even for the quarterly data, because each month the government uses new information to update and revise the quarterly data.

Chapter 16 turns to a group of monthly indicators that are not part of the National Income Accounting system. These indicators include some important labor market data, such as employment and unemployment, wages, and productivity. They also include the Index of Industrial Production, which supplements the production data in GNP on a monthly basis, and two widely cited price indices, the Consumer Price Index and the Producer Price Index, which compete with the GNP deflator as the primary indicators of inflation.

A regular rhythm of data releases is repeated each and every month. Chapter 17 introduces you to this rhythm by going through a sample month of regular and irregular economic news as reported in graphs, tables, and commentaries in the *Wall Street Journal.*

Chapter 18 is devoted to forecasting. It looks at how the forecasting problem can be approached from various angles and discusses the advantages and disadvantages of each approach. It also presents the Index of Leading Economic Indicators, a free forecasting service provided by the U.S. government. Chapter 18 concludes by discussing what goes on in a commercial economic forecasting firm and how managers can use these services.

13 MACROECONOMIC THEORY, DATA, AND SIGNALS IN MANAGERIAL DECISION MAKING

In its first issue of the year, the *Wall Street Journal* customarily presents a survey of macroeconomic forecasts by leading business economists. The persons surveyed are asked to present their best guesses for interest rates, real GNP growth, inflation, and the dollar exchange rate for the first and second halves of the upcoming year. The survey is updated at midyear. A table containing the forecasts published on January 2, 1990, is presented in Figure 13.1.

The average reader of the *Wall Street Journal* is not a professional macroeconomist but a member of the management team in some private business. Because the newspaper's marketing department surely must have researched thoroughly what its readers want, the publication of this survey should be a rather clear testimony to the relevance of macroeconomics for business managers. This chapter discusses the use of macroeconomic theory and data in management. We start by surveying the relationship between macroeconomic analysis and the various functional areas of management.

13.1 MACROECONOMICS AND THE FUNCTIONS OF MANAGEMENT

The usefulness of macroeconomics varies from one functional area to the next. It is perhaps most useful where the insights of all the areas are combined for purposes of strategic business decisions.

STRATEGIC MANAGEMENT

One of the most important tasks facing the manager of a company is setting an overall strategic direction for the firm. Formulating such a plan involves an evaluation of the company's internal strengths and weaknesses as well as the external environment. The company's internal strengths and weaknesses might include special resources, such as its work force, special patents or production processes, or special natural resources owned by the company.

A Sampling of Interest-Rate, Economic and Currency Forecasts

(In percent except for the dollar vs. yen)

	JUNE 1989 SURVEY					NEW FORECASTS FOR 1990									
	3-MO. TREASURY BILLS[1] 12/29	30-YR. BONDS 12/29	GNP[2] 2nd HALF 1989	CPI[3] 2nd HALF 1989	DLR. vs. YEN 12/29	3-MONTH TREASURY BILLS[1] 6/30	12/31	30-YEAR TREASURY BONDS 6/30	12/31	GNP[2] 1st HALF	2nd HALF	INFLATION RATE[3] 1st HALF	2nd HALF	DOLLAR vs. YEN JUNE	DEC.
Robert Barbera, Shearson Lehman	N.A.	N.A.	N.A.	N.A.	N.A.	6.75	7.00	7.85	8.00	1.3	3.2	4.1	3.5	128	133
David Berson, Fannie Mae	8.05	8.40	2.1	5.0	140	8.00	8.25	8.25	8.35	2.3	2.1	4.5	4.9	138	137
Paul Boltz, T. Rowe Price	8.00	8.25	1.8	4.8	135	8.00	8.50	8.25	8.75	1.7	2.5	4.5	4.8	140	130
Philip Braverman, DKB Securities	7.75	7.50	1.5	5.0	155	7.00	6.25	7.50	7.00	0.8	1.3	3.9	3.9	140	140
Kathleen Cooper, Security Pacific	8.00	8.25	1.8	4.5	135	7.00	6.75	7.50	7.25	1.6	1.5	4.0	4.1	135	130
Dewey Daane, Vanderbilt Univ.	7.75	8.00	2.0	5.3	120	7.00	7.75	7.50	8.00	1.7	2.3	5.0	5.5	120	130
Robert Dederick, Northern Trust	7.25	8.00	0.5	4.9	130	7.40	7.65	7.75	8.15	1.2	2.8	4.0	4.2	130	130
Lyle Gramley, Mortg. Bankers Assn.	8.00	8.00	1.9	4.7	130	7.20	7.10	7.40	7.30	1.5	2.1	4.1	4.0	135	132
Maury Harris, Paine Webber Inc.	8.00	8.00	2.0	4.0	135	6.25	7.00	7.00	7.50	1.3	1.8	3.3	3.5	135	140
Richard Hoey, Drexel Burnham	9.10	10.00	3.6	5.5	125	7.50	7.00	8.15	7.75	-0.5	-1.9	4.7	4.2	132	122
Stuart G. Hoffman, PNC Fin'l Corp.	7.70	8.15	0.6	5.1	140	6.60	7.30	7.65	8.15	-1.3	2.9	4.4	4.0	135	140
Edward Hyman, C.J. Lawrence	7.70	7.80	1.5	4.5	150	6.50	6.00	7.50	7.00	1.0	1.0	3.0	3.0	150	160
Saul Hymans, Univ. of Michigan	7.70	8.50	1.0	5.9	140	7.60	7.70	8.40	8.50	3.1	3.2	3.9	4.5	141	138
David Jones, Aubrey G. Lanston	7.75	8.00	1.8	5.8	138	7.00	7.50	7.75	7.95	1.0	2.0	4.5	4.5	140	145
Jerry Jordan, First Interstate	6.40	8.10	-0.7	5.2	123	6.75	7.23	7.85	8.00	1.9	3.0	4.3	4.2	135	130
Samuel Kahan, Fuji Securities	8.25	8.50	2.5	5.0	130	6.75	7.00	7.25	7.75	1.7	2.2	4.2	4.5	140	135
Irwin Kellner, Manufacturers Hanover	7.85	8.25	1.0	4.2	130	6.75	6.75	7.80	7.85	-0.2	0.9	2.9	3.6	135	125
Lawrence Kudlow, Bear Stearns	7.30	7.50	0.6	4.6	150	7.40	6.90	7.50	7.00	1.8	2.7	3.9	3.5	144	148
Carol Leisenring, CoreStates Fin'l	7.30	7.90	1.5	4.9	138	6.90	7.30	7.60	8.00	1.7	2.1	4.0	4.5	136	130
Alan Lerner, Bankers Trust	8.75	9.25	2.5	5.3	135	7.50	7.75	7.65	8.00	2.5	3.0	4.0	4.3	150	135
Mickey Levy, First Fidelity Bancorp	7.80	8.00	0.6	4.2	145	6.25	5.80	7.50	7.20	0.8	1.8	3.7	3.4	150	160
William Melton, IDS	7.30	7.80	1.8	5.3	130	6.60	7.00	7.20	7.60	1.1	2.7	4.4	4.5	134	129
Lynn Michaelis, Weyerhaeuser Co.	8.40	9.00	1.0	5.1	130	7.10	7.30	7.80	7.80	0.8	1.2	4.5	4.3	135	130
Arnold Moskowitz, County Nat West	7.40	7.90	1.1	4.8	145	7.45	7.55	8.20	8.20	0.8	1.7	4.3	4.0	140	160
Elliott Platt, Donaldson Lufkin	7.50	8.50	1.8	5.2	125	6.70	7.75	7.38	7.88	0.8	2.4	4.3	5.0	140	138
Donald Ratajczak, Georgia State Univ.	7.60	8.12	1.5	4.6	135	6.95	7.34	7.62	8.26	1.5	2.5	4.3	4.5	136	130
David Resler, Nomura Securities Int'l	7.75	7.75	1.5	4.8	135	6.88	6.38	7.10	6.90	1.3	1.8	4.0	3.2	140	145
Alan Reynolds, Polyconomics	6.80	7.40	2.2	3.7	140	6.90	7.20	7.40	7.70	1.8	3.2	3.2	3.7	141	146
Richard Rippe, Dean Witter	N.A.	N.A.	N.A.	N.A.	N.A.	6.80	6.90	7.25	7.50	1.2	2.4	4.4	3.9	133	125
Norman Robertson, Mellon Bank	7.75	8.10	1.6	4.9	135	7.50	7.70	8.00	8.30	1.9	2.3	4.4	4.5	138	136
Francis Schott, Equitable Life	7.60	8.10	1.0	5.3	135	7.10	7.60	7.50	8.00	1.2	2.2	4.6	4.4	140	135
A. Gary Shilling, Shilling & Co.	N.A.	N.A.	N.A.	N.A.	N.A.	5.50	4.00	7.00	6.50	-3.5	-2.5	3.0	2.0	135	175
Allen Sinai, Boston Co.	7.70	7.82	1.6	4.9	138	7.31	7.51	7.47	7.67	0.3	2.4	4.0	3.8	134	138
James Smith, Univ. of N.C.	9.10	7.85	3.6	4.1	145	6.75	6.25	7.15	6.75	2.8	2.3	3.7	3.4	151	158
Neal Soss, First Boston Corp.	8.00	7.75	2.2	5.0	150	7.00	6.75	7.75	7.50	2.2	1.6	4.5	4.0	140	130
Donald Straszheim, Merrill Lynch	7.59	8.00	-0.4	5.5	130	7.54	7.75	8.10	8.30	1.6	2.4	4.5	4.6	143	134
Joseph Wahed, Wells Fargo Bank	7.80	8.50	1.5	5.4	140	6.80	6.90	7.60	7.80	3.2	2.0	4.3	4.0	142	144
Raymond Worseck, A.G. Edwards	8.07	7.90	1.3	5.2	148	7.20	7.60	7.50	7.55	1.3	2.3	3.5	4.2	155	165
David Wyss, DRI/McGraw-Hill	7.50	8.10	1.1	3.8	125	7.70	8.00	7.70	8.10	1.5	2.0	4.2	4.3	135	120
Edward Yardeni, Prudential-Bache	8.00	7.75	3.0	4.0	150	7.30	6.80	7.30	6.80	2.5	3.3	4.0	3.5	150	160
Average[4]	7.76	8.12	1.5	4.9	137	7.03	7.12	7.62	7.71	1.3	2.0	4.1	4.1	139	139
Actual closing rates as of 12/29/89[5]	7.79	7.97	N.A.	N.A.	144										

N.A.—Not available. Messrs. Barbera, Rippe and Shilling were not polled in last June's survey, published July 5, 1989. [1]Treasury bill rates are on a bond-equivalent basis. [2]Gross national product, adjusted for inflation. Seasonally adjusted annual rate. [3]Consumer price index, annual rate. [4]Averages for the June 1989 survey are for the 38 analysts polled at that time. [5]The government will estimate second-half GNP later this month. Most analysts in this survey expect it to show inflation-adjusted growth of 1.5% to 2.0%. The CPI figure for the second half is expected to show an annual growth rate of about 3.4%, based on last month compared to June 1989.

FIGURE 13.1   Table of macroeconomic forecasts for 1990. Source: *Wall Street Journal*, 2 January 1990, p. A2.

The external environment consists first of the structure of the markets for the company's current or potential products. Managers must address such questions as the following: Who are the customers, and is price, quality, or advertising the primary determinant of demand? Who are the major competitors, and what form does competition take in these markets? What should the company's competitive stance be? The answers to these questions can be sought in the microeconomic field called industrial organization as well as in the management discipline called strategic management.

However, the external environment also includes those wider issues studied as parts of macroeconomic theory in the preceding chapters. The demand for a company's products ultimately is a function of the overall demand level in the economy. Thus, the trends in real GNP and overall income levels are important pieces of information for strategic planning.

Furthermore, since real GNP typically fluctuates with the business cycle, a sound business strategy should include *contingency plans* for how to deal with such fluctuations. One possible reaction is to respond passively by cutting production and laying off people in response to cyclical variations in demand. A more aggressive strategy is to cut prices and increase efforts to win over customers from competitors. A third strategy, a kind of "holding" strategy, is to accept the reduction in sales but keep most of the company's employees and let them produce for inventory or do maintenance work, in order to ensure that the company has a well-trained work force in place when the economy turns around. This strategy could be facilitated by a flexible compensation plan that varies with the company's fortunes, such as a system of bonuses determined by net earnings or an employee stock ownership plan. Because the formulation of such contingency plans involves important operational issues, we return to them below in our discussion of operations management.

However, a manager's understanding of macroeconomics can also help him or her devise a longer-run strategy to minimize the extent of fluctuations facing the firm. We saw in Chapter 5 that the demand for durable consumer goods and business investment goods fluctuates much more over the business cycle than the demand for nondurable consumer goods and consumer services. Moreover, among investment goods, residential investment fluctuates much more than the demand for business machinery. Thus, a company seeking to minimize the impact of business-cycle fluctuations might want to *diversify* its product portfolio between goods whose demands are stable over the business cycle and those whose demands are not. Determining such a strategy requires a thorough understanding not only of a company's own internal capabilities but also of these external macroeconomic relationships.

FINANCE

The finance function is another important determinant of the success of a business. It is responsible for managing the financial resources of the firm, including both securing sufficient resources to support the strategy of the company without placing it in too risky a position and overseeing the allocation of these resources. With regard to the former responsibility, managers must have an understanding of the effect of macroeconomic activity on sources of funds. One of the primary sources of capital is the stock market.

The performance of the stock market is influenced by news about the overall economy. Releases by government agencies that indicate strong real growth are signals suggesting that corporate profits may continue to be strong. Because corporate profits form the basis for the return on stock investments, such news can encourage investors to buy stocks. The resulting increase in stock demand buoys the price of the average stock, thus allowing the company to raise more money for the same number of shares sold.

Interestingly, however, the stock market often does not react favorably to encouraging news about economic activity. Instead, it frequently reacts as if "the good news is bad news and the bad news is good news." The reason for this seemingly perverse reaction is that news of strong economic activity also can be—and often is—taken as an indication that interest rates are about to rise. On one hand, higher activity levels also translate into a higher demand for money, which puts upward pressure on interest rates. On the other hand, news of increased activity tends to create expectations that the Federal Reserve will tighten monetary policy so as to keep the increased activity from resulting in inflation. We discuss these mechanisms further in Section 13.2.

Interest-rate increases tend to put a damper on stock prices for two reasons. First, higher interest rates mean increased costs of the physical investments that were supposed to generate further corporate profits. Consequently, stocks become less attractive investment objectives. Second, higher interest rates imply higher rates of return for money-market and other instruments whose returns follow interest rates. Thus, the *relative* attractiveness of stocks as investment objects declines as well. At such times, managers may postpone going to the stock market for funds.

In addition to deciding where and when to *obtain* funds, financial decisions must also be made as to how best to *invest* them. We discussed in Chapter 5 how an investment decision is made on the basis of a trade-off of the revenue it generates and the cost it incurs. In that chapter, we found that the cost of an investment project can be summarized in the form of the user cost of capital, the key ingredient of which is the real interest rate, defined as the difference between the interest rate and the expected inflation rate.

This insight brings two additional areas of macroeconomic analysis into the picture, namely, interest-rate analysis and inflation analysis. On one hand, the manager needs to know the facts about the current market interest rates and the latest inflation statistics. However, for long-term investment decisions, the current facts are not sufficient. The manager also needs to be aware of the forces affecting the future course of interest rates and inflation. Similarly, future trends in economic activity influence the prospective revenues generated by a potential investment project. The analysis of macroeconomic trends in part is a concern of macroeconomic forecasting, which we study in Chapter 18. However, to a large extent it is also a matter of interpretation of the signals contained in current data releases. The reading of these signals requires a combination of insights in macroeconomic theory and awareness of current data.

ACCOUNTING The accounting function is responsible for providing accurate and timely financial information for use in management decisions as well as for reporting purposes. Both the recording and the interpretation of these numbers and accounts require an understanding of macroeconomics. As an example, consider the use of accounting data in evaluating the success of an investment project. Most such projects require an early outflow of cash in return for a later inflow. A meaningful comparison of costs and revenues in this case requires that they be measured in the same units. Unfortunately, during times of inflation, normal accounting units such as the dollar lose their value over time. Consequently, a meaningful evaluation of the investment project requires correction for inflation.

In our discussion of macroeconomic theory, we have come across a number of cases in which nominal variables, such as the money supply, have been deflated. In such cases, we have divided by the overall price level. In theory, this is the correct procedure to follow. In practice, however, we need to decide which price index to use as our actual measure of the overall price level.

We will be better equipped to make this decision after we have studied the various indices for the overall price level in Chapter 16. However, we briefly introduced the three main measures—the Consumer Price Index, the Producer Price Index, and the GNP deflator—in Chapter 3. Which index is best suited for inflation correction in a company's accounts? Consumer prices are important, but the items going into the Consumer Price Index might not be representative of a given business company's sales and purchases. The Producer Price Index might be better for a number of business applications, but it does not reflect the prices of services or imports.

The preferable measure is probably a broad one that includes both consumer prices and the prices paid by business for investment goods, as well as prices paid by the government for the goods and services it needs. The implicit GNP deflator, which is computed as a by-product of the construction of real GNP data, satisfies these criteria. Unfortunately, however, it is not very timely, because it is issued quarterly and is subject to a number of revisions, although the revisions in the GNP deflator are usually small. Thus, the choice of index for inflation correction also involves a choice between reliability and timeliness.

In general, managers faced with making strategic decisions about investments and operational alternatives must be able to understand and interpret the financial statements given to them by their accounting departments. First of all, as mentioned in Chapter 1, managers must use financial measures to evaluate the performance of their businesses. However, the reporting and evaluation of a corporate profit report should also be read against the background of the overall performance of the economy. A company that reports a loss at the bottom of a recession may very well be financially sound. In fact, it may be carrying out expensive investments, with high start-up costs, in order to tool up for the rebound that should be expected once the recession has reached bottom. Losses or low profits incurred in an expanding economy, however, are signs of weakness. Indeed, slim profits after a long expansion period may be an indication that costs are getting out of control and may, in fact, signal the approach of the next recession.

Companies from time to time consider acquiring other firms. Thus, another use of macroeconomic insights in accounting is in predicting and reporting profits and losses for a business over the business cycle. Some financial analysts make a living predicting profits for individual companies for the benefit of parties who might be interested in buying those companies' stocks, either as passive investments or as part of a business strategy. Although the profits of many individual companies are only weakly correlated with the overall performance of the economy, the average correlation is very strong, because the economy is simply the total of all firms. This fact makes monitoring and forecasting of macroeconomic activity an integral part of the task of predicting individual corporate performance.

MARKETING

Marketing management involves a number of critical decisions, including which products to develop, how to price them, how to distribute them, and how to promote them. Business companies typically conduct extensive market research in order to obtain a better understanding of these issues. One component of this research is the analysis of demand. Though marketing research and marketing decisions usually deal with issues on a finer level of detail than does macroeconomic demand analysis, common themes arise.

First, as pointed out above, the demand for a *particular* product is usually related to the level of *aggregate* demand. This link is not always obvious. For example, the demand for microcomputers continued to grow right through the 1981–82 recession, which saw a considerable decline in the aggregate demand for *all* goods and services. However, because microcomputers are no longer a novelty, the computer industry cannot expect to be shielded from the effects of the next recession. Moreover, it is impossible for all products to be shielded all the time, because it is the fluctuations in the individual markets that add up to the fluctuations in aggregate demand.

Second, macroeconomic theory has contributed to the understanding of the demand for a number of individual products as well. In particular, the forward-looking hypothesis of consumer behavior, studied in Chapter 5, has given important insights into how people divide their income between spending and saving and how they react to income changes. Every marketing manager would do well to pay attention to the rule that people will spend most of permanent income increases but only a fraction of temporary gains. As a result, broad and lasting increases in consumer demand can be expected as a result of the substantial income gains over the last two decades in the so-called newly industrialized countries, such as South Korea, Taiwan, Hong Kong, and Singapore. Therefore, these countries should represent important markets for imported as well as domestic consumer goods. Following the same rule, the families of Appalachian coal miners could be counted on to continue their purchases of essentials throughout the strike against the Pittston Company in 1989. Even though the strike dragged on for many months, the income losses were temporary in the perspective of the miners' lifetimes. Such opportunities can be identified and taken advantage of by managers with an understanding of the relationship between income changes and spending.

Consumer demand may also react to changes in real interest rates. As in our discussion in Chapter 5, it is worth noting that any such reactions should be to *real* interest-rate changes, meaning that marketers should not have to worry about increases in nominal interest rates that appear to be purely the result of rising inflationary expectations. Moreover, for the case of nondurable goods and services, we also saw that changes in real interest rates could have both substitution effects and wealth effects and that these two effects could pull in opposite directions. Thus, a company producing nondurable consumer goods, such as food products, usually should not invest substantial resources in advertising campaigns or in special incentives to counter interest-rate changes.

The situation is different for *durable* goods, as noted in Chapter 5. The reason for the difference is that consumer decisions about purchases of durable goods resemble investment decisions. The essence of this resemblance is that the *consumption* of durable goods is separate from their *purchase*. Nondurable goods, such as groceries, are consumed shortly after their purchase—that's why they are called nondurable. For durables, however, we need to distinguish between the purchase of the good, such as a car, and the consumption of the services generated by the good, such as transportation.

If a person postpones the planned trade of an old car for a new car, the postponement represents a sacrifice, because a new car is more comfortable than an old one. However, that sacrifice is much smaller than it would have been if the person had had to stop driving altogether. In fact, postponing the replacement of a consumer durable may be seen as similar to the sacrifice involved in a modest reduction in the food budget achieved, say, by eating fish sticks instead of steaks.

For this reason, the cyclical fluctuations in the demand for durable consumer goods are particularly sharp. Any company producing for this market must be prepared for lean times every time a recession starts. It is important to prepare for this eventuality in advance, because the demand for durable goods is one of the first components of aggregate demand to drop in a recession. On the other hand, when the economy recovers from a recession, there is a pent-up demand for new durable goods, such as cars, by all those who had postponed their purchases. However, when this pent-up demand has been satisfied, there is no need for people to continue to buy more cars than normal. Thus, the level of purchases settles down to a normal rate after the initial surge following the recovery.

Because durable-goods purchases resemble investment decisions, marketers should also expect them to depend significantly on changes in real interest rates. The effect can be expected to be stronger the more durable the good. In particular, the demand for automobiles depends quite heavily on real interest rates. This means, on one hand, that higher nominal interest rates should be expected to soften the automobile market if the nominal rate increase is not believed to be matched by a corresponding increase in inflationary expectations. On the other hand, it means that expectations of rising prices can make consumers quite interested in buying durable goods. People usually think of this behavior as an attempt to beat inflation. That belief is correct, but it is worth noting that high expected inflation (for a given nominal interest rate) also means a low *real* interest rate.

OPERATIONS MANAGEMENT

Operations management is responsible for the day-to-day activities of a firm, such as purchasing, production, inventory control, warehousing, and shipping logistics. These functions have a macroeconomic dimension because they are related to interest rates and to the business cycle.

A boom may be good in terms of the demand for the goods or services the company produces; however, it also tends to increase costs, because shortages and wage increases tend to follow. Although it might be tempting to hire new workers at high wages in order to meet production demands, it is important to weigh the needs of meeting high demands against the long-term commitments that usually result from the hiring of new personnel.

Recessions present the opposite problem: Demand is low, but the company's work force, consisting perhaps of experienced and well-trained employees, represents an asset that the company should not dispose of easily. Again, the savings of wage costs resulting from laying off workers must be weighed against the long-term costs of losing experienced workers. This long-term dimension of employment relationships has led some economists to think of labor as a "quasi-fixed" input to the production process.* The tendency of many companies to "hoard" their labor during recessions has been used by macroeconomists as an explanation for the fact that measures of labor productivity tend to decline during a recession. We return to the topic of labor hoarding in our discussion of the labor market indicators in Chapter 16.

Inventory management is related to business cycles as well as to interest-rate fluctuations. The interest rate is an important component of the cost of holding inventories; therefore, operations managers should stay well informed about trends in the financial markets. However, inventory management is also a good example of a case in which the primary focus should be on the *real* rather than the nominal interest rate. During periods of high inflation, goods held in inventory should appreciate. The resulting capital gain represents a partial offset to the financing cost given by the interest rate. In this manner, the capital gain justifies the inflation correction that is undertaken in the transformation from the nominal to the real interest rate.

The business-cycle dimension of inventory management contributes an important element of uncertainty to this function. *Turning points* in the business cycle, such as the transition from an expansion to a recession, typically are occasions when demand levels change abruptly. Thus, it is easy for managers to be taken by surprise, especially if they have not paid sufficiently close attention to the macroeconomic signals indicating that a turning point might be imminent.

When unexpected shortfalls in demand do occur, unwanted pileups of inventories tend to result. On such occasions, the operations manager needs to decide whether to draw down the inventory gradually in order

---

*The classic reference is Walter Y. Oi, "Labor as a Quasi-Fixed Factor," *Journal of Political Economy*, December 1962, vol. 70, pp. 538–55.

to maintain a relatively steady production schedule or to halt production and perhaps lay off workers in order to deplete the unwanted inventory quickly. The fact that many managers choose the second alternative has in the past contributed to the abruptness of cyclical downturns in the economy.

INTER-NATIONAL MANAGEMENT

International management may or may not be a legitimate management area in its own right. However, it is becoming increasingly clear that almost all managers today need a broad understanding of the international arena, and the importance of macroeconomic insights for the management of international affairs should be clear.

International management requires international information. The apparatus to provide this information is not yet in place to the same extent as the corresponding apparatus that provides information about the U.S. economy. However, reports of foreign policy decisions, particularly in regard to monetary policy, are widely available and should be followed. These policies are important not only for how they affect interest rates, production activity, and inflation abroad but also for their effects on exchange rates. We saw in Chapter 10 that exchange-rate movements are sensitive to movements in monetary policy at home as well as abroad. Essentially, a widening of the difference, $i - i^*$, between home and foreign interest rates strengthens the home currency, just as a narrowing of this difference weakens the home currency. However, because exchange-rate movements are often unpredictable, following the rates themselves is equally important. Although exchange rates might seem somewhat abstract to people who are not used to dealing with them, they can be vitally important for any business involved in international transactions—and even for those that are not.

A few examples can illustrate the importance of exchange rates to international management. Suppose you manage a manufacturing company whose production facilities are in Japan but whose main market is in the United States. For this company, a rise in the yen (that is, a decline in the dollar relative to the yen) from ¥140 to ¥130 implies an increase in the dollar cost of production of about 7%. Such fluctuations can easily take place within a month and sometimes within a week. If your major competitors also produce in Japan, you might be able to pass on this cost increase to your U.S. customers, because your competitors will want to do the same. Suppose, however, that your competitors have their production facilities in the United States or in other locations, such as Canada or Mexico, that are better shielded against the fluctuations in the yen-dollar rate. Then you might be forced to absorb the cost increase in the form of reduced production. With luck, you will be able to recapture this loss when the yen falls again. However, such uncertainties should be calculated into the decisions of companies that consider moving their operations overseas.

As a second example, suppose you work for a British petrochemical company. The feedstock for your production process is crude oil, which you buy from British Petroleum, who extracts it from the bottom of the North Sea. Your customers are British manufacturing firms. Because both your suppliers and your customers are British, you might think your business is shielded from exchange risks. However, oil is priced in U.S. dollars on the international market, say at $18 per barrel. Suppose now that the pound declines from $1.60 to $1.55 per pound sterling. This means that the price you pay for oil rises from £11.25 to £11.61. That your supplier is British does not help you, because British Petroleum can sell its oil at the dollar price to other customers abroad if you are unwilling to pay more in pounds. On the other hand, it may well be that you are able to pass on some or all of this cost increase to your customers in the form of higher pound prices, because your competitors will have faced a similar cost increase. In particular, your competitors in the U.S. petrochemical industry will charge higher prices in pounds even though their costs in dollars are unchanged, precisely because the pound has fallen relative to the dollar.

As a final example, suppose you are part of the management team of a multinational company with headquarters in Switzerland and production facilities in many other countries, including the United States. Suppose your U.S. affiliate makes a good profit in dollars within a particular quarter but the dollar falls relative to the Swiss franc shortly before the end of the quarter. Obviously, this decline shrinks the value of these profits in Swiss francs. Note also that this shrinkage is real, and not only a quirk of the accounting system, as long as your main shareholders reside in Switzerland and ultimately want to take out their profits in Swiss francs. For them, the real value of the dollar profit has definitely declined; the exchange risk is part of the risk they take on by being involved in a global business.

To some extent, it is possible to insure against exchange risks by buying and selling foreign exchange in the forward market, as we discuss in the next chapter. However, the opportunities offered by this market are somewhat limited, because forward trading is organized only for a few currencies and usually only for contracts of up to 180 days. Other hedging possibilities exist. For example, if you need a certain amount of foreign currency in a year and want to make sure you get it at today's rate, you can borrow sufficient funds in your own currency in order to buy now the foreign funds you need in a year. However, you would not want to carry out such a transaction without being very well informed about likely trends in the foreign-exchange market. Thus, staying informed about this market is essential if you are engaged in international business and maybe even if you are not, as in the example of the British petrochemical company.

13.2 THEORY, FACTS, AND SIGNALS

The discussion in all of Part II dealt with macroeconomic *theory*. Section 13.1 identified certain direct applications of macroeconomic theory in management. We showed, for example, how macroeconomic theory can be used in marketing, where the forward-looking theory of consumer behavior can be used to model consumer demand. Furthermore, the macroeconomic theory of investment is also helpful in the analysis of a company's investment decisions, although more detailed methods have been developed in the theory of finance.

However, these direct applications are not the main reasons for going through a long exposition of macroeconomic theory. Rather, the theory was presented as a necessary background for putting macroeconomic *facts* in a meaningful perspective. The preceding section was full of references to such facts in various areas: real economic activity, interest rates, inflation, and exchange rates. The following three chapters study in detail how to obtain such facts from various kinds of data releases. We study how the various data series are defined, how they are constructed in practice, and what the schedules are for their releases to the public. Chapter 17 gives some further "feel" of how this system works by going through a typical month of regular and irregular data releases.

Current facts about the economy come closer to what a manager needs, but they are not sufficient. Management decisions are always directed toward the *future*, so decision makers need to have an idea of where the economy is going in the near as well as the more distant future. They need to know the current macroeconomic *trends* and the likely changes in these trends. This is why the *Wall Street Journal* publishes surveys of macroeconomic forecasts of the type displayed in Figure 13.1. Professional macroeconomic forecasting makes use of sophisticated statistical techniques as well as macroeconomic theory and data. We discuss some of these methods in Chapter 18.

Most companies do not have the resources to carry out their own macroeconomic forecasting efforts, nor do they find it worthwhile to subscribe to professional forecasting services. However, they can still detect important trends in the economy by reading the **signals** contained in current data releases. A macroeconomic signal is a piece of data that contains information about current and future economic developments, but in a somewhat disguised form because it is also influenced by less relevant current events. Thus, the reading of a signal requires more than simply keeping up on the facts. It also requires the interpretation of these facts in the light of macroeconomic theory and past economic experience. The rest of this section discusses a variety of macroeconomic signals a little more specifically. We suggest that managers who are able to recognize the signals and act on them before their competitors will enjoy a strategic advantage.

PERSISTENCE IN REAL ACTIVITY

Perhaps the most important trend to recognize is the state of the business cycle and the probabilities of recession, recovery, and expansion. A number of indicators provide facts related to this trend, including data on real GNP, employment, industrial production, retail sales and consumer spending, construction spending, automobile sales, and so on. These indicators are discussed in specific detail in Chapters 15 and 16. Each indicator typically is subject to its own disturbances and idiosyncrasies, which occasionally result in giving the impression that the signals conflict with one another. When the various indicators are considered together, however, a clearer picture often emerges. If it does not, the conflicting signals still provide useful information by suggesting that the economy's current direction is not settled.

When the *current* state of the economy has become reasonably clear, the next question to ask is what this information signals about *future* developments. In this regard, it is important to be aware of the fact that economic activity shows a substantial degree of **persistence,** meaning that a trend once begun tends to continue for some time. Past experience of such persistence is clear from the fact that recessions usually last from half a year to two years, while expansion periods may last for up to a decade. The theoretical explanation of persistence comes from two main sources: the accelerator process for investment and the sluggish adjustment of the price level in Keynesian analysis.

Chapter 5 analyzed how the accelerator principle shapes trends in the investment process. In this process, production changes are translated into new investment, which in turn spurs new production of investment goods. The persistent nature of this effect becomes even clearer when we look at the same process in a slightly longer perspective. Whenever the outbreak of a recession induces a decline in investment activity, the economy ends up with less capital equipment than it otherwise would have had. As a result, the productive capacity for future periods is impaired and aggregate supply contracts, which extrapolates the reduced production rate into the future.

The accelerator story spans across the schools of thought in macroeconomics. In particular, it is shared by both Keynesian and new classical analysis. As an additional explanation of persistence, Keynesian analysis adds the gradual adjustment of the price level that we studied as part of the Phillips curve dynamics in Chapter 7. If a shortfall in ag-

FIGURE 13.2

Persistence in real GNP growth caused by the sluggishness of the Phillips curve dynamics.

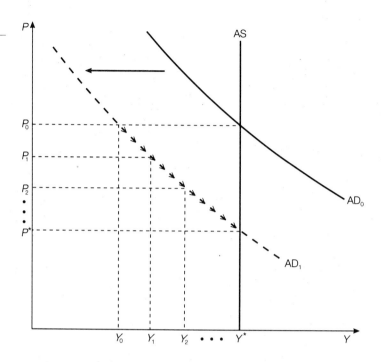

gregate demand drives the economy into recession, a dampening in the price level eventually pulls it out. However, since this process is sluggish, the movement toward recovery takes time. This mechanism is illustrated in Figure 13.2, where the recession is induced by a leftward shift in the AD curve from AD_0 to AD_1. Because the price level does not adjust immediately, the economy plunges into a recession as real GNP falls from Y^* to Y_0. As the price level declines gradually from P_0 to P_1, then to P_2, and eventually to P^*, real GNP moves back toward its original level. However, this process takes time. Thus, news about a pickup in economic activity, say, from Y_0 to Y_1 can be interpreted as a signal that the recovery process has started and can be expected to continue for some time.

REAL ACTIVITY AND INTEREST RATES

The formulation of the IS-LM model given in Chapter 6 emphasizes the fact that real GNP and the interest rate are determined jointly and simultaneously by the interaction of supply and demand in the money market and the market for goods and services. In this perspective, it does not make sense to say that an interest-rate increase causes a decline in real activity or that increased activity raises the interest rate, because *both* are driven by the exogenous forces that shift the IS and LM curves.

However, we must remember that these curves are analytical abstrac-

FIGURE 13.3

News of increased activity
signaling higher interest rates
when the higher activity reflects a rightward shift in the
IS curve.

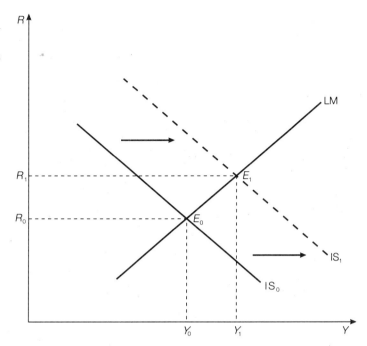

tions and cannot be observed directly. No report saying "the LM curve
shifted today" has ever come out of any news media! However, news
about real activity and about interest rates might tell something about
how the curves are moving. New data suggesting a strengthening of real
activity may be an indication that the IS curve is shifting to the right,
for example, because an innovation is raising profit expectations from
certain new kinds of investment in production equipment. This case is
illustrated as the shift from IS_0 to IS_1 in Figure 13.3. It leads to a rise in
the interest rate because the higher level of activity tightens the money
market as long as the money supply is unaffected. Thus, the news of increased production activity signals an increase in interest rates.

An alternative situation is illustrated in Figure 13.4. Here a monetary
expansion has shifted the LM curve to the right from LM_0 to LM_1. Eventually, this shift moves the equilibrium from E_0 to E_1, with a lower interest rate and a higher production level. However, while GNP changes
require adjustments in production schedules that take time to implement, the financial markets are able to react virtually instantaneously.
In other words, the money market stays in equilibrium all the time,
meaning that the economy stays "on" the LM curve, while the movement back toward goods-and-services equilibrium on the IS curve takes
some time. Thus, the likely order of events is that the interest rate first
"jumps" down to R'. Then, as the aggregate production level grows

FIGURE 13.4

News of increased activity signaling higher interest rates when the money market reacts faster to a monetary expansion than the market for goods and services.

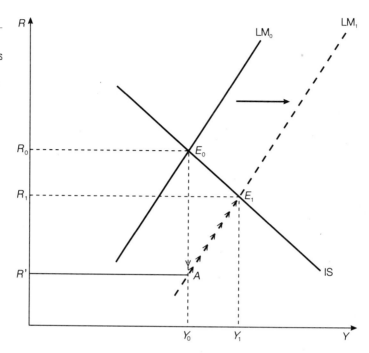

from Y_0 to Y_1, the interest rate is forced up again, from R' to R_1. Although this situation is somewhat different from that in which the IS curve shifts, the conclusion remains the same: *News about a strengthening of real activity signals an increase in the interest rate.*

Both of these cases represent dynamics along the LM curve. However, the dynamics along the IS curve should be noted as well. In Figure 13.4, the initial fall in the interest rate signals a pickup in real activity as firms planning investments and consumers wanting to buy durable goods react to the interest-rate decline. Foreign trade makes up another part of this mechanism, because the interest-rate decline will reduce the exchange rate and thus encourage net export demand. In short, *news about interest-rate reductions signals production increases.*

REAL ACTIVITY AND INFLATION

Inflation data are released every month in the form of the Consumer Price Index and the Producer Price Index for the preceding month, as well as the publication or revision of the GNP deflator for the preceding quarter.

Again, however, it is useful to notice the forces driving inflation rather than just inflation itself. Data related to these forces can be used as signals of upcoming inflation. Although we concluded in Section 8.1 that the ultimate source of inflation is growth in the money supply, we also found that the correlation between money growth (adjusted for real GNP growth) and inflation is not very close in the short run. For this reason, it is important to look for the driving forces that lie *between* money growth and inflation.

The empirical studies of the Phillips curve tell us that inflation, or at least unexpected inflation, tends to follow an increase in real activity. The Keynesian theory of the Phillips curve rationalizes that this observation is a reaction to disequilibrium in the form of a positive GNP gap. As we have seen, the validity of this mechanism is challenged by the real business cycle theory. However, if we adapt a balanced portfolio of approaches to macroeconomics, as suggested toward the end of Chapter 11, it would be prudent to expect some acceleration of inflation whenever real activity is picking up. Against this background, expecting that *news of increased real activity signals emerging inflationary pressures* has become common.

However, even in Keynesian theory, aggregate demand is not the only force that influences inflation. Chapter 8 also emphasized the role of inflationary expectations, which partly work via wage setting in the labor market. Thus, wage statistics are another signal of inflationary trends. Also, all kinds of inflationary shocks need to be watched. Extreme weather tends to drive up fuel prices and cause crop damage, which raises food prices. The price of oil was the most important source of inflationary shocks during the 1970s and 1980s. However, the prices of other commodities should also be monitored for possible similar signals. Finally, exchange-rate fluctuations tend to signal movements in the prices of imported goods. However, since foreign producers sometimes decide to absorb exchange-rate losses rather than passing them on to their customers, it is important to watch the prices themselves as well as the exchange rates.

EXCHANGE RATES

The importance of exchange-rate movements for business profits was emphasized toward the end of Section 13.1. The forces driving these rates were discussed in Chapter 10 and were identified as international exchange-rate differentials, international differences in inflation, and other factors that might influence expectations about future exchange rates. Trade imbalances are an important example of such factors, because a trade deficit, for example, indicates that the demand for foreign currency to pay for imported goods exceeds the corresponding supply arising from exports. Other examples are world political and military events. Increases in international tensions in the past have tended to strengthen the dollar, because people worldwide have wanted to transfer their funds to the United States as a "safe haven."

Above all, however, news about monetary policy—at home or abroad

—is the signal that needs to be watched by anyone interested in trends in exchange-rate movements. Monetary policy is of double importance, because it influences interest-rate differentials and inflationary expectations at the same time. This was the essence of the overshooting phenomenon discussed in Chapter 10. However, the monitoring of monetary policy has some problems of its own. This leads us to our last signaling area, signals sent by policy changes.

POLICY REACTIONS

All macroeconomic theory emphasizes the importance of monetary and fiscal policy. These policies move the LM and the IS curve, respectively, and they both move the aggregate-demand curve. Thus, news about policy changes is an important signal of changes in the economy. As long as at least some weight is given to the predictions of Keynesian theory, news about budget tightening in the government should create expectations of reduced interest rates and a slowdown in economic activity, because a fiscal tightening shifts the IS curve to the left. On the other hand, real GNP may benefit from the aggregate-supply side in the long run, as capital formation picks up when interest rates decline. A monetary contraction is also likely to slow real activity, but to raise interest rates, because it moves the LM curve to the left. Furthermore, a contractionary policy should be expected to reduce inflation, because it shifts the AD curve left, although perhaps with a longer lag than the effect on real activity.

Managers who are able to predict policy moves before they take place will be better prepared to adjust to the consequences. For example, if the manager of a company producing durable consumer goods is able to predict a monetary easing before it happens, that manager should have a head start on gearing up for the demand increase that is likely to follow from lower interest rates and increased incomes.

This insight seems fundamental. Notice, however, the results of the rational-expectations model for the case in which a monetary easing is anticipated. That model predicts that *no* real effects will occur and that the monetary acceleration will result only in inflation. This may seem like a paradox: The very attempt to take advantage of the situation will make the situation disappear. How can we reconcile this result with the recommendation just made to anticipate monetary policy?

The clue to understanding this apparent paradox is to realize that the rational-expectations model assumes that *everybody* expects the real effects of a monetary expansion to disappear. This expectation is rational because if everybody shares it the expectation will be fulfilled. Thus, the rational-expectations model of money and inflation implicitly assumes a little more than the fact that people are intelligent. It also assumes that they *all agree about what to expect*, namely, that the inflation rate will rise by the full amount of the increase in the money growth rate.* Suppose, however, that some people adjust their inflationary expectations by a more modest amount. Then, provided actual inflation depends on expected inflation, actual inflation will be lower as well. But then the real money supply rises, so the monetary expansion has real effects! In line with our discussion of a balanced portfolio of approaches, discussed toward the end of Chapter 11, it would seem prudent to recognize that this situation is a real possibility that a prudent manager would want to take into account. Then it remains true that the manager who can best predict these effects will be the one who can best take advantage of them.

Predictions about fiscal policy might be difficult to make for the long run because of the complexity of the fiscal decision process. For example, it is very difficult to know what the U.S. federal deficit will be five years from now. On the other hand, the same complexity causes the making of fiscal policy to proceed very slowly. Furthermore, this process is almost completely open to the public. Thus, figuring out what the fiscal policy stance might be for the next six months does not involve much mystery.

These matters are different in the case of monetary policy. Monetary policy moves in response to signals that the economy might not be strong enough, so a recession must be avoided, or that it might be moving too fast and setting off inflation. The policy moves can be swift, and in the United States they are mostly done in the dark, because the minutes of the Federal Open Market Committee are not released until six weeks after each meeting. Thus, making good guesses about likely monetary policy moves is an important part of smart decision making.

Since the late 1980s, the overriding concern of monetary policy in the United States as well as the other leading Western countries has been to contain inflation. However, these efforts could be abandoned at any time that the probability of a recession increases significantly. Although the central banks might not follow rules as rigid as those discussed in Section 12.3, the general guideline that monetary policy watches inflation except when recession becomes a threat is fairly typical.

Inflation indicators and indicators of real activity are thus the main signals about the likely course of monetary policy. This is the main reason why the financial markets almost always react favorably to good news about inflation. Low inflation may offer some advantages of its

---

* In technical language, the rational-expectations hypothesis implies that everybody knows what the "true model" of the economy is. If this assumption fails, rational expectations lose their usual meaning. A comprehensive but technical discussion of this issue can be found in M. Hashem Pesaran, *The Limits to Rational Expectations* (Oxford: Basil Blackwell, 1987).

own; however, many observers feel that its main advantage lies in removing the threat of monetary tightening and thus allowing low or moderate interest rates and real growth.

However, central bankers are well aware of the importance of making the right policy moves *before* inflation has manifested itself. Thus, they also look carefully at any signs of overheating, that is, at indications that aggregate demand is growing faster than aggregate supply, with the potential for a positive GNP gap and the formation of inflationary pressures. For this reason, seemingly good news about the economy might be reacted to as if it is bad news, as discussed in Section 13.1. Central bankers might view news of real growth as an indication of overheating and react by tightening monetary policy.

A weakening of real activity can be reason enough for an easing of monetary policy for the purpose of avoiding a recession. However, the central bankers are likely to weigh this concern against the danger of reigniting inflation. Part of this danger comes from the foreign-exchange market. Because an easing of domestic monetary policy will reduce the domestic interest rate, it is likely to bring down the exchange rate, which carries the danger of price increases for imported goods. The central bankers might also be interested in maintaining reasonably stable exchange rates for their own sakes. Thus, although a weakening of real domestic activity is a signal of a monetary easing, it is an ambiguous signal and should be read with some caution.

Nevertheless, it can hardly be overemphasized that the most central task of reading macroeconomic signals is to follow and interpret the forces influencing monetary policy. It is reasonable to assume that monetary policy has the power to make or break economic expansions. Those managers who can predict the policy moves will also be best prepared to take advantage of their outcomes.

CHAPTER REVIEW

1. Macroeconomic analysis has ties to most of the functional areas of management, although in varying ways.
2. In the area of strategic management, macroeconomic analysis covers part of the external environment for strategy decisions. A good strategic plan includes contingencies for recessions.
3. Finance and macroeconomics share a common focus on interest rates, money, and investment. The stock market may react positively or negatively to news of strength in the economy depending on its expectations about monetary-policy reactions. Trends in interest rates and inflation are important for investment decisions.
4. Accounting draws on macroeconomic analysis to account for inflation. Forecasts of company profits as well as their interpretation take into account the stages of the business cycle.
5. Marketing analysis has benefited from

the forward-looking theory of consumer behavior.

6. Operations management makes decisions about production and personnel over the business cycle. Inventory management depends on interest rates and is sensitive to business-cycle turning points.

7. International management depends on foreign as well as domestic macroeconomic information. Exchange rates are affected by monetary policy at home and abroad as well as by other events.

8. The main use of macroeconomic theory in management is as a background for the interpretation of economic data. A number of indicators serve as signals of economic trends; however, their interpretation requires knowledge of theory as well as the insights of former experience.

9. Indicators of strong (or weak) real growth serve as signals of further strength (or weakness) because of the persistence of macroeconomic activity, which is driven by the accelerator effect on investment and capital and by the sluggishness of price adjustment.

10. News of strengthening real activity serves as a signal of interest-rate increases, because higher activity raises the demand for money. At the same time, news of interest-rate reductions serves as a signal of higher real activity, because interest-rate reductions strengthen the demand for investment, consumer durables, and net exports.

11. Real activity serves as a signal of higher inflation via the dynamics of the Phillips curve. However, wage changes, oil-price changes, and changes in other commodity prices should be monitored as well.

12. Exchange rates are primarily driven by interest-rate differentials, so the indicators signaling interest-rate changes at home and abroad also signal exchange-rate changes.

13. Monetary policy typically seeks to tighten in response to signs of inflation, while at the same time seeking to avoid recessions. The most central task of macroeconomic signal reading is to follow and interpret the forces influencing monetary policy.

EXERCISES

1. Construct a matrix in which the rows are the functional areas of management and the columns are the main variables studied in macroeconomics. Evaluate the importance of each variable for the respective functional areas on a scale from 0 to 5. Enter the scores in the cells, and explain the reasons for your choices. Which area turns out to have the closest affinity to macroeconomics? Which variable is most important to management?

2. Your company started a new investment project six years ago, and you are being asked to evaluate the profitability of this project. You are given the following accounting data:

YEAR	NET CASH FLOW GENERATED BY THE PROJECT (MILLIONS OF DOLLARS)	CPI	PPI	GNP DEFLATOR
1	−2.0	106.0	105.0	105.5
2	−1.5	111.3	108.2	110.8
3	0.5	115.8	108.2	115.8
4	2.0	123.9	112.5	122.1
5	2.0	133.8	124.8	130.7
6	1.0	145.8	134.8	141.8

You want to use the evaluation method of net present value, which means that you divide the net cash flow for year t by $(1 + R)^t$ before you add up the values. You have been told to use an interest rate of 10%. However, the cash flow figures are nominal, so they need to be deflated. Try out each of the three price indices for this deflation. Does the result depend on which index you use? Considering the definitional differences between the three indices and the theory of the service price of capital in Chapter 5, which index would you recommend? What is your final evaluation of this project? What does this exercise tell you about the proper use of *real* interest rates?

3. Suppose you are involved with the marketing of a special brand of shoes. For the upcoming year, you are asked to estimate the

overall growth rate in the demand for shoes in several countries. You have been told that, although shoes are considered non-durable goods, their demand follows overall consumption demand pretty closely. You assume that the marginal propensity to consume is 1 for permanent income changes and 0.1 for transitory changes. You have the following information about real GNP growth in the respective countries: Country A is a developed country that has been growing steadily at an average rate of 3% per year, and growth at this rate is expected to continue into the following year as well. Country B has the same history, but for this country a recession is forecast with a real GNP decline of 1.5%. Country C has a history of growth between 7% and 10% per year but now seems to have settled down to a more steady growth rate of 4%, which is forecast for the following year. Country D is a developing country whose growth rate used to lie around 2% but has risen gradually over time. Next year's growth is predicted at 9%. Finally, country E is an industrialized country with a history of 2.5% growth per year. It is coming out of a recession, and for this reason growth is forecast as 6% for the upcoming year. Use your insights in macroeconomics to evaluate the prospects for the demand for shoes in each of these countries. Present your analysis and its conclusion in the form of a brief memo.

4. Suppose the past month has brought the following news: Industrial production is rising at 0.5% per month and retail sales at 0.3%, while the unemployment rate is holding steady. Producer and consumer prices are rising at 0.5% and 0.2% per month, respectively. Given these signals, how do you evaluate the prospects for inflation, interest rates, and real activity in the months ahead?

5. Consider the following hypothetical scenario: The Bundesbank and the Bank of Japan have both raised their discount rates by 1% each. In the United States, industrial production and retail sales have both shown modest declines, and the unemployment rate inched upward by 0.2 percentage points last month. The producer and consumer price indices have risen by 0.3% and 0.6%, respectively, while the numbers for the previous month were 0.1% and 0.3%, respectively. Evaluate the prospects for interest rates, exchange rates, and the business cycle for the next six months.

THINKING QUESTIONS

1. The discussion of the functional areas of management in this chapter did not go into management information systems or human resource management. Should they have been included? Why or why not?

2. Given that a good deal of signal reading involves guessing the future actions of the central bank, do you think it would be a good idea to lift some of the secrecy of central banking? Why or why not?

14 DAILY AND WEEKLY DATA

An abundance of *daily data* comes from the world's financial markets. The analysis of much of the information contained in these data belongs in a book on financial economics. However, a good deal of it is relevant to macroeconomics as well. Not many data are released on a *weekly basis* in the United States; the main sources are the Federal Reserve's estimates of weekly money supply and the Labor Department's tally of new claims for unemployment insurance. In a class by itself are automobile sales, which are released *every 10 days*.

In the world's financial markets, trades are carried out and prices change continuously. Modern communications technology has resulted in these markets being linked in what is very nearly one 24-hour market. People directly engaged in these markets follow them on a continuous basis. For these people, the ability to act properly within seconds—perhaps with the aid of supercomputers—may mean fortunes gained or lost. However, for most managers with other responsibilities, daily updates of the developments in the financial markets usually must suffice. Four markets are important: stock markets, bond markets, foreign-exchange markets, and commodities markets.

14.1 THE STOCK MARKET

Stock markets are organized in financial centers around the world. In the United States, the leader is the New York Stock Exchange (NYSE), followed by the American Stock Exchange (AMEX). Many stocks are also traded in the over-the-counter market organized by the National Association of Securities Dealers (NASD). Other important stock exchanges are located in Tokyo, Hong Kong, and London, as well as in other European cities. Every day, the American news media report the closing prices of important stocks on the NYSE. The prices of 30 large and frequently traded industrial companies are combined into the **Dow Jones Industrial Average.** A Dow Jones Utilities Average and a Dow Jones Transportation Average are computed as well. In the *Wall Street Journal*, the daily stock-market news is summarized briefly in the Business News section on page A1 and then presented in great detail in the paper's third section, "Money & Investing."

FIGURE 14.1

Presentation of the three Dow Jones averages on page C3 of the *Wall Street Journal*, 21 September 1989.

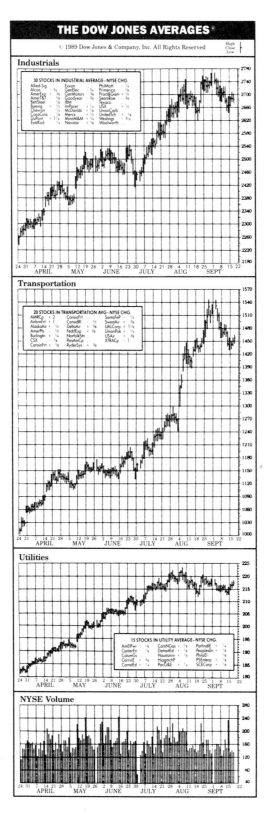

Figure 14.1 shows graphs of the three averages as presented by the paper, usually on page C3. In addition to the three Dow Jones averages, the figure also includes a graph of the trading **volume,** a measurement of the number of shares bought and sold on the stock exchange. The volume is interesting as an indicator of the level of activity in the stock market but contains no clear indication of the direction of the market or the economy. Another summary presentation, which also includes the bond market, the federal funds market, the foreign-exchange markets, and the commodities markets, is the "Markets Diary," usually presented on page C1. An example of this markets diary is shown in Figure 14.2.

In principle, it should be possible to extract a good deal of information from the stock market. According to the **efficient-market hypothesis** in finance, the market value of a company's stock should equal the *rational expectation of the present value of that company's present and future profits.* This rational expectation is sometimes referred to as "market fundamentals." A market whose prices move as indicated by fundamentals is an efficient market, while a market that strays from the fundamentals is not.

Now, since strong growth in real GNP is usually associated with healthy profits, it can be inferred from this hypothesis that an average of the stock prices of the nation's leading companies should provide an accurate picture of the economy's future health. The Dow Jones Industrial Average should be an excellent signal of real economic growth.

Empirically, it certainly is correct that the stock market reacts to news about the economy. As noted in Chapter 13, the market reaction to news of strong growth is sometimes positive, because strong growth indicates higher profits. Often, however, it is negative, because the growth is viewed as a signal of rising interest rates, either because strong growth raises the demand for money or because the news of rising activity levels is considered reason for the central bank to tighten monetary policy. Higher interest rates, whether engineered by the central bank or produced by market pressure, could spell leaner times for corporate profits as well as for the economy as a whole.

Either reaction to the news of higher growth can be equally rational depending on the attitude of the central bank. Similarly, the stock market reacts to new releases of other economic data, to political events that affect economic policy, to major accidents such as oil spills, and to natural events such as droughts. All such reactions are consistent with the efficient-market hypothesis.

However, the reliability of the stock market as a source of information is subject to some dispute. The fact that the market reacts to economic news is no guarantee that these reactions are the correct ones, nor does it ensure that the stock market does not also react irrationally to other events that have nothing to do with market fundamentals. If such is the case, the market movements may still contain valuable information

FIGURE 14.2

Summary presentation of the daily market figures for stocks, bonds, interest rates, exchange rates, and commodities as a "Markets Diary" on page C1 of the *Wall Street Journal,* 21 September 1989.

MARKETS DIARY 9/20/89

STOCKS Dow Jones Industrial Average

2683.89   −3.42

INDEX	CLOSE	NET CHNG	PCT CHNG	12-MO HIGH	12-MO LOW	12-MO CHNG	PCT PCT	FROM 12/31	PCT
DJIA	2683.89 −	3.42 −	0.13	2752.09	2038.58 +	593.39	+28.39 +	515.32	+23.76
DJ Equity	325.14 −	0.08 −	0.02	331.70	248.19 +	70.52	+27.70 +	64.40	+24.70
S&P 500	346.47 −	0.08 −	0.02	353.73	263.82 +	76.31	+28.25 +	68.75	+24.76
Nasdaq Comp.	466.72 −	0.33 −	0.07	471.86	365.07 +	81.81	+21.25 +	85.34	+22.38
London (FT 100)	2369.8 +	8.3 +	0.35	2426.0	1747.9 +	573.0	+31.89 +	576.7	+32.16
Tokyo (Nikkei)	34470.58 −	0.49 −	0.00	35140.83	27141.98 +	6757.92	+24.39 +	4311.58	+14.30

BONDS Shearson Lehman Hutton T-Bond Index

3309.27   −26.01

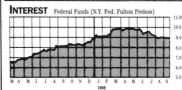

INDEX	WED	WED YIELD	TUES	TUES YIELD	YR AGO	12-MO HIGH	12-MO LOW
Shearson Lehman Hutton treas.	3309.27	8.37%	3335.28	8.29%	2822.46	3400.61	2793.95
DJ 20 Bond (Price Return)	92.97	9.36	92.89	9.37	89.12	94.15	87.35
Salomon mortgage-backed	500.61	9.60	501.60	9.55	447.02	502.06	447.02
Bond Buyer municipal	91-16	7.62	92-5	7.53	90-7	95-6	89-4
Merrill Lynch corporate	437.08	9.43	437.55	9.41	386.32	440.22	384.66

INTEREST Federal Funds (N.Y. Fed. Fulton Prebon)

9.50%   +0.60

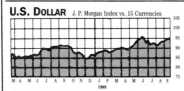

ISSUE	CLOSE	TUES	YEAR AGO	12-MO HIGH	12-MO LOW
3-month T-bill	7.78%	7.65%	7.18%	9.10%	7.18%
3-month CD (new)	8.15	8.21	7.79	9.52	7.78
Dealer Comm. Paper (90 days)	8.65	8.62	8.10	10.15	8.08
3-month Eurodollar deposit	8.88	8.88	8.31	10.63	8.04

U.S. DOLLAR J. P. Morgan Index vs. 15 Currencies

93.5   −0.5

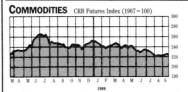

CURRENCY	LATE NY	LATE TUES	DAY'S HIGH	DAY'S LOW	12-MO HIGH	12-MO LOW —— LATE NY ——
British pound (in U.S. dollars)	1.5835	1.5700	1.5850	1.5658	1.8680	1.5120
Canadian dollar (in U.S. dollars)	0.8452	0.8440	0.8462	0.8452	0.8537	0.8097
Swiss franc (per U.S. dollar)	1.6820	1.6913	1.6770	1.6965	1.4370	1.7945
Japanese yen (per U.S. dollar)	145.13	145.85	144.70	146.45	121.03	149.46
W. German mark (per U.S. dollar)	1.9395	1.9545	1.9345	1.9600	1.7160	2.0340

COMMODITIES CRB Futures Index (1967=100)

225.28   +2.08

COMMODITY	CLOSE	CHANGE	TUES	YR AGO	12-MO HIGH	12-MO LOW —— AT CLOSE ——
Gold (Comex spot), troy oz.	$364.90	$+3.70	$361.20	$398.40	$431.70	$358.10
Oil (W. Tex. int. crude), bbl.	19.65	+0.10	19.55	14.55	24.65	12.60
Wheat (#2 hard KC), bu.	4.09	+0.01	1.08	4.03	4.72	3.99
Steers (Tex.-Okla. choice), 100 lb.	69.00	−0.25	69.25	68.25	79.75	68.25

NOTE Monthly charts based on Friday close, except for Federal Funds, which are weekly average rates.

about the market fundamentals, but the reliability of this information should be checked against other available facts. It is prudent to allow for the possibility that the stock market might be wrong; an outside observer should study the market-moving events themselves as well as the reactions they produce.

Research in this area has attempted to measure the market fundamentals and compare them to actual stock prices. The measurement method takes advantage of an important implication of the efficient-market hypothesis, namely, that the rationally expected present value of a company's profits should equal another rationally expected present value—that of future dividends and price increases for the company's stock. In other words, in an efficient market, stocks should be priced such that every shareholder is indifferent to the choice between selling the stock now and holding it for future dividends and capital gains.

Unfortunately, people's expectations cannot be observed directly. However, the *actual* dividends and capital gains can be observed easily enough. Moreover, if the expectations are rational, they should behave like efficient forecasts. Thus, the differences between the actual and the expected values should behave like *efficient forecast errors*. Although an analysis of efficient forecast errors lies beyond the scope of this exposition, we can at least note that a well-developed statistical theory is available for this purpose. Equipped with this theory, researchers have been able to estimate the relationship between stock prices and market fundamentals.

Many of these studies have been disappointing for the efficient-market hypothesis. What is typically found is that the actual stock prices fluctuate much more than the underlying fundamentals that should explain these fluctuations. This finding would seem to imply that other forces are present that make the stock prices move up and down to a greater extent than the market fundamentals would indicate.

However, it should be noted that these results are controversial. A common counterargument is that the methods used in the studies are valid only for data over very long periods and that the available data do not cover periods of sufficient length. Nevertheless, the evidence has been strong enough to convince a number of researchers that fundamentals are not the only force affecting the stock market. In the jargon of this research, the actual movements in stock prices also contain a good deal of "noise." *

---

*The expression is taken from sound engineering, where noise can make it difficult to discern the "signal" in sound reproduction. The analogy is that the stock market reproduces information about the economy but that this "signal" is disturbed by market "noise." For an attempt to measure the extent of stock market noise, see Steven N. Durlauf and Robert E. Hall, "Measuring Noise in Stock Prices," working paper from the National Bureau of Economic Research, 1989.

Other researchers have attempted to describe the factors other than fundamentals that affect the stock market. Some suggest that the behavior of investors follows fads and fashions, much as people buy clothes or choose leisure activities according to what is currently fashionable. Such fads may make the stock market move in unexpected directions.* If investor behavior is motivated by fads, substantial profits can be earned by anticipating other investors' expectations, whether or not these expectations are rational. In the words of Keynes, the point is "to guess better than the crowd how the crowd will behave."** If this is how behavior is motivated, the market can end up moving in a certain direction just because everybody expects it to move.

According to this view, a spectacular example of such behavior was the collapse of the stock market on Monday, October 19, 1987, when the Dow Jones Industrial Average fell over 500 points in one day. It is easy to argue that the market was too high relative to market fundamentals before the collapse and thus was due for a decline. It is also easy to point to certain events that could have triggered the fall, such as proposals for new legislation regarding corporate mergers or foreign trade policy. However, it is very difficult to justify how these events could have indicated such an enormous decline in earnings potentials on that particular day.

Despite such problems, the stock market can be a useful source of information when read with caution. A trained observer knows when important news has broken and has an independent understanding of what the news items mean. Nevertheless, because the stock prices reflect the actions of the financial community, the movements in these prices can tell something about how the members of the financial community interpret the news. This interpretation can be a valuable supplement to the observer's own interpretation.

14.2 BOND AND CREDIT MARKETS

The securities traded in the bond market are corporate bonds and government securities, such as Treasury bills and long-term Treasury bonds. Issuing bonds is a way to borrow money. In Section 6.2, we studied the

---

*An illuminating exposition of this view can be found in an article by Yale professor Robert J. Shiller, "Stock Prices and Social Dynamics," *Brookings Papers on Economic Activity*, 1984, issue 2, pp. 457–510.

**John Maynard Keynes, *The General Theory of Employment, Interest and Money* (London: Macmillan, 1936), p. 157. It is worth noting that Keynes's own investments made a fortune. An attempt to build a formal model of this kind of market can be found in J. Bradford De Long, Andrei Shleifer, Lawrence H. Summers, and Robert J. Waldmann, "Noise Trader Risk in Financial Markets," *Journal of Political Economy*, 1990, vol. 98, no. 4, pp. 703–38.

bond **yield rate** as the interest rate that effectively is paid for funds obtained by issuing bonds. Formula (6.7) showed how this rate can be computed from the bond's market price and its face value.

The yields on bonds issued by the U.S. Treasury make up one of the most eagerly watched barometers of market interest rates in the United States. They are often presented in the form of a graph called the **yield curve,** which compares the yield rates for bonds of similar risk with varying maturities. The **maturity** is the time that elapses from the time the bond is issued until the Treasury redeems the bond (that is, pays the face value to the person holding the bond). The maturity of a given bond is decided by the Treasury before the bond is offered on the market. As a result, separate markets have sprung up for bonds with different maturities.

An example of a yield curve with some accompanying statistics is presented in Figure 14.3. The horizontal axis in this graph represents the maturities of the various kinds of bonds, from 3-month Treasury bills to 30-year Treasury bonds. The vertical axis measures the yields, normalized to a per-annum basis.

The graph for this particular day indicates that the yield rises somewhat with maturity. This shape of the curve is considered normal, because the holders of long-term bonds must be compensated for the additional risk of tying up funds in longer-term instruments. Occasionally it slopes downward, a situation referred to as an **inverted yield curve.** Inverted yield curves are frequently interpreted as signals of upcoming recession. The logic behind this interpretation rests on an assumption that the recession is anticipated by the investors in the bond market. Investors realize that the recession will bring lower interest rates by re-

FIGURE 14.3

The Treasury yield curve with accompanying statistics. Source: *Wall Street Journal,* 2 January 1990, p. C17.

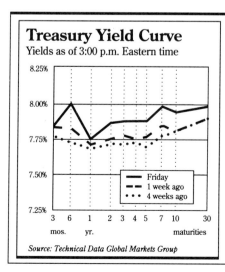

Treasury Yield Curve
Yields as of 3:00 p.m. Eastern time

Friday
1 week ago
4 weeks ago

Source: Technical Data Global Markets Group

YIELD COMPARISONS

Based on Merrill Lynch Bond Indexes, priced as of midafternoon Eastern time.

	12/29	12/38	High	Low
Corp. Govt. Master	8.36%	8.37%	9.99%	8.09%
Treasury 1—10 yr	7.98	7.96	9.89	7.65
10 + yr	8.18	8.16	9.51	7.99
Agencies 1—10 yr	8.26	8.25	10.19	8.01
10 + yr	8.61	8.56	9.82	8.41
Corparate				
1—10 yr High Qlty	8.97	8.97	10.28	8.57
Med Qlty	9.47	9.50	10.61	8.98
10+ yr High Qlty	9.21	9.20	10.32	9.05
Med Qlty	9.80	9.80	10.67	9.56
Yankee bonds (1)	9.07	9.08	10.28	8.77
Current-coupon mortgages				
GNMA 9.00%	9.36	9.32	10.63	9.17
FNMA 9.00%	9.47	9.44	10.46	9.10
FHLMC 9.50%	9.54	9.52	10.61	9.46
High-yield corparates	14.38	14.39	14.39	13.10
New tax-exempts	6.55	6.55	7.30	6.40
10-yr G.O. (AA)	7.00	7.00	7.60	6.70
20-yr G.O. (AA)	7.45	7.45	8.05	7.25
30-yr revenue (A)				

Note: High quality rated AAA-AA; medium quality,A-BBB/Baa; high yield,BB/Ba-C.
(1) Dollar-denominated, SEC-registered bonds of foreign issuers sold in the U.S.

ducing the demand for money for transactions purposes. If they hold short-term bonds now that come due when the recession starts, they will be forced to reinvest their funds then at low yields. In order to avoid this fate, they seek to transfer their funds to long-term bonds now. In so doing, they drive up the prices of long-term bonds, which lowers their yields and inverts the yield curve. Thus, in this view, an inverted yield curve is simply a representation of the bond investors' expectations of a recession.

Yield-curve inversions in fact have been followed by recessions on a number of occasions. However, it should be noted that yield-curve inversions are not a perfect signal. If our interpretation is valid, a yield-curve inversion predicts recessions correctly only if investor expectations are correct. For this to be true, the investors first must have rational expectations, which is an issue of some controversy. Second, even rational expectations are incorrect when truly unpredictable events occur. Third, investor expectations of future interest rates are influenced by forces other than business cycles. Because of these complications, the yield curve cannot be considered an infallible predictor of business-cycle movements.

In addition to publishing the Treasury yield curve, the *Wall Street Journal* includes an index of the Treasury bond market as part of its "Markets Diary" on page C1, which was reproduced in Figure 14.2. This display also includes the federal funds rate—the rate banks pay each other for funds they may use to satisfy reserve requirements—which the Federal Reserve has used as its target variable since the mid-1980s.

A selection of other interest rates is listed separately in the *Wall Street Journal*, as displayed in Figure 14.4. This list includes the federal funds rate as well as the discount rate, discussed in Chapter 4 as the rate charged by the Federal Reserve for loans to commercial banks. A number of bank rates are included as well, along with explanations of the kinds of loans or deposits to which they pertain. Finally, some foreign interest rates are included, such as the London Eurodollar rate, which is the interest rate paid by London banks on deposits denominated in U.S. dollars.

14.3 FOREIGN-EXCHANGE MARKETS

Foreign exchange is usually traded as bank accounts denominated in different currencies. Most of the trade takes place between the major banks (the "interbank" market) and between banks and their corporate customers. Modern communications make it a truly global market. The rates vary by the minute. The closing rates in each financial center are reported regularly in the media. Because of the substantial time differ-

FIGURE 14.4

Daily interest rate data.
Source: *Wall Street Journal*,
2 January 1990, p. C17.

MONEY RATES

Friday, December 29, 1989

The key U.S. and foreign annual interest rates below are a guide to general levels but don't always represent actual transactions.

PRIME RATE: 10½%. The base rate on corporate loans at large U.S. money center commecial banks.

FEDERAL FUNDS: 9¾% high, 6% low, 7½% near closing bid, 8½% offered. Reserves traded among commercial banks for overnight use in amounts of $1 million or more. Source: Fulton Prebon (U.S.A.) Inc.

DISCOUNT RATE: 7%. The charge on loans to depository institutions by the New York Federal Reserve Bank.

CALL MONEY: 10½%. The charge on loans to brokers on stock exchange collateral.

COMMERCIAL PAPER placed directly by General Motors Acceptance Corp.: 8.25% 30 to 44 days; 8.20% 45 to 59 days; 8.10% 60 to 89 days; 8% 90 to 119 days; 7.875% 120 to 149 days; 7.75% 150 to 179 days; 7.50% 180 to 270 days.

COMMERCIAL PAPER: High-grade unsecured notes sold through dealers by major corporations in multiples of $1,000: 8.65% 30 days; 8.45% 60 days; 8.30% 90 days.

CERTIFICATES OF DEPOSIT: 7.93% one month; 7.83% two months; 7.77% three months; 7.59% six months; 7.59% one year. Average of top rates paid by major New York banks on primary new issues of negotiable C.D.'s, usually on amounts of $1 million and more. The minimum unit is $100,000. Typical rates in the secondary market: 8.30% one month; 8.15% three months; 8.10% six months.

BANKERS ACCEPTANCES: 8.70% 30 days; 8.35% 60 days; 8.13% 90 days; 7.95% 120 days; 7.87% 150 days; 7.80%

180 days. Negotiable, bank-backed business credit instruments typically financing an import order.

LONDON LATE EURODOLLARS: 8⁷/₁₆% to 8⁵/₁₆% one month; 8⅜% to 8¼% two months; 8⅜% to 8¼% three months; 8⅜% to 8¼% four months; 8¼% to 8⅛% five months; 8¼% to 8⅛% six months.

LONDON INTERBANK OFFERED RATES (LIBOR): 8½% one month; 8⅜% three months; 8⁵/₁₆% six months; 8¼% one year. The average of interbank offered rates for dollar deposits in the London market based on quotations at five major banks.

FOREIGN PRIME RATES: Canada 13.50%; Germany 9.50%; Japan 4.875%; Switzerland 8.50%; Britain 15%. These rate indications aren't directly comparable; lending practices vary widely by location.

TREASURY BILLS: Results of the Tuesday, December 26, 1989, auction of short-term U.S. government bills, sold at a discount from face value in units of $10,000 to $1 million: 7.77% 13 weeks; 7.64% 26 weeks.

FEDERAL HOME LOAN MORTGAGE CORP. (Freddie Mac): Posted yields on 30-year mortgage commitments for delivery within 30 days. 9.77%, standard conventional fixed-rate mortgages; 8.25%, 2% rate capped one-year adjustable rate mortgages. Source: Telerate Systems Inc.

FEDERAL NATIONAL MORTGAGE ASSOCIATION (Fannie Mae): Posted yields on 30 year mortgage commitments for delivery within 30 days (priced at par) 9.75%, standard conventional fixed rate-mortgages; 8.60%, 6/2 rate capped one-year adjustable rate mortgages. Source: Telerate Systems Inc.

MERRILL LYNCH READY ASSETS TRUST: 7.81%. Annualized average rate of return after expenses for the past 30 days; not a forecast of future returns.

ence, the banks in Japan close before the start of business in the United States, so the closing exchange rates in Tokyo are reported on American radio and television in the early morning, often accompanied by midday quotes from Europe. The closing rates of the previous day are listed in the morning newspaper for leisurely reading.

Exchange rates are traded in both a spot market and a forward market. A **spot** transaction is a purchase for immediate delivery, while a **forward** transaction is a purchase of a contract for future delivery at a price that is predetermined in the contract. Forward transactions can be an important instrument for lowering risks of exchange-rate fluctuations for a company that anticipates payments or receipts in foreign currencies at certain points in the future. The prices of the forward deliveries reflect the market's expectations of the spot exchange rate at the time of delivery. We discussed some of the forces that influence these expectations in Chapter 10.

The "Markets Diary" (Figure 14.2) in the *Wall Street Journal* includes an index of the value of the U.S. dollar vis-à-vis a weighted average of 15 foreign currencies. This newspaper also publishes spot and forward exchange rates vis-à-vis a number of individual currencies. These are the rates of the so-called **interbank market** in New York, that is, the rates that the large banks pay each other. Figure 14.5 shows an example of how they are listed. The first two columns show the closing dollar prices of the respective currencies for the night before publication, in the

FIGURE 14.5

Typical presentation of spot
and forward exchange rates.
Source: *Wall Street Journal*,
21 September 1989.

EXCHANGE RATES

Wednesday, September 20, 1989

The New York foreign exchange selling rates below apply to trading among banks in amounts of $1 million and more, as quoted at 3 p.m. Eastern time by Bankers Trust Co. Retail transactions provide fewer units of foreign currency per dollar.

	U.S. $ equiv.		Currency per U.S. $	
Country	Wed.	Tues.	Wed.	Tues.
Argentina (Austral)	.001626	.001626	615.00	615.00
Australia (Dollar)	.7745	.7750	1.2911	1.2903
Austria (Schilling)	.07327	.07271	13.64	13.75
Bahrain (Dinar)	2.6521	2.6521	.3770	.3770
Belgium (Franc)				
Commercial rate	.02462	.02446	40.61	40.86
Financial rate	.02457	.02442	40.68	40.94
Brazil (Cruzado)	.30836	.30836	3.2429	3.2429
Britain (Pound)	1.5825	1.5715	.6319	.6363
30-Day Forward	1.5760	1.5648	.6345	.6390
90-Day Forward	1.5639	1.5529	.6394	.6439
180-Day Forward	1.5460	1.5349	.6468	.6515
Canada (Dollar)	.8455	.8453	1.1827	1.1830
30-Day Forward	.8430	.8429	1.1861	1.1863
90-Day Forward	.8384	.8371	1.1927	1.1946
180-Day Forward	.8322	.8321	1.2016	1.2017
Chile (Official rate)	.0037564	.0037564	266.21	266.21
China (Yuan)	.268716	.268716	3.7214	3.7214
Colombia (Peso)	.002444	.002444	409.00	409.00
Denmark (Krone)	.1325	.1317	7.5425	7.5895
Ecuador (Sucre)				
Floating rate	.001713	.001713	583.50	583.50
Finland (Markka)	.2282	.2269	4.3810	4.4065
France (Franc)	.152485	.151584	6.5580	6.5970
30-Day Forward	.152462	.151561	6.5590	6.5980
90-Day Forward	.152322	.151416	6.5650	6.6043
180-Day Forward	.152102	.151205	6.5745	6.6135
Greece (Drachma)	.005952	.005941	167.99	168.30
Hong Kong (Dollar)	.128090	.128073	7.8070	7.8080
India (Rupee)	.0597014	.0597014	16.75	16.75
Indonesia (Rupiah)	.0005633	.0005633	1775.00	1775.00
Ireland (Punt)	1.3772	1.3620	.726110	.734214
Israel (Shekel)	.5100	.5100	1.9607	1.9607
Italy (Lira)	.0007147	.0007097	1399.00	1409.00
Japan (Yen)	.006891	.006859	145.10	145.78
30-Day Forward	.006911	.006878	144.69	145.37
90-Day Forward	.006946	.00689655	143.96	145.00
180-Day Forward	.006997	.00696475	142.91	143.58
Jordan (Dinar)	1.6736	1.6736	.5975	.5975
Kuwait (Dinar)	3.3333	3.3333	.3000	.3000
Lebanon (Pound)	.001934	.001934	517.00	517.00
Malaysia (Ringgit)	.3710	.3707	2.6950	2.6975
Malta (Lira)	2.7855	2.7855	.3590	.3590
Mexico (Peso)				
Floating rate	.0003909	.0003909	2558.00	2558.00
Netherland (Guilder)	.4574	.4541	2.1860	2.2020
New Zealand (Dollar)	.5930	.5925	1.6863	1.6877
Norway (Krone)	.1413	.1404	7.0770	7.1185
Pakistan (Rupee)	.04773	.04773	20.95	20.95
Peru (Inti)	.0002388	.0002388	4186.00	4186.00
Philippines (Peso)	.046728	.046728	21.40	21.40
Portugal (Escudo)	.006131	.006143	163.08	162.78
Saudi Arabia (Riyal)	.26680	.26680	3.7480	3.7480
Singapore (Dollar)	.5053	.5053	1.9790	1.9790
South Africa (Rand)				
Commercial rate	.3574	.3558	2.7978	2.8103
Financial rate	.2475	.2475	4.0400	4.0400
South Korea (Won)	.0014974	.0014974	667.80	677.80
Spain (Peseta)	.008247	.008193	121.25	122.05
Sweden (Krona)	.1522	.1513	6.5700	6.6065
Switzerland (Franc)	.5948	.5915	1.6810	1.6905
30-Day Forward	.5956	.5922	1.6789	1.6886
90-Day Forward	.5966	.5931	1.6760	1.6858
180-Day Forward	.5983	.5947	1.6714	1.6813
Taiwan (Dollar)	.039108	.039108	25.57	25.57
Thailand (Baht)	.038476	.038476	25.99	25.99
Turkey (Lira)	.0004482	.0004482	2231.00	2231.00
United Arab (Dirham)	.2722	.2722	3.6725	3.6725
Uruguay (New Peso)				
Financial	.001489	.001489	671.50	671.50
Venezuela (Bolivar)				
Floating rate	.0261437	.0261437	38.25	38.25
W. Germany (Mark)	.5152	.5120	1.9408	1.9530
30-Day Forward	.5159	.5127	1.9381	1.9502
90-Day Forward	.5170	.5138	1.9339	1.9462
180-Day Forward	.5184	.5150	1.9288	1.9414
SDR	1.24669	1.24370	0.802127	0.804053
ECU	1.06667	1.05985	...	...

Special Drawing Rights (SDR) are based on exchange rates for the U.S., West German, British, French and Japanese currencies. Source: International Monetary Fund.

European Currency Unit (ECU) is based on a basket of community currencies. Source: European Community Commission.

Z-Not quoted.

newspaper and the corresponding price one day earlier. The comparison with the prices one day earlier helps the reader see the changes in the market and compare them to recent trends. The next two columns show the prices of the U.S. dollar in terms of each currency, which are simply the reciprocals of the numbers in the first two columns. This table can usually be found somewhere in the middle of the "Money & Investing" section of the *Wall Street Journal*.

The fluctuations in exchange rates can be substantial. For example, from 1985 to 1987 the value of the U.S. dollar in terms of Japanese yen fell from about ¥250 to about ¥125, a 50% decrease. We noted in Chapter 13 that these fluctuations can have a dramatic impact on earnings for companies that are involved in international transactions, and even for those that are not. Careful hedging of these risks, for example, through forward transactions, can be important.

Like stock and bond prices, exchange rates respond to major news items about the forces that affect them, such as interest-rate movements at home or abroad, new inflation figures, trade-balance figures, reports of central-bank intervention, and trade policy decisions, as well as to reports of other political events, such as the opening of the Berlin wall. Again, it is important to understand the events themselves, though the exchange markets may serve as gauges of how the events are interpreted in the international financial community.

14.4 THE COMMODITIES MARKETS

The main commodities markets in the United States are located in Chicago (the Chicago Board of Trade and the Chicago Mercantile Exchange) and New York (the New York Mercantile Exchange). In these markets, traders buy and sell staple commodities such as agricultural products (for example, wheat, corn, and pork bellies), metals (for example, gold, silver, copper, platinum, and palladium), and fuels (crude oil, gasoline, and heating oil). Both spot and futures transactions are undertaken. A **futures** transaction is the purchase of a contract specifying the delivery of a given quantity of a given commodity at a given price on a specified future date. It is similar to a forward contract, except that for a futures contract the daily price changes prior to the delivery date are actually paid by the party incurring a loss from the price change to the party making a profit. For example, if the market price of a contract for January delivery rises in December, the buyer pays the seller the amount of this increase in December. This feature of futures contracts is called **marking to market.**

The *Wall Street Journal* reports the daily closing commodities prices. The reports are usually found around the middle of the third section ("Money & Investing"). Figure 14.6 shows a sample of such a listing. For

FIGURE 14.6 Typical listing of commodities futures markets. Source: *Wall Street Journal*, 21 September 1989.

COMMODITY FUTURES PRICES

Wednesday, September 20, 1989

Open Interest Reflects Previous Trading Day.

—GRAINS AND OILSEEDS—

CORN (CBT) 5,000 bu.; cents per bu.

	Open	High	Low	Settle	Change	Lifetime High	Lifetime Low	Open Interest
Sept	235	239	230	234½	+ ¾	317¾	217	1,467
Dec	228	229¾	228	228½	+ 1¼	295	218½	96,537
Mr90	235¾	237	235¼	235½	+ 1	286¼	236	34,121
May	240½	242	237¾	240	+ ½	289½	230	9,026
July	243	244½	242	242	...	285	231	7,122
Sept	237	238	237	237	...	271	229	328
Dec	234	235¼	234	237	...	267½	222	3,318

Est vol 27,000; vol Tues 27,678; open int 141,919, −1,392.

OATS (CBT) 5,000 bu.; cents per bu.

	Open	High	Low	Settle	Change	Lifetime High	Lifetime Low	Open Interest
Sept	133½	135	133½	135	+ 1	243	130¼	51
Dec	141	141½	139½	139½	− ¾	247	139	8,065
Mr90	150½	151¼	149½	147½	− ½	234	149½	1,423
May	155	155	156	155	− ½	201	153½	189
July	158¾	140	150½	150½	+ ¼	179	157	326

Est vol 1,030; vol Tues 867; open int 10,054, +42.

SOYBEANS (CBT) 5,000 bu.; cents per bu.

	Open	High	Low	Settle	Change	Lifetime High	Lifetime Low	Open Interest
Sept	568½	570	564	568¼	+ 5¼	835	563	549
Nov	572	577	572	575½	+ 7	793	562	50,967
Ja90	583	587¾	583	585¾	+ 6¾	767	572	12,618
Mar	596	599	594¾	598¼	+ 7	774	581½	7,829
May	625	607½	633½	606	+ 6	778	509	4,943
July	608½	610½	607½	609¼	+ 4	778	593	2,233
Aug	...	...	...	602	+ 6	705	598	130
Sept	...	...	...	590	+ 6	660	578	143
Nov	582	589	582	586	+ 6	660	572	1,144

Est vol 31,000; vol Tues 29,158; open Int 83,576, +320.

SOYBEAN MEAL (CBT) 100 tons; $ per ton.

	Open	High	Low	Settle	Change	Lifetime High	Lifetime Low	Open Interest
Sept	206.00	206.50	282.90	205.60	+ 1.00	290.00	180.10	1,279
Oct	187.00	108.30	106.50	187.90	+ 1.10	237.00	176.50	12,561
Dec	182.08	183.40	182.00	183.20	+ 1.60	270.00	175.50	28,430
Ja90	181.50	182.20	181.08	182.10	+ 1.60	230.00	176.10	6,629
Mar	180.00	181.50	180.00	181.00	+ 2.00	230.50	178.00	4,185
May	179.00	180.50	179.00	180.20	+ .70	230.50	177.50	2,525
July	177.00	178.70	177.00	178.50	+ 2.00	203.00	175.00	2,417
Aug	176.00	176.00	176.00	176.00	+ 1.00	188.00	174.00	386
Sept	...	...	...	173.00	+ 1.00	186.00	171.50	237

Est vol 16,000; vol Tues 20,811; open int 58,640, +242.

SOYBEAN OIL (CBT) 60,000 lbs.; cents per lb.

	Open	High	Low	Settle	Change	Lifetime High	Lifetime Low	Open Interest
Sept	18.85	19.12	18.85	19.05	+ .25	28.70	17.65	390
Oct	18.95	19.25	18.92	19.11	+ .34	26.95	17.08	14,823
Dec	19.37	19.70	19.37	19.57	+ .36	28.05	18.33	28,780
Ja90	19.40	19.90	19.40	19.82	+ .37	25.45	18.55	12,147
Mar	20.08	20.30	20.00	20.23	+ .38	25.85	18.96	5,008
May	20.63	20.43	20.51	20.51	+ .30	26.05	19.30	1,362
July	20.00	21.00	20.00	20.92	+ .27	25.25	19.50	1,221
Aug	...	...	...	20.92	+ .25	22.10	19.60	191
Sept	...	...	...	20.92	+ .17	21.76	19.60	321
Oct	...	...	...	20.92	+ .17	21.28	20.45	115

Est vol 20,000; vol Tues 10,991; open int 62,527, −197.

WHEAT (CBT) 5,000 bu.; cents per bu.

	Open	High	Low	Settle	Change	Lifetime High	Lifetime Low	Open Interest
Sept	381½	381½	379½	300	...	429	330½	320
Dec	391	392	391	391¾	+ 1½	440½	378	36,530
Mr90	390	390¾	390	390¼	+ ¾	443	309	15,450
May	371	374	371	371¾	+ 1¼	432	370	3,962
July	363½	346½	363¼	343½	+ ¾	385	342¼	5,643
Sept	352	352	340½	340¾	+ ¾	377	348	1,336

Est vol 8,000; vol Tues 11,296; open int 62,241, −227.

HOGS (CME) 30,000 lbs.; cents per lb.

	Open	High	Low	Settle	Change	Lifetime High	Lifetime Low	Open Interest
Oct	41.40	41.87	41.25	41.77	+ .10	47.00	38.50	7,735
Dec	43.05	41.65	42.80	42.45	+ .16	47.25	40.55	10,955
Fb90	43.87	44.65	43.82	44.40	+ .42	48.05	41.75	5,081
Apr	41.85	42.52	41.85	42.45	+ .52	45.10	39.40	3,100
June	46.50	47.00	46.50	46.97	+ .42	40.70	44.25	934
July	46.00	47.00	46.00	47.65	+ .40	49.10	44.95	384

Est vol 7,958; vol Tues 13,386; open int 28,253, −60.

PORK BELLIES (CME) 40,000 lbs.; cents per lb.

	Open	High	Low	Settle	Change	Lifetime High	Lifetime Low	Open Interest
Feb	47.15	49.50	47.00	49.50	+ 2.00	61.60	38.30	9,236
Mar	47.30	49.62	47.20	49.62	+ 2.00	62.00	38.15	2,029
May	48.30	50.00	40.25	50.00	+ 2.00	61.00	39.50	514
July	48.00	51.00	48.60	51.00	+ 2.00	61.00	39.95	252
Aug	47.95	48.10	47.95	48.10	...	51.00	39.30	117

Est vol 3,872; vol Tues 2,997; open int 12,138, +25.

—FOOD AND FIBER—

COCOA (CSCE)—10 metric tons; $ per ton.

	Open	High	Low	Settle	Change	Lifetime High	Lifetime Low	Open Interest
Dec	1,055	1,062	1,048	1,051	+ 4	1,735	1,031	17,649
Mr90	1,065	1,060	1,048	1,048	+ 3	1,535	1,033	16,709
May	1,068	1,071	1,062	1,063	+ 4	1,465	1,648	6,185
July	1,087	1,087	1,083	1,081	+ 3	1,380	1,063	1,522
Sept	1,108	1,107	1,099	1,099	+ 6	1,609	1,000	4,464
Dec	1,125	1,140	1,129	1,129	+ 5	1,395	1,120	2,790

Est vol 2,783; vol Tues 2,578; open int 43,127, +90.

COFFEE (CSCE)—37,000 lbs.; cents per lb.

	Open	High	Low	Settle	Change	Lifetime High	Lifetime Low	Open Interest
Dec	81.00	82.90	79.80	82.74	+ 2.85	149.50	76.05	17,668
Mr90	82.34	85.00	82.15	84.75	+ 2.51	166.00	79.60	10,262
May	85.20	87.30	84.00	87.21	+ 2.81	124.50	82.25	2,532
July	87.30	90.00	86.25	89.56	+ 3.00	123.00	84.80	947
Sept	89.50	91.00	88.70	91.13	+ 1.00	120.00	87.00	551
Dec	92.50	92.50	92.50	93.08	+ 2.13	104.00	90.00	599

Est vol 6,457; vol Tues 4,835; open int 32,428, +304.

SUGAR—WORLD (CSCE)—112,000 lbs.; cents per lb.

	Open	High	Low	Settle	Change	Lifetime High	Lifetime Low	Open Interest
Oct	14.38	14.92	14.10	14.79	− .08	14.92	8.45	32,422
Mr90	13.82	13.90	13.60	13.49	− .07	14.03	8.75	104,607
May	13.63	13.48	13.42	13.45	−0.02	13.73	9.28	21,497
July	13.47	13.50	13.28	13.30	+ .03	13.50	10.55	8,850
Oct	13.10	13 .15	12.87	12.90	− .01	13.19	10.40	3,084

Est vol 32,287; vol Tues 32,928; open int 171,198, −1,017.

SUGAR—DOMESTIC (CSCE)—112,000 lbs.; cents per lb.

	Open	High	Low	Settle	Change	Lifetime High	Lifetime Low	Open Interest
Nov	22.66	22.71	22.65	22.70	+ .09	24.71	21.62	1,798
Ja90	22.35	22.40	22.25	22.43	+ .13	22.97	21.61	2,234
Mar	22.55	22.40	22.55	22.40	+ .10	22.95	21.90	1,614
May	...	...	...	22.73	+ .06	23.00	21.00	1,663
July	22 .81	22.81	22.81	22.81	+ .06	21.05	21.95	715
Sept	22.77	22.77	22.77	22.81	+ .02	22.95	21.65	768

Est vol 1,256; vol Tues 526; open int 8,627, +175.

PALLADIUM (NYM) 100 troy oz.; $ per troy oz.

	Open	High	Low	Settle	Change	Lifetime High	Lifetime Low	Open Interest
Sept	142.00	143.00	142.00	142.00	+ .75	180.00	119.00	12
Dec	143.50	145.75	143.50	145.10	+ 1.50	177.50	122.25	5,057
Mr90	144.00	145.25	143.50	145.20	+ 1.60	176.00	123.00	1,274
June	144.75	144.75	144.75	145.45	+ 1.35	175.00	133.00	685
Sept	...	...	...	145.80	+ 1.35	149.00	133.00	204

Est vol 691; vol Tues 418; open int 7, 257, +37.

SILVER (CMX)—5,000 troy oz.; cents per troy oz.

	Open	High	Low	Settle	Change	Lifetime High	Lifetime Low	Open Interest
Sept	508.5	514.0	508.5	511.9	+ 5.8	861.0	502.0	141
Dec	517.5	525.0	517.0	521.5	+ 5.5	806.0	511.0	57,125
Mr90	529.0	525.0	529.0	523.1	+ 5.6	910.0	522.0	11,557
May	542.5	542.5	540.0	541.2	+ 5.8	910.0	520.0	6,167
July	545.0	590.0	545.0	549.4	+ 6.0	761.5	537.5	4,944
Sept	...	...	...	550.1	+ 6.3	760.0	540.0	2,304
Dec	569.5	549.5	540.5	570.3	+ 6.6	742.0	542.5	1,471
Mr91	...	...	...	582.7	+ 6.7	666.0	575.0	579
May	587.0	587.0	587.0	591.1	+ 6.8	608.0	500.0	287
July	...	...	...	599.7	+ 6.9	593.0	593.0	102

Est vol 16,000; vol Tues 5,365; open int 84,757, +70.

SILVER (CST)—1,000 troy oz.; cents per troy oz.

	Open	High	Low	Settle	Change	Lifetime High	Lifetime Low	Open Interest
Sept	507.0	510.0	507.0	510.0	+ 4.5	548.0	501.0	24
Oct	509.0	515.0	502.0	512.0	+ 5.0	714.0	503.0	332
Dec	518.0	526.0	518.0	522.0	+ 6.0	735.0	510.0	9,191
Fb90	526.5	533.0	526.5	530.5	+ 5.5	694.0	522.0	294
Apr	537.0	543.0	537.0	539.0	+ 5.5	685.0	525.0	151
June	530.0	550.0	540.0	540.5	+ 6.5	685.0	538.0	307

Est vol 2,000; vol Tues 86; open int 10,330, +3.

CRUDE OIL, Light Sweet (NYM) 1,000 bbls.; $ per bbl.

	Open	High	Low	Settle	Change	Lifetime High	Lifetime Low	Open Interest
Oct	19.57	19.82	19.46	19.64	+ .08	20.09	12.75	20,100
Nov	19.42	19.78	19.30	19.68	+ .29	19.72	15.00	75,863
Dec	19.18	19.51	19.16	19.46	+ .32	19.51	12.87	45,123
Ja90	18.95	19.29	18.95	19.26	+ .34	19.29	15.67	23,095
Feb	18.83	19.14	18.80	19.11	+ .34	19.14	15.74	12,567
Mar	16.81	19.00	18.81	19.00	+ .33	19.00	16.10	16,737
Apr	18.75	18.89	18.75	18.94	+ .32	18.89	14.55	11,395
May	18.40	18.84	18.40	18.98	+ .31	18.84	14.25	9,893
June	18.66	18.76	18.66	18.83	+ .31	18.76	16.50	7,864
July	18.62	18.70	18.62	18.79	+ .31	18.70	16.60	5,683
Aug	18.63	18.60	18.43	18.75	+ .32	18.60	16.39	2,298
Sept	18.39	18.50	18.39	18.71	+ .32	18.50	16.50	1,963
Oct	18.53	18.53	18.53	18.68	+ .32	18.55	16.50	3,774
Nov	18.34	18.50	18.34	18.66	+ .32	18.50	17.30	2,341
Dec	18.35	18.50	18.35	18.66	+ .32	18.50	17.79	1,314
Ja91	...	...	...	18.65	+ .31	18.47	17.86	3,907
Feb	...	...	...	18.65	+ .31	19.06	18.15	317

Est vol 116,975; vol Tues 84,787; open int 244,939, −3,009.

HEATING OIL NO. 2 (NYM) 42,000 gal.; $ per gal.

	Open	High	Low	Settle	Change	Lifetime High	Lifetime Low	Open Interest
Oct	.5500	.5670	.5500	.5665	+.0160	.5700	.3720	12.275
Nov	.5585	.5725	.5585	.5709	+.0147	.5725	.3800	22,603
Dec	.5640	.5785	.5640	.5770	+.0150	.5785	.3785	22,879
Ja90	.5625	.5740	.5625	.5726	+.0125	.5740	.6660	14,134
Feb	.5625	.5605	.5525	.5616	+.0115	.5605	.4740	6,454
Mar	.5335	.5235	.5300	.5286	+.0105	.5380	.4640	3,183
Apr	.5130	.5150	.5130	.5186	+.0105	.5180	.4500	2,363
May	.5020	.5050	.4985	.5041	+.0105	.5070	.4450	1,412
June	.4910	.4910	.4910	.4951	+.0105	.5095	.6490	685

WHEAT (KC) 5,000 bu.; cents per bu.

Sept	399	399¾	392½	394	- .4	450	353	8
Dec	390¼	391¼	389¾	390¼	+ ¾	440	387	18,914
Mr90	308	308	306¼	387	+ 1	458	385	4,841
Mar	371	373	370	370	- 1	433½	370	1,011
July	342	345½	340	341	- ½	383	340	1,961

Est vol 3,102; vol Tues 6,756; open int 26,736, -246.

WHEAT (MPLS) 5,000 bu.; cents per bu.

Sept	385½	385½	385½	385½	...	440¼	379¼	144
Dec	306	306¼	385½	386¾	+ 1¾	445¾	384	6,618
Mr90	390¾	393	390¾	393	+ 3	415¼	381	1,667
May	386	386¼	385¼	385¼	+ 1½	308½	382	272
July	362	364	361	363	+ 1¼	406	358	127

Est vol 1,391; vol Tues 1,814; open int 8,828, +238.

BARLEY (WPG) 20 metric tons; Can. $ per ton

Oct	102.80	105.30	102.80	104.00	+ 1.00	140.00	98.50	4,022
Nov	107.00	107.00	104.00	104.00	+ 1.00	127.10	100.30	1,760
Dec	104.90	107.50	104.90	106.10	+ 1.20	128.40	101.70	4,522
Mr90	110.30	112.30	110.30	111.20	+ 1.30	118.00	106.00	2,782
May	113.00	114.00	113.00	113.50	+ .70	116.80	111.50	119

Est vol 995; vol Tues 497; open int 15,205, +436.

FLAXSEED (WPG) 20 metric tons; Can. $ per ton

Oct	372.50	377.80	372.50	377.80	+10.00	394.50	312.00	2,542
Dec	373.80	376.60	371.00	376.60	+10.00	434.00	316.00	4,102
Mr90	300.00	305.00	378.50	385.00	+ 9.93	306.90	317.00	1,660

Est vol 970; vol Tues 1,326; open int 8,171, -557.

CANOLA (WPS) 20 metric tons; Can. $ per ton

Sept	297.00	332.00	397.00	302.00	+ 6.20	379.50	278.50	57
Nov	303.00	308.30	333.00	308.10	+ 6.70	482.00	286.80	7,903
Ja90	321.40	317.00	312.20	316.90	+ 7.20	384.90	294.90	4,498
Mar	331.20	323.00	319.90	323.50	+ 5.70	391.50	332.50	1,597
June	330.00	333.50	329.90	333.20	+ 5.20	346.50	314.00	191

Est vol 1,470; vol Tues 2,544; open int 14,246, +253.

WHEAT (WPG) 20 metric tons; Can. $ per ton

Oct	128.50	132.00	128.50	128.80	+ .80	157.00	124.50	1,561
Nov	130.90	130.50	128.00	128.00	+ .90	156.00	126.50	787
Dec	127.50	130.50	127.50	128.70	+ 1.70	155.20	124.00	2,792
Mr90	132.90	136.00	133.90	134.10	+ 1.10	144.80	129.90	1,723
May	137.50	138.00	136.00	136.00	+ .50	140.50	132.50	465

Est vol 500; vol Tues 681; open int 7,308, +213.

RYE (WPG) 20 metric tons; Can. $ per ton

Oct	114.00	114.00	114.00	114.00	+ 1.50	154.00	110.50	811
Dec	114.50	117.50	114.50	117.50	+ 1.50	134.90	113.70	1,770

Est vol 68; vol Tues 165; open int 2,697, -291.

OATS (WPG) 20 metric tons; Can. $ per ton

Oct	98.50	100.50	90.50	100.50	+ 2.00	166.00	90.50	1,272
Nov	101.20	103.00	101.20	103.00	+ 2.00	146.00	108.00	1,957
Dec	106.00	106.30	105.00	105.30	+ 1.30	155.50	102.50	1,510
Mr90	...	...	...	110.00	+ 1.30	141.09	107.70	650

Est vol 100; vol Tues 964; open int 5,289, +3.

—LIVESTOCK & MEAT—

CATTLE—FEEDER (CME) 44,000 lbs.; cents per lb.

Sept	83.17	83.17	82.70	82.90	- .27	84.20	75.50	2,433
Oct	82.30	82.46	82.15	82.22	- .27	84.10	75.90	4,437
Nov	82.40	82.55	82.17	82.32	- .25	84.50	76.40	2,267
Ja90	82.35	82.50	82.10	82.22	- .37	84.35	77.30	2,656
Mar	81.55	81.40	81.30	81.50	- .25	83.06	77.40	769
Apr	89.65	80.65	80.45	80.45	- .30	82.45	78.85	223

Est vol 1,837; vol Tues 1,279; open int 12,862, -90.

CATTLE—LIVE (CME) 40,000 lbs; costs per lb.

Oct	71.15	71.35	70.87	71.15	- .10	76.90	68.20	22,809
Dec	73.10	73.25	72.82	73.17	- .07	75.36	69.40	22,686
Fb90	73.00	73.12	72.72	72.87	- .27	74.67	69.00	18,996
Apr	73.82	73.85	73.55	73.75	- .06	75.57	70.00	4,710
June	71.50	71.40	71.42	71.50	- .07	73.46	69.75	3,212
Aug	69.92	70.00	69.90	69.90	...	71.95	69.50	432

Est vol 17,785; vol Tues 18,910; open int 72,934, -564.

COTTON (CTN)—90,000 lbs.; cents per lb.

Oct	74.10	74.50	73.55	73.70	+ .65	76.40	50.35	3,830
Dec	74.50	74.90	74.21	74.25	+ .31	77.34	50.75	21,677
Mr90	75.40	75.00	75.40	75.40	- .01	78.00	53.40	9,521
May	76.20	76.60	76.16	76.23	- .31	78.20	59.75	7,181
July	76.70	76.75	76.20	76.27	- .35	70.10	64.70	3,033
Oct	70.10	70.40	70.00	70.40	+ .30	72.20	60.00	2,136
Dec	67.20	67.40	67.20	67.27	+ .07	69.20	65.00	2,413

Est vol 5,500; vol Tues 6,991; open int 49, 991, -146.

ORANGE JUICE (CTN)—15,000 lbs.; cents per lb.

Nov	134.00	135.00	134.10	135.15	- .75	176.75	129.00	3,792
Ja90	133.55	134.10	132.90	133.50	- 1.45	173.00	127.50	1,818
Mar	132.00	133.50	132.70	132.75	- 1.80	171.30	127.75	856
May	133.05	133.06	133.06	131.95	- 2.10	149.05	133.00	167

Est vol 1,088; vol Tues 802; open int 6,804, +76.

—METALS & PETROLEUM—

COPPER-STD/HIGH (CMX)—25,000 lbs.; cents per lb.**

Sept	136.20	138.00	136.08	137.30	+ .30	139.50	76.00	3,426
Oct	...	...	...	130.95	+ .60	135.50	123.50	123
Dec	125.30	127.00	125.10	126.70	+ .75	132.50	77.45	21,027
Ja90	127.50	127.50	127.50	127.50	+ 1.95	130.00	101.75	238
Mar	117.50	120.00	117.00	119.00	+ 1.50	125.00	98.50	1,836
May	115.25	115.25	115.25	115.25	+ 1.75	117.90	95.85	427
July	...	...	...	112.05	+ 1.75	113.00	93.25	521
Sept	.....	...	...	108.25	+ 1.75	110.00	94.00	414
Dec	103.00	106.75	103.00	104.45	+ 1.75	107.50	93.75	474

Est vol 7,100; vol Tues 9,650; open int 29,769, +634.

**1989 mos. are Standard grade—1990 forward are High grade. Vol. and Open int. reflect total of high grade and standard contracts.

GOLD (CMX)—100 troy oz.; $ per troy oz.

Sept	361.40	361.40	361.00	364.90	+ 3.70	382.00	399.00	123
Oct	362.40	369.00	362.40	365.70	+ 3.50	575.50	357.20	6,662
Dec	366.50	374.00	366.40	370.10	+ 3.90	514.50	360.60	77,902
Fb90	371.00	375.00	371.00	374.00	+ 3.90	516.00	364.70	12,725
Apr	374.20	381.00	374.20	378.10	+ 4.00	525.00	370.00	11,809
June	381.50	382.50	381.90	382.30	+ 4.00	497.00	372.90	11,196
Aug	...	...	...	386.40	+ 4.10	487.00	380.00	8,869
Oct	...	...	...	390.70	+ 4.10	472.00	384.50	2,410
Dec	396.00	396.00	393.00	395.00	+ 4.10	455.00	387.50	6,171
Fb91	420.50	400.50	408.50	399.30	+ 4.10	450.00	395.50	10,268
Apr	...	...	...	433.60	+ 4.20	415.50	400.50	3,005
June	404.00	404.00	404.00	408.00	+ 4.30	414.00	402.70	1,678

Est vol 50,000; vol Tues 21,516; open int 152,818, -921.

PLATINUM (NYM)—90 troy oz.; $ per troy oz.

Oct	476.00	479.90	475.00	478.20	+ 3.90	609.00	466.20	9,593
Ja90	479.00	421.00	479.00	481.60	+ 3.60	646.00	470.50	8,145
Apr	484.00	486.50	484.00	484.60	+ 3.60	567.00	475.00	1,093
July	...	...	...	487.60	+ 3.60	523.70	477.00	498
Oct	...	...	...	491.10	+ 3.60	500.00	483.00	283

Est vol 4,959; vol Tues 1,800; open int 19,495, -246.

EXCHANGE ABBREVIATIONS
(for commodity futures and futures options)

CBT–Chicago Board of Trade; CME–Chicago Mercantile Exchange; CMX–Commodity Exchange, New York; CRCE–Chicago Rice & Cotton Exchange; CTN–New York Cotton Exchange; CSCE–Coffee, Sugar & Cocoa Exchange, New York; IPE–International Petroleum Exchange; KC–Kansas City Board of Trade; MCE–MidAmerica Commodity Exchange; MPLS–Minneapolis Grain Exchange; NYM–New York Mercantile Exchange; PBOT–Philadelphia Board of Trade; WPG–Winnipeg Commodity Exchange.

July	.4850	.4900	.4850	.4926	+.0105	.4970	.4400	977
Aug	.4950	.4950	.4940	.4976	+.0105	.5000	.4700	346
Sept	...	...	...	.5036	+.0105	.5255	.4800	194
Oct	...	...	...	.5096	+.0105	.5200	.5200	151
Nov	...	...	...	.5156	+.0105	.5300	.5108	151

Est vol 29,904; vol Tues 24,198; open int 87,959, +193.

GASOLINE, Unleaded (NYM) 42,000 gal.; $ per gal.

Oct	.5700	.6020	.5780	.9974	+.0207	.6020	.4300	13,369
Nov	.5630	.5814	.5630	.5814	+.0200	.5814	.4125	15,672
Dec	.5425	.5570	.5425	.5555	+.0149	.5570	.4630	9,706
Ja90	.5240	.5370	.5240	.5350	+.0120	.5370	.4600	4,987
Feb	.5240	.5320	.5245	.5300	+.0100	.5320	.4710	2,773
Mar	...	...	...	.5245	+.0100	.5350	.4650	1,119
Apr	.5230	.5230	.5300	.5405	+.0100	.5400	.4850	1,155
May	.5550	.5550	.5550	.5605	+.0100	.5600	.5276	793
June	.5460	.5440	.5440	.5520	+.0100	.5500	.5250	484
July	...	...	...	.5420	+.0100	.5425	.5190	726
Aug	...	...	...	.5110	+.0100	.5325	.5265	190
Sept	...	...	...	.5200	+.0100	.5230	.5000	152
Oct	...	...	...	.4900	+.0100	.5000	.4870	509
Nov	...	...	...	.4800	+.0100	.4960	.4775	167

Est vol 33,479; vol Tues 16,299; open int 51,952, +431.

GAS OIL (IPE) 300 metric tons; $ per ton

Oct	166.00	168.00	165.50	166.25	- .25	170.00	100.00	16,035
Nov	164.25	166.00	163.50	164.75	+ .50	168.00	100.00	10,730
Dec	163.25	164.50	162.25	163.75	+ .50	166.75	136.25	10,439
Ja90	161.25	163.25	161.00	162.00	...	164.50	100.00	2,101
Feb	159.00	159.00	159.00	159.00	...	162.00	139.00	811

Actual Wed; vol 8,193; open int 40,585, -610.

—WOOD—

LUMBER (CME)—150,000 bd. ft.; $ per 1,000 bd. ft.

Nov	184.70	185.50	184.20	184.90	+ .20	190.60	176.30	2,950
Ja90	188.60	189.40	188.10	188.80	+ .10	192.00	181.20	1,856
Mar	191.50	192.00	191.10	191.40	- .20	193.90	185.00	728
May	194.50	194.90	194.20	194.70	+ .20	196.70	188.09	1,035
July	196.50	194.00	194.30	194.80	- .10	197.40	192.00	336

Est vol 532; vol Tues 349; open int 6,937, +35.

—OTHER COMMODITY FUTURES—

Settlement prices of selected contracts. Volume and open interest of all contract months.

Aluminum (CMS) 40,000 lbs.; cents per lb.
Dec 77.50 -1.00; Est. vol. 2; Open int. 95
Cattle—Live (MCE) 20,000 lb.; $ per lb.
Oct 71.15 -.10; Est. vol. 125; Open int. 424
Corn (MCE) 1,000 bu.; cents per bu.
Dec 228½ +1¼; Est. vol. 1,000; Open int. 5,966
Gold (CST) 100 troy oz.; $ per troy oz.
Oct 366.70 +3.50; Est. vol. 200; Open int. 502
Gold-Kilo (CBT) 32.15 troy oz.; $ per troy oz.
Oct 367.50 +4.30; Est. vol. 150; Open int. 372
Hogs—Live (MCE) 15,000 lb.; $ per lb.
Oct 41.77 +.10; Est. vol. 230; Open int. 750
Propane (NYM) 42,000 gal.; $ per gal.
Oct 22.15 +.05; Est. vol. 55; Open int. 551
Rice—Rough (CRCE) 2800 cwt; $ per cwt
Nov 8.11 -.14; Est. vol. 250; Open int. 2,785
Silver (MCE) 1,000 troy oz.; cents per troy oz.
Dec 521.5 +5.5; Est. vol. 50; Open int. 1,746
Soybeans (MCE) 1,000 bu.; cents per bu.
Nov 575½ +7; Est. vol. 4000; Open int. 18,025
Soybean Meal (MCE) 20 tons; $ per ton
Oct 187.90 +1.10; Est. vol. 15; Open int. 215
Wheat (MCE) 1,000 bu.; cents per bu.
Dec 391½ + 1½; Est. vol. 500; Open int. 21,196

each commodity, the first column shows the delivery months for the respective contracts. Thus, each line shows the market movements for a contract for delivery during one particular month in the future. The next four columns are prices. The first price is the opening price, that is, the price that was quoted at the time the market opened that morning. The second and third prices are the highest and lowest prices at which transactions took place during the day, respectively. The fourth price is the last price quoted before the market closed. This "closing price" is the price that is given the most attention in the media. The following column shows how much the closing price changed compared to the closing price of the previous market day. The next two columns show the highest and lowest prices, respectively, at which this contract has ever been traded. The last column, which is labeled "Open Interest," reflects the number of contracts.

Commodities prices are not always of interest to people outside the industries buying or selling the commodities involved, but sometimes the changes reflect trends that are interesting from the point of view of the overall economy. This is most often true of the gold market. Many investors consider gold, as a real commodity, a hedge against inflation. Thus, movements in the gold market may reflect shifts in investor expectations about inflation in the United States and the other Western economies. From another angle, it is sometimes argued that changes in the prices of commodities that are used as raw materials signal changes in inflationary trends for the rest of the economy. For this reason, macroeconomists sometimes consider these price changes early warning signs of inflation.

A particular role has been played by the spot and futures markets for crude oil. The movements in these prices are influenced by news about the weather and major accidents in the oil-importing countries, as well as by news about political, military, and economic events in the oil-exporting countries. For example, a speech by the Saudi oil minister threatening to flood the market with oil unless other OPEC countries stick to their quotas could cause a plunge in the futures prices of crude oil. These prices are important because of the central role oil plays in the Western economies. At least two recessions and much inflation have been blamed on oil prices. Although the typical manager outside the oil industry hardly needs to pay daily attention to oil prices, major events in this market should not be ignored, because they may have broader consequences.

14.5 WEEKLY DATA RELEASES

Each Thursday afternoon, right after the closing of the New York financial markets, the Federal Reserve releases its estimates of the **money**

supply (M1, M2, and M3) for the preceding week. In the early 1980s, these releases were given considerable attention by the financial community because the Federal Reserve then was known to use these aggregates as its intermediate targets. Stock prices and market interest rates would adjust to these news releases almost immediately. In fact, it is precisely in order to avoid violent market reactions that the releases are no longer made during the business day, as was done formerly. Interest in these figures reached its peak during the period in the early 1980s when the Federal Reserve deliberately tightened the supply of money in a successful attempt to ease inflationary pressures. However, interest has tapered off as the Federal Reserve has turned to the federal funds rate as its intermediate target.

Another reason for the loss of interest surely must have been the low reliability of the weekly money-supply estimates. These estimates are derived from a quick survey of the main items on the balance sheets of the member banks of the Federal Reserve system, while the balance sheets of the many smaller banks go unheeded. The Federal Reserve does not revise these figures. However, it prepares carefully revised estimates of the money supply for the end of each month that can be compared to the preliminary releases for the last week in each month. Recent research has suggested not only that the preliminary data contain considerable noise but also that filtering out some of this noise at an early stage should have been possible.*

A different type of weekly release is the Labor Department's report on **new claims for unemployment insurance,** or "jobless claims" for short. These data are also quite different from the monthly labor market data, which we study more closely in Chapter 16. An important drawback of the jobless-claims data is the fact that they cover only those jobless workers who are eligible for unemployment benefits. Even with this disadvantage, changes in the trends of these figures carry important information.

The jobless-claims figures are usually considered early-warning signs of changes in the overall unemployment data, because the people with new jobless claims are *recent entrants* to the pool of unemployed workers. Thus, for example, an increase in jobless claims is an indication of a quickening of the pace at which the number of unemployed increases. A little further down the road, then, we must expect higher unemployment rates. On the other hand, it should be remembered that these weekly figures are noisy because of their incomplete coverage, so the information that can be extracted from these data alone is somewhat limited.

---

* See N. Gregory Mankiw, David E. Runkle, and Matthew D. Shapiro, "Are Preliminary Announcements of the Money Stock Rational Forecasts?" *Journal of Monetary Economics,* 1984, vol. 14, pp. 15–27; and Knut Anton Mork, "Forecastable Money-Growth Revisions: A Closer Look at the Data," *Canadian Journal of Economics,* 1990, vol. 23, no. 3, pp. 593–616.

14.6 AUTOMOBILE SALES

Automobile sales, reported every 10 days, are an important indicator of consumer demand. They are not a perfect indicator, because they are easily influenced by temporary factors such as sales incentives offered by the automobile industry or temporary fluctuations in interest rates. They are also volatile for another reason. Because cars are among the most durable consumer goods, the auto sales statistics react much more strongly to news about income and other relevant information than other indicators of consumer spending.

To refresh your memory of our discussion of this phenomenon in Chapters 5 and 13, consider a situation in which the economy has just turned the corner of a recession, laid-off workers have been recalled, and the prospect of a continuing stream of future paychecks has returned. In this situation, many people who have managed with worn-out old cars during the recession will find they are able to trade them in for new ones. So auto sales will show a boom, which correctly reflects the improvement in the economy and an overall increase in consumer demand. However, after the first wave, the people with new cars will not need to trade them in again for quite some time. Thus, after the first recovery wave, auto sales might well decline again, although this decline has nothing to do with a downturn in consumers' general interest in spending money.

Even though they are volatile, the auto-sales data are useful as a general indicator of consumer demand because of the high frequency with which the reports are released. We should also note the large size of the automobile industry relative to the U.S. economy: For the years 1984–87, the category "motor vehicles and parts" on average made up 7% of total spending by U.S. consumers.

The data releases for auto sales are usually presented in two ways: as the absolute number of vehicles sold and as the change in sales from the corresponding period one year earlier. It is important to be aware that this is the basis used for comparison, because, for example, a decrease from the year-earlier period might be an increase from the preceding 10-day period. In the *Wall Street Journal*, the figures are typically presented in the form of a table as well as a graph illustrating the movements both during the current year and a year earlier, as shown in Figure 14.7. This graph allows the reader to look beyond the short-term fluctuations in automobile demand in order to get a more complete picture of the trend.

An article also accompanies this particular data release. When such articles are published, they usually appear on page A2 of the *Wall Street Journal* as part of the "Economy" section. The articles expand on such factors as whether special sales incentives were offered a year earlier or

FIGURE 14.7

Article reporting 10-day report on auto sales, with detailed table and graph. Source: *Wall Street Journal,* 21 September 1989, p. A2.

Car Sales in Early September Were Flat Following Sharp 13.1% Rise in August

BY GREGORY A. PATTERSON
Staff Reporter of THE WALL STREET JOURNAL

DETROIT—U.S. automobile sales lost some of their recent steam in early September, staying about flat with a year ago after a torrid August during which sales jumped 13.1%.

U.S. auto dealers sold 212,334 cars and light trucks in the first 10 days of September, compared with 244,173 vehicles the year earlier. This year's period included only seven selling days compared with eight last year and sales eased 0.6%.

Experts had been expecting softer sales in the wake of the August buying spree, which was fueled by hefty rebates and other "incentives" as well as fear of steep price boosts on the soon-to-debut 1990 models. But some analysts and dealers were surprised by the extent of the sales decline from August; they attributed it to shortages of some popular models and to continuing caution among some consumers.

Sales of North American–made cars alone—excluding trucks and vans—dropped 2.8% in early September, to 132,004 from 155,131 a year ago. That yielded a seasonally adjusted annual selling rate of 6.7 million cars, according to a Commerce Department formula. That's down sharply from an annual sales pace of eight million cars achieved in the final 10 days of August. Last year in early September, the car sales rate hit an annual pace of 7.3 million units.

"It looks like the fall collapse of auto sales is beginning early," said Dave Healy, an auto analyst with Drexel Burnham Lambert Inc. in New York. He noted that Ford Motor Co., which began September with the lowest inventories of any Big Three U.S. auto maker, also posted the biggest sales decline in early September. Ford's problem now is a shortage of such popular models as the basic Taurus sedan, Mr. Healy said, but soon the problem will be sticker shock on 1990 cars.

Ford, whose domestic car sales dropped 6.6%, had a 57-day supply of cars at the end of August, slightly below the 60- to 65-day supply considered ideal. Analysts said the auto maker's sales were stymied by the arrival at dealerships of more expensive 1990-model cars that don't carry the heavy incentives found on 1989 models—at least not yet.

"You've got to really want to be the first kid on the block [with a new-model car] to buy a 1990 Escort," said Ford analyst Joel Pitcoff. The 1989 Escort carries a rebate of $1,000, while the 1990 model hasn't any rebate.

Meanwhile, Ford's archrival, General Motors Corp., posted a 1.7% gain in domestic car sales. GM's performance was buoyed by availability, and a move the company made in late August that put incentives on its bread-and-butter Chevrolet Lumina sedan, analysts said.

Domestic car sales at Chrysler Corp. increased 6.7%. But the No. 3 auto

U.S. Auto Sales

Seasonally adjusted annual rate of domestic cars sold, in 10-day selling periods, in millions

Source: Commerce Department

maker's truck sales dropped 8.3%. Already Chrysler has begun offering incentives to dealers on some of its Jeep models.

Nissan Motor Corp. logged a big 79% decline in sales of its U.S.-made cars, and an accompanying 72% drop in sales of trucks made at its Tennessee plant. A company spokesman attributed most of the decline to the termination of dealer incentives that had ranged to $1,575 on its cars, and to $2,075 on its U.S.-made trucks.

Honda Motor Co.'s sales of U.S.-made cars dropped 36%. The company said it switched to producing 1990-model Civic subcompacts, but hasn't started selling them yet.

RETAIL U.S. CAR AND LIGHT TRUCK SALES-a	1989 Sep 1-10	1988 Sep 1-10	x-% Chg.
GM total vehicles	108,460	113,144	+ 9.6
Domestic car	66,445	74,640	+ 1.7
Imported car	2,834	4,309	– 24.8
Total car	69,279	78,949	+ 0.3
Domestic truck	39,052	34,195	+ 30.5
Imported truck	129	0	d
Total truck	39,181	34,195	+ 30.9
FORD total vehicles	63,625	79,574	– 8.4
Domestic car	37,044	45,318	– 6.6
Imported car	1,557	2,204	– 19.3
Total car	38,601	47,522	– 7.2
Domestic truck	25,024	32,052	– 10.8
CHRYSLER total veh	36,744	43,630	– 3.8
Domestic car	19,007	20,357	+ 6.7
Imported car	1,670	2,853	– 33.1
Total car	20,677	23,210	+ 1.8
Domestic truck	15,365	19,155	– 8.3
Imported truck	702	1,265	– 36.6
Total truck	16,067	20,420	– 10.1
NISSAN total vehicles	1,590	7,476	– 75.7
Domestic car	701	3,836	– 79.1
Domestic truck	889	3,640	– 72.1
HONDA domestic car	5,412	9,660	– 36.0
TOYOTA domestic car	1,917	814	+169.1
MAZDA domestic car	509	506	+ 15.0
MITSUBISHI-c	969	0	...
Total cars-b	138,065	164,497	– 4.1
Domestic-b	132,004	155,131	– 2.8
Imported	6,061	9,366	– 26.0
Total trucks	81,161	98,307	+ 2.7
Domestic	80,330	89,042	+ 3.1
Imported	831	1,265	– 24.9
Total domestic veh-b	212,334	244,173	– 0.6
Total vehicles-b	219,236	254,804	– 1.7

a-Totals include only vehicle sales reported in the period.
b-Includes Volkswagen domestic production to July 1988.
c-Domestic car.
d-Percentage change is greater than 999%.
x-There were 7 selling days in the most recent period and 8 a year earlier. Percentage differences based on daily sales rate rather than sales volume.

whether special holidays affected the number of trading days during the period. Import competition, quality issues, and legislation affecting the industry, such as environmental regulation or gasoline-mileage rules, may be discussed as well.

The unit of measurement for this series is an individual car, van, or pickup truck. The advantage of this choice is that it obviates the need for inflation adjustment, which always presents some problems. On the other hand, an automobile is hardly a well-defined unit, considering all the changes in quality and equipment that have taken place over the years. However, this problem is probably minor for short-term comparisons.

CHAPTER REVIEW

1. Daily data come from the world's financial markets. Although some of the interest in these data is limited to the participants in these markets, they also carry macroeconomic significance.

2. The efficient-market hypothesis suggests that the stock market should be a reliable indicator of the future course of the economy. However, the stock market also may be influenced by "noise" and other deviations from the efficient-market hypothesis. Thus, it is just as important to follow the events driving the economy and the market as the market's reactions to these events.

3. Because the yield on low-risk bonds is closely related to the interest rates on bank loans, the bond market carries information on interest-rate trends. The yield curve displays the yields on bonds with increasing maturities. A yield-curve inversion is a downward-sloping yield curve, which may signal recession.

4. The foreign-exchange market facilitates spot as well as forward transactions in foreign exchange. Forward transactions are important opportunities for hedging against the risks of exchange-rate changes for companies involved in foreign trade or international operations.

5. The commodities markets facilitate spot and futures transactions in a number of agricultural commodities, metals, and fuels. Movements in the prices of gold and commodities used as raw materials are sometimes associated with inflationary expectations or emerging inflationary trends. Oil prices are particularly important; at least two postwar recessions and much inflation have been blamed on oil prices.

6. The Federal Reserve issues weekly releases of the monetary aggregates. These figures are rather noisy and currently less important as indicators of U.S. monetary policy than is the federal funds rate.

7. The Labor Department's weekly releases of new claims for unemployment insurance are noisy but valuable early-warning signs of changes in employment trends.

8. Statistics for U.S. sales of cars and trucks are released every 10 days. Although volatile because of stock adjustments and other events, these figures are valuable indicators of the strength in consumer demand.

EXERCISES

1. If the 180-day forward exchange rate represents market expectations about the exchange rate six months into the future, can you use the interest parity condition in Chapter 10 to derive a relationship between

the spot exchange rate, the forward exchange rate, and foreign and domestic interest rates? Can you test this relationship empirically?

2. The following matrix shows how much must be paid by the currencies in each row for one unit of the currency in each respective column. This table reveals some opportunities for profitable arbitrage in the form of using one currency to buy a second currency, using that one to buy a third currency, and then using the third currency to buy back the first. Which are these opportunities?

	$	¥	DM	£
$	1	0.006892	0.5153	1.5825
¥	145.1	1	75.29	229.43
DM	1.9408	0.013281	1	3.0574
£	0.6319	0.004359	0.3271	1

3. You are an investor in the stock market and receive the news that both the index of industrial production and the consumer price index have risen by 0.5% over the last month. Both increases represent accelerations from previous months. However, you also know that this month experienced extraordinarily severe winter weather. How should you react to the news?

4. Suppose the government releases a report showing a sharp decline in the U.S. trade deficit. You are a trader in the foreign-exchange market. How should you react, and why?

5. Although the economy has been sluggish overall for a few months, the last two reports of auto sales have shown healthy increases from the year-earlier period. What can you conclude from these figures? What other information would you like to have in order to make this conclusion firmer?

6. Consider an economy that functions at three dates, which we call 0, 1, and 2. At date 0, you can choose between investment in a "short" bond, which matures at date 1, and

a "long" bond, which matures at date 2. Each bond has a face value of $1. Call their prices S_1 and L, respectively. At date 1, only short bonds are available. They all mature at date 2. Their face value is also $1, and their price is S_2. Suppose there is no uncertainty, so you know the value of S_2 for sure at date 0. You want to make an investment at date 0 and don't need your money out until date 2. However, you need to decide whether to buy long bonds at date 0 or to buy short bonds at date 0, redeem them at date 1, and then reinvest the proceeds in new short bonds. Derive the correct criterion for this choice in terms of the yield rates on the three bonds. What do you expect the relationship between these yield rates to be when the bond market is in equilibrium? What does your answer tell you about the yield curve?

7. The long-short interest differential, defined as the difference between the yield rates of 10-year Treasury bonds and 3-month Treasury bills, can be used as a rough measure of the slope of the yield curve, so an inversion of the yield curve corresponds to negative values of the long-short interest differential. Draw a curve to explain why this is so. Then compute quarterly data for the long-short interest differential from quarterly series of the yield rates of 10-year Treasury bonds and 3-month Treasury bills. Make a graph of these differentials. Also find the periods of recession in the U.S. economy from Table 3.1 and mark these periods on the graph. How many of the recessions have been preceded by yield inversions, and how many of the yield inversions have been followed by recessions?

8. Use the data for the long-short interest differential in exercise 7 together with data for quarterly real GNP growth. Run a regression with real GNP growth on the left and a distributed lag of the interest differential on the right. Use a maximum lag length of 4. What do the signs of the regression coefficients say about the relationship between yield-curve inversions and future real GNP growth? Compute an F-statistic to formally test the hypothesis that all the slope coefficients are zero at the same time. What are the results of the test, and what do they tell?

9. The efficient-market theory claims that the stock market should react to news about the economy and also foreshadow future business-cycle movements. Construct a graph of the quarterly changes in the Standard & Poor's index of 500 common stocks. On this graph, mark the periods of U.S. recessions from Table 3.1. Do you see a tendency for stock-market changes to signal turning points in the business cycle?

10. Run a regression of real GNP growth on a distributed lag of the stock-market data in exercise 9. Use a maximum lag length of 4. What do the regression coefficients tell about how the stock market signals aggregate economic performance? Compute an F-statistic to test the hypothesis that all the slope coefficients are zero at the same time. What is the result of the test, and what does it tell?

THINKING QUESTIONS

1. Suppose you are an institutional investor and are familiar with the fact that there are two competing hypotheses about the stock market: (1) the efficient-market hypothesis, which says that all movements are driven by market fundamentals, and (2) the view that investor behavior is driven by fads, fashions, and other social-psychological forces. You also know that the researchers are unable to agree on which hypothesis fits the data better. Because you are not a researcher, you cannot make your own determination. One morning, one of the stocks in your portfolio falls by 10%, while the others stay roughly unchanged. You have no other information about this particular company. How should you react?

2. Suppose that, in an attempt to relieve the environmental problem of CO_2 emissions, high taxes are imposed on cars and gasoline. What would you expect to happen to auto sales? What does this example tell about the reliability of auto sales data as an indicator of the overall health of the economy?

15 MONTHLY AND QUARTERLY INDICATORS IN THE NATIONAL INCOME AND PRODUCT ACCOUNTS

The **National Income and Product Accounts** (**NIPA**) are an information system created to keep track of important movements in the economy. Most countries have such an accounting system. The maintenance of the system is usually the responsibility of some government statistical agency. In the United States, this agency is the Bureau of Economic Analysis (BEA), which is part of the U.S. Department of Commerce. However, data are contributed by a number of other agencies as well.

The most important output from this system is the data for Gross National Product (GNP) and its components. The raw data used as input to the system come from a wide variety of sources, including surveys conducted by the Bureau of the Census, the Bureau of Labor Statistics, the Energy Information Administration, the Department of Agriculture, and other agencies; information from tax returns supplied by the Internal Revenue Service; and reports from industry trade associations.

All the NIPA data series are collected at least annually. Most are also available by quarter, and some are constructed monthly. GNP and its expenditure components (consumption, investment, net exports, and government expenditure on goods and services) are all available quarterly as well as annually. With regard to contributions to GNP by industry, annual data availability is the norm. For certain GNP components, most notably consumption, monthly data series are maintained.

15.1 REAL GNP—THE QUEEN OF ECONOMIC INDICATORS

The Gross National Product in constant dollars—real GNP for short—is the most comprehensive measure of the output produced by the economy and thus of the economy's activity level. This feature makes real GNP the most important economic indicator. It is no accident that the National Income and Product Accounts center around real GNP. A definition of GNP was given at the beginning of Chapter 3. It is repeated here to refresh your memory.

DEFINITION OF GNP

In *nominal* terms, the **Gross National Product,** or GNP, of the United States is defined as

> the total value of final goods and services, evaluated at market prices, produced by U.S. factors of production within a specified period of time.

The definition of **real GNP** is analogous, except that the term "market prices" is replaced by "base-period market prices."

Let us now look a little more closely at this definition. The first thing to note is that the term **total value** indicates the comprehensive nature of GNP as a measure of the country's production of goods and services.

Next we note that GNP is restricted to include only **final goods and services.** This qualifier means, for example, that if your company makes tires for delivery to a car manufacturer, your tire production is not included in GNP. However, the cars made with those tires are. The tires you make are referred to in the National Income and Product Accounts as **intermediate goods.** Intermediate goods are excluded from GNP in order to avoid double counting. After all, it would not make sense to add up both the tires and the cars with the tires and refer to the sum as total production.

However, there are circumstances in which your tires might be included in GNP. First, selling a tire to a consumer to replace a worn or damaged tire constitutes consumption and hence a final good. Second, selling tires overseas, whether to a car manufacturer or for direct consumption, constitutes exports, which are always considered a final good for the home country, even if used as an intermediate good abroad.

Goods made for use in production that are *durable* goods are considered investment goods, which are also counted as final goods. Naturally, this does not apply to tires but to the construction of houses, office and factory buildings, business machinery, and other similar items.

The evaluation **at market prices** reflects a belief that those prices are representative of the actual values of the various goods and services. However, this part of the definition raises a number of practical questions. First, when a good is sold subject to a sales tax or another indirect tax, such as the federal gasoline tax, should the tax be included as part of the market price? Although this is not a very deep issue, the accounts need to be consistent. The chosen convention is to include the indirect taxes.

A second question arises in regard to government services, which are not sold in markets and hence have no market price. For example, there is no market price for police protection or national defense. At this point, the National Income and Product Accounts use the next-best solution, namely, to value the services at the government's cost of providing them.

The issue of the market price of services arises in the private sector as well, most notably in regard to financial services, such as those provided by banks or securities brokers. These services are highly market-related, but the services themselves are not sold at specified prices. Rather, these institutions' revenues are obtained indirectly, for example, from the difference—or *margin*—between the interest rates on bank lending and bank deposits. In such cases, the same convention is used as for government services, namely, to evaluate the services at cost.

Nonmarket activities, on the other hand, such as homemaking, fall outside the National Income and Product Accounts. Be they ever so productive, they are not reflected in GNP.

The principle of evaluation at market prices is most easily applied to *nominal* GNP, which is evaluated as *current* market prices. In practice, this means that the government statisticians can add dollar amounts without worrying about correction for inflation. In the construction of *real* GNP, the same principle is modified to mean evaluation at the market prices that prevailed *in the base year*, which currently is 1982.

The specification that U.S. GNP be composed of goods and services **produced by U.S. factors of production** reflects a subtlety that is sometimes important in practice. It means, first, that work done abroad by U.S. residents (for example, management consulting for foreign clients) is included in U.S. GNP. It falls under the category of exports of services.

Second, it means that U.S. GNP includes the contribution made by U.S.-owned *capital* to the production at facilities in foreign countries. This contribution is measured as its market value, in other words, in the form of dividends or transfers of profits from foreign subsidiaries to their American parent companies, such as the profits that General Motors derives from its Opel subsidiary in Germany. This item is considered part of exports as well, specifically, exports of *capital services.* Conversely, the contribution to U.S. facilities by foreign-owned capital, such as the Japanese investment in Nissan's plant in Smyrna, Tennessee, is excluded from U.S. GNP. It is classified as imports of capital services.

You might wonder why we do not simply define GNP as the value of goods and services *produced within the country.* The answer is that this definition gives rise to an alternative measure of overall production, namely, **Gross Domestic Product,** or **GDP.** For large countries like the United States, GNP and GDP usually behave quite similarly. For smaller countries, this is not always the case, and GDP is often the preferred measure of economic output.

ANNUAL, QUARTERLY, AND MONTHLY LEVELS AND GROWTH RATES

The accounting system maintains the respective series in **level** form, such as the level of GNP and the level of consumption expenditure. For annual data, these levels are easily defined as the year's total production value for the goods included in GNP, and so on. However, if you look at the quarterly data for GNP levels, you will find that they are of the same order of magnitude as the annual levels. The explanation for this is simply that, whenever the BEA constructs quarterly level data, it takes the raw data and multiplies them by 4 so they can be compared more easily to the annual data. Similarly, for monthly data series, the raw level data are multiplied by 12.

For most of the data series in the National Income and Product Accounts, the **growth rates** have better intuitive meaning than the levels. For example, most people find it easier to grasp the fact that real GNP grew at an annual rate of 2.7% from the third to the fourth quarter of 1988 than an announcement that real GNP for the fourth quarter of 1988 was $4,059.3 billion in 1982 prices.*

We defined the *growth rates* for real GNP data in Chapter 3. For annual data, the growth rates are simple percentage changes from year to year. However, for quarterly growth rates, it is worth recalling from that discussion that the construction of quarterly growth rates gives rise to an issue similar to that for quarterly levels. If we use the straight percentage changes from quarter to quarter, we get numbers that are about one-quarter less than the annual growth rates on average. Actually, they tend to be a little *less* than one-quarter of the annual data. The reason is that the base for the percentage comparisons—last quarter's level—tends to grow throughout the year. In order to obtain comparable quarterly and annual growth rates, we therefore compute quarterly data according to formula (3.2). This formula includes compounding, which compensates for the growing base. We repeat formula (3.2) here for convenience:

$$(15.1) \quad \text{Quarterly real GNP growth rate at annual rate} = 100 \times \left[\left(\frac{\text{RGNP}_t}{\text{RGNP}_{t-1}} \right)^4 - 1 \right].$$

THE DEFLATION OF GNP

It is instructive to look a little more closely at the construction of real GNP, which is done by first constructing nominal GNP and then correcting it for inflation. This correction is referred to as **deflation.** (Obviously, the meaning of the word *deflation* is slightly different in this context from its other meaning of declining prices, that is, negative inflation.)

We have just seen that GNP figures can be constructed by adding up its spending components. In the actual accounting practice of the BEA, an even finer decomposition is used. For example, consumption expenditure is decomposed into durable goods, nondurable goods, and ser-

---

*There is also a deeper reason for being interested in growth rates. A number of the macroeconomic time series appear to be growing indefinitely. Application of advanced statistical methods to these series has suggested that they might be *nonstationary* in level form, which means, among other things, that the statistical variances of these level variables are infinite. This property can be quite awkward for statistical analysis. On the other hand, the growth rates for the same data series are usually *stationary*, which means that all the standard statistical methods, such as regression analysis, can be applied without problems being encountered.

vices, and durable-goods consumption in turn is decomposed into motor vehicles and parts, furniture and household equipment, and other durable goods. The decomposition sometimes goes even further. Let V_{it} denote the *nominal* expenditure on the ith component during period t. Suppose there are m such components altogether. Then nominal GNP during period t, Y_t^N, obviously is the sum of these components:

$$(15.2) \qquad Y_t^N = \sum_{i=1}^{m} V_{it}.$$

If the ith spending component consisted of only one good (say, for example, that all automobiles were Ford Escorts), it would be straightforward to decompose the nominal spending, V_{it}, into its price P_{it} and quantity X_{it} such that $V_{it} = P_{it}X_{it}$. If this could be done for all components, nominal GNP could be written as

$$(15.2') \qquad Y_t^N = \sum_{i=1}^{m} P_{it}X_{it}.$$

To construct *real* GNP, it would then be sufficient to replace all the current market prices, P_{it}, with their values in the base year, which we may denote P_{i0}, and construct real GNP as

$$(15.3) \qquad Y_t = \sum_{i=1}^{m} P_{i0}X_{it}.$$

In practice, however, the components do not consist of single goods. The category "automobiles" consists of many different brands and models, and even the subcategory of Ford Escorts contains many models with different prices. Thus, formula (15.3) cannot be applied directly. As a substitute, the BEA goes to other data sources, such as the data underlying the consumer and producer price indices maintained by the Bureau of Labor Statistics, to obtain a **price index** for each spending component of GNP. Thus, there is one index for automobiles, one for household appliances, and so forth. A price index, except for the customary factor of 100, has the dimension of a price now relative to the price in the base year. Thus, we can write the price index for the ith GNP component as $I_{it} = P_{it}/P_{i0}$, although it should be understood that the Ps here stand for the average price level for the different goods going into the component and not the price of an individual good. The BEA now uses these indices to **deflate GNP component by component.** Thus, the deflated ("real") spending for component i is defined as V_{it}/I_{it}, and real GNP is constructed as

$$(15.3') \qquad Y_t = \sum_{i=1}^{m} V_{it}/I_{it}.$$

To see that this method approximates the right answer, suppose again that each category consists of a single good. Then a little algebra shows that

(15.3'')
$$Y_t = \sum_{i=1}^{m} V_{it}/I_{it} = \sum_{i=1}^{m} \frac{P_{it}X_{it}}{P_{it}/P_{i0}} = \sum_{i=1}^{m} P_{i0}X_{it},$$

which is the same as the right side of (15.3). A small error is introduced by the fact that the BEA is unable to deflate every single good. However, this error can be ignored in practice.

THE GNP DEFLATOR

The ratio between nominal and real GNP is known as the **GNP deflator,** which is used as a measure of inflation. In order to see that it can be used this way, suppose that the volumes of all goods and services (X_{it}) stay unchanged but that all prices (P_{it}) rise by 5%. In this situation, it clearly makes sense that inflation has been 5%. Furthermore, it should be clear from (15.2') and (15.3) that nominal GNP rises by 5% while real GNP stays unchanged, so the GNP deflator has risen by 5%.

In general, however, volumes and the individual prices change in different proportions. To interpret the GNP deflator in this case, note that its definition implies

(15.4)
$$D_t = Y_t^N/Y_t = \frac{\sum_i V_{it}}{\sum_j V_{jt}/I_{jt}} = \frac{\sum_i (P_{i0}X_{it})P_{it}/P_{i0}}{\sum_j P_{j0}X_{jt}} = \sum_i w_{it}P_{it}/P_{i0},$$

where $w_{it} = P_{i0}X_{it}/\sum_j P_{j0}X_{jt}$ and where the last two formulae hold exactly if each spending component can be written as price times quantity for a single good. The last formula shows that the GNP deflator can be interpreted as a weighted average of the price indices for the individual components. Thus, the percentage change in the GNP deflator can be interpreted as a weighted average of the percentage changes in each individual price, which is exactly what we expect from a measure of inflation. The weights, w_{it}, are the shares of the respective goods in real GNP. These weights change each period, because the expenditure on each component changes in general. This feature makes the GNP deflator a **variable-weight** price index. In Chapter 16, we compare this index to **fixed-weight** indices, such as the Consumer Price Index and the Producer Price Index.

The order in which the deflation process takes place is worth noting. First, each spending component is deflated by means of component price indices. Second, real GNP is constructed as the sum of the deflated components. Then, as a final step, the GNP deflator can be computed. Thus, it would be incorrect to say that the GNP deflator is "used" to deflate GNP. For this reason, the deflator is referred to as the **implicit GNP** deflator. It deflates GNP in the implicit sense that real GNP equals the ratio of nominal GNP to the deflator; however, real GNP is always constructed first.

15.2 REVISIONS AND ERRORS IN GNP DATA

The first estimate of GNP for a given quarter or year is never completely accurate. It will be revised a number of times before the BEA statisticians feel confident that the number is as accurate as they can get it. Even then, errors may remain. This section explores the issue of data accuracy and its implications for management.

PUBLICATION SCHEDULE FOR THE GNP DATA

Nominal GNP and real GNP are published for each quarter as well as each year. However, instead of being computed and published once and for all, the data are published and revised in many steps as the BEA obtains access to new information.

A complete set of national income and product accounts is obtained only once every fifth year as a result of the quinquennial **economic census.** The census data take considerable time to process, so the exact figures are not known until several years after each census year. For example, the revisions of the GNP data based on the 1977 census were released in 1985, and the data from the 1982 census were scheduled to become available in 1990. The complete GNP estimates for the census years are used as **benchmarks** for the construction of GNP data for the intervening years. These data are constructed from a combination of data from **annual surveys** and interpolation between the census years, or extrapolation from the last census year, as the case might be.

In similar fashion, the *quarterly and monthly* data are based on a combination of interpolation between or extrapolation from the annual data and quarterly or monthly source data from surveys. The quarterly and monthly surveys use smaller samples than the annual surveys and thus are less reliable. Sometimes they also measure a slightly different variable than the corresponding NIPA concept, so that some kind of conversion is needed to construct the quarterly NIPA data. For example, the quarterly and monthly consumption data are derived in part from the monthly surveys of retail sales, as is explained further in Section 15.3.

A wide variety of quarterly and monthly surveys goes into the construction of quarterly GNP. Some take more time to process than others. Rather than waiting for all the data to come in, the BEA releases *preliminary* estimates based on the data that have become available at the time of the release. The article in Figure 15.1 provides a look at this process as it takes place in practice.

As more complete data arrive, more reliable estimates can be made.

FIGURE 15.1

Article describing the process behind the estimation of preliminary GNP data. Source: *Wall Street Journal,* 26 January 1990, p. A2.

ECONOMY

Eagerly Awaited GNP Is a Product Of Hours of Calls, Numbers Crunching

BY HILARY STOUT

Staff Reporter of THE WALL STREET JOURNAL

WASHINGTON—Yesterday afternoon, on a shabby street corner in the nation's capital, in dingy offices over a McDonald's restaurant, 25 economists and other bureaucrats completed weeks of effort totaling everything that the $5 trillion U.S. economy produced last quarter.

This morning, their report on the gross national product will cascade through the financial markets, which are eager for any indication of whether the economy is headed for a recession. Most analysts expect the Commerce Department report to show that the economy barely grew, or maybe even shrank a tad.

How on earth do these government economists figure it out?

It took hundreds of hours of pouring over government documents and scores of telephone calls to institutions as diverse as the New Jersey Gaming Control Commission and the New York Stock Exchange. And it requires lots of guessing—more guessing, in fact, than many people would imagine of a report released with multi-decimal precision.

Consider the quandary of pet services. When a veterinarian treats a cocker spaniel, that is economic output and should be included in the GNP. Buried under reams of computer printouts, the economists extrapolate the output of vet offices and pet stores across the land by looking at the American Kennel Club's latest yearly report on pure-bred dogs.

"We take the number of pure-bred dogs and multiply it by the consumer price index for pets and pet services," says Clinton McCully, who heads the group of six economists responsible for calculating the consumption portion of the GNP.

What about funeral services? That is economic output too.

The National Center for Health Statistics keeps numbers on "seasonally adjusted deaths," Mr. McCully says. And the economists multiply those by the appropriate component of the consumer price index.

Many of the calculations in the GNP aren't quite so sketchy. The Commerce Department's Bureau of Economic Analysis, which compiles the figures, draws most of its information from scads of other government reports—on the nation's trade, industrial production, retail sales, housing construction, federal spending and hundreds more. So in many cases, government economists are simply crunching numbers compiled by other government economists.

But some critical reports aren't available by the time—like this morning—that Commerce reports its first estimate of the GNP, the month after the quarter ends. For example, in producing today's report, the economists didn't have December's figures on U.S. imports and exports, nor the revised figures for November's trade. That means considerable guessing, for now, in one of the four main categories of the report.

Estimating is particularly tricky at the moment, some Commerce officials say. After several years of steady expansion, the economy is clearly switching gears. For a range of data only available on an annual basis—most notably, in the enormous service sector and state and local government spending—the department is accustomed to projecting a steady expansion based on the latest annual numbers. But such purely arithmetic projections may be impossible when the trendline is shaky. "It's very difficult to pinpoint the slowdown," says Robert Parker, associate director for national economic accounts.

Some projections are no more reliable than the weather—which, in fact, also figures prominently in the GNP report. A brutal cold wave clenched much of the country in December. But not so much as a decimal of consumption data is yet available from the Department of Energy and the American Gas Association, on which Commerce relies for energy-output statistics. For now, the Commerce economists must content themselves with analyzing figures on above-average and below-average degree days on the National Oceanographic and Atmospheric Administration.

Happily, today's GNP number won't be cast in stone. It will be revised twice in the next two months, and again in July, then again in 1995, as the department gleans more data.

A few years ago those revisions showed that the economy didn't grow at a 4.3% annual rate, as originally reported for the fourth quarter of 1984, but instead at 0.6%.

These estimates form the basis of the *revisions* to the estimates that are released later. The revisions continue in many rounds and are not completed until the census data for the year including the quarter in question or the first census year after the quarter have become available.

The publication of GNP data for a given quarter follows a set schedule, as follows:

1. The first estimate, called the **advance** estimate, is released on about the twenty-fifth day of the first month following the end of the quarter.

2. The second estimate, called the **revised** estimate, is released on about the twenty-fifth day of the second month following the end of the quarter.

3. The third estimate is released on about the twenty-fifth day of the third month following the end of the quarter. This estimate is officially called the **final** estimate, because it is the last estimate that is issued for this quarter in isolation. In fact, however, further revisions follow as the annual estimates are revised.

4. In July of each year, GNP for the preceding calendar year is updated on the basis of new, annual survey data. Because annual GNP data are constructed as interpolations between or extrapolations from benchmark years, GNP for the two years before the last are normally revised as well. The quarterly data for all three years are also revised in order to conform to the new annual figures. This revision is known as the **first July revision.**

5. The following year's July revision, by going three years back in time, will also affect the estimate for the quarter we are considering. This is the **second July revision.**

6. In the same way, there will be a **third July revision** a year later.

7. Finally, the **benchmark revision** based on new census data every five years completes the revision process.

PRESENTATION OF GNP DATA IN THE PRESS

Figures 15.2 and 15.3 give examples of how GNP releases are presented in the *Wall Street Journal*. On the front page of the newspaper, page A1, the release is reported in bulletin form under "Business and Finance" in the "What's News" columns (Figure 15.2). This bulletin is followed up with an article on page A2, which provides detail and commentary (Figure 15.3). The news on this occasion is the advance estimate of GNP for the second quarter of 1989. The graph shown with the article compares this estimate with the various estimates (advance, revised, and final) available for the preceding quarters. It shows that real GNP growth

FIGURE 15.2

Presentation of a GNP
release in bulletin form.
Source: *Wall Street Journal*,
28 July 1989, p. A1.

What's News—

* * *   * * *

Business and Finance

B RISTOL-MYERS AND SQUIBB
agreed to merge in a stock swap
valued at $11.52 billion, creating what
may be the world's second-biggest phar-
maceutical concern, after Merck. The
combination is the biggest in a recent
flurry of mergers that reflect the competitive pressures and huge costs in the
drug business.

(Story on Page A3)
* * *

Economic growth slowed to a 1.7%
annual rate in the second quarter, easing
fears of inflation without indicating a
recession. The GNP growth was much
smaller than the revised 3.7% rate in the
first quarter.

(Story on Page A2)
* * *

Ford Motor agreed to acquire Para-
mount Communication's consumer and
commercial finance unit, Associates Corp.,
for $3.35 billion.

(Story on Page A2)

World-Wide

MOSCOW'S PARLIAMENT ADOPTED
economic resolutions for the Baltics.
The legislature, the Supreme Soviet, approved two resolutions paving the way for
Lithuania, Latvia and Estonia to have greater
control of their economies. One resolution
would allow the three Baltic states to trade
independently with other Soviet republics.
The other supports the main provisions of a
draft law on economic independence for Estonia and Lithuania, which already have declared themselves sovereign states, the Tass
news agency said.

The paraliamentary action was con-
sidered a major victory for Baltic activ-
ists, who have accused Moscow of sap-
ping the republics' natural resources.

* * *

A Korean Air DC-10 crashed about a mile
short of a runway at Tripoli's airport. Officials
in Libya said at least 82 people were killed,
including four on the ground. The airliner,
carrying 199 people, was enroute to Libya
from Seoul. The cause of the crash wasn't
known, but dense fog at the airport was cited
as a contributing factor.

rates declined slightly over the calendar year 1988. The respective estimates appear to agree with respect to this tendency, even though they
tend to disagree somewhat among themselves. The first quarter of 1989
showed a rebound that might seem remarkable but in fact was due in
large part to the recovery of the farm sector from the drought in 1988.
The graph also suggests that *the revisions tend to go in the upward direc-*
tion, a phenomenon that we discuss a little further below. However, the
first quarter of 1989 was a notable exception to this rule.

The table at the end of the article in Figure 15.3 gives the details for
the expenditure components of the final GNP estimates for the first and
second quarters of 1989.* This information is given in level form, al-

---

*The column on the left is for the second quarter and that on the right is for the first
quarter. The identification of the quarters is incomplete because of a typographical error
in the newspaper.

FIGURE 15.3   Article reporting on a GNP release. Source: *Wall Street Journal*, 28 July 1989, p. A2.

Economic Growth in 2nd Quarter
Slowed to an Annual Rate of 1.7%

U.S. Report on GNP Eases Fears About Inflation; Recession Isn't Indicated

BY LAUREN COOPER

Staff Reporter of THE WALL STREET JOURNAL

WASHINGTON—The growth of the U.S. economy slowed considerably in the second quarter, the Commerce Department said, easing fears of inflation but stopping short of indicating a downturn.

Second-quarter estimates showed that real gross national product—the total output of goods and services, adjusted for inflation—rose at a 1.7% annual rate.

That is much smaller than the revised 3.7% rate of the first quarter, but the slowdown isn't as drastic as the numbers suggest. The government attributes 2.2 percentage points of the first-quarter growth to a return to near-normal output levels for crops and livestock affected by last year's drought.

"It is not a knockdown blow for the economy," said Campbell Harvey, an economist with Duke University. Other economists agreed, and many said that this latest measure of the economy is a direct effect of the Federal Reserve's economic restraint policies initiated over a year ago.

The annual rate of inflation, as measured by a broad GNP-based index, increased to 5.2% during the second quarter, up from a 4.6% rate in the first quarter. Increases in food and energy prices accounted for much of the first-quarter to second-quarter growth, the report said.

Michael Darby, undersecretary of commerce for economic affairs, was optimistic about reducing inflationary pressure. "Recent monthly price data . . . strongly suggests that the peak rate of inflation is now behind us. From here on, we expect that inflation will slow," he said.

Some other economists weren't as optimistic as Mr. Darby. "I think that is a bit bold," said Donald Straszheim, chief economist of Merrill Lynch Capital Markets in New York. "We could in fact see the inflation numbers a little bit higher."

The growth in personal consumption continued to slow during the period, increasing at a $7.2 billion annual rate after growing at a $13.3 billion pace in the first period. Personal income grew more slowly, as did exports. Imports jumped, fueled by larger oil shipments.

Business inventories rose at a $22 billion annual rate, $2.5 billion less than the first quarter rise. "We have got a lot better handle . . . on inventory management," said Moncure Crowder, executive vice president at First National Bank in Atlanta.

In a separate report, the department said GNP growth between 1985 and 1988 was stronger than previously estimated, averaging 3.6% a year rather than

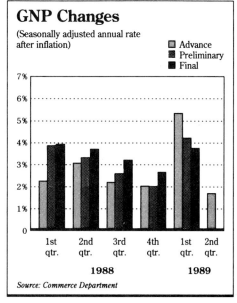

GNP Changes

(Seasonally adjusted annual rate after inflation)

▨ Advance
▧ Preliminary
■ Final

Source: Commerce Department

3.3%. A major factor in the revision was that exports averaged 2.1% higher over the period that previously estimated.

One of the most striking revisions was the one for 1988. The figure for economic growth from the fourth quarter of 1987 to the fourth quarter of 1988 was revised to 3.4% from 2.8%. Lesser increases in imports, decreases in nonfarm inventory investment and increased nondefense purchases were mainly responsible.

Not every economist was impressed by the revisions. "There is little importance in these numbers being released except to make the current slowdown that much more dramatic," said Alan Gayle, chief economist at Crestar Financial Corp.

No changes were made in the inflation estimates for the period, which averaged 3.7%.

GROSS NATIONAL PRODUCT

Here are some of the major components of the gross national product expressed in seasonally adjusted annual rates in billions of constant (1982) dollars:

	Qtr. 1989	Qtr. 1989
GNP	4,123.9	4,106.8
less: inventory chng	22.0	24.5
equals: final sales	4,101.9	4,082.3
Components of Final Sales		
Personal Consumption	2648.2	2641.0
Nonresidential Invest.	510.2	501.0
Residential Invest.	188.6	195.6
Net Exports	−52.6	−55.0
Gov't Purchases	807.6	799.7

In the second quarter, the implicit price deflator rose to 4.9% of the 1982 average, from 4.0% in the previous quarter.

though it is easy enough for the user to compute growth rates using formula (15.1). Note, however, that growth rates do not have real meaning for negative entries, such as net exports. They also tend to be volatile for small components of GNP, such as inventory changes.

This table also introduces the concept of **final sales,** which is defined as GNP less inventory accumulation. It measures that portion of output that is sold to a real customer and not just to the producing company itself in a dummy transaction. Thus, the figure for final sales is sometimes considered a better measure of the level of demand than real GNP itself. According to this report, the quarterly growth of final sales was $100 \times [(4,101.9/4,082.3)^4 - 1] = 1.9\%$, which is slightly higher than the estimated real GNP growth rate of 1.7%. This difference indicates that the level of demand strengthened slightly more than actual production.

The table also makes note of the GNP deflator, which rose at an annual rate of 4.9% from the first quarter, while the corresponding change during the preceding quarter was 4.0%, an indication—though weak—that inflation was on the rise.*

REVISIONS AND UNCERTAINTY IN THE EARLY GNP RELEASES

Considering that the early estimates are based on incomplete information, it is not surprising to find substantial revisions as more information arrives at the data constructors' desks. However, two important questions need to be asked. The first is whether the earliest estimates convey any useful information at all; the second question is whether the revisions follow a predictable pattern.

The answer to the first question is clearly in the affirmative. Some evidence to this effect can be found in Figure 15.4, which is reproduced from a recent study by BEA statistician Frank de Leeuw.** This figure shows an unambiguous, positive correlation between the advance estimates (called "preliminary" estimates in the graph) and the latest available estimates for all quarters between the second quarter of 1968 and the fourth quarter of 1986. The correlation coefficient is 0.83. This correlation is found even though the absolute revision in this estimate was as large as 2.0 percentage points on average. This result can be explained by the observation that the growth rates themselves varied more than the revisions. This pattern is quite apparent in both Figure 15.3 and Fig-

---

*The reference in the article to the 1982 average is misleading. It is true that 1982 is the base year for the GNP deflator, so its value was defined to be 100 during that year. Its level in the fourth quarter of 1988 was 123.4, which means that it was 23.4% above its average level during 1982. However, the inflation rates refer to the changes *from quarter to quarter,* not relative to 1982.

**Frank de Leeuw, "The Reliability of GNP," *Journal of Business & Economic Statistics,* April 1990, vol. 8, no. 2, pp. 191–203.

FIGURE 15.4

Growth rates, quarterly real GNP, 1968:2–1986:4, preliminary (horizontal scale) versus latest (vertical scale). The percentage of change at the annual rate is seasonally adjusted. Source: Frank de Leeuw, "The Reliability of U.S. Gross National Product," *Journal of Business & Economic Statistics*, April 1990, vol. 8, no. 2, pp. 191–203.

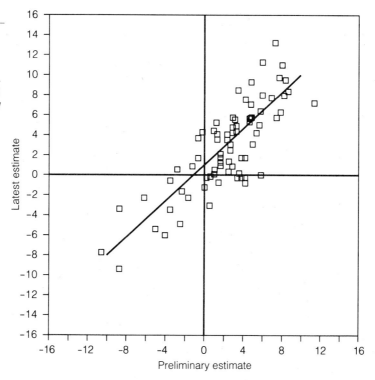

ure 15.4. Thus, even relatively inexact early estimates provide information about the *order of magnitude* of the final values.

In any case, it is possible that the *direction* of subsequent revisions can be predicted in advance. If that is so, it would be possible to make more accurate predictions of the final values than those given by the official preliminary estimates. In this regard, statistical tests seem to confirm the impression from Figure 15.3 that the revisions tend to go upward. Figure 15.4 reveals the same pattern by the fact that the estimated regression line crosses the *y*-axis a little above the origin, indicating that a 0% initial growth estimate tends to be revised upward to a few tenths of a percentage point. In fact, it seems prudent to assume that the eventual estimate of real GNP growth for a given quarter will be 0.3 to 0.5 percentage points higher than the advance estimate.*

---

*Knut Anton Mork, "Ain't Behavin': Forecast Errors and Measurement Errors in Early GNP Estimates," *Journal of Business & Economic Statistics*, April 1987, vol. 5, no. 2, pp. 165–75. Note, however, an opposing view presented by N. Gregory Mankiw and Matthew D. Shapiro in "News or Noise? An Analysis of GNP Revisions," *Survey of Current Business*, 1986, vol. 66, pp. 20–25.

ARE THE FINAL DATA RELIABLE?

In his recent study of the reliability of real GNP data, Frank de Leeuw* acknowledges that errors occur not only in the preliminary data releases but also in the final estimates. The errors in the preliminary data are observable in hindsight from the magnitude of the revisions. However, remaining errors in the final estimates present more of a problem.

Frank de Leeuw distinguishes between two types of errors, which he calls **gathering errors** and **adjustment errors.** The gathering errors include first of all *sampling* errors, which occur whenever the data are estimated from sample surveys rather than taken from a complete population count. However, the gathering errors also include problems such as interviewer bias and errors in the interview responses. Although these errors are unfortunate, statisticians at least have ways of estimating their magnitudes and sometimes of reducing them. We know, for example, that a small change in the GNP growth rate, say 0.2 percentage points from one quarter to the next, is well within such errors.

The adjustment errors are more difficult to deal with. An example might help explain their nature. In Section 15.3, we will see how monthly data for retail sales are used to estimate quarterly data for the consumption component of GNP. However, data for retail sales are collected by store and not by type of customer. Thus, if you buy a hammer from a hardware store to use in your home, that is consumption; however, if a contractor buys an identical hammer for use in the construction of a customer's house, that is a business purchase of an intermediate good for production. In order to determine how much of these sales is actually consumption, the BEA uses an *assumption* based on information on the relative magnitudes of consumption and business purchases at some time in the past, such as in the last economic census.

This is only one of many cases in which the surveys measure one quantity but data constructors use the numbers to estimate another related quantity. The errors arise because of the cost involved in obtaining complete data. As noted above, some of the quarterly GNP data are not even estimated at all but are computed as simple interpolations between the annual data. Without better methods, it is difficult to estimate the magnitudes of these errors. However, it would be imprudent—and implausible—to assume that the errors are negligible.

A third source of error is the process of **seasonal adjustment.** A number of economic data series show clear seasonal patterns, sometimes for obvious reasons. Consumer spending always rises before Christmas, construction activity is low during winter, and gasoline consumption peaks during the summer driving season.

---

* Frank de Leeuw, op. cit.

Because these fluctuations are not very interesting to most observers, the BEA seeks to weed them out through seasonal adjustment of the data. This process uses a complex but essentially mechanical statistical procedure that seeks to determine the average seasonal pattern in the data and remove this pattern from the movements in the data. The seasonally adjusted data are then used for comparisons over time. Thus, for example, if consumer spending is reported to have declined in December of a particular year, it usually means that spending actually rose but that the increase from November to December was less than normal for the season.

Errors occur in this process when the seasons—or their physical manifestations—vary from year to year. Although Christmas does not move around, Easter does, as does spring clothes shopping. Moreover, although the weather is seasonal, its pattern can vary from year to year. Thus, unusually warm winters often result in rosy reports from the construction industry.

The presence of errors in economic statistics adds to the difficulty involved in making unambiguous statements about the economy. We noted in Chapter 11 that it makes sense to listen to a variety of points of view in judging the performance of the economy, because we cannot know for sure which view is right. In Chapter 13, we noted the difficulty involved in reading economic signals because they often reflect irrelevant information, such as auto sales being used as a signal of consumer demand when the same sales have been boosted temporarily by special sales incentives. The errors involved in economic data present a third reason for caution in making decisions based on information about the economy.

Exercising caution is not the same as avoiding decisions, of course. Bold and aggressive decision making is a prerequisite for success in business. The point is rather that the decisions need to take into account the possibility that the economic data, signals, and predictions might turn out to be wrong. This is part of the risk of doing business. Good macroeconomic analysis can help reduce the risk, but the limitations of economic theory and data restrict that role somewhat.

15.3 CONSUMPTION, INCOME, AND SAVING

The consumption component of GNP is important not only because it indicates the strength of consumer demand but also because it alone makes up two-thirds of U.S. GNP. Although consumption expenditure tends to be a little smoother than GNP over the business cycle, as seen in Figure 3.7, changes in consumption trends are a good indicator of where the economy as a whole is going. Note that there is a good theoretical reason for this relationship: According to the forward-looking theory of consumption discussed in Chapter 5, consumers make their spending decisions based on their expectations about future income levels. Because the nation's overall income is generated by its production output, this theory suggests that consumer spending can be interpreted as a signal of people's expectations of future GNP movements. If people are good forecasters, paying attention to these expectations might be worthwhile.

Consumption is one of the GNP components for which data are reported on a *monthly* frequency, which brings it a good deal of attention. Many of the data that go into the monthly consumption statistics come from a related data series for **retail sales.** It might be useful to take a look at this data series first.

RETAIL SALES

The retail sales data are derived from monthly surveys of the nation's retailers conducted by the Bureau of the Census. Although participation in these surveys is voluntary, the majority of retailers participate.*

As mentioned in the last section, the retail sales data include some sales that are not consumption expenditures. For example, most of the sales at building material and supply stores are considered business purchases of intermediate goods rather than consumption. On the other hand, retail sales are a much narrower concept than consumption in the sense that their measurement includes only the sales of *goods* and excludes services. Thus, the percentage of durable goods is much higher in retail sales than in overall consumption. Since we know that the demand for durable goods is much more volatile than overall consumer demand, we then must expect the retail sales data to be more volatile than consumption. This is indeed the case, as illustrated by Figure 15.5. This figure shows the retail sales data for August 1989 as reported in the form of a graph in the middle column on top of the front page of the *Wall Street Journal.*

The retail sales data are released in *nominal* terms, that is, without adjustment for inflation. This makes them difficult to interpret when inflation is high or variable. To make the problem worse, the monthly retail sales data are released about a week *before* the release of the Consumer Price Index for that month, whose data could have been used for deflation. It comes shortly *after* the release of the Producer Price Index, but that index, by construction, reports prices on the wholesale rather

---

*For facts about the retail sales data, see David W. Wilcox, "What Do We Know about Consumption?" unpublished paper, Research Department, Federal Reserve Board, Washington, D.C., June 1988.

FIGURE 15.5

Graph accompanying the release of new data for retail sales. Source: *Wall Street Journal*, 15 September 1989, p. A1.

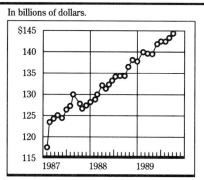

Retail Sales

In billions of dollars.

RETAIL SALES rose in August to a seasonally adjusted $144.29 billion from a revised $143.27 billion in July, the Commerce Department reports. (See story on page A2)

than the retail level. This means that the users of the retail sales data must make their own guesses about how to deflate them.

THE MONTHLY CONSUMPTION DATA

The retail sales data are a major input in the BEA's monthly estimates of consumption expenditures. However, it should be noted that the consumption data also include many items that are not covered by the retail sales survey, such as housing, health care, travel, and other services. Because the monthly data for these items are sketchy, we should emphasize that the factual base for the estimation of monthly data for the service component of consumption is weak. Consequently, most of the variation in the monthly consumption data comes from the spending on goods, which tends to be volatile because of the relatively large component of durable goods. Therefore, the monthly consumption data tend to contain a good deal of noise, which makes them volatile. For this reason, *it is unwise to attach too much meaning to a change in estimated consumer spending for an individual month.* Together, the monthly data are useful indicators of trends. However, changes in trends suggested by data for an individual month should be interpreted with caution.

Like the retail sales data, the monthly consumption data are released in *nominal* form. They are deflated later so that real monthly consumption data will be available for statistical analysis. However, at the time of the release, the user must make his or her own correction for inflation. This task is a little easier than in the case of retail sales, both because the consumption data are released shortly *after* the release of the Consumer Price Index and because the coverage of the CPI is much closer to the composition of the consumption data. A simple method for correcting for inflation is to subtract the monthly inflation rate from the monthly growth rate in nominal consumption. (You should be able to see by now why you need to subtract the inflation rate rather than, say, dividing by it.) While not exact, this method is unlikely to generate large errors.

Figure 15.6 shows a copy of an article that reports on a release of

FIGURE 15.6

Article reporting on consumption, personal income, and personal saving. Source: *Wall Street Journal*, 31 August 1989, p. A2.

Personal Income And Spending Rose By 0.7% in July

BY HILARY STOUT

Staff Reporter of THE WALL STREET JOURNAL

WASHINGTON—In another sign that the economy continues to perform at a healthy pace, the government said Americans' personal income and spending grew solidly in July.

Income and spending both increased 0.7%, the Commerce Department reported, their biggest gains in the past few months. The July gains follow revised increases of 0.5% in personal income and 0.2% in personal spending in June.

The new report came a day after the government sharply revised its calculation of the economy's growth in the second quarter, largely because federal analysts found increases in consumer spending to be double their original estimate.

Consequently, the new statistics on income growth and spending "certainly tell us that anybody who had some negative numbers for the second quarter or thought that this quarter might be the beginning of a recession might be premature," said Stuart Hoffman, chief financial economist at PNC Financial Corp. in Pittsburgh.

The new report showed that purchases rose across a spectrum of goods and services in July. At the same time, because of the larger income gain, the nation's savings rate stayed at 5.7% of disposable income, fairly high for recent years.

Overall, personal income expanded to a $4.449 trillion annual rate, while personal spending—which includes everything but interest payments on debt—increased to a $3.482 trillion rate.

Income from wages and salaries shot up 1.0%. "At least on the face of it, the income gains in July kept consumers above the inflation rate," Mr. Hoffman noted.

As with a string of recent indicators, these numbers were revised upward to show greater strength than the government initially reported. Originally, the department said personal income grew only 0.3% in June, while personal spending was unchanged.

All numbers were adjusted for seasonal fluctuations. After adjusting to remove the effects of inflation, personal spending grew 0.5% in July and 0.1% in June.

Here is the Commerce Department's latest report on personal income. The figures are at seasonally adjusted annual rates in trillions of dollars.

	July 1989	June 1989
Personal income	4.449	4.416
Wages and salaries	2.647	2.621
Factory payrolls	0.553	0.552
Transfer payments	0.634	0.631
Disposable personal income	3.804	3.776
Personal outlays	3.587	3.560
Consumption expenditures	3.482	3.457
Other outlays	0.104	0.104
Personal saving	0.218	0.216

monthly consumption data. As you can see, this release also contains information on personal income and saving, which we discuss next.

DISPOSABLE INCOME

Since income is ultimately generated by production, GNP can also be interpreted as a measure of the gross national income. Consequently, an alternative estimate of GNP is from the *income side*, that is, as the sum of all income earned in the country. Part of this income is **personal income**—income earned by households as opposed to corporations, institutions, and government agencies. Data for personal income are available monthly and are released together with the consumption data. Like the consumption data, they are released in nominal form, but again ad hoc deflation by the Consumer Price Index is a reasonable approximation. The personal income figure is reported both before and after tax. The after-tax figure is called **disposable personal income.** Both income concepts, as well as a breakdown of income according to source, are reported in the table at the end of the article in Figure 15.6.

The personal income figure is useful as a partial estimate of the economy's income-generating production activity. In other words, it is an indicator of the *production side* of the market, as opposed to the retail sales and consumption figures, which indicate spending demand. The difference between the movements in consumption and personal income thus serves as a measure of possible imbalances in the economy. This difference is summarized in the personal saving rate.

PERSONAL SAVING

Personal saving is defined as simply the difference between disposable personal income and consumer spending. Thus, it includes "passive" saving such as the equity portion of installment payments on home mortgages and consumer loans. It also includes contributions to pension funds that are deducted from employee wages and salaries. On the other hand, it does not include interest payments, which are counted as a negative contribution to income. Interest payments are netted against interest receipts to form net interest income, which is a component of personal income.

Personal saving computed as a percentage of disposable personal income gives the personal saving rate. Figure 15.7 shows the history of this rate over the last 35 years. Compared to some other countries, such as Japan and Germany, the U.S. saving rate has never been very high. However, the last decade has shown record low rates. Some improvement in the saving rate can be seen at the very end of the data series given in the figure, but these rates are still low by historical standards.

Personal saving is only one part of total **private saving.** The other part is corporate saving, which mainly consists of retained corporate earnings. Because a good deal of saving is done by corporations, total pri-

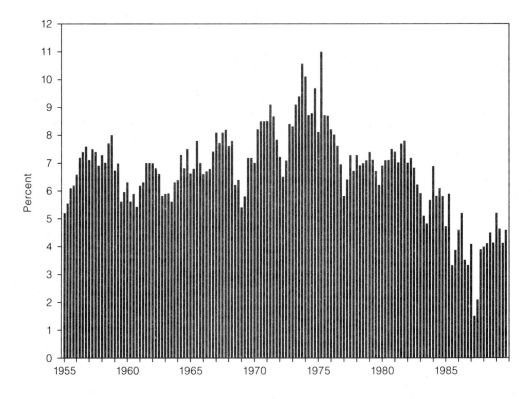

FIGURE 15.7

Data for U.S. personal saving as percent of disposable personal income, 1955–89.

vate U.S. saving as a percentage of GNP is significantly higher than the personal saving rate. Nevertheless, it has been smaller than the corresponding percentage for Japan throughout most of the postwar period.*

15.4   NET EXPORTS AND TRADE DATA

Quarterly data for net exports are released as part of the GNP releases, as shown by the table at the end of Figure 15.3. A related set of quarterly data is the **current-account balance** of the Balance of Payments Accounts, discussed in Chapter 9. Except for the fact that the current account also includes unilateral transfers, the data for net exports and the current-account balance should, in principle, be the same. In practice, because the Balance of Payments Accounts are kept separately from the

* For a careful but nontechnical comparison of these data, see Fumio Hayashi, "Is Japan's Saving Rate High?" Federal Reserve Bank of Minneapolis *Quarterly Review*, Spring 1989, vol. 13, no. 2, pp. 3–9.

National Income and Product Accounts, many details are treated differently, with the unfortunate result that the numbers often disagree. However, these differences do not affect the reading of important trends.

It is important to realize that both net exports and the current-account balance include trade in services as well as trade in goods (**merchandise trade**). An important component of these services is transportation, which is both a necessary companion to trade in goods and an important contributor to trade in its own right (for example, international air travel). In regard to other services, distinguishing between trade in labor services and trade in capital services is useful. Labor services are traded when Americans perform work abroad and vice versa, for example, in the form of consulting services. The services of guest workers are another example. The work of international commuters, such as those who cross the U.S.-Canadian border to get to and from work, is included in the category of labor services.

Capital services are another important category. Recall that GNP is defined as the output of U.S. factors of production, so the output generated by U.S. ownership in overseas facilities goes into the construction of U.S. GNP. As mentioned in Section 15.1, this output is defined as the return paid to U.S. capital owners and is accounted for as exports of capital services. Foreign ownership of production facilities in the United States is treated analogously. In previous years, the net export of capital services made a sizable contribution to net exports and hence to GNP for the United States. With growing foreign investment in the United States, this stream now very much goes both ways and has recently shown signs of turning negative.

Monthly trade data are available only for merchandise trade. It is important to know that these data are computed and released with a one-month reporting delay compared to the other major monthly series. Figure 15.8 shows how the **merchandise trade deficit** is typically reported by means of a graph in the *Wall Street Journal.* This particular report resulted from the release of the data for July 1989.

The graph first shows how large the U.S. merchandise trade deficits have been for the last three years. Note that these dollar amounts are *per month* and are not expressed at annual rates, so the annual data on average are 12 times as large. Second, a downward trend appears to have started around the end of 1987. This trend has a long way to go before it achieves balance, but at least the trade deficit is not widening.

Third, it is apparent from the graph that these monthly data are extremely noisy, as evidenced by the large month-to-month fluctuations. One reason for this noise is that the timing of individual shipments— that is, whether they arrive before or after the end of the month— is often quite arbitrary. In the case of some large shipments, such as the arrival of a supertanker carrying imported crude oil, insignificant

FIGURE 15.8

Graph accompanying the release of monthly data for the U.S. merchandise trade deficit. Source: *Wall Street Journal*, 18 September 1989, p. A1.

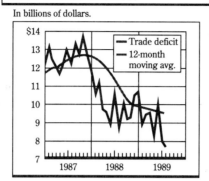

U.S. Trade Deficit

In billions of dollars.

Legend: Trade deficit; 12-month moving avg.

The U.S. merchandise trade deficit fell in July to a seasonally adjusted $7.58 billion, from a revised $8.01 billion in June, the Commerce Department reports. The 12-month moving average narrowed to $9.30 billion the previous month. (See story on page A2.)

events affecting the arrival date can have substantial effects on the monthly trade data. A second reason for the noise is that the timing of the *reporting* also may be somewhat inexact. In other words, a shipment that physically arrived at the end of one month may be reported as having arrived at the beginning of the following month. There is no reason to be disturbed by such noise in the data, but it underscores the need for caution in the interpretation of the trade data for individual months. To aid this interpretation, the graph in Figure 15.8 also shows a moving average of the figures for the last 12 months, which smooths out most of the noisy fluctuations.

CHAPTER REVIEW

1. The National Income and Product Accounts (NIPA) are an accounting system maintained by the Bureau of Economic Analysis (a U.S. government agency) with the intent of keeping track of important movements in the economy.

2. Real GNP is the most comprehensive indicator of overall economic activity. It measures the market value (in 1982 prices) of all final goods and services produced by U.S. factors of production.

3. All of the data series in NIPA are maintained

annually, most of them quarterly, and some monthly. Quarterly and monthly level figures are usually multiplied by factors of 4 and 12, respectively, in order to have the same order of magnitude as the annual figures. Changes from quarter to quarter or from month to month are usually expressed at annual rates, with compounding.

4. The deflation of GNP is made component by component. The GNP deflator is a by-product of this process. As a weighted average of individual prices, it serves as a broad

measure of inflation. Because the weights are current shares in real GNP, the GNP deflator is a variable-weight index.

5. The advance estimate of GNP for a given quarter is published toward the end of the month following the quarter. A revised estimate is issued a month later, followed by a "final" estimate one month later still. The annual July revisions, which are based on annual surveys with larger samples, are used to revise annual and quarterly GNP for the preceding three years. A benchmark revision is undertaken every five years as a result of the quinquennial economic census.

6. The preliminary estimates tend to give correct indications of the order of magnitude of real GNP growth. However, there is a tendency for the revisions to go upward. Even the final figures must be expected to contain errors and inaccuracies.

7. Data for consumption, personal income, and personal saving are published monthly. Some of the raw data for consumption comes from the monthly survey of retail sales, but the data for many other categories are less reliable. Because the best data are for durable-goods purchases, the monthly fluctuations tend to be dominated by movements in this component. The data for personal income give indications about the production side of the economy. The personal saving rate provides information about the balance between spending and production.

8. Net exports, along with the current-account balance, are published quarterly. They include trade in goods as well as services, where services include the yields on international claims. Only merchandise trade data are published monthly. These data tend to be quite noisy, because the exact timing of the trade flows—as well as their recording—is somewhat arbitrary.

EXERCISES

1. Consider a fictitious economy in which only three goods are bought and sold, namely, food, clothing, and machines. This economy has no government but trades with the rest of the world. You are given the following data for two years, year 1 and year 2. In year 1, consumer expenditure is $990 for food and $1,200 for clothing. Investment expenditure is $650, all for machines. Export revenues are $300 from food, $300 from clothing, and $130 from machines. The import bill is $190 for food, $450 for clothing, and $260 for machines. The prices for domestically produced goods in year 1 are $100 per unit of food, $150 per unit of clothing, and $130 per machine. The prices of imported goods are the same, except that imported food costs only $95 per unit. In year 2, consumption expenditure rises to $1,155 for food and $1,254.6 for clothing. Investment expenditure rises to $715, again all for machines. Export revenues become $440 from food, $306 from clothing, and $130 from machines. Imports change to $240 for food, $459 for clothing, and $390 for machines. Compared to year 1, the prices for domestically produced food and clothing rise by 10% and 2%, respectively. The price of imported food rises to $120 per unit. The price of domestic as well as imported machines is unchanged. Use year 1 as your base year. For each year, compute a set of National Income and Product Accounts, showing GNP, consumption, investment, and net exports in current as well as base-year prices. Also compute the GNP deflator, as well as growth rates from year 1 to year 2 of all the variables.

2. The table at the bottom of the article in Figure 15.3 provides level data for each component of real GNP for the second and first quarters of 1989.
   a. Compute quarterly growth rates for each component. Do these growth rates have meaning for every component?
   b. Compute annual growth rates for each component, using formula (15.1). Compare these rates to the rates you would have obtained if you had multiplied the respective quarterly rates by 4. Are the differences significant? Why or why not?
   c. Comment briefly on the differences and similarities among the growth rates of

the individual components. Do you see any signs of worsening or improving imbalances?

3. From back issues of the *Wall Street Journal* or another newspaper, collect data for the advance estimates of real GNP growth for every quarter from 1985 to the present. Compare this series to a standard series of real GNP growth that contains the last estimates available. Graph the two series and comment on your visual impression of their relationship. Also compare them statistically. Are the two series correlated? Are their means significantly different? Based on a regression, to what extent could the revisions have been predicted using only the information contained in the preliminary estimates? Comment on your results.

4. Construct three quarterly series for the growth in retail sales, defined as the monthly growth rates (at annual rates) for each of the three months of the quarter, respectively. Compute lagged values of each series as well, so that you have data for the growth rates in each month of the current and the previous quarter. Use these data to construct four regression-based prediction models for this quarter's real GNP growth, one using only retail sales growth from the previous quarter, one using retail sales growth from the previous quarter plus the first month of this quarter, and so on until you have used the data for all months in the current quarter. Comment on the fits of these models and on how you can use them to extract information from the monthly retail sales data about the current quarter's real GNP growth at different times during the quarter.

5. Compared to retail sales, consumption, income, and saving, the trade-deficit figures arrive one month late. Construct a model using current and lagged values of the former data that can be used to construct an earlier estimate of the expected trade deficit. Include the last month's trade deficit in the model as well. Does it fit significantly better than if only the lagged deficit is included? How can this model be used?

6. Construct a graph of U.S. government deficits and U.S. net exports. Do the two series tend to move together? If so, how? How high is their correlation? What do the results tell you?

THINKING QUESTIONS

1. When economic data undergo large revisions, the government statistical agencies are sometimes criticized for not having been careful enough in their construction of the preliminary data. Do you think that this is the correct basis for criticism? Why or why not? What criteria would you use to evaluate the work of these agencies?

2. Suppose you have a regression equation of the type in exercise 4 above that allows you to predict GNP revisions. Could you use such a model to your advantage in the stock market? Why or why not?

3. When countries are compared, countries with large government deficits tend to have high private saving, and vice versa. The United States tends to be an outlier in such comparisons, having both large government deficits and low private saving.

   a. What does the pattern for the non-U.S. countries tell you about the hypothesis of Ricardian equivalence introduced in Chapter 5?

   b. Why do you think the United States is different?

16 MONTHLY INDICATORS OF EMPLOYMENT, PRODUCTION, AND INFLATION

The U.S. government maintains a number of useful monthly indicators of economic activity. Some of these indicators, like those reviewed in Chapter 15, are directly or indirectly part of the National Income and Product Accounts. Other important indicators are not. This chapter reviews three groups of monthly indicators that are not part of the National Income and Product Accounts: indicators of movements in employment, industrial production, and inflation.

16.1 LABOR MARKET DATA

Labor market statistics are followed with keen interest from many quarters. Labor unions want high employment at wages that allow them to live comfortably. Managers prefer soft labor markets so they can attract the workers they want at wages they can afford. The participants in the financial markets look to the labor market for signs of emerging or easing inflation. Last, but not least, government policymakers follow labor market statistics eagerly because jobs, wages, labor cost, and productivity affect their constituents in profound ways.

The Bureau of Labor Statistics, or BLS, the data-collection branch of the U.S. Department of Labor, publishes a wide range of data relating to the labor market. On the first Friday of each month, it releases two sets of employment data, one based on a survey of households and one based on a survey of establishments. It also publishes data on wages and labor productivity.

THE HOUSEHOLD SURVEY: EMPLOYMENT, UNEMPLOYMENT, AND THE LABOR FORCE

Each month, the U.S. Bureau of the Census interviews people from a random selection of households. Some of the responses to these interviews are used by the BLS to put together data for *employment, unemployment,* and the *labor force.* A typical interview scenario follows. The interviewer rings the doorbell and makes sure that the person opening the door is 16 years old or over. If not, the person is not considered part of the **working age population,** and the interviewer needs to get another person to answer the list of questions.

When a member of the working age population has been found, the interviewer asks if the person was "gainfully employed" the preceding week. Being gainfully employed normally means having worked for pay for at least an hour. However, being self-employed, having worked without pay for a family business, and having been on vacation, sick leave, or strike count as well. After all the interviews are done, the BLS counts the people who answered yes to this question and blows up the figure by the ratio of the working age population to the sample size for the household survey. The resulting figure is the household survey's measure of **employment.**

Determining whether or not a given person is employed is usually pretty straightforward. The next issue to determine is whether a person who is not employed is **unemployed** or **not in the labor force.** This issue is much trickier. The basic idea is that unemployment should be defined such that only people actively seeking work should be counted as unemployed. Thus, if an interviewee answers no to the question about gainful employment, the interviewer goes on to ask a series of questions to see whether the person has engaged in any of a list of specific job-search activities. Such activities include making applications, distributing a resume, and visiting or calling potential employers. Just reading the want-ad section of the newspaper doesn't count. A person who has engaged in any of these activities is classified as **unemployed.** A person will also be classified as unemployed if he or she has been laid off temporarily and is waiting to be recalled. The number of unemployed now is blown up in the same way as the number of employed people to give an estimate of the number of unemployed people in the population.

The people who are employed or unemployed make up the **labor force.** The rest are classified as **not in the labor force.** This latter group includes retirees, full-time students, and homemakers. It also includes people who would like to hold jobs but have given up looking. This group of people is sometimes referred to as "discouraged workers." If a recession lasts for a long time, some workers usually become "discouraged" and leave the labor force, which may give the appearance of improvement in the unemployment statistics. As an offsetting effect, a recession also may spur the spouse of an unemployed worker to look for a job, even if the spouse was not previously in the labor force. This phenomenon is referred to as the "added worker" effect.

The **unemployment rate** is defined as the number of unemployed people *as a percentage of the labor force.* To express these relationships mathematically, let E denote the number of employed people and U the number of unemployed people. Then the labor force (LF) is

(16.1) $$LF = E + U,$$

and the unemployment rate is

(16.2) $$u = 100(U/LF).$$

The unemployment rate is a good gauge of labor market conditions. However, a couple of reasons why it is not a perfect measure are worth mentioning. First, people enter and leave the labor force according to their own decisions, so high unemployment may mean that jobs are scarce, that many people choose to look for jobs, or both. The unemployment rate does not by itself give any further information about what is going on. To find out more, it is usually useful to look at the *employment* data, which give more direct information about the development of job opportunities. Looking at the labor-force data might be informative as well, because they give some indication about trends in people's interest in holding jobs.

The other problem is that both the numerator and the denominator in formula (16.2) may vary. Thus, changes in the unemployment rate can sometimes be caused by factors other than changes in the number of unemployed. Suppose, as an example, that the same number of people are added to the number of employed as are added to the labor force. Then the unemployment rate declines because the labor force in the denominator has risen, even though the number of unemployed is unchanged. Another example is a case in which a number of people who have previously been outside the labor force start looking for work but are unsuccessful at first. Then the unemployment rate would rise even though nobody has lost his or her job.

Employment and unemployment statistics are broken down by age, sex, and race, which makes them useful for more specialized applications. Macroeconomists are especially interested in the unemployment rates for adult men and adult women. Adult men, in particular, as the traditional breadwinners, tend to be more stable participants in the labor force. For this reason, changes in the unemployment rate for adult men tend to be more reflective of the availability of jobs than of decisions to seek or not to seek work. Because it carries this information, the unemployment rate for adult men serves as an excellent signal of changes in the demand for labor.

Releases of unemployment rates are usually considered big news. Figure 16.1 shows the February unemployment rate for 1989 as displayed on the front page of the *Wall Street Journal*. Because of its widespread interest, news of unemployment rates usually is also reported widely in the less specialized media.

THE ESTAB-LISHMENT SURVEY: PAYROLL EMPLOYMENT

The establishment survey collects payroll information directly from employers. As a result, this survey gives no measure of unemployment, but it does provide much more detailed information about employment, hours, wages, and productivity. Because each company surveyed has many employees, this survey contains direct observations for many more workers than the household survey. The most important data to

FIGURE 16.1

Graphical presentation of the release of unemployment data for February 1989. Source: *Wall Street Journal*, 13 March 1989, p. A1.

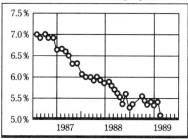

Unemployment Rate

Percent of labor force, seasonally adjusted.

UNEMPLOYMENT in February fell to a seasonally adjusted 5.1% of the civilian labor force from 5.4% the preceding month, the Labor Department reports. (See story on page A.2)

come out of the establishment survey is an alternative measure of employment, referred to as **payroll employment.**

Many analysts attach more significance to this figure than to the unemployment rate, because it is based on a larger sample of workers and because they believe the reporting to be a little more accurate. Furthermore, it is broken down by major industry at the time the data are released, so the analyst can find out how much of a given change comes from manufacturing, how much from other goods-producing industries (such as mining and construction), and how much from the service sector of the economy. The financial markets pay particular attention to payroll employment. If the movements in the payroll employment and the unemployment rate do not agree for a given month, the financial markets usually react on the basis of the movement in payroll employment.

A person who holds more than one job is counted twice in the establishment survey but only once in the household survey. Perhaps paradoxically, the double counting in the establishment survey is often considered an advantage, because it makes the payroll employment measure sensitive to changes in the *activity* levels of individual workers. The financial markets are more interested in activity than in how many people hold jobs per se; this is one reason why the financial markets pay close attention to the results of the establishment survey.

The data releases for payroll employment also present a problem, however. Because many firms in the sample don't submit their reports until the following month or later, the payroll data are often subject to substantial revisions. Moreover, as in the case of preliminary GNP or money-supply data, the revisions have been found to be somewhat predictable.* In contrast, the household survey is completed on time every month and does not present this problem.

Despite their importance, the payroll employment data tend to be reported with a little less fanfare than the unemployment rate. Figure 16.2 shows how payroll employment is typically reported along with details of the household survey in an article on page A2 in the *Wall Street Journal.*

THE ESTAB-LISHMENT SURVEY: HOURS, WAGES, AND PRODUCTIVITY

The payroll employment figure is counted in units of thousands of people. However, the establishment survey also collects data about hours and thus is used to construct data series for employment measured in employee hours. These data series are particularly useful for research, because an hour of work is a much better defined measure of labor input to the production process than one person working an unspecified amount of time.

As should be expected from a payroll survey, the establishment survey also collects wage data, referred to by analysts as "average weekly earnings" and "average hourly earnings." These data are important for inflation watchers, as we discuss further below.

Finally, the payroll employment data are combined with production data from the National Income and Product Accounts to construct measures of **labor productivity** in the form of *output per hour.* We discussed this measure of productivity in Chapter 7, as well as the alternative measure of total factor productivity. Data for labor productivity are constructed quarterly for the nonfarm business sector, the farm sector, and the manufacturing sector of the U.S. economy.

EXTRACTING SIGNALS FROM THE LABOR MARKET DATA

Employment and unemployment are measures of economic activity. For policymakers and public-interest groups with a strong interest in the creation of jobs, such as labor unions, the data on employment and unemployment are important in themselves. For marketing managers, they can serve as signals of income creation and hence indirectly of the demand for consumer goods. For financial and strategic analysts, the main point of interest is the close tie between employment and production levels, which we discussed in connection with the aggregate production function in Chapter 7. Coupled with the Phillips curve, the labor market data are usually considered important sources of information about possible inflationary pressures.

The link between employment and production has been verified em-

---

* David Neumark and William L. Wascher, "Can We Improve upon Preliminary Estimates of Payroll Employment Growth?" unpublished paper, Board of Governors of the Federal Reserve System, 1989.

FIGURE 16.2 Article providing details of the labor-market data presented in Figure 16.1. Source: *Wall Street Journal,* 13 March 1989, p. A2.

Fall in Joblessness Raises Inflation Fears;
More Fed Tightening Isn't Expected Soon

Unemployment in February Equaled '74 Low of 5.1%; Payrolls Grew by 289,000

BY HILARY STOUT
Staff Reporter of THE WALL STREET JOURNAL

WASHINGTON—February's drop in the unemployment rate to 5.1% brings the economy to what many economists consider "full employment," a level they view as a portent of escalating wages, faltering productivity and higher prices.

The civilian jobless rate, which was 5.4% in January, hasn't been lower since December 1973, when it reached 4.9% of the work force. Unemployment also stood at 5.1% in May 1974.

The Labor Department report confirmed the persistent strength of the economy, which last month generated an increase of 289,000 in nonfarm payrolls. The strong job growth followed

Stocks Confound Pessimists

The stock-market bulls really can't complain, but the bears and short-sellers are frustrated. They say they keep seeing the signals for a good downward 'correction,' such as Friday's report of high employment, but the market won't oblige. Story on page C1.

January's startling increase of 415,000, a revision from the 408,000 reported about a month ago.

The White House hailed the figures, with spokesman Marlin Fitzwater declaring, "Jobs are the best barometer of the economy."

Still, the low jobless rate and continued job growth will put pressure on businesses to raise wages to attract and keep workers. In addition, the shallower pool of available workers means companies in the job market may end up with employees who are less skilled.

February's labor report, said Allen Sinai, chief economist for Boston Co. in New York, "is terrific news for certain age groups and ethnic groups that had trouble finding jobs, but it does mean increased cost pressures . . . and inflation."

"In the short run, this is good," said Daniel Van Dyke, senior economist for Bank of America in San Francisco. "But in a longer-term sense, I think it portends additional risk to the economy. . . . Labor costs are about two-thirds of the whole economy, so when they go up you get additional price pressure."

Audrey Freedman, an economist at the Conference Board in New York, said, "They're reaching into every corner for additional workers."

Most of the decline in unemployment occurred in parts of the work force where jobless rates tend to be both higher and more changeable from month to month. Hispanics, who make up only 7.5% of the U.S. work force, accounted for nearly 40% of the February drop in unemployment. In addition, the jobless rate for teen-agers dropped 1.6 percentage points to 14.8%, and the rate among young adults—age 20 through 24 years—declined 1.2 points to 8.1%. Among people over 25, however, the rate barely changed.

Consequently, Janet Norwood, commissioner of the Labor Department's Bureau of Labor Statistics, cautioned in testimony on Capitol Hill, "sud-

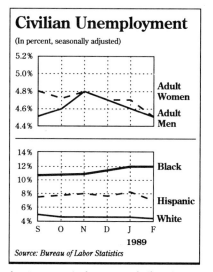

Civilian Unemployment
(In percent, seasonally adjusted)

Adult Women
Adult Men

Black
Hispanic
White

S O N D J F
1989

Source: Bureau of Labor Statistics

den movements in these more volatile series are frequently followed by similar movements in the opposite direction."

She added: "Additional data are needed to determine whether the February decline will be sustained."

The job growth in February came entirely in the services sector, which added 321,000 positions. Jobs declined by 32,000 in the goods-producing sector, largely because of a drop in construction employment amid harsh winter weather. The figures are adjusted for seasonal factors.

Jerry Jasinowski, chief economist for the National Association of Manufacturers, maintained that the drop doesn't signal weakness in manufacturing. "Apart from autos, manufacturers continue to see orders and production at a strong rate," he said.

Despite the concern over pressure on wages, pay was ltitle changed in February after increasing substantially in January. Average hourly earnings of production or non-supervisory workers edged up to $9.51 in February from $9.50 in January.

EMPLOYMENT
Here are excerpts from the Labor Department's employment report. The figures are seasonally adjusted.

	Feb. 1989	Jan. 1989
	(millions of persons)	
Total labor force	124.9	125.1
Total employment	118.5	118.4
Civilian labor force	123.2	123.4
Civilian employment	116.9	116.7
Unemployment	6.3	6.7
Payroll employment	108.3	108.1
Unemployment:	(percent of labor force)	
All workers	5.1	5.4
All civilian workers	5.1	5.4
Adult men	4.5	4.6
Adult women	4.5	4.7
Teen-agers	14.8	16.4
White	4.3	4.6
Black	11.9	12.0
Black teen-agers	32.4	34.5
Hispanic	6.8	8.4
Average weekly hours:	(hours of work)	
Total private nonfarm	34.7	34.8
Manufacturing	41.0	41.0
Factory overtime	3.9	3.9

pirically in a relationship called **Okun's law,** after the late Brookings Institution economist who made the relationship between GNP and employment famous.* Okun ran a regression of the changes in the unemployment rate on the growth rate of real GNP on quarterly data from 1947:2 to 1960:4 and got the following result:

$$(16.3) \qquad \Delta u_t = 0.30 - 0.30 y_t,$$

where Δu_t is the quarterly change in the unemployment rate in percentage points and y_t is the real GNP growth rate (at a *quarterly*, not annual, rate). Although the exact values of the coefficients in this regression have changed a little over time, the slope coefficient of Okun's law remains representative of the current relationship between real GNP changes and changes in the unemployment rate on average. For example, a regression using data only for the 1980s yields an intercept of 0.20 and a slope coefficient of -0.32. Thus, a 1% increase in real GNP on average translates into about three-tenths of a percentage point decline in the unemployment rate. Equivalently, it takes about a three percentage-point improvement in real GNP to reduce the unemployment rate by one percentage point.

The labor market statistics take on special significance as indicators of production activity, because they are the first data for such activity released for any given month. However, it is important to bear in mind that the correspondence between employment and production is not quite one-to-one. Strong employment growth most often means strong output growth. However, it can mean weak productivity growth: more people may have been hired without much more being produced. At the time of the release of the employment data, it is impossible to tell which is the case. Since higher employment *most often* means higher output, this is the most likely outcome, but the possibility of weaker productivity performance is always worth keeping in mind.

The labor market data are also followed as *signals of inflation,* for three reasons. The first reason is simply the Phillips curve, according to which higher activity means rising inflationary pressures, whether this activity is measured by output or employment. The second reason is that the labor market seems to have served as an important link in the inflation process. When inflationary pressures are building, they often start in the labor market. For example, when managers have a hard time hiring all the workers they need to fill the demand for their products, they are likely to offer higher nominal wages. However, higher

---

*Arthur M. Okun, "Potential GNP: Its Measurement and Significance," *American Statistical Association, Proceedings of the Business and Economic Statistics Section,* 1962, pp. 98–104.

wages mean higher nominal production costs, which may be passed through to customers as higher nominal prices. The third reason is that the wage data in the labor market statistics give direct information about inflationary forces in the labor market. Wage inflation was followed with especially keen eyes in the late 1960s and the 1970s, when inflation was perceived by many as driven by wages—"cost push" inflation. In contrast, the rising inflation in the late eighties has not been characterized by strong wage increases. This experience serves as a reminder that wage inflation, though useful as a signal, is not the ultimate measure of inflation.

16.2 INDUSTRIAL PRODUCTION AND CAPACITY UTILIZATION

The **Index of Industrial Production** is a monthly indicator of production activity that is maintained outside the National Income Accounting system. The data are collected and released by the Federal Reserve System. The index measures changes in the physical volume or quantity of output in manufacturing, mining, and electric and gas utilities. Thus, it can be used directly as a real variable without adjustment for inflation.

Although it is not a substitute for GNP, this index is a widely used alternative measure of overall production activity. Part of the reason for this prominence is the timeliness of the index. It is published monthly, only a couple of weeks after the end of the month whose activity it measures. Thus, the release of the Index of Industrial Production follows by only about a week the release of the labor market data. It supplements it in an important way, because it measures production directly rather than indirectly via employment.

The Index of Industrial Production follows the trends in real GNP but is somewhat more volatile. Part of this volatility can probably be explained by the fact that the economy fluctuates more from month to month than from quarter to quarter; the quarterly construction of the GNP data smooths over the monthly fluctuations. Another reason is that the index has a bias toward the production of goods as opposed to services. In fact, utility services are the only services included. Because goods production contains a larger percentage of investment goods and consumer durables than total production, it is more inclined to be dominated by the movements in these components. We know they are more volatile than overall output, so it is not surprising to see that this index fluctuates more than GNP.

Normal seasonal patterns in industrial production are removed by seasonal adjustment of the data before their release. However, the word *normal* is important, because changes in the seasonal pattern can distort the index, as in the case of retail sales. For example, extreme cold or hot weather boosts the output of the utility sector for heating or air-conditioning, respectively, and gives a spurious impression of healthy economic growth. When the weather returns to normal, the index gives an equally spurious impression of decline.

Figure 16.3 presents an article from page A2 of the *Wall Street Journal* reporting and commenting on the change in this index for February 1989. For that month, the overall index showed no change from the month before, which was viewed as a sign of slowing of the overall economy. Although this was discouraging news by itself, it was greeted with some relief, because people thought that it also signaled an easing of inflationary pressures. Comments to this effect implicitly rely on the Phillips curve mechanism studied in Chapters 7 and 8. The breakdown into components shown in the table at the end of the article was also of some interest. For the overall index, the major weakness was in defense and space, which fluctuates with government contracts. The production of consumer goods showed slow growth, while the production growth in business equipment was a vigorous 0.8% monthly, corresponding to an annual growth rate of 10%. At the time, many people considered this bias a good sign in an economy that had been characterized by strong consumption growth and modest investment activity.

Capacity utilization is a by-product of the industrial production index and is often issued a day or two later. In addition to collecting data on production volumes, the Federal Reserve also estimates capacity levels in the companies it surveys and publishes a series of average capacity utilization for the entire economy. This series is useful because it indicates the presence of idle capacity as well as the possibility of bottlenecks, which might slow further expansion and lead to inflationary pressures. It can also be read as a signal of the demand for investment goods that could be used to eliminate such bottlenecks.

The weakness of this series is that production capacity is not a well-defined concept. The maximum level of output from a given plant depends not only on the plant size but also on the number of workers, how many shifts per day, and how much is used of other inputs, such as energy and raw materials. Furthermore, a physical definition of maximal capacity might not correspond to the desirable level of operation from an economic point of view. Costs and profitability will be affected by factors such as overtime pay, downtime for desirable maintenance, and time taken to assure quality. Such considerations suggest that production at less than physical capacity might be desirable and that the optimal utilization of the physical capacity varies from plant to plant and from industry to industry. Nevertheless, as a rough measure, the capacity utilization index provides information about the business-cycle movements in idle capacity and the likelihood of bottlenecks in industry.

For February 1989, the capacity utilization rate was reported as

FIGURE 16.3

Article reporting on the Index of Industrial Production for February 1989. Source: *Wall Street Journal*, 17 March 1989, p. A2.

Industrial Output Was Flat in February; Operating Rate, Housing Starts Dropped

By HILARY STOUT
Staff Reporter of THE WALL STREET JOURNAL

WASHINGTON—Three new government reports show further signs of slowing in major sectors of the economy.

U.S. industry in February failed to increase its production for the first time in a year, the Federal Reserve reported. At the same time, the Fed said, the nation's factories, utilities and mines used a slightly smaller portion of their capacity than in January. And new housing construction plunged 11.4% in February, the Commerce Department reported.

Earlier this week, the government reported that retail sales dropped in February and that U.S. exports and imports both declined in January. All the figures suggest that economic activity is slowing down.

The latest reports follow a set of economic statistics for January that showed widespread strength in the economy. But a number of economists said the new figures, combined with other economic data for February, are leading them to forecast with increasing confidence that the economy is beginning to slacken.

"My sixth sense from all the numbers is that three or four months ago you were hard pressed to find any indications of slowing," said Joel Prakken, vice president of Laurence H. Meyer & Associates Ltd., an economic consulting firm in St. Louis. "Now almost every report has some tidbit suggesting moderation of growth. I think the tide has turned a little."

Many economists have been hoping for slower economic growth, contending that the economy has expanded to the point where rapid advancement is breeding inflation. The Fed has been actively trying to rein in the economy by coaxing up interest rates. But until recently, report after report had signaled persistent vigor in the economy.

Operating Rate Off

The leveling-off of industrial production in February followed a 0.4% rise in December, according to the Fed's report. Meanwhile, industry's operating rate fell to 84.3% of capacity from 84.5% in January, the first decline since September, the Fed said.

February's decline in housing starts means that work was begun on new houses at an annual rate of 1,498,000. The drop followed a revised 8% jump during January, an increase most analysts said was stimulated by unseasonably mild weather. All three reports are adjusted for seasonal changes. Originally, the Commerce Department calculated a January rise of 7.2%.

"Certainly the February number was a more real number than January," said Robert Sheehan, economist for the National Apartment Association, although he added that "February was certainly affected by very lousy weather."

Mr. Sheehan and other economists said the housing industry is feeling the effect of rising mortgage rates.

"I think you will continue to see—as long as inflation paranoia continues—a decline in housing starts," said Kent Colton, executive vice president of the National Association of Home

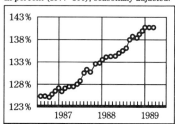

Industrial Production

In percent (1977=100), seasonally adjusted.

Builders. The Fed's policies, he said, "are having an impact on the economy now. My concern is we will talk ourselves into a recession. The housing sector is clearly slowing down."

The issuance of building permits for future construction declined 6.8% in February to a 1,404,000 annual rate after falling 3.8% in January.

Problems for Bush

The prospect of a slowdown in the economy poses some problems for the Bush administration, which is counting on vigorous economic activity to generate enough tax revenue to shrink the federal budget deficit.

But Edward Yardeni, chief economist at Prudential-Bache Securities Inc., said that although the numbers show the economy "isn't booming," it's "expanding in the right places."

The industrial production figures, for example, reflected declines in production of automobiles and construction supplies but a rising level of output of business equipment.

The growth in business equipment "confirms the view that capacity is expanding . . . and the fact that the capacity utilization rate is down in the face of flat production shows that capacity is expanding," Mr. Yardeni said.

Tight capacity is worrisome because it can lead to production bottlenecks and shortages, which can drive prices up.

In the area of production, Mr. Yardeni said, "A lot of weakness was in car sales. I have no problem with an economy where we have consumer spending growing at a slower pace and capital spending at a faster pace."

He added: "If we keep this up, we'll start looking like Japan."

INDUSTRIAL PROTECTION

Here is a summary of the Federal Reserve Board's report on industrial production in February. The figures are seasonally adjusted.

	% change from	
	Jan. 1989	Feb. 1988
Total	0.0	5.0
Consumer goods	0.1	5.8
Business equipment	0.8	8.5
Defense and space	-0.2	-5.4
Manufacturing only	0.0	5.7
Durable goods	0.1	6.1
Nondurable goods	-0.1	5.0
Mining	-1.8	0.0
Utilities	1.9	1.2

The industrial production index for February stood at 141.1% of the 1977 average.

84.3%, a slight decline from 84.5% the month before. A rate around 85% is usually considered rather high. Utilization rates near 90% are considered by many as indicative of an overheating economy, while rates in the seventies and upper sixties are typical of recessions.

16.3   INDICATORS OF INFLATION

The rate of inflation is a measure of the average change in prices from one period (year, quarter, month) to the next. Computation of the inflation rate requires some measure of the overall or average *level* of prices. Such a measure is called a **price index.** Suppose the value of some index for year t is P_t. Then, as we have noted before, the inflation rate for year t is

$$(16.4) \qquad \pi_t = 100 \times (P_t - P_{t-1})/P_{t-1} = 100 \times (P_t/P_{t-1} - 1).$$

Of course, P_{t-1} denotes the price level the year before.

The inflation rates for quarterly price indices are usually expressed at annual rates with compounding. Thus, if P_t and P_{t-1} denote the price levels for two consecutive quarters, the inflation rate for quarter t is usually expressed as

$$(16.5) \qquad \pi_t = 100 \times [(P_t/P_{t-1})^4 - 1].$$

This is done routinely for data releases of the GNP deflator (discussed in Chapter 15), which are made quarterly.

For monthly price indices, such as the Consumer Price Index and the Producer Price Index, the data are often released as *monthly* rates of change. In other words, formula (16.4) is used with the times t and $t - 1$ denoting two consecutive months. Under this convention, inflation rates from 0.1% to 0.3% are usually considered moderate, since they correspond to annual rates of about 1% to 4%. However, the monthly data are also sometimes expressed at annual rates, that is, based on formula (16.5) with t and $t - 1$ indicating consecutive months and 12 used instead of 4 as the exponent for P_t/P_{t-1}.

The exact number used for the inflation rate depends on which measure is used for the overall price level. We consider three common measures: the Consumer Price Index (CPI), the Producer Price Index (PPI), and the GNP deflator.

THE CONSUMER PRICE INDEX

The basic idea behind the construction of the CPI is quite simple. First, a list of goods and services that the average household buys is defined and the average quantities purchased are determined. This information is extracted from the Consumer Expenditure Survey, which is conducted by the U.S. Bureau of the Census under contract with the Bureau of Labor Statistics.* After this shopping list has been determined, price data are collected each month to find out its current cost. The CPI is simply the ratio of this current cost to the cost of the same shopping list in some base period (called period 0), normalized by multiplication by 100:

$$(16.6) \qquad P_t^{CPI} = 100 \times \frac{\text{cost of shopping list at time } t}{\text{cost of shopping list at time } 0}.$$

If P_{it} is the current (period t) price of item number i on the list and X_{i0} is the amount of that good on the list, then an equivalent formula is

$$(16.6') \qquad P_t^{CPI} = 100 \times (\sum_i P_{it} X_{i0})/(\sum_j P_{j0} X_{j0}).$$

Define I_{it} as P_{it}/P_{i0}. Except for the customary factor of 100, this is a price index for the ith good (or service) on the list. You should now be able to show that the CPI can be written as a weighted average of these individual indices:

$$(16.6'') \qquad P_t^{CPI} = 100 \times \sum_i w_{i0} I_{it},$$

where the weights are

$$w_{i0} = P_{i0} X_{i0}/(\sum_j P_{j0} X_{j0}).$$

In other words, the weights are the respective items' shares in total expenditure at base-period prices. Because these weights do not change from one month to the next, the CPI is called a **fixed-weight index.**

Following is a list of some useful things to know about the CPI:

1. The CPI is defined for a shopping list made up of the consumer goods and services bought by the typical household. Consequently, it is not a general index of overall inflation. In particular, it ignores inflation in the prices of investment goods as well as intermediate goods and raw materials used by business. However, it is a good gauge of the inflation facing consumers and wage earners.

2. The CPI includes the prices of *imported* goods that consumers typically buy. This feature makes the index sensitive to fluctuations in foreign prices and exchange rates.

3. The CPI reflects inflation only as it is faced by *urban* households. The shopping list is based on the buying habits of urban households, and only the prices of urban establishments are sampled each month.

---

*The first such survey was conducted in 1888–91. Since the 1930s, new surveys have been carried out about every 10 to 12 years. Starting in 1979, the Consumer Expenditure Survey has been an ongoing effort, with data produced annually.

Rural households have historically been excluded, because the collection of prices paid and received by farmers has been the responsibility of the Department of Agriculture.

4. The use of fixed weights is both good and bad. On the good side, they permit quick calculation of the CPI once the individual prices are known, as is apparent from formula (16.6″). On the bad side, they can cause the CPI to overstate the increase in the cost of living when the prices of some items increase more than others, because the fixed weights ignore the potential savings to consumers of changing their consumption pattern away from those items that have become more expensive. For example, in the 1970s, the contribution to inflation of rising energy prices was exaggerated, because the index ignored energy conservation. The contribution from gasoline prices was computed as if people continued to drive "gas guzzlers" when in fact they had traded these vehicles for small, fuel-efficient cars.

5. The CPI is widely used as a basis for cost-of-living adjustment (COLA) clauses in labor contracts and for Social Security benefits. In this connection, it is useful to note that there are, in fact, two consumer price indices with slightly different shopping lists. Contract wages are often tied to the CPI-W, whose shopping list is typical of urban *wage earners*. However, the index given the most publicity is the CPI-U, whose shopping list represents the average buying habits of *all urban households*.

6. The CPI can be broken down into a number of component indices representing food, housing, clothing, medical care, and so on. Perhaps the best-known breakdown is the CPI excluding food and energy. Because the movements in the prices of food and energy during the 1980s tended to be somewhat more volatile than prices overall, this index is considered by some to give a more correct picture of the underlying inflationary trends in the economy. However, it is important to keep in mind that food and energy prices can also dominate the overall inflationary picture, as they did in the 1970s.

7. Special CPI indices are also available by region and by major metropolitan area.

8. The CPI for a given month is released toward the end of the following month, usually around the twentieth.

The monthly announcements of CPI releases are met with great interest by policymakers and financial-market participants, as well as the general public. In the *Wall Street Journal*, the CPI is usually presented as a graph in the middle of the top of the front page. The graph for the February 1989 CPI is shown in Figure 16.4. In addition, the monthly per-

FIGURE 16.4

Graphical presentation of release of the Consumer Price Index for February 1989. Source: *Wall Street Journal*, 22 March 1989, p. A1.

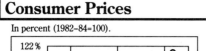

Consumer Prices

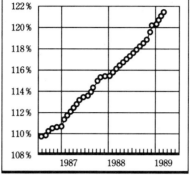

In percent (1982–84=100).

CONSUMER PRICES rose in February to 121.6% of the 1982–84 average from 121.1% in January, the Labor Department reports. (See story on page A2)

centage increase is presented in bulletin form in the "What's News" section. A follow-up article in the "Economy" section on page A2 almost always provides further detail and comment. A typical article (again for the February 1989 CPI figure) is shown in Figure 16.5. This follow-up article usually ends with a table giving detailed statistics, as shown in the figure.

THE PRODUCER PRICE INDEX

Mechanically speaking, the PPI is constructed in a manner similar to the CPI. That is, a list of goods and quantities is used to define a shopping list, and the PPI is then constructed as a fixed-weight index of the prices of the items on this list. Thus, the formulae for the PPI are the same as for the CPI. However, the information contained in the PPI is quite different from that of the CPI. The PPI measures the prices of goods that are typically bought by businesses rather than by consumers. By measuring prices on the *wholesale* level, it excludes the contribution to prices from the services rendered by the retail industry. Therefore, the PPI is not so much a measure of current inflation as it is a measure of the cost of doing business. As such, it is often read as an early warning sign of upcoming price trends that might reach consumers in the months ahead.

Following are some other points worth noting about the PPI:

1. The coverage of the PPI in one sense is broader than that of the CPI, because it includes investment goods. In fact, there are at least three PPIs: one for raw materials, one for intermediate goods, and one for

ECONOMY

Consumer Prices Rose 0.4% Last Month And Fears of Rampant Inflation Let Up

Modest Rise Is Below January's, Far Below Producer-Price Jump

By HILARY STOUT

Staff Reporter of THE WALL STREET JOURNAL

WASHINGTON—Consumer prices rose 0.4% in February, slower than their January pace and far below the February jump in producer prices, the Labor Department said.

The report brought cautious relief to the financial markets, which were alarmed by the department's report Friday that prices producers charged for finished goods soared 1.0% in February for the second month in a row. That was the largest two-month increase since early 1981.

"I think the inflation statistics have returned to sanity," said Michael Evans, president of Evans Economics, an economic forecasting firm here.

The Bush administration said the new price report "should calm inflation fears." According to Marlin Fitzwater, the White House spokesman, the consumer price report "showed inflation moderated in February."

But many economists remained wary that the low unemployment, high demand and tight productive capacity in the economy will continue to generate pressure on prices.

"The financial markets were pleased because it was not similar to the horrific producer price index, but I think it suggests that while inflation is not galloping upward it is still creeping," said William Dudley, senior economist at Goldman, Sachs & Co.

February's climb in the prices consumers paid for a variety of goods and services follows an increase of 0.6% in January, the largest monthly rise in two years. So far in 1989, consumer prices have risen at an annual rate of 6.1%, well above the 4.4% increases posted for 1988 and 1987.

No Worst-Case Scenario Seen

Many economists said there is no doubt inflation will continue at a quicker clip than during the past few years, though they said the latest consumer price numbers suggest the country isn't in danger of tumbling into an inflationary spiral.

"Certainly 1989 will deliver a noticeably higher inflation rate than 1988," said William Dunkelberg, dean of the Temple University School of Business and Management and chief economist of the National Federation of Independent Business.

But Jerry Jasinowski, chief economist of the National Association of Manufacturers, said the latest consumer price numbers show, "in essence, fears of inflation getting out of control look premature."

"After the temporary spike in the first quarter," he added, "inflation should settle into the 5% (annual) range by midyear."

Except for medical care and housing, inflation slowed in every category of the consumer price report. Medical costs rose 0.8% for the second month in a row. Energy and transportation costs both rose 0.6%, smaller than the January increases in both those categories.

Even excluding food and energy, where wide price swings can distort the overall index, consumer prices rose 0.4% during the month.

The Labor's Department's consumer price findings for February stood in stark contrast to those in its producer price report, which spread grim fears of renewed inflation through the financial markets.

Often increases in producer prices take a few months before they show up at the retail level. "We won't see the effect of the high PPI (producer price index) inflation until about six months from now," Mr. Dunkelberg said. Also, the consumer price index includes prices of services and imported goods; the producer price index does not.

Weekly Earnings Decline

"I think the producer price report overstates the magnitude" of inflation, Mr. Dudley said. "But at the same time, it doesn't change any of the fundamentals that inflation is accelerating."

Yet, in a sign that inflation pressures may not be as great as some analysts fear, the Labor Department also said that the average weekly earnings of U.S. workers dropped 0.6% in February, after adjusting for inflation. Even without taking inflation into account, average weekly earnings slipped to $330.00 from $330.60.

Some economists also maintain that February's producer price report contained some "fluky" numbers. The report said the price of tomatoes, for example, skyrocketed 158% in February, accounting for nearly half of a 1.2% leap in producer food prices. But a Labor Department analyst acknowledged that tomato prices fell the day after the department took its price sample.

"Wages are not accelerating, and to me that's a lot more important than the price of tomatoes," Mr. Evans said.

All the Labor Department's figures were adjusted for seasonal variations.

Another price measure, the consumer price index for urban wage earners and clerical workers, also grew 0.4% in February. This narrow gauge is used in calculating cost-of-living adjustments to Social Security and a number of other benefit programs.

CONSUMER PRICES
Here are the seasonally adjusted changes in the components of the Labor Department's consumer price index for February:

| | % change from | |
	Jan. 1989	Feb. 1988
All items	0.4	4.8
Minus food & energy	0.4	4.8
Food and beverage	0.5	6.0
Housing	0.3	3.9
Apparel	-0.2	4.6
Transportation	0.6	4.5
Medical care	0.8	7.2
Entertainment	0.4	5.1
Other	0.6	7.4

Consumer price indexes (1982–1984 equals 100), unadjusted for seasonal variation; together with the percentage increases from 1988 were:

All urban consumers	121.6	4.8
Urban wage earners & clerical	120.2	4.8
Chicago	122.2	4.8
Detroit	120.1	5.6
Los Angeles	125.5	4.8
New York	127.6	5.4
Philadelphia	125.4	5.1
San Francisco	124.0	5.2
Dallas-Fort Worth	117.5	3.1
Detroit	120.1	5.6
Houston	112.7	4.4
Pittsburgh	117.9	4.1

FIGURE 16.5

Article commenting on the CPI release in Figure 16.4.
Source: *Wall Street Journal,* 22 March 1989, p. A2.

finished goods. However, the index publicized in the media is the PPI for finished goods.

2. However, the coverage is narrower in the sense that the PPI covers *only goods and no services.* This is a major limitation, considering the growing importance of the service sector of the economy. Because the prices of services also tend to fluctuate less than the prices of goods, this index is more volatile than the CPI. A typical example is the effect of the oil-price decline in 1986, which produced a plunge in the

PPI that lasted for several months, while the effect on the CPI was much more moderate.

3. The PPI *excludes the prices of imported goods.* This feature shields the PPI from foreign prices and exchange rate fluctuations to some extent. Quite often, however, a price change for an imported good is accompanied by similar ("sympathetic") price changes for competing domestic goods, so the shielding is not complete. However, at times this feature can distort the information carried by the PPI. In the 1970s, when crude oil produced in the United States was subject to price controls, the PPI ignored the much higher prices of imported oil on the world market.

4. The PPI is released on about the fifteenth of each month, which means that it is released about a week before the CPI for the same month. This timing adds to the attention given to the release of PPI data.

Figure 16.6 shows the news of the February 1989 PPI as presented on the front page of the *Wall Street Journal,* with a top story in the "Business and Finance" column of the "What's News" section as well as a graph. This particular release received unusual attention, because the monthly increase was as large as 1% and followed on top of an equally large increase the preceding month. With surges this large, compounding matters; therefore, it is common to translate the monthly increase into a compounded annual rate, as was done in this news bulletin. Concerns were also raised this particular month that the price increase seemed to extend beyond the traditionally volatile components of food and energy. These concerns were discussed further in an article on page A2 of the paper, the beginning of which is reproduced in Figure 16.7.

THE GNP DEFLATOR

The GNP deflator is the third major indicator of inflation. It is released quarterly together with the GNP figures. In Chapter 15, we discussed its definition and some of its features. Formally, it was defined in formula (15.4) as the ratio of nominal to real GNP. Some manipulation of this formula showed that it can be interpreted as a weighted average of the price indices of the individual goods included in GNP. Specifically, the formula derived was

$$(16.7) \qquad D_t = Y_t^N / Y_t = \sum_i w_{it} P_{it} / P_{i0},$$

where the weights are the individual goods' shares in real GNP. These shares contrast with those of the CPI and the PPI in that they can change in each period.

The **variable weights** have the advantage of taking into account substitution away from goods and services whose prices have risen more

What's News—

* * *

* * *

Business and Finance

FED EFFORTS TO DAMP inflation have had little effect so far. Friday's report that producer prices jumped 1% in February, or at a 12.7% annual rate, alarmed economists and sent financial markets reeling. The surge in prices, which affected a broad range of items, makes it likely the Fed will push up interest rates even further, fueling recession fears.

The **Dow Jones industrials** skidded 48.57, or 2%, to 2292.14, the worst drop in nearly a year. Bonds plunged, sending long-term Treasury yields to six-month highs. The dollar surged.

(Stories in Column 6 and on Page A2 and C1)

World-Wide

SALVADORANS VOTED for a new president amid widespread combat.

Leftist revolutionaries opposed to the election attacked military posts and army troops countered with rockets and rifle fire as Salvadorans cast ballots for a successor to Duarte, who is constitutionally barred from seeking re-election. His term ends June 1. At least five guerrillas and two soldiers were reported killed in fighting in nine provincial towns. Two journalists also were reported killed. Early voter turnout appeared diminished by the violence and a guerrilla-imposed transport ban.

Polls showed the candidates of the Christian Democrats and the right-wing party, known by its Spanish acronym Arena, leading the field. A runoff election is expected next month.

Producer Prices

In percent (1982=100).

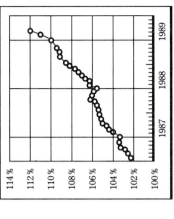

PRODUCER PRICES on finished goods in February rose at a seasonally adjusted rate of 112.1% of the 1982 average, vs. 111% in January, the Labor Department reports. (See story an page A2.)

ECONOMY

Producer-Price Jump of 1% in February Fuels Inflation Fears and Rocks Markets

Spurt, After January Surge, Costs Stocks 48.57 Points And Sets Bonds Reeling

By David Wessel
And Hilary Stout

Staff Reporters of The Wall Street Journal

WASHINGTON—Inflation is busting out all over.

In February, for the second month in a row, producer prices rose 1%, the equivalent of a 12.7% annual rate, the Labor Department said. Not only were there sharp rises in food and energy prices, which sometimes show wide swings from month to month, but prices of other finished goods from flatware to pharmaceuticals also shot up.

Although the Bush administration contiued to predict that inflation will abate, private economists expressed alarm, and prices on financial markets plunged. The Dow Jones Industrial Average fell 48.57 points Friday. Bond prices plummeted, pushing up long-term yields on government bonds to their highest level in more than six months.

Price increases of this magnitude, if they continue, "cannot be absorbed by the economy without tremendous negative consequences," said Dirk Van Dongen, president of the National Association of Wholesalers-Distributors.

But Michael Boskin, the chief White House economist, said he expects the inflation figures "to subside to more-reasonable levels in the coming months." He emphasized the need to "remain vigilant" against

inflation, but said, "We had expected a couple of bad months of inflation numbers."

Inflation specialist Donald Ratajczak, a Georgia State University economist, didn't react so calmly. "Back-to-back double digits! If that's not inflation, I'm going to send them a pair of glasses."

He warned, "We're starting to get what I call me-too pricing." Producers in some industries where cost pressures aren't substantial are raising prices anyhow—simply because everyone else is, he explained. "That's a sign that inflationary expectations are greater than we thought," he said.

Signs that inflation is accelerating—and the strong reaction from financial markets to Friday's report—increase the chances that the Federal Reserve will raise interest rates further in order to slow the economy and relieve pressure on prices.

The producer-price report capped a week of confusing economic data for February. A week earlier, the government said unemployment fell to 5.1%, a 15-year low, and employers added 289,000 jobs. A few days later, however, other reports showed retail sales falling in February, industrial production unchanged for the first time in a year and factories' use of capacity declining, all hints of an economic slowdown that would lessen the chances of an inflationary outbreak.

The government's index of consumer prices rose 0.6% in January, the fastest clip in two years. The report for February comes out tomorrow.

The February increase in producer prices was more widespread than in January. Excluding volatile food and energy prices, producer prices climbed 0.6% in February,

Fastest Rising Prices

Increase in producer price of selected consumer goods

	FEBRUARY*	PAST 12 MONTHS
Vegetables	35.3%	38.1%
Processed turkeys	5.3	28.8
Household flatware	4.1	12.4
Gasoline	4.1	5.6
Consumer paper goods	2.9	8.0
Prescription drugs	1.5	10.0
Books	1.2	6.6
Natural gas	1.9	9.3
All consumer goods	1.2	5.9
All finished goods	1.0	5.3

*Seasonally adjusted, except books and natural gas
Source: Bureau of Labor Statistics

compared with 0.4% in January and 0.7% in December.

Prices of household flatware, for instance, climbed 4.1% in February, and stand 12.4% higher than a year earlier. Producers blame higher prices for nickel and chrome. These increases have forced up stainless-steel prices by 50% over the past year, said Peter Fobare, vice president, sales, at Oneida Ltd. Silversmiths. Oneida absorbed the higher costs through the end of 1988 and had planned on doing the same through this spring. "The increases became too large to not pass along," he said.

Prescription-drug prices rose 1.5% in February after rising 1% in January. Drug companies, which have been raising prices 8% or 9% a year, now are charging fully

Continued on Page A4, Column 4

FIGURE 16.7

Beginning of article commenting on the PPI release in Figure 16.6. Source: *Wall Street Journal*, 20 March 1989, p. A2.

than the average. Thus, the problem posed by energy conservation in the 1970s was alleviated. On the other hand, the variable weights also mean that the index moves not only in response to price changes but also—at least potentially—in response to changes in the weights. Thus, even if no prices change, it is possible for the GNP deflator to move if the relative contributions to GNP by the respective components change. Fortunately, this feature does not usually cause major problems.

A much more important difference between the GNP deflator and the two other inflation indicators is the **broad coverage** of the GNP deflator. Because it reflects the prices of all goods that go into GNP, it covers all sectors of the economy. It is the most comprehensive measure of inflation available. At the same time, it is important to be aware of the fact that the GNP deflator leaves one area uncovered—the prices of imported goods. Just as imported goods are excluded from GNP, so also are their prices excluded from the GNP deflator.

The third difference between the GNP deflator and the two other indices, which arises in regard to **timing,** works to the disadvantage of the GNP deflator. The CPI and the PPI are computed quickly each month and are not subject to substantial later revision. In contrast, the GNP deflator is constructed only quarterly and is subject to many subsequent revisions. The reason for this delay is the use of variable weights, which are determined as a by-product of the estimation of real GNP. Because of these variable weights, the GNP deflator cannot be computed from the price observations alone; it is necessary to wait for the computation of the weights. As a result, the GNP deflator is released with the GNP data and is subject to as many revisions.

The GNP deflator is the preferred measure of inflation for many observers because of its wide coverage and variable weights. However, as we have just seen, these advantages are somewhat offset by the lack of timeliness. In data construction, as elsewhere, quality carries a cost.

CHAPTER REVIEW

1. The monthly data on employment and unemployment, industrial production, and inflation are important economic indicators, though they are not included in the National Income and Product Accounts.
2. The household survey of labor market conditions provides data for employment, unemployment, the labor force, and the unemployment rate. Unemployed workers are people who do not hold a job but are actively seeking a new one. The labor force is the total of employed and unemployed. The unemployment rate is the number of unemployed as a percentage of the labor force.
3. The establishment survey provides an independent measure of employment, called payroll employment. It also provides data for hours, wages, and productivity.
4. The labor market data for any given month are released on the first Friday of the following month.
5. The Index of Industrial Production is a monthly indicator of production activity maintained by the Federal Reserve. It is a

measure of the physical output of manufacturing, mining, and utilities. The Federal Reserve also maintains data for productive capacity in the same industries. The ratio of industrial production to productive capacity (as a percentage) is called capacity utilization. Both measures are released around the middle of the following month.

6. The rate of inflation is the rate of change of the price level, as measured by some index. Inflation for a quarter is usually expressed at a compounded annual rate. Inflation for a month is expressed sometimes at a monthly rate, at other times at a compounded annual rate.
7. The CPI is a fixed-weight index, that is, it measures the current cost of a fixed shopping list (representative of urban households) relative to the cost of the same list in some base period. The CPI covers imported consumer goods as well as services. The fixed weights may bias the CPI upward when some prices increase much more than others. The CPI is often used for cost-of-living adjust-

ments. Many subcomponents and special indices are available. The CPI for any given month is released on about the twentieth of the following month.

8. The PPI is a fixed-weight index as well, but it measures prices paid by business establishments. It has several versions, the best known being the PPI for finished goods. The PPI covers investment goods as well as consumer goods but does not cover services or imported goods. It is released around the middle of the month following the month to which the data pertain.

9. The GNP deflator is issued quarterly with GNP. Its coverage is as broad as that of GNP. Import prices are excluded. As a variable-weight index, it avoids the bias of the CPI and the PPI when some prices rise much faster than others. However, because its publication schedule follows that of GNP, it is slow and subject to many revisions. Nevertheless, many observers consider this deflator their preferred measure of inflation.

NUMERICAL AND ANALYTICAL EXERCISES

1. For a given month, you have the following information about movements in the labor market. Twenty-four million workers were fired or laid off permanently. Another 1 million were laid off temporarily, while 0.5 million workers who were laid off temporarily last month were recalled. In addition, 32 million new workers were hired, 7 million people retired, another 1 million quit their jobs voluntarily for other reasons, 5 million finished full-time studies and either got or looked for new jobs, 2 million teenagers turned 16 without being in school full time, 0.5 million people who had been in the labor force went back to school full time, 2 million workers who previously had been unemployed gave up looking for a job, and 3 million people who previously had been homemakers entered the labor force. The previous month had a labor force of 116 million, 6 million of whom were unemployed. Com-

pute the level of employment, the labor force, and the unemployment rate for the current month.

2. For the economy in Chapter 15, exercise 1, suppose the CPI covers food and clothing, with weights given by consumption in the base year. The PPI covers food, clothing, and machines; the weights are the domestic production levels in the base year. For machines, the producer price is the same as that used in the National Income and Product Accounts. However, for food and clothing, the producer prices are $90 and $145, respectively, in the base year and $95 and $150, respectively, in year 2. Compute the CPI, the PPI, and the GNP deflator for this economy. Compare the inflation rates implied by the three indices. How do you explain the differences?

3. In the open-economy IS-LM model, the overall price level serves two roles. The first role is to influence the nominal demand for money, while the second is to serve as a component in the relative price of domestic goods on the world market. Which price index— the CPI, the PPI, or the GNP deflator—comes closest to serving each of these respective roles? Would you use the same index for both roles? Why or why not? Can you suggest any changes that could be undertaken in the model to better distinguish the two roles?

DATA EXERCISES

1. Construct quarterly data for the level of Industrial Production (IP) as averages of the monthly levels. Use these quarterly levels to compute quarterly IP growth at annual rates. Regress data for quarterly growth in real GNP (also at annual rates) on the quarterly IP growth. What do the results tell you about the empirical relationship between these two variables?

2. Construct three quarterly series for IP growth, defined as the monthly growth rates (at annual rates) for each of the three months of the quarter. Compute lagged values of

each series as well, so that you have data for the growth rates in each month of the current and the previous quarter. Use these data to construct four regression-based prediction models for this quarter's real GNP growth, one using only IP growth from the previous quarter, one using IP growth from the previous quarter plus the first month of this quarter, and so on until you have used the data for all months. Comment on the fits of these models and on how you can use them to extract information from the monthly IP data about the current quarter's real GNP growth at different times during the quarter.

3. Assume, as a simplification, that one month's annualized growth rate for a series x_t can be written as $12 \cdot (x_m - x_{m-1})$, where m stands for individual months. Let $\bar{x}_q$ denote the quarterly average for the same series, defined as an unweighted arithmetic average of the values for each month of each quarter. Finally, define the annualized quarterly growth rates as $4 \cdot (\bar{x}_q - \bar{x}_{q-1})$. Show how this quarterly growth rate can be written as a weighted average of the monthly growth rates for the current and the previous quarter. Use this result to add to your interpretation of the empirical regression coefficients in data exercise 2.

4. Repeat data exercise 2, but this time include the monthly growth rates for payroll employment in addition to industrial production. Experiment with the two variables to see which is the better predictor. Carry out F-tests to determine whether payroll employment contributes significantly to the prediction given that industrial production is being used, and vice versa.

5. Observers sometimes disagree as to which labor market statistic (payroll employment, employment as measured by the household survey, or the unemployment rate) is the best indicator of the economy's level of activity or inflationary pressures. Can you use regression analysis to shed some light on this issue? Can you combine the statistics to obtain an even better indicator?

6. The PPI is often considered an early-warning sign of inflation in consumer prices. Test this claim by regressing monthly data for CPI inflation on a distributed lag of PPI inflation as well as lagged CPI inflation rates. Do some experimentation to find a suitable maximum lag length.

7. Suppose you accept the claim that the GNP deflator is the best measure of overall inflation but feel handicapped because it arrives later than the CPI and the PPI. Using the same procedure as in data exercises 2 and 4, construct a model that allows you to extract information contained in the CPI and the PPI about the likely change in the GNP deflator before the last is released. Is the output of this model superior to the information obtained by just looking at the CPI or the PPI?

THINKING QUESTIONS

1. Government agencies all over the world spend large sums of money on data collection. Considering this cost but also the value of these data, would you argue for a curbing or an expansion of these data-collection efforts?

2. Many people argue that tasks traditionally performed by the government, such as mail delivery, could be done more efficiently by private companies. Would you apply the same argument to the collection of economic data? Why or why not?

3. In the data collection process for the United States, a good deal of effort is put into getting the data out fast. Considering the margin for error in early releases as well as the cost of data collection, state which of the following alternatives you think is better and why: (a) hire more people to make the process more accurate in the time now available, (b) postpone the releases, (c) leave things the way they are.

17
A WALK THROUGH A MONTH OF DATA RELEASES

The announcements of most economic data releases in the United States follow a regular, predictable pattern. News on the financial and commodities markets is reported daily. Weekly money-supply figures are reported after the closing of the New York Stock Exchange every Thursday afternoon. New jobless claims are also announced on Thursdays. The various monthly indicators are released at the same time every month, allowing for weekends and holidays. The employment and unemployment data come the first Friday of each month, the industrial production index around the fifteenth, and so on. Finally, the quarterly data from the National Income and Product Accounts follow their own monthly routine, with new or revised estimates for the preceding quarter for GNP, its major components, and the GNP deflator being released around the twenty-fifth of each month.

Because of this regularity, each data release is anticipated by all those who depend on the information for their business transactions. For these people, life becomes an endless repetition of a familiar monthly rhythm. There is something curiously permanent about this cycle. Individuals and generations are born and die, wars are won and lost, the economy goes from recession to recovery, and political administrations move in and out of power, but the monthly rhythm of economic data releases goes on undisturbed. This permanency serves as an almost eerie reminder that the economic system moves on, independent of its individual members.

However, not all economic news follows a regular schedule. Policy initiatives, especially in monetary policy, can appear at any time. Wars, accidents, natural disasters, and the weather can all disrupt markets and production schedules. These unexpected events, as well as the occasional unexpected turns in the regular indicators, add spice to the lives of economy watchers.

This chapter takes you through the movements of a typical month. We give special attention to the big news items and note some of the less important ones. We focus on the information contributed by each figure to the understanding of the overall trends in the economy. At the end of a month of indicators, a picture usually emerges of strong or slow economic activity, of declining or rising interest rates, of the U.S. dollar's position among the world's currencies, and of rising or falling inflation.

We follow the news releases week by week as they are reported in the *Wall Street Journal.* Of course, the exact division of a month into weeks varies from month to month. We use as our example the month of April 1989, which happened to start on a Saturday and end on a Sunday, a fact that helped us divide it neatly into four business weeks.

17.1 FIRST WEEK: PRELIMINARIES, THEN THE EMPLOYMENT DATA

On Mondays, the *Wall Street Journal* usually presents, on page A2, a summary table of the data releases of the preceding week as well as a list of the expected releases for the upcoming week. This table, as it appeared on April 3, 1989, is reproduced in Figure 17.1. The list of upcoming releases starts with a number of relatively minor items: construction spending on Monday, the 10-day report on auto sales on Tuesday, and sales of major chain stores on Thursday. These are followed by the regu-

FIGURE 17.1

Weekly overview previewing the data releases of the first week of April 1989. Source: *Wall Street Journal,* 3 April 1989, p. A2.

CLOSELY WATCHED REPORTS

Statistics Released in the Week Ended March 31

	TOTAL	CHANGE (from prior period)		TOTAL	CHANGE (from prior period)
Money supply			**Manufacturers' shipments**		
M1 Week ended March 20 (in billions)	$786.8	+$2.7	February (in billions)	$227.61	−1.7%
M2 Week ended March 20 (in billions)	$3,085.3	+$7.5	**Purchasing managers' index**		
M3 Week ended March 20 (in billions)	$3,965.7	+$14.5	March	50.4	−2.6%
			New homes sold		
Leading indicators			February, annual rate	626,000	−9.4%
February index	145.2%	−0.3%	**Farm prices**		
			March, index	149%	+0.7%
Manufacturers' orders			**New jobless claims**		
February (in billions)	$230.68	−2.3%	Week ended March 18	322,000	−4.2%

Statistics to Be Released This Week

Construction spending (Mon.)
February

Auto sales (Tues.)
March

Money supply (Thurs.)

Chain store sales (Thurs.)
Paine Webber Index, March

New jobless claims (Thurs.)

Unemployment rate (Fri.)
March

Employment, payroll (Fri.)
March

Consumer credit (Fri.)
February

lar weekly releases of money supply and jobless claims. This listing is typical of the beginning of the first week of the month. The first major item comes at the end of this week in the form of data on employment and unemployment, which are always released on the first Friday of the month.

However, another news item reported on this Monday was also worth noting. The **federal funds rate** had suddenly risen by 0.2 percentage points on the preceding Friday. This change can be read off the "Markets Diary" graph in Figure 17.2, taken from page C1. Because this interest rate was known to be the intermediate target variable for U.S. monetary policy, speculation arose immediately as to whether this increase reflected a deliberate tightening by the Federal Reserve. Monetary policy had, in fact, been tightened considerably in the months prior to April 1989 in an attempt to alleviate some perceived inflationary pressures. This policy had followed the Phillips curve prescription of using monetary policy to let higher interest rates reduce aggregate demand, thus allowing the inflationary pressures to ease as the economy moves down the Phillips curve. The question raised this particular Monday was whether the Federal Reserve had now decided to tighten the screw by another turn, as it were. The *Wall Street Journal* devoted a special article to this issue, which is reproduced here as Figure 17.3. However, anonymous "government officials" were quick to deny these rumors. Instead, the run-up in the federal funds rate was explained as a random event without further significance. We discussed some of the random elements in the money-supply process toward the end of Chapter 4. The financial markets appeared to believe the government explanation, as the stock and bond markets both rose and the exchange rates were mostly unchanged. As it turned out, the explanation was confirmed by a commensurate decline in the federal funds rate on the following day.

The article in Figure 17.3 also offers a look into the proceedings of the Federal Open Market Committee, as the minutes of its early February meeting were released just before the publication of this article. These minutes revealed a clear resolve to tighten monetary policy in order to counter inflationary pressure, although some disagreement existed within the committee as to the timing of the response.

The tightening of monetary policy and the resulting rise in interest rates during the winter months appeared to have put a damper on the construction industry, according to the reports on **construction spending** and **building contracts** that were released this Monday. The 7% decline in construction contracts was particularly spectacular. The steady rise in interest rates can be read off the graph for the federal funds rate in Figure 17.2. However, some observers noted that the slowdown in construction spending in February, as well as the preceding strong in-

MARKETS DIARY — 3/31/89

STOCKS — Dow Jones Industrial Average — 2293.62 +12.28

INDEX	CLOSE	NET CHNG	PCT CHNG	12-MO HIGH	12-MO LOW	12-MO CHNG	PCT	FROM 12/31	PCT
DJIA	2293.62 −	12.28 +	0.54	2347.14	1941.48	Closed		+ 125.05 +	5.77
DJ Equity	276.90 −	2.30 +	0.84	280.94	235.47	Closed		+ 16.16 +	6.20
S&P 500	294.87 −	2.35 +	0.80	299.63	250.56	Closed		+ 17.15 +	6.18
Nasdaq Comp.	406.73 −	2.17 +	0.54	409.51	347.07	Closed		+ 25.35 +	6.65
London (FT 300)	1707.9 +	21.2 +	1.26	1761.1	1382.9	Closed		+ 252.6 +17.36
Tokyo (Nikkei)	32838.68 +	12.55 +	0.04	32838.68	26282.12	+ 6734.46 +25.80	+	2679.68 +	8.89

BONDS — Shearson Lehman Hutton T-Bond Index — 2932.50 +15.24

INDEX	FRI	FRI YIELD	THU	THU YIELD	YR AGO	12-MO HIGH	12-MO LOW
Shearson Lehman Hutton treas.	2932.50	9.27%	2917.26	9.33%		2978.95	2648.95
DJ 20 Bond (Price Return)	87.59	10.23	87.44	10.25		90.62	87.18
Salomon mortgage-backed	454.93	10.65	454.95	10.65	431.58	460.17	426.83
Bond Buyer municipal	90	7.89	90	7.89		99	86-25
Merrill Lynch corporate	397.64	10.38	398.27	10.34		400.40	366.13

INTEREST — Federal Funds (N.Y. Fed. Fulton Prebon) — 10.08 +0.19

ISSUE	CLOSE	THU	YEAR AGO	12-MO HIGH	12-MO LOW
3-month T-bill	8.87%	8.95%		9.10%	5.78%
3-month CD (new)	9.50	9.50		9.52	6.45
Dealer Comm. Paper (90 days)	9.95	9.95		10.15	6.70
3-month Eurodollar deposit	10.31	10.31		10.63	7.06

U.S. DOLLAR — J. P. Morgan Index vs. 15 Currencies — 90.6 −0.1

CURRENCY	LATE NY	LATE THU	DAY'S HIGH	DAY'S LOW	12-MO HIGH	12-MO LOW — LATE NY —
British pound (in U.S. dollars)	1.6858	1.6870	1.6910	1.6855	1.9005	1.6475
Canadian dollar (in U.S. dollars)	0.8387	0.8380	0.8389	0.8375	0.8477	0.8004
Swiss franc (per U.S. dollar)	1.6630	1.6485	1.6458	1.6670	1.3605	1.6630
Japanese yen (per U.S. dollar)	132.83	131.95	131.95	132.86	121.03	136.53
W. German mark (per U.S. dollar)	1.8983	1.8897	1.8865	1.8994	1.6522	1.9210

COMMODITIES — CRB Futures Index (1967=100) — 242.06 +0.41

COMMODITY	CLOSE	CHANGE	THU	YR AGO	12-MO HIGH	12-MO LOW — AT CLOSE —
Gold (Comex spot), troy oz.	$385.00	$+ 2.80	$382.20		$467.00	$380.80
Oil (W. Tex. int. crude), bbl.	20.20	−0.60	20.80		20.80	12.60
Wheat (#2 hard KC), bu.	4.40	−0.01	4.41		4.60	3.02
Steers (Tex.-Okla. choice), 100 lb.	79.75	+0.25	79.50		79.75	65.25

NOTE: Monthly charts based on Friday close, except for Federal Funds, which are weekly average rates.

crease in January, could have been related to an unusual weather pattern. If so, this decline was an example of the distortions that arise when the seasonal factors don't follow their regular patterns, as we discussed in relation to retail sales and industrial production in Chapters 15 and 16, respectively.

FIGURE 17.3

Article discussing monetary policy and a run-up in the federal funds rate. Source: *Wall Street Journal,* 3 April 1989, p. A2.

Fed Policy-Makers Decided Last Week Not to Tighten Credit Now, Officials Say

By David Wessel

Staff Reporter of The Wall Street Journal

WASHINGTON—Federal Reserve policy-makers decided last week against boosting interest rates any higher, at least for now, according to government officials.

A surge in a key interest rate Friday sparked some speculation in financial markets that the Fed had tightened monetary policy, but government officials dismissed the increase as a short-term fluctuation that didn't signal any change in Fed policy.

The federal funds rate, the interest rate over which the Fed has the most direct control, climbed above 10% Friday after hovering at 9⅞% for the past few weeks. The federal funds rate is what banks charge each other for overnight loans.

The Fed has been raising interest rates and tightening its grip on credit for the past year in an attempt to slow the economy and thus avoid an acceleration of inflation. Short-term interest rates are more than three percentage points higher than they were a year ago.

But with economic indicators signaling that the economy may have begun to cool, even some outspoken advocates within the Fed of tighter policy are saying that the central bank now should wait to see how the economy is performing before tightening further.

Separately, newly released minutes of the February meeting of the Fed's policy-setting open-market committee show that the members agreed then to tighten credit only if new signs of inflation emerged. Just two days after the meeting ended, the government reported that producer prices rose a substantial 1% in January—and the Fed tightened policy in response. A week later, the Federal Reserve Board boosted the closely watched discount rate, the rate it charges on loans to banks, half a percentage point to 7%.

The minutes of the Feb. 7 and 8 meeting were released Friday after the customary six-week lag. The committee met again last Tuesday.

At the February meeting, the minutes say, "Members generally felt that there should be a clear presumption of some further firming if the incoming information tended to confirm expectations of growing inflationary pressures."

Most members argued against tightening monetary policy immediately to see what effect a year of tighter credit and higher interest rates was having. "Recent information had given a somewhat mixed picture of economic and private developments, and these members preferred to wait for further confirmation of inflationary pressures before additional firming of monetary policy was taken," the minutes say.

A minority wanted to tighten immediately, arguing that delay "would only worsen such [inflationary] pressures and could greatly increase the difficulty and ultimate cost of achieving the committee's anti-inflationary objectives."

The committee voted 10–2 to hold policy steady, but to lean toward tightening. Lee Hoskins, president of the Cleveland Federal Reserve Bank, and Robert Parry, president of the San Francisco Fed, dissented because they wanted immediate tightening. In the end, the differences were inconsequential because of the tightening triggered by the Feb. 10 producer-price report.

The voting members of the open-market committee include the seven Federal Reserve Board governors, the president of the New York Fed and four other regional Fed bank presidents.

The latter four seats rotate annually among the other 11 regional Fed presidents. The February meeting was the last at which Messrs. Parry and Hoskins served as voting members during this rotation. They will continue to participate in committee deliberations, however. Their turn as voting members comes up again in 1991.

Construction is normally a useful signal of overall trends in aggregate demand and production activity. As such, it signaled some weakening at this time. However, the uncertainties arising from the weather rendered this indication somewhat ambiguous.

Monetary policy also played a role in the **foreign-exchange market** during this week. Prior to April, the rise in U.S. interest rates contributed to a rise in the U.S. dollar that started in December (see the "Markets Diary" in Figure 17.2). This rise conflicted, at least to some extent, with the stated intentions of the leaders of the so-called Group of Seven (the United States, Japan, West Germany, France, Britain, Canada, and Italy). On Monday, April 3, the rise in the dollar prompted an intervention by the Bank of Japan, which succeeded in reducing its value somewhat. These events were reported in an article on page C1 of the April fourth issue of the *Wall Street Journal*, the beginning of which is reproduced in Figure 17.4.

A second sign of slowdown as a result of higher interest rates appeared in the report on **auto sales** for the last third of the month of March, which showed a decline of 17.8% from the same period the previous year. The article reporting this release on Wednesday, April 5, is reproduced in Figure 17.5. Such dramatic changes must always be interpreted with considerable caution because of the strong and frequent fluctuations in the auto sales statistics. However, the comparison of the graphs for the two years in Figure 17.5 leaves a rather clear impression of a slowing trend compared to the year before as well as to the preceding months.

A confirmation of this trend arrived with the March sales reports from the **major retail chains,** which showed an average increase of 4.1% from the same month a year earlier but a 1.3% decline from February. Because these data cover only the major chains, they are incomplete as measures of overall retail sales. Their value lies in the fact that they arrive a week before the official retail sales figures released by the Bureau of Economic Analysis (BEA).

Among all these signs of slowdown, the Thursday report on **new claims for unemployment insurance** for the last full week of March suggested a slight tightening of the labor market. However, this report was given very little attention in anticipation of the release the following day of the overall employment and unemployment statistics for March.

Somewhat surprisingly, the **unemployment rate** for March continued its previous decline, settling for the moment at 5% of the civilian labor force. The graphical presentation of this rate on page A1 of the April tenth issue of the *Wall Street Journal* is reproduced in Figure 17.6; the more complete report in the "Economy" section on page A2 is shown in Figure 17.7. To some extent, this report contradicted the earlier impres-

FIGURE 17.4

Beginning of an article reporting on intervention in the foreign-exchange market by the Bank of Japan. Source: *Wall Street Journal*, 4 April 1989, p. C1.

Intervention by Bank of Japan Helps to Drive the Dollar Lower

FOREIGN
EXCHANGE

By MICHAEL R. SESIT
Staff Reporter of THE WALL STREET JOURNAL

The Bank of Japan backed up tough talk from finance ministers and central bankers by intervening against the dollar in world currency markets.

It was the first time in 3½ years that Japan's central bank has sold dollars directly in an effort to break the U.S. currency's climb, according to traders in Tokyo. Though the amount involved was small—estimates ranged from $5 million to something less than $50 million—the intervention was effective.

"It seems to be that the dollar's ascent has been capped, at least temporarily," said Norio Nakajima, a senior vice president at the Industrial Bank of Japan in New York.

In late afternoon New York trading, the dollar stood at 1.8760 marks and 131.75 yen, down from 1.8983 marks and 132.83 yen late Friday. The pound rose to $1.6912 from $1.6858 on Friday.

Despite the success of the intervention, however, traders emphasized that demand for the U.S. currency remains buoyant. They added that a major test of central-bank strength could come if U.S. interest rates continue to rise and if foreigners' appetites for dollar-denominated investments increase. Higher interest rates usually increase a currency's allure.

On Sunday, finance ministers and central-bank heads from the Group of Seven major industrial countries meeting in Washington issued a statement emphasizing that a further climb in the dollar would be counterproductive. They also

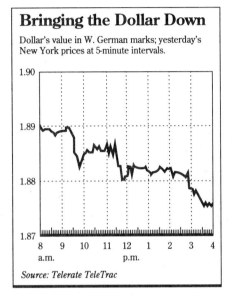

Bringing the Dollar Down

Dollar's value in W. German marks; yesterday's New York prices at 5-minute intervals.

Source: Telerate TeleTrac

reaffirmed their commitment to stable exchange rates.

A strong dollar threatens to undermine the nearly four-year-long efforts of the U.S. and its major industrial partners to reduce the large U.S. trade deficit and correspondingly big Japanese and West German surpluses. That is because a rising dollar makes U.S. products more expensive in world markets, and reduces the cost of imports for U.S. consumers.

A strong dollar also worsens inflationary pressures in Europe and Japan and increases pressure on those countries to raise rates to fight that inflation. That, in turn, can further damp the attempt to correct international trade imbalances, because weak currencies mean foreigners will buy fewer imports.

FIGURE 17.5

Report on automobile sales for the last 10 days of March 1989. Source: *Wall Street Journal*, 5 April 1989, p. A2.

Car, Truck Sales Skidded 17.8% In Late March

Sluggish U.S. Auto Market Is Fresh Sign Economy May Be Slowing Down

By Joseph B. White
Staff Reporter of The Wall Street Journal

U.S. domestic car and light truck sales skidded 17.8% in late March, a fresh sign the economy may be slowing down.

The Big Three auto makers, anxious to support their ambitious production plans, didn't wait for the official results to crank up efforts to reinvigorate the sluggish market. **Ford Motor** Co., followed by **General**

U.S. Auto Sales

Seasonally adjusted annual rate of domestic cars sold, in 10-day selling periods, in millions

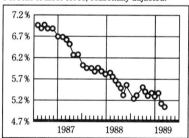

Source: Commerce Department

Motors Corp. and **Chrysler** Corp., are all trying to lure customers back to showrooms with cut-rate financing deals and big rebates on most car and truck models.

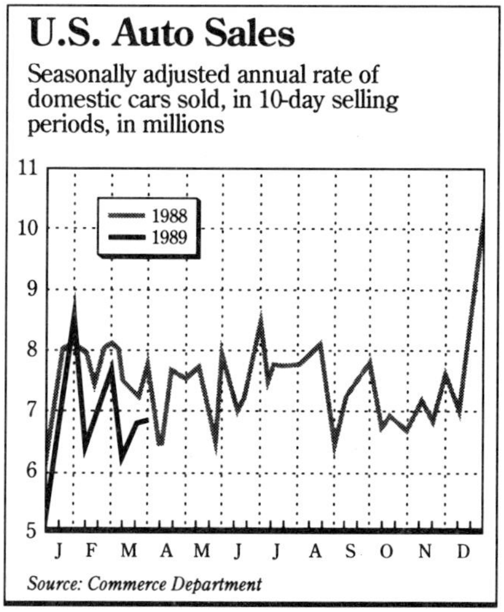

FIGURE 17.6

Graph reporting the unemployment rate for March 1989. Source: *Wall Street Journal*, 10 April 1989, p. A1.

Unemployment Rate

Percent of labor force, seasonally adjusted.

UNEMPLOYMENT in March fell to a seasonally adjusted 5% of the civilian labor force from 5.1% the preceding month, the Labor Department reports. (See story on page A.2)

sion of a slowdown. However, some balance was provided by the **payroll employment** figures from the establishment survey. Although this employment measure increased by 180,000 workers, the increase was considerably lower than in previous months, for example, 400,000 in January and 280,000 in February. Thus, whether the statistics reflected a

ECONOMY

Jobless Data Only Hint at a Slowdown

Unemployment in March Declined to 5%, but Some Detect Easing of Growth

By HILARY STOUT

Staff Reporter of THE WALL STREET JOURNAL

WASHINGTON—The latest employment figures contain hints of economic softening amid considerable strength.

Compared with recent months, the number of new jobs created in March was low. Businesses outside of agriculture added 180,000 workers to their payrolls last month after increases of 280,000 in February and more than 400,000 in January, the Labor Department reported.

Yet the languid employment growth reflected some special factors. The strike at Eastern Airlines reduced payroll growth by 25,000, Labor Department analysts said. Excluding that, job growth would have exceeded 200,000, within the range posted last year, when the economy grew a strong 3.8%.

Moreover the nation's civilian unemployment rate dropped to its lowest level since December 1973—just 5% of the work force, down from 5.1% in February. By another measure, which includes the military, the jobless rate fell even lower, to 4.9% from 5.1%.

"I think the bottom line is that labor conditions are tight, but there are indications that a more moderate pace of activity is in the offing," said Samuel Kahan, chief financial economist at Kleinwort Benson Government Securities in Chicago.

However, he said: "I think it's important to realize that you're not getting a collapse. I think the real question is, is the forward momentum intact, or are there some signs of unraveling? I think there is enough in the wind to suggest some unraveling."

Securities markets, which had been looking for the report to confirm a recent stream of economic data showing a slowing in the economy, seemed unsure what to make of the numbers; stock prices rose Friday, while bond prices slumped.

"I'm afraid it was another inconclusive economic statistic," said Norman Robertson, chief economist at Mellon Bank in Pittsburgh. "On balance it does [indicate] perhaps some moderation in economic growth but certainly not enough to lower the inflation rate."

But Gary Ciminero, chief economist at Fleet/Norstar Financial Group in Providence, R.I., said wage data in the report suggest inflation isn't heading out of control. Hourly wages rose two cents in March, to $9.56 from $9.54. Average weekly earnings increased to $328.86 from $327.22, but that was still below the January level of $329.13.

"If you want to find something to worry about [regarding] inflation, it's not wage gains," Mr. Ciminero said.

Many analysts expect the Federal Reserve Board to sit tight and leave interest rates where they are in the wake of the report. The governors of the nation's central bank had been nudging up interest rates to increase the cost of borrowing and try to head off inflation.

Thomas F. Carpenter, chief economist for ASB Capital Management, an investment advisory service in Washington, predicted that the Fed won't raise short-term rates over the next 30 to 60 days. However, he said, the Fed "will not be inclined to ease monetary policy either."

The bulk of the March job growth came in services. Manufacturing employment increased slightly, but construction jobs were down 50,000.

EMPLOYMENT

Here are excerpts from the Labor Department's employment report. The figures are seasonally adjusted.

	March 1989	Feb. 1989
	(millions of persons)	
Total labor force	124.9	124.9
Total employment	118.8	118.5
Civilian labor force	123.3	123.2
Civilian employment	117.1	116.9
Unemployment	6.1	6.3
Payroll employment	108.5	108.3
Unemployment:	(percent of labor force)	
All workers	4.9	5.1
All civilian workers	5.0	5.1
Adult men	4.2	4.5
Adult women	4.6	4.5
Teen-agers	13.7	14.8
White	4.2	4.3
Black	10.9	11.9
Black teen-agers	31.6	32.4
Hispanic	6.5	6.8
Average weekly hours:	(hours of work)	
Total private nonfarm	34.6	34.6
Manufacturing	40.9	41.1
Factory overtime	3.9	3.9

FIGURE 17.7

Article discussing the labor market report for March 1989. Source: *Wall Street Journal*, 10 April 1989, p. A2.

continuing tightening or a leveling off in the labor market was somewhat unclear. Moreover, wage inflation was limited to 0.2% on a monthly basis, which gave only a weak signal of overall inflation. In fact, the modest wage increase suggested a *real wage decline.*

Figure 17.8 shows the following Monday's summary of this week's reports, which confirms the impression of mixed signals. In addition to the data discussed above, it shows the **money supply** figures for the last week in March. The decreases in M2 and M3 and the slight increase in M1 indicated that the monetary tightening was not over.

The preview part of this table suggested a quiet week until Thursday, which was to bring reports of monthly retail sales and business inventories in addition to the 10-day auto sales and the usual weekly reports on money supply and jobless claims. Friday promised to be even more eventful, with the release of four major indicators: the monthly trade deficit, industrial production, capacity utilization, and the Producer Price Index.

FIGURE 17.8

Weekly overview of data
released during the first
week of April 1989. Source:
Wall Street Journal, 10 April
1989, p. A2.

CLOSELY WATCHED REPORTS

Statistics Released in the Week Ended April 7

	TOTAL	CHANGE (from prior period)		TOTAL	CHANGE (from prior period)
Money supply			**Employment, payroll**		
M1 Week ended March 27 (in billions)	$787.1	+$0.2	March (in millions)	108.5	+0.2%
M2 Week ended March 27 (in billions)	$3,079.9	−$5.4	**Chain store sales** Paine Webber Index March vs. year ago	+4.1%	$12.42
M3 Week ended March 27 (in billions)	$3,962.8	−$3.0	**Auto sales** Late March, total vs. year ago	272,520	−18.1%
Unemployment rate March, change in percentage points	5.0%	−0.1	**Consumer credit** February (in billions)	$669.3	+$4.22
Construction spending February, annual rate (in billions)	$423.0		**New jobless claims** Week ended March 25	317,000	−1.6%

Statistics to Be Released This Week

Retail sales (Thurs.) March	**Business inventories** (Fri.) February	**Capacity utilization** (Fri.) March
Auto sales (Thurs.) Early April	**Trade deficit** (Fri.) February	**Producer price index** (Fri.) March
Money supply (Thurs.)	**Industrial production** (Fri.) March	
New jobless claims (Thurs.)		

17.2 SECOND WEEK: THE MAJOR MID-MONTH INDICATORS

The early part of this second week proved to be as quiet as the preview suggested. However, the importance of the news released on its last two days made it well worth the wait. First, **retail sales** proved almost flat, showing a monthly increase of 0.1% from February to March, following an actual decline of 0.6% the month before. This news item was presented in a graph on page A1 of the *Wall Street Journal* and commented on in a follow-up article on page C1, shown in Figures 17.9 and 17.10, respectively.

This data release was the first *broad-based* indicator of the strength of the *demand* side of the economy during the month of March. The auto sales figures were indicative of broader trends but directly representative of only a small segment of aggregate demand. The sales reports of the major retail chains were incomplete, because they exclude smaller establishments. The employment figures are a broad-based measure of economic activity but from the production side rather than the spending side. The BEA report on retail sales is thus the first reasonably solid indicator of the strength of aggregate demand to be released each month. Read together with the employment figures and the production figures that come a little later, it carries information about the overall strength of the economy as well as possible imbalances between spending and production, which are capable of affecting the saving rate, the trade balance, and the inflation rate.

At the time of their initial release, the retail sales data are adjusted for normal seasonal variation but not for inflation. The latter feature is important for interpretation of the 0.1% monthly increase in March. Although March inflation rates were unknown at the time the retail sales data were released, that they would be less than 0.1% was very unlikely. Thus, it seemed likely that the 0.1% nominal increase represented a real decline, on top of the February data, which showed a decline even in nominal terms.

Did this report imply a severe reversal of the previously strong growth in aggregate demand? That seemed possible at the time but far from certain. It must be borne in mind that most of the variation in the retail sales data comes from durable goods purchases, which are known to fluctuate a good deal. Thus, the declines might well have been a temporary phenomenon. On the other hand, the flat report obviously did not signal continued strength. The retail sales data thus were added to the other indications of a slowdown, in contradiction to the relatively upbeat unemployment data. If the retail sales figures are taken as representative of spending and the employment figures as representative of income, the implication is an increase in saving. As we will see below,

FIGURE 17.9

Graph reporting on retail sales for March 1989. Source: *Wall Street Journal*, 14 April 1989, p. A1.

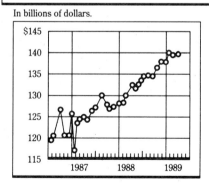

Retail Sales

In billions of dollars.

RETAIL SALES rose in March to a seasonally adjusted $139.42 billion from a revised $139.26 billion in February, the Commerce Department reports. (See story on page C10.)

FIGURE 17.10

Article discussing report on retail sales for March 1989. Source: *Wall Street Journal,* 14 April 1989, p. C1.

Retail Sales Inched Up 0.1% During March

Data Hurt by Auto Sector; Many Types of Stores Also Report Declines

By HILARY STOUT
Staff Reporter of THE WALL STREET JOURNAL

WASHINGTON—Retail sales were weak again in March, reflecting the third consecutive month of falling auto purchases, the Commerce Department reported.

Overall, sales inched up 0.1%, to $139.42 billion, but declines were widespread. Department, furniture, hardware, clothing and drug stores all saw business drop during the month. Sales rose at food stores and gasoline service stations, but a number of analysts attributed much of those boosts to price increases.

The feeble retail sales growth in March follows a slide of 0.6% in February and a jump of 0.6% in January. While the figures clearly represent a slackening in the economy's vast retail sector, analysts generally said they need at least another month's numbers to determine whether the slowing is a clear trend.

"The question is whether something fundamental is going on or this is just a hiatus," said Robert Dederick, chief economist at Northern Trust Co. in Chicago and a former Commerce Department official.

The White House called the retail sales report "further evidence of a pattern of slower consumer spending in recent months."

Marlin Fitzwater, the White House spokesman, said, "We continue to believe the economy is sound, showing steady growth with low inflation."

Consumer spending has choked and spurted before. After showing some sluggishness in the fall last year, for instance, retail sales soared in the final few months.

Not since July, August and September of 1984 have car sales slumped three months in a row. But last month they slipped 0.1% after tumbling 2.5% in February and 1.9% in January.

Rising interest rates could be hindering car buying, some economists suggested, but most said the lack of special sales incentives at the start of the year has probably been a bigger factor. U.S. auto makers now have launched new incentive programs, however, and analysts predicted that car sales will improve this month.

Recent reports have showed activity easing in key areas of the economy, from home construction to factory orders. But at the same time, record numbers of Americans have jobs, personal income continues to expand and surveys show consumer confidence is still strong.

"The momentum has slowed in the economy, but how much it has slowed and if this is going to be a significant slowdown, at this point I can't tell," said Ira Silver, chief economist for J.C. Penney Co. in Dallas.

Economists would like the economy to slow. They believe its recent pace—with consumer demand high, labor markets tight and productive capacity squeezed—is increasing the likelihood of accelerating inflation.

But none of them wants to see the economy slow so far or so fast that it topples into a recession. "The cooler spending pace is certainly good news unless it's too cool," Mr. Dederick said. "The authorities are hoping, like everyone else, that consumers don't storm out of the stores but just be more subdued in their spending."

All the retail sales numbers are adjusted for seasonal fluctuations but not for inflation.

this indication was in fact confirmed when the personal saving rate was released near the end of this month.

Much of this slowdown came from the automobile component of the retail sales data. This fact is hardly surprising against the background of the 10-day report from the last third of March, which we looked at above. However, the corresponding figures for the first 10 days of April appeared to show renewed strength, as indicated in Figure 17.11. The

Incentives Lift Car Sales 28.3% For Early April

Year-Earlier 10-Day Period Was Weak; Annual Rate Is Less Than Impressive

By Bradley A. Stertz
Staff Reporter of The Wall Street Journal

DETROIT—U.S. auto makers showed in early April that they can still entice buyers back into showrooms with generous incentives, but it seems the old trick is losing some of its appeal.

Sales of North American–built cars and trucks jumped 28.3% in the first 10 days of April. The increase isn't as impressive as it seems, however, because the year-earlier period was one of the weakest in 1988.

What's more, the seasonally adjusted sales pace for the latest period was just 7.6 million domestic cars. While that's well above the anemic 6.6 million annual rate during March, it's also far below the pace generated by sweeping low-interest financing programs in recent years. When the Big Three offered 2.9% financing in August 1986, for

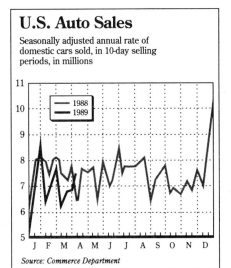

U.S. Auto Sales

Seasonally adjusted annual rate of domestic cars sold, in 10-day selling periods, in millions

Source: Commerce Department

example, sales immediately surged to an annual pace of 11.5 million domestic cars.

But to manufacturers that had seen sales dragging in prior weeks, the early April gains were a welcome sign that consumers are still willing to make big purchases.

data showed almost a 30% increase from a year earlier. However, there turned out to be less to this figure than met the eye. For one thing, the base for this comparison, the first 10 days in April 1988, happened to have been unusually weak. For another, because of the earlier weakness in the automobile market, the big U.S. automakers had introduced special incentives—2.9% or interest-free financing—in early April 1989. Given this background, it was not surprising to see some improvement. In fact, according to some observers, the response to the special incentives was weaker than expected. The reason might have been that most of the pent-up demand for automobiles had already been met and the market was becoming somewhat saturated for the time being. These figures provide an interesting illustration of the volatility in the demand for consumer durables that we studied in Chapters 5 and 13. In this regard, they did not shatter the impression that the economy was losing some steam at this time.

Somewhat by coincidence, Friday, April 14, offered releases of three major indicators, which were reported in the following Monday's newspaper. The most attention was given to the **Producer Price Index,** which was reported to have risen at a monthly rate of 0.4% from February to March, as shown in Figure 17.12. This report was greeted as good news by those who had feared a return to very high inflation rates—the two

FIGURE 17.12   Bulletin and graph reporting on the Producer Price Index for March 1989. Source: *Wall Street Journal*, 17 April 1989, p. A1.

What's News—

* * *

* * *

Business and Finance

A MILD INFLATION REPORT for March triggered stock and bond rallies Friday, though analysts say inflation may worsen again soon. Producer prices rose 0.4% last month after surging 1% in the two previous months. But rising oil prices are expected to drive up wholesale and retail prices in the months ahead. Still, other signs that the economy may be slowing could help damp inflation.

Stock and bond prices posted their biggest gains of the year, though analysts say the rally probably is temporary. The Dow Jones industrials soared 41.06, or 1.8%, to 2337.06.

(Stories on Pages A2 and C1)

World-Wide

SPAIN'S ENVOY WAS KILLED in Christian-Moslem fighting in Beirut. Madrid's ambassador to Lebanon and 17 other people were killed as Christians battled an alliance of Syrian and Moslem gunners in residential areas in and around the Lebanese capital. Police also said that at least 90 people were wounded in the weekend blitz, raising the casualty toll from 40 days of factional fighting to at least 234 dead and 847 injured. France began evacuating some of the wounded to a hospital ship, but a mission to bring food, fuel and medical supplies was blocked by the shelling.

The latest offensive in the 14-year-old conflict erupted after Christian army units blockaded militia-run harbors along Lebanon's Mediterranean coast.

* * *

Producer Prices

In percent (1982=100).

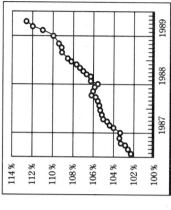

PRODUCER PRICES on finished goods in March rose at a seasonally adjusted rate of 112.6% of the 1982 average, from 112.1% in February, the Labor Department reports. (See story an page A2.)

preceding months had shown increases of the order of magnitude of 1% per month. The stock market apparently breathed a sigh of relief, as the Dow Jones Industrial Average rose over 40 points. Most likely, investors felt that the news of more moderate inflation removed some of the pressure on the Federal Reserve to tighten the supply of money, so interest rates could be allowed to decline or at least stay flat. However, this sentiment was not universal; some analysts expressed expectations of further inflation ahead. These views are reported in the accompanying article on page A2 of the *Wall Street Journal*, reproduced in Figure 17.13.

The table at the end of this article also gives some details of the PPI release. First, we note that the inflation rate would have been recorded as being somewhat lower (4.5% over the preceding 12 months as opposed to 5.6%) if food and energy goods had been excluded. This might have been considered good news, since these two categories typically show more erratic fluctuations than the other categories. However, oil prices were still rising at the time the PPI was released, so the energy price increase was not quite temporary. Second, the table gives the PPI inflation rates for intermediate goods and for crude goods. At 6.6% and 9.6%, respectively, since March 1988, these rates were both higher than the rate for finished goods. Both no doubt reflected the steady increase in oil prices during this period and were possible signals of higher inflation ahead. However, because crude goods and even intermediate goods are relatively modest components of the cost of final goods and services, this prospect was uncertain.

Figure 17.13 also contains a report on the **Index of Industrial Production** and **capacity utilization** for March. For the third month in a row, industrial production showed no change—definitely an indication of a slowdown in activity. The decline in capacity utilization (also called the operating rate) from 84.2% to 84.0% confirmed this impression. This slowdown was considered further good news by those who had feared an acceleration of inflation, because it suggested that the economy might be moving down along the Phillips curve. This interpretation probably contributed to the 40-point rise in the stock market noted above.

However, the details in the table at the end of the article in Figure 17.13 suggested that the truth was a little more complicated in this case as well. The decline in industrial production was concentrated in defense and space, always a volatile component, and consumer goods. The latter was to be expected given the weak reports of car sales and retail sales in general. Another contributing factor appeared to have been the unusually mild winter, which helped contract the output of the utilities sector. This decline was yet another example of seasonal adjustment gone slightly wrong. At the same time, however, the production of business equipment showed a modest increase, which suggested that business might be gearing up for further production increases ahead.

ECONOMY

Producer Prices Increased 0.4% in March

Economists Still See Signs Of Approach of Inflation Due to Higher Oil Costs

By HILARY STOUT

Staff Reporter of THE WALL STREET JOURNAL

WASHINGTON—Though wholesale price increases eased in March, many economists still expect some bleak inflation numbers in the coming months.

These analysts look for climbing oil prices to make their way to the gas pumps and rising costs for intermediate and crude materials to pass through to consumer goods.

Economists, as well as financial markets, were relieved by the Labor Department's report showing that the producer price index for finished goods climbed 0.4% in March, after two previous months of 1.0% rises.

But Evelina Tainer, senior domestic economist at the First National Bank of Chicago, warned: "I would view this as sort of a reprieve but not a sign that inflation pressures are abating."

Nevertheless, evidence mounted that the economy is slowing, suggesting some additional easing of inflationary pressures. The Federal Reserve Board's report on industrial production for March showed that it hasn't changed since January, while U.S. factories, mines and utilities were using less of their capacity in March—the second month in a row that the industrial operating rate has declined.

However, a number of economists expect rising oil prices will drive both wholesale and retail prices up in the coming months. And they expect that tight labor markets will push up the cost of many services and boost consumer prices.

In the first quarter of 1989, the producer price index increased at an annual rate of 10.2%, the largest quarterly rise since the first three months of 1981.

Still, the White House welcomed the latest price figures. Spokesman Marlin Fitzwater said the 0.4% increase in March was "encouraging compared to increases of the last couple months." (See chart on page one.)

"I think we can safely say the economy is slowing," said Cynthia Latta, senior financial economist at DRI/McGraw Hill Inc., an economic forecasting firm in Lexington, Mass.

Industrial Production

In percent (1977=100), seasonally adjusted.

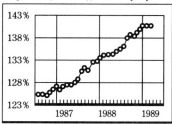

Nevertheless, she added, "Inflation is not slowing yet, so far as I can tell. But it's not getting as bad as fast as the January and February numbers perhaps indicated."

The Fed's report showed that factory production actually slipped 0.1% in March, while mining production rose 0.5% and utility output dropped 0.5%, leaving total industrial production unchanged for the second consecutive month. Meanwhile, the industry operating rate fell to 84% of capacity from 84.2% in February and 84.4% in January.

When factory operation creeps too close to full capacity, manufacturers have trouble producing enough to meet demand and are often led to raise prices.

Americans may now be confronted with the possibility of a slowing economy but continuing rises in inflation, some analysts said.

That puts the Fed in a delicate situation. The nation's central bank has been nudging up interest rates for more than a year now in hopes of restraining economic activity and warding off inflation. But the Fed wants to guide the economy through a careful slowdown, not knock it into a recession.

Wayne M. Ayers, senior economist at the Bank of Boston, said the latest economic reports show the Fed may well succeed. "I think this is the best evidence to date that the Fed is going to be able to pull off this soft landing," Mr. Ayers said.

However, another government report wasn't as encouraging. The Commerce Department said

business inventories climbed 0.5% in February while sales plunged 0.9%. If businesses and factories don't balance their inventories with sales they will cut back on orders and production to whittle their excess stock. The chain reaction can lead to a recession.

Excluding the volatile categories of food and energy, producer prices increased 0.3% in March compared with 0.6% in February and 0.4% in January. Energy prices climbed 0.9% last month after soaring 2.4% the month before. Food prices rose 0.8% after jumping 1.2% in February.

The prices of intermediate and crude goods climbed faster than those of finished goods, suggesting that increased materials prices could later show up in the price tags of finished products. Prices of intermediate materials, which have had some processing, rose 0.7% in March; the price of crude goods leaped 2.3%.

The price of tomatoes, which catapulted by more than 150% in February, plummeted almost 48% last month.

INDUSTRIAL PRODUCTION
Here is a summary of the Federal Reserve Board's report on industrial production in March. The figures are seasonally adjusted.

	% change from	
	Feb. 1989	March 1988
Total	0.0	4.6
Consumer goods	−0.4	5.5
Business equipment	0.1	8.0
Defense and space	−0.4	−5.8
Manufacturing only	−0.1	5.3
Durable goods	−0.1	5.6
Nondurable goods	0.0	4.8
Mining	0.5	−0.6
Utilities	−0.5	2.0

The industrial production index for March stood at 141.0% of the 1977 average.

BUSINESS INVENTORIES
Here is a summary of the Commerce Department's report on business inventories and sales in February. The figures are in billions of dollars, seasonally adjusted.

	(billions of dollars)		
	Feb. 1989	Jan. 1989	Feb. 1988
Total business inventories	763.62	759.80	707.89
Manufacturers	359.09	357.46	335.42
Retailers	224.27	222.58	205.61
Wholesalers	180.27	179.76	166.86
Total business sales	507.29	511.88	466.05
Inventory/sales ratio	1.51	1.48	1.52

PRODUCER PRICES
Here are the Labor Department's producer price indexes (1982 = 100) for March, before seasonal adjustment, and the percentage changes from March, 1988.

Finished goods	112.2	5.6%
Minus food & energy	120.9	4.5%
Intermediate goods	111.6	6.6%
Crude goods	103.1	9.6%

FIGURE 17.13

Article discussing the reports on the Producer Price Index and the Index of Industrial Production for March 1989.
Source: *Wall Street Journal*, 17 April 1989, p. A2.

The final item worth noting this week was the report of a worsening of the U.S. **trade deficit** from $8.68 billion in January to an estimated $10.50 billion in February. Note that this figure arrives a month later than most of the other monthly indicators. Note also that it is reported as a raw monthly total without being multiplied by 12 so as to correspond to the annual data. The trade deficit is adjusted for seasonal variation but not for inflation. Because of the plenitude of statistical releases on this date, this normally important information was relegated to an article on page A3 of the *Wall Street Journal*, shown here as Figure 17.14.

FIGURE 17.14   Report on the U.S. merchandise trade balance for February 1989. Source: *Wall Street Journal,* 17 April 1989, p. A3.

U.S. Trade Deficit Widened in February As Appetite for Imports Stymied Progress

By HILARY STOUT
Staff Reporter of THE WALL STREET JOURNAL

WASHINGTON—America's appetite for imported products, from video cassette recorders to office machines, underlies the widening of the nation's merchandise trade deficit in February and will continue to stifle progress on the trade front, many economists say.

New figures from the Commerce Department show the deficit widened $1.81 billion in February, to $10.50 billion. While exports during the month climbed slightly—to $28.91 billion from $28.75 billion—imports rose far more, to $39.40 billion from $37.42 billion.

"Major improvement in trade continues to be held hostage to our addiction to imports of both consumer and industrial products," said Jerry Jasinowski, chief economist of the National Association of Manufacturers.

The White House called the import figure disappointing, but said, "We still believe the long-term trend is for a decreasing trade deficit."

Many economists, however, see little sign that the boom in exports, which helped narrow the annual trade deficit $32.36 billion last year, to $119.76 billion, will even come close to its 1988 pace.

"Even if the dollar depreciates further, we haven't got the capacity to increase exports," said Sung Won Sohn, chief economist at Norwest Corp. in Minneapolis. A Federal Reserve report released Friday, for example, showed that the paper industry, where export demands are particularly strong, was using more than 93% of its production capacity in February.

A lower dollar helps exports because it makes U.S.-made products cheaper for customers abroad. It was a fall in the U.S. currency that helped propel the export surge last year, but the dollar has been stable recently.

"Given that the dollar has stayed within a range for the past year, it's not surprising to see improvement in

U.S. Merchandise Trade Deficits

(In billions of U.S. dollars, not seasonally adjusted and including insurance and freight costs)

	FEB. '89	JAN. '89	FEB. '88
Japan	$4.65	$3.53	$4.25
Canada	0.82	1.81	1.18
Western Europe	0.62	0.05 (surplus)	1.20
NICs*	1.77	2.40	2.62

*Newly industrialized countries: Singapore, Hong Kong, Taiwan, South Korea

Source: Commerce Department

the deficit stabilize," said Kathryn Eickhoff, president of Eickhoff Economics in New York.

And the imbalance might get worse for a while. Petroleum imports edged down in February, but with the price of oil rising in

March and April, petroleum import totals may jump, analysts said.

Moreover, while a series of recent reports suggests the economy is slowing, a damping of consumer demand probably won't slash imports to the levels needed to make a dent in the trade deficit.

"For a lot of imported items—VCRs, cameras—we don't really have any good domestic substitutes," Mr. Sohn explained. "When you look at electronic goods, there really isn't any choice" but to buy imports.

The trade picture worsened with many of the country's major trading partners in February. After improving markedly in January, the deficit with Japan increased more than $1 billion in February, to $4.65 billion. And January's rare trade surplus with Western Europe slipped back into a $624.4 million deficit in February.

The Commerce Department reported January's trade deficit at $8.68 billion, a steep revision from its original calculation of $9.49 billion.

All the numbers were adjusted for seasonal fluctuations.

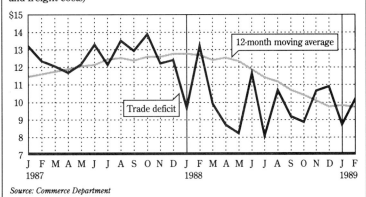

Tracking the Trade Deficit

(In billions of U.S. dollars, not seasonally adjusted and not including insurance and freight costs)

Source: Commerce Department

The graph at the bottom of this article explains why the trade deficit worsening caused no great alarm. Substantial month-to-month fluctuations are normal for this variable and relate to random factors in both the timing of the arrivals and departures of shipments and the timing of their recording. Furthermore, these monthly figures have been subject to rather substantial and seemingly unpredictable revisions. From this perspective, the February increase seemed no different from the previous pattern of monthly rises and falls. A clearer picture emerges if the figures for the last 12 months are averaged, eliminating some of the random fluctuations in the data. This 12-month moving average is shown as a shaded line in the graph. It indicates a steady decline since the beginning of 1988 but also some signs of flattening out at around $10 billion per month in the months prior to February 1989.

The table at the top of the article in Figure 17.14 shows the bilateral trade balances with the United States' major trading partners. Interestingly, the trade with Western Europe as a group was in rough balance even though the balance with West Germany showed a substantial deficit. Trade with Canada showed a deficit, which might not have been large in an absolute sense but certainly was large relative to the size of the Canadian economy. The trade with Japan remained the major point of imbalance, as it had been in previous months and years, while the deficit vis-à-vis the newly industrialized countries showed signs of improving. Perhaps their strong income growth had induced growth in imports from the United States as well.

Figure 17.15 shows the summary table of the second week's statistical releases, as presented on page A2 on the following Monday's *Wall Street Journal*. Although nuances were hidden in the details, the overall impression remained that of a slowing economy, as indicated by the declines or modest improvements in retail sales, industrial production, capacity utilization, new jobless claims, and money supply. This weakness on the real side did not prevent a sizable increase in the PPI, but the potential for a slowdown in inflation seemed to be present.

17.3 THIRD WEEK: CONSUMER PRICES, OIL PRICES, AND GERMAN INTEREST RATES

Against the backdrop of a frenzy of data releases at the end of the second week, the third week of the month promised relative calm, with the Consumer Price Index the only major regular indicator. However, this week also happened to bring some other surprising news of substantial interest to economy watchers. A change in the West German discount rate affected the value of the U.S. dollar. More dramatically, an increase in consumer gasoline demand, tightened environmental standards, OPEC discipline, a major oil spill in Alaska, and a "blowout" resulting in the

FIGURE 17.15

Weekly overview of data released during the second week of April 1989. Source: *Wall Street Journal,* 17 April 1989, p. A2.

CLOSELY WATCHED REPORTS

Statistics Released in the Week Ended April 14

	TOTAL	CHANGE (from prior period)		TOTAL	CHANGE (from prior period)
Money supply			**Business sales**		
M1 Week ended April 3 (in billions)	$781.1	−$6.1	February (in billions)	$507.29	−0.9%
M2 Week ended April 3 (in billions)	$3,083.9	+$5.2	**Industrial production index** March	141.0%	Unch.
M3 Week ended April 3 (in billions)	$3,959.5	−$2.4	**Capacity utilization** March, change in percentage points	84.0%	−0.2
Merchandise trade deficit February (in billions)	$10.50	+$1.82	**Business inventories** February (in billions)	$763.62	+0.5%
Producer price index March	112.2%	+0.4%	**Auto sales** Early April	295,735	+28.3
Retail sales March (in billions)	$139.42	+0.1%	**New jobless claims** Week ended April 1	318,000	+0.3%

Statistics to Be Released This Week

Consumer price index (Tues.) March	**Housing starts** (Tues.) March	**Money supply** (Thurs.)
		New jobless claims (Thurs.)

closing of an important platform in the North Sea all converged to give a substantial, though temporary, boost to the price of oil. With fears of inflation already high, this news was potentially alarming.

The story started with a report on page C12 in the *Wall Street Journal* for Tuesday, April 18, about a surge of 2¢ per gallon in the futures price of unleaded gasoline for May delivery. The beginning of this report is reproduced in Figure 17.16. The increase was attributed in part to OPEC's success in enforcing its production quotas, which would limit the supply of crude oil, and in part to a very strong consumer demand for gasoline. Crude oil prices followed suit with an increase of 53¢ a barrel to $21.22 per 42-gallon barrel in the futures market for May deliveries of the main American type of crude, called West Texas Intermediate.

The following Thursday brought news of an accident in the Brent oil field in the British sector of the North Sea. The supply disruptions caused by this accident raised the spot price of Brent crude oil, which had already been following an upward trend, as shown in Figure 17.17. The U.S. markets followed suit, as shown in the commodities-price tables in Figure 17.18. West Texas Intermediate crude oil rose another $1.10 to $22.61 per barrel, while May deliveries of heating oil and unleaded gasoline rose by 0.57¢ and 0.76¢ per gallon, respectively. The reaction in the financial market indicated an expectation that these increases, even though they reflected temporary supply problems, would prevent an

FIGURE 17.16

Report on oil price increases.
Source: *Wall Street Journal,*
18 April 1989, p. C12.

COMMODITIES

Gasoline Leads Petroleum Futures to 3-Year High As Benchmark Crude Breaks $21-Barrel Barrier

By JAMES TANNER
Staff Reporter of THE WALL STREET JOURNAL

Propelled by gasoline, U.S. petroleum futures surged yesterday to the highest level in more than three years.

West Texas Intermediate crude for May delivery broke through the important technical level of $21 a barrel to settle 53 cents higher at $21.22.

The jump was said to be attributed in part to a report from the Organization of Petroleum Exporting Countries that most OPEC members were holding output within their quotas. Although OPEC only reported March figures for 11 of its 13 members, some traders immediately concluded that total OPEC output was only around 19 million barrels a day. Since that was lower than the 20 million-plus barrels a day estimated by outside sources, the OPEC report was interpreted as another bullish factor in what already was a strong oil market.

But analysts generally agreed the chief catalyst for yesterday's big rally on the New York Mercantile Exchange for most fuels, including heating oil and crude oil, was gasoline. "This is a gasoline-driven market," said Nauman Barakat, a Prudential-Bache Securities vice president.

May delivery gasoline was up more than two cents a gallon to settle a fraction above 72.1 cents. That was the highest close for near-month deliveries for both gasoline and crude oil since January 1986—the month that launched that year's oil-price crash.

Ironically, the big increase in gasoline futures came just after Exxon Corp. and other industry officials testi-

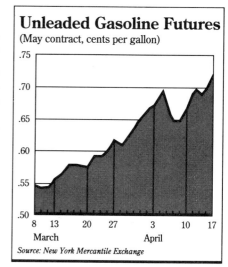

Unleaded Gasoline Futures
(May contract, cents per gallon)

Source: New York Mercantile Exchange

fied before a U.S. Senate subcommittee hearing on the Alaskan oil spill, saying that the spill hadn't caused the runup in motor fuel prices. They noted that the rise in gasoline prices was because of increased costs, including higher crude oil prices and new environmental standards.

Oil economists and others do agree that fuel prices to consumers have been increasing recently, mainly because of the big runup in crude oil prices that was launched last November by OPEC's production accord. Nevertheless, in futures trading, gasoline now is pulling up crude, instead of the other way around.

"One thing or another makes gasoline strong, and that keeps crude oil up there," said Eric Bolling of Edge Trading Corp.

FIGURE 17.17

Graph of spot prices for crude oil from the Brent field in the British sector of the North Sea. Source: *Wall Street Journal*, 20 April 1989, p. A3.

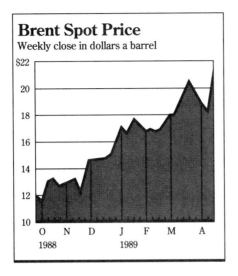

Brent Spot Price
Weekly close in dollars a barrel

early easing of U.S. inflationary pressures and force the Federal Reserve to maintain a tight monetary policy. The federal funds rate rose by 0.2 percentage points, and the bond market declined slightly.

The story continued into the following day, with no less than a $2.04 increase in the price of May deliveries for West Texas Intermediate. However, because this was the last trading day for contracts with May delivery, the increase could be attributed to the extraordinary volatility in the market that is normally observed on final trading days. The prices for deliveries in June and later months moved much less, and by the end of the day the dramatic events in the oil market were over for this time.

The middle of this week also experienced the effects of another international event—an increase in the discount rate of the Bundesbank, the central bank of West Germany, from 4.0% to 4.5%. Although this was not a major event, it illustrates the workings of the international monetary system. Figure 17.19 reproduces the first part of a report on this event on one of the "International" pages (A8) in the *Wall Street Journal* for April 21. As expected, several other central banks in continental Europe followed suit. These countries maintain fixed or near-fixed exchange rates vis-à-vis the deutsche mark. Thus, if they had not followed the move of the Bundesbank, capital would have flowed out of their respective countries and into D-mark-denominated assets, which would have raised the market supplies of their currencies and hence made the exchange rates slide vis-à-vis the D-mark. Since the central banks of these other countries didn't want that to happen, they had no choice but to let their discount rates move with that of the Bundesbank.

No similar move was made by the Federal Reserve in the United States. Thus, the difference between U.S. and West German interest

FIGURE 17.18 Futures prices on the New York Mercantile Exchange, April 19, 1989, showing the movements for crude oil (West Texas Intermediate), heating oil, and unleaded gasoline. (For directions on how to read these tables, see the text that accompanies Figure 14.6). Source: *Wall Street Journal*, 20 April 1989, p. C14.

COMMODITY FUTURES PRICES

Wednesday, April 19, 1989

Open Interest Reflects Previous Trading Day.

—GRAINS AND OILSEEDS—

CORN (CBT) 5,000 bu.; cents per bu.

	Open	High	Low	Settle	Change	Lifetime High	Lifetime Low	Open Interest
May	276	276¾	269½	273	– 2½	369	207½	55,258
July	278	279¼	270½	274¾	– 3	360	233	54,403
Sept	271	271¾	264	267¼	– 3¾	317¾	245	12,337
Dec	270	271	262¾	266	– 4	295	235	46,260
Mr90	275½	276¾	269	272½	– 4	286½	257½	5,818
May	277¼	277¾	271	273¼	– 4¼	289½	260	1,301
July	279½	279¾	273	275	– 4½	284	261½	385

Est vol 45,000; vol Tues 46,083; open int 175,762, –2,727.

OATS (CBT) 5,000 bu.; cents per bu.

	Open	High	Low	Settle	Change	Lifetime High	Lifetime Low	Open Interest
May	202½	202½	194	197	– 1¼	340	179	3,161
July	209½	210	199½	202¾	– 2¼	277	187	4,325
Sept	212	212	203	205½	– 2¾	243	193½	1,331
Dec	218	218	208	212½	– 1½	247	200½	1,500

Est vol 1,000; vol Tues 1,611; open int 10,400, +134.

SOYBEANS (CBT) 5,000 bu.; cents per bu.

	Open	High	Low	Settle	Change	Lifetime High	Lifetime Low	Open Interest
May	751	758½	734	745	– 3½	1003	647	28,820
July	760	766½	743	752¼	– 6¼	986	684	32,009
Aug	759	763	741	749½	– 7	951	712¾	5,785
Sept	746	748	729	735	– 9¼	835	695¼	5,221
Nov	740½	740½	722	728¼	– 9¼	793	663	25,983
Ja90	748½	748½	730½	736¾	– 9½	767	684	2,916
Mar	756½	756½	740	745	– 10	774	700	1,118
May	761	761	746	750	– 9	778	711	471

Est vol 55,000; vol Tues 44,146; open int 102,419, +1,439.

SOYBEAN MEAL (CBT) 100 tons; $ per ton.

	Open	High	Low	Settle	Change	Lifetime High	Lifetime Low	Open Interest
May	231.50	233.50	225.20	227.80	– 2.80	304.00	200.50	20,999
July	230.00	231.80	223.50	226.00	– 2.90	300.00	215.50	16,233
Aug	228.50	229.50	221.70	224.00	– 2.70	298.00	214.00	5,631
Sept	226.00	226.00	219.50	221.00	– 2.70	290.00	210.50	3,995
Oct	223.00	223.00	215.00	217.20	– 3.50	237.00	203.00	2,920
Dec	221.00	221.50	214.00	215.90	– 3.60	270.00	199.50	5,565
Ja90	220.50	220.50	215.00	215.00	– 3.00	230.00	207.00	764
Mar	220.00	220.00	215.00	215.00	– 3.00	230.50	208.00	341
May	...	...	...	215.20	– 2.80	230.50	209.00	506

Est vol 24,000; vol Tues 17,160; open int 56,954, +147.

SOYBEAN OIL (CBT) 60,000 lbs.; cents per lb.

	Open	High	Low	Settle	Change	Lifetime High	Lifetime Low	Open Interest
May	23.30	23.38	23.02	23.21	– .05	33.00	21.56	24,382
July	23.95	23.98	23.62	23.81	– .08	32.50	22.08	28,008
Aug	24.22	24.23	23.90	24.07	– .09	32.05	22.30	7,071
Sept	24.40	24.40	24.12	24.33	– .07	28.70	22.49	5,838
Oct	24.60	24.60	24.40	24.50	– .10	26.95	22.60	3,092
Dec	24.95	25.00	24.70	24.83	– .09	28.05	22.80	6,541
Ja90	25.08	25.08	24.90	25.00	– .10	25.30	23.40	830
Mar	...	...	...	25.47	– .08	25.40	24.00	320

Est vol 16,500; vol Tues 27,713; open int 76,146, –99.

WHEAT (CBT) 5,000 bu.; cents per bu.

	Open	High	Low	Settle	Change	Lifetime High	Lifetime Low	Open Interest
May	409	415	408½	411¾	+ 4¾	445	330	11,010
July	400½	401¾	397	401¼	+ 2	422	327	31,450
Sept	408	409	404	408¾	+ 1¾	429	350½	11,235
Dec	420	421	416½	420¼	+ ¾	440½	378	6,688
Mr90	425½	426½	422½	425	...	443	403½	1,090
May	418½	418½	418½	418½	– 1	432	403½	404

Est vol 12,000; vol Tues 15,334; open int 61,877, –157.

HOGS (CME) 30,000 lbs.; cents per lb.

	Open	High	Low	Settle	Change	Lifetime High	Lifetime Low	Open Interest
Apr	40.65	40.80	40.40	40.42	– .37	51.65	39.35	1,056
June	46.35	46.65	45.40	45.90	– .60	56.25	42.50	14,084
July	46.85	47.05	46.10	46.42	– .57	56.00	45.20	7,999
Aug	45.80	46.00	45.00	45.30	– .80	51.00	43.80	3,877
Oct	42.50	42.55	41.85	42.07	– .50	47.00	40.80	2,645
Dec	44.40	44.40	43.80	43.82	– .67	47.25	42.52	1,416
Fb90	45.70	45.70	45.20	45.30	– .30	47.20	43.70	260

Est vol 7,601; vol Tues 5,215; open int 31,414, –367.

PORK BELLIES (CME) 40,000 lbs.; cents per lb.

	Open	High	Low	Settle	Change	Lifetime High	Lifetime Low	Open Interest
May	32.50	32.90	31.40	31.57	– 1.72	65.50	31.40	5,600
July	32.55	33.20	31.70	31.82	– 1.85	64.50	31.70	9,441
Aug	32.75	33.00	31.30	31.32	– 1.87	58.25	31.30	6,505
Fb90	48.00	48.70	47.35	47.62	– 1.25	61.60	42.00	1,071

Est vol 6,627; vol Tues 3,378; open int 22,667, +354.

—FOOD AND FIBER—

COCOA (CSCE)—10 metric tons; $ per ton.

	Open	High	Low	Settle	Change	Lifetime High	Lifetime Low	Open Interest
May	1,332	1,346	1,324	1,327	– 31	2,088	1,152	3,226
July	1,235	1,249	1,235	1,243	– 17	1,985	1,172	11,033
Sept	1,230	1,242	1,226	1,238	– 12	1,850	1,205	8,906
Dec	1,243	1,258	1,240	1,255	– 10	1,735	1,225	5,968
Mr90	1,255	1,257	1,250	1,256	– 14	1,535	1,230	4,061
May	1,262	1,265	1,255	1,264	– 13	1,465	1,240	2,219
July	...	...	...	1,271	– 6	1,280	1,240	331
Sept	...	...	...	1,286	– 6	...	...	220

Est vol 5,154; vol Tues 4,953; open int 35,964, –149.

COFFEE (CSCE)—37,000 lbs.; cents per lb.

	Open	High	Low	Settle	Change	Lifetime High	Lifetime Low	Open Interest
May	138.00	139.60	138.00	139.45	+ 1.45	159.20	112.13	6,103
July	134.50	135.99	134.50	135.47	+ 1.79	155.25	114.00	11,262
Sept	129.80	130.50	129.50	130.45	+ 1.27	152.90	114.00	6,116
Dec	124.80	126.00	124.75	125.93	+ .93	149.50	114.75	3,320
Mr90	122.75	122.75	122.00	122.38	+ .13	146.00	114.75	948

Est vol 8,450; vol Tues 9,592; open int 27,806, +813.

SUGAR—WORLD (CSCE)—112,000 lbs.; cents per lb.

	Open	High	Low	Settle	Change	Lifetime High	Lifetime Low	Open Interest
May	12.35	12.60	12.35	12.55	+ .29	13.64	7.87	41,978
July	12.27	12.50	12.27	12.47	+ .33	13.40	8 .10	39,128
Oct	12.15	12.33	12.15	12.31	+ .25	13.30	8.45	59,721
Mr90	11.73	11 .90	11.73	11.90	+ .23	11.90	8.75	14,630
May	11.74	11.85	11.74	11.85	+ .22	11.83	9.20	1,735
July	...	...	...	11.81	+ .18	11.65	10.68	214

Est vol 32,770; vol Tues 25,898; open int 157,411, –687.

SUGAR—DOMESTIC (CSCE)—112,000 lbs.; cents per lb.

	Open	High	Low	Settle	Change	Lifetime High	Lifetime Low	Open Interest
July	22.34	22.35	22.34	22.34	– .03	22.60	21.80	2,920
Sept	22.43	22.45	22.43	22.45	+ .01	22.60	21.95	2,226
Nov	22.06	22.07	22.05	22.07	+ .01	22.50	21.62	751
Ja90	...	...	...	22.03	+ .01	22.18	21.61	123
Mar	...	...	...	22.05	+ .01	22.10	21.80	150

PALLADIUM (NYM) 100 troy oz.; $ per troy oz.

	Open	High	Low	Settle	Change	Lifetime High	Lifetime Low	Open Interest
Apr	169.50	169.50	165.00	167.55	+ 2.55	185.00	157.60	82
June	162.00	168.75	161.00	167.05	+ 1.40	184.00	114.00	5,212
Sept	158.10	167.00	157.00	164.55	+ 2.65	180.00	119.00	2,210
Dec	157.00	164.50	156.50	162.55	+ 3.15	177.50	122.25	2,095
Mr90	156.25	163.00	156.15	160.55	+ 3.40	176.00	123.00	417
June	160.00	162.00	158.00	159.55	+ 3.35	175.00	155.00	101

Est vol 2,682; vol Wed 3,236; open int 10,117, +231.

SILVER (CMX)—5,000 troy oz.; cents per troy oz.

	Open	High	Low	Settle	Change	Lifetime High	Lifetime Low	Open Interest
Apr	578.5	578.5	575.0	575.0	– 1.3	618.5	572.0	0
May	579.0	581.9	574.0	576.5	– 1.5	965.0	574.0	44,206
July	590.5	592.5	585.0	587.2	– 1.5	985.0	585.0	23,667
Sept	601.0	602.0	594.5	597.7	– 1.5	861.0	594.5	7,932
Dec	615.0	619.0	611.0	612.9	– 1.5	886.0	611.0	10,269
Mr90	632.5	632.5	627.5	628.0	– 1.5	910.0	627.5	6,839
May	640.0	640.0	640.0	638.2	– 1.5	910.0	640.0	3,715
July	654.0	654.0	650.0	648.6	– 1.5	761.5	650.0	2,511
Sept	...	...	...	659.5	– 1.5	760.0	665.0	771
Dec	667.0	680.0	677.0	675.0	– 1.5	742.0	677.0	580

Est vol 17,000; vol Tues 17,096; open int 100,516, +307.

SILVER (CBT)—1,000 troy oz.; cents per troy oz.

	Open	High	Low	Settle	Change	Lifetime High	Lifetime Low	Open Interest
May	580.0	580.0	576.0	576.0	– 2.0	628.0	576.0	12
June	584.0	587.0	580.0	582.0	– 1.0	865.0	580.0	6,129
Aug	596.0	598.0	592.0	593.0	– 1.0	700.0	592.0	620
Oct	607.0	607.5	604.0	604.0	– 1	.0716.0	604.0	137
Dec	618.0	621.0	615.0	615.0	– 1.0	735.0	615.0	1,689

Est vol 500; vol Tues 563; open int 8,826, +39.

CRUDE OIL, Light Sweet (NYM) 1,000 bbls.; $ per bbl.

	Open	High	Low	Settle	Change	Lifetime High	Lifetime Low	Open Interest
May	22.40	22.90	23.30	22.61	+ 1.10	22.90	12.52	30,773
June	20.90	21.15	20.60	20.81	+ .47	20.66	12.60	82,861
July	20.01	20.18	19.70	19.86	+ .27	20.18	12.65	47,951
Aug	19.35	19.45	19.05	19.18	+ .20	19.63	12.60	27,277
Sept	18.97	18.97	18.55	18.69	+ .15	19.28	12.68	14,801
Oct	18.45	18.55	18.15	18.32	+ .12	18.93	12.75	14,183
Nov	18.34	18.35	17.90	18.03	+ .10	18.67	15.00	10,300
Dec	18.00	18.00	17.71	17.79	+ .08	18.50	12.87	12,892
Ja90	17.45	17.69	17.35	17.57	+ .06	18.10	15.67	4,033
Feb	17.50	17.60	17.40	17.40	+ .04	17.95	15.74	1,674
Mar	17.35	17.40	17.15	17.23	+ .02	17.80	16.10	1,138
Apr	...	...	...	17.08	– .01	17.35	16.70	239
May	17.40	17.40	17.10	16.93	– .04	18.17	16.25	367

Est vol 151,618; vol Tues 138,138; open int 248,527, –4,945.

HEATING OIL NO. 2 (NYM) 42,000 gal.; $ per gal.

	Open	High	Low	Settle	Change	Lifetime High	Lifetime Low	Open Interest
May	.5400	.5480	.5290	.5333	+.0057	.5650	.3520	11,400
June	.5280	.5330	.5165	.5226	+.0071	.5475	.3665	21,197
July	.5190	.5220	.5080	.5145	+.0060	.5380	.4575	9,957
Aug	.5200	.5200	.5090	.5145	+.0053	.5400	.3545	7,918
Sept	.5240	.5240	.5145	.5205	+.0053	.5450	.3640	2,384
Oct	.5300	.5300	.5210	.5260	+.0053	.5490	.3720	2,742
Nov	.5330	.5350	.5250	.5315	+.0053	.5550	.3800	2,191
Dec	.5415	.5425	.5330	.5370	+.0053	.5605	.3785	1,296

Est vol 20,660; vol Tues 24,194; open int 59,125, +1,597.

WHEAT (KC) 5,000 bu.; cents per bu.

May	425	427	424¼	426½	+ 2¾	443	324	6,694
July	419½	420½	417¾	420¼	+ 3	436	331	11,802
Sept	426	427	424	426	+ 2	443	353	2,393
Dec	436	438	434¼	437	+ 2	453	387	1,097

Est vol 5,903; vol Tues 5,522; open int 22,046, +18.

WHEAT (MPLS) 5,000 bu.; cents per bu.

May	422	425¼	422	424½	+ 2½	436¼	399	3,090
July	418	421	418	419½	+ 1½	433½	380	1,680
Sept	416	418½	415¾	417	+ 1½	428½	388	2,115
Dec	424½	424½	424½	424½	+ 2½	428	405	144

Est vol 1,244; vol Tues 1,938; open int 7,030, +217.

BARLEY (WPG) 20 metric tons; Can. $ per ton

May	118.20	118.40	113.50	116.00	− 1.90	148.51	112.40	4,633
July	123.00	123.10	118.50	120.50	− 2.20	147.00	117.50	4,678
Oct	124.80	125.30	121.00	123.00	− 1.80	140.00	117.60	2,900
Nov	126.40	126.40	123.00	124.00	− 2.00	127.10	119.20	136
Dec	127.40	127.40	124.10	124.50	− 2.70	128.40	120.70	809

Est vol 1,645; vol Tues 631; open int 13,156, −55.

FLAXSEED (WPG) 20 metric tons; Can. $ per ton

May	389.80	389.80	380.80	383.50	− 7.30	490.00	366.00	1,885
July	394.50	395.00	384.80	387.50	− 6.00	492.00	368.00	1,748
Oct	378.50	378.90	372.00	374.50	− 3.50	394.50	326.50	866
Dec	375.50	375.50	372.00	374.50	− 2.50	434.00	319.00	1,328
Mr90	383.00	383.00	380.50	383.00	− 2.50	383.00	370.00	151

Est vol 890; vol Tues 789; open int 5,978, −183.

RAPESEED (WPS) 20 metric tons; Can. $ per ton

June	348.00	349.00	338.60	340.80	− 6.30	490.00	323.60	14,382
Sept	361.00	361.50	352.00	354.50	− 5.20	390.50	333.00	3,816
Nov	368.00	369.00	360.10	362.00	− 5.20	482.00	261.80	4,666
Ja90	374.50	375.20	366.30	369.00	− 4.80	375.90	357.10	828

Est vol 3,510; vol Tues 3,512; open int 23,723, +1,195.

WHEAT (WPG) 20 metric tons; Can. $ per ton

May	145.50	145.90	140.20	142.00	− 3.20	168.50	135.50	2,425
July	149.90	149.90	145.00	147.10	− 2.10	167.00	144.30	2,059
Oct	152.50	152.50	147.20	150.00	− 2.20	157.00	144.80	1,523
Nov	154.00	154.00	148.70	149.40	− 4.30	156.00	145.30	837
Dec	152.00	152.00	148.70	149.50	− 4.20	154.50	146.00	257

Est vol 1,020; vol Tues 558; open int 7,101, −31.

RYE (WPG) 20 metric tons; Can. $ per ton

May	144.80	144.80	141.50	141.50	− 3.30	171.50	134.90	394
July	141.00	141.00	140.50	140.50	− 4.00	164.00	134.90	664
Oct	...	...	...	140.00	− 4.00	154.00	133.00	533

Est vol 25; vol Tues 33; open int 1,591, −3.

—LIVESTOCK & MEAT—

CATTLE—FEEDER (CME) 44,000 lbs.; cents per lb.

Apr	76.25	76.25	75.30	75.40	− .97	84.50	74.40	1,131
May	76.35	76.35	75.45	75.55	− .90	84.15	75.45	5,268
Aug	76.60	76.60	75.90	75.92	− .92	83.27	75.80	4,196
Sept	76.70	76.70	75.80	75.85	− .90	83.10	75.50	1,231
Oct	76.50	76.50	75.90	75.92	− .85	83.00	75.90	1,492
Nov	77.32	77.32	76.82	77.15	− .57	83.50	76.60	676
Ja90	78.00	78.00	77.50	77.65	− .60	83.75	77.30	333

Est vol 2,485; vol Tues 2,135; open int 14,328, −309.

CATTLE—LIVE (CME) 40,000 lbs; costs per lb.

Apr	77.10	77.15	76.72	77.10	− .10	78.90	67.20	3,756
June	71.15	71.20	70.25	70.50	− 1.02	75.90	68.75	36,813
Aug	67.65	67.65	66.50	66.87	− .90	73.80	66.50	16,799
Oct	68.95	68.95	68.20	68.27	− .75	74.00	68.20	17,606
Dec	70.10	70.30	69.62	69.95	− .60	73.95	69.40	3,952
Fb90	70.90	70.90	70.40	70.50	− .60	73.70	69.90	804
Apr	71.75	72.00	71.60	72.00	− .20	74.00	71.00	166

Est vol 26,882; vol Tues 12,877; open int 79,953, −1,716.

May	22.04	22.04	22.04	22.04	− .02	22.05	21.80	155

Est vol 82; vol Tues 216; open int 6,437, +28.

COTTON (CTN)—50,000 lbs.; cents per lb.

May	65.70	65.75	64.90	65.13	− .44	68.70	49.03	5,983
July	66.35	66.50	65.76	66.07	− .36	68.53	49.26	12,919
Oct	65.80	65.95	65.40	65.75	+ .15	65.95	50.35	3,758
Dec	64.85	64.98	64.55	64.95	+ .20	65.50	50.75	11,019
Mr90	65.30	65.35	65.01	65.35	+ .22	65.35	53.60	1,228
May	65.25	65.25	65.20	65.29	− .10	65.70	59.75	785

Est vol 6,000; vol Tues 9,731; open int 35,737, −677.

ORANGE JUICE (CTN)—15,000 lbs.; cents per lb.

May	177.50	179.40	175.00	178.00	+ .75	179.40	132.00	2,314
July	179.75	182.00	177.30	180.30	+ 1.15	182.00	132.00	2,702
Sept	174.85	176.65	173.05	175.80	+ 1.20	176.65	132.00	1,662
Nov	164.50	164.50	162.50	164.40	+ .90	166.50	129.40	773
Ja89	158.00	158.00	156.80	156.95	− .40	158.00	127.50	302

Est vol 2,000; vol Tues 1,125; open int 7,846, +65.

—METALS & PETROLEUM—

COPPER-STANDARD (CMX)—25,000 lbs.; cents per lb.

Apr	142.00	143.00	140.50	140.65	− 2.15	146.55	125.00	233
May	141.00	142.50	138.70	138.90	− 2.00	146.00	73.15	18,487
July	133.30	134.60	131.20	131.50	− 1.70	138.50	76.00	13,839
Sept	126.50	128.00	124.70	125.00	− 1.40	131.50	76.00	2,632
Dec	121.00	121.40	118.80	119.00	− 1.50	126.00	77.45	2,276

Est vol 7,500; vol Tues 7,402; open int 37,467, −507.

GOLD (CMX)—100 troy oz.; $ per troy oz.

Apr	384.00	385.20	383.00	383.40	− .10	550.00	381.00	678
May	...	...	...	384.30	− .30	...	...	228
June	387.30	389.20	385.70	387.10	− .30	570.00	385.30	74,246
Aug	392.50	393.50	391.00	391.70	− .40	575.00	390.00	22,621
Oct	398.50	398.90	396.80	397.00	− .40	575.50	396.50	7,928
Dec	403.50	404.30	401.80	402.30	− .40	514.50	401.80	19,542
Fb90	...	...	...	407.50	− .50	516.00	407.50	5,457
Apr	413.50	413.50	413.50	412.70	− .60	525.80	413.50	6,125
June	...	...	...	418.10	− .60	497.00	420.50	10,484
Aug	...	...	...	423.50	− .60	487.00	428.30	6,524
Oct	...	...	...	428.90	− .60	472.00	434.30	1,886
Dec	...	...	...	434.30	− .60	455.00	437.50	2,808
Fb91	441.00	441.00	441.00	439.90	− .60	450.00	441.00	551

Est vol 32,000; vol Tues 40,149; open int 159,078, +1,225.

PLATINUM (NYM)—50 troy oz.; $ per troy oz.

Apr	550.00	551.00	543.00	545.50	...	643.50	482.00	211
July	549.00	554.80	545.50	548.00	− .50	640.00	505.00	13,849
Oct	549.00	554.00	543.00	546.50	− 1.00	609.00	501.00	4,867
Ja90	553.50	553.50	552.00	547.50	− 1.00	646.00	459.00	1,675
Apr	552.00	552.00	552.00	549.50	− 1.00	557.00	517.00	101

Est vol 3,886; vol Tues 5,613; open int 20,703, −859.

EXCHANGE ABBREVIATIONS
(for commodity futures and futures options)

CBT–Chicago Board of Trade; CME–Chicago Mercantile Exchange; CMX–Commodity Exchange, New York; CRCE–Chicago Rice & Cotton Exchange; CTN–New York Cotton Exchange; CSCE–Coffee, Sugar & Cocoa Exchange, New York; IPE–International Petroleum Exchange; KC–Kansas City Board of Trade; MCE–MidAmerica Commodity Exchange; MPLS–Minneapolis Grain Exchange; NYM–New York Mercantile Exchange; PBOT–Philadelphia Board of Trade; WPG–Winnipeg Commodity Exchange.

GASOLINE, Unleaded (NYM) 42,000 gal.; $ per gal.

May	.7600	.7670	.7455	.7462	+.0076	.7670	.3740	14,434
June	.7100	.7190	.6980	.7023	+.0090	.7190	.3850	20,150
July	.6740	.6780	.6620	.6650	+.0077	.6780	.4050	16,847
Aug	.6430	.6458	.6315	.6335	+.0076	.6467	.4020	13,466
Sept	.6010	.6150	.6000	.6020	+.0075	.6150	.4000	4,656
Oct	.5750	.5760	.5600	.5640	+.0115	.5760	.4380	1,730
Nov	.5550	.5550	.5370	.5420	+.0120	.5550	.4125	992
Dec	.5300	.5360	.5280	.5290	+.0090	.5390	.4675	404

Est vol 29,897; vol Tues 31,472; open int 72,679, −1,214.

GAS OIL (IPE) 100 metric tons; $ per ton

May	156.00	159.00	155.50	157.25	+ 4.25	160.25	115.00	17,680
June	153.00	155.75	152.25	153.25	+ 3.50	158.25	112.75	11,412
July	152.75	154.00	151.50	151.75	+ 2.50	158.25	112.75	5,502
Aug	152.00	153.75	151.50	152.00	+ 2.50	159.00	110.75	1,483
Sept	154.00	154.00	154.00	154.00	+ 3.50	165.00	136.50	298
Oct	154.50	157.00	154.50	156.75	+ 3.50	168.00	138.00	269
Nov	156.00	157.00	155.00	157.00	+ 4.00	168.00	137.00	699
Dec	158.00	159.00	158.00	159.00	+ 3.00	169.00	149.50	363

Actual Wed; vol 15,017; open int 37,706, +1,301.

—WOOD—

LUMBER (CME)—150,000 bd. ft.; $ per 1,000 bd. ft.

May	176.70	177.50	175.00	177.40	+ 1.10	194.50	170.10	3,277
July	180.20	181.50	179.70	181.30	+ .70	196.00	175.10	2,405
Sept	181.50	182.60	181.10	182.50	+ 1.00	194.70	175.10	1,212
Nov	179.50	180.40	179.40	180.40	...	190.60	176.70	895
Ja90	186.00	186.20	185.80	185.90	+ .20	192.00	181.20	175
Mar	189.00	189.00	188.70	189.00	+ .40	192.40	185.00	320

Est vol 832; vol Tues 1,870; open int 8,343, +68.

—OTHER COMMODITY FUTURES—

Settlement prices of selected contracts. Volume and open interest of all contract months.

Aluminum (CMX) 40,000 lbs.; cents per lb.
May 96.00 ; Est. vol. 0; Open int. 155
Cattle—Live (MCE) 20,000 lb.; $ per lb.
Jun 70.50 −1.02; Est. vol. 245; Open int. 507
Corn (MCE) 1,000 bu.; cents per bu.
May 273 −2½; Est. vol. 900; Open int. 6,568
Gold (CBT) 100 troy oz.; $ per troy oz.
Jun 387.00 −.50; Est. vol. 500; Open int. 1,819
Gold (MCE) 33.2 troy oz.; $ per troy oz.
May 384.30 −.30; Est. vol. 15; Open int. 152
Gold-Kilo (CBT) 32.15 troy oz.; $ per troy oz.
Jun 387.50 −.20; Est. vol. 100; Open int. 492
Hogs—Live (MCE) 15,000 lb.; $ per lb.
June 45.90 −.60; Est. vol. 205; Open int. 492
Propane (NYM) 42,000 gal.; $ per gal.
May 22.00 +.10; Est. vol. 90; Open int. 764
Rice—Rough (CRCE) 2000 cwt; $ per cwt
May 7.70 +.12; Est. vol. 425; Open int. 2,104
Silver (CBT) 5,000 troy oz.; cents per troy oz.
May 576.0 −2.0; Est. vol. 10; Open int. 68
Silver (MCE) 1,000 troy oz.; cents per troy oz.
May 576.5 −1.5; Est. vol. 80; Open int. 892
Soybeans (MCE) 1,000 bu.; cents per bu.
May 745 −3½; Est. vol. 4,500; Open int. 13,766
Soybean Meal (MCE) 20 tons; $ per ton
May 227.80 −2.80; Est. vol. 20; Open int. 729
Wheat (MCE) 1,000 bu.; cents per bu.
May 411¾ +4¾; Est. vol. 800; Open int. 5,960

FIGURE 17.19

Beginning of an article reporting on an increase in the discount rate of the Bundesbank, the central bank of West Germany. Source: *Wall Street Journal,* 21 April 1989, p. A8.

West Germany Raises Discount, Lombard Rates

―――――

Boost Is Quickly Matched By Some Other Nations; Moves Depress Dollar

―――――

By Terence Roth
Staff Reporter of The Wall Street Journal

FRANKFURT, West Germany—The Bundesbank surprised financial markets yesterday with half-point increases in West Germany's discount and Lombard rates to 4.5% and 6.5%, respectively, ending a wait-and-see policy on inflation.

The sudden tightening in monetary policy by West Germany's central bank was quickly matched by the central bank of the Netherlands, which boosted its discount rate to 5.5% from 5% and a key money-market intervention rate to 6.7% from 6.5%. The Austrian central bank followed suit, raising its discount rate to 5% from 4.5% and its Lombard rate to 6.5% from 6% to maintain parity with West Germany. The National Bank of Denmark also raised its discount rate by a half-point, to 9%.

The Bundesbank's Central Bank Council increased West German interest rates to curb monetary growth and support the weakening mark, which fuels inflation by boosting import prices.

Effect on Dollar

The moves sharply depressed the U.S. dollar in foreign-exchange trading. The dollar, trading at about 1.86 marks just before the afternoon announcement, dropped to 1.844 marks at the close only two hours later, its lowest level since March 6. It recovered slightly in New York, trading at around 1.847 in midafternoon.

The Bundesbank's discount facility, under which banks borrow short-term funds using securities as collateral, sets the floor for West Germany market rates. The Lombard rate is a penalty rate and serves as the ceiling for bank borrowings.

Earlier in the day, the Bundesbank said West Germany's money supply rose by 6.2% in March, continuing to exceed the bank's 5% target for the year.

The Bundesbank said in a statement that its decision "was guided in particular by the consideration that monetary expansion in Germany continues to be stronger than is consistent with stability policy requirements." West Germany's leading interest rates were last increased in January, also by a half-point each.

rates declined. Because the dollar–deutsche mark exchange rate depends directly on this differential, the dollar fell. In other words, the U.S. dollar suffered the same fate that the other European currencies would have suffered had their discount rates not been raised. This change produced expectations of either further inflation in the United States, as imported goods became more expensive, or further tightening by the Federal Reserve to prop up the dollar. Either prospect was unpalatable to the financial markets, so the stock and bond markets both fell.

The only really important statistical release during the third week was the **Consumer Price Index** for March. The monthly increase in the CPI was 0.5%, which was right in line with the 0.4% rise for February and the 0.6% rise for January (Figures 17.20 and 17.21). These figures

FIGURE 17.20   Bulletin and graph reporting on the Consumer Price Index for March 1989. Source: *Wall Street Journal*, 19 April 1989, p. A1.

What's News—

* * *

* * *

Business and Finance

CONSUMER PRICES ROSE 0.5% in March, led by soaring energy costs. Though economists said the report signaled worsening inflation, financial markets rallied amid relief the increase wasn't bigger. A 5.4% drop in housing starts also was considered bullish. The January-March rise in consumer prices was the biggest quarterly advance in two years.

The Dow Jones industrials surged 40.14, to 2377.93, in heavy trading. The yield on 30-year Treasury bonds fell below 9% for the first time in over two months. The dollar declined.

(Stories on Pages A2 and C1)

World-Wide

CHINESE STUDENTS STAGED a pro-democracy demonstration in Beijing.

As many as 10,000 protesters, using the death Saturday of former Communist Party chief Hu Yaobang to challenge authorities with demands for democracy and freedom, paraded in and around the capital's Tiananmen Square. Hundreds of police moved in to end a five-hour sit-in at the party's headquarters, and troops repulsed several thousand students who tried to force their way into the compound, where China's highest-ranking leaders live and work.

The demonstration was considered the biggest in Beijing since clashes following the death of Chou En Lai, when many were killed by security forces.

* * *

Consumer Prices

In percent (1982-84=100).

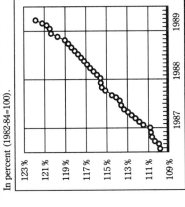

CONSUMER PRICES rose in March to 122.3% of the 1982-84 average from 121.6% in February, the Labor Department reports. (See story on Page A2)

FIGURE 17.21 ———— Article discussing the Consumer Price Index for March 1989. Source: *Wall Street Journal*, 19 April 1989, p. A2.

Consumer Prices Increased 0.5% During March

Quarterly Rise Was Biggest In 2 Years; Economists Are Gloomy on Inflation

By HILARY STOUT

Staff Reporter of THE WALL STREET JOURNAL

WASHINGTON—Pushed by soaring energy costs, consumer prices climbed 0.5% in March, completing their largest quarterly increase in two years, the Labor Department said.

A number of economists saw the report as grim evidence that inflation continues at a significantly higher rate than the economy has seen through most of the 1980s.

But the financial markets, bruised by two months of bad inflation numbers,

Housing Starts

Annual rate, in millions of dwelling units.

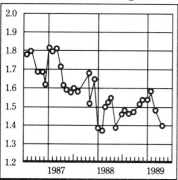

seemed relieved that the price rise wasn't bigger. Traders also appeared to welcome a second government report—that housing starts dropped 5.4% in March to an annual rate of 1,397,000—as another in a string of recent studies suggesting that the economy is slowing,

which could ease inflationary pressures. Consequently, the Dow Jones Industrial Average climbed 41.61 points and long-term bond prices jumped more than a point, or over $10 for each $1,000 face amount.

But A. Gary Shilling, president of an economic consulting firm in New York, said of the March price increase: "There is nothing to suggest this is acceptable."

The latest jump in the consumer price index—though only slightly higher than February's 0.4% rise and slightly lower than January's 0.6% jump—was greater than any monthly advance last year. Not since Januray 1987, when the index grew 0.7%, have consumer prices risen as fast as they did in January and March of this year.

And in the first three months of 1989, consumer prices climbed at an annual rate of 6.1%, the fastest pace since the 6.3% rate in the first quarter of 1987 and well above any yearly inflation rate since 1981.

"By no means is this a good number on inflation," said Stephanie Murphy, an economist at Carroll McEntee & McGinley, a brokerage firm in New York. And she added: "We know there's more inflation in the pipeline waiting to come out."

Energy prices, for example, leaped 1.1% last month, and the price of crude oil has continued to climb into April. That paves the way for further price rises in gasoline, home-heating oil and other fuels.

But perhaps more disturbing is that the cost of products made with petroleum, including plastics, chemicals, pharmaceuticals and artificial fibers, is likely to grow if oil prices continue to rise.

Some economists like to discount energy, as well as food, from inflation measures because pricing is so volatile in those areas that they can distort the overall inflation rate. But even excluding food and energy, consumer prices increased 0.4% last month.

Along with the decline in housing starts, the issuance of building permits tumbled 13.7% to a 1,221,000 annual rate, the Commerce Department said. In February, housing starts plunged 12% but in January they rose 6.4%. But January's rise and February's fall were

propelled by sharp changes in the weather, many analysts believe.

"March just feels like pretty typical weather," said David Seiders, chief economist at the National Association of Home Builders. "Now it truly does feel like the economic fundamentals are really the things to worry about."

For over a year the Federal Reserve Board has been trying to slow the economy, and stave off inflationary pressures, by boosting interest rates. Mr. Seiders said the housing numbers suggest the Fed is succeeding, at least in that interest-sensitive area.

In addition to energy costs, growing food and clothing prices pushed up the consumer price index in March. Food prices escalated 0.7% after jumping 0.5% in February. Clothing costs zoomed 1.4%, after falling 0.2% in February. But price increases slowed for medical care and entertainment, while they held their February pace for housing and transportation.

For the markets, the March consumer price figures were doubly sweet coming less than a week after a report showing producer prices rose 0.4% in March. That followed two months of alarming 1.0% jumps in producer prices. But many analysts expect the relief to be short-lived.

Mr. Shilling put it this way. "It may be a relief, but it's the same kind of relief you get after hitting your head against a stone wall. It may feel good, but that doesn't mean you're restored to full health."

CONSUMER PRICES

Here are the seasonally adjusted changes in the components of the Labor Department's consumer price index for March.

	% change from	
	Feb. 1989	March 1988
All items	0.5	5.0
Minus food & energy	0.4	4.7
Food and beverage	0.7	6.3
Housing	0.3	3.8
Apparel	1.4	4.4
Transportation	0.6	5.1
Medical care	0.5	7.2
Entertainment	0.3	4.8
Other	0.6	7.3

March consumer price indexes (1982–1984 equals 100), unadjusted for seasonal variation; together with the percentage increases from March 1988 were:

All urban consumers	122.3	5.0
Urban wage earners & clerical	120.8	5.0
Chicago	123.0	5.2
Los Angeles	126.2	4.6
New York	128.9	6.1
Philadelphia	126.0	5.4
San Francisco	125.9	5.7
Baltimore	122.8	4.3
Boston	129.7	6.2
Cleveland	121.5	5.6
Miami	119.8	4.1
St. Louis	119.4	4.6
Washington, D.C.	126.1	5.8

FIGURE 17.22

Weekly overview of data released during the third week of April 1989. Source: *Wall Street Journal*, 24 April 1989, p. A2.

CLOSELY WATCHED REPORTS

Statistics Released in the Week Ended April 21

	TOTAL	CHANGE (from prior period)		TOTAL	CHANGE (from prior period)
Money supply			**Housing starts**		
M1 Week ended April 10 (in billions)	$781.5	+$0.5	March, annual rate	1,397,000	−5.4%
			Building permits		
M2 Week ended April 10 (in billions)	$3,084.3	+$2.0	March, annual rate	1,221,000	−13.7%
			Consumer price index		
			March	122.3%	+0.5%
M3 Week ended April 10 (in billions)	$3,966.3	+$7.7	**New jobless claims**		
			Week ended April 8	320,000	+0.6%

Statistics to Be Released This Week

Durable goods orders (Tues.) March	**Personal income** (Thurs.) March	**New jobless claims** (Thurs.)
Real GNP (Tues.) First quarter, advance	**Savings rate** (Thurs.) March	**Farm prices** (Fri.) April
Personal consumption (Thurs.) March	**Money supply** (Thurs.)	**Leading indicators index** (Fri.) March

signified steady inflation of around 5–6% per year. Even excluding food and energy, the monthly change was 0.4%; in other words, the sources of inflation were definitely not limited to these two volatile components. However, the financial markets took this news in stride, apparently because the expectations had been even more pessimistic. The Dow Jones Industrial Average rose by over 40 points, bond prices increased, and interest rates declined. Interestingly, the dollar also declined, apparently responding more to the decline in interest rates than to the lower-than-expected inflation figures.

The easing of inflationary expectations was also helped by the 5.4% monthly decline in housing starts from February to March, which is reported in the article in Figure 17.21. Although this series is always highly volatile, the decline did indicate that yet another section of the economy was slowing down.

Figure 17.22 presents the *Wall Street Journal* summary table for the third week, which restates the 0.5% increase in the CPI. In terms of real activity, it contains only housing starts, building permits, and new jobless claims, all of which suggested a slowdown. The growth in M1 and M2 remained modest, with both indicating about 3% annual growth.

17.4 FOURTH WEEK: GNP, PERSONAL INCOME, CONSUMPTION, AND SAVING

The summary table in Figure 17.22 also previews the indicators that will round out the month's events in the fourth and final week. Of these, the greatest interest was centered on the release of the advance estimate for first-quarter GNP, the first estimate for that quarter. However, the monthly figures for March for personal income, consumption, and the

FIGURE 17.23

Report on the advance estimate of GNP for the first quarter of 1989. Source: *Wall Street Journal*, 26 April 1989, p. A2.

Economy, Propelled by Farm Recovery, Grew at Vigorous 5.5% Rate in 1st Period

Some Economists View Pace As Snappy, but Others See Clear Slowing Trend

---

ECONOMY

By HILARY STOUT
Staff Reporter of THE WALL STREET JOURNAL

WASHINGTON—A return to normal farm production following last year's devas-

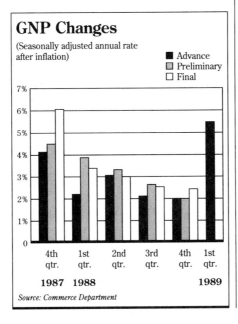

GNP Changes

(Seasonally adjusted annual rate after inflation)

■ Advance
▨ Preliminary
□ Final

Source: Commerce Department

tating drought propelled the U.S. economy to a vigorous expansion in the first quarter at a 5.5% annual rate, the Commerce Department reported.

Outside of the farm sector, the economy slowed from its fourth-quarter clip, but the pace was still faster than some inflation-conscious Federal Reserve officials have said they would like to see.

Discounting the statistical catch-up from the drought, the gross national product—the value of the nation's output of goods and services—grew at a 3% annual rate in the first three months of 1989, the Commerce Department said. In the fourth quarter, GNP expanded at an annual rate of 2.4%, but the pace would have been 3.5% had it not been for the drought's effects.

All the numbers are adjusted for inflation and for seasonal changes.

The department also revised its estimates of U.S. corporate profits in the fourth quarter, reporting that after-tax profits grew 3.2% during the period, compared with its initial estimate of 2.8% reported last month and a 3.9% increase in the third quarter. Before taxes, fourth-quarter profits climbed 2.1% instead of the original estimate of 1.8%; the third-quarter increase was 2.6%. For all of 1988, U.S. corporations posted a 14.7% increase in after-tax profits and a 10.1% increase before taxes.

Mild Surprise

Some economists expressed mild surprise that the underlying economic growth continued at so snappy a pace, given the Fed's efforts to curb economic activity by pushing up interest rates. But many others said the GNP numbers show the economy is following a clear slowing trend.

"I think this slowdown is precisely what

personal saving rate also carried important information both about the overall strength of the economy, as indicated by income and consumption, and about the balance between income and spending, as indicated by the saving rate.

The GNP report for the first quarter, shown in Figure 17.23, turned out to be somewhat confusing and contradictory. On one hand, the advance estimate of the overall real growth rate was 5.5% at an annual rate. That rate was the highest in over a year, hardly sustainable without generating inflation, and was quite at odds with the many other sig-

FIGURE 17.23

(continued)

the doctor ordered," said Lyle Gramley, chief economist of the Mortgage Bankers Association and a former Fed governor. "We were in great danger of the pot boiling over."

Many analysts have feared that the economy's pace was generating inflationary pressures by absorbing too much of the country's industrial capacity and using nearly all of the available work force. Some policy makers at the Fed have made it known they would like to see the economy expand no more than 2.5% this year.

Nevertheless, Mr. Gramley predicted that the central bank will refrain from further tightening because a number of recent economic indicators point to continued slowing n the economy. "The Fed is not going to tighten further," the former Reserve Board member said. "I don't often make flat statements like that, but it is virtually impossible to imagine that the Fed will tighten further given the pervasive signs of a slower economy."

'Tiny Bite'

But Alan Sinai, chief economist at Boston Co. in New York, said the Fed's policies appear only to have taken "a tiny bite" out of the economy. Noting that most of the first-quarter slowing came in consumer spending—particularly on big-ticket items like cars—and in home construction, Mr. Sinai said: "A small part of the economy was in a slowdown for the first part of this year."

It was precisely this composition that cheered many analysts, however. While consumer spending slowed, business investment grew by $11.4 billion after falling $3.6 billion in the fourth quarter. Exports continued to grow while imports slowed. And the government's defense spending dropped off by $6.6 billion.

"A pattern of growth that favors exports and investment in plant and equipment is a desirable one for the sustainability of the economic expansion," Commerce Secretary

Robert Mosbacher said in a statement issued shortly after the report was released.

Laying Groundwork

Expansion of business investment and sales of products overseas don't generate the worrisome pressures on prices that come from voracious consumer demand. Indeed, investment in new facilities and equipment can ease inflation by laying the groundwork for gains in productivity and efficiency.

Consequently, the GNP report "was basically good news," said James F. Smith, a professor of finance at the University of North Carolina Business School in Chapel Hill. "You've got consumers backing off and businesses continuing to modernize and serve or regain foreign customers."

Yesterday's GNP report contained a historic footnote as the economy, before adjustment for inflation, passed the $5 trillion mark for the first time, hitting a $5.117 trillion annual rate in the quarter. On that unadjusted basis, the economy grew at a 9.7% annual rate in the first quarter.

The report did include evidence that inflation is rising. A price index that measures the change in costs of a fixed basket of goods and services increased to a 5% annual rate in the first quarter from 4.2% in the fourth. Another price measure—known as the implicit price deflator—dropped to 3.9% from 5.3%. Commerce Department economists say the first measure is a more meaningful gauge of inflation because it isn't influenced by changes in the mix of goods and services produced in any one quarter.

GROSS NATIONAL PRODUCT

Here are some of the major components of the gross national product expressed in seasonally adjusted annual rates in billions of constant (1982) dollars:

	1st Qtr. 1989	4th Qtr. 1988
GNP	4,088.2	4,033.4
less: inventory chng	53.8	29.1
equals: final sales	4,034.5	4,004.4
Components of Final Sales		
Personal Consumption	2,634.8	2,626.2
Nonresidential Invest.	502.8	491.4
Residential Invest.	194.8	196.6
Net Exports	−95.6	−105.4
Gov't Purchases	797.7	795.5

In the first quarter, the implicit price deflator fell to 3.9% of the 1982 average, from 5.3% in the previous quarter.

nals of a slowdown. On the other hand, the numbers were accompanied by a statement by the Commerce Department to the effect that almost half the estimated first-quarter growth was due to a rebound in agriculture from the drought of the previous year, which had reduced the growth estimates for the two preceding quarters. Taking this information into account, we can see that the GNP report indicated continued moderate growth, with neither accelerating nor decelerating tendencies.

However, the component figures contained some interesting details. First, the growth in consumption, which had been exceptionally strong for some time, slowed to an annual rate of 1.3%. Meanwhile, nonresidential investment, which adds to the economy's productive capacity, expanded at an annual rate of almost 10%, and net exports improved considerably. These details were consistent with previous indications in the reports on industrial production, retail sales, and automobile sales. All suggested a slight shift in activity from consumption to investment in new equipment and expansion in foreign markets. Although minor, this change could mean some relief from the imbalances, characterized by too much consumption and too little saving and investment, that had plagued the U.S. economy.

The following day brought the monthly report on disposable income, consumption, and saving for March as shown in Figure 17.24. This report largely confirmed the impression left by the quarterly GNP report. Household income continued to grow faster than inflation, before as well as after taxes. However, consumer spending grew by only 0.2% in nominal terms and was reported as declining in real terms. Consistent with the auto sales reports, the slowdown was greatest in consumer durables, which showed a nominal monthly decline of 1.5%.

That income outpaced consumption implied, of course, an improvement in the saving rate. At 6.3%, it reached a four-year high. This report confirmed the impression gained from the retail sales and employment releases earlier in the month, which had indicated faster increases in income than in spending.

Figure 17.25 shows the fourth weekly summary, published on May 1. It included a 0.7% decline in the **Index of Leading Economic Indicators,** which is maintained by the BEA as an average of 11 different indicators believed to signal overall real growth. We take a closer look at this index as part of our discussion of macroeconomic forecasting in the next chapter. For now, we note that it confirms the overall impression received from the other indicators of some slowdown in real growth.

The following week, the monthly cycle started all over again, as May took over from April. The regular rhythm of data releases continued, month in and month out.

FIGURE 17.24

Report on personal income, consumer spending, and personal saving for March 1989. Source: *Wall Street Journal,* 28 April 1989, p. A2.

Rise in Consumer Spending Slowed In March; Savings Rate Rose Again

Increases in Interest Levels Appear to Have Damped Big-Ticket Buying Plans

By HILARY STOUT
Staff Reporter of THE WALL STREET JOURNAL

WASHINGTON—The rise in consumer spending slowed in March as higher interest rates appeared to crimp people's plans for big-ticket purchases, new Commerce Department figures suggest.

The department said consumer spending edged up 0.2% last month to an annual rate of $3.39 trillion, after climbing 0.5% in February and 0.7% in January. Purchases of durable goods—cars, appliances and other products expected to last at least three years—were the weakest, falling 1.5%. Spending on services slowed, while spending on nondurable goods increased at about its February pace.

Adjusted for inflation, consumer spending actually dropped 0.4% after climbing 0.3% in February and holding steady in January. All the numbers are adjusted for seasonal fluctuations.

Americans' income continued to rise during the month but also at a slower rate. Personal income expanded 0.8% to an annual rate of $4.350 trillion after increasing 1% in February and 1.7% in January (see chart on page one). Reflecting an increased caution in buying, the personal-savings rate continued to rise, hitting 6.3% of after-tax income, the highest level since May 1985.

Economic analysts said the numbers back up a government report Wednesday that showed the economy outside the agriculture sector slowing, in large part because of slackening consumer spending. Many economists took that to mean that the Federal Reserve's campaign to slow the economy and reduce inflationary pressures by increasing the cost of borrowing is having an effect.

"It's essentially showing the economy sloping off but still going," said Charles Renfro, chief economist at Alphametrics Corp., an economic-analysis company near Philadelphia. "The good news is in the bad news, in that we really don't want the economy too strong."

Part of the growth in personal income last month came from a large increase in retroactive Social Security benefits and profit-sharing payments to auto-company employees.

But wages and salaries also picked up, rising 0.8% in March after growing 0.5% in February.

But Americans' after-tax, or disposable, income tapered its expansion. It grew 0.8%, to an annual rate of $3.729 trillion, after rising 1.1% in February.

Here is the Commerce Department's latest report on personal income. The figures are at seasonally adjusted annual rates in trillions of dollars.

	Mar. 1989	Feb. 1989
Personal income	4.350	4.316
Wages and salaries	2.592	2.571
Factory payrolls	.552	.543
Transfer payments	.623	.616
Disposable personal income	3.729	3.701
Personal outlays	3.495	3.487
Consumption expenditures	3.390	3.383
Other outlays	105	104
Personal saving	234	214

FIGURE 17.25

Weekly overview of data released during the fourth week of April 1989. Source: *Wall Street Journal,* 1 May 1989, p. A4.

CLOSELY WATCHED REPORTS

Statistics Released in the Week Ended April 28

	TOTAL	CHANGE (from prior period)		TOTAL	CHANGE (from prior period)
Money supply			**New jobless claims**		
M1 Week ended April 17 (in billions)	$781.6	−$0.4	Week ended April 15	288,000	−10.0%
M2 Week ended April 17 (in billions)	$3,087.1	+$3.5	**Real corporate profits** Fourth quarter, revised, annual rate (in billions)	$174.5	+3.2%
M3 Week ended April 17 (in billions)	$3,971.1	+$5.5	**Personal income** March, annual rate (in trillions)	$4.35	+0.8%
Real GNP First quarter, advance, annual rate (in trillions)	$4.088	+5.5%	**Personal consumption** March, annual rate (in trillions)	$3.39	+0.2%
Durable goods orders March (in billions)	$124.87	+0.8%	**Savings rate** March, change in percentage points	6.3%	+0.5
Purchasing managers' index April	53.0%	+2.6	**Leading indicators** March, index	144.4%	−0.7%

Statistics to Be Released This Week

Construction spending (Mon.) March	**New home sales** (Tues.) March	**Employment, payroll** (Fri.) March
Manufacturers' orders (Tues.) February	**Auto sales** (Wed.) April	**Consumer credit** (Fri.) March
Manufacturers' shipments (Tues.) February	**Unemployment rate** (Fri.) March	**Money supply** (Thurs.)
		New jobless claims (Thurs.)

CHAPTER REVIEW

1. The releases of macroeconomic data in the United States follow a regular, predictable pattern of releases from month to month. This chapter reports, as an example, the releases made during April 1989.
2. The regular releases are occasionally interspersed with news of policy initiatives and market reactions to wars, accidents, natural disasters, and the weather.
3. The main data release during the first week is the labor market report from the Bureau of Labor Statistics, released on the first Friday of each month. For March 1989, the unemployment rate fell, but payroll employment showed some deceleration.

4. Four major indicators are released around the fifteenth of the month: retail sales, industrial production, the Producer Price Index, and the trade balance (from two months earlier). The trade balance for February was consistent with recent trends of a monthly deficit of around $10 billion. For March, the increase in the PPI slowed somewhat, industrial production was flat, and retail sales rose only slightly. The economy appeared to be headed down the Phillips curve.
5. The Consumer Price Index, released on April 18, indicated continued inflation, contrasting somewhat with the Producer Price Index data.

6. The advance GNP estimate showed very strong growth for the first quarter of 1989; however, about half of it was attributed to one-time forces in agriculture. Personal income rose substantially for March, while consumer spending hardly moved, resulting in a higher rate of personal saving than in earlier months.

7. News other than data releases included some intervention in the foreign-exchange market by the Bank of Japan aimed at bringing the dollar down; a discount rate increase by the German Bundesbank, which also weakened the dollar; and a combination of accidents and consumer demand that produced a substantial but temporary increase in the price of oil.

8. Overall, the news released during April 1989 pointed in the direction of some slowing or leveling off in real growth. Inflation showed some signs of slowing as well, although less unambiguously so.

EXERCISES

1. Go through the data releases for last month. Write an essay evaluating what these releases imply about the current state of the economy as well as its likely course in the near future. Describe how you could use this information as a manager in (a) manufacturing, (b) the retail business, (c) the airline industry.

2. Go through several months of data releases and make notes of the dates when the respective data series are released. Construct a calendar of the regular data releases.

3. The discussion in this chapter suggested that the personal saving rate could be predicted by the releases for employment and retail sales. Go through six months of data releases and see if you can find such a pattern. Then locate data for longer time series of the same data and run a regression of the changes in the saving rate on the changes in the two other variables. What do you find?

4. Month-to-month changes in economic data are often attributed to one-time events, such as extreme weather, natural disasters, accidents, and strikes. Go through three months of newspaper reports of data releases and see how often this argument has been used by commentators. With the benefit of hindsight, what do you conclude about the validity of those comments?

THINKING QUESTIONS

1. Critics sometimes challenge the validity of government data. Budget cuts for data-collection agencies have added fuel to this criticism. Supposing the critics are right, what would you propose as an appropriate management response to this problem? Is there any way the private sector can verify the government data? Would such efforts be worth the cost?

2. People who pay close attention to the government data releases are sometimes accused of becoming obsessed with minute short-term changes while losing sight of the big picture. How would you respond to this criticism?

3. Modern technology has made it possible to design a system of data releases whereby all subscribers to the system would receive the data at the instant they are released. Do you think such systems are good investments for society as a whole? Would you find it worthwhile as an entrepreneur to design and market such a system?

18 MACROECONOMIC FORECASTING

The basic managerial use of macroeconomics is the regular monitoring and interpretation of macroeconomic data releases. In many cases, this level of use is sufficient. However, because managerial decisions are directed toward the future, the most important aspect of economy watching is to detect trends and turning points. In Chapter 13, we discussed how to detect trends by interpreting data releases as signals of coming events. This chapter addresses the same issue in the form of forecasting.

The history of macroeconomic forecasting has paralleled that of the electronic computer. After modest beginnings in the 1940s and 1950s, macroeconomic forecasting has now become big business. Modern forecasting firms maintain and simulate econometric models with literally hundreds of equations and issue forecasts for equally as many variables. Large numbers of people are involved: Ph.D. economists, statisticians, and mathematicians; business consultants and marketing specialists with MBAs; computer programmers, technical writers, graphic designers, and production workers. Major investment in computers and communications technology is required.

Two large firms today dominate the commercial forecasting market in the United States. One is Data Resources, Incorporated (DRI), which is headquartered in Lexington, Massachusetts, and which grew out of the intellectual environment of Harvard and MIT. Its founder, Otto Eckstein, was a Harvard economics professor, a position he continued to hold until his untimely death in 1984.* This firm was bought in 1979 by McGraw-Hill, whose ownership is reflected in the firm's current name, DRI/McGraw-Hill.

The other major firm is Wharton Econometrics Forecasting Associates (WEFA). This firm grew out of the circle surrounding Lawrence Klein at the University of Pennsylvania's Wharton School of Business. Until 1987, Chase Econometrics was a third major player in the commercial forecasting industry. At that time, however, the activities of

---

*The structure of the DRI model has been published in book form in Otto Eckstein, *The DRI Model of the U.S. Economy* (McGraw-Hill, 1983). This chapter has benefited from that book.

Chase and WEFA were merged under the ownership of the Swiss corporation WEF Associates, A.G., whose U.S. subsidiary is WEFA, Inc.*

These industry leaders are not without competition, however. A number of smaller forecasting outfits are affiliated with major universities, such as the University of Michigan; the University of California, Los Angeles; and Georgia State University. In addition, the Federal Reserve Board maintains its own forecasting model, known as the MPS model. A forecasting model maintained by the Federal Reserve Bank of Minneapolis is of particular interest because despite being very small it has often proved capable of outperforming many larger models.**

18.1 FORECASTING WITH STRUCTURAL MODELS

Structural macroeconomic forecasting makes direct use of macroeconomic models. We studied a prototype of such a model in Chapters 5–8. Its main building blocks were the IS-LM model, which represented aggregate demand; aggregate supply; and the Phillips curve as the link between aggregate demand and aggregate supply. This model sought to tell a story about human behavior in regard to economic decisions for various players involved in decision making: for consumers, about how much to spend or save; for firms, about how much to produce and invest and what prices to charge; and so on. This story outlined a description of the *structure* of the economy—hence the term **structural model.**

The forecasts generated by a structural model represent the equilibrium—or disequilibrium—**solution** to that model. For example, the forecasts generated by the IS-LM model were the values of real GNP and the interest rate compatible with simultaneous equilibrium in the goods market and the money market. Graphically, we found these solutions to be the coordinates of the intersection of the IS and LM curves. Numerically, they were the solution values for the IS and LM equations. Given this solution for real GNP, as well as information about past inflation, the Phillips curve then produced a solution—generally a *dis*equilibrium solution—for the price level.

In order to find this solution, we needed to know the money supply

---

* The WEFA group's most recent model of the U.S. economy—called Mark 9—is described in *The WEFA Group April 1988 U.S. Economic Outlook.* This firm has also invested heavily in international forecasting, including a world model.

** Until very recently, the U.S. Commerce Department's Bureau of Economic Analysis maintained its own forecasting model, known as the BEA model. This model was used to generate economic projections for use in the construction of the administration's budget proposal. In February 1990, this effort was discontinued in order to free up resources for improvements in the construction of economic statistics.

and the level of government spending on goods and services. In a slightly more general version of the IS-LM model, we would also need to know various tax rates. Given these assumptions for the *exogenous* variables, the model would provide a solution for the *endogenous* variables. Thus, the forecasts depend crucially on the policy assumptions. For this reason, structural forecasting is also called **conditional forecasting:** The forecasts are made conditionally given the policy assumptions, and they are likely to fail if these assumptions prove incorrect.

THE MAIN BUILDING BLOCKS OF A LARGE-SCALE FORECASTING MODEL

For all their differences and innovations, the major macroeconomic forecasting models continue to use the simple structure of this essentially Keynesian textbook model as a common foundation. Amid a myriad of added complications, consumption and investment basically remain functions of income and interest rates, and net export demand remains a function of income and the exchange rate, with the exchange rate in turn a function of the international interest-rate differential—hence the IS curve. Though broken down into many components, the demand for money remains an increasing function of real GNP and the price level and a decreasing function of various interest rates—hence the LM curve. Finally, although prices and wages are modeled separately, inflation is ultimately a function of the imbalance between aggregate demand and aggregate supply and some approximation of inflationary expectations—hence the Phillips curve.

The reliance on this simple framework is important conceptually. However, if you take a casual look at some of the 700-plus equations in a typical large-scale macro model, you will probably find the framework difficult to recognize, because the large-scale models add a lot of detail and sophistication. This is what makes them large-scale.

ADDED DETAIL

Extensions of the simple IS-LM–Phillips-curve framework take four main forms. First, detail is added by **disaggregation,** which means taking the whole and breaking it into parts. For example, rather than one money-demand equation being specified, a number of demand functions are specified for a variety of liquid and less liquid assets, ranging from stocks and bonds to checking accounts and cash. Monetary policy is specified not simply as a change in any of the monetary aggregates but by the target range for the federal funds rate, or perhaps as a change in bank reserves (or a related variable), while the money supply is predicted by means of an explicit model of the money-multiplier process. Net export demand is split into export and import demands for a number of different categories of goods. Government purchases are separated at least into military and civilian spending on the federal level, while attempts might be made to predict spending by state and local governments from the various factors influencing their revenues.

Second, a number of **supportive features** are added, such as demographic trends and energy and raw-materials prices. These features may be specified as additional exogenous variables or as simple submodels whose results are used as exogenous inputs to the macro model.

Third, **dynamics** are added by including lagged effects in the various behavioral relationships. In our model, the only really dynamic element was the sluggish price adjustment implied by the Phillips curve. Large-scale macro models incorporate other dynamic elements as well. For example, consumption might be related to a weighted average of current and past income levels as an approximation of the forward-looking theory, but with adaptive rather than rational expectations. Similarly, the modeling of investment demand typically includes lagged production and interest-rate levels, reflecting the time required to complete an investment project as well as expectations of the future.

The fourth type of extension is to add **industry detail.** This addition is often done as an add-on to the macro structure. For example, after the model has determined real GNP, it goes on to predict how this overall production level will be divided among the various industries. This extension is important for most clients in private industry, whose ultimate interest is not in the overall economy but rather in the business climate of their particular industries.

ESTIMATION AND DATA

A large-scale macro model contains literally hundreds of *equations*, each of which contains a number of *coefficients*, such as the marginal propensity to consume. The values of these coefficients must be *estimated* from historical data. The standard estimation method is ordinary least squares, which we studied in Chapter 2. When complications arise such that the assumptions underlying ordinary least squares are not satisfied, more advanced methods are substituted.

Fortunately, this substitution presents no significant problem for the trained econometrician. Nevertheless, the task of estimating all the parameters of a large-scale macroeconometric model is a major undertaking because of sheer size. Moreover, the estimations procedure must be repeated regularly as new data become available, because estimates based on more and newer data are always more accurate.

An additional problem is collecting the data and transforming them into forms suitable for estimation. Most of the data come from government statistics, although some also come from private agencies, for example, stock prices and the University of Michigan's index of consumer expectations. The commercial forecasting firms maintain their own **data bases.** These data bases are extraordinarily rich. In order to facilitate frequent reestimation, they are also kept up to date, with new updates every time a new statistic is released or an old one revised.

From the forecasting firm's point of view, the data base is a highly marketable by-product of the forecasting activity. Subscription to a firm's services usually includes on-line access to its data base. This access is important whenever the client wants to carry out analyses in-house or simply wants to get a "feel" for past trends and correlations.

SOLVING THE MODEL

After all the parameters have been estimated, the model is ready to be *solved* for future periods. These solutions, which are also referred to as **simulations,** produce the numbers that form the model's forecasts. Naturally, this task is done by computer. The inputs to the solution process are the estimated parameter values, the projected values of the exogenous variables (such as the policy variables and demographic trends), and the actual data for all the variables whose lagged values appear in the equations.

The model is solved for one period at a time. Suppose you have a quarterly model and the time is February 1991. You have data through the fourth quarter of 1990 and want to generate forecasts for the first two quarters of 1991. You start by solving the model for the first quarter of 1991, given the parameter values, the policy assumptions for the first quarter of 1991, and the data through 1990 for all the lagged variables. This solution defines your forecasts for the first quarter of 1991. Next you add the solution values to your data set and use them as part of the lagged data that you need as inputs to the solution for the second quarter. This solution also requires assumptions for the second quarter about policy and other exogenous variables. The resulting solution becomes your forecast for the second quarter as of February.

REVISING THE FORECASTS

However, this solution will not be your ultimate forecast for the second quarter. When the data for the first quarter start coming in, you will find that your forecasts for that quarter were not entirely accurate, because the future is always uncertain. However, the forecast errors for the first quarter mean that the second-quarter forecasts are based on somewhat inaccurate assumptions. When enough of the first-quarter data have come in, you will want to *revise* your second-quarter forecast, just as the weatherperson on your local TV news station updates his or her own five-day forecast each day. These updates are an important part of the forecasting companies' function of keeping clients abreast of current events.

JUDGMENTAL ADJUSTMENTS

In practice, however, very few forecasters ever issue the forecasts directly as they come out of the computer the first time. Before the forecasts are issued, they are subject to intense scrutiny by the professional forecasting staff as well as the firm's top executives. These forecasts are the firm's "bread and butter" and better look right. They need to be more than technically correct; they also need to *make sense*. Computer models are extremely useful for processing large amounts of information, but they lack human intuition. Trained and experienced economists can detect when and where a forecast is unreasonable or unlikely. Whenever this happens—and it almost always does—some further work must be done before the forecast is issued.

It is not enough just to change the forecast of one or more variables judgmentally, because the forecasts for the respective variables need to be consistent with each other, and the preservation of consistency for hundreds of variables at the same time goes beyond normal human capacity. Thus, the forecasting staff goes back to the model and looks for ways to modify it that would bring the forecasts in line with the forecasters' professional judgment. If the model is not the problem, the next step is to adjust the model's **add factors,** which are constants that are added to each equation. They can be interpreted either as judgmental adjustments to the intercept terms or, viewing the equations as regression equations, as assumptions that the residuals are expected to take values other than zero. Add factors are commonly used by all macroeconomic forecasters and are one reason why the forecasts are as accurate as they are. Although the add factors might seem arbitrary, they in fact appear to work well as summaries of the forecasters' professional insights that go beyond the formal model.

COMMUNICATING THE FORECASTS

Professional forecasting involves more than simply imparting a series of numbers. One of the main reasons for a business to subscribe to a forecasting service is to receive well-informed, verbal evaluations of current trends. In response to this need, the forecasting firms issue **monthly reviews** to their clients containing broad but concise articles with evaluations of the current situation and discussion of important current economic issues. These reviews are issued exclusively to the clients, at a stiff price. The actual forecasts are included as an appendix. The add factors may be listed as well.

ADVANTAGES AND DISADVANTAGES OF STRUCTURAL FORECASTS

Structural forecasts take full advantage of the insights that have been formulated as the macroeconomic *theory* that underlies the model. Thus, if you accept the theoretical basis, you can be confident that the forecast is sound. Although the quality of a forecast unavoidably depends on the ability and philosophy of the individual forecaster, the adherence to a widely accepted body of theory provides a certain stamp of approval. Furthermore, at least ideally, the reliance on accepted macroeconomic theory should keep the structural forecasts from relying on any accidentally discovered—and perhaps spurious—correlation.

Unfortunately, these strengths are also weaknesses. By relying on the theory, the forecasts share the theory's limitations. It can sometimes be dangerous to rely on one particular view of the economy. New intellectual developments, such as real-business-cycle analysis or the coordination-failure models discussed briefly in Chapter 11, can be missed. Furthermore, by focusing particularly on the mechanisms that have already been built into the model, forecasts can easily ignore new forces that might have entered the scene. In his critique of structural models, discussed briefly in Section 8.4, Robert Lucas emphasized that observed patterns of behavior could reflect established policy patterns rather than fundamental characteristics of human behavior.

The problem of ignoring new developments turned into an embarrassment for most modelers in the mid-1970s. The then-used versions of the Phillips curve came under heavy attack for failing to foresee the combination of inflation and weak or moderate real performance. In particular, the existing models at the time did not include any mechanisms for shocks of the type that occurred when the world price of oil quadrupled. Many forecasts, in fact, predicted that this price increase would *stimulate* the U.S. economy in 1974–75!

An additional problem of structural forecasting is that the model's solutions are always sensitive to the assumptions the forecaster needs to make about the exogenous variables. This problem became acute in the early 1980s, when the Reagan administration and the Federal Reserve announced an attack on inflation with a monetary tightening as its main instrument. Most major forecasters failed to take these announcements seriously and assumed a considerably easier monetary policy than the one that in fact was followed. As a result, they failed miserably at predicting the 1981–82 recession.

18.2 ATHEORETICAL FORECASTING

When forecasts are generated by structural models, they are accompanied by a story—implicit in the model—about the mechanisms that generate the predicted effects. However, in an important paper published in 1980,[*] Professor Christopher Sims of the University of Minnesota argued that the economists' current body of knowledge was too limited for any such story to be really credible. Sims's point was not so much that the stories were wrong as that they were overpretentious. Other assumptions could give rise to alternative stories that could be equally consistent with the data. However, rather than pondering which model might be the most correct, Sims argued that macroeconomists should give up the hypocrisy of structural modeling. Giving up structural models also could mean better forecasts if the forecaster, freed from the straightjacket of macroeconomic theory, were able to make use of empirical correlations not clearly implied by any theory.

The alternative forecasting method that emerges from this argument

---

[*]Christopher S. Sims, "Macroeconomics and Reality," *Econometrica*, January 1980, vol. 48, pp. 1–48.

is called **atheoretical** forecasting. As the name suggests, this method does not make use of macroeconomic theory, at least not in a direct sense. It uses a formal model, but one based on *statistical* theory rather than economic theory. The basic idea is to identify strong *empirical regularities* in the data whether or not the forecaster is able to tell a good theoretical story about them. Let us look at how this can be done in practice.

BUILDING AN ATHEORETICAL MODEL

Atheoretical forecasting models contain no *simultaneity*. This principle differentiates such models from, say, the IS-LM model, which solves simultaneously for real GNP and the interest rate. The simultaneity in that model followed from the fact that the IS curve defined real GNP as a function of the interest rate *during the same period*, while the LM curve, in turn, defined the interest rate as a function of real GNP, also during the same period. Thus, in order to avoid simultaneity, *the atheoretical model must define each variable as a function of lagged variables only*. We studied a simple example of such a model in Chapter 2 when in equation (2.16) we specified real GNP as a function of the real money supply with a one-year lag.

The explanatory variables in the model should be chosen so as to obtain the best possible fit. It does not matter in this context whether you can explain this fit, as long as it is there. Nevertheless, you must check that it does not show up by mere coincidence. A common way to carry out such a check is to estimate the model with only part of the available data and see how well the model predicts beyond the estimation sample. For example, if you have time-series data going through 1990, you might estimate the model on data through 1985 and see how well its forecasts for 1986–90 fit the actual data for those years. Once you are satisfied with this forecasting performance, you will, of course, want to estimate it again using *all* the available data.

One atheoretical model that has become particularly popular is the **vector-autoregressive model (VAR).** In order to understand this expression, note first that an **autoregressive** model specifies the current value of a variable as a linear function of its own past values. For example, an autoregressive model of the real GNP growth rate could specify this quarter's growth rate as a linear function of the same growth rate one, two, and three quarters ago.

However, to qualify as *vector*-autoregressive, the model must contain more than one variable. You are probably familiar with the concept of a vector as a pair or an *n*-tuple of real numbers. For example, the pair of the two variables of real GNP and the interest rate can be thought of as a vector whose first element is real GNP and whose second element is the interest rate. A VAR model is an autoregressive model for such a vector of variables. Specifically, it is a model consisting of two or more variables, where each variable is specified as a linear function of its own past values as well as the lagged values of all the other variables in the model.

A SIMPLE VAR MODEL

As a simple example, consider a quarterly VAR model for the real GNP growth rate and the yield rate on 3-month Treasury bills (T-bills). These variables are chosen because they correspond to the two central variables in the IS-LM model. (Note that we use the growth rate rather than the level of real GNP and the nominal rather than the real T-bill rate. The reason is simply that these choices result in somewhat better forecasts, which agrees with the spirit of atheoretical modeling.)

Call the two variables y and i, respectively, and include lags of up to three quarters in the model. It then consists of the following two equations, which here have been estimated by ordinary least squares on quarterly data for 1955–85:

$$y_t = 3.70 + 0.22y_{t-1} + 0.19y_{t-2} - 0.07y_{t-3} - 0.12i_{t-1}$$
$$\quad\ (0.97)\ \ (0.09)\qquad (0.09)\qquad (0.09)\qquad\ (\ .42)$$

(18.1a)

$$\quad - 1.31i_{t-2} + 1.15i_{t-3} + e_t,\quad SER = 3.85,\quad R^2 = 0.22;$$
$$\qquad (0.62)\qquad (0.43)$$

$$i_t = -0.11 + 0.03y_{t-1} + 0.04y_{t-2} + 0.01y_{t-3} + 1.11i_{t-1}$$
$$\quad\ (0.21)\ \ (0.02)\qquad (0.02)\qquad (0.02)\qquad (0.09)$$

(18.1b)

$$\quad - 0.50i_{t-2} + 0.38i_{t-3} + u_t,\quad SER = 0.82,\quad R^2 = 0.93;$$
$$\qquad (0.13)\qquad (0.09)$$

where e_t and u_t are the stochastic disturbance terms for the first equation and the second equation, respectively.

The coefficients of VAR equations do not always have clear interpretations. However, some patterns are worth pointing out. First, for both variables, there is some indication that the observations in subsequent quarters are similar to each other. This tendency means that the variables show some *persistence*, as discussed in Section 13.2. This persistence is reflected in the positive coefficients for lagged GNP growth in the first equation. Because these coefficients are much smaller than 1, we can infer that the persistence in GNP growth is not very strong. However, for the T-bill rate it is very strong indeed, as indicated by the large coefficient for the first lag of the T-bill rate in equation (18.1b).

Second, there is some tendency for high interest rates to signal declining growth rates for real GNP. This tendency is reflected by the first two lag coefficients for the T-bill rate in equation (18.1a). Similarly, we also see a tendency, though a much weaker one, for high GNP growth rates to signal rising interest rates. These results are quite in line with our discussion of signals in Section 13.2.

At the same time, we can hardly avoid noticing that the overall pattern of these coefficients is somewhat unwieldy. An atheoretical forecaster will not worry about such issues, however, because the purpose is only to find a good forecast, not to tell a good story.

How good are the forecasts generated by this model? First, within the estimation period 1955–85, the fit for the T-bill equation appears to be excellent, with an R^2 well above 90%, while the fit for the equation for real GNP growth is much poorer, with an R^2 of only 22%. However, to an experienced forecaster, this relatively poorer fit would come as no surprise but would be seen as a reflection of the well-known fact that accurately forecasting real GNP growth is extremely difficult.

Figure 18.1 illustrates the forecasts of the model for real GNP growth for the period 1986–89. These forecasts were constructed by substituting the actual data for the lagged values of real GNP growth and the T-bill rate on the right side of each equation and thus computing a fitted value for the variable on the left. Clearly, the forecasts are much better for the last two years of this four-year period. On the other hand, the model faced a much more difficult task for the first two years, because some large changes were then taking place in the economy.

FIGURE 18.1

Forecast and actual values of U.S. real GNP growth, 1986–89, using two-variable VAR model.

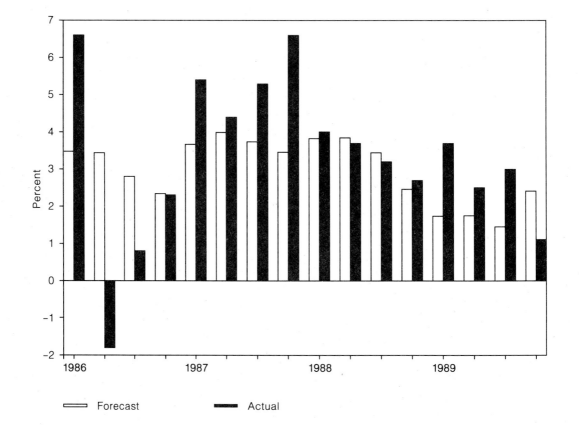

There is a general lesson here, namely, that all forecasting models tend to perform much better during smooth times, when no big surprises happen. The most difficult periods to forecast are the *turning points* in the business cycle, which we mentioned briefly as part of our discussion of operations management in Section 13.1. The second quarter of 1986 almost became an example of such a turning point, but not quite, because what followed turned out not to be an actual recession.

However, we also notice that the model underpredicts real GNP growth for three of the four quarters in 1989. The Federal Reserve pursued a tight monetary policy that year, and the model predicted the dampening of real activity that typically followed such moves in the past. However, for some reason the reaction in 1989 turned out to be much milder than predicted. This event suggests a weakness of atheoretical forecasting models. They derive all their power from past regularities in the data, without consideration for whether these regularities might have changed over time. Predicting such changes usually requires some insights from macroeconomic *theory*, but such insights are not incorporated into the atheoretical models.

Figure 18.2 compares the actual and forecasted T-bill rates. This

FIGURE 18.2

Forecast and actual values of the 3-month U.S. Treasury-bill rate, 1986–89, using two-variable VAR model.

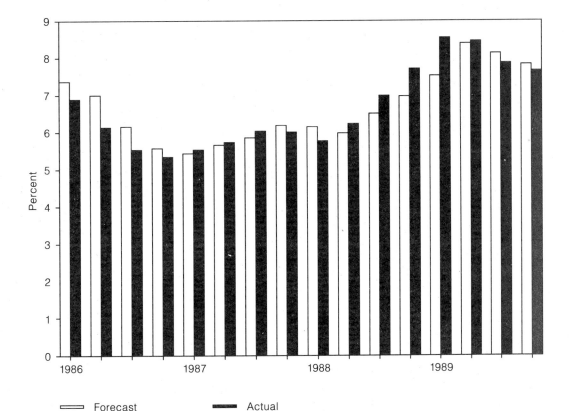

model is obviously much more successful, even in predicting the increases leading up to the high rates in 1989. Thus, we see again that other variables can be much easier to forecast than real GNP growth.

ATHEORETICAL MODELS IN PRACTICE

Better success in predicting real GNP growth requires a larger model. Some commercial forecasting firms now offer sophisticated atheoretical models as alternatives to their structural models. One empirical VAR model deserves special mention. It goes under the name BVAR and is maintained by the Federal Reserve Bank of Minneapolis. Its forecasts are generated from the lagged values of six variables: real GNP, the GNP deflator, nonresidential fixed investment, the unemployment rate, the T-bill rate, and the money supply. In Section 18.3, we look at a comparison between the forecasting performance of the BVAR model and the leading commercial structural models.

VAR FORE-CASTS AS UN-CONDITIONAL FORECASTS

Recall from Section 18.1 that structural forecasts are *conditional* in the sense that they are sensitive to the particular assumptions the forecaster makes about future monetary and fiscal policy as well as other exogenous variables, for example, the world price of oil. VAR forecasts, on the other hand, suffer from no such sensitivity. If policy variables are included in a VAR model, they are not singled out as exogenous but are treated like any other variable. Thus, for example, lagged values of the money supply may be included among the variables used to predict real GNP growth.

Note further that this treatment is symmetric in the sense that the model then also yields a forecast for the money supply, based on the lagged values of real GNP growth, its own lagged values, and the lagged values of the other variables in the model. Thus, the model carries implications about central bank behavior. This feature is very similar to the art of reading signals about monetary policy, which we discussed toward the end of Chapter 13.

ADVANTAGES AND DISAD-VANTAGES OF ATHEORETICAL FORECASTING

The ability to issue unconditional forecasts can be an advantage. Note, however, that this advantage holds only as long as the policymakers follow their past behavioral patterns, because these are the patterns that the model will predict from past correlations. Abrupt policy changes, such as the sharp monetary tightening in the early eighties, can give the advantage back to the conditional forecasters, provided they are able to detect the change in policy patterns in time to incorporate them into their forecasts. However, most structural forecasters in fact missed this opportunity in the early eighties by refusing to believe that the tightening would go as far as the policymakers had announced.

Being independent of theory also may give the atheoretical forecaster a philosophical advantage. The forecasts then are not the products of

Keynesian, monetarist, or new classical philosophy. This independence can be a great advantage for anyone who works with people who are skeptical of one or more macroeconomic theories or who disagree with the forecaster or each other philosophically.

However, this independence can be a disadvantage as well. Because no theoretical considerations are involved, the forecasts do not take advantage of the insights of macroeconomic theory, and important information can be ignored. Worse, if the forecaster truly has no idea about how the macroeconomy works, he or she will also have no idea about which variables to include in the model. Of course, it is possible to look for statistical correlations, but the trick in atheoretical forecasting is not just to find single variables that correlate with the one to be forecast but to find *combinations* of variables that *together* can help forecast a particular variable. Anyone who starts to look blindly for such combinations will soon discover that the number of possible combinations is enormous.

Thus, in practice, atheoretical modeling is an art that is best practiced by people who have both good theoretical insights in macroeconomics and a good deal of experience with real-world data and correlations. Given that this is the case, it is also well worth looking at forecasting methods that rely on macroeconomic theory explicitly, in other words, structural forecasting.

18.3 THE TRACK RECORD

Since the ultimate proof of the pudding is in the eating, we now look at the actual performance of some U.S. forecasting models. As a numerical measure of forecasting performance, we use a measure called the **root mean squared forecast error,** or **RMSFE.** It is analogous to the concept of a standard deviation and is defined as follows: Let F_t denote the forecasted growth rate for quarter t and A_t the growth rate that actually materialized. Then

$$(18.2) \qquad \text{RMSFE} = \left[(1/n) \sum_{t=1}^{n} (A_t - F_t)^2\right]^{\frac{1}{2}},$$

where n is the number of periods for which the forecasts are studied.

Obviously, a low value for the RMSFE is preferable to a high one. Thus, if we compare the forecasts of a number of firms, the firm with the lowest RMSFE can be declared the winner. But how high is high? As a benchmark, we can define the RMSFE of a **naive forecast,** which simply predicts that the variable in all periods will be equal to its past average value. Such a forecast would be naive indeed, and it seems highly reasonable to expect that any respectable forecast would have a substantially lower RMSFE than this naive forecast.

For a number of years, Dr. Stephen K. McNees, vice president and economist at the Federal Reserve Bank of Boston, has examined the forecasting performance of a number of leading forecasting outfits. The results of his studies have been published in a series of articles in the bank's quarterly review.* Table 18.1 reproduces his estimates of the RMSFE for some selected models as well as the naive forecast defined above.

The Chase, DRI, and WEFA forecasts are conditional forecasts based on structural models with some judgmental adjustments. Each of these models contains hundreds of equations. The BVAR forecasts are generated by the six-equation VAR model maintained by the Federal Reserve Bank of Minneapolis. The BVAR forecasts have *not* been adjusted judgmentally. All the forecasts have been made during the quarter being forecast but before the release of the quarterly data for that quarter. Because the forecasting firms usually update their forecasts during the quarter, the table presents different forecasts made early in the quarter, in the middle of the quarter, and late in the quarter.

These results show first of all that the forecasters do better than the naive rule that the immediate future is going to be like the average past, as seen from the fact that the naive forecast always has a larger RMSFE than all the model-generated forecasts. However, sometimes the difference is not spectacular. In particular, the early-quarter real GNP forecasts are not much better than the naive ones. This result is a reflection of the fact, noted in Section 18.2, that real GNP growth actually is very hard to predict. In contrast, the model-based forecasts do much better in predicting the unemployment rate and the interest rate. Part of the difficulty for the GNP data studied here is that the period 1980–85 contained no fewer than *four* cyclical turning points as the economy went in and out of the 1980 and 1981–82 recessions. We have already seen that such turning points are particularly difficult to predict.

The improvements made as the quarter proceeds are not surprising, because the forecasters benefit from the information contained in the monthly economic indicators, even if these indicators contain some noise. In fact, it is remarkable that the late-quarter GNP and inflation forecasts do not perform better, considering the fact that two months' worth of monthly data is known by the time these forecasts are released.

---

*For example, "Which Forecast Should You Use?" *New England Economic Review*, July/August 1985, pp. 36–42; "The Accuracy of Two Forecasting Techniques: Some Evidence and Interpretation," *New England Economic Review*, March/April 1986, pp. 20–31; and "Why Do Forecasts Differ?" *New England Economic Review*, January/February 1989, pp. 42–54.

TABLE 18.1 ROOT MEAN SQUARED ERRORS OF MACROECONOMIC FORECASTS: RESULTS OF ONE-QUARTER-AHEAD FORECASTS FOR THE SECOND QUARTER OF 1980 THROUGH THE FIRST QUARTER OF 1985[a]

FORECASTER	REAL GNP GROWTH	UNEMPLOY-MENT RATE	INFLATION (GNP DEFLATOR)	3-MONTH T-BILL RATE	MONEY SUPPLY
Early Quarter					
Chase[b]	4.4	0.4	1.4	1.4	4.3
DRI	4.0	0.3	1.6	1.5	4.0
WEFA	4.2	0.3	1.7	1.5	4.2
BVAR	4.2	0.4	2.1	1.6	4.8
Mid-Quarter					
WEFA	3.1	0.2	1.9	0.4	2.5
BVAR	3.6	0.2	2.0	0.4	3.0
Late Quarter					
Chase	2.4	0.2	1.4	0.2	2.6
DRI	2.0	0.2	1.4	0.1	2.1
BVAR	2.8	0.2	2.5	0.1	2.1
Naive	5.4	3.2	3.2	6.5	6.8

SOURCE: Stephen K. McNees, "The Accuracy of Two Forecasting Techniques: Some Evidence and an Interpretation," *New England Economic Review*, March/April 1986, pp. 20–31. (The naive forecasts were not studied by McNees.)

[a]All forecasts are one quarter ahead, i.e., forecasts for the current quarter before the actual data are released.

[b]Abbreviations of forecasters:
Chase: Chase Econometrics (merged with WEFA in 1987)
WEFA: Wharton Econometric Forecasting Associates (merged with Chase in 1987)
DRI: Data Resources, Inc.
BVAR: Bayesian Vector Autoregressive Model, maintained by the Federal Reserve Bank of Minneapolis
Naive: Forecast equal to average value from the first quarter of 1954 through the first quarter of 1980 (growth rates except for unemployment rate and T-bill rate)

By and large, the differences between the models are not large. Among the forecasts based on structural models, the DRI model tends to perform somewhat better when it comes to forecasting real GNP and the money supply, while for inflation the Chase model does a somewhat better job and the WEFA model matches the DRI model quite closely.

Interestingly, the performance of the atheoretical model BVAR is quite similar to that of the structural models for real GNP, the unemployment rate, and the Treasury-bill rate, especially early in the quarter. Its performance in terms of inflation forecasting is not quite as good. These results indicate on one hand that it is not easy for an atheoretical model to outperform the structural models. On the other hand, it should be noted that the VAR model is much smaller and correspondingly cheaper to maintain. Furthermore, the VAR forecasts are presented "as is," without adjustments by the forecaster. Because this procedure deprives the client of the insights that the forecaster possesses outside the model, it might not serve the client best. However, we should note the possibility that the VAR-based forecasts could have performed even better if such adjustments had been undertaken.

The examination of the money-supply forecasts provides an interesting opportunity to compare conditional and nonconditional forecasts. In the VAR model BVAR, the money-supply forecasts are generated in the same unconditional way as for the other variables. In contrast, the structural models use specific assumptions about monetary policy. These assumptions pertain to the Federal Reserve's direct actions, so the models' solutions for the money-multiplier process lie between these assumptions and the forecasts for the money supply. Thus, although the money-supply forecasts are not assumed directly, very few steps come between the policy assumptions and the actual forecasts.

Overall, the VAR-based forecasts of the money supply do a little more poorly than the conditional forecasts. However, when we consider the historical circumstances, the difference is not great. The early 1980s were a period of rather abrupt changes in monetary policy. An atheoretical model should not be expected to do well in such a situation, because it implicitly assumes that no abrupt changes take place in the pattern of economic policy making. The makers of the structural models, on the other hand, follow the current policy debate and can incorporate the latest signals from the Federal Reserve in their forecasts. The signals from the Federal Reserve were, in fact, quite clear during this period. The structural forecasters' failure to read these signals might be an important reason why their forecasts for real GNP did not do better during this period.*

18.4 THE INDEX OF LEADING ECONOMIC INDICATORS

The U.S. government—specifically, the Bureau of Economic Analysis— offers a special free forecasting service. Its results are released to the public at the very end of each month under the name of the **Index of Leading Economic Indicators,** or **ILEI.**

---

*This point is discussed more fully in Stephen K. McNees, "The Accuracy of Two Forecasting Techniques: Some Evidence and an Interpretation," *New England Economic Review*, March/April 1986, pp. 20–31.

THE COMPONENTS OF THE ILEI

The ILEI is an average of 11 different economic indicators, all of which have tended in the past to signal future trends in real economic activity. The ILEI consists of the following indicators:

1. The length of the average workweek in manufacturing

2. Average weekly initial claims for state unemployment insurance

3. Manufacturers' new orders for consumer goods and materials in 1982 dollars

4. Vendor performance (an index in which a high value means a slow-down in delivery times)

5. New contracts and orders for plant and equipment in 1982 dollars

6. New building permits

7. Change in manufacturers' unfilled orders for durable goods in 1982 dollars

8. Changes in sensitive materials prices

9. Stock prices (Standard & Poor's index of 500 common stocks)

10. Money supply (M2) in 1982 dollars

11. Consumer expectations (index of changes in consumer sentiment, based on a survey by the University of Michigan Survey Research Center)

The ILEI is reported as a monthly percentage change. It is not a forecast of any particular variable. Rather, it is intended to signal the overall climate of economic activity in the months ahead. The monthly percentage change in the overall index is a weighted average of the change in each of the respective components. Note that some of the components are already in the form of percentage changes. For those components, the changes in these percentage changes contribute to the percentage change in the overall index. The unemployment-claims component is "inverted," that is, included with the opposite sign of the actual change, because high claims indicate a weak economy, and vice versa. In contrast, the index of slower deliveries is not inverted, because slow deliveries reflect high activity.

This index can be viewed as an exercise in atheoretical forecasting, because it relies on correlations that are not completely explained theoretically. However, its reliance on statistical methods is much less formal than in most other atheoretical models. It is also worth noting that the thinking behind the construction of the index draws to a great extent on macroeconomic theory, which makes it somewhat related to structural forecasting as well.

WHY DO THE COMPONENTS LEAD?

We can distinguish four categories of ILEI components in explaining why the components tend to lead economic activity. First, some of them reflect **commitments** to future activity, such as the three order-related components (indicators 3, 5, and 7) and building permits. A commitment is not a sure signal that the intended transaction will be carried out. If abrupt changes take place, people may find it better not to live up to their commitments. However, because changing a commitment, such as canceling an order, can be costly, the parties have an incentive to live up to the commitment, which makes commitment-related variables useful as predictors.

Second, two indicators reflect people's **expectations,** namely, the stock market and consumer expectations. To the extent that these people are right, their expectations should be useful predictors. Furthermore, consumer expectations are likely to influence today's spending according to the forward-looking theory of consumer behavior. The stock market is a reflection of the stock investors' expectations of future dividends and stock prices. In our discussion of the value of the stock market as a signal of economic activity, we noted that some doubts have been raised about its reliability. Nevertheless, the stock market's performance is likely to influence corporate decisions and hence future activity.

Third, one indicator reflects **policy,** namely, the money supply. This component is the indicator most clearly related to the macroeconomic theory studied in this book. Against the background of that theory, the claim that growth in the real money supply should foreshadow real expansion should require no further explanation.

Fourth, the remaining components are included because they are general indicators of a tightening economy and because they have tended to be **early signals** of expansions and contractions in the past. Whenever production rises or falls in response to demand changes, companies need to decide whether to hire or lay off people or to change the work hours of the existing work force. During the early stages of a contraction or expansion, they often choose to change the hours, because this can be done more cheaply and quickly while management waits for indications of whether the slowdown or pickup in demand is going to last.

The change in initial unemployment claims tends to lead because it reflects *changes* in the labor market. People filing new claims have just been added to the pool of the unemployed. Over time, such additions translate into changes in the unemployment rate, which are known to be closely correlated with changes in production.

The vendor performance is an early signal of tightness in the markets for intermediate goods. The idea is that when demand increases, orders in these markets will back up and take more time. Thus, longer delivery times indicate a tighter economy. In the markets for raw materials, however, increased demand tends to be reflected first in higher prices. This is why materials prices are included as a component of the ILEI.*

WHY A WEIGHTED AVERAGE?

Each ILEI component can be used as a signal of future economic activity. However, all are somewhat unreliable. For example, faster deliveries might be due to increased supply or to improved procedures for delivery of inventories, such as a Just-In-Time delivery system, which you may have studied as part of Operations Management. Materials prices might rise because supply is curtailed by wars, natural disasters, or political decisions. Building permits might be influenced by the weather, the money supply by random shifts in the money multiplier, and the workweek by strikes. In this fashion, every component contains a good deal of noise.

Using an average of the individual components filters away some of this noise. If one component behaves erratically in one particular month, another component might make up for it by being erratic in the opposite direction. At least, the averaging minimizes the influence on the index of the errors in the individual components. This process is similar to choosing a balanced portfolio. If one security does not yield a good return, chances are that the other securities in your portfolio will. By choosing a portfolio of many securities, you make sure that bad developments for individual securities have minimal effects on the return on your entire portfolio.

IS THE ILEI USEFUL?

The practical usefulness of the ILEI has been examined by a number of economists. These examinations invariably conclude that the index is valuable but also somewhat unreliable because it tends to issue some false signals.

In a 1982 article, Professor Alan Auerbach of the University of Pennsylvania undertook a rigorous study of whether the changes in the ILEI could help predict the unemployment rate or growth in industrial production.** (These two variables were chosen over real GNP because they, like the ILEI, are released monthly.) After having studied the historical data carefully, Auerbach concluded that the ILEI was in fact a

---

*It is worth noting that oil prices are *not* included in this index of materials prices. They have been excluded in order to avoid the large fluctuations that have been common in the oil market.

**Alan J. Auerbach, "The Index of Leading Indicators: Measurement Without Theory, Thirty-five Years Later," *Review of Economics and Statistics*, 1982, vol. 64, pp. 589–95.

good predictor for both the unemployment rate and the growth in industrial production.

These results confirmed that the ILEI is helpful in forecasting economic activity in an *overall* sense. However, most people look to the ILEI for a more specific purpose, namely, to predict *turning points* in the business cycle. In other words, they want to know when recessions are likely to begin and end.

This issue has been explored by a number of economists. One of the most recent attempts is a study by Gerald H. Anderson and John J. Erceg, economists at the Federal Reserve Bank of Cleveland.* Using past data, these authors try out several rules for using the ILEI to predict business-cycle turning points. For business-cycle **peaks,** that is, beginnings of recessions, their preferred rule is the following. If the ILEI has declined in four of the last seven months, a recession is likely to start within the next 13 months after the release of the ILEI for the last of these seven months. This rule would have predicted all the postwar recessions. Unfortunately, however, on four occasions it also would have given out false signals of recessions that failed to materialize. Thus, this rule is only about two-thirds reliable.

For business-cycle **troughs,** that is, ends of recessions, Anderson and Erceg suggest looking for two consecutive increases in the ILEI. This rule would have given two false signals and missed the recoveries in 1970 and 1975. Otherwise, however, it would have led to correct predictions.

Anderson and Erceg also point to another source of ambiguity in the index. Its first release for a given month gives a *preliminary* figure, which is often revised later. An interesting case of revision occurred in 1989. According to the data released by the end of August of that year, the ILEI had declined in four of the last seven months, which would indicate an upcoming recession. However, on September 1, two of these declines were revised to indicate an increase and a case of no change, respectively. This revision thus canceled the prediction of an upcoming recession.

The composition of the ILEI has changed somewhat over time. For example, M2 was substituted for M1 as the monetary variable in the early 1980s. The first figures based on the list given above were released on March 3, 1989. Further changes may be undertaken from time to time whenever BEA statisticians believe that alternative components are more helpful in predicting general economic activity.

Further impetus for change comes from a recent research project at

---

*Gerald H. Anderson and John J. Erceg, "Forecasting Turning Points with Leading Indicators," *Economic Commentary*, Federal Reserve Bank of Cleveland, 1 October 1989.

the National Bureau of Economic Research.* This project has utilized highly sophisticated atheoretical forecasting methods. Its outcome is worth watching.

18.5   DEALING WITH FORECASTERS

Professional macroeconomic forecasting can be both fascinating and extremely useful to managerial decision making. However, it is also very expensive. Thus, a number of considerations should be taken into account before a decision is made about subscribing to a forecasting service.

WHAT TO EXPECT OF A FORECASTER

First, you want a forecasting firm to reduce your uncertainty about the future by providing **accurate macroeconomic forecasts.** Accuracy varies somewhat from firm to firm, so it can be useful to shop around and check the forecasting accuracy among the competing firms. We saw in Section 18.3 that accuracy is a multidimensional concept, because a macro forecast involves a number of variables. Different clients have different needs in this regard. For example, a primary need of a financial institution might be to obtain accurate interest-rate forecasts, while for a clothing manufacturer the forecasts of consumer demand and competing imports take center stage. Thus, you should identify the variables that are most important to your company and check the accuracy of these forecasts.

Second, the forecasts need to be **timely.** For example, are the forecasts issued once a quarter, or are they updated monthly? Naturally, you can expect more frequent services to be more expensive. You will have to decide how valuable timeliness is to your company. If you use the forecasts to guide decisions about day-to-day operations, frequent updates will be more important than if you use them mainly for long-term strategy discussions.

Third, the forecasts should be **presented in an informative manner.** The raw forecasting figures are barely meaningful to outside forecasting experts not familiar with the idiosyncracies of the particular model being used. Because most managers do not have such expertise, they rely heavily on the forecasters' presentations of their own results. Managers need forecasts to be accompanied by a story that gives the num-

---

*A report on this effort can be found in James Stock and Mark Watson, "The Revised NBER Indexes of Coincident and Leading Economic Indicators," in *NBER Macroeconomics Annual 1989*, edited by Olivier-Jean Blanchard and Stanley S. Fischer (M.I.T. Press, 1989).

bers meaning in a decision-making context. Sims's critique notwith-standing, such stories play an important role for managers as mental frameworks for the intuitive understanding they need in order to make decisions. However, it is worth keeping in mind that the mental frame-work provided by one particular model can also become a straight-jacket. Good macroeconomic forecasters need to remain open to new ideas even as they base their analyses on the old ones.

Fourth, a good forecasting firm should be able to go beyond macro-economic forecasting to provide **tailor-made consulting services.** One step toward such services is taken by the industry details contained in most large-scale models, which facilitate forecasts of what is likely to happen in your particular industry. However, in addition, you should be able to call on your forecasting company whenever you have special needs. For example, if you are considering a joint venture in Indonesia, your forecasting firm should be able to provide a special study of the state of the Indonesian economy, even if it does not maintain a regular forecasting model for Indonesia. If you are negotiating with state or local authorities about the location of a new facility, you should be able to have your forecaster prepare a special study of the impact your new operations would have on the local economy.

Finally, the relationship with your forecaster should be flexible enough to allow you to coordinate the outside forecasting services with your own **in-house analyses.** For this purpose, you will need as a minimum to have access to the forecaster's data bank. In some cases, you might want the opportunity to carry out your own simulations with the full macro-economic model in order to study particular scenarios you are inter-ested in. For example, you might want to study the macroeconomic effects of a proposed new set of environmental regulations. In practice, this can be done via a data network even if the model continues to reside in the forecasting firm's computer. Alternatively, you can purchase the right to install and simulate the entire model on your own computer. An increasingly popular alternative is to construct the model such that it can run on the client's personal computer.

LOWER-COST ALTERNATIVES TO LARGE-SCALE FORECASTING

Most businesses can benefit from keeping abreast of macroeconomic trends. However, the cost involved in acquiring this information makes consideration of alternatives to large-scale forecasting services important.

First, a good deal of information can be obtained for free. All **govern-ment data** are released to the public. We discussed in Chapter 13 how to interpret these data releases as signals of trends and turning points. In Chapters 14 through 17, we studied in detail how to obtain this informa-tion essentially for free from the **daily press.** It is worth adding that the press usually offers some additional free forecasting advice. The reports of the data releases are always accompanied by comments by leading economists. More formal surveys of economic forecasts are also presented, such as the semiannual survey in the *Wall Street Journal* that we looked at in Chapter 13.

For many companies, going beyond this level of information does not justify the cost. Note, however, that the acquisition of this information is not free in terms of your own or your staff's time, especially if staff members are untrained. A **short course** teaching your staff how to read and interpret current information might be well worth the cost. You might also consider paying an **economic consultant** to come in and brief you and your staff on current developments, say once a week.

Other low-cost sources of information are available as well. A number of financial institutions and accounting firms circulate economic **newsletters** among their clients. The staffs of the **Federal Reserve district banks** keep continuous watch over the economic trends in their respective districts. Some of this information is published in the respective district banks' quarterly reviews, which are available free of charge. More detail can be found in the district banks' briefings to the meetings of the Federal Open Market Committee eight times a year. This briefing, popularly known as the "Beige Book," is in the public domain and available from the Federal Reserve. Also, information about the local economy is usually available from the economic research centers of leading **public universities.**

Before we complete our list of free or relatively inexpensive information, it is worth making separate note of the **Index of Leading Economic Indicators.** We have seen that users of this index should be warned against the possibility of false signals. However, when read critically in conjunction with other economic data and the public comments of professionals, this index can provide useful information about the general economic climate a few months ahead.

If you are willing to pay a little more, you can obtain some of the services that the large-scale forecasters provide at a lower cost. For example, you might not need a full-scale forecast of the whole economy but would like some fairly detailed information about interest-rate trends. Then you could go to a number of financial consultants who carry out this type of analysis. As another alternative, you could go to one of the large-scale forecasting firms and purchase a subset of their services. You might be able to buy and receive regular updates of a personal-computer model that predicts only interest rates. If your needs are more in the direction of analysis than forecasts, you can use the services of economic or management consultants that provide such analysis on a one-time or continuing basis.

INTERNAL AND EXTERNAL EXPERTISE

Yet another alternative is to hire your own staff for macroeconomic analysis and forecasting. This is not unusual in many large companies, both in the financial industry and in industries such as manufacturing. For good reason, members of this staff sometimes take on a central role in the company's strategic planning.

Maintaining an internal staff can be quite expensive, easily more expensive than the standard subscription rate for the basic services of a large-scale forecasting company. On the other hand, you gain the advantage of having exclusive access to a staff whose energies are directed solely toward the issues facing your company.

External and internal expertise can interact in important ways. Maintaining an internal staff does not necessarily mean that your need for external services goes away. The internal staff will want to know what is going on among the professional forecasters. The output of the external forecasting company becomes input to the internal analysis. The internal staff might want to perform its own analyses using the outside model or their own tailored version of that model.

Even if you cannot afford to maintain a large internal economics staff, it might be worthwhile to make sure your company has someone with the skills needed to read the material you receive from the forecasting firm. Like any supplier, a forecasting firm needs to be watched for possible errors and misjudgment. Access to internal expertise can help you retain a sense of skepticism while at the same time making sure you benefit from the outside analyses.

CHAPTER REVIEW

1. Structural forecasts are generated by theory-based macroeconomic models. They are usually conditional in that they depend on the forecaster's assumptions about monetary and fiscal policy and other exogenous variables.

2. The typical large-scale macroeconomic model starts with the IS-LM–Phillips-curve model, then adds disaggregation, exogenous variables, dynamic lag structures, and industry detail.

3. The data used to estimate large-scale models are available to clients as valuable data bases.

4. Given assumptions about policy and other exogenous variables, raw forecasts are generated by solving the system of equations that define the model. These raw forecasts are usually adjusted judgmentally by means of add factors. Releases of the forecasts are accompanied by verbal analyses available exclusively to clients.

5. Structural forecasts take full advantage of the theory underlying the model. However, the tie to the theory may sometimes prevent the forecasters from taking advantage of new developments.

6. Atheoretical forecasting makes no use of macroeconomic theory but relies extensively on statistical methods. Vector-autoregressive models are often used. Atheoretical forecasts are typically unconditional.

7. Atheoretical forecasts are not bound by any particular economic philosophy, but they

also do not take advantage of the insights of macroeconomic theory.

8. The track record of macroeconomic forecasters is quite good overall, although some important events have been missed. Real GNP growth is very difficult to forecast. The performance of structural and atheoretical models is not very different.

9. The Index of Leading Economic Indicators (ILEI) is an average of 11 components. The indicators tend to lead real economic activity because they reflect commitments, expectations, policy, and early signals of change. The averaging of the individual components filters out noise.

10. Statistical studies have found the ILEI to be useful overall. It is used especially for predicting business-cycle turning points, although it has occasionally given off false signals.

11. Forecasters should be expected to provide accurate forecasts in a timely manner, presented in an informative way. In addition, they can provide tailor-made consulting services and facilitate clients' in-house analyses.

12. Low-cost alternatives to large-scale forecasting include the reading of government data releases, such as the Index of Leading Economic Indicators, financial newsletters, Federal Reserve publications, and the services of public universities.

13. Internal expertise can be a substitute for an external forecasting service. More often, however, it supplements external assistance and tailors the analysis to the needs of your own firm.

EXERCISES

1. The survey of forecasts shown in Figure 13.1 is published in the *Wall Street Journal* twice a year. From back issues of that newspaper, obtain copies of this survey for the last five years. Identify five forecasters that have been part of the survey each time. For these forecasters, as well as the survey average (at the bottom of the table), compare the forecasts to the actual data. Compute and compare the root mean squared forecast errors. Comment on the results.

2. Add the rate of growth of the money supply to the VAR model of real GNP growth and the T-bill rate studied in this chapter. Continue to include lags of up to three quarters. Estimate the model with data through 1985 and compute forecasts for all the variables from 1986 to the present in the same way as in the text. Comment on the results. Does it make any difference whether you use M1 or M2 to represent the money supply?

3. Construct a VAR model for inflation, a short-term interest rate, and the money supply. Make your own choices of specific data series for each variable and choose how many lags you want to include. Estimate the model with data through 1985 and study its forecasts from 1986 through the present. Comment on the results. Why would you want to choose these particular variables?

4. Auerbach's test for the ILEI's usefulness in predicting the civilian unemployment rate was based on an F-statistic for the hypothesis that the parameters $b_0, \ldots, b_{10}$ are all zero at the same time in the regression equation
$$u_t = a_0 + a_1 u_{t-1} + a_2 u_{t-2} + \cdots + a_{10} u_{t-10}$$
$$+ \, b_1 \ell_{t-1} + b_2 \ell_{t-2} + \cdots + b_{10} \ell_{t-10} + e_t,$$
where u is the unemployment rate, ℓ is the rate of change in the ILEI, and all the data are monthly. The testing equation for the growth in industrial production was analogous. Find data for these variables. With these data, which will be more recent than those used by Auerbach, follow Auerbach's lines in testing how well the ILEI can predict future activity.

5. Auerbach did not test how well the ILEI could forecast real GNP growth, because the ILEI is released monthly and GNP quarterly. Try to construct a model with which this hypothesis can be tested. [Hint: Construct three quarterly variables for the rate of change in the ILEI, one taking the value of the rate of change in the ILEI for the first

month of the quarter, another the corresponding value for the second month of the quarter, and so on.] Report and comment on your results.

THINKING QUESTIONS

1. Suppose you manage a consumer retail business in a metropolitan area of about one million people. For planning purposes, you are interested in forecasts for the local economy. No such service is currently available, but two competing consulting companies have made one proposal each. The first company offers to build a fairly large structural model, which it claims will help you understand, not just forecast, the local economy. The other company offers to build a five-variable VAR model of the economy in your area. The latter alternative is about one-third the price. Which one would you choose, and why? Given a sufficient budget, would you see any reason for buying both?

2. Forecasts for states and local areas often rely on outside forecasts of national variables (such as real GNP and interest rates). The outside forecasts are used as exogenous variables in the local forecasting model. What do you see as the strengths and weaknesses of this approach?

3. Noting that the ILEI is a reasonably good guide for predicting business-cycle turning points, why would you want to pay large fees for a commercial forecasting service? Why do you think so many companies do?

4. Refer back to the discussion of the Lucas critique in Chapter 8. What does this critique imply about the reliability of atheoretical models?

5. Some macroeconomic modelers have supplemented the IS-LM–Phillips-curve framework with forecasting equations for economic policy. For what purposes do you think this is a good idea?

6. Macroeconomic forecasters are sometimes criticized for not fully disclosing the extent to which their forecasts are adjusted judgmentally. How valuable would you find this information from a managerial point of view?

7. Atheoretical models claim to be independent of economic theory and particularly of the various schools of thought in macroeconomics. Remember, however, that the atheoretical models and forecasts are produced by people who on one hand hold opinions like everybody else but on the other hand want to maintain a reputation for good forecasts and perhaps make money from them. Considering these factors, how credible do you find the claims of independence?

8. Forecasting accuracy has a number of dimensions. From the point of view of the industry you are in or expect to go into, state what is more important to you in terms of (a) which variables are forecast the most accurately, (b) accuracy for forecasts for the near term versus the remote future, and (c) average accuracy versus accuracy at business-cycle turning points.

APPENDIX

TABLE 1   THE F DISTRIBUTION

SIGNIFICANCE LEVEL 1% (p = .01)

n_2 \ n_1	1	2	3	4	5	6	8	12	24	∞
1	4052	4999	5403	5625	5764	5859	5981	6106	6234	6366
2	98.49	99.01	99.17	99.25	99.30	99.33	99.36	99.42	99.46	99.50
3	34.12	30.81	29.46	28.71	28.24	27.91	27.49	27.05	26.60	26.12
4	21.20	18.00	16.69	15.98	15.52	15.21	14.80	14.37	13.93	13.46
5	16.26	13.27	12.06	11.39	10.97	10.67	10.27	9.89	9.47	9.02
6	13.74	10.92	9.78	9.15	8.75	8.47	8.10	7.72	7.31	6.88
7	12.25	9.55	8.45	7.85	7.46	7.19	6.84	6.47	6.07	5.65
8	11.26	8.65	7.59	7.01	6.63	6.37	6.03	5.67	5.28	4.86
9	10.56	8.02	6.99	6.42	6.06	5.80	5.47	5.11	4.73	4.31
10	10.04	7.56	6.55	5.99	5.64	5.39	5.06	4.71	4.33	3.91
11	9.65	7.20	6.22	5.67	5.32	5.07	4.74	4.40	4.02	3.60
12	9.33	6.93	5.95	5.41	5.06	4.82	4.50	4.16	3.78	3.36
13	9.07	6.70	5.74	5.20	4.86	4.62	4.30	3.96	3.59	3.16
14	8.86	6.51	5.56	5.03	4.69	4.46	4.14	3.80	3.43	3.00
15	8.68	6.36	5.42	4.89	4.56	4.32	4.00	3.67	3.29	2.87
16	8.53	6.23	5.29	4.77	4.44	4.20	3.89	3.55	3.18	2.75
17	8.40	6.11	5.18	4.67	4.34	4.10	3.79	3.45	3.08	2.65
18	8.28	6.01	5.09	4.58	4.25	4.01	3.71	3.37	3.00	2.57
19	8.18	5.93	5.01	4.50	4.17	3.94	3.63	3.30	2.92	2.49
20	8.10	5.85	4.94	4.43	4.10	3.87	3.56	3.23	2.86	2.42
21	8.02	5.78	4.87	4.37	4.04	3.81	3.51	3.17	2.80	2.36
22	7.94	5.72	4.82	4.31	3.99	3.76	3.45	3.12	2.75	2.31
23	7.88	5.66	4.76	4.26	3.94	3.71	3.41	3.07	2.70	2.26
24	7.82	5.61	4.72	4.22	3.90	3.67	3.36	3.03	2.66	2.21
25	7.77	5.57	4.68	4.18	3.86	3.63	3.32	2.99	2.62	2.17
26	7.72	5.53	4.64	4.14	3.82	3.59	3.29	2.96	2.58	2.13
27	7.68	5.49	4.60	4.11	3.78	3.56	3.26	2.93	2.55	2.10
28	7.64	5.45	4.57	4.07	3.75	3.53	3.23	2.90	2.52	2.06
29	7.60	5.42	4.54	4.04	3.73	3.50	3.20	2.87	2.49	2.03
30	7.56	5.39	4.51	4.02	3.70	3.47	3.17	2.84	2.47	2.01
40	7.31	5.18	4.31	3.83	3.51	3.29	2.99	2.66	2.29	1.80
60	7.08	4.98	4.13	3.65	3.34	3.12	2.82	2.50	2.12	1.60
120	6.85	4.79	3.95	3.48	3.17	2.96	2.66	2.34	1.95	1.38
∞	6.64	4.60	3.78	3.32	3.02	2.80	2.51	2.18	1.79	1.00

Values of n_1 and n_2 represent the degrees of freedom in the numerator and in the denominator, respectively. Adapted from Fisher and Yates, *Statistical Tables for Biological, Agricultural, and Medical Research*, Sixth Edition, 1974.

TABLE 1   THE *F* DISTRIBUTION (*Continued*)

					SIGNIFICANCE LEVEL 5% ($p = .05$)					
n_2 \ n_1	1	2	3	4	5	6	8	12	24	∞
1	161.4	199.5	215.7	224.6	230.2	234.0	238.9	243.9	249.0	254.3
2	18.51	19.00	19.16	19.25	19.30	19.33	19.37	19.41	19.45	19.50
3	10.13	9.55	9.28	9.12	9.01	8.94	8.84	8.74	8.64	8.53
4	7.71	6.94	6.59	6.39	6.26	6.16	6.04	5.91	5.77	5.63
5	6.61	5.79	5.41	5.19	5.05	4.95	4.82	4.68	4.53	4.36
6	5.99	5.14	4.76	4.53	4.39	4.28	4.15	4.00	3.84	3.67
7	5.59	4.74	4.35	4.12	3.97	3.87	3.73	3.57	3.41	3.23
8	5.32	4.46	4.07	3.84	3.69	3.58	3.44	3.28	3.12	2.93
9	5.12	4.26	3.86	3.63	3.48	3.37	3.23	3.07	2.90	2.71
10	4.96	4.10	3.71	3.48	3.33	3.22	3.07	2.91	2.74	2.54
11	4.84	3.98	3.59	3.36	3.20	3.09	2.95	2.79	2.61	2.40
12	4.75	3.88	3.49	3.26	3.11	3.00	2.85	2.69	2.50	2.30
13	4.67	3.80	3.41	3.18	3.02	2.92	2.77	2.60	2.42	2.21
14	4.60	3.74	3.34	3.11	2.96	2.85	2.70	2.53	2.35	2.13
15	4.54	3.68	3.29	3.06	2.90	2.79	2.64	2.48	2.29	2.07
16	4.49	3.63	3.24	3.01	2.85	2.74	2.59	2.42	2.24	2.01
17	4.45	3.59	3.20	2.96	2.81	2.70	2.55	2.38	2.19	1.96
18	4.41	3.55	3.16	2.93	2.77	2.66	2.51	2.34	2.15	1.92
19	4.38	3.52	3.13	2.90	2.74	2.63	2.48	2.31	2.11	1.88
20	4.35	3.49	3.10	2.87	2.71	2.60	2.45	2.28	2.08	1.84
21	4.32	3.47	3.07	2.84	2.68	2.57	2.42	2.25	2.05	1.81
22	4.30	3.44	3.05	2.82	2.66	2.55	2.40	2.23	2.03	1.78
23	4.28	3.42	3.03	2.80	2.64	2.53	2.38	2.20	2.00	1.76
24	4.26	3.40	3.01	2.78	2.62	2.51	2.36	2.18	1.98	1.73
25	4.24	3.38	2.99	2.76	2.60	2.49	2.34	2.16	1.96	1.71
26	4.22	3.37	2.98	2.74	2.59	2.47	2.32	2.15	1.95	1.69
27	4.21	3.35	2.96	2.73	2.57	2.46	2.30	2.13	1.93	1.67
28	4.20	3.34	2.95	2.71	2.56	2.44	2.29	2.12	1.91	1.65
29	4.18	3.33	2.93	2.70	2.54	2.43	2.28	2.10	1.90	1.64
30	4.17	3.32	2.92	2.69	2.53	2.42	2.27	2.09	1.89	1.62
40	4.08	3.23	2.84	2.61	2.45	2.34	2.18	2.00	1.79	1.51
60	4.00	3.15	2.76	2.52	2.37	2.25	2.10	1.92	1.70	1.39
120	3.92	3.07	2.68	2.45	2.29	2.17	2.02	1.83	1.61	1.25
∞	3.84	2.99	2.60	2.37	2.21	2.09	1.94	1.75	1.52	1.00

Values of n_1 and n_2 represent the degrees of freedom in the numerator and in the denominator, respectively. Adapted from Fisher and Yates, *Statistical Tables for Biological, Agricultural, and Medical Research*, Sixth Edition, 1974.

TABLE 2 THE *t* DISTRIBUTION

df	LEVEL OF SIGNIFICANCE FOR ONE-TAILED TEST				
	.10	.05	.025	.01	.005
	LEVEL OF SIGNIFICANCE FOR TWO-TAILED TEST				
	.20	.10	.05	.02	.01
1	3.078	6.314	12.706	31.821	63.657
2	1.886	2.920	4.303	6.965	9.925
3	1.638	2.353	3.182	4.541	5.841
4	1.533	2.132	2.776	3.747	4.604
5	1.476	2.015	2.571	3.365	4.032
6	1.440	1.943	2.447	3.143	3.707
7	1.415	1.895	2.365	2.998	3.499
8	1.397	1.860	2.306	2.896	3.355
9	1.383	1.833	2.262	2.821	3.250
10	1.372	1.812	2.228	2.764	3.169
11	1.363	1.796	2.201	2.718	3.106
12	1.356	1.782	2.179	2.681	3.055
13	1.350	1.771	2.160	2.650	3.012
14	1.345	1.761	2.145	2.624	2.977
15	1.341	1.753	2.131	2.602	2.947
16	1.337	1.746	2.120	2.583	2.921
17	1.333	1.740	2.110	2.567	2.898
18	1.330	1.734	2.101	2.552	2.878
19	1.328	1.729	2.093	2.539	2.861
20	1.325	1.725	2.086	2.528	2.845
21	1.323	1.721	2.080	2.518	2.831
22	1.321	1.717	2.074	2.508	2.819
23	1.319	1.714	2.069	2.500	2.807
24	1.318	1.711	2.064	2.492	2.797
25	1.316	1.708	2.060	2.485	2.787
26	1.315	1.706	2.056	2.479	2.779
27	1.314	1.703	2.052	2.473	2.771
28	1.313	1.701	2.048	2.467	2.763
29	1.311	1.699	2.045	2.462	2.756
30	1.310	1.697	2.042	2.457	2.750
40	1.303	1.684	2.021	2.423	2.704
60	1.296	1.671	2.000	2.390	2.660
120	1.289	1.658	1.980	2.358	2.617
(Normal) ∞	1.282	1.645	1.960	2.326	2.576

Adapted from Fisher and Yates, *Statistical Tables for Biological, Agricultural, and Medical Research*, Sixth Edition, 1974.

INDEX